THE CHEROKEES

The Cherokees

———•———

In War and at Peace
1670–1840

DAVID NARRETT

THE BELKNAP PRESS OF
HARVARD UNIVERSITY PRESS
Cambridge, Massachusetts
London, England
2025

Copyright © 2025 by David Narrett
All rights reserved
Printed in the United States of America

FIRST PRINTING

Library of Congress Cataloging-in-Publication Data

Names: Narrett, David E., 1951– author.
Title: The Cherokees : in war and at peace, 1670–1840 / David Narrett.
Description: Cambridge, Massachusetts ; London, England : The Belknap Press of
Harvard University Press, 2025. | Includes bibliographical references and index.
Identifiers: LCCN 2024022188 | ISBN 9780674258204 (cloth) |
ISBN 9780674299641 (epub) | ISBN 9780674299672 (pdf)
Subjects: LCSH: Cherokee Indians—History. | Cherokee Indians—
Government relations—History. | Cherokee Indians—Social life and customs. |
Cherokee Indians—Wars—History. | Cherokee women—Social conditions. |
Cherokee Nation—History.
Classification: LCC E99.C5 N37 2025 | DDC 975.004/97557—dc23/eng/20240724
LC record available at https://lccn.loc.gov/2024022188

To the memory of Michael Kammen

friend, mentor, and extraordinary historian

Contents

Introduction: Cherokees in a Changing World	*1*
I Cherokees in Their Homeland and Beyond, 1670–1730	*13*
1 Cherokee Culture and Lifeways	*15*
2 South Carolina and the Native Southeast	*40*
3 "Not Like White Men"	*68*
4 A Cherokee Voyage to London	*100*
II Cherokees, Native Peoples, and Empires, 1730–1762	*119*
5 Warfare and Peace Quests across Half a Continent	*121*
6 Confronting Colonialism and the Creek Nation	*155*
7 Tempests of the French and Indian War	*187*
8 Prelude to the British-Cherokee War	*224*
9 Carnage and Peace Diplomacy	*257*
III Upheavals and the Will to Live, 1762–1795	*291*
10 The Politics of Alliance and Survival	*293*
11 Cherokees and the American Revolution	*328*
12 Bloodshed and Quests for Peace	*364*
13 An Unbroken People	*397*

Conclusion: Washington's Farewell and Cherokee Paths   *439*

    Abbreviations   *469*
    Notes   *477*
    Acknowledgments   *573*
    Index   *575*

THE CHEROKEES

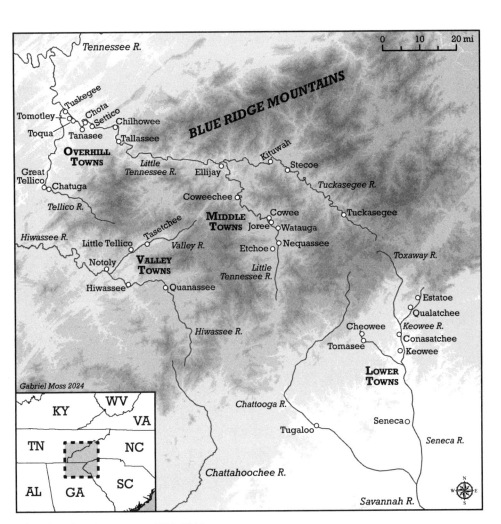

The Cherokee Country, ca. 1720–1740

INTRODUCTION

Cherokees in a Changing World

Like many other Native American peoples, the Cherokees were masters of metaphor when it came to negotiation with European colonial authorities. Examples abound across generations, expressed in periods of crisis and less momentous occasions. For illustrative purposes, consider a speech made by chief Kanagatucko (Standing Turkey) in September 1761 when Cherokees moved toward peace with the British, South Carolina, and Virginia after a brutal war of two years. Kanagatucko forwarded his talk to Colonel Adam Stephen of the Virginia militia, then quartered east of Cherokee territory and seemingly poised to invade unless English treaty demands were met. The chief's remarks were put to paper by interpreter John Bench, a corporal who had lived among the Cherokees for several years. So, the written text approximates rather than captures precisely what Kanagatucko spoke.[1]

Kanagatucko respectfully addressed the English, former Cherokee allies before a breakdown in relations and the war's ensuing destruction. He hoped for "a peace that is never to be broke, for all our men are tired of fighting with our Elder Brother the English." In typical Native manner, Cherokees understood kinship, or its absence, as the core of relations. Kanagatucko was pleased to have received "a good talk from our Brother the Governor in Charlestown [Charleston, South Carolina], & now the Path is Streight, and our hearts are Clear, & the Chain is bright, which has been for long black, & we shall live like one people as formerly." Brotherly bonds with the English could be honorary and emblematic and not literally biological in the sense of sharing a mother's blood—the life source of Cherokee kinship.[2]

Kanagatucko returned to the idea of light: "now as our Eyes are opened, & the Sky Clear, & we can see our faults." The intent was not to assume or assign blame but for belligerents to move beyond the war: "We have had a great deal of mischief done on Both Sides, but let it not be thought on. . . . We [Cherokees] have Enemies enough of our own Colour, without fighting the White People." The Cherokee peace talk, he continued, "is spoke by one and all, and the Hatchet is now buried under ground never to be seen by the English again."[3]

Kanagatucko's identification of the English as "the White People" was commonplace among Cherokees and other Native peoples of southeastern North America by the 1720s. This fact is not itself surprising since the English frequently identified themselves as "white" in conferences with those they styled "Indians," who increasingly referred to themselves as "red" by comparison. Cherokee headman Attakullakulla, a foremost peace advocate in 1761, said to a British officer: "I am a red Man and you are white, but I hope all will be well again."[4]

When Cherokees referred to individuals as "white" or "red," they were using words signifying skin pigmentation of contrasting hues rather than making any obvious judgment as to what might be called "race." Native peoples took pride in their own physical appearance, to be sure. Writing in the 1760s, trader James Adair, who lived for several decades among southeastern Indians, described Native skin tone as "of a copper or red-clay colour." He added: "All the Indians are so strongly attached to, and prejudiced in favour of, their own colour, that they think as meanly of the whites, as we possibly do of them."[5] Adair's assessment does not mean that Cherokees saw skin color as a barrier to mutual respect with colonials. In fact, the movement to peace was one of bridging divides. Attakullakulla relayed Kanagatucko's wish to the English that "the road will be clear to white and red" people. A "clear road" meant an open trading path that reflected harmony and goodwill between nations. Attakullakulla's optimistic view was not universally shared in Indian country. As expansive white settlements became more threatening to Native peoples, the latter increasingly saw their "red" skin as a mark of supernatural favor, a call to unity among themselves and resistance against the colonials.[6]

When the Cherokees made peace with the British in 1761, it did not mean that they would be free of conflict. As Kanagatucko said, "We [Cherokees] have Enemies enough of our own Colour, without fighting the White People." To place his words in context, we need first to locate the speaker more precisely. Kanagatucko was *uku* or priest-chief of Chota, the single most influential Cherokee town lying west of the Appalachians. As will be discussed in greater detail, Cherokee villages were situated in widely dispersed river valleys, extending from the foothills of the Blue Ridge, in what is today's far western South Carolina, to the Great Smoky Mountains of the Appalachians, and still farther west to the Cumberland Plateau in eastern Tennessee. Beyond these areas, there was a vast Indigenous geography that impinged on Cherokee lives in war and at peace. Cherokee diplomacy itself had a remarkable physical range and a level of sophistication that were linchpins of communal strength.[7]

In eighteenth-century Cherokee society, peace and war both partook of the sacred but in different ways. To the Cherokees and numerous American Indian nations, for example, white was the color of peace, while red signified war. Both colors, as well as others, had multiple uses in ritual and ceremony. At conferences with colonial officials, Cherokee headmen invariably distributed strings of wampum beads to signify and speak their intent. "Good talks" were "made fast" or strengthened by gifts of white wampum. Fashioned from mollusk shells, wampum was essential to messaging across ethnic bounds. As James Merrell has written, "no frontier negotiator" of colonial stripe could succeed unless knowing "the language of beads," whether expressed in simple form or in elaborately woven wampum belts. The Cherokees sometimes placed black beads, signifying darkness or death, on a string with white shells when something was amiss but not at the stage of war. This type of symbolism was well understood when Native peoples communicated in person or dispatched items to friends or foes. In 1726, for example, Cherokees and Creeks inched from war to truce talks by exchanging white bird feathers. The Creeks, meanwhile, sent a string of red wampum to the Chickasaws. The "red" signified Creek hostility aroused by recent Chickasaw attacks.[8]

"White" and "red" were powerful forces in social and cultural counterpoise. As Steven Hahn tells us, these colors had meaning beyond peace and war. To the Creeks (Muscogees), "white signified peace, age, wisdom, and deliberation," while "red" represented "war, youth, passion, and bold action." Creek *talwas* (towns) were traditionally considered either "white" or "red" in character. "White" towns had a reputation as being fit places for consultation and the settlement of disputes among Muscogee factions. "Red" towns customarily leapt to the fore in war deliberations, though all Creek communities had warriors prepared to fight enemies and protect native ground. The symbolic

Introduction　　　　　　　　　　　　　　　　　　　　　　　　　　　3

meanings of "red" and "white" shaped communal identity, though without necessarily dictating a particular course of action.[9]

European colonial officials readily picked up on Indigenous metaphoric speech even if its subtleties were often missed in translation. While conferencing with Native headmen, provincial governors talked of brightening "the Chain of Friendship," clearing "the path," and called on Indian allies to "take up the hatchet" in war. Shared rhetoric did not itself create trust across cultural bounds. Actions counted. Cherokees were acutely cognizant of what colonial officers had pledged in the past and were expected to fulfill. Indigenous historical memory was an integral part of diplomacy.[10]

Speech and ritual gesture were commonly fused when Cherokee headmen negotiated with colonials over trade, war and peace, territorial bounds, and sovereignty. Performance and protocol were embedded in diplomatic conferences, not unlike formal exchanges between emissaries at European courts. Throughout southeastern North America, British interpreters commonly referred to a Native headman's speech as a "talk"—a word connoting formal political discourse in which the speaker's words, gestures, and bearing were the medium of exchange. Native peoples were attuned to implicit questions raised in diplomatic communication. Would the recipients of a talk bring to mind and heart what was said? Would listeners believe in the speaker's sincerity, strength of character, and capacity to represent his people? Words had power. So, too, did gifts that spoke in pragmatic and spiritual ways. Gifts displayed generosity while entailing obligations on recipients and expectations of mutual respect. Certain gestures had broad cultural meaning in Indigenous North America. For example, women sometimes accompanied men on peace missions with the intent of showing the hosts that the visitors meant goodwill—and not war.[11]

Diplomatic acuity encompassed the ability to dissimulate as well as to speak literal truth. To palliate wrongs committed by one's own group—or even to conceal them—was quite as much an Indigenous as a colonial approach to compromising situations. The resolution of crises between ethnicities often called on interested parties to accept half-truths or fictions for the larger purpose of avoiding blowups and escalating violence. Quests for the diplomatic "middle ground," which Richard White has richly described for French-Indian relations in the Great Lakes region, depended on a rough equivalence of power between contending groups that bargained with some understanding

4   *Introduction*

of one another. Significantly, White's "middle ground" was a precarious state, shaken episodically by interethnic instability and violence. The restoration of balance and harmony often came about through negotiated compromise rather than by an overwhelming military victory or a defeat among the contending parties.[12]

Eighteenth-century Europeans commonly had the idea that American "Indians" were constantly at war with one another. After all, were not young boys in numerous Indigenous nations customarily trained for war? Yes, that was the case, but it did not mean that fighting between ethnicities followed any simple pattern or fell into what could be called a Hobbesian war of all against all. In Indigenous North America, bloody conflicts might be short-lived or persistent affairs, and truces brief or long-lasting. Alliances were subject to change. Diplomacy was often as important as warring prowess to group cohesion and survival. These facts of life were present for centuries prior to European arrival and persisted under new and drastically changing conditions long afterward.

Cherokee relations with intersecting Native and colonial worlds were characterized by assertions of power, tempered by acute awareness of vulnerability. Edward Countryman is on the mark in writing that "whatever value [American] Indians placed on autonomy, they understood that the weak needed the strong." The Indigenous tenaciously guarded independence and resisted subordination—and for this very reason often sought powerful allies within frameworks of respect and reciprocity. To the Cherokees, such relationships were ideally a bond, implicitly covenantal and not merely contractual.[13]

While historical literature on the Cherokees is voluminous, there is still a great deal to be learned about their lives in war and at peace from the 1670s, when they had their first encounters with the English, to the agonizing era of forced removal and the Trail of Tears in the 1830s. This is not at all to suggest that Cherokee history begins with English colonialism. Native traditions and beliefs, long predating European arrival in the Americas, are an essential part of this story. So, too, are archaeological and anthropological insights that tell us about lifeways that developed over time and often had roots centuries before the written historical record begins. Living in an interior and mountainous continental zone, Cherokees had tenuous contacts with British colonials until the dawn of the 1700s—long after many other Indigenous nations were convulsed by the spread of "Old World" diseases, the

Introduction

5

competition for guns and goods in the fur and deerskin trades, and the havoc wrought by the traffic in Indian slaves. This was a new world in turmoil for Native peoples and not simply for colonials.[14]

Historians of the Native American past face the challenge of getting the big picture right while offering a sense of the daunting complexity encountered along the path. For example, to write of "the Cherokees" as a single nation making decisions regarding war is a simplistic idea for much of the 1700s. Given the dispersed situation of Cherokee towns over a broad landscape, kin and village loyalties governed much of social life. Warriors gave priority to protecting those closest to them. The diffusion of authority made it difficult for disparate regions to unify in warfare. Paradoxically, Cherokee society drew strength from its customary allowance for local autonomy, its capacity to absorb diverse perspectives, and to seek consensus on war and peace through persuasion.[15]

This book is not simply about what Europeans "did" to "Indians" as victims of colonialism. It concerns the changing and often tumultuous relations between Native peoples as they variously fought, made peace, or allied with one another in the light of new and often unprecedented challenges. As Daniel Richter has written, European imperial clashes in North America interfaced with "indigenously" spawned wars "that grew from longstanding home-grown conflicts." Well into the eighteenth century, Native peoples adeptly leveraged Europeans for advantage in their own interethnic rivalries.[16] The Cherokees' evolving relations with Native ethnicities—Creeks, Shawnees, Iroquois, and other Indian groups—were integral to shaping their diplomacy with colonials well before the birth of the United States.

Crises were part of Cherokee life through most of the eighteenth century. In 1715, Cherokees faced the difficult choice of which side to take in the Yamasee War, an uprising of Native peoples against English South Carolina. The Cherokees knew little peace over decades from the powerful Creeks and Iroquois. Then there was the British-Cherokee War of 1760–1761, the dramatic upsurge of white settlers intruding into Cherokee territory from 1763 to 1775 and the ravages of the American Revolutionary War that followed. That war, in which many Cherokees aligned with the British, witnessed scorched-earth invasions by Southern state militias. Widespread destruction spurred a geographic reorientation of Cherokee communities, marked by the rise of the militant Chickamauga movement that battled American settlers into the 1790s. Given this history of conflict, it is no wonder that "peoplehood and perseverance" is a vital theme for Cherokees and other Native Americans, who continue to draw strength from shared memories of courage and survival against all odds.[17]

Cherokee warfare and peace-making strategies evolved in tandem rather than in separate spheres. The white path of peace counterbalanced the red path of war for nearly the entire eighteenth century. This does not mean any simple equilibrium existed between war and peace, but rather that many Cherokees weighed the destructiveness of warfare, its costs in lives to themselves, and the need to dampen the flames when conflagration threatened chaos and exacerbated internal divides. Choices on the war and peace fronts were often wrenching and difficult, especially when increasingly aggressive settler colonialism became an overhanging danger to the Cherokee way of life in the mid- to late eighteenth century. Cherokee responses to this threat were variable and fluid, involving political and diplomatic strategizing, and not militant resistance alone.

A great deal of Native diplomacy in the early colonial era had the object of acquiring sufficient supplies of European trade goods and munitions—resources vital against Indigenous adversaries. We may deplore the arms race in retrospect, but that begs the issue. To assume that Cherokees and Creeks should have halted their battles of the period 1715–1750 is no more realistic historically than imagining sweet peace between Great Britain and France or Spain in that era. Indigenous conflicts went hand and hand with diplomacy involving the quest for wartime allies or mediators that might further truce talks with foes. Cherokee headmen strived for British mediation at certain critical junctures, while relying on Native friends in other instances. Negotiation was a multifaceted tool, employed as in other cultures to keep enemies at bay as well as to reduce tensions and curtail hostilities. Through the 1700s, Cherokee peacemaking had a spiritual component—an ideal of reconciliation with adversaries through mutual and purposeful forgetting of past wrongs inflicted on one another. The capacity of Native peoples to forget no less than to remember eased communal healing amid strife, bloodshed, and loss. On occasion, new social bonds arose to signal the close of war. In the mid-1750s, the Creeks and Cherokees solidified a recent peace by recognizing a headman of the opposing nation as one of their own adopted and honorary chiefs. Variations on this theme are evident among numerous Native American peoples for

Introduction

7

whom condolence ceremonies, gift exchange, and ritual feasts were part of making peace.[18]

Cherokee diplomatic approaches, honed within the Native world, had direct relevance to negotiating postures toward European colonials and later with American state officials and federal authorities. When facing danger, it made sense for Cherokees to seek protection from powerful forces beyond their country. A belief in the "Great King George" as a shielding power was later echoed by the hope that Congress and President Washington would act as the new "father."[19] Cherokees were not naïve when they collectively decided on what they hoped would be a lasting peace with the United States in 1794 after years of conflict. They harbored few illusions that land-hungry, Indian-hating American settlers would suddenly change their ways. The war's end came when Cherokee peace factions found common ground with militants that had themselves suffered stinging defeats at the hands of white militiamen. What is remarkable about this state of affairs is that differing Cherokee groups, living at considerable distance from one another, reached a consensus by consultation in the face of peril. Persuasion, not diktat, was the operative rule.

Until the 1790s, the great portion of written documentation on Cherokee diplomacy comes via British or Anglo-American interpreters who made their livelihood as traders in Indian country. These men, who often had Native wives or mistresses, were essential participants at parleys between Cherokees and colonial officials in Charles Town (later Charleston), Williamsburg, and other venues. Interpreters transcribed Cherokee "talks" sent from Indian country to colonial capital towns, not infrequently at distances of 300 to 500 miles. Interpreters were similarly vital when translating governors' written messages forwarded to Cherokee headmen and warriors. Trader-interpreter Robert Bunning accompanied seven Cherokee men who made a voyage across the "great Water" (the Atlantic) in 1730 to visit London and see the king. While the work of colonial interpreters was imperfect and subject to misinterpretation of Native meanings, it is still an indispensable historical source. Translation to French or Spanish naturally came into play when Cherokee delegates visited New Orleans or other Gulf Coast venues. This book makes use of all three European languages, English being the most important because of the sheer depth of Cherokee relations with the British and later the Americans. French documents are significant for broadening our geopolitical framework. In a Native world of intricate ties among many nations, French negotiations with the

Choctaws, Chickasaws, Creeks, and Iroquois shed light on developments in Cherokee country.[20]

North America's Native peoples generally lived without centralized and coercive structures of governmental power at the time that the first European settlements appeared on the continent. Authority within Cherokee society operated through customs and rituals by which individuals, depending foremost on their age and gender, assumed certain duties and responsibilities. Loyalties were founded on kinship, clan identity, and locality. The shared myths and stories told in Cherokee communities deepened cultural allegiance. Like other Indigenous groups, Cherokees believed themselves to be the "real people," or the true human beings—*Ani-Yunwiya*. Their sense of the world will be discussed more fully in the chapters to follow. One may begin with a simple statement: Cherokee peoplehood was far from static; it evolved in response to rivalries with other Indigenous groups and the pressures of colonialism.[21]

Bonds of "peoplehood" are not precisely the same as modern nationalism with its diverse components, variously embracing culture, politics, language, ethnicity, and religion. Peoplehood is a way of human connectedness through common beliefs, ancestral myths and narratives of shared origins, and a deep sense of communal belonging and place, often expressed in ceremonial rites. It is generally, though not always, inbred in early youth and passed from generation to generation in lineages and communities, and it is not dependent at its roots on imposition by state or governmental authority. Peoplehood has tribal or particularistic elements, distinguishing one group from another, though it may also have universal qualities. It is fundamentally felt by individuals rather than simply "imagined."[22]

Cherokee peoplehood had various levels of social obligation, depending on the closeness of kin and clan ties between persons living within a certain geographic compass. For example, blood law was a motive force in warfare between Native peoples. If a Cherokee man's kin were slain by an enemy, his first obligation was to wreak vengeance on the foe. A warrior necessarily harkened to female kin when the latter demanded retaliation for blood relatives who had suffered death in an enemy attack. A victim's spirit was literally believed to "cry blood" and to haunt his still living clan members; the dead gained rest only when a surrogate visited like punishment on the slayer or someone symbolically standing for him. The same held true among the Creeks

Introduction

and many other Indigenous societies. The ritual torture and execution of enemy captives was only one facet of retributive justice in Native American cultures. Quite as notable was a markedly different choice—the adoption of prisoners by the will of the captors.[23]

Adopted captives, requickened as kin in a new social matrix, had a notable role in Native diplomacy. Whether male or female, they were well positioned to serve as go-betweens because of their broad kin ties and linguistic skills—the ability to speak in both their native language and the tongue of their adopted nation. The Indian adoption of child captives, including whites, is well known. In some cases, children born of an enemy foe even rose to become leaders of their adopted society. By one account, which is admittedly speculative, the renowned Cherokee headman Attakullakulla ("The Little Carpenter" by English name) was a native Nipissing of Canada who was captured as a young boy by Cherokee warriors (or otherwise came into their hands). In midlife, a reverse twist of fate occurred when Attakullakulla was seized by Canadian Indians who, by his good fortune, adopted him rather than put him to the stake.[24] This story is but one example of the rich human dimension of Native American history that often raises enigmas and unanswerable questions.

Cherokee women had a significant influence in war and peace—an impact that receives close attention in this book. The role of women on these critical matters appears unevenly in the written historical record. For some periods, there is episodic information, while for others such as the British-Cherokee War the sources are astonishingly rich, telling us of individual women who acted according to their understanding of communal needs and often did so autonomously from men. Cherokee women were actively involved in crisis decision-making long before the remarkable Nan-ye-hi (Nancy Ward) became the first Cherokee woman to offer a public address at a formal conference with colonials, in this case Virginia and North Carolina officials, during peace negotiations in 1781. She did so again four years later, appealing to congressional commissioners: "I am fond of hearing that there is a peace, and I hope that you have now taken us by the hand in real friendship. . . . I look on you and the red people as my children. . . . I am old, but I hope to yet bear children, who will grow up and people our nation, as we are now to be under the protection of Congress, and shall have no more disturbance."[25] Tragically, there was no true peace, and congressional protection proved a phantom when it came to upholding Native rights.

10   *Introduction*

Nan-ye-hi became known to white Americans of her era as "Nancy Ward" through her marriage to trader Bryant Ward, who lived with her only a few years. Before becoming a "beloved woman" advocating peace, Nan-ye-hi was a "war woman" honored for her bravery in fighting the Creeks in the early 1750s after seeing her Cherokee husband, her first spouse, killed in battle. Living into the 1820s, Nan-ye-hi took part in great changes in Cherokee life during her later years.[26] This was an era in which the Cherokees formed their own National Council and subsequently developed a constitution written both in English and in their own language through Sequoyah's genius in creating a syllabary for his people's native tongue. There was now a Cherokee nation with a central government, something virtually unthinkable just a generation before. A Cherokee elite, composed largely of men with some white ancestry, came to the forefront in diplomacy. Wealthy Cherokees commonly owned enslaved Blacks even if the great majority of the nation did not. Gradations in wealth and status in Cherokee society arose that were foreign to tradition. By 1820, a substantial minority of Cherokees, influenced by U.S. inducements and pressures, had migrated west of the Mississippi. And yet the idea of Cherokee peoplehood, transcending government and even a single national home, endured through unremitting convulsion and turmoil.[27] It is this phenomenon that *The Cherokees: In War and at Peace* identifies and traces from the late 1600s to the 1830s. The book is undertaken in an open-ended quest for knowledge and understanding, and with a fitting measure of humility.

Introduction

I

Cherokees in Their Homeland and Beyond

1670–1730

1

Cherokee Culture and Lifeways

The Cherokees were among many Native American peoples who attached a primal significance to their own humanity. They were Ani-Yunwiya, "the people" or "the real people." *Cherokee* may not have been their original term for themselves. According to some scholars, English colonists picked up "Cherokee" from Creek Indians living south of the Appalachians. In the Creek (Muscogee) language, *chilokee* refers to "people of a different speech." The Cherokee equivalent is *Tsalagi*, the national name of today's Cherokees in the Eastern United States, Oklahoma, and elsewhere. *Ani-Tsalagi* are the Cherokee people.[1]

The enigmatic origins of "Cherokee" are more than a curiosity. It speaks to Indigenous histories not easily recoverable from the precolonial past and the unpredictable circulation of tribal names, which proliferated once Europeans appeared on the scene. One of the earliest English references to "Cherokee" dates to 1674, when Dr. Henry Woodward, an enterprising trader venturing from Virginia to newly founded Carolina, wrote of the "Chorakae Indians" living northwest of the Savannah River's headwaters. In an old and since-defunct Cherokee dialect, *Tsaragi* (i.e., Cherokee) was pronounced with a rolling "r" instead of a near "l" as a middle consonant. British colonials had difficulty in distinguishing between these sounds, quite foreign to English. In brief, *Tsaragi* and *Tsalagi* made their way into English as *Cherokee.*[2]

The Cherokees were among the most populous Native peoples in southeastern North America at the beginning of the eighteenth century. Their towns, which numbered approximately sixty-five, had some 16,000 to 20,000 persons. Cherokee towns and fields hugged river valleys and streams below hillsides and mountains. The Cherokees were too practical to place their villages on steep heights. They made use of the earth's bounty in various forms. Women took responsibility for cultivating the soil and tending corn, peas, beans, squash, and other food crops that nourished communities. They were also gatherers of nuts, berries, and grasses and tenders of mulberry and plum trees in and about villages. This was both "a mothered" landscape and a "forest community," as one astute historian has written. Men ranged far beyond towns in their role as hunters and warriors. The division of labor by gender was a rule of life, if not ironclad. Men helped in clearing ground and planting crops, just as women went beyond the village to be of service to hunters or warriors.[3]

A Sense of Place

Cherokees lived in a vast Appalachian homeland from the Blue Ridge Mountains' eastern foothills in today's South Carolina to the Cumberland Plateau in mid-Tennessee. Historical geographer Donald Edward Davis writes that the Cherokee "cultural hearth" of the early 1700s covered approximately 40,000 square miles. This figure is astounding; today's Ohio is of similar breadth. But there is no exact measure of early eighteenth-century Cherokee territory. If outlying hunting grounds are brought into view, Cherokee country extended "from the mountains of northern Georgia to southwestern Virginia and from western North Carolina to central Tennessee, an area encompassing more than 70,000 square miles."[4] The region abounded in oak, hickory, chestnut, and hemlock along with firs and spruce at higher elevations. Some old-growth forests still tower in the heart of old Cherokee country. Caves are embedded in craggy limestone ridges and hillsides. Waterfalls plunge from the Blue Ridge's steep escarpment to the piedmont below. The eighteenth-century Cherokee environment was wilder than today. Bison, bear, and wolves were plentiful besides deer and other creatures. With the damming of rivers during the twentieth century, the sites of many Indigenous towns of the colonial era lie under water. This is true of Tanasee—a village on the Little Tennessee River—a place that lives through Cherokee memory and the name of an American state.[5]

The Cherokees took their identity from their immediate landscape and the region in which their villages were situated. Issues of war, trade,

Site of Tanasee. © *David Narrett*.

and sustenance played out in particular settings. British traders who lived in the southern Appalachians usually identified four to five major Cherokee regions by the mid-1700s. Cherokees themselves distinguished between geographic areas in their country. Language expressed this fact. Cherokee speech of the eighteenth century had eastern, middle, and western dialects and even sub-dialects in particular locales.[6]

Cherokees commonly relocated from one village to another or abandoned certain sites in favor of new ones long before their first contact with the English in the mid- to late 1600s. Group migration expressed deliberate choices about the circumstances best calculated to sustain community. Cherokees built and rebuilt connections to place and tradition. For example, the village of Kituwah by the Tuckasegee River retained its "beloved" status as a "mother" or ancestral town well after it fell sharply in population. Many Cherokees still refer to themselves today as *Ani-Kituwagi*—"the people of Kituwah." Cherokee "mother" towns, venerated as "ancient," stood in several regions, befitting a people who viewed hearth communities as giving life and sacredness to places across the land.[7]

Cherokee Culture and Lifeways

Kituwah's status reminds us of Neal Salisbury's extrapolation of the Indians' "Old World," which was adaptive and innovative over millennia. The Indian peoples that resided in certain locales when the Spanish, French, Dutch, and English first arrived in the "New World" were not necessarily those who had lived in those same locales from time immemorial. Some Indigenous groups were rooted in particular areas over centuries and others for far briefer periods. Their history was marked by similar forces that have shaped the human past in a global sense—war, trade, migration, cultural evolution, intercultural borrowings, and ethnic intermixture.[8]

English understandings of Cherokee geography were initially simple, distinguishing between Lower, Middle, and Upper Towns as colonial observers moved northwest from South Carolina. From this perspective, the most striking distinction was between the "Lower Towns" and the "Upper" or "Overhill Towns"—the latter literally seen by British colonials as "over the hills"—the Appalachians. The Lower Towns were situated by the Savannah River's headwaters that fan across today's far northwestern South Carolina and neighboring Georgia. These communities stood below the eastern face of the Blue Ridge Mountains, whose daunting summits rise above 6,000 feet in height. The Savannah River's western tributaries race from high ground in the Blue Ridge and slow as they descend from the piedmont to the coastal plain and finally the Atlantic. Upper Cherokee Towns lay in a quite different watershed, west of the "Great Smokies" with their misty and cloud-shrouded sky tops. "Overhill" villages clustered along the Tellico and Little Tennessee Rivers that flow north into the great Tennessee River whose winding westerly course finds an outlet in the Ohio River close by the Mississippi. Regional geography had a major impact on Cherokee relations with outsiders. The Lower Towns' southeasterly position meant that they were the first to encounter English South Carolina's expansive settlements by the late 1740s. The Overhill communities had a far-ranging view of French and Indian maneuvers in the continental interior.[9]

The Cherokee "Middle Towns" were perched below the Great Smoky Mountains' southern rim within present-day North Carolina. The "Valley Towns" lay south of the Unicoi Mountains—a rugged and stunningly beautiful portion of the Appalachian Highlands. (*Unicoi* is derived from the Cherokee word *unega* or "white.") The Valley Towns are nestled by the gentler portions of the Hiwassee River and its tributaries, whose waters plunge from mountainous terrain to a fairly level landscape before racing ahead again. One far eastern portion of Cherokee territory was dubbed "the Out Towns" in British parlance. Of course, the Native inhabitants of these communities, hugging the Tuckasegee River in the Great Smokies, regarded themselves as living at the center of things and not in a remote area, as the colonials had it. Hilly and steep terrain intersected Cherokee regions, making it difficult for far-flung towns to unite against enemies. These barriers were not insurmountable, however. The Cherokees used numerous pathways, streambeds, and mountain passes to maintain connections with one another.[10]

Trader James Adair, who dwelt among Southern Indian peoples for nearly three decades during the mid-1700s, wrote that the Cherokees were "strongly attached to rivers," which they used not only for ritual purification but also for "the services of common life, such as fishing, fowling, and killing of deer, which come in the warm season, to eat the saltish marsh and grass." Naturalist William Bartram, who toured Cherokee country in 1776, delighted in the resplendent trees, flowering plants, and strawberries along the Keowee River in springtime. Tragically, Keowee Town (literally "Mulberry Grove Place") was no longer standing when Bartram came upon the scene. Largely abandoned during the British-Cherokee War of 1760–1761, the town was resettled toward the conflict's close only to see its residents flee once more as hostilities mounted between Cherokees and white Americans in 1775 and 1776.[11]

Many Cherokee purification rites required "going to the water"— dipping or washing in flowing streams. There are literally thousands of verb forms in Cherokee language for the English "to wash" or bathe. Cleanness as opposed to uncleanness was a fundamental spiritual distinction as was the difference between animals proper to be eaten and those considered taboo. The landscape spoke with deep meanings to those who understood and felt its force.[12]

Like other Native American groups, Cherokees had a spiritual sense of mountains, rivers, animal life, and much else from the earth below their feet to the sky above. Myth and legend were alive in the present. James Mooney, a renowned anthropologist of the late nineteenth and early twentieth centuries, identified scores of Cherokee place names suffused with mythic or historic meaning. *Datleyastai* on the Tuckasegee River literally means "where they fell down," referring to the stream's depressed bed where two *uktenas*—horned snake monsters—fought each other so furiously that they rose above the water and crashed down

Cherokee Culture and Lifeways

with sufficient force to carve a hole in the stony bottom. *Gakatiyi*—
"place of setting free"—is a spot on that same river where the Cherokees
are said to have released war prisoners.[13]

The Cherokees did not presume safety from living within mountainous terrain. In one of their creation myths, people beg the Great
Buzzard to flap its wings and flatten the land so that they and other
creatures may have more space to live. The Buzzard harkens not to
human voices, however, and instead flies away. Dangerous beings lurk in
the mountains—such as the cannibal monster dressed in stone who lusts
after hunters but weakens to helplessness at the sight of menstrual
women. Another menacing creature is Ustutli—a giant footed snake
that crosses ravines and rivers in pursuit of human prey. The hunter
must tread nimbly to escape Ustutli's grasp. He falls prey by running
fearfully up a summit; he saves himself by following mountainside
ridges the monster cannot reach.[14]

Cherokees shared a widespread Native belief that a people's safety
rested on a precarious cosmic balance between an underworld, a realm
of change and chaos below the earth's surface, and an upper world of
grandeur and order above the sky vault. Benign and hostile forces inhabit the middle earthly realm in which humans dwell along with animals, themselves spiritually potent beings if not so powerful as their
primordial ancestors. In one Cherokee myth, the earth slowly emerges
above watery depths after the little beetle dives into the lower sphere
to gather mud that forms an island for animals to inhabit before humans
appear on the land. Animals speak, bargain, and negotiate with one
another over the type of world they desire. Humans do not hold sway.
They learn from animals about the nature of things. The supernatural
is part of the here and now. Cherokees believed in mysterious spirit
people—the Nunnehi—who live in the highlands and may suddenly
appear as warriors coming to the aid of towns beset by foes. Turning
invisible at their pleasure, the Nunnehi have the power to devastate
an enemy with arrows that swirl about rocks to find their mark. These
occurrences were mythic precisely because they were unpredictable
and beyond human capacity to control.[15]

The Cherokee worldview connected nature and spirit, myth and
daily existence, ancestral creation with the present and future. Selu,
the first human mother, is a corn giver, while the primal father Kanati is
a hunter. Their one son and his companion "Wild Boy" are entranced by
Selu's power but fear her as a witch. Killing her at her own command,
they drag Selu's body in a circle, drawing the blood that fertilizes the

20   *Cherokees in Their Homeland and Beyond, 1670–1730*

earth from which corn grows. The Cherokees and many other Native American peoples held a belief in blood as life source. Theda Perdue writes that "the distinct ways in which Cherokees encountered human blood helped define them as women and men. Menstruation and childbirth, hunting and warfare deeply embedded a person in a category: these were the times when women were most female and men were most male." Blood was associated with life-giving fertility and also with danger. Menstruating women abstained from normal labors and secluded themselves in small huts lest their blood pollute others and endanger the community. Men fasted, purged themselves, and avoided sexual intercourse for days before going on a war party. On their return, they gave their spoils to a near kinswoman, joined in communal song and dance, and purified themselves.[16]

Sacred rituals were a critical social bond. A high point of the year was the Green Corn Ceremony—a communal festival of four days whose elaborate rites preserved harmony between humankind and the cosmos. Fittingly, hunters provided a buck's tongue for the festival while women and their households offered corn, beans, and fruits. In Cherokee country, the ceremony occurred in late July or early August—just as the new harvest ripened. Similar seasonal observances were practiced by numerous Native American societies whose rich ceremonial life, suffused with music and dance, went hand in hand with respect for diplomatic protocol.[17] Joy, jest, or what might be called serious play had a place in many Cherokee rituals, while others had a predominantly solemn or somber tone.

As a peace emissary to the Cherokees in 1762, Lt. Henry Timberlake of Virginia was welcomed to the town of Settico by headman Cheulah (Fox), who led a procession of 300 to 400 Cherokee men, "ten or twelve of which were entirely naked, except a piece of cloth about their middle." Six of this group were fully body-painted and had "eagle tails in their hands, which they shook and flourished as they advanced," all the while dancing and singing "in concert" with beating drums. Cheulah, himself "painted blood-red, except his face, which was half black," held a sword of war in his right hand and an eagle tail in the left as a peace emblem. After a joint shout of the entire Cherokee assemblage, the chief waved the sword over Timberlake's head and then "struck it into the ground" just a few inches from the lieutenant's left foot. Cheulah presented Timberlake with a string of beads and then held him by both arms and led him as a guest into the village townhouse where a fire was symbolically rekindled. Four male dancers appeared once more, this

Cherokee Culture and Lifeways

time with bodies painted "milk-white" to signify peace. Though the lieutenant understood little of the eagle tail dance, which seemed to him "a violent exercise," he was glad to be treated in friendly fashion. Timberlake was less comfortable when successively given 170 to 180 peace pipes to smoke, which, as he recalled, "made me so sick, that I could not stir for several hours." He nonetheless quite admired the beauty of the pipes, whose bowls were carved of red or black stone, "extremely pretty when polished," and with stems three feet in length and "finely adorned with porcupine quills, dyed feathers, deers hairs, and such like gaudy trifles."[18]

Timberlake was a curious observer of Indian country. He arrived at a charged time because of the just-concluded British-Cherokee War. Cheulah put a sword of English manufacture into the ground as he symbolically buried war and declared peace. One imagines that similar rites, if performed with a different war instrument, had been conducted for centuries.[19]

Peoplehood and Clan

By the early eighteenth century and certainly well before, Cherokee peoplehood was characterized by overlapping allegiances and obligations—felt most centrally to kin, clan, locality, and more loosely to what we might call the nation as a whole. In this era, Cherokee men, women, and children belonged to one of seven matrilineal clans—each of which had a place in every town in the nation. (Seven was a sacred number in Cherokee culture and cosmology.) By belief and custom, clan members were of common blood and descent. They shared traits associated with a particular totemic creature, natural force, or quality. The seven clans were wolf, deer, bird, long hair or "twister," wild potato, the color blue, and paint. (Some authors believe that "paint" meant "red paint," though this point remains unclear.) In no small part, Cherokee social ties reached beyond the local level because all clans were represented in each town. The clan system, as one scholar has aptly written, "linked the Cherokees not as a political state but as an ethnic nation of shared experience and common culture." Similar ways of conceiving social bonds permeated diverse Native American peoples. Among the Creeks, writes Charles Hudson, the clan "was the most important social entity to which a person belonged. . . . An alien had no rights, no legal security, unless he was adopted into a clan."[20] Few persons in Creek (Muscogee) society were more wretched than the individual who was disowned for a serious offense and therefore could not expect kinsmen to avenge his death. To the Creeks, writes Robbie Ethridge, this was "a horrifying thought," no less than soul-murder without release from suffering.[21]

The clan was an emblem of profound social affinity that paralleled the obligation of blood revenge. Cherokee men were known to show special courtesy and favor to fellow clansmen who came to their villages in travel. Unfortunately, European colonial observers wrote very little about southeastern Indian clanship. Its deeper meanings may be gleaned from Native folklore passed across generations. Considered to be of common blood, men and women within a single clan were forbidden to marry one another lest they be guilty of incest. It was not uncommon for young persons to wed an individual from a grandfather's clan. A grandfather was likely to be of a different lineage than a grandchild whose blood was believed to come solely from the mother and her maternal ancestors.[22]

Clan ties permeated Cherokee society on a town, regional, and still broader national level. In daily life, kinship had its deepest meaning in village settings or closely related communities within the same river valley or nearby ones. If we think of Cherokee blood relations, the bonds between sisters and brothers of the same mother were especially close. Boys were apt to rely on a maternal uncle, their immediate blood elder, as a foremost protector and guide. The ideal Cherokee man was one who acted judiciously and above all avoided face-to-face clashes within his social circle and was apt to withdraw physically, if not emotionally, to avoid aggressive encounters with others in the community. While young males were instructed in these attributes and learned them by example, they were not expected to realize at once the elder's steady demeanor. Disciplining the wayward was often a matter of teasing or chiding rather than harsh action, apart from heinous societal breaches such as incest or murder. In a tightly bound community, shaming did not have to be rigidly punitive to be effectual.[23]

Native American kinship systems were often an elaborate interweaving of age groups and genders in which relationships were understood fluidly and symbolically and not only on a literal plane. For example, a Cherokee referred to a mother's sister as "mother" in common parlance. The Indigenous capacity to respect duties and responsibilities among clan, kin, and community was an asset in diplomatic engagements with outside forces. Similar to other Native peoples, Cherokees customarily listened carefully to one another in councils, patiently

Cherokee Culture and Lifeways

awaiting turns to speak, and seldom interrupting those addressing the group. This traditional practice had the effect of avoiding slights and harmful speech that could rend the communal social fabric. What applied on the town level operated through clanship across far-flung regions. Cherokee deputies who met with British officials commonly took one night's time before responding to an initial proposition. This pause in negotiation allowed for consultation and consensus when a headman spoke for a delegation. While Cherokee diplomacy evolved over time, it had strong customary foundations.[24]

Non-State Societies

Cherokee myth reflects a worldview that was fundamentally antagonistic to imposed authority from a superior social order. Well into the nineteenth century, Cherokees recounted the legend of the Ani-Kutani, a hereditary priestly caste that lorded over ordinary people and seized a beautiful woman from her young husband for their own pleasure. By one version of the story, the aggrieved man led a revolt against the Ani-Kutani in which the haughty sect was wholly destroyed. Many Cherokee myths or legends speak of "animal or human protagonists" that, in anthropologist Raymond Fogelson's words, "set themselves above their fellows through arrogance . . . and then are brought down through retributive reaction."[25]

The legend of the Ani-Kutani rings true metaphorically. Cherokee society was not a simple unity when the English came upon the southern Appalachians in the late seventeenth and early eighteenth centuries. No single paramount chief existed for the Cherokees at that time, though some headmen had considerably more prestige and influence than others. Authority was diffuse rather than centralized, and it remained that way for much of the 1700s.[26]

Similar to other Indigenous societies in southeastern North America, Cherokee towns had "white" and "red" social orders, respectively symbolizing peace and war. Distinctions between the two orders were not hard and fast. For example, head warriors had significant civil obligations beyond their leadership in war. As men aged, their role commonly shifted from a "red" stance, characterized by aggressiveness, to a "white" one associated with wisdom and experience. The "white" order was generally headed by an *uku* (priest-chief) who was believed to possess special access to the spirit world and whose incantations proverbially had the power to heal or kill. Nutsawi, a Cherokee man of the early 1800s, relayed that an uku traditionally took an eight- or nine-year-old boy to a secluded mountainous place and initiated him in the mysteries attached to his sacred office. The priest-chief was aided by councilors, ideally composed of a shaman and seven men representing each of the seven clans. The holding of councils of local, regional, and occasionally of still greater breadth was an essential feature of Cherokee life and common to Native American societies where consultation was all-important to consensual decision-making.[27]

Every Cherokee town of any size had a council house that was a political, social, and religious ceremonial center. Built atop earthen mounds, these structures were part of the southern Appalachian Indigenous landscape by the early 1600s and possibly well before then. On his visit to Cherokee country in 1762, Henry Timberlake described one council house as "raised with wood, and covered over with earth" and resembling "a sugar loaf," with a circular floor and pitched roof. With a narrow door and tiers for seating around the inner wall, the council house had sufficient size for as many as five hundred persons—a typical population of a large village. While Timberlake viewed the townhouse as "extremely dark" inside, he observed the glow of a fire kept at the center of the dirt floor. In each town, the uku had the duty of preserving the sacred fire. Sharing a central hearth was a foundation of Cherokee community—and vital to many other Native peoples. A Cherokee site of the late 1600s shows graves placed below and about the townhouse, signifying connections between the living and the dead.[28]

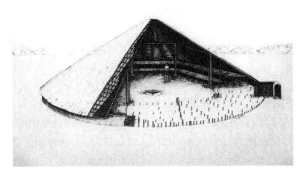

Drawing of a Cherokee council or townhouse. *Frank M. McClung Museum, Volunteer Voices, University of Tennessee, Knoxville.*

Cherokee Culture and Lifeways

Pragmatic and communally oriented, Cherokees often had open and rectangularly framed summer town structures for gatherings in the warm season besides the council house where the sacred fire was kept. Households, too, often had summer and winter dwellings. Timberlake lodged at the winter "hot-house" of priest-chief Kanagatucko while at the principal town of Chota. The hut's intense heat and smoky air induced Timberlake, nearly "suffocated," to throw off his blanket. While Cherokees had a sense of owning personal ornaments and clothing, they regarded land as serving the needs of the whole. Women had a role in preserving part of the corn crop for communal feasts and needs.[29]

When Cherokees met in town councils, women had the right to speak as well as men. This was not a universal practice among Native peoples. For example, Muscogee women were not allowed to enter the town plaza or rotunda when men were meeting in council. In some Cherokee town meetings, the entire community was present. In others, which Timberlake observed, "chiefs" or "headmen" were the foremost participants as well as "war women" whom he described as "powerful in the council." A war woman was one who distinguished herself by some extraordinary action when fighting an enemy or assisting warriors in battle. While war women might be few at any single time, their presence attests to the Cherokee capacity to transcend strict gender roles for the communal good. Cherokees honored wise, older women as "beloved"—the same title of respect afforded male elders.[30]

Cherokee women's role in diplomacy was more subtle than that of men since it was largely exercised in town councils and through social networking rather than in formal negotiations with colonials or consultations with other Indigenous people. Women advised warriors and "beloved men" on negotiation with their people's allies and enemies. Cherokee women not infrequently urged men to avoid hostilities in unfavorable circumstances or to secure a truce when warfare become overly damaging. In this sense, female sagacity was critical in negotiating the precarious ground between the red and white spheres of war and peace. As in other Native societies, Cherokee women called on male kin to avenge the slain, but they also wielded an undoubted influence to curtail bloodshed that ravaged their communities.[31]

Women anchored Cherokee households. A young man left his mother's house to marry and reside in his wife's household, though without becoming part of her clan and lineage. English colonials had difficulty understanding this facet of Cherokee life. Trader Alexander Longe once asked a Cherokee priest-chief why a man and his wife were *not* considered to be of "one flesh" or "akin" to one another. The priest found the idea incomprehensible. If he were "one flesh" with his wife, his situation would be no different than if he had breached the incest taboo by marrying his own mother or sister—a woman of his own flesh and blood.[32]

The Cherokee notion of correct human behavior centers on what one scholar has called "the harmony ideal" of "balance, order, and sharing" fundamental to a people's well-being. This principle should not be confused with individual "equality"—a concept eighteenth-century Cherokees would have found difficult to comprehend given their ethos based on gender and age-specific roles and responsibilities. Males commonly spoke of themselves as acting as "men" or "warriors" and distinctly not as "women." For a man to be called a "woman" or an "old woman," as we shall see, was considered a grave insult. In a male world of hunting and war-making, this fact should not surprise us. Cherokee men saw no contradiction in respecting women—beings with life-giving procreative power—while believing that male warriors were by nature the protectors of women and children.[33]

Cherokee women exercised considerable autonomy in choosing sexual partners before marriage so long as incest taboos were not violated. Marriage customs were quite simple. After consultation with kin, a young couple was free to marry, with the groom bringing firewood or venison to his female companion while she gave him corn or food to eat. Married persons freely separated from a spouse if their present mate was unsuitable or if they discovered a more agreeable companion. Custom constrained men somewhat more than women in this respect; the community frowned on males who jumped about too freely among female partners. The maintenance of group harmony and the avoidance of discord were, again, of profound social importance. Unlike the Choctaws, Chickasaws, and Creeks, the Cherokees had no obvious rule for punishing adultery and disciplining either men or women who committed that offense. Commenting on these various customs, James Adair avowed that Cherokees had a "petticoat-government" when it came to marriage and divorce.[34] From another view, a male hunter-warrior culture was balanced by female corn-givers and life-sustainers, who aided the community in war but were ready to warn against entering or perpetuating hostilities when conflict threatened ruin.

Cherokee women's broad sexual freedom was critical to interethnic relations, trade, and diplomacy. A young woman's autonomy allowed her to form liaisons with colonial traders who resided in Cherokee

Cherokee Culture and Lifeways

country. The Cherokees were by no means singular in this respect. Creek, Choctaw, and Chickasaw headmen often encouraged their marriageable female kin to form unions with colonial traders who supplied goods and munitions. A headman's influence and prestige came from his capacity to distribute resources to kin and fellow villagers rather than to amass wealth for himself alone.[35]

John Lawson, an astute English observer who toured the Carolina piedmont in the early 1700s, commented on colonial-Native marital ties:

> The [European] *Indian* Traders are those which travel and abide among the *Indians* for a long space of time; sometimes for a Year, two, or three. These men have commonly their *Indian* Wives, whereby they soon learn the *Indian* Tongue, keep a Friendship with the Savages; and, besides the Satisfaction of a She-Bed-Fellow, they find these *Indian* Girls very serviceable to them, on Account of dressing their Victuals, and instructing 'em in the Affairs and Customs of the Country.

Lawson's commonplace use of the term "savage" should not obscure his genuine respect for Native peoples, whom he remarked "are really better to us, than we are to them." Tragically, Lawson was slain by Indians during the Tuscarora War in 1711.[36]

Liaisons between colonial traders and Native women varied greatly in character. Relationships of brief duration were common but so, too, were long-lasting unions in which Cherokee women were clearly partners and not subordinates. Of great import, the children whom Native women had by colonial men were invariably raised as Cherokees. By the principle of matrilineal descent, such children were considered Native regardless of their "mixed" ancestry and despite their being condescendingly styled "half-breeds" by Anglo colonials. The "mixed-blood" occupied an increasingly important place in Cherokee kin networks during the mid- to late 1700s.[37]

Localism and regionalism were built into the Cherokee geopolitical and cultural landscape. The absence of a unitary command structure in war and peace may appear a weakness in retrospect, but the situation was not so simple. The diffusion of authority in towns and regions allowed individuals, kin groups, and communities to act flexibly, moving between war and peace, and avoiding severe disputes when taking diverse paths. It is no coincidence that the Cherokee movement toward a national government in the early 1800s, undertaken during an era of unrelenting stress, was fraught with social discord and occasional inter-necine violence.[38]

The Cherokees were not a simple "tribe" during the eighteenth century because of their multifaceted loyalties across an extensive homeland. One should not discount, however, Cherokee tribal affini-ties in which individuals experienced a profoundly emotive connected-ness to kin, clan, community, and the natural-supernatural environs in which they resided. One anthropologist has written of Indian "tribal repertoires," ways in which particular groups recognized their own customs as distinctive, if not wholly dissimilar from those of other Na-tive peoples.[39]

Cherokees dared not naively trust those outside the web of people-hood. Strangers of human form were presumed to be dangerous; they were not of the "real" people. This fact did not, however, consign out-siders to permanent enemy status. Strangers could be treated as if they were kin for trade and diplomatic purposes and even adopted and honored. Negotiation depended on such understandings. As one scholar explains, truces or peace accords among Native American peoples were based not on formal legal codes but rather on pledges "to think good thoughts of one another," and to forget past wrongs inflicted by the other party. The lessening of apprehension and fear was a foremost aim, even if trust was less than complete in reality.[40]

Cherokee men applied ritual understandings of brotherhood among themselves and in diplomacy with other peoples. By custom, young men who felt a special bond of friendship ceremonially exchanged garments piece by piece with one another. Connectedness was shown through gestures of affection. When Cherokee youths spiritually bonded, the boys were said to have realized "Ah-nah-tawh-hano-kah"—"peace is about to happen amongst them." The phrase also implies "one has turned around," suggesting a circle of wholeness.[41]

Hunting and War

Hunting and war were quintessential male pursuits among a myriad of North American Indian cultures. In Cherokee myth, the hunter's test of manhood is similar to that posed by war. In one epic tale, primordial Wild Boy and his companion-brother leave home in quest of game. The two youths follow their father Kanati ("the Lucky Hunter") into a swamp and see how he fashions reeds to make arrows. The boys later survive by cagily slaying wolves and withstanding a panther. They then

Cherokee Culture and Lifeways

shout, "We are men!" Their greatest ordeal comes when they are cornered by "Roasters" or "cannibals"—members of a hideous enemy tribe. The Roasters seem to be fully in command. Wild Boy is seized and thrown into a boiling pot. Instead of being frightened, his brother puts more kindling into the fire. Just when the cannibals lift the pot for their feast, they are struck dead by lightning. When father Kanati again sees the boys, he is much surprised. The youths exclaim, "Yes, we never give up. We are great men!"[42]

The danger in the hunt comes not only from an unpredictable animal world but through confrontations with enemies met on the journey. Manhood is not simple triumph; it requires self-control, the capacity to endure pain and to defy the enemy to the end. There is a stark separation from the female world when Wild Boy and his brother slay corn-giving mother Selu and sprinkle her blood on the earth. The youths repeatedly go out from the village and return, epitomizing what men do in the course of hunting and warring. Life comes full circle when Wild Boy and brother eventually come to the world's end and are welcomed by Kanati and Selu before heading, too, toward the darkening land.[43]

If hunting and war depended on similar skills, they differed in certain fundamental ways. Deer were respected creatures that helped to feed and clothe people; they were not akin to enemy warriors. In Cherokee belief, there was a mythic "Little Deer," chief to all its kind and invisible to all but the most experienced and knowledgeable hunters. When any deer was slain in the hunt, Little Deer overlooked the killing site and saw whether the hunter propitiated the fallen animal and its spirit. If he failed to do so, the Deer spirit tracked and tormented the hunter with crippling rheumatic pain. Southeastern Native peoples generally cooked venison and other game thoroughly so as to draw out the blood before eating. Blood was an animate force, essential but dangerous, not unlike the hunt and war.[44]

The propitiation of the spirit world was essential to life. Cherokees relied on shamans to use their special arts to forestall a bad dream's power. Men aired incantations and songs before going on a hunt or leaving town with a war party. Both hunting and war partook of the Sacred Fire and its power. The night before a hunt, a man might take ashes from the council fire and rub it on his chest as a good omen. By Cherokee tradition, warriors did not go to war before the priest-chief gave them a small red clay pot whose flame was kindled from the town's sacred fire. Keeping the pot's embers alight was believed essential for warriors to defeat the enemy. Besides the fired pot, one shaman or his helper carried a divining stone wrapped in seven deerskins. Warriors watched for portents of victory or defeat.[45]

While certain war rites had a distinct Cherokee character, others were more widely shared among American Indian peoples. Warriors drew strength from denizens of the animal world. In Cherokee war parties, the Raven was thought of as a Great Warrior aided by Owl and Wolf on his flanks and Fox at the rear. Fighters wore skins of these creatures and even imitated their sounds to communicate with one another. Approaching an enemy encampment, warriors not uncommonly stripped, going nearly naked even in the coldest weather, before yelling the shrill war cry and attacking the foe. On returning to their village after successful combat, warriors hallooed and whooped to announce their arrival. The entire town celebrated if the men brought in enemy scalps as war trophies—physical and spirit-infused emblems of the vanquished. Once taken at killing sites, scalps were handled with great care. Observing this practice firsthand, James Adair described how southeastern Indian warriors tied a scalp on a pole "with bark or deer's sinews," and secured it in "a small hoop to preserve it from putrefaction." Scalps were valued and preserved as evidence of bravery and triumph."[46]

Young Cherokee men were trained for war partly through sport and ritual—overlapping arenas. Prior to a ceremonial ball game, youths observed dietary restrictions and held off from touching a woman for at least seven days. Men and women danced in a common area (but as part of separate groups) the night before a match. As competition approached the next day, conjurors of rival towns readied their players by chanting and casting spells on opponents. Still more ritual preliminaries followed. Priest-chiefs employed sharp stones to scrape the youths' bodies until blood appeared on chests, limbs, and backs. Players washed their wounds before beginning the game, in which each side used sticks to carry and shoot a ball toward goals marked by posts with emblems. While pledged to rules, contestants battled roughly and hit each other hard enough that injuries were commonplace. Native groups in much of North America played variants of the ball game that tested the hardiness of boys and young men.[47]

Male youths in Native societies were customarily honored with a new name or title after proving their mettle in war. For example, the Chickasaws extolled the very brave; a warrior who slew a formidable foe won acknowledgment as *Minggáshtàbe*—"One Who Killed a Very

Cherokee Culture and Lifeways   31

Great Chieftain." The Muscogees (Creek Indians) ranked warriors' prowess not only by scalps taken but also by swiftness, stealth, and "a certain recklessness," in the words of one historian. Native peoples dispensed with euphemism when it came to war. Cherokees called a great warrior *Outacite*—"Mankiller" in the English rendering. The ideal warrior had a deep sense of communal obligation and responsibility. Without formal command, he sprang into action when impelled by kin, fellow warriors, and his own courage.[48]

Significantly, Cherokee head warriors assumed a more direct and substantial role than priest-chiefs in negotiations with the English, French, and Spanish for the greater part of the eighteenth century. Warrior-diplomats were commonplace in Native American societies, which undercuts stereotypes about wholly warlike "Indians" that persist in popular culture to the present day. We should also note a common life course in which youthful warriors rose to prominence through martial prowess before becoming beloved men and town counselors in their later years. We see an innovative adaption of this tradition in 1795 when Cherokee men deliberated in a national council on a proposition by the United States to build a trading post and garrison by the Tennessee River. The chiefs met in two groups—one each of "Beloved Men" and "Warriors" before giving a joint answer to the federal agent.[49]

Cherokee head warriors came to the fore through local recognition and respect. Besides the title *Outacite*, another common honorific for a head warrior was *Askiyvgvsta*, or "skiagusta" in English transliteration. Skiagusta, wearing an eagle tail on his scalp, was accompanied by an attendant holding a red-painted pole with a similarly dyed deerskin. The assemblage also included a chief speaker (*Skalioski*), who by tradition was not to eat a frog or an animal tongue, evidently lest his speech be impaired. In the 1820s, Cherokee men spoke of their forefathers who purified themselves, after shedding blood in war or coming into contact with the dead, by plunging twice daily in water over a seven-day period and not touching a woman for at least four days. One account put the ritual time of abstinence at twenty-four days. The number seven, itself sacred, figured in many ceremonies in war and peace, as did four, which represented the cardinal directions.[50]

There was no single Cherokee way of war because of the different levels of clashes between Indigenous foes. Young men who set out on small raids for revenge did not necessarily follow detailed war protocol that might be employed when a larger force was assembled for more sustained fighting. Moreover, distinct portions of the Cherokee nation might be concurrently in conflict with different adversaries. E. Wayne Lee contends that Native American warfare often fell between war and peace, in which periods of relative quiet were punctured by sudden outbursts—strike and counterstrike—before some measure of calm might be restored. War was a combustible force whose flames were not easily controlled, since blood feud waxed with the warrior's pursuit of status. Small-scale clashes could escalate into broader conflicts, though restraints on Native warfare also existed. War parties might be put off by bad omens. Perhaps most important, communities paid heed to war losses, which were keenly felt in towns with limited populations.[51]

The interdependent roles of Cherokee men and women were apparent in virtually all spheres of life, not least war. In the "scalp dance," women celebrated a battle victory by rhythmically circling a fire and extolling the warriors, who in turn boasted of valorous deeds and delivered scalps, war trophies, and prisoners to their closest female kin. It was common for women in southeastern tribes—and the Cherokees were no exception—to take the lead in lashing, beating, and torturing captives consigned to death. Prisoners were tied to poles and poked and singed with flaming sticks until they howled, only to be revived by caring female attendants before being tormented in still grosser fashion. The entire village viewed the spectacle, mocking and ridiculing the victim, who cursed his tormentors as long as he had the least ounce of strength. American Indian societies might inflict great cruelties on the captured warrior but still respect his spirit, especially if the victim exhibited hardiness during torture. Not all captives suffered a grisly fate. Child and female prisoners had a greater likelihood than enemy men of having their lives spared. Some captives were adopted as full members of Cherokee clans. Others remained as permanent outsiders—slaves entirely under the master's will, which extended to the power of life and death.[52]

While the custom of blood vengeance operated against foreign or external enemies, it was also invoked when a clan member's relative was slain, whether purposely or not, by a Cherokee belonging to another clan. By custom, the kin of the victimized clan could avenge the wrong either by taking a life or accepting a gift or token in satisfaction of their loss—a resolution somewhat like the old Anglo-Saxon custom of wergild. In Cherokee society, an accord between the slayer and the aggrieved party had the effect of "covering the bones of the dead," allowing the unquiet soul to rest in peace. Honor, integrity, and a sense

Cherokee Culture and Lifeways

of rightness were on the line for both sides in the negotiation, not unlike the situation when warring Indigenous nations considered a truce. As one might expect, bloodletting across ethnic boundaries tested peacemaking skills to a far greater extent than disputes between Cherokee clans or villages. In a world of recurrent though not continual violence, outsiders loomed as enemies absent cooperative understandings or alliance.[53]

From the Pre-Contact Era to the Colonial Period

It is a daunting challenge to understand how Native American ways of warfare carried over from the immediate "pre-contact era," the phase just prior to European exploration and colonization, into the period in which colonial records supply written documentation on events. The Cherokees' deep history relative to other Native peoples is particularly difficult to assess. Archaeologists and other scholars do not even agree on the era *when* the Cherokees developed as an ethnicity within the southern Appalachians. One important clue is evident from linguistic studies. Along with the Tuscaroras of North Carolina, the Cherokees are the only southeastern Native group of the colonial era whose speech is within the Iroquoian language family.[54] The Cherokees' forebears probably migrated southward from a region in the Iroquois heartland that once stretched from the St. Lawrence River to the southern shores of Lakes Ontario and Erie. About 1720, an elderly Cherokee priest-chief recounted to Alexander Longe that his people's ancestors had come from a far distant land. At a crisis point, the group passed over mountains of snow and ice to come closer to "the sun setting" and warmer weather. By this legend, the Cherokees were once a people speaking the same language but had lost that ability through internal conflict and group dispersion. The priest-chief's story suggests a southwesterly migration and also expresses the ideal of an irretrievable ethnic and linguistic unity.[55]

Hernando de Soto's expedition of 1539–1542 was the first European incursion deep into interior southeastern North America. The aspiring conquistador and his men cut a bloody path as they marched through Indigenous territories from the Gulf Coast to the Appalachians and west to the Mississippi Valley. While an abject failure, the expedition had horrific consequences for Native peoples struck by smallpox and other pathogens. Some of the hardest-hit Indian groups lived in areas within today's Mississippi, Alabama, the Carolinas, and Georgia. Subsequent Spanish expeditions of Tristán de Luna (1560) and Juan Pardo (1566–1568) may have intensified epidemics in areas through which de Soto passed.[56]

De Soto's impact on the Cherokees is not entirely clear. We learn more of the Cherokee presence from Pardo's expedition. His mission was to discover a land route from Santa Elena, an outpost along today's South Carolina coast, to Mexico's silver mines. Not surprisingly, the task proved impossible given the continent's breadth, which the Spaniards grossly underestimated. Pardo and his men still managed to cross the Blue Ridge and to enter Appalachian valleys. The Spanish came across several Cherokee towns, including one they spelled *Quetua*—most probably ancestral Kituwah.[57]

Roughly 130 years passed between de Soto's expedition and the English colonization of South Carolina in 1670. The interim period, as Charles Hudson has written, is a kind of historical "black hole" for much of southeastern North America apart from Spanish Florida. Archaeological findings indicate enormous changes in certain areas—the abandonment of towns and a slew of group migrations, most likely caused by disease, subsistence crises, political breakdown, and warfare.[58]

Southeastern Indigenous societies were prone to fissure even before the Spanish appeared on the scene. This was especially true of paramount chiefdoms belonging to "the Mississippian" cultural tradition, which originated in the middle to lower Mississippi Valley (circa 1000 CE) and later spread well eastward. Mississippian rulers of cities and towns exacted tribute from subordinate villages. Power flowed from the top down in hierarchically ranked systems subject to periodic crisis and breakdown, caused in part by tensions between centralized control and counterthrusts toward independence and local autonomy. Over time, most paramount chiefdoms devolved into small, localized tribes that might form consensual alliances with neighboring groups for mutual protection. This was a dynamic process of change and adaptation that was part of the Indigenous cultural arsenal long before de Soto entered the scene.[59]

Threatened and vulnerable groups had a strong tendency to relocate to places where they could find security. There were numerous variations on this theme in sixteenth- and seventeenth-century eastern North America where numerous Indigenous societies evolved through migration and the *coalescence* of communities or ethnic groups. "Coalescence" im-

Cherokee Culture and Lifeways

plies a melding of cultures in which distinct peoples aligned or merged with one another for subsistence and mutual aid against common foes.[60] Group migrations might cover either short or long distances. There was no single rule that dictated survival.

The reestablishment of order in the wake of dispersal was neither a simple nor a uniform process. Some groups adapted by developing political and social understandings suitable to their new environs. Steven Hahn contends that while the Creeks were heirs to the Mississippian tradition, they "de-emphasized the cult of the chief" and instead put great stock in "the harmony and balance of the group." Life centered on individual towns (*talwas*) tied to nearby communities with analogous clan structures. Political skill among affiliated groups was a precursor of Native diplomatic adeptness with European colonials. Indigenous customs of negotiation were as deeply rooted as ways of warfare.[61]

The name "Creek" was itself of British origin. It arose by happenstance during the early 1700s when English Carolinians used that name to identify a Native people living by the Ocmulgee River and its tributary creeks (in today's Georgia). In actuality, the Creeks had far deeper and more complex origins than the English perceived. While Muscogees were the predominant ethnolinguistic group among the Creeks, the latter included Hitchiti, Yuchi, Kosati speakers and other ethnicities. "Muscogee" is therefore an incomplete shorthand for describing the Native groups described as "Creek" by British colonials. The Alabamas—a distinct Native people living by the river that bears their name—formed close ties with nearby Creek towns during the first half of the eighteenth century.[62]

The linguistic map offers insight into dramatically altered Native environments. For example, there are many place names of Muskogean origin in eighteenth-century Cherokee territory. Yet few Muscogees lived there at the time, reflecting a substantial population shift in the not-too-distant past. Muscogees of the Appalachians appear to have migrated southward after being depleted by disease following Spanish incursions, which left them quite exposed to Indigenous foes. The Cherokees took advantage of this circumstance to become the dominant force in many hillside and mountain valleys. The Cherokees built some council houses on or near old mound sites, apparently to demonstrate their possession of scared places previously under the control of other Native groups.[63] Did Cherokee-Creek conflicts of the 1700s have roots in the era well before English traders arrived

36   *Cherokees in Their Homeland and Beyond, 1670–1730*

in their territories? That is quite likely from what is known and may be inferred.

Population Loss, Disease, and Warfare

Native peoples lacked immunity to smallpox, measles, influenza, and other diseases Europeans unknowingly carried to the Americas. The results were most catastrophic in "virgin soil epidemics" in which regional populations were initially infected, creating dangerous conditions for themselves and for those who came into contact with them. Epidemics spread from hand to hand or mouth to mouth into regions in which no Europeans had yet set foot. Pigs as well as humans were vectors of disease.[64] Successive generations were susceptible to epidemics. Within a half century (1610–1650), the Five Nations of the Iroquois League were reduced from above twenty thousand persons to less than half that number. Significantly, the League reached the apex of its military strength during the mid-seventeenth century. The impetus came from the desire for war honors, control of the beaver trade, and the urge to gain captives to replace the dead among their own ranks.[65]

The Cherokees certainly suffered substantial population loss, which can be estimated for the eighteenth century. While there were some 16,000 to 20,000 Cherokees around the year 1700, there were only about 9,000 by the mid-1750s. Their towns, which formerly numbered sixty to seventy, were reduced to no more than forty to forty-five by the latter point. Disease was no doubt the major cause of decline, though warfare with other Native groups was a significant contributing factor. So, too, was the susceptibility of Cherokee men to illness and death from increased dependency on colonial rum. A diminished population weighed heavily on the Cherokees, augmenting perils in both diplomacy and warfare.[66]

Cherokee population decline has to be measured relative to other Native groups, some of which suffered to an even greater extent through European entry, the ravages of smallpox and other diseases, and warfare. Many small tribes in coastal and piedmont zones from Virginia to South Carolina were reduced to tiny numbers from the 1660s through 1710s. A pall of death hovered about the inland slave trade in which Indian men bartered captured tribal enemies to colonials.[67]

Cherokee Culture and Lifeways

37

The impact of contagious disease cannot be fathomed solely by statistics. Native women's roles as childbearers and horticulturalists weakened as lives were broken. The deaths of tribal leaders damaged the transmission of tradition, knowledge, and power from one generation to the next. Certain epidemics victimized the elderly and children in disproportionate ways that tore at the social fabric. Patricia Galloway has astutely written, "As the death of the old is the death of the past, so the death of the young is the death of the future." That Indigenous societies survived under altered and trying circumstances attests to human resilience and adaptability.[68]

The most numerous southern Indian peoples—the Creeks and the Choctaws—suffered significant population loss through disease but were abler than others to rebuild or at least hold their own by absorbing weak tribes that settled near them for security. In absolute terms, Creek and Choctaw numbers were small in comparison to eighteenth-century Eurasian or African population centers. The Creeks appear to have totaled about 10,000 persons in 1715 but increased to 13,000 by 1760. The Choctaw population was above 20,000 in the late seventeenth century, declined to perhaps 17,000 in 1715, and numbered above 13,000 in 1760.[69]

Native ways of life were transformed in the wake of European colonialism and its enormous shock on the Indigenous world. Here one calls to mind the triad of "guns, germs, and steel," in Jared Diamond's striking phrase. Dependency on European trade goods and gifts, not least guns and ammunition, became a fact of daily life. Rum and other liquors exacted a terrible toll on Indian men over generations. Even taking all this into account, many Indigenous societies remained viable and potent forces. Interior Indian peoples such as the Cherokees, Creeks, Choctaws, and Chickasaws faced little danger from white settlement on their lands for decades after colonial enclaves were founded in coastal or riverine zones. Early European colonies in southeastern North America were small in population and vulnerable for decades. The Spanish, French, and English all understood that they required Native alliances to defend themselves and to achieve the upper hand over European rivals. Moreover, British Carolina and French Louisiana were potential powder kegs because of their dependence on African slavery. Colonial officials quite deliberately fostered divisions between enslaved Africans and Indians whenever possible.[70]

Besides the enormous changes wrought by colonialism, the Cherokees confronted the rise of the Creeks as the most powerful Indian society in southeastern North America by the mid-eighteenth century. In a still broader sense, Cherokees felt the swirl of events from Canada and the Great Lakes to the Iroquois country of the Mohawk River and to Chickasaw and Choctaw lands where rivers flow into the Mississippi or Gulf of Mexico. This was a world in which Native men engaged in warfare across scores and hundreds of miles. Mountains provided only limited security because the Cherokees' adversaries knew waterways, valleys, and passes that were routes of attack. Colonialism heightened the deadliness of intertribal conflicts, though it did not alone dictate the choices Native peoples made about the pursuit of war and peace.

Cherokee Culture and Lifeways

2

South Carolina and
the Native Southeast

Violent upheavals were part of Native America long before an entire hemisphere came to bear the name of an Italian explorer. What is astonishing about the early colonial era is how Indigenous conflicts intensified in far-flung continental regions where Europeans might be few in number but had extensive influence—especially by the traffic in guns, gunpowder, and lead. To be sure, Native peoples valued European goods beyond munitions. By offering furs and deerskins to colonial traders, they acquired woolen and cotton blankets, brass cooking pots, iron hatchets, ornamental glass beads, and much else besides liquor. Indian nations with a leg up in trade had advantages over less resourceful rivals.[1]

Indigenous economies were noncapitalist, oriented toward the accumulation of goods rather than individual monetary gain and the use of earnings to generate more profit. Economic competition still heated up in Indian societies. Headmen who had a trading edge gained prestige by distributing goods among their people. Redistribution brought honor to the giver and bolstered communal strength. It is no wonder that Native leaders in eastern North America frequently welcomed colonial traders to their villages and encouraged the visitors to wed their young female kin.[2]

Trade was a matter of survival when muskets and munitions were on the line. Any Indigenous group lacking such firepower was at risk of being decimated by tribal foes. The rapidity with which many Native peoples became skilled in the use of muskets is remarkable. Loading and firing European flintlocks were hardly simple tasks. From Iroquois to Creek country and far west to the Comanches, Native men came to prefer the use of the gun over bow and arrow for sheer military prowess. The noise and smoke produced by "thundersticks"—as one Native group called muskets—added a shock value to their lethal force. David Silverman aptly describes destructive "arms races" spreading throughout the continent. As he writes, "the gun never displaced the bow and arrow, hatchet, or club, but it did become an essential part of the Indian arsenal." Native reliance on musketry heightened dependence on colonials for the repair of old weapons and new supplies of guns, gunpowder, flints, and lead.[3]

The gun trade in southeastern North American during the late seventeenth and early eighteenth centuries went hand in hand with the traffic in Indian slaves. Warriors of various nations seized Indigenous enemies for the purpose of selling the prisoners to colonials—and reaping guns and goods in the process. British traders had a foremost place in the Indian slave trade, and nowhere more so than in early South Carolina, which surpassed Virginia's head start in this gruesome business. Alan Gallay estimates that at least twenty-four thousand southern Indians, and perhaps twice that number, were sold in the British colonial slave trade from 1670 to 1715. Most of the captives were transported from Charles Town (today's Charleston) to English colonies from the Caribbean to New England.[4]

The colonial marketing of slave captives was impelled by voracious profiteering and the pervasive view of Indians as "savages," beings scarcely worthy of respect unless they belonged to useful and powerful ethnicities. British Carolinians had the habit of setting Native groups against one another and of ditching erstwhile Indian allies when the latter appeared troublesome and expendable. In the struggle for European guns and goods, Indian warriors' captive-taking veered from its traditional use in war to something far more deadly and massive in scope.[5] Colonial power was far from absolute, however. Native peoples often took to slaving warfare on their own terms. This was certainly true of the Creeks, Chickasaws, and Yamasees whose ties to Charles Town's traders solidified during the 1680s and 1690s. It took another twenty years for Carolinians to enter the mountainous Cherokee homeland on a regular basis. The Cherokees then proved willing participants in the hunt for captives and the goods reaped by their sale.

English Carolina dominated the southeastern Indian trade by 1710, though its power had a paradoxical weakness. British profiteering knew few restraints, triggering a backlash among Native peoples infuriated by spiraling debts to colonial traders. The Yamasee Indians are

South Carolina and the Native Southeast   41

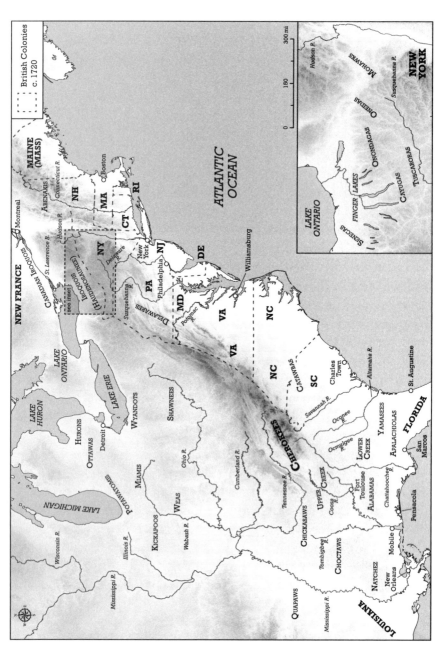

Eastern North America, ca. 1720

the most striking example. While in cahoots with English slave traffickers for over two decades, they finally recoiled from dependency and spearheaded a great Indian uprising in 1715 that threatened South Carolina's very existence. Some Cherokees made a fateful choice during that war to befriend the English and take on the potent Creeks in the process. By 1720, the Cherokees occupied a very different place in the continental scheme of things than had been the case just two decades earlier. In this new world of turmoil, the winds of change were of tornadic force, producing storms of furious intensity and duration.

The Emergence of South Carolina

Among all English North American colonies, South Carolina had the most geographically far-ranging impact on Indian peoples during its first half century of settlement. Scarcely beholden to imperial government, British Carolina settlers pursued individual pathways to wealth and power. Weak metropolitan oversight gave colonials broad latitude in fashioning relations with Native peoples, though nothing close to dictatorial power over populous and potent Indigenous groups.

South Carolina's origins date to the restoration of the monarchy under Charles II, many of whose high-ranking supporters bid for emoluments in an expansive empire. In 1663, eight nobles and gentlemen received the king's imprimatur to oversee colonization in newly proclaimed Carolina. By royal charter, these Lords Proprietors and their heirs obtained the right to possess and govern all North American lands between the 31st and 36th parallels from the Atlantic to the "South Sea"—the Pacific Ocean. Just three years later, the king expanded the grant, at least on paper, to the 29th parallel, thereby taking in much of Florida.[6] When Carolina was chartered, the English had only the dimmest conception of the continent's breadth or its Indigenous peoples. Governor William Berkeley of Virginia, an enthusiast for western exploration, imagined that an expedition setting out from Jamestown might reach the Pacific in only two weeks.[7]

While Carolina was conceived as a single colonial entity, the dispersal of settlers along its lengthy coastline led to new political arrangements. By the mid-1670s, North and South Carolina were already emerging as distinct jurisdictions, though it was not until 1712 that the Lords Proprietors appointed a separate governor for each region. Both Carolinas developed representative assemblies that vaunted high notions of their liberties and frequently vied with executive authority.[8]

South Carolina and the Native Southeast

South Carolina rapidly surpassed its northern neighbor as a center of Indian trade, diplomacy, and imperial strivings. Geography had much to do with the difference. Charles Town, nestled on a spit of land between the Ashley and Cooper Rivers, had the makings of an Atlantic seaport and provincial capital. North Carolina's shoreline was not so favorably situated since it juts sharply to the northeast above Cape Fear, placing the coast at considerable distance from the piedmont, let alone the faraway Blue Ridge. The Outer Banks' shifting sands and exposure to hurricanes were continual hazards. Coastal rivers were too short or shallow to offer navigable access to the interior.[9]

Carolina's Proprietors conducted affairs from London, which compromised their ability to control overseas events. They failed in their design to monopolize the inland deerskin trade and were powerless to curb practices that eviscerated their ideal of peaceful colonial-Native relations. Proprietary orders to restrict the Indian slave trade had gaping loopholes that unscrupulous men exploited at will. The Proprietors' influence was still felt in various ways. As advocates of population growth, they encouraged Scottish settlement and welcomed French Huguenots, who assumed a major place in Charles Town's Indian commerce. The Scottish presence made South Carolina a de facto *British* colony before Parliament's Act of Union of 1707, which integrated Scotland into what had hitherto been an English overseas empire. Adding to this diversity, by the early 1700s several Jews were living in South Carolina, and more would follow by the mid-1700s. In 1695, Governor John Archdale relied on an unnamed Sephardic Jew in Charles Town to act as interpreter in a conference with Spanish-speaking Indians.[10]

While critical of ignoble conduct toward Indians, the Proprietors had no similar objections to African slavery, which rose to the fore in South Carolina from its earliest years. Black laborers became a majority of the population in the colony's coastal area by about 1700, and 60 percent of the whole thirty years later. The human landscape changed in profoundly disruptive ways for coastal Indigenous groups such as the Sewees, who endured by diplomatic finesse—a tradeoff in which they gained colonial protection at the price of acknowledging English sovereignty and accepting reduced living space.[11]

South Carolina's growth was slow, confined almost entirely to the "low country," with its swampy, mosquito-breeding grounds that sent many colonials to early graves from malaria, yellow fever, and other ailments. Few English newcomers could imagine the coastal plain's breadth, which extends some 120 to 150 miles inland before giving way to the piedmont's undulating grasslands and forests. According to a census of 1708—taken nearly four decades after South Carolina was founded—the colony had 4,080 white inhabitants and 4,100 enslaved Blacks. About 1,400 Indian slaves, victims of the traffic in captives, lived in white households that year.[12]

Though small in population, South Carolina quickly acquired strategic weight as a frontier colony directly at odds with Spanish Florida. (Georgia would not be founded until 1733.) Regional competition heated up in the 1680s when Britons and Spaniards clashed over influence in bordering Native territories.[13] Imperial rivalry grew still more complex when France founded its first settlements along the Gulf Coast just before century's close. In 1699, the French established a precarious foothold by Biloxi Bay. The colonists, beset by disease and hardship, decamped to Mobile three years later. The tiny French enclave was the creation of Pierre Le Moyne, a native Canadian who carried the noble title sieur d'Iberville for his past exploits against the British.[14]

At Iberville's death in 1705, his younger brother, Jean-Baptiste Le Moyne, sieur de Bienville, took charge of governance, Indian diplomacy, and the struggle for survival. Mobile was a garrison that scarcely merited the name. In 1708, it had the grand total of seventy-seven colonists (largely Canadian by background) and 122 sailors and soldiers—nearly all of whom depended on food supplied by nearby Native groups. The settlement also had eighty Indian slaves—an astonishingly large number given the tiny French population. While an adroit diplomat, Bienville showed an iron fist when dealing with obstreperous Indians. In 1707, the French and their Native allies decimated the small Chitimacha tribe in response to the murder of a Catholic missionary. Bienville meanwhile wooed the powerful Choctaws as essential allies against the English.[15]

A Changing Continental Landscape

While initially on the margins of Carolina's interior Indian trade, Cherokees learned something of the English when a couple of Virginia explorers crossed the mountains in their neighborhood in 1673. Most importantly, the Cherokees absorbed lessons as they viewed the broader scene in which certain Native peoples rose in power while others fell in intertribal conflicts whose outcome hinged on access to European munitions and goods. To the north, formidable Iroquois war parties

South Carolina and the Native Southeast

devastated Indigenous nations of the Great Lakes, Ohio Valley, and the upper Mississippi from the mid- to late 1600s. In Richard White's words, the attacks left a "fragmentary, distorted world" that had to be rebuilt from "shattered pieces." The Cherokees knew, too, of weakened peoples who revived by migrating, incorporating with other tribes, and cultivating colonial trade in new environs.[16]

Indigenous adaptation in the wake of warfare often occurred out of colonial view. European records give little hint of the origins of the Yamasees, an amalgam of migrant and refugee groups that lived for some time among the Cherokees. While most Yamasees migrated to Florida around the 1670s, a small portion kept a foothold in Cherokee territory. Fifty years later, Cherokees still regarded the Yamasees as a type of kin whom they were loath to fight.[17]

Once in Florida, the Yamasees settled by Franciscan missions above St. Augustine before moving north and entering trade with South Carolina. From 1685 to 1710, Yamasee bands grew in power by attacking the missions, killing scores of Florida Indians, and seizing a still greater number for sale to British Carolinians. The Yamasees' dramatic turnabout defies simple explanation, though it was unquestionably motivated by disgust with proselytizing friars and a desire for enhanced trade. Well stocked with goods, Britons readily sold guns to Indian allies, while the Spanish were reluctant to provide muskets, not least out of concern that Native men might one day turn those weapons against colonial patrons.[18]

Indigenous decisions to invite colonial trade were a linchpin of exchange and diplomacy. After all, South Carolina adventurers could not have trekked far westward without Indian cooperation along the way. A key point came in 1685 when British traders were welcomed by the Muscogee towns of Coweta and Cussita by the Chattahoochee River— villages whose people desired to strengthen their hand against Apalachee Indian foes and their Spanish patrons. Madrid's regional officers did not tolerate this state of affairs. In 1686, Spanish soldiers and their Native allies attacked several Muscogee towns, uprooting the inhabitants and putting villages to the torch. The refugees migrated toward Carolina, deepened their English ties, and awaited opportunities for revenge. British colonials soon referred to the new communities as "Creeks"—a name that became an English commonplace over time.[19]

Fiercely competitive among themselves, South Carolina's traders relied on a host of Native peoples to learn the lay of the land and where best to ford rivers in dry summers and winter's rains. Muscogee villages by the Tallapoosa and Coosa Rivers entered British trade, as did the Chickasaws further west by the Tombigbee River's headwaters. Before the dawn of the 1700s, the Chickasaws added English arms to their arsenal to become the most audacious slave raiders of the Lower Mississippi Valley, Arkansas country, and Gulf Coastal plain. The typical Chickasaw war party attacked enemy villages with the aim of killing men and abducting women and children. These assaults met reprisals but nevertheless continued over years.[20]

The Cherokees learned the human price of letting down their guard against well-armed foes. In 1692, Savannah Indians ambushed a Cherokee town when the village's warriors were absent. The attackers killed several old men and carried off women and children as slaves for sale to English traders who marketed the captives in Charles Town. The Savannahs were themselves a branch of the Shawnees, a people compelled to disperse after being shattered by Iroquois attacks in the Ohio Valley. By the 1680s, Shawnees could be found within South Carolina's trading perimeter, in other environs such as the Susquehanna River, and as far west as Illinois. To say that the Native world of eastern North America was under great stress during this era would be an understatement.[21]

The Savannah attack on the Cherokees would probably be lost to history had it not come to the attention of colonials who reported the episode to Governor Philip Ludwell in Charles Town. While Ludwell was disturbed by anarchic slaving warfare, South Carolina's provincial assembly (the colonial legislature) saw no reason why Savannah allies should be discouraged from making war on Indian foes. The legislators' indifference was a matter of geopolitical calculation. The Savannahs occupied a strategic gateway for Carolina traders en route to the Creeks and Chickasaws. The Cherokees in their mountain homeland barely figured in Charles Town's compass.[22]

Native peoples were acutely sensitive to a changing human landscape. The Cherokees could not have been blind to the fact that the Muscogees, Yamasees, and others grew in power through their links with the English. This budding trend burst into full view once England came into war against Spain and France in 1702. Most Indian peoples hardly knew of the conflict across the ocean, but they certainly felt its effects. In Europe, nations fought in the War of the Spanish Succession (1702–1713), ignited by Louis XIV's drive to place his grandson on the throne in Madrid. English colonists called the conflict Queen Anne's War after their monarch.[23]

South Carolina and the Native Southeast

James Moore, one of Carolina's largest Indian slave traffickers, was in the governor's chair in Charles Town at the imperial war's outbreak. His first object was to capture St. Augustine, which Carolinians had coveted for years. In September 1702, Moore led a force of five hundred colonials to lay siege to St Augustine's fortress, the formidable Castillo de San Marcos. Much to his chagrin, the governor found "ye Castle much Stronger than it hath been represented to us." The English withdrew when a Spanish naval flotilla approached with reinforcements.[24]

Moore's campaign had Indian support, but not the kind that aided his objective. While 270 Yamasee warriors allied with the English, they fought quite independently, navigating Florida's waterways by canoe in their hunt for Indian slaves. Captain Thomas Nairne, who accompanied Yamasee fighters, marveled at the warriors who swam across a "Deep River," seized thirty-five captives, and killed numerous foes. The haul of Indian slaves in the fighting grew to several hundred—and Yamasee men gained a windfall for their cache by selling directly to English colonists and not bowing to South Carolina's government that ached for first purchase.[25] Reeling from the defeat in Florida, South Carolina soon resorted to new taxes, which included *import* duties on African slaves and an *export* duty on enslaved Indians. Black labor was in high demand; Indigenous captives were shipped out along with deerskins and furs.[26]

After the abortive St. Augustine campaign, South Carolina's budding imperialists counted on Indigenous allies as their predominant striking force. They had no other military option. Their province's white population was too small, and its enslaved Black population too great, for the colony to conduct a sizable offensive into the continental interior. These circumstances were the background to South Carolina's notorious campaign of 1703–1704 in which the prime object was the capture of Spanish-allied Indians above the Gulf Coast. No longer governor, Colonel Moore equipped fifty white volunteers at his own expense, headed southwest, and gained some 1,000 to 1,300 Muscogee, Yamasee, and other Native fighters for assault. While these warriors were auxiliaries from a colonial perspective, their own choice to join Moore should not be minimized. The invaders killed hundreds of Apalachees and carried off a great, if an unknown number of Indian slaves toward Charles Town. All was accomplished, Moore wrote, "without one penny Charge to the Public."[27]

The toll of war wore a different face in Florida than Carolina. As Muscogee warriors and Carolina men approached one Spanish mission, Father Juan de Parga summoned Apalachee Catholic converts to battle and marched alongside them, only to be killed with many of his charges. Even in defeat, Apalachees proclaimed their faith and cursed their captors. Colonel Moore stood aside while Muscogee warriors tied Apalachees to the stake, burning and mutilating as many as forty prisoners at one locale.[28]

When Moore headed back to Carolina, he marched with untold hundreds of Apalachee slaves. As a measure of English self-interest, three hundred Indian captives were granted freedom to live within South Carolina's trading orbit by the Savannah River.[29] Curiously, Moore complained that the long column of Indians on his return trek prevented him from riding into "the Cherokee Nations"—a region he had long supposed rich in mineral wealth. As early as 1690, he suffered a setback in his first visit to the "Appalatheean Mountains," where he had a tiff with Cherokee men who refused to guide him to a place where the Spanish had supposedly once mined. By Moore's account, which is unverifiable, the Cherokees claimed to have killed the Spaniards for fear the latter would, in time, make them slaves. Moore's visit may have sparked similar Cherokee fears of the English.[30]

Moore died in 1706 of an unnamed "distemper," probably yellow fever, just as English South Carolina seemed on the verge of dominating far inland territories through economic might and strategic Indian alliances. Appearances were deceiving. Most South Carolina landholders were immersed in daily tasks of estate-building and managing enslaved African labor. Only a small coterie of provincial imperialists, themselves prone to political infighting, aggressively aimed to push their colony's bounds to the Gulf Coast. Moreover, these men could count only so much on Indian nations that had their own agendas. Thomas Nairne, the veteran of Florida slaving warfare, learned this lesson in 1708 when he journeyed to Muscogee towns and on to Chickasaw country but failed to gain sufficient Native support for an intended assault on French Mobile. The powerful Choctaws pointedly rejected Nairne's overtures in favor of retaining their French ties.[31]

A native of Scotland, Nairne was a crucial figure in shaping South Carolina's imperial ambitions. Ruthless in war, he was a keen observer of Native customs despite his biases and the pride he took in the destruction of enemy "Barbarians." Paradoxically, Nairne regarded himself as

South Carolina and the Native Southeast

an upholder of law. As a magistrate, he arrested trader James Child in 1707 for arming Cherokee fighters who seized and enslaved 160 Indian foes, likely Creeks, who were themselves friends to South Carolina. The captives were sold to English colonials, much to Nairne's disgust. While no humanitarian, he believed South Carolina's affairs would descend into chaos if traders failed to distinguish between Indigenous friends and enemies. Cherokees must have seen the issue differently. They cared simply about procuring guns, no matter the individual colonial trader with whom they dealt.[32]

At Nairne's behest, South Carolina enacted its first substantive legislation regulating Indian trade in 1707. Significantly, the law prohibited colonials from selling "free" Indians into slavery but did not prohibit the capture and enslavement of Native foes at war with the province. The new regulatory regime, supervised by Indian Trade Commissioners, had limited efficacy. Colonial legislators banned liquor sales to Indians but their mandate was hardly enforced beyond Charles Town. Private profiteering outpaced government oversight, undermining South Carolina's Indian trade laws over decades.[33]

Nairne was a spirited fellow, unafraid to criticize South Carolina governor Nathaniel Johnson for taking his cut from the illicit sale of Indian slaves. Incensed, the governor struck back by jailing Nairne on a treason charge in 1708. In this duel of nerves, the savvy prisoner won out by slipping the hoosegow in a year's time, sailing to England, and putting his case to British worthies.[34] While still in prison, Nairne sketched a remarkable map of southeastern North America that he later refined and had published in London. His is the first English colonial map with a clear reference to the Cherokees, depicted as living in mountainous country above the Savannah River's headwaters. Indicating Native fighting strength on the map, Nairne listed the Cherokees at three thousand men or warriors—a roughly accurate estimate. The mapmaker's knowledge extended only so far, however, as he grossly underrated the pro-French Choctaws at 700 men when they actually embraced over five thousand fighters.[35]

Nairne initially dispatched his map to London along with a bold exegesis on American affairs to the Earl of Sunderland, the queen's secretary of state. In a bid for imperial backing, he advocated a new British colony above the Gulf Coast, which he envisioned as a base for forays against the Spanish realm. With keener insight, Nairne elaborated on the English need for a "Common defence against the French and their party [of Indians]" in eastern America. In his view, the Cherokees were natural allies in that struggle, though he described them as currently hamstrung, being "Miserably harassed" by northern Iroquois raiders. Nairne wished the governors of New York and Maryland to use their diplomatic influence to restrain the Five Nations of the Iroquois League, themselves English allies by treaty. Though his advice had little immediate impact, it anticipated British endeavors over decades to reduce intertribal hostilities that compromised imperial interests. The Cherokees would have their say in this diplomacy.[36]

Nairne imagined South Carolina as a bedrock of what he called the "English American Empire." His map was a futuristic outline, showing South Carolina extending from the Atlantic to the Gulf Coast and north to the Appalachians, of which he knew precious little. Eager to impress London, Nairne boasted to Sunderland that the "Chericke nation" is "now Entirely Subject to us." His braggadocio was far from true, but how could Sunderland know the situation in distant America? The Cherokees did not compose a single polity, nor were they altogether committed to the English. Returning to South Carolina in 1711, Nairne plunged again into the business of furthering a well-ordered Native trade. He could scarcely imagine the terror that would engulf South Carolina in just a few years when the Yamasees, former English allies, turned violently against the British.[37]

Cherokees and the Web of Violence

In the fall of 1711, Charles Town received news that the Tuscarora Indians were at war with North Carolina's expansive settlements. Tuscarora warrior bands, aided by nearby Native groups, struck hard at German and Swiss immigrant communities, and the entire colony was thrown into chaos.[38] South Carolina quickly decided on a military response once learning of the breakdown to the north. Charles Town employed its timeworn strategy, enlisting Native allies who hungered for captives and plunder by taking on the Tuscaroras. In an offensive of 1712, Colonel John Barnwell had 240 Yamasees as his stoutest fighters—"my brave Yamassees," as he called them. The next year, Colonel James Moore Jr., son of the late slave-dealing magnate, commanded a motley army of one hundred Carolina militiamen, strengthened immeasurably by 760 Native warriors, including many Cherokees. Prior to the climactic battle, the invaders' encampments on March 20, 1713, ringed the Tuscarora fort. The "Charike [Cherokee] Camp," as shown in a colonial sketch, alone had a strength of "310 Indians," with only two Carolina

South Carolina and the Native Southeast

captains and "10 White men." In a furious assault on the palisaded village, the English and their Native allies killed more than five hundred Tuscaroras and captured four hundred men, women, and children. Several hundred Tuscaroras who escaped the slaughter migrated far northward to settle among their Iroquois kin. Others relocated at short distances, achieving a measure of security by acknowledging subordination to North Carolina and Virginia authorities. No single strategy governed remnant Native groups in crisis. Some Tuscaroras and their tribal allies retained a precarious footing by sheltering in swamps, forested hideaways, and marginal lands where they stayed clear of whites.[39]

Cherokees, Yamasees, and other Indian victors sold their Tuscarora captives to the English for munitions and goods. Something more was at stake. Before the war, the Yamasees were reputed to be 100,000 deerskins in debt to South Carolina traders. In brief, Yamasee involvement in slaving warfare had become a ruthless necessity for an Indian people at once dependent on English trade and ensnared by it. Aware of Native dissatisfaction, South Carolina's Board of Indian Commissioners admonished colonial traders "to be kind and loving" to the Yamasees, and "not to abuse them by beating or any other Way oppressing them." These instructions were readily given, but scarcely enforced.[40]

Native dependency on colonial trade carried the seeds of violence in the early eighteenth-century Southeast. Some Cherokees felt they had little choice except to war for slaves to satisfy traders' demands and insure the flow of goods. A prime case occurred about 1713 when a group of Middle Town Cherokees ravaged the Yuchi Indian village of Chestowe at the behest of traders Alexander Longe and Eleazar Wigan, who supplied gunpowder and bullets for a devastating assault. Some Chestowe residents killed themselves rather than fall into the enemy's hands. Longe and Wigan obtained six Yuchi slaves—one woman and five children as a payoff.[41]

The Chestowe massacre was a flagrant breach of South Carolina law, as it had no government authorization and targeted a friendly tribe. The colony's Board of Indian Trade Commissioners questioned Longe and Wigan in Charles Town, and found them culpable, but the two roustabout traders suffered no discernible penalty. Both were soon back in Cherokee country where they were quite welcome. Longe subsequently wrote a sensitive and detailed account of Cherokee customs. Wigan was among the most important interpreters and couriers of his era between the Cherokees and Charles Town. Cherokees dubbed

52   *Cherokees in Their Homeland and Beyond, 1670–1730*

him "Old Rabbit" for his agility in negotiating mountain pathways well into his mature years.[42]

Two Cherokee men, called Cesar and Flint by the English, collaborated closely with Longe and Wigan in the Chestowe massacre. Both Cherokees were present when Longe and Wigan appeared before the Board of Indian Commissioners in Charles Town to account for their actions. Longe showed no remorse whatsoever, and talked of his having settled scores with Yuchis who had torn off his hair a few years before. Additional testimony, offered by several white traders, made clear that the Yuchis were resentful at Longe over his demand for debt payments. This train of events escalated to terrible bloodshed once Longe and Wigan procured Cherokee fighters for a price.[43]

Flint and Cesar lived in Euphasee, a Hiwassee Valley town that inclined toward the English because it was exposed to attack by "French Indians" to the west and north. Both men exhibited strong local loyalties, deliberately keeping their gains in slaving warfare close to home and not sharing their stash of munitions with Cherokees outside their region. The lines between freedom and slavery were permeable in this tumultuous era. Cesar was himself a victim of the Indian slave trade before he became a broker in that same business with Longe and Wigan. A shrewd individual, he learned some English while laboring for his white Carolina master, and then absconded in quest of freedom. Teaming with his friend Flint, both men traveled to Charles Town in 1713, and presented letters to the governor in which Alexander Longe, not yet in ill repute, attested to their good character. The upshot was that colonial officials confirmed Cesar's freedom. South Carolina dared not alienate the powerful Cherokees, who might be susceptible to French influence if their needs were not met. Cesar and Flint deliberately exploited this circumstance to advantage.[44]

The Yamasee War

South Carolina's government was not blind to the dangers of a loosely regulated Indian trade but failed to mitigate deep-seated intercultural clashes. Indian men bristled when their women were abused by traders whom they regarded as their guests and even as kin. The promiscuous dispensing of liquor became par for the course in violation of a South Carolina law prohibiting such sales. Colonial traders' habits of marking up prices and selling goods on credit were systemic ills. Indian deer kills in winter might be plentiful but somehow came up short when hunters

South Carolina and the Native Southeast

brought in their peltry to traders in the spring. Debt bred an explosive mix of humiliation and desperation. Natives hardly knew that traders operated under pressure from Charles Town merchants who equipped them on credit extended by London suppliers.[45]

The combustible elements of South Carolina-Indian trade burst into flames on Good Friday, April 15, 1715, when Yamasee warriors, living by the colony's southern coastal frontier, attacked nearby English settlements in full force. The uprising's sudden outbreak gave little hint of its deep causes. Yamasee fears of enslavement grew with colonial encroachments on Native land, staggering debt, a diminished Carolina market for the sale of Indian slaves, and the ravages of disease. There are ironies to the war's explosive beginnings. On the eve of conflict, commissioner Thomas Nairne strived to resolve Native grievances by negotiations at Pocotaligo, a leading Yamasee town. While chieftains received him and other Carolina officers politely on April 14, they were inwardly suspicious and dogged by loose rumors of English designs to kill them. Early the next morning, red-and-black-painted warriors fell upon Nairne and his companions before talks were supposed to resume. Yamasees killed the Carolina men, except for one hideout who told of Nairne's execution by fire and torture at the stake over several days.[46]

The Yamasee War was the first broad assault that Indian peoples had ever aimed against South Carolina's low country settlements. Yamasees and their Creek allies cut into the colony's southern margins, killing sixty and capturing another fifty in the first shock wave. While most of the dead were whites, there were Black victims as well. Indian success in one quarter inspired attacks across a broad arc. Catawbas and other piedmont tribes struck from the north while Apalachees and others raided from the west. Some Cherokees joined, too, though not in large numbers, which was small comfort to white Carolinians beset on nearly all sides. Hundreds of colonists, especially women and children, fled to Charles Town for safety.[47]

Two geographic sectors were at the war's core. The first was the low country—the heart of colonial settlement. The second spread across Indian territories where Carolina traders did business, usually far from English settlements, sometimes 300 to 400 miles distant. There was no battle in such places. Native warriors simply cut down colonial traders in a sudden and bloody reckoning. Traders were killed across Muscogee country from the Ocmulgee to Chattahoochee Rivers and west to the Tallapoosa and the Coosa. The Alabamas took vengeance, too, for the wrongs they felt. Ironically, all these peoples had been

Cherokees in Their Homeland and Beyond, 1670–1730

English allies in slaving warfare but now revolted against entrapment. A slain trader could collect no debts. Perhaps only ten of a hundred South Carolina traders escaped death by fleeing Indian territories. Native violence was not wholly indiscriminate. The Catawbas killed several South Carolina traders in their villages but sold horse loads of deerskins to two Virginia traffickers who possibly dispensed gunpowder and shot in exchange. The Native war coalition was makeshift, with particular groups collaborating but also fighting for their own objectives. Several militant Indian groups remained open to considering a diplomatic settlement with the English.[48] This was a far more nuanced geopolitical environment than what may simplistically appear as a steadfast pan-Indigenous union.

At the height of Indian attacks during the spring of 1715, South Carolina whites feared their colony to be at the edge of disaster. Rumors spread of a far-flung and even "universal" Native conspiracy set in motion by the Spanish and French. While the mainsprings of conflict lay in Indian country, Carolina whites were not off base about Spanish and French exploitation of English vulnerability. Some five hundred Yamasees found refuge near St. Augustine during the war's first year. Spanish officers armed the Yamasees, while the French at Mobile dispatched munitions to the Creeks and Alabamas.[49]

South Carolina colonials were few in number, and quite aware of their vulnerability. In 1715, about 7,000 white residents lived in the entire province, compared to 8,000 to 10,000 enslaved Blacks. Governor Charles Craven believed his colony had no more than 1,500 white men capable of bearing arms. The Indian nations that struck colonial traders and settlers had at least 3,000 warriors. To desperate colonials hugging the low country, Native foes appeared closer to 12,000 for being widespread and mostly beyond view. John Tate of Charles Town bemoaned that the enemy "won't appear to come to a decisive battle" but rather "pursue their old method of bush fighting." Warriors hid in thickets, patiently awaiting the appearance of whites by watering holes to "pour in their Volley and then Scour off into ye woods." White Carolinians meanwhile felt abandoned by their colony's absentee Proprietors, whose contributions to provincial defense were considered wholly inadequate. All the political cry in Charles Town was for South Carolina to become a royal colony directly under the king's authority and protection.[50]

While war raged in 1715–1716, South Carolina's commanders mustered a mixed array of fighters to combat Native foes. Whites were

South Carolina and the Native Southeast

aided by a number of enslaved Black men who feared Indian invasion. Carolinians found allies, too, among small coastal tribes that had previously made peace with the English in the interest of survival. Stretched to the limit, South Carolina summoned enough firepower to defeat piedmont Indians and compel the Yamasees to retreat southward by the late summer of 1715.[51] There was no sudden end to the fighting, however. Yamasees and allied bands remained unbowed. They continued to harry plantations, abducting Blacks or helping the enslaved to find shelter in Spanish Florida. White Carolinians complained of the Yamasees' "robbing them of their Slaves, Cattle &c, which they carry to St. Augustine, & are there openly bought by the Spaniards." Some Black escapees, though not all, gained freedom in Florida and its environs.[52]

An Uptick in Cherokee Diplomacy

In June 1715, Captain George Chicken's Carolina militia defeated a Catawba war party near Wassamassaw swamp in the low country. According to one colonial report, seventy Cherokee fighters in the Catawba camp exited the battle zone on the eve of the clash, just after learning of a Carolina peace overture. The story is intriguing since it suggests a fluid situation in which Cherokees debated and reconsidered their stance in the broad Yamasee War. Thus far, only a small portion of Cherokees had joined the fight against the English. Others were in a mode of wait-and-see, monitoring the war's course and likely outcome. Cherokees knew that the Creeks, their traditional foes, were a major force in the anti-English uprising. In these circumstances, some Cherokee communities decided to tap the English for munitions to strengthen their position relative to Native adversaries.[53]

Cherokees relied on British trader-interpreters as their conduits to Charles Town. This was a marriage of convenience. Trader Eleazar Wigan, who had earned Cherokee trust, leapt to the fore as diplomatic courier with the intent of personal gain as much as any public motive. In the summer of 1715, Wigan and companion Robert Gilchrist set out on a daring journey that took them from the Appalachian highlands to the war-torn low country. Appearing before the South Carolina assembly on August 6, the two men were confident of pulling off a deal that would seal an English-Cherokee alliance. The legislators enthusiastically embraced the idea. The assembly awarded £50 to each trader, with the promise of a hefty £500 bonus provided the pair could persuade

56 *Cherokees in Their Homeland and Beyond, 1670–1730*

the Cherokees to join South Carolina against enemy Indians—Yuchis, Apalachees, and Yamasees.[54]

Wigan and Gilchrist were received warmly when they returned to Cherokee country. In October 1715, a Cherokee delegation arrived in Charles Town for talks with colonial authorities. An Anglican missionary put the number of Indian visitors at twenty "Kings and great Warriours" with one hundred other men. Wigan accompanied the group as interpreter. One of the Cherokee deputies on hand was Cesar, the same headman who had worked with Wigan and Longe in executing Chestowe's destruction. Cesar and other headmen doubtless anticipated greater gains through stronger English connections.[55]

The citizens of Charles Town saluted the Cherokee delegates as deliverers in wartime. Here were Cherokee friends—an antidote to "Savage" Indians who had "so cruelly and treacherously murdered" the king's subjects. Colonial onlookers were incredulous to see Cherokee men dance, and then suddenly "stript themselves, and laid their Cloaths by Parcels at the feet of some of our most considerable Men, who in turn must do the like to them." Sharing garments had meaning in Native culture as a bond between "blood" brothers. Though colonists were initially befuddled by the Cherokee display, they responded in friendly fashion. All participants smoked the peace pipe. Many colonists felt relieved and joyful to have a powerful Native nation ready to aid them when survival appeared at stake.[56]

Not all was so simple as colonials hoped. Nearly all Cherokee visitors returned from Charles Town to their country over the next month. Anxious not to lose an opportunity, South Carolina's government determined on an unprecedented follow-up mission by tasking Colonel Maurice Moore with leading three hundred newly raised militiamen to Cherokee country. No English colonial force of such size had ever before journeyed so far inland from the Atlantic coast. The purpose was not to invade but to show colonial strength. By this logic, the Cherokees would be so impressed with English power that they would join in war against the Creeks, Yamasees, and other Carolina foes.[57]

The colonials, whose ranks included at least forty-five Blacks, took nearly a month to trek from their base camp in the coastal plain to the Lower Cherokee town of Tugaloo. The troops met with Cherokee friendship along the way. Indian hunters shared their barbecued venison with colonials. Cherokees supplied corn bread and flour as the soldiers negotiated progressively hilly terrain. Native elders greeted Carolina officers with a show of eagle feathers when colonial troops

South Carolina and the Native Southeast

approached Tugaloo on December 29. The officers took "the black drink"—a strong herbal tea with emetic quality believed by many southern Indian groups to be endowed with purifying, health-giving properties. Tugaloo's priest-chieftain Charitey-Hagey, whom the English called "the Conjuror," accepted two white flags given by the Carolina men as a peace offering. One of the banners was put atop the town council house.[58]

Captain George Chicken, a veteran fighter in the colonial force, kept a journal that is an invaluable source on the expedition. One question loomed at the outset: Would Cherokees trust English strangers and take their hand in war? Charitey-Hagey avoided any full-throated commitment while pledging that his men would no longer fight the English, as had been the case the previous spring. He rejected any strike against the Yamasees, whom he called "his ancient people" by kinship. The English learned, too, that Cherokees and Muscogees were considering a truce with one another. Here were hints of intertribal conflicts and diplomatic exchange quite independent of colonial influence. Chicken was only beginning to grasp that Cherokee towns in different regions might not act in unison and that their full geographic compass was well outside of Carolina's view. In Charitey-Hagey's telling, a Cherokee war party of fifty men had recently traveled west by canoe, killed sixteen Frenchmen and fifty Illinois Indians in a fight, seized trade goods, and brought back French colonial women and children as slaves. Cherokees looked west and not only east as they weighed an English alliance.[59]

Chicken's education in Cherokee country proceeded with assistance. Like other Carolina officers, he relied on Native guidance and a few trader-interpreters such as Wigan. Leaving Tugaloo on January 1, 1716, Chicken joined officers and some militiamen on a twenty-mile march west to the town of Soquee and traveled the next day a dozen miles further along "a verry hilley and stoney" trail to Nacoochee and nearby Chottee. Both villages, situated in today's northern Georgia, lay by the Chattahoochee River's headwaters in southwesterly Cherokee territory. It is a beautiful land, though on the frigid winter days Chicken was little inclined to note the scenery. Other sites caught his attention. Headman Cesar, now living at Chottee, stirred young men with talk of taking on the Creeks. Cherokee youths joined in a war dance all night, ignoring older men's cautionary words.[60]

Cherokee leaders appeared eager to strengthen bonds with Carolina officers. The priest-chief of Coosawattee, a Cherokee town, voiced his love for "white" men, that is, the English, though he complained of abusive traders. The priest-chief further explained how he had taken two English traders under his wing, but both men had been killed by Creeks while he was out hunting. The story was plausible, but how could the English know if it was true or was instead a Native leader's way of avoiding responsibility for ill tidings that could imperil his community? Captain Chicken had much to ponder as the political climate seemed to change within a few days. A Cherokee courier brought word that the Lower Creeks favored peace with "the white men." Chicken now saw an English peace settlement with the Creeks as preferable to an escalation of war. A Creek-Cherokee truce, too, might be in the offing.[61]

Carolina officers changed their tune from sounding the drumbeat of war to tamping down Cherokee bellicosity. With Colonel Moore ill, Captain Chicken shouldered the burden of persuasion when he met with Cesar and other headmen at Quanassee, a Hiwassee Valley town, on January 23, 1716. Cherokee leaders expressed an unflinching will to go to war alongside the English against their old enemies—"the Southward Indians," meaning the Creeks. Chicken asked the headmen about the number of warriors they had as a whole. Their answer was a substantial 2,370 men. When Chicken asked how many of these were "Gun men," the Cherokee deputies said that about half possessed guns. The headmen deliberately gave the impression of belonging to a powerful and unified people when it was in their interest to attract English support. There may have been about 2,500 males of fighting age in the Cherokee population of roughly 11,000 at the time.[62]

Cherokees had little doubt what they wanted from the "white men." According to Chicken's account, headmen answered him "in a great passion" when the captain advised against war with the Creeks. The Cherokees said they had no other way than war of "getting of Slaves to buy ammunition & Clothing." Headmen were puzzled by Chicken's insistence that "they were not to make war or peace without ye Consent of ye English." The captain invoked the governor's authority but to little effect. Cherokees remembered quite clearly how Craven had urged them to fight English enemies.[63]

Four days after the deadlocked meeting, Chicken was on the trail back to Tugaloo when he heard startling news. Cherokee warriors had killed twelve Creek men who had arrived at the town just a few days before. Most astonishingly, the victims had come with the intent of discussing peace. While Carolina troops were not at the massacre site, their

South Carolina and the Native Southeast

nearby presence certainly influenced events. Some Cherokee men evidently decided that killing the Muscogee emissaries was the most effective way to settle old scores and display prowess to the English. Cherokee-Carolina ties were now "sealed in blood," in Steven Oatis's striking phrase.[64]

Much about the Tugaloo massacre remains enigmatic and unknowable. We have little evidence about the Cherokee groups that urged the slaughter or about those who might have been of a different mind. Did Tugaloo men and others take up the war hatchet for revenge? Cherokee headmen had told Chicken that they were at war with "the Southward" Indians quite recently, as if "it was but as yesterday." In brief, some Cherokees saw an opportunity to "cut off" the enemy and to exact more damage if the English would then fight alongside them, as previously pledged. Priest-chief Charitey-Hagey quite probably consented to killing the Creek emissaries. Though not exercising coercive power over warriors, he still had undoubted prestige in his own community.[65]

Cherokee men spoke of fighting the "Southward" Indians who were among the first to strike the English in the Yamasee war. The prime targets were Ochese Creeks, whose chief was the formidable Brims, a shrewd diplomat who ironically saw little value in a prolonged battle with the English, especially once the latter recouped from the war's heaviest blows. Brims's fighters had closely tracked the Carolina militia's northward course to Cherokee country but did not attack. Peace feelers followed, sent by two Creek couriers who told an English captain of Brims's goodwill. Having given advance notice of their pacific intent, the Muscogee emissaries doubtless felt safe to proceed to Tugaloo.[66]

The Tugaloo killings were a stunning blow to the Muscogees but did not dissuade Brims from carrying out broad strategic goals. At the time of the massacre, the Ocheses were about to move south to their ancestral Chattahoochee homeland that they had fled under Spanish attack thirty years before. The migration went ahead as planned. The ancient town of Coweta would rise again to prominence by courting the English, while upping its political leverage by cultivating the French and Spanish. In 1717, Coweta and the English of Carolina made peace through negotiations between Brims and trader John Musgrove, who had a Muscogee wife and son. The path was open for a renewed deerskin trade that brought English goods ranging from weaponry to women's sewing needles to the Chattahoochee. Not all was whole, however. The blood spilled at Tugaloo was deeply embedded in Creek consciousness—and Cherokees would pay a heavy price for their temerity.[67]

Consequences

The South Carolina militia's stay in Cherokee country had far-reaching consequences that can scarcely be measured by its brevity. The great portion of the militia departed southward in early February 1716, little more than a month after arriving at Tugaloo. In a final meeting with Colonel Moore, Charitey-Hagey asked that thirty Black troops, whom Cherokees respected as able scouts, remain. Moore granted the request; he had already decided that fifty white militia would stay for a time. Black men had a freedom in army service that was tragically lacking in the colonial society to which they returned only months later as slaves. Before the colonial pullout, Moore recompensed the Cherokees by ordering that they receive two hundred muskets as well as gunpowder and bullets.[68] In effect, Cherokees had English arms but were now on their own in defending against the Muscogees and other Native enemies.

In the wake of the Yamasee uprising, the South Carolina Assembly reviewed its previous failures in regulating the Indian trade. Legislative reform had one main purpose—to prevent private traders' cutthroat practices from provoking another Native war. In June 1716, the provincial assembly mandated that a government board have exclusive authority to purchase deerskins, market goods at set prices, and appoint agents to conduct business with inland Native peoples. Economically hard hit by war, South Carolina intended to restore its competitive edge over Virginia, which was boosting its trade with the Cherokees and piedmont groups such as the Catawbas.[69]

Charles Town's new Board of Indian Trade Commissioners attempted a radical change by foreclosing Native purchases by credit, initially even to the value of a single animal skin. (This regulation was subsequently modified, in the case of the Cherokees, to allow an individual Indian to obtain credit to the value of one to three skins.) If Indians could not accumulate debt, it was reasoned, they would be unlikely to become ensnared in unpayable sums that bred resentment and resistance. In retrospect, we know that South Carolina's public monopoly over Indian trade lasted only a few years. In 1721, the government exited the business, undone by expense and the difficulty of disciplining wayward agents and preventing interlopers from intruding on business.[70] Adapting to changing conditions, Cherokees maneuvered inside and outside Carolina's trading regime. They frequently negotiated with Charles Town, bargaining on the diplomatic and economic fronts to achieve their ends.

Cherokees moved to set the terms of exchange even before South Carolina established a government monopoly on the interior Indian trade. In April 1716, Charitey-Hagey of Tugaloo visited Charles Town to fix a price schedule for "his people" with Colonel James Moore Jr., son of the late magnate. The priest-chief was quite eager to be a foremost negotiator with the English. His arrival in South Carolina's capital came only three months after the Creek emissaries were killed in his town. By his agreement with Moore, Cherokees were to give thirty deerskins or beaver pelts for a gun or broadcloth coat, the most expensive items on the price schedule. An English hatchet cost three skins, and thirty bullets could be had for a single skin. Significantly, women's items also figured on the list. A calico petticoat had a price of fourteen skins, and pair of scissors cost a single skin.[71]

When back at Tugaloo, Charitey-Hagey cooperated on the trade front with Colonel Theophilus, a Carolina agent. By late June 1716, the two men arranged that twenty Cherokee "Burdeners" would carry 473 beaver skins in fifteen packs to Charles Town. When the Cherokees set about their return trip about a month later, they brought a large quantity of gunpowder, bullets, flints, and other wares for distribution at Hastings's storehouse. The allotment of goods followed a rule satisfactory to Cherokees and English. By Charles Town's order, Hastings was to earmark half the ammunition for "the Upper Charikees" so that all should not go to Tugaloo and other Lower Towns. Woolens would be similarly distributed if the "lower [Cherokee] People" consented to share the cloth with kin to the north. In short, the commissioners recognized that the Cherokees were a nation of communities with regional loyalties. Trouble could arise if some regions benefited disproportionately compared to others.[72]

South Carolina agents soon established depots ranging from Keowee, east of the Blue Ridge, to Tanasee and Tellico west of the Appalachians. These last towns were among those the English called "Overhill," or "ye other side of ye hilles" people, as George Chicken wrote in his simple and earthy style. Tanasee and Tellico were 500 miles from Charles Town. South Carolina's trade commissioners ruled in June 1717 that all "Guns, Ammunition and Goods" sent to the Cherokees "be shared as equally

Section of "Map of the southeastern part of North America," 1721, by William Hammerton (and John Barnwell), showing Overhill Cherokee towns of "Terequa" (Great Tellico) and "Tarnasee" (Tanasee). *Yale Center for British Art, Yale University.*

as may be, amongst the whole Nation." All towns again desired to be in the distribution loop for sustenance and security.[73]

We gain a sense of government-sponsored trade by following one large circuit of exchange. In 1717, thirty-one Cherokee bearers delivered nine hundred skins and twenty-one Indian slaves to Charles Town, where commissioners dispensed "sundry Arms, Ammunition, Goods and Utensils" for the Native men to carry to their homeland for distribution and sale at colonial trading houses. (The peltry and slaves brought to Charles Town were evidently in payment for previously dispatched English goods.) Cherokee bearers faced the threat of Creek attack, whether traveling east or west across the piedmont. The commissioners provided gunpowder and shot to each bearer who owned a musket so that the group could defend the return cargo. The large convoy apparently made do without horses, though pack animals may have helped in other cases. Remarkably, Cherokees carried heavy packs of pelts on their backs several hundred miles to and from colonial outposts or Charles Town.[74]

Indian slaves were still a commodity in colonial trade, though on a reduced scale after 1715, given the disruptive Yamasee War and the lessening demand in other English colonies for such labor. Not all had changed. South Carolina's trade commissioners countenanced the purchase of Indian slaves if the latter belonged to nations outside the colony's treaty networks and presumably under French or Spanish influence. Colonial agents were not, however, to buy any male slaves above fourteen years old, undoubtedly because those individuals were difficult to control and were not easily marketable to whites. Agents were prohibited from enslaving any "free" Indian, a person who adhered to a "Nation that is in Amity and under the Protection of this Government." This was a bow to the late Thomas Nairne's advice on fairly treating Indigenous nations whose support was vital for security and trade.[75]

The Cherokees had a stake in the capture and sale of slaves because they were in strife with a slew of pro-French Native peoples of the lower Great Lakes, the Ohio Valley, and Illinois. Besides Indian captives, Cherokees seized Frenchmen for ransom payments by the English. Since Britain and France were now at peace, Charles Town felt obliged to redeem French captives held by their Indian allies. Charitey-Hagey was awarded a coat and hat for delivering a French prisoner to Charles Town. Another Cherokee man released a French captive in exchange for a gun. Enemy Indian captives were meanwhile sold at Charles Town to fill government coffers.[76]

Women were part of exchange networks in Cherokee towns. Peggy, a Cherokee woman married to Carolina trader John Sharp, came to Charles Town in 1716 to exchange a Frenchman for optimal price. (Peggy gained the captive from her brother, who had purchased him from another Indian man for a gun, cutlass, three coats, and some gunpowder and paint.) Relying on Eleazar Wigan as interpreter, Peggy asked the commissioners to give her cloth as a substitute for the gun in barter for the Frenchman. Interestingly, she requested payment in strouds, the cheap European woolens that were a staple of the southern Indian trade. A resourceful woman, Peggy made out even better than she asked. Carolina's commissioners valued her friendship and wished to keep it for the future. The Board ordered that she receive a new hunting gun besides the eight yards of strouds and a calico suit for herself in addition to clothing and a hat for her son. Peggy had a corn house at Tugaloo that her husband used for storing goods, but it was her domain, dubbed "Peggy's Corn House." Communal life hinged on women as corn growers and preservers of the harvest.[77]

A few Cherokee wheeler-dealers emerged in the pursuit of special English favor. Headman Cesar of Chottee is a notable example. Having previously partnered with Longe and Wigan in slave-dealing, he offered his services in a similar vein to trade commissioners at Charles

Town. In June 1717, he and his Cherokee companion, a man called Partridge, offered to raise a war party to attack the Yamasees. Cesar asked for rum and sugar besides guns so that he and his fellows could drink "a Bowl of Punch, in Commemoration of the English." His offer was a token of diplomatic finesse besides acculturative mastery. Though Cesar's expedition did not come off, colonial officials still gave cloth to nine Cherokee women who had agreed to accompany the warriors on their trek. Women's interests counted in Cherokee society. Cesar himself did not make out so well on his return to Chottee, as he was beaten by warriors who resented his self-interested machinations. He nevertheless remained an influential figure for years. In 1751, "old Captain Cesar," fluent in English, served as an interpreter and mediator in Cherokee-Carolina diplomacy.[78]

While the Creeks bargained for Carolina trade, they had no hesitancy in attacking Cherokees en route to Charles Town. In September 1717 a Coweta war party attacked twenty Cherokee deerskin bearers on the trail, killed several men, and made off with 770 skins. Cherokee headmen repeatedly pressed the English to fulfill their need for arms. Significantly, South Carolina was determined to keep the Cherokees in their camp so that they could face down various Indian enemies. The Creeks were by no means the only threat. In late 1717, Charitey-Hagey received word from Carolina officials that munitions and guns were forthcoming "to all the Charikees" in light of a rumored invasion, said to be coming "five Moons hence" from the north and west: Nottawegas, Senecas, Cahokias, "and several other Nations combined." "Nottawega" was a common Cherokee name for northern Indians of the Iroquois country, Great Lakes, and Canada. [79] The Cahokias were an Illinois tribe, while the Senecas were the most French-inclined of all the Iroquois. Although the rumored offensive did not eventuate, the list of Native foes is telling about the daunting and dangerous geography in which Cherokees lived. There was a constancy about certain threats. Illinois tribes, Great Lakes Indians, and the Iroquois continued to bedevil the Cherokees for decades. Cherokees struck back, though the colonial record tells us little of particular engagements until the 1740s.

South Carolina's commitment to the Cherokees had limits. To supply goods and share intelligence was in the cards, but providing direct military aid was not, except under special circumstances. By Governor Robert Johnson's order of 1718, Carolina would join the Cherokees in war only if the French were themselves engaged as adversaries. The

South Carolina and the Native Southeast

government would not "intermeddle" if the Cherokees were attacked by Indians alone.[80] If this was alliance, it was asymmetrical, rather than strictly reciprocal, at the fundamental level. Codependency was the actual state of affairs. Cherokees and English had need of one another but did not want to be tied down by binding obligations to the other.

For all of Charles Town's attempts to build an orderly and equitable trade after the Yamasee uprising, there remained sore points that wounded Indian sensitivities. Cherokee bearers, none too pleased about hauling heavy deerskin packs above a certain norm, were understandably annoyed when colonial agents shortchanged them at journey's end. In one instance, seventy Cherokee men each carried a load of fifty skins to a piedmont outpost, only to receive duffel (woolen) blankets cut four inches short of what they believed their due (one yard and three-quarters for each bearer). Native men invariably compared their treatment at English hands to the manner in which other Indian nations fared. Cherokees bristled when one piedmont garrison commander kept them ill fed outside his fort when Catawba visitors had free ingress and regress, and decent provision. Cherokee headmen in this group suffered the further indignity of being told to sleep outside of Charles Town after they had treated with the governor in the city. The visitors were then harried in the middle of the night, forced to move by truculent landowners who cursed their government for putting "Damned" Indians in the neighborhood. Other problems festered. Cherokees found Virginia prices fairer than South Carolina's. By the close of 1720, Cherokees were furious enough to break into Carolina storehouses and rifle goods. According to agent William Hatton, "All their cry was that the Virginians was very good, but they valued us of Carolina no more than dirt."[81]

By the time South Carolina's government left the Indian trade in 1721, individual traffickers were only too glad to have the field to themselves. Operating under loose legislative oversight, Carolina traffickers flooded Indian country with goods, outdueling Virginia for the Cherokee trade. For all the instances of routine exchange, there were periodic crises in which Cherokees became incensed at British traders and the latter felt their lives under threat. As will be seen, Charles Town responded with temporary embargos on trade in 1734 and 1751, with threatened cutoffs in other years. The English-Cherokee bond, often called an alliance of forty years' duration, was not so ironclad or constant as some historians have implied.

Cherokee trust was razor-thin at times. In 1721, Tugaloo's people were shocked to learn that Charitey-Hagey had been slain by Mukogees while returning with a large cargo from Charles Town. Cherokee bearers in the vicinity, who came under attack, suspected the English of conniving with the Creeks to kill their honored leader. In truth, there was no such plot, but that meant little at the moment. Charitey-Hagey was cut down close to colonial settlements and seemingly under the white people's protection. Once news spread to Tugaloo, the priest-chief's kinsmen appeared ready to take vengeance on the first Englishman they could lay hands on. Trader William Hatton quivered when bereaved warriors came "within a Bow's shot" of his house but finally held their fire. He believed his life spared only by the intervention of "some Head men who was my friends."[82]

Few persons at Tugaloo could then have known that Charitey-Hagey's death signaled a turning point. No single Cherokee priest-chief or headman succeeded him in overseeing trade negotiations with Charles Town. The Cherokees were too geographically spread out and too wary of hierarchy to accept one leader's dominance in such an important sphere. With a few notable exceptions, head warriors rather than priest-chiefs took the diplomatic lead for the rest of the century. This was the case when Cherokee-Creek conflict waxed hotly during the 1720s. It was then that the Long Warrior of Tanasee in Overhill country emerged as the savviest Cherokee spokesman-diplomat strategizing on widespread geographic fronts.

South Carolina and the Native Southeast

3

"Not Like White Men"

In September 1725, Colonel George Chicken, South Carolina commissioner of Indian affairs, was in his third month of a visit to Cherokee country. Traveling hundreds of miles, he held meetings with headmen from Lower Town Keowee to Overhill Tanasee and back again. Besides monitoring the deerskin trade, Chicken explored whether the Cherokees would make peace with the Creeks, with whom they had been at war at least since the Tugaloo massacre nine years before. No truce was forthcoming, however. In mid-September, Chicken received word from Captain Tobias Fitch, his colleague among the Creeks, that the Muscogees and Choctaws were planning a major assault against the Cherokees.[1]

Warning Cherokee headmen at Tugaloo of the impending threat, Chicken urged them to reconnoiter and launch a full-fledged offensive. Speaking through an interpreter, he contended that the Cherokees would have a formidable "Army" by raising only ten men from each of their roughly sixty towns. The plan seemed logical enough to a colonial officer accustomed to a militia draft. The headmen had other ideas. Thanking the colonel for his consideration, they put a premium on scouting and vowed to defend their own towns to the death. Local security took priority over all else.[2]

A few days later, Chicken visited the Cherokee town of Estatoe, where he was impressed by the village palisades and the perimeter ditch filled with wooden spikes. He was far less pleased by Keowee, where villagers dallied at fortification. Inaction seemed unfathomable when the enemy might be daily expected. Chicken critically addressed the situation with Keowee headman Crow, who answered that he could not command in

English style. "The people," he remarked, "would work as they pleased and go to War when they pleased. . . . and that they were not like White Men." These words came from a chief whom South Carolina commissioned as "king" of Lower Cherokee towns. His title, bestowed by outsiders, had little meaning in Cherokee society. Only hours after Chicken and Crow conversed, Keowee villagers heard a celebratory whoop from a Cherokee fighter bringing in a single Creek scalp, or more precisely the piece of a scalp. The scalp was divided so that it could be shared by several Cherokee towns that celebrated their common foe's death and humiliation. Small-scale fighting between Cherokees and Creeks persisted for the time being. There was no major Creek-Choctaw assault on the Cherokees as rumored.[3]

Crow's observation that Cherokees were "not like White Men" had a cultural meaning transcending skin color itself. His message was that the Cherokees would war in their own way and not necessarily follow an English military plan. Crow's perception of the English as "white" was commonplace—and for good reason. Carolina officers routinely referred to their country folk as "the White People" or "English" during meetings with American Indians. They avoided talk of being "British" lest they confuse Indians on the matter of nationality. A "British empire" was growing in power, but that concept lay outside the Native American political vocabulary.[4]

Some Cherokees spoke of themselves as "red" in comparison to "the White People." Long Warrior of Tanasee, a foremost chief of the 1720s, did so on several occasions when he negotiated with South Carolina officials. His words, as we will see, were careful. He did not put all red people in a single category. The Creeks were not to be trusted even if their skin color was much like that of the Cherokees. There were different kinds of white people, too. Long Warrior told the English that he might consider a truce with pro-French Indians but not with their "white" friends—in this instance the French.[5]

Like other North American Indians, Cherokees conceived of human relationships through kinship. While the English were a different people, Cherokees could still regard them as honorary kin—"Brothers" and even "their Eldest Brothers"—if they acted in a collaborative way.[6] In that regard, skin color was irrelevant. Brotherly affection was steeled through the crucible of war. Those who fought and died together were united as if they were of common blood. The English had quite a different idea of Indian friendship. South Carolina officials expected Native allies to be part of a chain of command in which the English stood at the highest

"Not Like White Men"

level. Gifts and trade goods flowed from Charles Town with the presumption that Native recipients would perforce show gratitude and dutifully follow the English lead.

Had South Carolina been able to dictate events, Indians would obediently align in strategic place. The Muscogees would give up warring with the Cherokees and instead smash the Yamasees—British South Carolina's most adamant Native foes. The Cherokees would then be free to guard against French and "French Indian" intrusions from the west and north. Charles Town's political designs often went awry despite its economic clout in Indian country. Indigenous peoples not only made war for their several purposes but also had their own manner of negotiating peace with one another in circumstances beyond colonial control.

The Commission Business and Native Leadership

Francis Nicholson, South Carolina's first royally appointed governor, busily engaged in Indian diplomacy after arriving in Charles Town in May 1721. A veteran colonial administrator, he pursued a vigorous course despite his sixty-five years. A keen imperial strategist, he intended to bring order to the Indian trade, confine the Spanish, and surpass the French in the continental interior. Britain was not then at war with France, but peace was hardly taken for granted. Anglo-Spanish relations were tense in the broad expanse of Native lands bordering Carolina and Florida.[7]

Ensconced in his capital, Nicholson welcomed a slew of Native delegations that met with him and council. Cherokees, Creeks, Chickasaws, and Catawbas had their own reasons for journeying to Charles Town. The visitors aired their people's needs, commonly pledged goodwill, and expected English reciprocity in kind. Nicholson made it a practice of commissioning Native leaders as official chiefs or "kings" within their respective regions. Not acting on whim, he took account of headmen who enjoyed prestige and respect among their people. A commissioned chief received a document bearing the governor's signature and a red wax seal, which likely appealed to Native men for whom red signified warlike power.[8]

In July 1721, Nicholson entertained a Cherokee delegation, smoked the calumet with his visitors, and offered them pictures of the royal family and His Majesty's coat of arms. The gifts had an obvious purpose. The governor wished for Indians to see him as a direct representative of the English monarch. Early the next year, Nicholson showed his penchant for hierarchy by appointing Keowee's head warrior as "King" of "the lower Nation of the Charikee Indians." An unusual request followed. The provincial council asked the chief to choose a few Cherokee men who might voyage with him to England and see the British monarch. By extending the invitation, Nicholson reprised a stratagem he used in 1710 as a military officer in New York when he promoted a Mohawk voyage to England. That visit came off well, strengthening Iroquois ties to the Crown. Nicholson had no such luck with the planned Cherokee excursion. The Cherokee "king" was not eager to cross the sea, and the Carolina legislature was doubtful of the idea. Besides, no reliable interpreter was available since Eleazar Wigan, the veteran in that field, declined a return to old England.[9]

While Nicholson's commissions made little impression on Cherokee communities, his policy had a deeper meaning to the Creeks who had a custom of hereditary leadership, which allowed headmen of certain lineages to adopt and name successors. Believing his town supreme, Brims of Coweta, the Creek "Emperor" by South Carolina's reckoning, became miffed when Nicholson moved to commission other Muscogee headmen without his approval. In 1725, he told one Carolina envoy that several recent honorees were no better than "Dogs." "I am Old," he declared, "yet I am the head of this Nation and my mouth is good." After all, he was Coweta's *mico*, the town's foremost civil or "white" chief, and particularly jealous of his influence in the diplomatic-political realm. Even Brims, however, recognized limits to his power. In Muscogee society, the lines of authority operated through consultation and persuasion rather than dictation—and this same rule was even more pronounced among Cherokees.[10]

Cherokees and Creeks—Confederations?

The English idea of a "Cherokee Nation" was still in its genesis during the 1720s. Charles Town distinguished between "Lower," "Middle," and "Upper" Cherokees—broad geographic designations that actually encompassed a labyrinth of local loyalties. Nicholson's plan of centralizing Cherokee authority met some opposition from influential colonists in his bailiwick. The South Carolina assembly was apprehensive lest a unified and powerful Cherokee nation emerge that was less amenable to colonial control. Legislators declined to endorse "any An[n]ual or Oftener meeting of the three districts of upper Middle &

lower Charikees." Such gatherings could be of "Dangerous Consequence" if perchance the entire nation united against "this Government." South Carolina's elite had little faith in the Cherokees or any Indians, for that matter.[11]

From a Cherokee viewpoint, English favoritism to certain chiefs was a sensitive matter. In November 1723, Keowee's head warrior, the commissioned "king" of the Lower Towns, visited Charles Town to complain of a local rival who claimed the same honor. While in the city, he took the opportunity to iron out a problem that threatened a halt in colonial trade in his neighborhood. Orderly commerce was thrown off when an English trader, a fellow by the name of Hunt, treated his Cherokee female helper—a woman tasked with looking after his house—in a manner upsetting to several Native women who thought him "too familiar" with her. The discontented females not only chased out the housekeeper but also persuaded Cherokee men to "jeer" Hunt at his residence. What was the upshot of this seemingly minor affair? South Carolina's council issued a warning in which the commissioned Cherokee "king" was advised to punish any Lower Town men who behaved with "insolence" toward English traders. In fact, the head warrior was constrained by communal sentiment, not least by women's say over town affairs.[12]

Cherokees had a deep sense of kin and local loyalties amid a more diffuse feeling of peoplehood across regions. Cherokee polity on a national level was consensual, contingent, and provisional. Interregional collaboration came to the fore in crisis periods. It sprouted from time to time and quickened by the mid-1700s as towns in several regions gathered more frequently to plot strategies toward the English and their French rivals as well as the Creeks, Shawnees, Iroquois, and other Indigenous groups.

Cherokee collaborative endeavors appear in both subtle and dramatic ways. In November 1723, the Long Warrior of Tanasee, a head warrior in his own right, arrived in Charles Town while Keowee men were in the city, as noted above, to air their concerns over chieftainship and trade. It is possible that Long Warrior may have joined the Keowee deputies en route to Charles Town. While there, he too raised trade issues, especially the high price of colonial goods. He listened patiently while the provincial council explained that private traders, and not the governor, established the terms of exchange. Cherokees should therefore seek "the best agreement" they could on prices. The council subsequently observed that Long Warrior "required no Commission for his being General." This declaration is curious, suggesting that Long Warrior was strongly respected by his people and that he saw no need for an English honor to secure his status. Many Cherokee towns called on his leadership when conflict and negotiation with the Creeks came to a crisis point a few years later.[13]

Town, regional, and kin-based decision-making were vital to both the Cherokees and the Creeks. Achieving consensus by deliberation and not coercion was the rule. The Creeks differed most strikingly from the Cherokees in their multiethnic and multilingual alliance-building. Diversity did not mean equality across the board. Muskogean-speakers were most influential in both population and power among

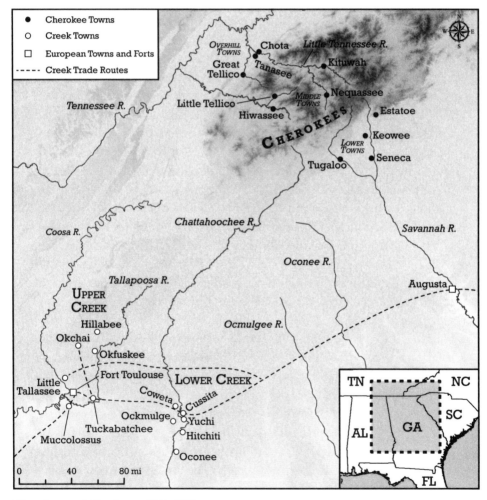

Cherokees and Creeks, ca. 1720–1750

"Not Like White Men"

"Creeks" in the "Lower" (Chattahoochee) towns and in "Upper" (Tallapoosa and Abeika) communities.[14] Coweta itself had an outsized role in Muscogee legend; it was considered an "ancient town" whose warriors had proverbially come to the rescue of other villages under enemy threat. In one tale, the Cowetas arose from "the bowels of the earth" and saved neighboring Cussita by slaughtering Cherokee assailants. Muscogee-Cherokee warfare grew to mythic status and probably well before the English set foot in Carolina.[15]

In the Creek world, certain communities believed themselves entitled to primacy above others. Similar rivalries existed in Cherokee society, but seldom in such sharp relief. Steven Oatis writes that Muscogee leaders of "founding towns" wielded "influence beyond their own settlements" even before extensive contact with Europeans. Colonials reinforced this tendency by relying on high-status communities as "trade depots" and centers of authority. Status rested concurrently on legend and fact.[16]

Through the 1720s, South Carolina had no more important goal than gaining Native assistance against the Yamasees, who persistently hewed to Spanish Florida, raided English settlements, and encouraged the southward flight of enslaved Blacks. In May 1722, Nicholson and council made a blunt case to visiting Creek chiefs, including Brims's son Ouletta. The Creeks were given the option of persuading the Yamasees to migrate well north of Florida or, failing that, to attack and destroy them. Charles Town preferred the latter outcome. The provincial assembly offered Theophilus Hastings, its own agent to the Creeks, the hefty sum of £1,000 for achieving the Yamasees' annihilation, as opposed to £500 for their resettlement within Carolina's orbit.[17]

While Brims resisted English pressure on the Yamasee issue, chiefs of other towns struck their own deals with Carolina, mainly to gain munitions and to avoid a trade embargo. During the spring of 1723, chief Cusabo of Cussita vaunted his town's independence from Coweta by fighting the Yamasees and gaining Charles Town's hearty approbation. The colonial assembly showered Cusabo with gifts, sending him a gun and sword, a laced hat, six yards of "Scarlet broad Cloth," and some gunpowder and shot. His town gained a further supply of gunpowder, bullets, flints, and a small English flag. Later that year, Tallapoosa headmen were similarly rewarded for boasting of war exploits against the Yamasees. Coweta and other recalcitrant Chattahoochee towns were meanwhile subject to an English trade cutoff. The pro-French Alabamas suffered the same punishment.[18]

Did confederation exist in any meaningful way when Muscogee communities and affiliated groups took diverse and even opposing diplomatic paths during crisis? While addressing this question, we may be misled if we apply European political conceptions of confederation to Native American societies. Creek confederacy did not mean a union in which various towns, let alone regions, walked in step while dealing with external pressures and threats. There was instead an implicit understanding that allied peoples would not war against one another and, should a common danger arise, would consult and possibly take joint action. Disagreement was a given. The challenge was for various leaders and their communities to keep their differences in bounds and accept disagreement for the sake of avoiding internecine violence. For example, Coweta chose self-restraint after learning that Cussita had talked down Brims to the English. There was no onrush to violence in response to the reported insult. Reading between the lines, one senses that Creek communities often talked frankly with one another but employed a different discourse, more calculatingly self-protective, when speaking in conference with colonials. Politics were fluid and contingent, varying with circumstance and audience. A Tallapoosa headman told an English officer of his community's readiness to stand tall against Coweta, even to the death, but the situation may not have been as dire as described.[19]

Brims was open to negotiation with the English despite being elderly and forgoing travel to Charles Town. Standing for him, Ouletta and two other high-ranking Coweta men revisited Carolina's capital in November 1723 following a testy meeting the previous month. Pitting Creeks regions against one another, Nicholson touted Tallapoosa and Abeika friendship for the English compared to Coweta's recalcitrance on the Yamasee question. Cooperative headmen had even told the governor that Brims had badmouthed "the English Talk" as "rotten at the Root." Ouletta answered coyly, telling Nicholson that he was disturbed by "the many Divisions among those of our own Colour." He pledged to give his people a "streight Talk"—to persuade them to assist the English, though he could not "force" them to do so. Compulsion was not in the cards.[20]

Tallapoosa towns were not as gung ho for a Yamasee war as their headmen intimated to Charles Town. According to an English trader, two hundred Tallapoosa warriors set out against Yamasee villages in the summer of 1723 but turned back when they found the towns abandoned; the inhabitants had gone to the Spanish post of San Marcos

"Not Like White Men"

on the Gulf Coast. The Tallapoosas killed one Yamasee woman and brought her scalp in several pieces to Charles Town as proof of supposed kills. This was a pittance compared to the destruction of the Yamasees as a people, the stated goal of the English whose animus in this case bordered on genocide.[21]

South Carolina's trade embargo on resistant Creek Lower Towns was potent, though not inexhaustible. Colonial deerskin traders did not relish being shut out of business; some traffickers circumvented government restrictions by setting up shop outside embargoed villages. South Carolina officials worried that the Creeks would stomach only so much economic punishment before turning to the French and Spanish. Charles Town's embargo of 1723 petered out within a few months. For the moment, Brims and his allies held on.[22]

Many Creeks shunned South Carolina's demand for war against the Yamasees because they had other needs and priorities. Creek-Cherokee conflict raged through the 1720s. Most of the fighting consisted of guerrilla raiding, with quite deadly outcomes for both adversaries. Not all war parties were small; larger forays numbered from fifty to a few hundred men. In the fall of 1724, Creek fighters, said to be two hundred strong, assaulted trader John Sharp's storehouse near Tugaloo. The raiders shot Sharp in the leg and grabbed all they could, making off with a large bundle of "heavy drest Deer Skins," along with "light skins" and some beaver. The windfall also included all manner of pistols, gunpowder, bullets, and saddles, along with Sharp's "Slave Woman" and her two children. The wounded trader was stripped nearly naked. All this occurred, as Sharp wrote Nicholson, "whilst the Cherikees kept themselves secure in their Forts." Tugaloo and neighboring towns were less than enamored of Sharp, known for his hot temper and bossy manner.[23]

Trader William Hatton, living at Tomotley twenty miles away, first heard of the raid from Cherokees who sounded "the War-whoop," expressing their alarm that Tugaloo might be "cut off" by the enemy. Tomotley quieted once it became clear that the Creeks had robbed Sharp but done little else. Reaching Sharp's residence with fellow traders, Hatton questioned local headmen on why they did nothing to help "the White Man." Several Cherokees offered a common face-saving answer: their people had been out hunting when the attack occurred. The true reason for inaction went deeper. Cherokee leaders had become frustrated by empty English promises. Had not the governor in Charles Town sent papers pledging that "white men" would join them to fight the Muscogees if the latter acted badly? It seemed to them that the English were "much afraid of the Creeks." Only a few years earlier, Creek warriors killed three Englishmen in an attack on Nacoochee, a Cherokee town, which itself suffered losses in dead and others carried off as slaves.[24] Cherokees expected strict reciprocity. They were ready to shed their blood for the English if "white men" acted in kind. Friends took risks for one another.

Diplomacy in Cherokee and Creek Country

Arthur Middleton, president of the South Carolina council, assumed the role of acting chief magistrate when Francis Nicholson departed for England in May 1725. Once at the helm, Middleton called on the colonial assembly to forge an activist diplomacy toward the "difficult" task of "Settling & Securing the Interest of this Province . . . with the Creeks and Cherokees." Middleton admitted that South Carolina "has long Strug[g]led with the Various Humours and Interests of those Nations."[25] The present state of confusion was unacceptable.

The assembly took up the charge by appointing two emissaries to negotiate with Cherokees and Creeks on Native ground. Colonel George Chicken would visit Cherokee country while Captain Tobias Fitch journeyed to the Muscogees. In South Carolina's ideal scenario, Fitch would persuade the Creeks to make peace with the Cherokees and then turn in full force against the Yamasees. Charles Town proceeded with caution on the volatile Muscogee front. The assembly advised Fitch not to venture to Creek country until colonial traders assured him that the path was clear.[26]

Colonel Chicken's mission was less risky than Fitch's because of Cherokee friendship for the English, notwithstanding trading disputes and misunderstandings. Chicken was accompanied on his westward path by veteran trader-interpreter Eleazar Wigan. Joseph Cooper, another skilled interpreter, was also on hand when Chicken arrived at Keowee to a warm welcome on July 5, 1725. Following festivities in the town plaza, "king" Crow ceremoniously led the colonel by the arm to Cooper's nearby house, where headmen smoked pipes with their distinguished English visitor. This was communal diplomacy; no single Native leader held sway. After the colonel's stay in Lower Cherokee villages, both colonial "linguisters" accompanied him by horseback on an arduous trek to the Cherokee Middle Towns before setting out for Tanasee in Overhill country, where Wigan had his storehouse and intimately

"Not Like White Men"

knew the local scene. Interpreters were vital to diplomacy at all stages. Since Wigan remained at Tanasee once at home, Chicken relied on Cooper on his return to Keowee. It was there that the colonel had an especially frank exchange with Crow, who insisted, as mentioned previously, that his people could not be expected to fight "like White Men" and would go to war as they pleased.[27]

While Chicken had absorbed something of Cherokee ways from his previous visit to the southern Appalachians in the winter of 1715–1716, he still had a great deal to learn about Native customs and diplomacy. At a meeting with the headmen of twenty-one towns at Tugaloo in mid-July 1725, the colonel, having declared that he had come a long way "with a great talk from the English," asked if all in the assembly knew who he was. The Cherokees said they knew him "very well" and expressed their readiness to listen carefully to "the English talk." Chicken regarded the meeting as a stepping stone to a conference with "the head Men of the whole [Cherokee] Nation," but such a gathering would not easily materialize. Cherokee geographic dispersion and local loyalties complicated the colonel's task. So, too, did the spread of rumors that clouded the atmosphere.[28]

While at Tugaloo, Chicken was surprised to learn that Cherokee headmen expected English troops to aid them in their war with the Creeks. The colonel felt bound to set the record straight: Charles Town's policy was to supply the Cherokees and cultivate their loyalty but not to intervene directly in their conflict with the Muscogees. In fact, South Carolina was eager to encourage a Cherokee-Creek truce for colonial purposes, not least to counter French and Spanish influence in Indian country.

Since South Carolina did not have a government agent in Cherokee and Creek territory on a continual basis, it is not surprising that diplomacy did not proceed as smoothly as Chicken desired. Besides the challenge of gaining Cherokee trust, the colonel entered an environment in which colonial traders had personal agendas at variance with the government in Charles Town. Months before Chicken's tour of the Lower Towns, Cherokee hopes of English military assistance were fanned by trader William Hatton, who spread the idea through Peggy, an influential Cherokee woman of Tugaloo. Though Hatton's motive can only be surmised, he likely aimed at enhancing his standing with the Cherokees by circulating reports that the latter wished to hear, namely that Charles Town was ready to send them as many as three hundred soldiers to fight the Creeks. Peggy, a well-versed liaison with

English traders, had credibility among her people. Chicken worked against the rumor mill while staying outwardly calm. He had as yet not absorbed much of Cherokee perspectives.[29]

As Chicken traveled in Cherokee country, he glimpsed the interconnectedness of Indian peoples over a broad compass. Choctaw-Chickasaw warfare to the west, for example, influenced conflict between Cherokees and Creeks. Chicken found Cherokee headmen stubbornly localist and not easily persuaded to obey English-appointed "kings" or to travel to particular venues for general meetings. Being tactful, they tended to avoid sharp disagreement with an English "beloved man" when the latter meant well but was short of understanding. A Cherokee grunt of assent meant the white man's "talk" was sensible, not that a course of action was necessarily at hand.[30]

In late July, Chicken, Wigan, and Cooper followed Native trails as they trekked southwest below the Great Smoky Mountains, crossed the eastern continental divide, and headed north to Great Tellico, a sizable Cherokee town of 340 inhabitants. Chicken remarked on how the village was "very Compact and thick Settled," with two fortified council houses and dwellings constructed to be "Musket proof." While Muscogee foes loomed to the south, Tellico commonly warred with French-allied Indians to the north and west. Tellico and Tanasee, sixteen miles apart, were both within short distance of the Great Tennessee River, with its lengthy passage to the Ohio and the continental interior.[31]

English-Cherokee diplomacy reached a critical point when Chicken, aided by Wigan and Cooper, met with Tanasee's Long Warrior, who served as communal spokesman while addressing his English visitors before the entire town. In a dramatic scene, Long Warrior now told of the great changes that had occurred in his lifetime. His people "must now mind . . . that all their Old men were gone, and that they have been brought up after another Manner than their forefathers." The truth had to be recognized that "they could not live without the English." Long Warrior was glad the English had sent up Chicken, "one of their beloved men," whom Tanasee's "Young Men had never seen before." It was necessary for youths to absorb all that they heard and witnessed. Calling to mind the inevitable passage of time, Long Warrior hoped that Tanasee would follow his example after he died by choosing a headman "that will talk to you for your own good . . . and that will always Stick Close to the English."[32]

Once Long Warrior had finished speaking, all of the townspeople—men, women, and children—took the English visitors "by the hand as Brothers and fathers to them." By this emotive gesture, which Long Warrior encouraged, Tanasee's villagers accepted the English as protectors within their circle of kinship. The communal greeting took place in the open, close by the council house, where the sacred flame burned. That evening, Long Warrior supped with his Carolina visitors and joined them in smoking two or three pipes of tobacco. He recounted how "French Indians" to the west had recently seized a Cherokee woman just outside Tanasee. About one moon before, Cherokee hunters had spied "a great body of their Enemies" along a nearby river, possibly the Tennessee. Cherokee warriors pursued their foes by canoe but could not catch them. Long Warrior concluded his story with an astute political observation. Making peace with the Creeks, "the Southward Indians," might be wise since the Cherokees were "hemmed in all round with their Enemies." A pause in hostilities with the Muscogees might give some breathing room. Tanasee's people would then have no enemy except "the French Indians" and could "leave their Women and Children at home . . . and have room to Hunt." Chicken was understandably impressed with Long Warrior, describing him as "the Most Noted Man in the [Cherokee] Nation."[33]

Peace feelers had their own dynamics among southeastern Native peoples. In the absence of national governments, particular towns and regions frequently took the initiative in dealing with adversaries. Leading headmen seldom undertook diplomatic missions into hostile territory, evidently out of fear that their own lives could be at risk. Various couriers, including women, had a role in communication across ethnic lines. George Chicken learned as much during his journey of 1725, seemingly by happenstance. While he was in Overhill country, a Creek man of Coosa brought a Cherokee woman with him to Great Tellico. The woman was herself a Creek war captive and the daughter of Tellico's head warrior. After a parley with the Cherokees, the Coosa man ran off while his female prisoner stayed with her kin. Her release was evidently a sign that Coosa's chiefs desired a truce with the Cherokees. Coosa was a town within the Abeika region—the Upper Creek area that happened to be closest geographically to the Cherokees. Both peoples commonly hunted in the Coosawattee Valley that served as a loose border region between them.[34]

Curious about the Cherokee woman's story, George Chicken questioned the former captive. Unnamed in his journal, she was obviously intelligent. Since living among the Muscogees, she had learned their language and spoke confidently of what she knew and inferred. By her account, Upper Creek chiefs were offering the Cherokees a peace from the current summer to the next springtime. The Abeikas had decided to curtail hostilities because they believed "French Indians"—and not Cherokees—were responsible for quite recent killings of their people. In the Indigenous world, a message's power often depended not so much on its exact truth as on the willingness of the recipients to accept its intended meaning. Honorable propitiation of a foe—in this case by denying harmful purpose—was a way toward mutual understanding and, sometimes, toward a truce, if not a long-lasting peace.[35]

Chicken was puzzled by what might result from Coosa's overture to Great Tellico. By all appearances, the Abeikas had sent their truce proposal out of fear of being attacked by South Carolina troops and the Cherokees. While Great Tellico's bruited leaders deliberated peace, some of the town's warriors made their way to raid Upper Creek territory. Chicken did not understand why Tellico's head warrior had allowed youthful fighters to go to war when peace seemed in the offing. The headman's reply was simple: "Young Men" would "do what they pleased." The colonel conjectured that Tellico had a generational divide, with the town's elders favoring the truce but unable to persuade young warriors. His guess was a stab at deciphering Indigenous ways that baffled English colonials.[36]

Peace talk was all but dead in the wake of Cherokee raids into Muscogee territory. In mid-September 1725, Captain Fitch reported from Creek country that the Abeikas were "Dayly Terrified" by their Cherokee enemies. In one foray, four "Young Lads" of Tellico, Chicken learned, scouted Coosa's margins. One of the warriors shot dead two Coosa women in a cornfield and carried their scalps back to his town. The victims' kin surely cried for vengeance. Indian fears of having their women and children killed or taken captive were all too real. Earlier that year, a Chickasaw man brought word to Keowee that "French Indians" west of the Appalachians had recently killed two Cherokee women and seventeen of his own people (six men, four women, and seven boys and girls). In intense intertribal warfare, no person was safe.[37]

Chickasaws and the Broader Canvas

The idea of an enemy-of-an-enemy being a friend was as true in Indian country as anywhere else on the globe. Chickasaws and Cherokees were drawn together in just such a fashion. Both were enemies of the

French and French-allied Indians. The Chickasaws had the unenviable position of drawing French ire because of their proclivity to host Carolina and Virginia traders. In 1721, Jean-Baptiste Le Moyne, sieur de Bienville, the commandant-general of Louisiana, armed the Choctaws to the teeth in order to break the Chickasaws of this habit. In the spring of 1722, the Choctaws and allied tribes reaped French rewards by bringing in scores of Chickasaw scalps and one hundred slaves. Bienville boasted that he had achieved victory in proxy warfare without the loss of a single French soldier. It was to Louisiana's benefit, he wrote, if "barbarians" destroyed themselves in the process. In August 1723, he advised his council that Chickasaws were like "a bone" the Choctaws had to "gnaw" for contentment. It was not until 1725, just before Bienville's departure for France, that he helped bring about a Choctaw-Chickasaw truce. By then, Choctaw assaults had forced a few hundred Chickasaws to migrate east to Cherokee territory and beyond to the Savannah River. This was not an inconsiderable number since the Chickasaws had a total population of about two thousand at the time.[38]

George Chicken was frustrated by events beyond his control. His attempts to lessen Cherokee-Creek antagonism was complicated by Chickasaw involvement on the Cherokee side in the conflict. He struggled, too, in persuading Cherokees of various regions to meet with him in a general conference. In August 1725, Chicken's prodding finally produced a substantial gathering in which "all the Upper Settlements" and twenty-four Lower Towns were represented at Ellijay. The colonel's perseverance paid off, aided by the fact that Cherokees had reason to strengthen English bonds in the face of external foes.[39]

The Cherokee assemblage chose Long Warrior of Tanasee to be its spokesman—a sign of the broad respect that he held. His talk began with tough words but did not rule out peace with the Muscogees. There were still stumbling blocks, however. Long Warrior observed that the Creeks had not been punished for killing Englishmen and Cherokees who traveled together on the trading path. If the Creeks did not offer satisfaction for past wrongs, the Cherokees were "ready to go against them as they did against the Tuskerorees [Tuscaroras]." This last war, in which Cherokees aided the English, was thirteen years past and still fresh in memory. It was out of respect for English friends that Long Warrior and his people would consider a truce with the Creeks—a people not to be trusted. To palliate Charles Town was a shrewd tactic in the tricky business of interethnic diplomacy. The Cherokees took the English as "their Eldest brothers" for supplying them with goods and all that was necessary for war. After Long Warrior finished speaking, Chicken asked if the Cherokee assembly agreed with the chief's words. The headmen voiced their approval.[40] At that moment, a Cherokee nation came to life through a consensus achieved through careful consultation. The path appeared open to an English-mediated truce between Cherokees and Creeks.

A negotiated settlement was still in its incipient stages and was easily undone. A few weeks after Chicken met the Cherokee assembly, he received discouraging news by packet from Charles Town. The bundle included Captain Fitch's report of his ongoing mission to the Muscogees. In a blow to the peace prospects, Abeika and Tallapoosa Creek leaders voiced their resolve to avenge lethal Cherokee raids. The headmen would consider a truce only after the corn harvest—when their warriors had an opportunity to strike the enemy. Brims of Coweta was more adamant, vowing that there would be no peace with the Cherokees as long as a single man in his town was alive. He could not forget how the Cherokees had slain his emissaries when the Carolina militia ("the White people") stood nearby at Tugaloo nine years before. His course was fixed no matter what the Tallapoosas and Abeikas decided.[41]

While Cherokees expressed confidence in English goodwill, Muscogees in the fall of 1725 were distrustful. In fact, Upper Creek headmen had cause to believe that Fitch had himself forewarned Cherokees of the Creek war plans. How else could it be explained that forty Muscogee fighters had stalked a Cherokee town for fifteen days but brought off no scalps? Cherokee scouts closely guarded the area. When Creek men returned home, they questioned Fitch on the matter, correctly suspecting that the agent had sent advance word of the Muscogee offensive to Charles Town and then to Colonel Chicken in Cherokee country. In a tight spot, Fitch fibbed, saying that his message was intended solely for South Carolina's governor and that the news had wafted west by a wayward trader. Fortunately for Fitch, the Creeks let the matter drop, but not before scolding him for English favoritism to the Cherokees. As one Creek headman asked Fitch rhetorically, "Since You [the English] Call yourselves our friends, why do you not give us an account of the Cherokeys Designe against us? But that you never do."[42]

For all this wrangling, Upper Creek headmen did not exclude English mediation of peace with the Cherokees. There was one new condition, however. The Cherokees would have to expel all Chickasaws from their

"Not Like White Men"

territory before serious talks could begin. The Creeks knew that some Chickasaws filtered into Cherokee country and were in league with their foes. Although George Chicken initially dismissed talk of Chickasaw-Cherokee collusion, the alliance solidified over months.[43] In March 1726, a combined force of Cherokee and Chickasaw warriors attacked Lower Creek Cussita. The attackers carried the Union Jack as an emblem of power. Cussita's defenders boasted their own small British flag, also courtesy of Carolina! Cherokees and Chickasaws were probably unaware that Cussita happened to be in good standing with the English.[44] And they would have cared little had they known it. Their offensive was a mark of autonomous Indian warfare. Indigenous combatants fought with scant regard for British aims even though English weaponry and emblems were evident on both sides.

The attack on Cussita generated shock waves in Charles Town. South Carolina's stock was plummeting among Creek headmen, who suspected the English of aiding the Cherokee and Chickasaw invaders. This rumor was amiss, but that nebulous point hardly lessened the political fallout. The French and Spanish were exploiting the situation to draw the Creeks, especially the Chattahoochee towns, into their good graces. In May 1726, South Carolina's assembly called again on the services of Chicken and Fitch, and this time, both envoys received explicit instructions to mediate a Cherokee-Creek peace. The adept Chicken journeyed once more to the Cherokees, while feisty Fitch grudgingly accepted his assignment to the Creeks.[45]

The making of a Cherokee-Creek truce had complexities that differed in kind from a peace accord between two European monarchies. For example, the British and French had a clear conception of when a state of war, as opposed to peace, stood between their nations. But Native societies operated according to different assumptions. Peace and war might be partial in scope, and even exist side by side, between rival ethnicities that were not wholly unified among themselves. Interestingly, the loosely knit Cherokees came closer to consensus when tested by South Carolina's diplomacy compared to the more complex Muscogee world with its rival power centers.

The Duress of Peacemaking

Tobias Fitch thought he had gained appreciable insight into Creek ways during his diplomatic tour of 1725. When setting out for Muscogee lands the next summer, he sensibly planned to begin his mission at Upper Creek towns, which were more receptive to English influence than Coweta. He even managed to convince Hobohatchey, an influential Abeika headman then on the path to Charles Town, to change course and join him for talks with other Creek chiefs at Okfuskee.[46] Interestingly, Upper Creek headmen appeared outwardly gleeful that Lower Town Cussita had taken its comeuppance from the Cherokee-Chickasaw attack the previous spring. By Fitch's account, the message was clear. The Upper Creeks expected the Lower Towns to come to their senses by agreeing to an English-mediated peace with the Cherokees.[47]

Fitch had little choice but to sound out the Creeks before he learned what Colonel Chicken had achieved in talks with the Cherokees. The news, which took about a month to reach Fitch, seemed promising. On July 27, 1726, Chicken had a favorable meeting with Cherokee headmen at Tuckasegee, a town deep within the Smoky Mountains. Deputies of thirty-eight towns were present, representing some two-thirds of all Cherokee communities. Most important, the assemblage assented to Chicken's proposal for peace talks with Creek leaders at a colonial frontier outpost in the presence of South Carolina's governor and his beloved men. Cherokees pledged to deliver their Creek captives if the Muscogees would act in kind. However, there was still considerable suspicion. Cherokee headmen declined Chicken's request that their couriers, accompanied by a white man, carry his message to Captain Fitch in Creek territory. That path was reckoned too dangerous.[48]

Chicken had a steady and confident manner that earned respect. Cherokees had seen the previous year how the colonel admonished colonial traders who belittled and deceived them. The colonel even told Cherokee men that they should feel free to shoot white men's horses when they strayed into their fields and trampled corn. Chicken took his usual stance in his mission of 1726, warning Cherokees not to rob traders, while also taking their complaints with due seriousness.[49]

The Tuckasegee conference was amicable, though Chicken was chagrined that no representatives of five Overhill Towns attended the meeting. The absence of Tanasee's Long Warrior especially worried him. Could a Cherokee-Creek peace be secured or stand without the prestigious headman's consent? Eager for information, Chicken dispatched interpreter Wigan to speak to Long Warrior and test Overhill opinion. Wigan's message was promising. Long Warrior welcomed "the English Talk" and was willing to enter into a peace with the Creeks,

"Not Like White Men"

provided a suitable prisoner exchange could be made with the enemy. There was still one trouble spot from the English perspective. Long Warrior had recently met with a deputy of "French Indians" to discuss the release of his nephew who had been captured by an unnamed tribe. Carolina's officials immediately feared that Long Warrior might be open to French machinations.[50]

The Cherokees and Muscogees acted as national polities—however provisional in character—when headmen of numerous towns gathered to decide issues of war and peace. The Cherokee-Chickasaw threat loomed over Muscogee towns. All had an interest in seeing what they might gain by negotiating with Fitch when the latter called for a general conference in late September 1726. The site was Tuckabatchee, a prominent town on the Lower Tallapoosa that was suitably located, being about halfway between the Chattahoochee and the northern Abeika villages. Reporting to Charles Town, Fitch wrote rather vaingloriously that "the whole Nation of Creek Indians" was represented at the gathering. In reality, a sufficient array of Native men attended to give that impression. During the talks, The Abeika and Tallapoosa towns each had their own spokesman. Chigelly of Coweta, representing the Lower Creeks, took center stage in sharp exchanges with Fitch. A younger brother of Brims, he stepped to the fore with his elder's blessing.[51]

Fitch's record offers a glimpse of Creek politics, despite more being concealed from his view than what he could glean. As negotiations proceeded, it became clear that Coweta intended to restore its prestige by forging a common Muscogee stance toward Cherokee and Chickasaw adversaries. Brims had been stung badly during the previous several years when various Creek towns went their own way and gained Carolina's favor by spilling Yamasee blood. The Coweta chief did not let the deaths of his previously appointed successors, Ouletta and Chipacasi, halt what needed to be done. Now was the time for Chigelly to reassert Coweta's leadership in negotiation.[52]

As the talks opened, Chigelly told Fitch that matters would have to change before any truce: "It is not the Cherokees that we Contend so much with as the Chickasaws who they Harbour that comes daily & kills & takes our People." A Tallapoosa headman supported Chigelly by arguing that even if his people made peace as Fitch desired, the Chickasaws would still do "Mischief" and then blame the Cherokees for the harm done to the Creeks.[53] In their customary manner, Creek chiefs consulted with one another before presenting their common

86   *Cherokees in Their Homeland and Beyond, 1670–1730*

stance the next day. Chigelly was again prime spokesman. His position admitted little bargaining room. The Muscogees would accept Carolina's mediation of peace only on the condition that the Cherokees killed or drove out all Chickasaws from their country. A small window for future talks was left open. Chigelly sent a white feather as a gesture of goodwill to the Cherokees. A string of white and red beads was also forwarded—with the message that the white or peace beads were solely for the Cherokees with the red or "bloody" being for the Chickasaws. Chigelly added that "our People" entertained a Cherokee negotiation out of respect for the English. The Muscogees wished to keep the trading path open to South Carolina more than they cared about satisfying Cherokee foes.[54]

Fitch was pessimistic in the aftermath of the talks. Chigelly said that the Cherokees "were not like People" in light of the Tugaloo massacre. Desperate to mollify Creek anger, Fitch went to the extreme of saying that Carolina's soldiers had urged the Cherokees to kill the Creek deputies eleven years previous. Chigelly was unpersuaded, though he admitted it was best to put aside "what was done so long ago" since talking would not bring the dead back to life. Revenge was not the sole motive for Muscogee policy, which aimed to break the Chickasaw-Cherokee alliance.[55]

Chigelly showed aplomb in his initial round of talks with Fitch before the Creeks made their peace overture. He listened patiently while the South Carolina captain blamed Brims for dallying with the Spanish in St. Augustine when Cussita was hit by the large Cherokee-Chickasaw attack. Chigelly warded off the criticism with a few words. He would not air differences among Muscogee towns to an English outsider, especially since the headmen of various communities were immediately present. He spoke instead of how the Cherokees had violated "Custom" by not sending a "small Present"—a token with their apparent peace talk. How could his people know that the Cherokees were "willing to be friends"? Chigelly said that he had sent gifts to other Indian nations—Senecas, Shawnees, and Tomahitans—all Cherokee foes. He needed to hear from them before giving an answer on a Cherokee peace. The Tomahitans, an obscure group, had apparently come from the Appalachians to live in Creek territory, while the Shawnees dwelt in the Susquehanna, Ohio, and Cumberland Valleys.[56]

It was no coincidence that Chigelly paid heed to the Senecas, members of the Iroquois Confederacy. All knew that Iroquois warriors persistently raided into Cherokee country. Little more than a year before,

"Not Like White Men"

the Cowetas engaged with Senecas in a round of long-distance diplomacy, even though the two peoples lived a thousand miles apart! After a visit to Iroquois country, Coweta deputies returned home with five Seneca men as honored guests. Fitch happened to be at Coweta when the Senecas were present. The Senecas talked bluntly, advising the Muscogees to settle their differences with the English but never make peace with Cherokees, or else be considered enemies, too. The Seneca emissaries added: "We have no people to war Against nor yet no Meal to Eat but the Cherokeys." These words had an eerily literal quality since the Iroquois had the custom of feasting on the flesh of captured warriors put to ritual execution.[57]

The Creeks were not wholly united in diplomacy. Speaking for Chattahoochee towns, Chigelly was adamant that Cherokees sever their Chickasaw connections. Taking a softer line, Abeika headmen, keen on a Cherokee peace, shouted their contempt for one Lower Creek town known for its anti-English conduct. The target was "the Stinking Lingo people," peripheral members of the Creek confederacy often mocked for speaking a seemingly dissonant or impure dialect. In this case, the put-down was about political affinity and not simply language.[58]

Frustrated by Chigelly's obdurate stance, Fitch shot back that Coweta was reluctant to make peace because it was a "Bloody Town"—by nature "red" and prone to war, as compared to the "white" peacemaking towns in the Creek social order. The colonial agent strained for a political argument based on a simplistic reading of Muscogee customs. While Chigelly belonged to a red town, that fact hardly precluded him as a civil chief (mico) from negotiating a truce with external foes. Various towns—and the white and red lineages within them—had a place in deciding on a common course of action. The Creek white and red beads, sent respectively to Cherokees and Chickasaws, would speak for the whole. Fitch was pessimistic precisely because he believed the Cherokees would never accept the Creek demand that they drive out or kill their Chickasaw friends.[59]

George Chicken jumped into action once he received Fitch's dispatch by urging a general Cherokee meeting to address the smoldering Creek conflict and a possible way to truce. Cherokee leaders were responsive, no doubt because they believed English propositions important to hear during crisis. On October 25, 1726, deputies of Cherokee communities met with Chicken at Nacoochee. Long Warrior was present and served again as chief spokesman for the headmen of various regions. All listened carefully while Chicken relayed the Creek messages. The Muscogee tokens, now visibly displayed, spoke quite as forcefully as any words. It was clear that the red beads were for the Chickasaws and the white feather and beads for the Cherokees. Chicken conveyed the Creeks' insistence that the Chickasaws be expelled from Cherokee territory. He was tactfully mum about Chigelly's demand that the Chickasaws otherwise be destroyed.[60]

After confidential deliberations, Cherokee headmen accepted negotiations with the Creeks under Carolina's auspices. The talks would be open-ended, with no advance commitments regarding the Chickasaws. Cherokee reliance on English trade was a spur to negotiation, though not the sole factor at hand. Worn down by years of battling enemies from the Wabash to the Chattahoochee, Cherokees were anxious for a respite on their southern front. Long Warrior said his people made their decision solely out of respect for the English and not for their Indian adversaries. Chigelly's message to Fitch was no different. Neither Indian leader wished to show weakness before critical negotiations began. Long Warrior signaled goodwill by sending two gifts to the Creeks—a "very white" bird wing and a string of beads of even greater length than his people had received from the Muscogees. The Cherokees were not to be outdone by their adversaries in gift-giving. Keowee sent a pipe, earmarked for whichever Creek headman "loves the English the best." The pipe's smoke would itself "give out" the Cherokee peace talk.[61]

For all of Carolina's diplomacy, there would have been no Cherokee-Creek peace conference without Native initiative. This was not only a matter of decision-making but one of travel. On September 1, 1726, President Middleton and council decided that it would be too onerous for them to journey roughly 130 miles to meet Cherokee and Creek headmen at Savano Town, the frontier outpost initially designated for negotiation. If a parley was to take place, it would have to be in Charles Town. Carolina's leaders justified their reluctance to travel by stating that their capital alone had the capacity to accommodate numerous Indian visitors.[62]

The Cherokees had little hesitancy about setting out for Charles Town. Long Warrior expected the path southeastward to be "white," that is, free of menace. The Cherokees would regard any Creeks who crossed their way to be enemies. Not all was tough talk; peace required reciprocity as well as strength. Long Warrior relayed that all Cherokees, and the Chickasaws among them, would refrain from war with the Muscogees until negotiations were concluded. He satisfied Chicken by pledging to seize any Frenchmen who came among his people.

"Not Like White Men"

Carolina could not hear enough times that the Cherokees were on their side against the French and their Indian allies.[63]

The Charles Town Conference

By December 11, 1726, the Long Warrior, along with nineteen other Cherokee headmen and thirteen male attendants, arrived at George Chicken's Goose Creek estate after a long trek. The group stayed with the colonel through Christmas and New Year's before heading to Charles Town. In contrast to the Cherokees, the Creeks were slow to set out for Charles Town, and those who made the journey were relatively few in number. One can only surmise if the Muscogees deliberately made their Native adversaries wait on them. Several Abeika headmen, led by Chief Hobohatchey, entered Charles Town on January 10, showing again that they were the Creek group most eager for a Cherokee peace. However, this small regional delegation had limited negotiating clout until Coweta leaders arrived on the scene. Impatient with delay, the Cherokees were loath to wait longer in the city to meet their dreaded Lower Creek foes. The Carolina government's food and drink alone kept them in town. A modest Lower Creek delegation led by Chigelly, with only four other headmen, finally arrived on January 24 and was ceremoniously received by Middleton and council. Chigelly's slim cohort implies that there was no broad Creek consensus for peace with the Cherokees.[64]

The Cherokees were unquestionably South Carolina's most valued Indian friends. While on their way to the capital, the provincial assembly ordered frontier guards to be on the lookout lest Tuscarora and Iroquois warriors, said to be lurking to the north, target the invitees on their trek.[65] In early January 1726, Chicken and his militia escorted Cherokee emissaries into Charles Town, where they were welcomed with a salute of "Small Arms." While the assembly ordered similar honors for the Creeks, it reserved the discharge of "great Guns" for the Cherokees alone. The legislative committee on Indian affairs carefully assigned the same gifts to Cherokee and Creek headmen and followers according to rank. Long Warrior and Chigelly were each singled out for the most elaborate presents—a blue broad cloth coat with lace and brass buttons, a shirt, a laced hat, a pair of Indian stockings, and a flap in addition to a blanket and gun. The Carolina assembly enumerated gifts prior to the conference with delivery at the meeting's

90   *Cherokees in Their Homeland and Beyond, 1670–1730*

end. This customary colonial practice was an inducement for Indian cooperation.[66]

Business moved ahead quickly once Chigelly and company finally reached Charles Town. The next day, Middleton, his council, and the House committee on Indian affairs held two separate meetings—the first with Chigelly and fellow Creeks and the second with Long Warrior and Cherokee headmen. These preliminaries set the stage for the drama of January 26, when both Native delegations confronted one another before the entire provincial assembly gathered in the legislative chamber. All Cherokee and Creek attendees respectively took their seats in rows at opposite sides of the hall. It was an extraordinary scene. Men of two warring Native peoples wore feathered headdresses and ornamental beads, jewelry, and earrings or pendants hanging from stretched earlobes. Their cloaks and leggings were often styled of English cloth, while their deerskin moccasins were of Indigenous fashion. The Indians' tattooed faces and skin were in contrast to the colonial gentlemen in fine jackets and waistcoats above tight-fitting shirts, breeches, stockings, and buckled shoes or boots. Several colonials may have worn wigs to lend dignity and authority to their presence. Indian chiefs wore especially elaborate headdresses as a mark of prestige. In this respect, Natives and colonials were not so different.[67]

Middleton began the session by asking Chigelly why so few Lower Creeks were present. The Coweta chief answered that some of his people had gone hunting while others had fallen ill. Middleton questioned why the Tallapoosas were not represented in the Creek delegation. Chigelly stood his ground. "I have their Talk with me. . . . I talk for all," he affirmed in proud Coweta fashion. He next rose from his chair and held up a "white large Wing" as a peace gesture before laying his offering on a table. Addressing the Cherokees, he declared, "I stand here before you all as friends. . . . If the Peace is made Our grounds will all be as one, and our Children will all have the Benefit and not be destroyed as they have been."[68] Here was diplomatic finesse and magnanimous display lauding peace across national territories.

Long Warrior did not respond kindly to Chigelly's words. Keeping his seat at first, he rose to chide the Creeks for sending so few deputies and breaking past promises. The Cherokees could not imagine a peace with the Muscogees unless the latter were "good to the white People," meaning the English. Long Warrior again thought it important for the Cherokees to have a better reputation with Carolina than the Creeks,

"Not Like White Men"

who had done "Mischief" to the English since the peace made after the Yamasee uprising. He did not bother to name the misdeeds.[69]

Long Warrior's talk to Chigelly was emphatic: "It is now come to this. We the Red People are now met together. Our flesh is both alike but we must have further Talk with you[.] We shall see when we go home, whether any of our People have been Killed [by yours], and whether You are Rogues. If so, we Shall Know what to do." The idea of sharing "red" skin was part of Cherokee and Creek consciousness, though it did not create unity across the ethnic divide. Long Warrior objected strongly when Chigelly blamed the Chickasaws for stirring up problems between Creeks and Cherokees. Calling himself "King" over Chickasaws in his nation, Long Warrior declared his prowess in battling obstreperous Creeks: "I laid them all in Their Blood."[70]

The Charles Town conference played out as theater. Long Warrior was as harsh as Chigelly was high-minded. A slight turn came when Abeika headman Hobohatchey faced Chigelly and said, "Here is talk enough . . . we can talk together hereafter." Long Warrior then berated Chigelly one more time while the Creek leader repeated his desire for friendship with the Cherokees and "with all these white People." At last, Long Warrior picked up the Creek white eagle wing, declaring that he received it to please the English governor. He remarked: "All Shall be well, If you [the Creeks] be good," adding that he would be glad "to talk further to you when we meet and Eat together in the Woods." A true peace between Native peoples, in other words, would be built over time in their own environment and not simply in a meeting in a colonial city.

The conference neared its culmination when Chigelly raised his wine cup, turned to Long Warrior, and toasted Middleton for his good services in bringing about a peace. Chigelly and Long Warrior then shook hands, as did all the Creeks and Cherokees with one another, and finally all Indian men with the English. The entire assemblage then walked to the fort, where they drank the king's health to the boom of cannon fire. Middleton hailed the proceedings, written into the official record, as binding on all parties. Long Warrior still carped at the Creeks. Chigelly suggested that Creeks and Cherokees go to smoke tobacco together. The peace pipe was a perfect antidote to ill feelings.[71]

The South Carolina president described the agreement as if it were a treaty to endure as long as Indian signatories kept to their word.

92   *Cherokees in Their Homeland and Beyond, 1670–1730*

The Creeks and Cherokees more likely regarded their understanding as a truce that would require further give-and-take if it were to last. There is no evidence that Long Warrior and Chigelly ever met again after returning to their respective countries. The Creek-Cherokee truce of January 1727 was short-lived. Violence between the two nations abated for a brief time but tensions remained high. The conflict reignited by 1730, flaring up periodically over the next decade and reaching its hottest point from the mid-1740s to 1753.[72]

If hardly bringing a close to Cherokee-Creek enmity, the Charles Town conference is significant for showing how Native peoples conducted diplomacy concurrently with the English and with one another. Indigenous perspectives come into view, notably when Cherokee and Creek delegations met separately with Middleton in preliminary talks. In both meetings, Middleton aired his province's resolve to suppress the Yamasees. The Cherokees offered no help to the English in this way. While admitting that the Yamasees had once lived in their country, headmen explained that those bonds were a thing of the past. South Carolina pushed the Muscogees, especially the Chattahoochee towns, to distance themselves from the Spanish and migrate north so as to be closer to the English. In conference, a Coweta head warrior rejected the idea as preposterous and told Middleton as much: "If we should remove to a fresh Settlement, It would Kill all our People." Did his statement reflect the Creek fear of contagious disease or the dread of dependency on Carolina and its trade? Perhaps the warrior had both menaces in mind.[73]

Middleton presumed that potent Indian nations were as hungry as ever to wage war for the purpose of gaining slaves. If the Cherokees made peace with the Creeks, he questioned, would they next fight the Choctaws? Long Warrior answered vaguely that his people would war against "French Indians" without identifying the precise enemies to be confronted. Perhaps he felt no need to be pinned down when the Cherokees, especially those living west of the Appalachians, were frequently in conflict with French-allied tribes from the Wabash to the Mississippi. As will be seen, this state of warfare was episodic and did not rule out negotiation for truce.[74]

Long Warrior consistently maintained that his people were far more reliable English allies than the Creeks. He hewed to this tactic whenever white Carolinians were in earshot and even after handshakes and toasts were shared by all assembled. In one notable instance, two Muscogee men expressed their wish for an enduring peace, only to be upbraided by

"Not Like White Men"

Long Warrior, who slammed the Creeks for trading with the French and Spanish rather than entirely with the English. His lecture to the Creeks came in a flurry of unanswerable questions: "Why do you go to the French & Spaniards? What do you get by it? How can you go to so many of the white People? This great Town is able to Supply us with every thing we want more than all the French or Spaniards."[75] These assertions of English economic prowess might be expected from a South Carolinian, not a Native leader! One wonders if Long Warrior's declamation carried a touch of envy. While the Creeks were geographically positioned to extract favors from different colonial nations, the Cherokees had little opportunity that way. South Carolina's traders far surpassed the French, besides besting Virginia competitors in the southern Appalachians, giving the Cherokees little choice except to embrace Charles Town.

Long Warrior could not have appeared more of a pro-English stalwart than he did at Charles Town. Sitting in the assembly room and looking for George Chicken, he asked, "Where is my Country Man?" When the colonel finally entered, the Tanasee leader called him "one of my People." He wished Middleton to know that the Cherokees were good to Carolina's "beloved men"—and, again, far better than the Creeks. Long Warrior was sincere in his friendship for Chicken, but that did not make him a puppet of the colonial regime. He was no such thing. After returning to his homeland, he continued to cultivate contact with the group of "French Indians" that held his nephew as a hostage. Chicken's journal identifies those Indians as "Nitteragers" and "Notoyaws"—names reflecting how Cherokees identified Indians living to the far north. According to Long Warrior, the group that captured his nephew lived near a French "town"—quite the vague description. Tanasee's chief was clearly reluctant to inform Carolina in any detailed manner about his independent diplomatic track that possibly reached to Montreal.[76]

Long Warrior carefully weighed the options of continuing his northern Indian contacts without alienating the English. During the summer of 1727, he sent a peace pipe from an unnamed pro-French Indian group to Charles Town as a goodwill gesture. Hardly pleased, the South Carolina committee on Indian affairs returned the pipe to Long Warrior, recommending that he give it back to whichever nation had offered it. No peace between Cherokees and French-allied Indians was acceptable to Charles Town.[77]

Retribution and Survival

Carolina's jousting with Long Warrior occurred just as the colony faced a new crisis to the south. In July 1727, a band of Yamasee and Lower Creek warriors murdered six Carolina men and seized several others at a trading store by the Altamaha River. The perpetrators left behind signs of contempt for the dead traders—an abundance of deerskins burnt and cut to pieces. It is not clear if Chigelly encouraged or ordered the raid. While a principal Coweta headman, he did not control the entire Chattahoochee region, let alone outlying villages or the Yamasees with their own ties to the Spanish at St. Augustine and San Marcos.[78]

South Carolina's response to the Altamaha River killings was punitive, if wavering about the utility of military force. On August 25, 1727, the provincial assembly ordered a trade embargo on all Creeks, with the idea of swaying the Upper Towns to take Carolina's side in return for a resumption of commerce. Within the next month, the government considered a thrust against the Yamasees as a prelude to a much larger offensive aimed at Coweta and the Lower Creeks. After a spirited debate, the assembly finally decided to proceed against the Lower Creeks, but only if it could secure military support from the Cherokees and Catawbas.[79] The colony, with its large Black population, was again unable to field a militia that could carry the fight alone against a populous Indian nation on its own ground.

South Carolina managed only one small-scale if significant military offensive in the aftermath of the Altamaha killings. With one hundred white troops and another hundred Indian auxiliaries, Colonel John Palmer wreaked havoc on the Yamasee villages near St. Augustine in March 1728. Palmer's Indian allies belonged mostly to small coastal Carolina tribes such as the Edistos and the Cussoes, whose way of life depended on cooperating with English authority. To encourage Chickasaw recruitment by the Savannah River, the colonial assembly allotted bounties: £20 for every enemy Indian scalp with attached ears and £30 for each enemy brought in alive. Ears, with hair and skin, were grisly proofs of authentic kills. A live prisoner had a higher valuation than a scalp because the captive could be sold into slavery. While South Carolina's Indian slave trade had diminished, colonial authorities still regarded the enslavement of Yamasees as a more or less routine form of retribution.[80]

"Not Like White Men"

There was little pity shown a weakened and vulnerable people. South Carolina's victory over the Yamasees raised English prestige among the Creeks, who saw that the Spanish failed to protect their Indian allies. Some Creek warriors had already begun to hunt for Yamasee scalps in order to restore their Carolina trade. By the spring of 1728, Muscogee towns that went against the Yamasees received fresh supplies of English gunpowder and bullets. Fighting continued sporadically over years. By the mid-1730s, the Yamasees suffered mounting losses at the hands of Creek foes and smaller tribes that befriended the new English colony of Georgia. Though battling gamely, the Yamasees barely held on amid the ravages of disease and war. There was no going back—the Yamasees and their children deepened their Spanish alliance and never bowed to the English after their people's fateful decision of 1715.[81]

Muscogee decision-making was more intricate than a brief summation suggests. Colonel Charlesworth Glover, Carolina's emissary to the Creeks in 1727–1728, was baffled by Muscogee resistance to a unified stance on war with the Yamasees. The colonel warned Chigelly that an entirely new order was necessary: "Your Towns can never mend unless you are of one mind one Tongue and one people." If not, "you must fall to the ground like a House that is Supported by Some piece of Rotten Wood."[82] The bonds of Creek confederation were nuanced and variable—and barely visible to colonials who yearned for Indian predictability. The Muscogees and allied groups would not behave as one nation, as Glover consistently urged. The Creeks' allowance for local autonomy appeared chaotic, but it enhanced interregional comity and helped to keep disagreements from degenerating into internal strife and bloodshed. Though not of one view, Lower Towns cooperated sufficiently to forestall South Carolina's demand for the surrender of "Tyger King," a presumed murderer of whites.[83]

Glover was finally smart enough to realize the limits of South Carolina's influence. Wary of a Muscogee turn to the French, he allowed trade to be resumed with Coweta in April 1728 before Charles Town officially approved the measure. Brims was courted even if he no longer had the pull he once did. "The old man," as Glover remarked, was one at "heart" with the Spaniards who sent him "now and then a Cag of Molasses & a little Chocolate and Sugar." To his dying day in 1731, in short, Brims would not be won by the English.[84]

Long Warrior's Last Years

In 1725, Long Warrior advised his people to stay close by the English after he was gone. Within three years, he was not so sure. After discussing peace with the Creeks in Charles Town, the English seemed to pay him little respect. The Carolina assembly refused to accept the French Indian peace pipe that was his gift. While not abjuring the English, Long Warrior continued his gambit for a truce with French-allied Indians. One of these groups lived near "a French town." Was that unnamed place the outpost Detroit or perhaps Montreal? Long Warrior saw beyond the Ohio and the Great Lakes to the French along the St. Lawrence and Mississippi from his view west of the Appalachians. He saw, too, the forests, savannahs, and swamps of the Lower Creek country. His responsibility as Tanasee's head warrior was to weigh dangers and opportunities from all directions.[85]

Eleazar Wigan was an old and knowledgeable hand in Cherokee country. Once a buyer of Indian slaves from the Cherokees, he grew in empathy for the people among whom he lived and traded. In October 1727, he warned Charles Town that all was not right in Cherokee country. Wigan predicted "great distraction" in the Cherokee "Nation" unless "imprudent" English traders stopped driving Indian hunters into debt to the value of "16 or 18 hundred [deer] Skins." The letter closed on a poignant note. Wigan confessed that weak eyesight prevented him from writing as much as he wished.[86] He was now old and had gained wisdom with experience.

George Chicken died in 1727. One of his last acts as commissioner of Indian affairs was to help the Chickasaws redeem one of their women from slavery in South Carolina. The purchase price was set at either ten blankets or a hundred deerskins. Beyond a capacity to address Indian grievances, Chicken understood something of the importance that Indigenous peoples attached to communal preservation and prowess. While a thoroughgoing imperialist, he saw a confluence between Cherokee strength and English containment of French advances. That is why he echoed Long Warrior's words that Cherokees avoid situations in which they were subject to attack on all sides. The purpose of a Creek peace, as Chicken told headmen, was so the Cherokees would enjoy "free hunts and get great Quantitys of Skinns To Cloath your Women and Children and in Time will be a rich and great People, which will make your Enemies dread you."[87] This was language that Indians

"Not Like White Men"

readily grasped, for it was their own strategic outlook, even if colored by an Englishman's sense of national grandeur.

Cherokee peoplehood was multifaceted, expressed through town and regional bonds along with kin and clan ties seldom conveyed in the colonial record. Diplomacy was consultative within a broad matrix. Colonel John Herbert, Chicken's successor as commissioner, discovered this fact when he journeyed to Cherokee territory in November 1727. South Carolina was still reeling from the Lower Creek killing of white traders and was desperate for Cherokee warriors to join a prospective colonial strike on Coweta and allied towns. Herbert had little luck as he traveled from the Lower to Middle Cherokee towns. A few headmen talked of supporting the English but made no commitments. The colonel was advised to consult Long Warrior. Herbert met rebuff when finally reaching Tanasee on December 20. Long Warrior thought little of Carolina's plans to attack the Creeks. The Muscogees, he predicted, would hide in swamps and "draw down to the Rivers & Sea side" to evade colonial troops. Cherokee leaders were not about to leave their women and children in the lurch by fighting alongside the English against a distant and powerful enemy. Stung by Long Warrior, Herbert took some comfort on hearing that Tellico's warriors had just returned home after killing six "French Indians" and taking three enemy captives. The colonel sent a message to Long Warrior asking if the Tanasee leader would follow the same course. No reply came.[88]

Tanasee's stance was not the same as Great Tellico's. The two towns were just sixteen miles from each other but did not see matters exactly the same way. Their differences were not unlike Creek towns that followed their own paths in war and diplomacy. South Carolina encouraged Tellico's recent forays by presenting a gift to the town's head warrior. Long Warrior was no French ally, but he did not wish to see his people blindly beholden to the English. As he told Wigan, his motive in negotiating with Indian enemies was to gain a respite from war. The tribes he negotiated with were accustomed to "doing us mischief." His peace initiative was only with "Red people, and that as I am Red, it is only with them that I talk & eat with." Indian peoples negotiated with one another by sharing food and gifts. This practice did not assure lasting amity but created a friendly atmosphere where a truce might follow. Long Warrior distinguished between the Indian adversaries whom he hosted and "the white people"—that is, the French—who lived near them. The French, he claimed, "never shall come here."[89]

98   *Cherokees in Their Homeland and Beyond, 1670–1730*

Long Warrior of Tanasee apparently died about 1729. There is no record of his presence the next year when momentous events occurred in Cherokee country. In March 1730, Scots adventurer Alexander Cuming came to the southern Appalachians and managed to persuade seven Cherokee men to join him in a voyage to England. One of the travelers was White Owl—the future Attakullakulla who grew up near Tanasee. The visit across the "great Water" quite possibly would not have occurred if Long Warrior was still Tanasee's senior war chief. Long Warrior's words of the past were true. The "Old men were gone," and the Cherokees could not live without the English. How the Cherokees would retain their freedom, while being dependent, remained an open question.

"Not Like White Men"

4

A Cherokee Voyage to London

White Owl was the youngest of seven Cherokee men who journeyed to England in 1730 and spent nearly four months in London and vicinity. The visit is remarkable for bringing Native American men to the heart of the British Empire. It was not the first such "transatlantic encounter" of the era. The journey to London of four Mohawk "kings" in 1710 was an important occasion; Native American headmen were welcomed to Britain, wined and dined, and brought into a closer bond with the English. One of the four guests that year was actually of the Mahican tribe, but that detail was overlooked in imperial circles. What counted was that Mohawks of the Iroquois Confederacy, the mighty Five Nations, were present to be honored. Mohawk chief Theyanoguin ("Hendrick" in colonial parlance) treasured his time in England and became a significant figure in Iroquois-colonial diplomacy over four decades. During the French and Indian War, he led Mohawks in battle alongside the British, only to be killed near Lake George in 1755.[1]

The Mohawk and Cherokee visits had quite different antecedents. As early as the 1670s, the Five Nations entered a "Covenant Chain" with New York's governor—and through him to the British monarch. Iroquois headmen regarded the "Chain" as a mutual pledge of "good understanding and friendship" so strong, as sachems said, that it was "not in the power of men or Devils to break it." Spokesmen of the Five Nations repeatedly renewed the Chain, expressing their people's sense of rights and obligations while avoiding subordination to any European power. By contrast, the Cherokees through the 1720s had little sense of a British monarch. Their experience with the English centered on South Carolina and its trading network. The Cherokee visit to England of

1730, which included a royal audience at Windsor, brought King George directly into view. All seven Native men who made the voyage returned safely to their land and spread word of what they had experienced to their people. Rather than fade over time, memories of the king assumed a nearly legendary aura by the 1750s and became a defining element in Cherokee diplomacy, bringing the distant monarch into the Indian world as if he were physically present.[2]

The voyage across the Great Water in 1730 came about by events defying all probability. It was not the work of royal officials but instead the result of individual colonial adventurism—a lone man's search for honor, glory, and wealth in Indian country. Sir Alexander Cuming, an eccentric Scots baronet of thirty-eight years, was the principal in the unfolding drama. A newcomer to the colonies, he sailed from England to Charles Town in 1729, inspired by his wife's dream that he would make a fortune in America. A lone ranger at heart, Cuming left his lady behind in Britain and, once in Carolina, indulged in financial confidence games before sidestepping legal trouble by setting out west. While in the low country, Sir Alexander heard of mineral riches lying in what he called "the Cherrokee Mountains."[3] Ambition, shrewdness, and opportunism drove his quest.

Cuming arrived in Charles Town at a fortuitous time for adventurist gambits. South Carolina in 1730 was in a political waiting mode. Robert Johnson, the colony's newly appointed royal governor, was in England and was not expected to sail for several months. There was no strong hand in Charles Town to guide Indian policy. Colonel George Chicken, Sr. had died a few years before. One doubts that the highly experienced colonel, an officer who brooked no insubordination, would have allowed an upstart like Cuming to leap suddenly to the fore in Native diplomacy.[4]

In March 1730, Cuming cleverly attached himself to a small group of South Carolinians on an official mission to the Cherokees. George Chicken Jr., son of the late colonel, was head of the entourage, while surveyor George Hunter charted the route to the Lower Cherokee Towns. Cuming went his own way as soon as the travelers reached the piedmont. Racing ahead on horseback, he persuaded Joseph Cooper, colonial trader and Cherokee interpreter, to ride alongside him at the breakneck pace of nearly forty miles a day. The pair reached Keowee only four days after beginning their jaunt.[5]

Cuming next launched a whirlwind diplomatic tour that took him to Cherokee towns on both sides of the Appalachians and then back again

A Cherokee Voyage to London

to Keowee in the astonishingly brief span of two weeks. During this whirlwind of conferencing, he scouted for Native volunteers to undertake a voyage with him to England. Six Cherokee men agreed, and a seventh joined the group en route to Charles Town. On May 4, 1730, Cuming and his Cherokee companions embarked for England on the H.M.S. *Fox*. After a month's ocean crossing, the ship arrived at Dover. Two weeks later, the Cherokee visitors saw King George II and Queen Caroline at Windsor Palace, certainly a highlight of their lengthy stay in England.[6]

All of this is recorded in Cuming's brief account published in London in 1731. Not surprisingly, the author made himself the central character, invariably referring to himself in the third person. He is "Sir Alexander," a figure describing his exploits in Cherokee country in the manner of Julius Caesar recounting his campaigns in ancient Gaul. In Cuming's case, the object was a type of conquest—not by force of arms but by persuasive power to convince the Cherokees to pay homage to the British Crown.[7] Curiously, Cuming ended his narrative with an episode from Tacitus in which Roman legionnaires conspire to kill their commanders but are suddenly quieted by a lunar eclipse. To Sir Alexander, the eclipse's bedazzlement of superstitious soldiers was analogous to the Cherokees' readiness to follow his leadership after a violent thunderstorm struck during his stay at one Native town. In his view, "a barbarous [Indian] People" was swayed into "Submission"—vassalage to King George—by the need to propitiate higher powers. Imbued with notions of British superiority, Cuming interpreted Cherokee conduct by an imperial script. He was impervious to the fact that Cherokees had ways of honoring useful English allies without yielding their culture and independence. Their homeland was their own and not the king's.[8]

Let's turn briefly to one more story in Cuming's narrative. While at the town of Joree, Sir Alexander asked a warrior to find some "good Iron Ore" for him. Several days later, the man climbed "a steep and craggy Mountain" and gave Cuming what appeared to be a genuine sample of ore. The warrior said that he performed the deed though it raised bad omens that could bring death. Cuming was impressed, imagining that the Cherokee man desired to please him at great personal risk. Did the climber have some foreboding about ascending to heights where Ustutli, the monstrous horned foot snake, lurked to prey on humans entering its domain? The Cherokee sense of awe and wonder, of living amid supernatural forces that variously comforted or wounded, was part of the Indigenous response to colonialism in ways scarcely fathomable to Sir Alexander and not easily discerned by twenty-first-century historians. Cherokees listened to Cuming's speech and observed his bearing and gestures, though without necessarily absorbing the message he intended. Much the same could be said of the written British treaty to which the seven Cherokee visitors later put their marks in London. Cherokee assent in this formalized European manner did not signal any obvious subordination to empire.[9]

Colonial Opportunism / Native Purpose

Long Warrior had once told his people to "stick close the English," but persistent Cherokee discontent with South Carolina's traders undercut that advice. Just before Cuming came to the mountains, rumors spread that the Cherokees were plotting to expel or kill white traffickers. Sir Alexander was unfazed. On his first evening at Keowee, he carried a gun, a cutlass, and two pistols on his person while entering the town council house for a talk with Native headmen. Cavalierly strutting into sacred communal space, Cuming gave a declamatory speech and supposedly obtained the headmen's pledge of fealty to King George. Ludovick Grant, a resident Scots trader to the Cherokees, recalled his amazement at Cuming's eccentric behavior a quarter century later. In Grant's recollection, Cuming bragged to fellow Britons that he would have taken a brand from the Keowee council fire, burned all to the ground, and blocked the exit of Cherokee men, women, and children at the door had Indian leaders refused to drink to King George's health. Unsure of Sir Alexander's sanity, Grant chose to watch over Cuming when the latter headed deep into Cherokee country. A temperamental adventurer could bring disaster to British traders.[10]

There is a strange mix of empirical observation and fantasy in Cuming's journal. Fortunately, the Scots adventurer took detailed notes on his stay in Cherokee country, indicating the towns he visited and the headmen whom he met. Grant remembered that Cuming "seldom stayed above two or three hours, never above a night at any place." His route was strenuous by any judgment. Journeying northwest from Joree to Great Tellico, he negotiated mountain defiles and sinuous pathways as if in his native Scottish Highlands. Along with interpreters Cooper and Grant, he followed a trail to the heights of "Ooneekawy Mountain" and a descent of twelve miles to the valley below. Cuming's ear was alert to Cherokee place names. For example, his "Ooneekawy

A Cherokee Voyage to London   103

Mountain" is in today's Unicoi Range. Unicoi ("Unaka") means "white" in Cherokee speech, perhaps suggesting whitish clouds or snow hovering at summits.[11]

Cuming's narrative relates events in quick succession, as if no other outcome were imaginable. The adventurer will attain his end by sheer force of will. At Great Tellico, Cuming conversed with head warrior Moytoy, whom Sir Alexander imagined as leader of the entire Cherokee nation. Moytoy seems to have played along with the stranger's idea of a supreme Native potentate. And why should he not, if gaining in the process? Perhaps the stranger would funnel munitions and goods his way.[12]

Cuming learned of Great Tellico's stance at the forefront of Cherokee conflict with French-aligned Indians. Ludovick Grant, fellow Scotsman and trader at Tellico, was a useful interpreter there. Further to the east at Tanasee, Cuming met the elderly Eleazar Wigan, who struck him as "the complete Linguist" for his knowledge of Cherokee language. Sir Alexander, impressed by military prowess, observed that Tanasee warriors had just carried fifteen enemy scalps to their town. If Cuming is to be believed, Tanasee's "king" went on his knee that evening, just as other Cherokee leaders had done at his command, to "do Homage to King George II." Hurrying back that same night to Great Tellico, Sir Alexander was an honored guest in the town house. In his telling, "the *Indians* sung Songs, and stroaked his Head and Body over with Eagles Tails." Unfortunately, Cuming did not comment on Cherokee women. His interest was solely with headmen, pillars of his idealized Native polity.[13]

Compared to the late George Chicken's steady diplomatic pace, Cuming worked with frantic alacrity. By April 3, 1730, just ten days after reaching Keowee, he managed a general meeting with Cherokee headmen, "assembled from the different Towns of the Nation," at Nequassee, a prestigious village of the "Middle Settlements." Cherokees were evidently as fascinated by their visitor as he was with them. It was at Nequassee that Cuming climbed to the height of fantasy about Native ceremonial gestures. Perhaps all headmen there went on their knees, at his request, to pay respect to the British king, "the great Man on the other Side of the great Water." Even if this courtesy took place, Cuming's interpretation of Cherokee politesse is dubious. All that he saw in strictly hierarchical and even feudal terms could not have had that same meaning to Cherokees. In his mind, the headmen at Nequassee had made a "Declaration of Obedience" to George II and admitted his "Sovereignty over them." The same assembly supposedly accepted Cuming's appointment of Moytoy as their "Emperor" answerable to Sir Alexander himself.[14]

Cuming may not have been a mountain chieftain, but Scottish heritage was still in his blood. In his telling, the Cherokees might as well have been a Highlands clan with dual allegiances, first to its own chief and second to a superior chief duty bound to protect and aid all his clansmen. (In the Highlands, this last figure was "the Supreme Chief of the Clan or Kindred.") Cuming grew up in Culter in Aberdeenshire, a county whose western portions fell within the Highlands. In his generation, the great political test was whether a Highlander would offer fealty to the reigning British monarch or align with the "Jacobites"— those who remained loyal to the ousted Stuart dynasty—James II and his heir, James Edward of Scotland. Cuming proved where he stood by his youthful service as a British soldier in Flanders and later by his loyalty to George I and the Hanoverian succession.[15]

Cuming did not encounter any English naysayers to his Scots patriotism in the Cherokee mountains. All seemed to fall in place when Overhill headmen satisfied his desire for an honorary gift—a warrior's "crown"—a headdress of dyed possum hair bedecked with five eagle tails and the scalps of four enemies. It was the type of decoration that a highly esteemed Cherokee "beloved man" received on assuming his station. Cuming called the headdress "the Crown of Tannassey" since it came from that town. Once the headdress was brought to Nequassee, Moytoy presented it to Sir Alexander before the assembled headmen. Cuming described the "crown" as nothing less than an "Emblem" of the Cherokees' willing obedience to George II. He would carry the headdress to England as proof of his endeavors.[16]

All of this raises the question of how Cherokees understood Cuming's declamations, which perforce had to be conveyed by colonial interpreters in a Native language of which he scarcely knew a word. One imagines that his gestures and mannerisms were quite as important, if not more so, as the words he spoke to Native men. Cherokee visitors in London respectfully referred to him as "the Warrior." This point is critical since Cuming's manly bearing carried weight with Cherokees who did not see him as an ordinary colonial trader.[17]

Cherokee hospitality to Cuming was sensible. He appeared to be a stouthearted warrior who respected them and could be serviceable in kind. His journal does not once use "savage" in reference to Indians. He courted Cherokee friendship and offered protection by the English

A Cherokee Voyage to London   105

king. Cherokees could not afford to dismiss the Scots adventurer; they had Muscogee enemies to the south and other Native antagonists aligned with the French. The Overhill Towns, which were especially helpful to Cuming, faced the brunt of attack from the north and west. Moytoy and other Upper Town headmen acted pragmatically by choosing to meet with Cuming at Middle Town Nequassee, which was far closer to the Overhill region than the Lower Cherokee Towns. Nequassee had been the gathering place just four years earlier for a large array of Cherokees who decided under Long Warrior's leadership to attempt peace negotiations with the Creeks. That effort failed, making Sir Alexander's appearance all the timelier.

Cuming's forthright manner earned a respectful Native hearing, though it hardly guaranteed that he would gain Cherokee voyagers to Britain. There is only one Cherokee account of the recruitment of volunteers for the oceanic passage. The oral recollection is that of the mature Attakullakulla, who had several Cherokee names during his life besides the White Owl of his youth. In 1755, Attakullakulla delivered his reflection on events of a quarter century past during a visit to Charles Town. He did so at the request of Governor James Glen of South Carolina, who was interested in magnifying his own accomplishments in Cherokee diplomacy and discrediting what Cuming had allegedly achieved. The governor posed questions to Attakullakulla, his closest Cherokee ally, who answered through a colonial interpreter.[18]

Attakullakulla spoke confidently of the past, saying that he remembered "everything as if it had happened yesterday." His memory was precise on one key point. He recalled that many Cherokee headmen met with Cuming in a town (i.e., Nequassee) "near the middle of our nation." Stating he was present then, Attakullakulla remembered Cuming saying "that We [the Cherokees] were so poor & naked, that he was sure if the Great King George knew it, He would take pity on our condition & would give us Some Cloaths." In all probability, Attakullakulla was referring to the Cherokee need for English aid in the present and not only about what was wanted in the past.[19]

Cuming's narrative corroborates Attakullakulla's on the theme of royal protection. At Nequassee, Sir Alexander spoke of "the Power and Goodness of his Majesty King George," who viewed "all his Subjects" as "Children." Attakullakulla recalled that Cuming referred to himself as "one of King George's Children." There was honor, and no disgrace, in being under a great ruler's protection. In Attakullakulla's telling, Cuming was "the Warrior," a man worthy of respect. As for the invitation to

106   *Cherokees in Their Homeland and Beyond, 1670–1730*

England, not a single Cherokee man at the Nequassee meeting initially volunteered to "go over the great Water." Attakullakulla recalled that he was finally convinced to travel by Eleazar Wigan, who told him that the distance to England was not so great and that "the Warrior" (Cuming) desired his company. This point is interesting since Wigan lived in or about Tanasee, close to the village where Attakullakulla grew up.[20]

Attakullakulla's oral account was politic, aimed at satisfying his friend, Governor Glen. In response to one set-up question, Attakullakulla unequivocally denied that Cuming had any plan by which the Cherokees surrendered or gave their lands "to the Great King" for protection in return. Glen alone wanted to take credit for that supposed achievement in a quite recent treaty, which was itself ambiguous in meaning. Attakullakulla added his own take on the agreement with English officials in 1730. To Cherokees, the treaty came down to one simple statement: "that we would be one with the white people in War, That is if they assisted us in our Wars against our Enemies We would assist them against their Enemies." This was the test of true clan brotherhood, whether in the Cherokee mountains or the Highlands of Scotland.[21]

Attakullakulla likely erred on one point in his recollection. Asked about the six Cherokees who had been with him in London, he answered that all were dead; he was the only Cherokee "now alive who was in England or that Saw the Great King George." Nearly three years after Attakullakulla gave his account, Tistoe of Hiwassee told Governor William Henry Lyttelton in Charles Town that he "was one of the Chiefs of the Cherokees who went to see the Great King George." In fact, he gave a string of wampum to Lyttelton, explaining that one part of the belt was "an Emblem of the Great King" and the other part a symbol of the Cherokee nation and that both sections were tied together "for their Mouths were as one." This was "performative" utterance in which speech infused a gift with life. The wampum belt was a Cherokee statement of connection with the English king. As long as all was right, both parties would speak with a single voice and spirit. Tistoe's remembrance of being in England seems credible. If he spoke truly, why did Attakullakulla state that he was the only Cherokee man alive who had seen King George? Attakullakulla's claim was likely a point of pride, reflecting his desire to take the lead in negotiation with the English during the 1750s.[22]

The Cherokee men who accompanied Cuming to England chose to go voluntarily. At least two of the seven voyagers clearly came from

A Cherokee Voyage to London

Tasetchee, a smallish village situated in southwesterly Cherokee territory. It was at Tasetchee that the village priest-chief, who did not himself journey to England, was supposedly persuaded by a violent storm to encourage headmen to join Cuming for the voyage. Two Tasetchee voyagers were head warrior Skaygusta Oukah Ulah and second warrior Scalilosken Ketagusta. Attakullakulla recollected that he and his companions undertook the trip for "pleasure" rather than to deliver any message to the king. One imagines that more was at stake than simple curiosity, though. On the path to Charles Town, the Cherokee travelers discussed the question of who would be their spokesman. Attakullakulla recalled that he immediately deferred to others since he was the youngest of the group, a statement entirely consistent with Cherokee custom.[23]

To England

Sir Alexander was not one to share credit with others. His account makes no mention of trader Robert Bunning, who served the Cherokees as interpreter during the voyage to England, their lengthy stay in Britain, and the return trip. Cuming's record is unfortunately silent about how the seven Cherokee voyagers experienced the ocean crossing, which took thirty days, a quick-paced transatlantic voyage for the time. It is doubtful that any in the group had ever previously been out to sea. After all, they belonged to an interior people who lived from 250 to 500 miles from the ocean. One Cherokee myth said that the earth was originally "a great island floating in a sea of water" and suspended by four cords hanging from a rocky vault in a higher realm. In time, when the world grew old, the cords at the four cardinal points would break and the earth would sink entirely beneath the water. Given this cosmography, it is remarkable that seven Cherokee men braved the voyage.[24]

H.M.S. *Fox*, the vessel that carried Cuming and the Cherokees, must have seemed a marvel to its Indian passengers. Riding the waves at full sail, the ship carried hardened sailors who may have been amused at the Cherokees on board. With England at peace, there was little danger of enemy vessels bearing down on the *Fox*, which safely put into Dover on June 5, 1730. Bidding his Cherokee companions goodbye for the moment, Sir Alexander hurried by coach to London so that he could spread word of the Indians' arrival to the government. The seven

108   *Cherokees in Their Homeland and Beyond, 1670–1730*

Cherokee men remained on ship several days after the *Fox* reached Deptford on the Thames just east of London. The great metropolis of six hundred thousand residents at last came into view. There was nothing remotely like it in North America. The Cherokees thought of Charles Town, with its four thousand inhabitants, as a large city. Now they witnessed the imperial capital's grand edifices, St. Paul's Cathedral and Parliament, teeming streets, and innumerable dwellings in crammed alleys.[25]

Cuming was in his glory at the beginning of the Cherokees' stay. On June 18, Sir Alexander presented the Indian guests to King George II and Queen Caroline at Windsor Castle. It was a day of pomp and ceremony. Courteously kneeling before the king and queen, the Cherokee men stood by while the Duke of Cumberland, son of the royal couple, and two other nobles were installed as Knights of the Garter. Trumpets blared as prelude to the play of fifes and drums while the procession of king and knights walked solemnly to St. George's Chapel.[26]

Four days later, Cuming and the Cherokees came before the king for a brief audience. Sir Alexander knelt, as did the Indians who were becoming expert in that British practice. Cuming laid the crown of eagle tails with enemy scalps at His Majesty's feet. The Cherokee visitors were seemingly in awe of the British monarch, whom they likened to the sun. Their respect did not necessarily mean the type of absolute obedience Cuming intended. Cherokees were curious about their surroundings. One Indian visitor asked if he might shoot an elk in the royal park at Windsor, though he was not allowed that privilege. The request was quite natural considering that Cherokee hunters had developed fine skills in the use of guns over the previous twenty years.[27]

A British writer in the London press perceived the Cherokees as "Blacks" by skin color, reflecting the English tendency to differentiate starkly between "white" skin tone and darker shades. Except for Oukah Ulah, who wore a "Scarlet Jacket," the Indian men were described as "naked, except [for] an Apron about their Middles, and a Horse's Tail hung down behind." The Cherokees' faces and bodies "were painted and spotted with red, blue, and green, &c. [with] painted Feathers on their Heads."[28] Cherokees had tattoos applied by having their skin pricked by a sharp object and then rubbing soot or gunpowder with dye into the wound. Men favored designs that reflected their courageous deeds in war. What the English observer saw as a Cherokee "apron" was probably a breechclout. Traditionally made of leather, this

A Cherokee Voyage to London

article was often fashioned from imported woolen cloth obtained through the Carolina trade. A yard in length and up to eighteen inches wide, the breechclout was strung about the waist and belted, with flaps in front and back. (Perhaps the British observer saw the back flap as something like a horse tail.) Had the Cherokees made their visit in autumn or winter, they would have carried loosely draped mantles or cloaks for everyday use. Indian men put great stock in having free movement and not being constrained by tightly fitting garments, even while adopting British cloth. Trader James Adair recounted being told "discreetly" by southern Indian women that "as all their men sit down to make water, the ugly [European] breeches would exceedingly incommode them."[29]

Later in their visit, the Cherokee men received clothing out of the royal wardrobe and donned vests or waistcoats and knee-length broad breeches. In one English engraving, the group poses in decorative garb before a garden landscape. There is little at first glance to distinguish them as American Indians apart from the central figure's feathered headdress, the side locks of several others, and the darkened facial skin tones of a few men that are in contrast with their companions' blanched appearance. A close view shows the Cherokees wearing just enough English garb to please their hosts. The men seem bare-legged below the knee and wear moccasins. By artistic design, they are positioned according to relative status. "King" Oukah Ulah, the group's most prestigious member, stands proudly at the center, grasping the handle of a sheathed sword with one hand and a musket with the other. (The firelock appears unthreatening as its butt rests on the ground and its muzzle points upward.) Oukah Ulah's companions pose with various items that might amuse and surprise English viewers. Scalilosken Ketagusta, whom English newspapers labeled "the Prince," holds a whitish feather, a symbol of spiritual power. One Cherokee man has a bow and arrow while another lifts a gourd rattle to ward off evil spirits. Each Cherokee visitor is identified by name according to a small number drawn at his feet with an explanatory table below. White Owl (here spelled "Ukwaneequa") stands on the far right with a sheathed dagger at his side. He is short and slender and appears to be the youngest of the group.[30]

Invited to a Windsor inn, the Cherokees were treated to a dinner by English merchants engaged in the Carolina trade. Here the company feasted on "a good old English Dish of Beans and Bacon," followed by "a substantial Leg of Mutton" and "a capacious Bowl of Rum-Punch."

Cherokee Delegation to England, 1730. *Yale Center for British Art, Yale University.*

Wearing an officer's blue coat, Oukah Ulah was said to look "as soldierly as the King of Sweden, having as many Scarifications in his swarthy Face as there are Bars in a Gridiron." In a more complimentary manner, the English writer admitted that the chief "had a Great deal of Sagacity in his Looks as well as Majesty in his Deportment." The Cherokee headman seemed to show "the modern World a true Copy of a primitive King in the simple State of original Government." This was a romanticized view, consciously likening the Cherokee leader to an ancient "*British* King" with simple and uncorrupted manners.[31]

While still at Windsor, five of the Cherokee men witnessed a grand review of British cavalry regiments before the royal family and other English worthies. This was a novel scene for Native American onlookers, some of whom had encountered colonial militia but seen nothing like professional troops riding in full regalia. As their Windsor stay approached six weeks, the Cherokees eagerly awaited an opportunity to see London again. Once back in the city on July 31, the seven

Cherokees enjoyed a plethora of entertainment. They were regaled at the Carolina Coffee House in Birchin Lane, where they again dined with merchants who traded with Charles Town and had a stake in Indian goodwill. Well-to-do city dwellers jumped at the opportunity of hosting the Cherokees at dinners for pleasure and prestige. Newspapers advertised the Indians' coming visits to raucous popular theater in order to boost ticket sales. At the height of summer fairs in August 1730, Oukah Ulah and company were guests at Tottenham Court's "theatrical booths" or playhouses where they took in farces such as "Mad Tom of Bedlam." One imagines English audiences chuckling and howling at puns and satire that the Cherokees could only interpret through the actors' grimaces, smiles, and gestures. English theatergoers meanwhile gaped at the Cherokees. Interpreter Bunning, himself a Lincolnshire native, doubtless offered a verbal synopsis to Cherokee men, though his words could only go so far in translating the untranslatable. The Cherokees dined with Mr. James Figg, a sports impresario, before viewing "Mad Tom," so they suffered no pangs of hunger during that performance. The next day, they went by boat on the Thames to Richmond Wells for the diversion of a ball. A week later, the Cherokees witnessed a display by the Archery Society, though they felt awkward when given a try at the English long bow and arrows, which were unlike their own weaponry. Private individuals and associations set the tour's pace with little government involvement. City folk of various ranks found the Cherokees to be curiously exotic, well-mannered, and not at all threatening despite their reputation as fearsome warriors. An American Indian delegation's visit to London was rare enough to gain widespread public attention.[32]

Cuming was chagrined to see Britons welcome the Cherokees without paying due respect to his initiative in bringing the guests to England. Quartered in Windsor Castle's cloister during the Indians' stay in the vicinity, he received an unwelcome note from innkeeper J. A. Crowe, who would no longer tolerate the Cherokees in his house. The Indians had a falling-out among themselves the previous night; two chiefs caused a ruckus by fighting each other. Crowe demanded Cuming pay the guests' bill of £41 and change. This unusual disturbance shows that not all went smoothly during the Cherokees' sojourn. When the Native men came to London, they were put up at the same undertaker's house near Covent Garden where Mohawk and Mahican guests had lodged twenty years before. The government footed the bill, relieving Sir Alexander of further personal liability.[33]

Diplomacy and a British-Cherokee Treaty

While Cuming had flouted formal structures of empire, his opportunism allowed British officials to propose a treaty to the Cherokees. The Duke of Newcastle, secretary of state, assigned this responsibility to the Board of Trade and Plantations, the advisory body on colonial affairs to the Privy Council and Parliament. The Lords Commissioners—as Board members were styled—dispensed with Cuming, who lodged nearby. Imperial issues were the business of the king's government.[34] His personal pretensions notwithstanding, the Scots adventurer was pushed aside.

Based on intelligence from South Carolina, the Board characterized the Cherokees as "a Warlike People" that "can bring Three Thousand fighting Men, upon Occasion, into the Field." Here again was a rather simplistic assumption of Cherokee national cohesion and coordinated military strength. The Cherokees, observed the Board, could be the empire's "Frontier Guards" on the southern continental front as the Iroquois were in the north. By negotiating a treaty with Indian delegates, the Board might enhance His Majesty's title "in those Parts, even to all the Lands which these People [i.e., the Cherokees] now Possess." The object was Native "Dependence upon the Crown of Great Britain" rather than a precipitous land grab.[35]

On September 7, 1730, the Cherokee visitors suddenly entered a dramatic stage of their English stay. Just after noon, two coaches arrived at their lodgings and carried them to the Plantations Office at Whitehall Palace at the invitation of the Board of Trade. Grenadiers accompanied them along the way, and other soldiers guided their walk to the meeting hall. The Cherokees were now guests before high-ranking English gentlemen in a building that must have struck them as a very great council house.[36]

Three Lords Commissioners presided, assisted by Robert Johnson, South Carolina's newly appointed governor, and William Keith, former governor of Pennsylvania. Johnson's presence was important because it gave voice to the province that took the lead in English relations with the Cherokees, Creeks, Chickasaws, Choctaws, and other southern Indian groups. British authorities presented the Cherokees with a treaty ("Articles of Friendship and Commerce") that was put to paper after preliminary discussions—and explained through interpreter Bunning. The seven Cherokee representatives, who included the most prominent headmen in the delegation, were scarcely prepared to enter a negotiation,

A Cherokee Voyage to London   113

let alone agree to a treaty proffered to them that they had had no hand in making. They were voyagers to England but not ambassadors with authority to bind their people without consent. Interpreter Bunning had his work cut out for him given the treaty's numerous details. The Articles identified the Indian visitors as "deputed" by their "whole Nation" to treat with the British monarch through the agency of Sir Alexander Cuming and by "express Authority" from chief Moytoy and "all the Cherokee People." Of course, Cuming was not present in the hall; Moytoy was at Tellico across the Great Water. The Cherokee men at Whitehall were suddenly transformed by British sleight of hand into the august status of spokesmen for their entire people. The Cherokee "Crown" of scalps and feathers, which Cuming had laid a few months before at His Majesty's feet, was again said to be a "Token" of Indian "Obedience." In fact, imperial authorities desired both Cherokee alliance and subordination—goals not easily reconcilable.[37]

Speaking in the "Words of the Great King," the Board announced that the English and Cherokees were bound by an unbreakable "Chain of Friendship . . . like the Sun, which both Shines here, and also upon the great Mountains, where they live." This stylized phrasing, appealing to Indian sensibilities, echoed the Covenant Chain that the British had forged with the Iroquois. The King was said to fasten one end of the new chain to "to His own Breast" and desired the other end to be similarly bound to Moytoy along with the Cherokees' "old Wise Men, your Captains, and all your People." The Cherokees and the English of Carolina were henceforth to "live together as the Children of one Family" under a benevolent kingly father. Future colonial expansion was permissible, if ambiguously described. The English would "Build Houses, and . . . plant Corn, from Charles Town, towards the Town of the Cherokees, behind the Great Mountains." Paradoxically, colonists were prohibited from settling "near any Indian Town." Most important, royal sovereignty was affirmed. Just as the monarch allowed his English "Children" to live on "His Land on both Sides of the great Mountains . . . so he now gives to the Cherokee Indians the Priviledge of living where they please."[38] This provision would have baffled the Cherokees had they understood the English words. How could their ancestral soil be a gift from the British monarch?

The Board of Trade envisioned "the great Nation of Cherokees" working in concert with South Carolina, which was to take the colonial lead in executing the treaty. At the South Carolina governor's command, Cherokee "Brethren" would be ready to fight any foes, whether "White

Men or Indians, who shall dare to molest or hurt the English." Significantly, the Board referred to the Cherokees as brothers rather than children when they took up arms for "the Great King" and his people.[39] In the main, the treaty's operative principle was royal gift-giving—a purchase of alliance in all but name.

The Cherokees garnered presents for every treaty requirement they accepted. For example, gunpowder and bullets were allotted, provided the Cherokees neither trade with any "White Men" apart from the English nor allow such persons to build any fort or settlement in their territory. The treaty offered incentives for Indian cooperation on the capture and return of runaway slaves. Each Cherokee man who seized and delivered a Black fugitive would receive a gun and a matchcoat (long cloak). The Board of Trade added other emoluments to encourage compliance in this business—a box of vermilion, ten thousand gunflints, and six dozen hatchets. This munificence attests to how strongly white Carolinians counted on Indians as slave catchers.

By the formal treaty, colonial magistrates were to resolve disputes when either an Englishman killed a Cherokee or an Indian slew an Englishman. In the latter case, the accused party was to be delivered to South Carolina's governor for judgment. Cherokees were subject to colonial justice, but Englishmen were not to be put before an Indian tribunal. This subject had yet to arise as a source of conflict in Cherokee-English relations. In 1730, most contact between Cherokees and colonials came through trade in Indian country. Few Cherokees could foresee how critical the issue of retributive justice would become when clashes between white settlers and Natives escalated during the 1750s.

Carefully enumerating all presents, the Board stored the entire trove of gifts pending Cherokee assent. Samples of the presents were shown, dangled before the visitors, before any were dispensed. These included "several fine Firelocks, with Shot, [and] Powder and Ball in Casks." The king's representatives asked for an answer to their treaty in just two days. The Cherokee delegation's chief spokesman consented, adding that his people "were not come hither as enemies but as friends." This phrase tactfully kept the door open to agreement based on Cherokee expectations of reciprocal amity and not obeisance.[40]

There is one retrospective account, recorded years after the London voyage, indicating that several Cherokee visitors were angered by the treaty's language in which the English king claimed possession of their country. In this story, told by one Englishman to another, at least a few

A Cherokee Voyage to London

115

Indian deputies in London felt bitter after they left the Board of Trade to consider the propositions. The dissatisfied Cherokees were supposedly of a mind to kill the warrior and his interpreter who had given verbal assent to the Board.[41] However, any disputes that the Cherokees may have had among themselves were kept under wraps in London. There was a strong Cherokee custom of keeping internal disagreement within limits and preventing destructive internecine violence.

All was peaceful when the Cherokee men appeared before the Board of Trade after the two-day hiatus. The Lords Commissioners dispatched a guard of two sergeants and twelve grenadiers to Whitehall to impress the visitors. Scalilosken Ketagusta of Tasetchee served as the group's spokesman when the Cherokees affirmed the agreement. He respectfully explained how much he and his fellows had gained from their visit to the land across the Great Water: "We are come hither from a dark Mountainous Place, where nothing but darkness is to be found; but are now in a place where there is light." His statement was politic, voicing appreciation of newly discovered abundance, wonders, and hospitality. In Cherokee belief, mountain caves were entrances to a dangerous underworld closed to brightness and warmth. Speaking for his fellows, Scalilosken accepted bonds of kinship between "red" and "white" people in which the Cherokees would be nurtured and protected and therefore would be loyal in kind: "We look upon the Great King George as the Sun, and as Our Father, and upon Ourselves as his Children. For tho' We are red, and you white, yet Our Hands and Hearts are joined together." The strongest bond was one of mutual security: "In War We Shall always be as one with you. The Great King George's Enemies Shall be Our Enemies. His people and Ours shall be always one, and die together."[42] The British monarch's stature appealed to Cherokees who welcomed a powerful fatherly protector against enemies. In their matrilineal society, it should be recalled, a father was a respected elder rather than a patriarchal overlord.

On the surface, all appeared harmonious between the Cherokees and British authorities. Scalilosken placed feathers on the table before the Board to signal his people's assent to the accord. He did not publicly object to any part of the agreement, apart from stating that the Cherokees could not be expected to return runaway Blacks as strictly as Carolina demanded. Gesturing with a small rope in hand, he explained that the English shackled their slaves with iron chains while Indians used no such means with captives. This matter was not itself a stumbling block toward an agreement. The Lords Commissioners pledged the Cherokees would receive the official treaty with the king's seal. Oukah Ulah and companions exchanged kisses with Board members and then serenaded the assemblage. The Cherokee chant or song is fascinating to imagine, though it not surprisingly went unrecorded.[43]

There was no finished deal quite yet, however. Only six days after the treaty appeared final, the Board received a formal letter from Cuming stating that the Cherokees would not put their marks to the official document without their trusted benefactor, Sir Alexander, present. What had led to the impasse? Cuming desperately wanted official recognition and preferment. Besides, the Cherokees wanted assurance that all would go right. The Board of Trade had little choice but to bend. On September 29, the commissioners sent for Cuming to secure his support. That evening, the Cherokees made their marks on the treaty at Cuming's lodgings in Westminster. They then sang and danced with gratitude.[44]

Cherokee respect for Cuming was genuine. When Scalilosken spoke at Whitehall on September 9, he told the Board of Trade that Cuming "came to us like a Warrior. . . . A Man he was, his talk was upright. . . . We shall never forget him." In his own world, Cuming had little such respect. Some Londoners suspected him as a scheming Scots Jacobite. In response, Cuming touted his patriotism in a London newspaper. No, he had not gone "up to the Cherokee Mountains, in order to find a Refuge for the [Stuart] Pretender." Nor was he a "Cheat" who dealt falsely in promissory notes, as was asserted in the colonies. He rather deserved "Credit" for bringing the Cherokees to honor His Majesty.[45]

Cuming had a hand in publishing the Articles of Friendship and Commerce in the London press. Just below the document, he inserted a declaration, certifying that he approved the agreement, "to which the Indians . . . have, by my Advice, given their Consent." There is no such statement included in the official British record. The imperial government had little tolerance for Sir Alexander and dismissed his petition that one of the Cherokee men stay with him in London. In early October 1730, the Cherokees sailed for home with Robert Bunning and Governor Johnson on the same ship that had brought them to England a few months earlier. Still in London, Cuming did not give up but pleaded for a three-year appointment as royal deputy to the Cherokees. He was willing to "run all risks" by leading the Cherokees in war and giving them "Such Rules for their obedience, as should make them a Great and good People, if your Majesty consented to the

A Cherokee Voyage to London

same." There was no reply from court. Sir Alexander would not be the supreme tribal chieftain he imagined.[46]

Cuming never again ventured to America, while his restless mind gave him no peace. Nearing sixty years of age in 1750, he addressed a most unusual plea to the Duke of Bedford, secretary of state, in which he aspired to found a colony of three hundred thousand Jewish families in the Cherokee homeland, which would not only be beholden to the "British Nation" but to God "when his Kingdom, the Kingdom of righteousness shall at last be established upon Earth." Cuming's imperial quest was now transformed into a millennial vision for the end of days. He also had a more prosaic end in mind—release from debtor's prison, where he had wallowed for some years. In 1766, he was mercifully taken in by the city's charterhouse. He died there in 1775.[47]

In December 1730, the seven Cherokee voyagers arrived in Charles Town from their eventful English visit. They now faced another challenge—how to return safely to their country when their people were in conflict with the Creeks. All goods and munitions brought from England had to be transported across territory that was vulnerable to attack. Johnson suggested that some Cherokees journey from the mountains to Charles Town and serve as bearers during the long trek back. Oukah Ulah and his fellows rejected the idea as too risky. A workable solution was then found. The governor offered a small colonial escort and supplied packhorses for carrying the goods. The cavalcade was soon on its way.[48]

The Cherokee men asserted their independence on a most important matter. They insisted on carrying the royally sealed treaty to their people; they would not entrust it to a colonial courier, as Johnson had proposed. The special paper appeared to promise amity, ample trade, and the supply of munitions—and not a mark of subordination. That message was carried to all Cherokee regions.[49] Cherokees presumed English support would be forthcoming whether they warred with the Creeks or French Indian adversaries. A path to King George was open, notwithstanding the distance across the Great Water. Attakullakulla clung to this idea when his people were called on to aid the English decades later in what is customarily called "The French and Indian War." To understand the Cherokee position at that time, it is essential to trace the upswing of Anglo-French rivalry across eastern North America in the decades prior to that conflict.

Cherokees in Their Homeland and Beyond, 1670–1730

II

Cherokees, Native Peoples, and Empires

1730–1762

5

Warfare and Peace Quests across Half a Continent

The 1730s and 1740s are too often overlooked in the history of warfare and diplomacy in the Native American southeast. These decades were dramatically eventful, given Anglo-Spanish clashes on the Florida frontier, the fallout from French-Chickasaw conflicts, and upheavals in Indian country when Great Britain and France were at war from 1744 to 1748. The choices that Native peoples faced in this era were not simply about playing off imperial powers against one another or deciding to align with either the French or British. These matters counted greatly, but so, too, did keeping abreast of Indigenous allies and adversaries across a broad geographic sphere. Some intertribal enmities appeared irreversible while others were amenable to negotiation and resolution. The red path of war was too costly to be continually pursued. Respite was needed, too, for communal recovery and replenishment.

Given the decentralized character of Indian societies, there was no single Cherokee perspective any more than there was a unitary Creek or Iroquois approach. In 1740, Lower Town Cherokees felt the impact of Anglo-Spanish war in Florida while the Overhill Towns west of the Appalachians were embroiled in conflict with the French and their Native allies about the Ohio, the Great Lakes, and Canada. Connections proliferated far and wide between Indigenous peoples. Cherokees felt the impact of the Natchez uprising against the French in 1729, the Chickasaw fight to stave off French domination, and the Shawnee quest to unify Native peoples seeking security from Anglo-French contention during the 1740s.

For all the accommodations between French colonials and Native peoples from the St. Lawrence to the Great Lakes, the southeastern portion of the continent tells a very different story. Like their British counterparts, French officials perforce worked as eighteenth-century imperialists did by pressing Native peoples to do their bidding and serve as auxiliaries or proxies in war. Potent Indigenous nations, loath to accept subordination, strove to preserve their freedom of maneuver in both the commercial and the political realms. This was a continual struggle in which some Native peoples fared far better than others, and few could rest easy for any length of time.

The Limits of British Alliance

Historians commonly write of a Cherokee-British alliance that lasted with little interruption from the 1710s well into the 1750s. The reality was not so straightforward. The Cherokee visit to England in 1730 came off well but hardly foreclosed contention. In 1733, the South Carolina council weighed rumors that the Lower Cherokees were plotting to kill British traders in their towns. The next year, the provincial government imposed a trade cutoff on the Cherokees for their alleged "Insolence" toward Anglo traffickers. Governor Robert Johnson attributed the unrest to "young ungovernable fellows" who grabbed traders' goods and threatened violence over high prices. The troubles died down in several months when sixty Cherokee men visited Charles Town, pledged good conduct, and won Carolina's assurances of renewed trade. This scenario was par for the course—a cycle of disturbance, diplomacy, and restored calm of uncertain duration. Not all disputes were fully resolved. Four years after the London visit, Cherokees complained of not receiving all of the royal presents shipped from England for their benefit. Searching for an excuse, Governor Johnson admitted to headmen that "some small things were lost in the Path" from Charles Town. Colonial teamsters and others may have picked up their share along the way.[1]

The colonial imperative to project strength was a frequent response to Native unrest. During the squabble over trade, Johnson lectured Cherokees that he was unafraid of Indians "because I have men and arms enough without sending to my King for any help." This was a rather empty boast. South Carolina remained militarily weak and internally vulnerable. In 1730, the colony had some 10,000 white inhabitants, outnumbered by 20,000 enslaved Blacks. Johnson vigorously promoted European Protestant immigration to lessen the demographic imbalance. Though his policy yielded long-term gains, he did not live to witness the results. Johnson died in 1735 just as Swiss newcomers settled Purrysburg by the bluffs along the lower Savannah River.[2]

In 1733, South Carolinians welcomed the founding of Savannah, the first settlement in Georgia, which appeared well situated to strengthen the British position vis-à-vis Spanish Florida. Charles Town aided its new colonial neighbor, only to be miffed when Georgia became an aggressive competitor in the deerskin trade. James Oglethorpe, Georgia's moralistic governor, felt duty bound to ensure fair Indian commerce in his province's jurisdiction, which by royal charter of 1732 extended from the headwaters of the Savannah and Altamaha Rivers to the "South Seas" or Pacific Ocean! On paper, the grant cut deep into South Carolina's prospective western domain.[3] Oglethorpe's deputies went on the offensive in 1735 by evicting a dozen Carolina traders from Creek, Cherokee, and Chickasaw territories for the dubious offense of trafficking without a Georgia license in that colony's supposed bounds. Carolinian John Gardiner had his Tanasee storehouse broken open by Georgia men who chalked a large "R" (for "rex") on his front door, indicating his property was forfeit under the king's authority.[4]

Cherokees in the neighborhood of Tanasee were peeved by the intercolonial ruckus that interrupted customary exchange. Some Native men talked of killing the Georgia intruders if the latter harmed resident traders. Gardiner, the ousted Carolina man, dissuaded his Cherokee friends from violence, advising them that the Georgia fellows were "white People" and the king's subjects. From the prevailing British perspective, Cherokees were expected to show a certain respect to all English—no matter if whites were at odds with one another.[5]

The spat between South Carolina and Georgia raised issues of Native sovereignty and freedom of commerce. In an appeal to the Board of Trade, the South Carolina assembly contended in 1736 that four major southern Indian nations—Catawbas, Cherokees, Creeks, and Chickasaws—had negotiated treaties as "Allies but not as Subjects of the Crown of Great-Britain," and should be free to trade with whichever province they chose. (This argument conveniently bypassed South Carolina's past attempts to exclude Virginia traders from its domain.) The four Native nations, declared the Carolinians, "have maintained their own Possessions and Preserved their Independency; Nor does it appear . . . that they have by Conquest lost, or by Cession, Compact, or otherwise, yielded up or parted with those Rights to which by the Laws of Nature and Nations they were and are entitled." For wholly self-interested purposes, Charles Town invoked natural

Warfare and Peace Quests across Half a Continent   123

rights theory, quite as if it accorded Indians the same liberties that European nations asserted by law.[6]

In 1738, the Privy Council bowed to Charles Town by allowing South Carolina's Indian traders to traffic in Georgia's bounds with a license obtained from either province. Imperial authorities had far greater concerns that year. Britain neared war with Spain. Oglethorpe, no political slouch, had recently scored a coup while in England by being appointed commander of both South Carolina and Georgia troops on the front with Florida. Just as important, he secured more than six hundred regular troops for the impending campaign, by far the greatest British military commitment in the region to that time.[7]

The English colonial agenda put a premium on gaining Native support in advance of war. In March 1737, the South Carolina assembly set the goal of bringing as many as five hundred Creek warriors to the Florida frontier and summoning three hundred to four hundred Cherokees to guard "the out settlements of this Province" and "to be ready to march on an hour's warning." White Carolinians had more than the Spanish in mind. Lieutenant Governor Thomas Broughton desired some Cherokee men "to Come down to the Settlements" and "be an Awe to the Negroes" by seizing Black escapees heading to Florida. Little came of this plan, however, since the Cherokees remained aloof, preoccupied with their own affairs.[8]

Since Georgia banned African slavery from its founding, Oglethorpe looked beyond the issue of slave-catching that troubled white Carolinians. Putting great stock in Indian fighters, he journeyed to Coweta in the summer of 1739 in a bid for Creek support in the impending war with Spain. The upshot was ambiguous. Oglethorpe conceived of organizing a Creek "Regiment" of four hundred men, while Muscogee leaders offered aid in a looser and more open-ended manner. The governor was certainly eager to satisfy Indian concerns. By treaty, he affirmed respect for all Creek lands "as high as the Tide flows," implicitly as far west as the Atlantic's surge drove Georgia's coastal waterways inland. The Creeks would have been all too pleased if this rule were made permanent.[9]

While Oglethorpe engaged in Indian diplomacy, South Carolina was suddenly shaken by slave revolt. On September 9, 1739, twenty African men rose in rebellion by the Stono River about fifteen miles southwest of Charles Town. Blacks timed the revolt to exploit wartime confusion and took courage from a newly promulgated Spanish royal edict granting freedom to English slaves who reached St. Augustine.

With numbers rising above sixty, the rebels headed south and killed twenty-one whites before being repelled in a sharp fight with the South Carolina militia.[10]

Oglethorpe continued on his Indian recruitment drive, regardless of the Stono revolt. On September 17, he met with thirty-four Cherokee men at Fort Augusta on the Savannah. His appeal for military support met pushback. One chief said that his people had been struck by two deadly ills—smallpox and foul English rum that had killed as many as a thousand warriors and hunters since the previous winter. The death toll was severe, if possibly overstated by Cherokees who were cool to participate in an English invasion of Florida. Headmen dampened the atmosphere, saying that some of their towns had turned to French traders out of disgust with British traffickers.[11]

Oglethorpe brushed off this bad news, acting as if the Cherokees could still be persuaded to contribute mightily to the British war effort. Thomas Eyre, the governor's deputy to the Cherokees, was tasked with raising 600 to 1,000 warriors, a wildly unrealistic number. He accomplished little during the fall-winter hunting season when most Cherokee men were far from their towns. While at Tugaloo, he met headmen who again brought up their people's severe losses from smallpox. Carolina deerskin traders meanwhile threatened Eyre for meddling in their neighborhood and attempting to draw off Native hunters. Traders had their own business—to hell with that of the king! After five tiresome months, Eyre gained 106 Cherokee volunteers, doubtless enticed by munitions and emoluments. Trekking southeast from Keowee, the warriors arrived at Savannah on April 15, 1740, and were huzzaed by colonials, serenaded with honorary cannon fire, and warmly greeted by Oglethorpe. William Stephens, a Georgia official on the scene, described the Cherokees as "a Body of lusty, lively Fellows, with all their Faces most dismally painted with Vermillion and Blue, variously, as each fancied, to make himself appear terrible (as is their usual Custom) and well armed with Firelocks and Hatchets."[12]

The next month, 90 Cherokees saw their first action in Florida where they joined 200 British troops, 100 colonial militiamen, and a few Creek warriors in the capture of a Spanish blockhouse below the St. Johns River. The Cherokees had no joy in the battle's aftermath when scrupulous General Oglethorpe chided them for killing the enemy's cattle. One Cherokee warrior said, "it was a strange Thing that they were permitted to kill the Spaniards, but not their Beef."[13] Other Indians found Oglethorpe's war code just as peculiar. Eastern

Warfare and Peace Quests across Half a Continent

Chickasaw men danced and whooped before they entered the general's tent and presented him with the severed head of a "Spanish Indian." Oglethorpe was aghast. He refused the gift, calling it a "Barbarity." Taken aback, the Chickasaws said they would never have been so badly treated if giving an Englishman's head to a French commander.[14]

Oglethorpe's difficulties with Indians transcended cultural differences over atrocities. The Creeks had their own way of war and much preferred to fight Florida Indian foes than to assist the English siege of St. Augustine's fortress. In July 1740, the British withdrew in the face of Spanish reinforcements from Cuba. With defeat, South Carolina and Georgia leaders traded recriminations over the responsibility for failure.[15]

Cherokee warriors suffered gravely during their Florida venture; many died of disease. As surviving fighters trekked home, they clashed with Muscogee men and their Yuchi allies. In early 1741, a Yuchi-Creek band killed two Cherokees and took three as prisoners near the Savannah River. A Georgia settler vainly attempted to ransom the captives. Rejecting the offer, a Yuchi man vowed to have one of the prisoners burned alive because Cherokees had "cut his Uncle to pieces." This was likely payback for the Cherokee massacre of Yuchis in 1713–1714. Intertribal conflicts again had their own life outside of imperial battles.[16]

Parameters of Anglo-French Rivalry

Britain and France were at peace from 1714 to 1743, by far the lengthiest interval without war between the two nations from the reign of Louis XIV through the French Revolution and Napoleonic era. In North America, the formal state of peace scarcely diminished adversarial scheming by rival colonial camps, which competed strenuously for the upper hand in Indian country. Imperial antagonists believed it only a matter of time before partial jousting gave way to full-scale war ignited by European hostilities. For all the bad blood on both sides, British and French officials shared a similar line of thought—the surest way of securing an Indigenous nation's support was to gain mastery over its trade and supply. Conversely, the loss of trade to colonial opponents could spell disaster. The French felt especially vulnerable on this front, but the English were not without their concerns.

Colonial insecurity waxed hot for a simple reason. Neither Britain nor France had a sure position in vast stretches of interior North America. In 1734, the South Carolina Assembly petitioned King George II to heed the threat of French expansion. Charles Town identified two points of danger. The first was a French military buildup by the Mississippi, which seemingly brought the Choctaws, numbering some five thousand fighting men, within Louisiana's grasp. A second concern was Fort Toulouse, a strategic if lightly manned French fort on the Coosa River just above its confluence with the Alabama. The common French name for the fort—"Le Post aux Alibamons" ("the Alabama Fort" to the English)—underscores the garrison's dependence on nearby Native communities. The outpost was a diplomatic center, a source of intelligence, and a delivery point for Indian trade goods and presents transported by galley boats from Mobile. The Alabamas and nearby Muscogee villagers valued Fort Toulouse as a counterpoise to English influence. As early as 1720, Colonel John Barnwell of South Carolina wrote that all Indians west of the Alabama fort were essentially "frenchified." In reality, the small French garrison depended on Native goodwill. In 1721, Fort Toulouse's commandant called on Alabama fighters to pursue and kill about twenty mutinous French soldiers who deserted the post and headed for Carolina. The Alabamas fulfilled the mission without difficulty, slaying eighteen mutineers, while one poor deserter was executed by his countrymen.[17]

The British drew little comfort from this episode. English colonial anxieties intensified during the early 1720s when the French launched their first major thrust at colonization in the Lower Mississippi Valley. Imperial France vaunted its North American ambitions by maps that aroused foreign astonishment and jealousy. Few maps of the era drew more British scrutiny than cartographer Guillaume Delisle's published masterpiece of 1718: *Carte de la Louisiane et du cours du Mississipi* (Map of Louisiana and the course of the Mississippi). Besides offering a trove of information about Native peoples, Delisle asserted France's immense territorial claims by writing "LOUISIANE" in bold letters from Apache country to the Appalachians and even further east.[18]

With Delisle's work in view, the British Board of Trade called on governors of all of the North American colonies to forward maps of their respective provinces and interior territories. Early in 1720, Lieutenant Governor Alexander Spotswood of Virginia informed London that he had rough maps of inland regions but no individual who could "put them in a proper Dress or copy them exactly." Frustrated by this deficiency, Spotswood expressed a geographic truism that would be repeated over decades. The French would soon be poised to surround "all the British Plantations in America" by "Communication . . . between

Warfare and Peace Quests across Half a Continent

Canada and [the] Mississippi, by the conveniency of the Lakes . . . and the many Rivers running into them and into the Mississippi." Exploiting these strategic routes, France would engross Indian trade and be well equipped for the offensive. The French or "their Indians" might readily descend on Virginia "by possessing themselves of the Passes of the Great Mountains, which lie between us and the Lakes." Interestingly, Spotswood believed South Carolina to be in danger from French intrusions among the "Coosta" Indians (the Coosas in Upper Creek country), opening passage to "the Great Nation of the Cherokees."[19]

British views changed little even though Louisiana hardly thrived as the English feared. Among the roughly seven thousand French immigrants who arrived in Louisiana from 1717 to 1721, no more than half were alive or remained in the colony by 1726. Enslaved Africans, who were transported to Louisiana in large numbers through the 1720s, suffered horrifically from disease and maltreatment, and consequently had a high mortality rate. Louisiana's frontier garrisons were often miserable places for ill-provisioned soldiers. French missionary efforts had notable success in the St. Lawrence Valley and the Great Lakes but gained relatively few converts among southeastern Indigenous peoples. These shortcomings were blurred to English colonial officials who viewed French power as menacing because of limited British influence in Indian country from the Great Lakes to the Gulf.[20]

Tugs of Will and Quests for Survival

In late 1729, Louisiana officers anxiously bid for Choctaw aid after a Natchez Indian revolt devastated the colony's most promising plantation district above New Orleans. The uprising, provoked by fears of French domination and land engrossment, was extraordinarily bloody. In just four hours on November 28, Natchez fighters killed 145 European men, 36 women, and 56 children. The Natchez captured another 150 colonial women and children, at least some of whom were tortured and slain. Innocents were cut down no less than French officers known for their abuse of Indians. Blacks in the vicinity had a varied role in these events. Some Africans joined the uprising, while others were seized as Natchez prisoners.[21]

The magnitude of the French disaster cannot be measured by numbers alone, though the death toll is astonishing when one considers that all Louisiana had about 2,000 white residents at the time; the black population was perhaps 4,000. Determined to suppress the Natchez, French officers called on the Choctaws as their essential striking force. Colonial pledges of munitions and trade goods were the price of support. In January 1730, five hundred Choctaw warriors dealt the Natchez a heavy, if not crushing blow. A month later, desperate Natchez escaped a Franco-Choctaw siege by fleeing their palisaded fort in the middle of the night and evading foes. The Choctaws closely measured their own interests, declining further involvement in the offensive unless the French delivered on supplies and favorable trade terms.[22]

The French-Natchez War had no definite end point. Bent on retribution, the French went about executing or enslaving those of the enemy that fell in their grasp. Natchez survivors fled both west and east of the Mississippi and targeted the French and their Indian allies. Within a few years, scores of Natchez exiles settled in Chickasaw territory, while smaller numbers reached Cherokee and Creek country. The French demanded that the Chickasaws kill or surrender the Natchez or face destruction.[23]

In the wake of the Natchez uprising, the French imperial government instituted two momentous changes to Louisiana's administration. First, Paris placed the colony directly under royal rule, ending governance by private companies that were ill equipped to carry a heavy financial burden. Second, the king called on Jean-Baptiste LeMoyne, sieur de Bienville, who was in France during the Natchez revolt, to return to the Mississippi and take the helm as provincial governor in New Orleans. The choice was fitting, as Bienville had been a driving force in Louisiana since the colony's inception at the dawn of the eighteenth century. Fifty-five years old on his return in 1733, he believed himself the only leader with sufficient knowhow to restore Indian relations to a proper course. Bienville's goals transcended the neutralization of the Chickasaws for harboring the Natchez and refusing to renounce English trade. All Indian peoples under Louisiana's government should know that it was "dangerous" to offend the French.[24]

Red Shoe (Soulouche Oumastabé), a formidable Choctaw warrior who had fought the Chickasaws and Natchez in the past, stirred the waters by testing an English trading option in 1734. That summer, he reached Savannah with six other Choctaw men and several women after a trek of six hundred miles. Red Shoe pointed to the women's presence as a sign of his people's "good hearts" in peacemaking. He hoped to meet Oglethorpe but could not because the governor was then in England

Warfare and Peace Quests across Half a Continent   129

on a lobbying mission.[25] After a short stay in Savannah, Red Shoe and company returned to their country with a load of presents. The chief carried a British musket, a Union Jack, and a gold-laced scarlet suit, itself an English emblem. Commenting on Red Shoe's maneuvers, Father Michel Baudouin, an astute Jesuit priest perched in Choctaw country, minimized the threat to French interests. From all he saw, the Choctaws were not about to take a sudden turn toward the English. That was indeed true, but Baudouin underestimated Choctaw disaffection with French authority. Many Choctaws chafed at being treated as Bienville's underlings. They worried that the governor might dispense with their services, effectively throwing them to the dogs if the Chickasaws were wholly destroyed. French officials complained of Choctaw men demanding high prices for Chickasaw scalps while also insisting on having their firearms repaired gratis at Mobile.[26]

French and English officials had little tolerance for Native diplomacy based on self-interest, especially freedom of trade and association. Despite knowing the risk of alienating European powers, American Indians were natural free traders attracted by the best bargain wherever it could be found. Provincial governors struggled to impose uniformity in Native commerce by repeated calls on Indians to toe the line.[27]

The Chickasaws Hold the Line

The Chickasaws of the Upper Tombigbee were as staunch fighters as any southeastern Native nation in the mid-1700s, especially when measured by their small population. It seems to defy all odds that they managed to repel successive French and allied Indian assaults from the Illinois country and Mobile in 1736. The southern invasion force alone, under Bienville's command, was composed of 500 French troops and colonial militia, about 100 free Black and African slave conscripts, accompanied by 600 Choctaw warriors. Defying the invaders, 300 to 400 Chickasaw fighters, aided by 40 Natchez warriors, shocked the enemy with withering gunfire from palisaded strongholds. At the height of battle on May 26, the Choctaws held back and watched in amazement as Bienville's soldiers continued their advance as their comrades were felled by an entrenched enemy. In several hours, French losses mounted to 37 dead and 117 wounded, besides captives. As night fell, Chickasaw women taunted the French by banging a large pot and ridiculing the foe's weakness and hallooing their own men's strength.

Adding to insult, a British flag defiantly flew atop one Chickasaw fort throughout the day.[28]

Fifteen Anglo traders were with the Chickasaws during the engagement. When news of the battle reached Charles Town, Carolina assemblymen were elated but dumbfounded since they did not see how this small Indian nation, fighting virtually on its own, could stave off more French assaults. In December 1737, South Carolina's government advised the Chickasaws to move east for their own survival and live among the Cherokees. Stalwart Chickasaw headmen shelved the idea. War chief Mingo Ouma derided some of his fellows as "women" for even considering flight from the homeland.[29]

Despite holding their ground, many Chickasaws badly wanted a French peace and a respite from Bienville's practice of inciting the Choctaws against them. Communal survival was on the line. Under these conditions, Chickasaw headmen discussed the idea of appeasing the French by evicting or killing the Natchez who lived in their midst. Talk of this kind was no secret. As word got around, many of the Natchez no longer felt secure among the Chickasaws. During the summer of 1736, 150 desperate Natchez, mostly women and children, headed east from Chickasaw territory toward Cherokee country. The journey was perilous. As the exiles neared the Tennessee River, they were attacked by Mascouten and Kickapoo warriors returning to Illinois from the previous spring's battle with the Chickasaws. Natchez men fended off the attackers, losing two dead and three captured in the skirmish. By 1737, 30 Natchez women, 100 children, and an unknown number of men were living among the Cherokees. Their motive was group survival. Some Natchez, meanwhile, remained with the Chickasaws through mutual if tenuous accommodation.[30]

Natchez reliance on new Cherokee hosts brought uncertainty. The hosts, having their own mouths to feed and their own kin to safeguard, might renege on taking in a small group with powerful enemies. In 1737, four unnamed Cherokee headmen arrived at Fort Toulouse to hold talks with French commandant, Lieutenant Erneville. Beset by conflict with pro-French Alabamas, the Cherokee envoys offered a quid pro quo. Their people would observe strict neutrality in French-Chickasaw conflict provided they gained a letup in Alabama enmity. A chilling proposal followed. The Cherokees stated their willingness to kill the Natchez in their territory if it would bring peace with the Alabamas and satisfy the French. Before leaving the fort, Cherokee men told Erneville that they would return the next spring and bring several Natchez

Warfare and Peace Quests across Half a Continent

scalps with them. Fortunately, this bloodcurdling offer was not executed. The Natchez evidently had Cherokee protectors whose goodwill was literally a breath of life. Safety did not come from benevolence alone. Some Cherokees valued the Natchez for being willing friends in the fight against the French and their Native allies.[31]

The Cherokees were highly interested in the ongoing French-Chickasaw hostilities. During the summer of 1736, a Cherokee war party killed four French voyageurs along the Ohio. As the Cherokees headed south, they came under attack by one hundred Miami and Wea fighters of the Wabash who wounded one man and took three prisoners, one of whom was a Natchez warrior. Bienville paid close attention to this news. The Natchez would fight the French in all quarters.[32]

Bienville repeatedly wrote the French ministry that he was determined on the "destruction" of the Chickasaws. Did he mean the total elimination of a people—genocide? That question is not easily answered. Bienville certainly believed that the Chickasaws must be wholly destroyed as a military force and uprooted from their territory. The French goal—little different from the English, in the case of the Yamasee—was to reduce the Chickasaws through war and enslavement to little more than a remnant people.[33]

There is another question worth posing. Would Bienville have been satisfied if the Chickasaws had turned on the Natchez, as he urged? That bloodshed would have closed one chapter but not another in the governor's book. Bienville had his own domino theory. The Chickasaw preference for English trade, unless arrested, would inevitably spread to the Choctaws, thereby dooming Louisiana. It should be said that Bienville did not fanatically hate the Chickasaws, but indeed admired them for their love of country, expert musketry, and bravery. His logic was coldly imperial. "Barbarians" could not be tolerated if they posed a danger to a fragile colonial enterprise whose purpose was to stave off English continental expansion.[34]

Not desiring continual war, Chickasaw leaders weighed a French peace and tested negotiation toward that end. In 1737, Mingo Ouma, a foremost headman, called on a deerskin artist to represent his people's diplomatic stance to the French. He meanwhile enlisted the Pakana captain, an Alabama chief, to carry the deerskin to Mobile and to explain its meaning to colonial officers. The choice of an intermediary was critical to bridge divides. Trusted by Mingo Ouma, the Pakana captain was also on good terms with the French. From Mobile, the deerskin map was sent to New Orleans, where it was copied by engineer Alexandre de Batz, who added a written title and notations based on what Pakana relayed.[35]

The map, drawn with circles depicting nations, places the Chickasaw at the center. Seven major pathways or lines emanate from Chickasaw country. Five of these are "red" warpaths symbolized by their brokenness; these lines do not connect peoples in unity or harmony. There are two unbroken "white" or peace paths—one to the Abeika Creeks and the other to the Cherokees, peoples that shared the Chickasaws' trading ties with English South Carolina. Interestingly, the map depicts two Cherokee circles—one larger than the other. The western one has greater prominence, telling us that the "Upper" or Overhill Cherokees were more important to the Chickasaws than the distant Lower Towns. Like the Chickasaws, Overhill Cherokees commonly sent war parties to the west and north against French-allied Indians. They, too, were hit by "French Indian" attacks initiated from the Great Lakes region and Canada. Mingo Ouma's declared hope was that the red lines would become white and the broken lines whole through peace. Left unresolved was the question whether the Natchez, who had no place on the map, would be sacrificed toward that end.[36]

Though intrigued by Mingo Ouma's diplomacy, Bienville had already decided on a large multi-pronged offensive to crush the Chickasaws. The campaign was finally launched during the summer of 1739 when five hundred troops put into New Orleans from France, with transport ships bearing enormous quantities of weaponry and supplies. This level of imperial engagement in North American Indian warfare far exceeded any instance in the British colonies to that time. French military assistance to the colonies had precedents dating to the 1660s when Colbert, Louis XIV's first minister, dispatched soldiers to the St. Lawrence that saved fledgling New France in its decades-long battle with the Iroquois.[37]

Bienville's grand campaign of 1739–1740 failed for many reasons. One major error was his decision to transport hundreds of French troops up the Mississippi in summer's torrid heat and lethal disease environs. Scores of soldiers either died or fell gravely ill and were rendered hors de combat. Black slave deck hands suffered, too. The governor still managed to assemble a formidable force of French regulars, colonial militia, and a daunting array of Native warriors at Fort Assumption (the site of modern Memphis, Tennessee) during the fall of 1739. At one point, there may have been as many as seven hundred French and perhaps a similar number of allied Indians in the locale. The largest

Warfare and Peace Quests across Half a Continent

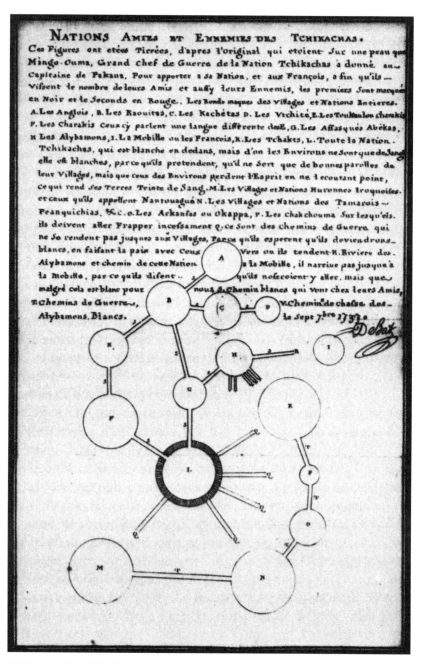

Chickasaw Map. "Nations Amies et Ennemies des Tchikachas" (Friendly and Enemy Nations of the Chickasaws) by Alexandre de Batz, 1737. *Archives nationales d'outremer, Aix-en-Provence, France, ANOM.*

northern Indian contingent—160 men alone—consisted of Canadian Iroquois who dwelt in mission villages near Montreal. Another hundred warriors of Illinois, Arkansas, and other regions joined the Native encampment. At one feast, Missouri Indians smoked the calumet with the Iroquois and regaled them with war chants. Warriors of the two nations, living more than one thousand miles apart, spoke no common language but understood one another perfectly.[38]

Bienville's designs went awry during the winter months, when heavy rains made the terrain nearly impassable, food and supplies ran short, and the French ranks were sapped by disease. The governor belatedly discovered that Chickasaw villages lay considerably farther east of the Mississippi than he had thought. By the time the French finally launched the offensive, many allied Indian fighters had left for home. Other warriors sallied forth in raids on the Chickasaws independent of French command. Only about sixty Choctaws joined the campaign rather than the hundreds that were anticipated by Bienville. Captain Céleron de Blainville's striking force, composed of 200 French soldiers and 330 warriors, finally neared the Chickasaws' prairie towns in late February 1740. The invaders reconnoitered snow-covered terrain and skirmished with well-fortified defenders for a week before a truce was arranged. Chickasaw chiefs journeyed to Fort Assumption for parleys with Bienville. A peace deal followed, but nothing was resolved in any lasting sense.[39]

The French failure of 1739–1740 had far-reaching implications for southeastern North America. Bienville's reverse meant that English traders would continue to embed themselves among the Chickasaws. French prestige diminished even though Louisiana's officials spared no effort to keep the Choctaws in their camp. Choctaw social unrest grew, with internal rifts over whether villages and kin groups should back the French or turn toward the English. By 1746, the Choctaws were plunged in a deadly civil war.[40]

Cherokee Warfare and Diplomacy

The Cherokees took heart from the Chickasaws' repulse of invasion in early 1740. That spring, a band of Cherokee warriors numbering thirty to seventy men attacked a small French convoy headed up the Ohio River toward the Wabash. The assailants struck by surprise when Canadian voyageurs put ashore to rest and left their camp unguarded. Several French traders were struck dead as they slept; others fled for their lives with African laborers and Indian guides. The Cherokees captured two Frenchmen and seized two pirogues. When news of the episode reached New Orleans, colonial officers could only speculate on which Indian group had conducted the attack. Bienville initially suspected the Sioux of the Great Plains; others believed the Chickasaws to be the main culprits. A half-year passed before the French learned from their Alabama allies that the Cherokees had been responsible. Reconnoitering the killing site after the attack, Illinois colonists found war clubs, rattles, and food pouches purposefully left by Cherokee warriors announcing their triumph. Battle remains told a highly intentional story—enemies beware! Cherokees in disparate regions were pulled in differing directions. While Overhill fighters took an aggressive course to the west, Lower Town hunters were being recruited by Oglethorpe to battle Spaniards in Florida.[41]

Cherokees built on their successes on the western waters. During the fall of 1740, 140 Cherokee warriors targeted a convoy of twenty-four French and Canadian traders moving up the Ohio near its confluence with the Tennessee. Caught in a small cove during bad weather, the defenders fought bravely against the odds. By the attack's end, sixteen colonial hunters and traders were dead besides a woman and one girl who was said to have passed gunpowder to comrades until her last breath. Five wounded colonials and three others managed to escape. Having full command, Cherokees took a haul of furs, tobacco, lead, and gunpowder. The warriors passed the news to British traders, who sent word to Charles Town. Successful attacks on the French brought English gifts of munitions—just as the victors expected.[42]

Unfortunately, French records do not disclose the particular Cherokee towns or war chiefs that led these attacks. From all that can be gathered, there is little doubt that Overhill Cherokees led the way in northwesterly attacks. They dwelt west of the Appalachians and were well abreast of developments in Chickasaw country and along the Ohio-Tennessee-Mississippi Rivers. Moytoy of Great Tellico, who had been honored by Alexander Cuming in 1730, remained the single most prestigious Cherokee war leader through the next ten years. In March 1738, he led seventy-three Cherokee men to South Carolina's capital, where the provincial assembly doled out a coat and breeches to each Indian visitor and presented the entire group with sixty-four guns and ammunition. Moytoy received singular honors—"a Scarlet Coat and Breeches of Broad Cloth trimmed with Gold" as well as "a good Gun" and "a Tie Wig"—this last gift mirroring the English gentlemanly fashion of wearing a wig with curls tied in the back.[43]

On November 15, 1741, a Cherokee war party again targeted French river craft, in this case just when boats passed from the Mississippi to the Ohio after a long voyage out of New Orleans. Eighty to ninety Cherokees approached one boat's crew that rested along the riverbank. The Frenchmen were at first unafraid because they took the Natives for Illinois and Missouri Indian friends. A minute later, the Cherokees let loose musket fire that killed three Frenchmen and wounded two others. The attackers took five captives, including a Black man. All the prisoners were bound and collared as slaves. The war party seized all goods on the enemy boat and then embarked in twenty-two canoes with plunder and captives up the Ohio for the "Cherokee River" (the Tennessee) and their country. Interestingly, several Natchez Indians guided the Cherokees to the attack site.[44]

We know a good deal about the episode from the journal of Antoine Bonnefoy, a French trader who was taken prisoner in the assault. Bonnefoy's first Indian master sold him to another Cherokee man, who treated him as a brother. Other Cherokees adopted French captives, though the Black prisoner, suffering from a festering musket wound, received no favor. Once reaching a Cherokee village, warriors handed the ailing man to Indian youths, who promptly killed and scalped him. Was this a mercy killing or instead a training for war—perhaps something of both? The record does not say.[45]

Bonnefoy's Cherokee brother trekked beside him on the final leg to Overhill country. The Frenchman carried a gun, gunpowder, and bullets, just as his master did. On the way, Cherokees met Chickasaws with whom they smoked pipes, traded goods and slaves, and then went on their separate paths. The Cherokee party and its captives renewed their journey until reaching Great Tellico. The French prisoners, including Bonnefoy, were again collared and ordered to strip, given a rattle and stick for each hand, and made to sing for hours until the town's women served them a savory meal of corn porridge, buffalo and bear meat, rabbit, and sweet potatoes. The next morning the captives once more acted out ceremonial roles as slaves before being de-collared and fully adopted—born anew after the old self was spiritually laid to rest. Bonnefoy's Cherokee brother took him into his cabin and washed and ate with him. Both men were soon hunting together for days at a time.[46]

Warfare and Peace Quests across Half a Continent

Great Tellico's involvement is a sure sign of Overhill Cherokee warfare against the French and their Native allies. Bonnefoy saw British traders supplying Cherokees with guns and munitions for use against his countrymen. The French captive became aware of an Indian world far beyond Louisiana's control. Fifteen Natchez men were in the village, some having come as far as the Ouachita River west of the Mississippi. With their kin in mind, they departed Tellico to search for refugees among their dispersed nation.[47]

Bonnefoy and two compatriots themselves fled Great Tellico one night when the Cherokees were having a drunken revel. Making their way west by land and water, the three men were separated when their makeshift raft plunged over river rapids gushing in springtime. Alone and struggling over days, Bonnefoy trekked south toward Fort Toulouse but was seized by Alabama warriors and brought to an Indian town where fifteen Chickasaw men were present along with English traders. The Chickasaws taunted the Frenchman in the Mobile Indian tongue—a regional patois that Bonnefoy and the British visitors understood. In this intricate social environment, travelers of different nationalities crossed paths in various guises—as freemen and slaves, allies and foes, and bargainers for advantage. Two Alabama men escorted Bonnefoy to Fort Toulouse and received the commandant's present for his return.[48]

During his time in Tellico, Bonnefoy's most intriguing acquaintance was Christian Gottlieb Priber, a German legal scholar and religious mystic who flouted all colonial norms. After emigrating to South Carolina, he cast aside his worldly goods, set out for the Appalachians, and came to live at Great Tellico about 1736. Priber earned his hosts' respect by learning their language and adopting their dress. According to Scots trader Ludovick Grant, Priber "trimm'd his hair in the Indian manner & painted [himself] as they did going generally almost naked except [for] a shirt & a Flap." Priber dreamed of forming an ideal community in the borderland between Cherokee and Creek territories where Indians and whites could live together harmoniously and where both French and English traders would be welcome. As Grant related the plan, Priber's "Society" would admit not only Cherokees but "Creeks & Catawbas, French & English, [and] all Colours & Complexions."[49] This was a truly otherworldly vision for its time and place—and perhaps for any other.

Priber's presence among the Cherokees did not sit well at Charles Town. In October 1739, Lieutenant Governor William Bull reported to

London that Priber, "a Saxon" (German), was a probable French agent who might sway Indians in dangerous ways. Without swift English action, Bull imagined a French fort soon arising in Cherokee country, hastening the enemy's "grand design in Surrounding the British Colonies." Charles Town countered with its own means of persuasion. At Bull's behest, trader Grant offered Moytoy "a great present" if he handed over Priber. Moytoy refused, explaining that his people believed it wrong to surrender someone who had taken shelter among them. The Tellico chief was no one's tool even though he held the English title of Cherokee "emperor."[50] Priber ventured toward Fort Toulouse and Mobile in 1743, only to be captured by Creek warriors, who delivered him to an English officer. The German mystic's next stop was a prison barrack at Fort Frederica on the Georgia coast. Tragically, he took ill and died there a year later.[51]

Priber passed from the scene just as the French took severe measures against the Cherokees for targeting their river convoys. In this case, retaliation came by willing proxies. In 1742, the marquis de Beauharnois, governor-general at Quebec, ordered his officers from the St. Lawrence to the Great Lakes to arm Native allies for attacks on the Cherokees, Chickasaws, and Natchez. In warfare that reached its height about 1743, the Cherokees were hit by the same nations that were customary foes: Miamis and Weas, Hurons and Ottawas, Canadian Mohawks and their kin of the Iroquois League.[52] In many cases, we cannot identify the specific Indian nation that dealt the blows. Moytoy of Tellico was killed in battle in 1741. Georgia records disclose that he died at the hands of a "back Enemy," implying an assault by Native foes to the west or north.[53]

The Cherokees and the Iroquois

British officials from South Carolina to New York were frustrated by Indian allies that acted contrary to imperial interests. Particularly vexing were hostilities between the Iroquois (now Six Nations) and their southern foes—the Cherokees and Catawbas—since all were supposedly English friends. From an imperial perspective, this kind of petty, nagging warfare vitiated a common front against the French.[54]

Given complementary interests, New York and South Carolina sought to mediate an Iroquois peace with southern Indians during the late 1730s. Virginia entered the diplomatic arena, too, since its burgeoning settlements in the Shenandoah Valley stood astride time-tested trails used by Indian war parties. The Shenandoah's "Great Wagon Road," which grew appreciably in the 1730s and 1740s, became an artery for colonial immigrants who entered the valley after putting into Philadelphia, traveling west, and then following a well-worn path to the Potomac with ferry service to Virginia. Extensions of Virginia's wagon road soon reached into the Carolinas and then Georgia.[55]

The changing human landscape carried portents of violence. In 1738, Lieutenant Governor William Gooch of Virginia was at his wit's end as he dealt with the consequences of an Iroquois attack on the Catawbas followed by a Catawba counterraid that struck the enemy near the Potomac. In the conflict's aftermath, a band of Iroquois warriors killed eleven Virginia settlers "on the back of the mountains," that is, west of the Blue Ridge, as Gooch reported. When the governor pressured several Iroquois towns to surrender the "murderers," the village chiefs claimed that "French Indians," and not their own people, had killed the colonists. This was standard self-protective diplomacy.[56]

While upset at the killings, Gooch was even more troubled by the Iroquois League's position relative to the British Empire. In a letter to the Board of Trade, he maintained that the Six Nations were bound by treaty with "His Majesty's Government." They accordingly stood "if not as [British] Subjects, at least as Allys," and had no right to "employ their Force to destroy other [Indian] nations under the same Protection with themselves." In short, Indian nations had obligations toward one another when they dwelt under the British imperium. If Gooch had his way, the empire rather than its Indigenous allies would call the shots. The Six Nations had a quite different idea, believing they had dominion over previously conquered lands—an indeterminate expanse across Pennsylvania, Maryland, and Virginia to the Ohio country and even to regions south of the Ohio. Gooch rejected the Iroquois conception while realizing it could not be brushed aside without new treaty arrangements. The governor looked forward to the day when "the [white] Subjects of His Majesty would soon extend their Settlements beyond the mountains," thereby warding off the French "on this side [of] the Lakes, and the River Missisippi."[57]

Powerful Indigenous nations were wooed by provincial governments but were not as easily swayed to swallow their pride and relinquish a smidgen of independence. The Iroquois coyly put off Virginia's offer of 1738 to mediate peace talks with Cherokees and Catawbas at Williamsburg. Two years later, Governor George Clarke of New York asked

Cherokees, Native Peoples, and Empires, 1730–1762

Iroquois deputies at Albany to broaden the Covenant Chain by entering friendship with "all the Nations of Indians under his Majesty's protection who live to the Southward and Westward . . . even as far as the great River Mississippi." In that event, Cherokees, Catawbas, Chickasaws, and others would be brought into peace with the Six Nations through their common bond with the British Crown.[58]

Iroquois spokesmen replied that they were not yet ready to "be united as one body, one heart and one flesh" with southern foes. The Six Nations offered a window of two years for the Cherokees and Catawbas to send emissaries north to confirm a truce or treaty. Dissatisfied with the delay, Clarke insisted that he could not give presents to the Iroquois unless they acknowledged southern Indians as "Brethren" out of respect for "the [English] King," their "Father." The Iroquois deputies consented. A tactful bow to King George did not lessen their freedom of action. Before the Albany meeting concluded, Iroquois emissaries presented a wampum belt to New York officials so that it could be sent to Virginia's governor and then passed to Charles Town for presentation to the Cherokees and Catawbas. Indigenous messaging ran through colonial capital towns as necessary.[59]

Long-distance diplomacy was never a speedy matter. Eight months elapsed between Clarke's conference with the Six Nations and a follow-up in Charles Town, where Cherokee and Catawba deputies met with Lieutenant Governor Bull. The Cherokees responded favorably to the Iroquois wampum belt. In return, they requested that Bull forward gifts to the Six Nations. The items included beads, a pipe, and an eagle's tail along with a captured French flag, all intended to display peaceful intent along with strength. While the Catawbas also sent presents northward, they were less eager for peace and insisted on a prisoner exchange as part of any truce with the Six Nations. They blamed "Northern Indians," presumably Iroquois, for recently killing two of their men and capturing four women and three children. Guerrilla raiding had a searing impact on victimized groups beyond what can be measured by any single clash.[60]

French officials in Canada looked askance at a potential peace between the Six Nations and southern tribes. English machinations in Indian country were to be thwarted if at all possible. The French accordingly urged the Senecas, their stoutest Iroquois friends, not to heed British designs. In this instance, the Senecas chose their own course. In 1743, they welcomed Cherokee emissaries to their country and escorted them to Onondaga, the site of the Iroquois Confederacy's council fire,

Warfare and Peace Quests across Half a Continent

where a truce was made. The talks proceeded quite independently of any colonial power. Our limited evidence of the negotiation comes from the journal of Conrad Weiser, Pennsylvania agent to the Six Nations, who briefly remarked on the Cherokee visit. While warming to the Cherokees, the Iroquois staunchly opposed peace with the Catawbas, who had not even deigned to send emissaries to the haughty northern confederacy. One Iroquois spokesman at Onondaga vowed to fight the Catawbas "to the End of the World."[61]

Imperial War and the Cherokees

The French and British vigorously bid for the American Indian allegiance during "King George's War"—the English colonial moniker for the conflict triggered by Europe's War of the Austrian Succession (1744–1748). The fighting in Europe began months before the declaration of formal hostilities. On June 27, 1743, George II, king of Great Britain and elector of Hanover, commanded an army of forty thousand Hanoverian, British, and Austrian troops that defeated French forces at Dettingen by the River Main in Germany. Little more than a year later, the governors of Pennsylvania, Maryland, and Virginia explained their wartime perspective to the Six Nations at a momentous conference held in Lancaster, Pennsylvania. On July 3, 1744, Governor George Thomas of Pennsylvania told Iroquois deputies of George II's triumph: "The Great God covered the King's head in that Battle, so that he did not receive the least Hurt, for which you, as well as we, have Reason to be very thankful." The next day, Iroquois spokesman Canassatego replied that he was not surprised by the outbreak of war. The Six Nations had already informed "*Onontio*, our Father"—meaning the governor of New France—that the French should not traverse Iroquois lands to hurt "our Brethren the *English*," while there was "Room enough at Sea" for the European combatants to wage war. Canassatego's rejoinder was nothing less than a Native American dream, a vision commonly expressed over decades: It would be a good day when European belligerents battled one another on the ocean or in any case far from Native soil.[62]

The heating up of Anglo-French hostilities was a boon to Cherokees because their Iroquois and Canadian adversaries were too preoccupied with northern continental affairs to focus on southern raiding. At the war's beginning, the French upped the flow of arms to numerous allies, including Canadian Iroquois, Abenakis, Nipissings, and Ottawas for

142   *Cherokees, Native Peoples, and Empires, 1730–1762*

strikes on New England and New York frontier settlements. The results were devastating for dispersed and weakly defended communities beset by Indigenous shock parties, commonly bolstered by French troops.[63]

In the broad continental expanse between South Carolina and Louisiana, there was no conflict of this character. Heavily dependent on African slave labor, white populations were wary of internal security; provincial governments were poorly positioned to embark on long-distance offensives. Both the French and English were preoccupied with strengthening existing Native alliances and preventing defections to the rival imperial camp. Little was taken for granted. The threat of invasion hovered in the mind, a fear of attack by enemy soldiers and Indians. Rumors of hostile movements circulated widely. Discerning credible news was a quandary for Natives as well as colonials.

Native peoples were acutely sensitive to shifts in the balance of power in both Indigenous and colonial spheres. Because populous Indian nations were composed of diverse local and regional centers, with a maze of kin-based loyalties, they did not speak in a single voice. In unstable, dangerous times, Native societies were challenged to maintain confederative cohesion, that is, to hold together by finding common ground and avoiding factional rifts that could spawn confusion and internecine bloodletting.

The rhythms of Indigenous conflicts and diplomacy did not neatly align with the timeline of European colonial warfare. Many Cherokees leaned toward peaceful accommodation with the French well before the official outbreak of war between France and Britain in 1744. The reason was clear. The Cherokees, especially the Overhill Towns, were prepared to quit their fight with the French on western rivers in the wake of punishing blows by Canadian and Great Lakes tribes. Cherokee peace feelers reached New Orleans in the summer of 1742 and continued the next year when Bienville returned to France to live out the rest of his years.[64] He was replaced as governor by Pierre François de Rigaud, the marquis de Vaudreuil-Cavagnial. Proud of his aristocratic and Canadian parentage, Vaudreuil felt confident in managing Indian relations, provided Paris fulfill his requests for huge royal subsidies to compete with the English in trade. He was the type of governor who dined amiably with Choctaws at Mobile while privately airing his distaste for Native men, whom he regarded as slovenly, gossipy, and insupportable when drunk.[65]

Provincial governors had a great deal to do with setting the tone of colonial-Indian relations. Of course, they could seldom pull the strings

Warfare and Peace Quests across Half a Continent

without assistance. French frontier commandants were critical players in Indian affairs. Vaudreuil had officers by Mobile Bay, at the Tombigbee and Coosa Rivers, and in Arkansas and Illinois to be his eyes and ears. These men, along with missionaries, were intermediaries between the Crown and Indigenous peoples. By comparison, South Carolina had occasional agents but virtually no administrative reach into the continental interior over decades. Georgia's most outward post was Fort Augusta on the Savannah. British colonial governors were overwhelmingly dependent on traders for information on doings in Indian country.[66] French sources of intelligence were appreciably more diverse.

In the summer of 1743, Vaudreuil learned of a Cherokee peace offer from a Shawnee man who passed word to Fort Toulouse's commandant. As customary, the initiative took the form of quid pro quo. The Cherokees were ready for peace provided the French used their clout to restrain Canadian Indians from hostile southerly incursions. Vaudreuil was impressed that the Cherokees wished to bury the hatchet so soon after a skirmish in which they got the better of pro-French Illinois Indians. Looking beyond small-scale violence, the governor resolved to pursue détente. If all went right, France could conceivably build a post on the Cherokee (Tennessee) River to contain English advances and safeguard communication between Louisiana, Illinois, and Canada.[67]

Indigenous diplomatic networks had their own life, frequently relying on intermediaries that traversed spaces between ethnicities. Dubbed "the greatest Travellers" by one colonial observer, the Shawnees were notable go-betweens because of their wide-ranging geography, with towns centered in the Ohio country and other villages located as distant from one another as Canada and Creek country. Skilled in intertribal diplomacy, Shawnees assisted the Cherokees when the latter opened direct talks with the Iroquois in 1742–1743.[68] Though the Shawnees and Cherokees were former adversaries, their old enmity was not a barrier to cooperation when both parties had something to gain.

Creative Native diplomacy came to the fore as a counterweight to chaos, displacement, and violence. Uprooted by Pennsylvania's territorial expansion during the 1730s, many eastern Shawnees moved from the Susquehanna River to the Ohio country where they joined others of their people. The Ohio country, with its rich hunting grounds, fertile soils, and slight European presence, held strong appeal to numerous Native groups. While not free of intertribal contention, it was

Cherokees, Native Peoples, and Empires, 1730–1762

a place of renewal, a land where neither the French nor the British dominated.[69]

The chief Shawnee liaison to southern Indians was Peter Chartier, son of a French father and Shawnee mother, who despised the English for stratagems that tore his family from its Pennsylvania land during the 1720s. An adroit trader, Chartier built a devoted Native band that migrated west to the Ohio country. During King George's War, he and his followers were staunchly pro-French, robbing British traders and holding several as prisoners. In 1745–1746, Chartier set out on an audacious mission that carried him far south from the Wabash, his most recent abode. He visited Cherokee, eastern Chickasaw, and Upper Creek villages and, according to Carolina trader Ludovick Grant, spread word of "a general peace [among Indians] with the Crown of France."[70]

Shawnee loyalty was broadly pro-French while at heart strongly "Nativist," favoring Indigenous unity across ethnic lines and burying old enmities when possible. In November 1745, Shawnee men told French Illinois officers that their people had spread a peace message to the nearby Mascoutens and Kickapoos, and well south and east to Cherokees, Chickasaws, Creeks, Alabamas, and their own kin by the Alabama River. Each nation received proof of the talk through gifts—talismanic animal entrails, mollusk shells, wampum belts, and pipes—an array of spirit power. A common Native yearning was for trade with security, without being beholden to any one European power. With Shawnee help, Cherokees passed word to New Orleans of their continuing desire for "peace with the French and the Nations of the North."[71]

When Chartier visited Overhill Cherokee country in March 1746, he was accompanied by one Frenchman and twenty-two Indian men, most of whom were Shawnees. British traders in the vicinity feared that the visit was a prelude to something terrible, no less than a French invasion. Imagining the worst, trader Robert Bunning sounded the alarm, notifying Charles Town that "a Great Body of French and Indians" was approaching the Upper Towns. One "Peter Shirty" (Peter Chartier), a "half French, half Savanah" man, was already winning friends at Chota by promising gunpowder and bullets for fowl hunting. Bunning and friends saw themselves as likely sitting ducks. Word spread that five hundred Frenchmen were camped with their Indian allies by the Tennessee River and poised to advance to the southeast. The rumor, perhaps deliberately circulated by Cherokees to put the English on guard, was false, but that was hardly obvious to frightened British traders ready to scurry southeast should the French suddenly

Warfare and Peace Quests across Half a Continent

appear. Chartier and his band scared the hell out of English South Carolina simply by being welcomed by several Cherokee towns when France and Britain were at war.[72]

French documents tell a similar story, if from an opposing perspective. In early 1746, Shawnee men guided two French deputies of Illinois who traveled up the Tennessee River to visit Overhill country. The Cherokees greeted the visitors and made good on a promise to release two French captives. Ludovick Grant got nowhere when he demanded that Cherokees surrender the Frenchmen for a price. One Cherokee chief invited a French officer to his cabin for a smoke and called on his dogs to scare off an Englishman who tried to interfere. French visitors and their Shawnee companions received Cherokee peace pipes and ample provisions for their return western journey.[73]

Chartier's appeal was strongest in Overhill Towns that desired a cessation of attacks from the north. The most welcoming community was Chota, an ancestral "mother town" in Cherokee tradition, though virtually unmentioned in Carolina records of the 1710s to 1730s, which refer frequently to neighboring Tanasee as a sizable town and trading venue. It may be that many Tanasee villagers relocated to Chota at some time during the 1730s. If so, they would not have been moving far; Chota was situated just across a stream from Tanasee. In May 1741, Cherokee deputies told Lieutenant Governor Bull that they intended to lodge their newly received Iroquois wampum belt at Chota—only a prestigious town would have been considered suitable for the belt's reception.[74] Quite as significant, Connecorte, Chota's priest-chief, steered his town's diplomacy without bowing to South Carolina's dictation. Trade with the English was welcome, but Chota paid little heed to Charles Town's admonishments about rejecting French or pro-French Indian visitors. In this respect, Connecorte was following in the tradition of Tanasee's Long Warrior of the 1720s. Connecorte was politic, wielding his persuasive power largely outside of English view in the 1740s. His influence would become far more apparent in the next decade.[75]

Governor Glen and Southern Indians

South Carolina experienced a political watershed when James Glen, a native Scotsman, took the helm as South Carolina's new royal governor in December 1743. Hardly of aristocratic rank, he was a former judicial magistrate catapulted to his Carolina post through patronage, the usual means of royal preferment in the colonies. While Charles

Town's white inhabitants warmly greeted the new governor, not all were pleased, as Glen had received his appointment in 1738 but delayed his passage to America for five years, reaping all the while a large share of the chief executive's salary.[76]

Glen took the occasion to remind Carolinians that Scots were as stout British patriots as Englishmen. In 1746, he publicly heralded the suppression of Scots Jacobite rebels whose army, bereft of expected French support, had been smashed by British forces. To Glen, the conflict with France in southeastern North America was no less vital than in Europe, though it would have to be waged by different means. Burdened by debt after a trying battle with Spanish Florida, South Carolina had no prospect of targeting Mobile or New Orleans. Along with Georgia, it had a paltry assortment of British troops committed to guard duty in coastal forts.[77] By comparison, Vaudreuil had 586 French and 150 Swiss troops at his disposal in 1745, spread among far-flung garrisons, with New Orleans having the largest single contingent. French officials complained interminably about the poor quality of troops and their habits of thievery, insubordination, and desertion. Without these soldiers, however, Louisiana could scarcely have retained its Indian trade and diplomatic influence and kept the British on their guard. The entire colony had 1,700 white men among its 4,000 European inhabitants in 1746. The Black population, nearly all enslaved, amounted to 4,730.[78]

Once at Charles Town, Glen instantly became an ardent imperialist and seldom let up during his dozen years in office. Haughtily overconfident at the outset, he badly misjudged British influence relative to the powerful Creeks and distant Choctaws. The governor's first setback came in 1746 when he pressed the Creeks to oust the French from Fort Toulouse and to welcome a new British garrison in its stead. That autumn, Glen put the matter directly to Muscogee headmen in Charles Town. Though some Creek deputies appeared receptive, the governor's démarche was scotched by Malatchi, Coweta's powerful chief who followed the path forged by his predecessor Brims of not conceding predominance to any single colonial power. As Malatchi told Glen and council, a Muscogee attack on the Alabama fort "would occasion the spilling of Blood," provoking "the French and their Indians" to "fall upon them [i.e., the Creeks] on all sides, so that they would no longer be a people."[79] This was an artful and strategically acute explanation. The Creeks wanted no part of an Anglo-French conflict lest they be attacked by belligerents and risk a falling-out among

Warfare and Peace Quests across Half a Continent

themselves. Fort Toulouse remained French in no small measure because Muscogees and Alabamas desired a check to overweening British trading clout.

While immersed in Creek diplomacy, Glen concocted a scheme of drawing the Choctaws entirely out of French alliance and into the English camp. The idea was not wholly unrealistic, though it was dependent on a fortuitous scenario. Glen counted on prestigious Choctaw chief Red Shoe, already restive under the French, to be the pro-English colossus among his people. The governor, meanwhile, licensed a private trading firm (in which his brother had an interest) as the sole authorized company to transport munitions and supplies to the Choctaws—a people living more than six hundred miles from Charles Town. Red Shoe was certainly willing to move ahead. During the summer of 1746, he had three Frenchmen killed in retaliation for the slaying of two Englishmen by pro-French Choctaws the previous year. Red Shoe and fellow warriors cut the victims' scalps and sent pieces of the flesh to Chickasaw headmen, English traders, and the Upper Creek Abeikas. The bloodstained offerings cried out for friends to join the red path against the French.[80]

Red Shoe's bold overture failed, largely because it was rejected by the Abeikas, who had no intention of becoming involved in internecine Choctaw conflict. Refusing to keep the scalps, Abeika men covered the flesh in white skin and sent the wrapping to an Alabama chief, the Pakana captain, who passed it to a French officer. The Pakana captain, himself a wily diplomat, was just the type of man to be entrusted with this weighty responsibility. The respectful handling of scalps was a potent peace gesture, a way for the Abeikas to demonstrate concern for the aggrieved French. Indigenous diplomacy was in dynamic motion, churning within and outside the struggle between imperial powers. The Abeikas, who had been at war with pro-French Choctaws a few years earlier, were loath to renew hostilities when the scalps came their way. Peace between Native peoples came through common interests and understandings, not by pacifism as an absolute principle. In 1747, Alabama Shawnees put aside their peace message and slew a group of pro-English Choctaws and Chickasaws that had ventured into their territory.[81]

By the time of the Shawnee attack, Choctaw country was convulsed by infighting. Headmen and communities clashed over allegiance and leadership as well as the choice of keeping French ties or opening the door to the English and a potentially more plentiful trade. Under

148   *Cherokees, Native Peoples, and Empires, 1730–1762*

pressure from New Orleans, one Choctaw war band in June 1747 killed Red Shoe and two Englishmen. Vaudreuil remained unsatisfied, however, demanding that Choctaws prove their loyalty by rooting out and destroying the pro-English among their people. The results were horrific. Hundreds of Choctaws died in a calamitous civil war, which reached its height in 1748–1749 just after a smallpox epidemic raged in the area. The pro-English faction finally succumbed, left virtually defenseless because of delayed munitions from Charles Town. Glen's Choctaw gambit was a stunning political defeat. By far the heaviest loss was borne by the Native dead and their kin. As the fighting died down in Choctaw country, Vaudreuil worked to restore peace among rival factions by urging them to join in war against the Chickasaws.[82] In this last respect, little had changed over forty years.

The Choctaw civil war lingered after France and Great Britain arrived at a peace settlement in 1748. Neither empire achieved a clear victory in the European theater that engaged a host of nations and principalities. The results in North America were no more decisive. The French and their Indian allies carried the fight to the English quite successfully along the New England–New York frontier. In other respects, the war exposed the weakness of French colonialism. With British naval power ascendant, France could not sufficiently supply its Native allies in North America. By 1747, Indigenous nations of the Ohio country and Upper Great Lakes were in near revolt against the French over this deficiency. France had only a small settlement on the Wabash and had yet to establish a fort on that river or the Tennessee. British colonial traders made western inroads, and Virginia's elite looked to expand to the Ohio and Mississippi. The roots of the future French and Indian War were becoming evident.[83]

The Cherokees' Situation

Being at a distance from imperial warfare, Cherokees had some space in the mid-1740s for recovery, which was sorely needed given the depletion of population due to disease and intertribal clashes. By a de facto peace with the French, Upper Cherokee towns experienced a letup in hostile Native forays from the north. Nearly all Cherokees benefited from the English perception of their importance in fending off French inroads. Some degree of colonial respect was in order, especially in wartime. James Glen, who courted the Cherokees quite early on in his governorship, drove his efforts into high gear when Peter Chartier

Warfare and Peace Quests across Half a Continent

and Shawnee friends were welcomed at Chota and other Cherokee venues in 1746.

Glen had little cause to anticipate such challenges in April 1745, when 130 Cherokee headmen and warriors traveled to Charles Town for their first conference with the governor. Ammouiscossitte of Great Tellico, himself a youth, served as lead spokesman, undoubtedly because he was son of the late Moytoy, the former Cherokee "emperor" by English reckoning. As talks began, he addressed Glen as his people's "Eldest Brother" and unfurled the Cherokees' copy of the treaty made in London in 1730. The paper, he added, said that "the king's Enemies shall be my Enemies." This was true remembrance. As a further sign of respect, Ammouiscossitte knelt and placed his own headdress of silk and badger's skin at the governor's feet—just as Cherokee men had once delivered a "crown" to King George at Windsor Palace. Glen was asked to send the gift to the English monarch as a token of lasting friendship.[84]

In this uncanny diplomatic sequence, Cherokees signaled their intent by coupling markedly different objects—an English parchment treaty bearing the royal seal and a Native headdress. The treaty was evidence of the king's fatherly protection—a point that the new English governor should see with his own eyes. Skiagusta (Skaygusta) of Keowee, an experienced head warrior, elaborated on this theme once Ammouiscossitte had finished his talk. As a sign of trust, he deposited his old English commission at the governor's feet. Glen did his part by pledging new gubernatorial commissions to Skiagusta and two other principal headmen. While Cherokees were averse to steep social hierarchy, over time they became increasingly desirous of special English honors.

While valuing his commission, Skiagusta admitted that he was often perplexed by letters dispatched by colonial governors to Indian country. As he told Glen and council, "It is a Pity we Red Men cannot write and read as the white Men do, for when we see a Letter, it is like a Darkness to us ... for we do not know the Meaning of it." While speaking these arresting words, he placed his hands over his face and eyes to signify blindness. By comparison, it brought light to see Glen in person and listen to him—and that even in translation. Skiagusta remarked that headmen had brought "a great many young People to hear the Governor's Talk, so that they might know what he delivers to us ... that they may tell it to the other Young people when they return Home." Words lived on as passed from one generation to the next. Skiagusta talked of how the Cherokees had first learned of "the great King George" from a "great and beloved white Man" who had come to "our Nation." The allusion was to Sir Alexander Cuming, whose visit of fifteen English years past had made a lasting impression. In Skiagusta's memory, Cuming had said: "You Red Men are all of you Brothers of the White Men," worthy of the king's care in the same way "though the white Men are great and numerous as the sands on the Sea shore." Equal treatment under royal authority was much on Skiagusta's mind. As a Lower Town leader, he was highly sensitive to the current growth of white settlement in the Cherokees' piedmont hunting grounds.[85]

Glen felt satisfied with his first Cherokee conference. The Cherokees had accepted his words along with Catawba headmen who were in Charles Town at the same time. Both Native peoples were advised to end quarreling among themselves and to stand together with English friends. The governor stated that England was at war. He expected Native allies to answer his call for aid during the conflict and not to admit French visitors or their Indian allies to their territories. The Cherokees departed for home quite pleased with Glen's presents, though not all was as rosy as the governor thought.[86]

Within months of the Charles Town meeting, Glen was taken aback when he learned of Chartier's visit to the Overhill Towns. Not wasting time, he extended invitations to Catawba, Cherokee, and Creek headmen to meet with him at separate gatherings in the piedmont during the spring of 1746. The Cherokee conference was held nearby Ninety-Six, a newly settled frontier district by the Saluda River. Glen's venture was virtually unprecedented for South Carolina chief magistrates, who seldom ventured into Indian country and were accustomed to receiving Native delegations that traveled several hundred miles to Charles Town. The governor set out in style, accompanied by 250 paid horsemen, fifty gentlemen volunteers, and servants.[87]

In late April, sixty Cherokee headmen greeted Glen at the Saluda, but his correspondence unfortunately does not disclose their names, with the exception of Ammouiscossitte, the so-called emperor whose English title far exceeded his stature in Cherokee country. The attending headmen gave no outward sign of deserting the British. They referred to the French as "Strangers" as compared to old English friends. In a tactful manner, the emissaries explained why some Overhill Towns could not help but entertain talks with the French. Glen himself neatly summarized the Cherokee talk to London. As he wrote, the Upper villages,

Warfare and Peace Quests across Half a Continent

"situated upon the Rivers that Run into the Mississippi," lay "quite open and exposed, and at the Mercy of the French and their Indians, who quite frequently visit them in their Canoes." Did Glen relay a precise Cherokee message or fashion his own rendering to alert London that more royal assistance should come his way? Certainly, he latched onto the trans-Appalachian region for broad strategic reasons. While at Saluda, Glen posed a lead question to Cherokee deputies on whether they desired an English fort in the Overhill region. The headmen listened carefully without a hasty answer. Glen was careful not to press too hard on a sensitive subject. In his dispatch to the Duke of Newcastle, minister for the colonies, the governor aptly described the Cherokees as being "pretty jealous of their Liberty." In his view, that love of freedom was best kept under guard. A British Overhill fort "would effectually bar the Door against the French and would prove such a Bridle in the Mouths of the Indians themselves, that would forever keep them ours."[88] The object was British imperial control.

Glen's Saluda River conference was a temporary salve that did not heal restiveness in Chota and neighboring Tanasee, which within a few months pressed Charles Town for the delivery of munitions. Anxious to counter French influence, the governor and assembly appointed Colonel George Pawley as special agent to the Cherokees. In early 1747, the colonel made his way to Keowee, where he negotiated the first significant land cession from Lower Cherokee Towns to the English. The agreement, to be discussed at greater length below, was amicable on the surface but aroused keen Cherokee discontent despite the munitions and goods given for the land.[89]

Pawley next headed for the Overhill Towns, which he reached in late February 1747 with his small party of about ten white men and several Black servants—enslaved men who were aides on the journey. When the Carolinians approached Tanasee, a few Shawnee men came out in the open and taunted Pawley with a mocking dance. The atmosphere took a friendlier turn a few days later. Cherokee headmen greeted Pawley with their English flag in hand and invited him for a talk in Tanasee's council house. The colonel asked the Cherokees to surrender Chartier, who was at Chota. The headmen balked, citing their obligation to Shawnee visitors who "loved the French man" so much "that they would die" before returning to the Ohio country without him. Pawley repeated his demand the next day and received a blunter "no." Cherokee men said the Shawnees would split the colonel's skull if he persisted. Pawley then backed off.[90]

Blood ties solidified Cherokee-Shawnee collaboration. Cherokees relied on a man of their own nation who had lived among Shawnees as their interpreter across tribal lines. In a variation on this theme, Shawnees told French Illinois officers that they would serve as mediators with the Cherokees only if joined by "Kind Heart" (*Joly coeur*), a former French soldier who had deserted and lived with them for at least six years. The request was granted, with approval from Governor Vaudreuil, who referred to Joly Coeur as part of Chartier's family. Adoption was a powerful bond in Native American societies.[91]

While stymied on bagging Chartier, Pawley conducted lengthy discussions with several Cherokee headmen on the key issue of building an English fort in Overhill country. Chief Black Dog answered in a politic way. He wished to see forts situated near both Great Tellico and Tanasee, thereby protecting towns in the two main Overhill river valleys (today's Tellico and Little Tennessee Rivers). If the English were to build the posts, his people would gladly provide corn to colonial workmen for two years and build fences to protect the white people's hogs and cattle. Black Dog's most fervent appeal to Pawley was one of kinship: "We are all Brothers and live like Brothers." The visit to England of 1730 was recalled: "some of our head men have been over the greate water with the greate King George who is our Father, and we his Children." Black Dog displayed "a roll of parchment," which was kept at Chota, and was nothing less than the Articles of Friendship and Commerce concluded in London by the seven Cherokee visitors. This was the same document that Cherokees had previously shown to Glen in Charles Town. In Black Dog's words, "The good Talk which he [the King] gave us in this Paper we keep fast and shall never drop it out of our h[e]arts."[92]

Black Dog clearly inclined toward a reciprocally advantageous Cherokee-English bond. He explained, too, that his people's hunting grounds were now safer because of Shawnee friendship that cemented a truce with eleven unnamed enemy towns or "tribes." He saw nothing incongruous in French boats coming up the Tennessee to trade while English traders had a clear path to Carolina. Black Dog bemoaned the toll of war, especially in the seven Overhill Towns that were his homeland: "We were once a great people but are now reduced to a small number by the force of our Enemies."[93]

The prospect of a British fort was controversial to Cherokees. Ostenaco, a head warrior of Chota, relied on a secret courier when notifying Pawley of his support for an English garrison. The fort, he

Warfare and Peace Quests across Half a Continent

stated, "will protect our wives and children and the Traders that Comes [*sic*] among us." Above all, Ostenaco explained that Cherokee friendship with pro-French Indians should not be equated with fondness for the French themselves. By his own admission, he had visited the towns of "French Indians" the previous summer and had then welcomed their residents. He did not hold the French in his "heart," but "as to the Peace with the Red people it is what we love."[94] Long Warrior of Tanasee had said virtually the same words twenty years before. Love of "Red people" resonated among Indian groups that were once enemies but called a halt to bloodletting against one another.

Ostenaco longed to treat with other Native groups—"the red" in contrast to "the white"—outside the bounds of Anglo-French hostility. His diplomatic stance was pragmatic and subtle, the product of Cherokee experience in dealing with Europeans and a multiplicity of Indian ethnicities. Stasis was a luxury not to be had. Chickasaw and Natchez refugees had entered and crossed Cherokee lands in the recent past. By the late 1740s, diverse northern Indians increasingly frequented Cherokee country. As we will see, these newcomers were prone to use the southern Appalachians as a base to attack the Creeks and Catawbas. The Muscogees, holding the Cherokees responsible, strongly retaliated. These hostilities escalated in a trying period, just as Cherokees confronted growing white settlement on their eastern borderlands and hunting grounds.

6

Confronting Colonialism and the Creek Nation

In March 1748, Captain George Haig and two assistants, Billy Brown and William Wrightknower, were on a trading mission to the Catawba nation. After concluding their business, the threesome set up camp by nightfall but toward dawn had a rude awakening. Fifteen armed Indian men burst into their tent, took their guns and pistols, and grabbed their clothes and caps. Haig, a piedmont landowner, pleaded for freedom by offering three horses to the intruders, but the latter refused. The Indian men shot down the horses with arrows, tied Haig and Brown with "Slave strings" around their necks, and brought the two men with them to the north. The assailants released Wrightknower, a German immigrant servant, giving him a tomahawk to show colonials as proof of the capture. The warrior then pronounced "Nattooyaw," at least as Wrightknower heard it.[1]

Colonials were puzzled by the tribal identity of these "Nattooyaws." The captors seemed to belong to a broad group of "northern Indians"—Nottawegas in common Cherokee parlance. The abductors were a nervy bunch and had friends in some Cherokee towns. Two weeks after the capture, six Nottawega men appeared at Keowee with Haig's coat, jacket, and hat. A few days later, a Nottawega war party harassed a Catawba village, leaving behind a large cane stalk marked with the likenesses of Haig, Brown, and five other white prisoners, two of whom were shown headless, a sure sign of death. Drawings of colonial hats, shoes, and buckles punctuated the grisly message.[2]

White Carolinians recoiled at the abduction of Haig and Brown. They were at a loss to explain why the Cherokees, ostensible allies, had not come to the captives' aid but rather had welcomed and hosted enemies. Colonials were especially concerned with Keowee, one of the foremost Cherokee towns east of the Blue Ridge. Strange Indians from the north appeared there weeks after the capture. Keowee men told Carolina traders that they would rather die than turn against their northern Indian friends. Not all Native villages in the area were of this mind. Tugaloo's leaders offered to help the English, but their efforts were to no avail.[3]

Elizabeth Haig, wife of the abducted captain, knew little peace at her home in the frontier settlement of Saxe-Gotha. Preparing for the worst, she asked a merchant to send her some "Light and Coarse" cloth suitable "for every day's Wear and very Grave." In a formal plea, Mrs. Haig went so far as to urge Governor Glen to impose a trade embargo of eighteen months on the Cherokees unless they secured the captain's return. She had already called on fellow settlers to raise a rescue posse but was discouraged by neighbors who worried that hostile Indians would retaliate by stealing Black slaves in their households.[4]

Since the Indian captors had headed well north, Glen wrote Pennsylvania's government for information on the two missing Carolina men. An answer came months later. In September 1748, Pennsylvania agent Conrad Weiser encountered a band of Senecas holding Billy Brown in the Ohio country. The Indians released the shaken captive, who later spoke haltingly of his experience before the provincial council in Philadelphia. By Brown's recollection, Haig had "high words" with his captors and could barely keep up with their pace. An Indian man tomahawked the captain to death, displaying his bloodstained weapon and the slain man's clothes to Brown.[5]

Seneca leader Tanaghrisson, who was not present at the killing, sorrowfully informed Weiser of Haig's murder. The chief admitted that some of his people had been moved by an "evil Spirit," which he hoped would not sunder "the Chain of Friendship" between the Iroquois and English. The killers had "struck the Hatchet into our own Body" by slaying an English brother. Tanaghrisson spoke with authority as chief Iroquois emissary in the Ohio country. Giving a wampum belt to Weiser as a sign of good intent, he requested that the governors of New York and Pennsylvania spread his peace message to Charles Town. While tactful, Tanaghrisson confessed that Senecas had targeted Haig for supplying munitions to their Catawba foes. In this instance, which was far from unique, intertribal conflict spilled into violence against colonials.[6]

156   *Cherokees, Native Peoples, and Empires, 1730–1762*

Haig's abduction put Skiagusta, the "Old Warrior" of Keowee, in a tight spot. Though an avowed friend to South Carolina, he had failed to prevent his townsmen from aiding the captors. Questioned by one trader, he remarked that the Nottawegas were "very dreadful People" who could not be swayed to release Haig and Brown. The old chief was otherwise coyly mum on the Nottawega men and their tribal background.[7]

Nottawegas in Cherokee territory appear to have numbered in the scores of warriors rather than in the hundreds at any one time, but that fact was unknown to those who felt threatened. When Haig and Brown were captured, one Carolina trader feared that northern Indians were about to "Spirit up" the Cherokees to kill all of his compatriots. A band of thirteen Nottawegas was spotted in Lower Cherokee territory in April 1748. Three hundred more were said to be on the way that spring "as soon as the Leaves on the Trees are about half Grown." No such large war party eventuated, but that was little comfort to white traders in Cherokee country. English fears were magnified because Great Britain and France had not yet reached a peace settlement. Glen imagined the French were responsible for inciting Indigenous war parties, but the situation was not so simple. Well after the European peace of October 1748, northern Indian bands continued to filter southward not solely for war but for trade and sustenance. In 1750, a British trader at Tomasee in Cherokee country wrote that the Nottawegas in that town "behaved themselves very Honest and is our friends Seemingly."[8] The word "seemingly" speaks volumes about colonial uncertainty—a feeling shared in Native communities endangered by "red" people and not only whites.

Northern Indian incursions add a measure of complexity to our understanding of the Cherokee world of the mid-1700s. While British colonial expansion was an unquestionably disruptive force, it was not alone responsible for unsettling Cherokee lives. Nottawega sojourners in Cherokee territory frequently targeted Catawbas, Savannah River Chickasaws, and the powerful Creeks who retaliated against Cherokees for harboring the assailants. By the early 1750s, the Creeks got much the better of this fighting, impelling hard-hit Cherokee communities to lean on English South Carolina to mediate a truce. Cherokee-English relations were scarcely stable. It took strenuous diplomacy—on the part of Cherokee leaders and Governor Glen—to keep a lid on hostilities amid mounting distrust between Indians and whites.

Confronting Colonialism and the Creek Nation

Expanding White Settlement

Given Charles Town's need for Cherokee friendship, South Carolina's government was careful not to license overly aggressive or hasty colonizing endeavors. In 1743, the provincial Commons House (the lower chamber of the legislative assembly) blocked an attempt by two colonial deerskin traders and associates to purchase forty-eight square miles of Cherokee land for mining supposed lodes of silver and other ores. Legislators feared that the Cherokees might be provoked to war by an onrush of fortune seekers onto Native soil. Georgia, meanwhile, apprehended illicit ventures in its presumed western territories. On receiving reports of the affair, the Board of Trade nixed the project. The decision reinforced a principle that dated to the 1630s but was often bypassed or finagled by self-interested colonials. Private purchases of Indian land were not considered legally valid unless authorized or confirmed by provincial governments or the Crown.[9]

Rather than barge into the mountains, South Carolina's white settlers trudged gradually into the piedmont, whether traveling south via the Shenandoah Valley's Wagon Road, relocating from the coastal low country, or shipping into Charles Town before heading west. The newcomers were of various ethnic backgrounds—Scots and Scots-Irish, English and Welsh, as well as Germans and Swiss. The piedmont was by no means vacant land, though its Native population had diminished greatly since 1650. The Catawbas, whose villages clustered by the current North Carolina–South Carolina state line, had 300 to 500 warriors and a total population of perhaps 1,500 during the period 1730–1750. Known for their fighting prowess and alliance with South Carolina, they were lauded by James Glen as "the Bravest Fellows on the Continent of America."[10]

Chickasaws were also denizens of the piedmont, even though the great portion of their nation lived far to the west. The Savannah River Chickasaws, pushed east by Choctaw attacks, numbered about three hundred persons in 1750 and carried diplomatic weight in both Georgia and South Carolina. As intermediaries in the deerskin trade, they honed the art of self-protection by passing intelligence on political doings and war threats to Indian peoples and colonials.[11]

The movement of white settlers into upland South Carolina centered on several areas. German newcomers began to colonize "the Congarees" (in and about present-day Columbia, South Carolina) in the 1730s. By

158   *Cherokees, Native Peoples, and Empires, 1730–1762*

the close of the next decade, the settler population in that neighborhood numbered perhaps five hundred persons. Fifty miles to the northwest, colonials seated themselves in Ninety-Six by the Saluda River—a district named for its distance in miles from Keowee, the nearest Cherokee town. The district militia mustered only twelve men in in 1748. Some 180 settlers were living in the area four years later. While white colonials predominated in the piedmont, enslaved Blacks were frequently present in well-to-do settler households.[12]

South Carolina's low country and its western frontier districts were quite different worlds. The province's Black population, concentrated in the coastal region, approached 50,000 in 1750; whites accounted for only 25,000 inhabitants throughout South Carolina. Fear of Black preponderance induced the colonial assembly to steer customs duties on imported Africans to a fund that aided poor European Protestant arrivals and helped them on their way to inland townships. In this budgetary shuffle, imposts on slave labor boosted the prospects of non-slaveholding white immigrants.[13]

The growth of South Carolina's white piedmont population was fairly modest in 1750, amounting to roughly two thousand non-Indians living between 60 and 150 miles of Cherokee towns. Of course, Cherokees looking *east* saw the white colonial approach as threatening, especially since an increasing number of footloose frontiersmen were arriving in and about Native villages to hunt and trade. In 1745, Keowee's Skiagusta rather gingerly expressed concern about colonial settlement to Glen: "We Red Men live a great Way from the White People, yet we live all upon the same Land; tho' the white People every Day come nearer and nearer and settling up toward us, yet it is all our Land, and therefore we are all King George's Children." Skiagusta's meaning, not easily captured in translation, breathes unease. While there was something good in being under the English king's protective mantle, the head warrior was clearly disturbed by the implacable advance of colonials on his Native ground.[14]

Keowee and other Lower Towns east of the Blue Ridge were far more anxious about white settlement than Cherokee villages situated well to the north and west. It may seem surprising, therefore, that in February 1747 headmen of twelve Lower Towns approved a substantial land cession to South Carolina. The agreement, negotiated at Keowee, was unprecedented. No Cherokee group had ever previously offered anything more than a smidgen of Native ground to a colonial government.

Confronting Colonialism and the Creek Nation   159

While Cherokee headmen granted some land for a colonial garrison ("Strong House") near Lower Town Chauga in 1734, the treaty was not executed. In 1747, circumstances were different. South Carolina, hungering badly for more piedmont land, achieved a Native land cession by a treaty in which Cherokees received 400 lbs. of gunpowder, 800 lbs. of bullets, 20 lbs. of vermilion, and 200 lbs. of beads, with one fowling piece, a type of shotgun. The munitions were by far the most important commodity in the purchase, suggesting the Lower Towns' priority on defense above the use of shot and powder for hunting. The single fowling piece thrown into the deal may have been intended as an honorary gift as much as a valued weapon.[15]

The treaty of 1747 outlined a northern perimeter for white settlement, roughly one hundred miles in length from the Savannah River east to the Saluda and Broad Rivers. The line intersected the "Cherokee Path," a major deerskin trading route, about sixty miles from Keowee. Significantly, the treaty's fine print was heavily tilted to colonial advantage. The Cherokees were said to have yielded their land for all future generations, while the northern colonial borderline was implicitly provisional and open to renegotiation over time. For white settlers, the purchase's prime asset was "the Long Canes"—a fertile area abutting Long Cane Creek flowing southwest from the hilly terrain above Ninety-Six to the Savannah River. Colonists prized the region for its rich bottomlands, grazing meadows, salt licks, and abundant wild game. The popular name "Long Canes" pithily captured the thickets of hard stalk grasses that grew plentifully by waterways in the Carolina piedmont.[16]

Why did Cherokee headmen agree to a cession that would soon place white settlers within sixty miles of their homeland? Besides the need for munitions, Cherokees possibly calculated that colonials were already filtering into the ceded region and that a fixed border would be better than none at all. Keowee's Skiagusta, who was generally well disposed to Charles Town, again captures our attention for assuming a leading role in the negotiation. His name sits first on the written treaty, above marks made by thirty-three other "principal Men." The cession stirred Cherokee dissent, which burst to the surface just a year later when Keowee men stood aside while Nottawega warriors seized Captain Haig and Billy Brown. Some Cherokees were clearly upset by what they had already lost in hunting lands; they were even more apprehensive about all that seemed building against their people.[17]

Cherokees, Native Peoples, and Empires, 1730–1762

Fear, Retribution, and Accommodation

Mrs. Elizabeth Haig characterized the Cherokees as "brutish Creatures" for their complicity in her husband's capture. Her grievance did not, however, stop her from doing business with Indians. She had children to raise, and her work as an innkeeper brought in money. In 1749, the provincial assembly reimbursed the widow Haig £46 for supplying provisions and liquor to Catawba and Cherokee deputies on their way to and from Charles Town.[18] Amicable and routine encounters between Cherokees and white frontier folk were not uncommon, even though these instances were increasingly overshadowed by rising tensions in both camps, which by 1751 had reached panic stage.

The Lower Cherokee region witnessed scenes of violence in early 1748 even before Captain Haig's capture. On February 4, an Indian man of Euseteestee, a small village, shot packhorseman Edward Carroll dead after calling him "a Devil and a Witch." That same day another Cherokee man went to James Butler's store at Cheowee, only four miles from Euseteestee, and asked for goods on trust or credit. When Butler refused, the man dragged him out of the store and beat him badly. Lower Town leaders decided over the next two weeks that the man who had shot Carroll should pay with his life when he returned from war. Many Cherokees wanted to end trouble and put things right. Colonial traders in the vicinity asked Glen to see that the sentence was carried out lest the Cherokees, whom they claimed daily insulted them, lose all respect for "the White People." The implication was that all English colonists had a stake in the traders' security.[19]

Glen responded with two letters. The first, sent to the traders, insisted that justice would be done only if the Cherokees themselves killed the culpable Indian in the presence of white men. The second admonished Cherokee headmen that they would have to give "Satisfaction" if they wished to brighten "the Chain of Friendship" with the English. In a striking metaphor borrowed from Indigenous speech, Glen signified what the Cherokees must expiate: "the path betwixt your Nation and us, is spoiled by the Blood of a White Man." The governor, ever the benevolent paternalist in Indian relations, did not simply threaten but also reminded Cherokees how he befriended them at Ninety-Six two years earlier, when all had slept in the woods and eaten and imbibed together. Glen was himself the Cherokees' "Friend & Loving Brother."[20]

Confronting Colonialism and the Creek Nation

Cherokee towns consulted about the English packhorseman's killing weeks before the governor's message arrived in their locales. The fear of a retaliatory English trade cutoff was rampant. By one colonial trader's account, seven Overhill Towns threatened to destroy Euseteestee unless the town offered satisfaction to Glen. This was an extraordinary warning, at odds with the Cherokee custom of town autonomy. Euseteestee's people protested an injustice. Why should they put one of their honored warriors to death for killing some lowly English hired man who was not even a trader? By this argument, retribution might be fair, but only if there was an equivalent sacrifice by the respective parties. The odds soon mounted against a bloodless resolution. Raven, the Hiwassee Valley's most prestigious head warrior, trekked 100 miles to Euseteestee to see that satisfaction was given. Tugaloo headmen accompanied him for like purpose. When Euseteestee's villagers balked, Raven answered that there was no escape. His people could not live apart from the English who supplied them with woolens and other goods. Raven feared that Glen would cut off all trade unless the manslayer paid with his life. Euseteestee's headmen relented, calling on four warriors to dispatch the culprit. Finding the condemned man hiding in a tree hollow, they dragged him out by the heels and cut off his head with a hatchet.[21]

Did the retributive killing transpire in exactly the way recorded in English South Carolina? That is unknown. Glen certainly took pleasure in relaying the story to London. Through his influence, a Cherokee town had put to death one of their own, "a great Hunter and Warriour," for killing an Englishman who "was but a worthless drunken fellow, a Packhorseman." In Glen's view, "the Affair was managed by the Indians with great circumspection, prudence, and justice." In the governor's telling, the Native man's corpse was laid out on the ground to rot so that all passing Englishmen would know that the Cherokees had fulfilled their duty. Glen aired a European sense of superiority: "It is a great Step toward civilizing savage and barbarous Nations when they can be brought to do Public Acts of Justice upon their Criminals." The Cherokees had a very different view. The manslayer's death assuaged an English governor, resolving a crisis that might have brought a trade embargo and other punitive action. Cherokee honor was shown by fulfilling obligations to English allies. Enemies went to war over killings; kin negotiated solutions to lethal violence among one another.[22]

162   *Cherokees, Native Peoples, and Empires, 1730–1762*

Glen's Bid for Cherokee Allies

Rising tensions between Indigenous peoples and colonials raised dilemmas for both South Carolina and neighboring Georgia. Provincial governments increasingly demanded that Indians give "satisfaction" for violent acts, especially killings of white traders and settlers. But how was this to be done? Glen weighed two main factors while addressing the quandary. First, South Carolina did not possess the military means to force Cherokees to deliver suspected Indian killers of colonials into British hands. Second, the governor did not want to alienate valued Native allies whose cooperation was necessary for British fort construction in their country.[23]

The issue of "satisfaction" played out during the crisis over Haig's abduction. In June 1748, Cherokee deputies from several towns—Overhill and Lower villages—arrived in Charles Town for deliberations at Glen's invitation. While the governor desired a modus vivendi, the provincial assembly proposed a trade stoppage with "the whole Cherokee Nation" unless Keowee and two nearby towns gave "Satisfaction to this Government." Glen cast aside the projected sanctions by proroguing (suspending) the Commons House. He strengthened his position by soliciting a letter from William Stephens, president of Georgia's council, who doubted the feasibility of an embargo, which might provoke Cherokees to disturb colonial commerce with the Creeks. It was better, wrote Stephens, to have the Cherokee nation as "a Lukewarm Friend than an open and avowed Enemy, there being no other Barrier betwixt us and the French."[24]

Glen won this political battle, but he could not stave off the assembly's desire to give visiting Cherokees, especially Keowee's Skiagusta, a tongue-lashing in the government house. By South Carolina custom, Glen read the legislative committee's draft speech, in this instance a rebuke to his Native guests. Perhaps he enjoyed the opportunity to play "good cop" even while giving the assembly's lecture, a sequence of biting rhetorical questions:

> We therefore wish to know what Mark of friendship you receive from the French? Have they assisted you with Arms and Ammunition to defend you against your Enemys? Do you think they are able to supply you with Goods to cloath Your People as we have always done? You know they cannot. You have Enemys already. The Creeks

Confronting Colonialism and the Creek Nation

are at War with You and are angry that You suffer the French Indians to come thro' your Nation to War against them. Do you think we have not Men and horses enough with Arms to March . . . into your Nation if we was your Enemies? You know we have. Do you see such a Town and so many People and Ships amongst the French as you see here? We know you do not. Why then . . . [do you] seem to want to throw away the English and to shake hands with the French?[25]

Glen soothed this tough message by meeting privately with Cherokee deputies before the latter left Charles Town. Presents were distributed to cooperative Cherokees visitors such as the Tugaloo Warrior and "Half-Breed" Johnny of Tanasee. Glen may have offered some tokens to the Keowee guests, too. His aim was to keep lines of communication open, restore stability, and sell his fort-building plan to the Cherokees.[26]

Besides conferencing with visiting southern Indian delegations, Glen commonly forwarded long-distance written talks to Cherokee and Creek headmen. The governor's words were dispatched to colonial trader-interpreters for oral translation to Native leaders, who responded in kind by having their talks transcribed and sent on to Charles Town. This form of communication obviously depended on trust between Native men and the interpreters who worked with them. During the height of crisis in 1751, the Raven of Hiwassee called on veteran trader Robert Bunning to forward a reassuring talk to Glen by letter. The message itself voiced Raven's praise for Bunning's "great help on both Sides." The chief's "beloved men" said "that one half of Mr. Bunnion [Bunning] belonged to them, and the other half to the White[s], and his Tongue for both." Bunning, who had accompanied Cherokees to England in 1730, was an old trusted hand. Could he help it if Raven's missive spoke of the interpreter's services in such glowing terms?[27]

When trouble loomed after Haig's capture, Raven responded warmly to one of Glen's letters. Giving his talk to Ludovick Grant, the Hiwassee leader assured the governor that "all the Bad Talks" lately "spread up and down the Nation . . . were but Boys talks and not Men's." As long as his generation of warriors lived, "there should be no harm come to any English in his Nation." Knowing what played well in Charles Town, the Raven cited Cherokee enmity to the French whom he claimed were arming the Creeks. The chief spoke, too,

164   *Cherokees, Native Peoples, and Empires, 1730–1762*

about the past, when "the over hills [Cherokee] people" killed the French "upon the River."[28] Glen should not forget that the Cherokees merited favor for all the battles they had waged against English enemies.

In this same exchange of 1748, Raven courteously declined Glen's invitation to visit Charles Town, given his illness and widespread hunger among his people. The chief's explanation, by its general tenor, was a tactful headman's way of declining a friend's hospitable request. Raven doubtless dreaded the prospect of traveling to Charles Town during the oppressive summer season. He enlisted his own son, along with headman Tistoe and two companions, for the long journey. Once reaching the low country, the travelers stayed at a plantation and an inn until trader-interpreter James Beamor joined them on the final leg to Charles Town. Beamor was initially reluctant to comply because of ill health, but the Cherokee men prevailed on him, insisting that they did not want to "look like Fools if they have nobody to talk for them." Amicably received by the assembly, the visitors returned with gifts of colored coats, ruffled shirts, breeches, laced hats, stockings, shoes, and of course flints, gunpowder, bullets, and body paint. Face-to-face diplomacy was again important for reciprocal exchange in the truest and most rewarding sense.[29]

Glen cultivated understandings with Native headmen for British imperial purposes, which in his view were consonant with the well-being of the Great King George's Indian "Children." Cherokee leaders did not mind the governor's conceit as long as it brought them protection and supply. Proudly independent, priest-chief Connecorte of Chota referred in one talk to King George as "his Father" and Glen as "Brother." Sending a lengthy message to Glen in 1752, he was glad that the previous summer's "Troubles" between colonials and Cherokees had quieted, just like a "strong Gale of Wind which blew hard . . . but is now all over and calm again." He had since asked nearby Overhill Towns "to be careful of their white People, and not to hurt any of them, though he knew they were, but as Swine Herds or Hog Cleaners in Regard of the great beloved Men below," that is, the planters in the low country. Connecorte, nicknamed "Old Hop" by British traders because of his age and limp, had an acute understanding of colonial hierarchy. While he thought disparagingly of ruffian packhorsemen and the like, he had sincere respect for the governor and the "Great King" across the Great Water.[30]

Confronting Colonialism and the Creek Nation   165

Bad Blood and Distrust

The "strong Gale" Connecorte spoke of was the result of "bad talks" that swirled out of control in a tempestuous human landscape. Colonial rum sellers, horse rustlers, and other unruly fellows were common intruders into Cherokee territory. Whites in the Carolina piedmont meanwhile fretted about the "strange Indians" whose tribal affiliation was unclear but who left unmistakable signs of hostility by destroying settlers' livestock and damaging or robbing farmsteads. Were the perpetrators Nottawegas, Cherokees, or others? None of the colonials had a satisfying answer.[31]

In 1750, Glen offered his own take on the Nottawega situation in a letter to Governor George Clinton of New York. In his view, the Native intruders, who "pass under the general Name of Nottawagees," appeared a medley: "Some times called Seneca, but it is certain that besides the Five Nations, there are the Delaware, and some of the Indians on the Ohio, as well as the Susquehanna, and Virginia Indians." Glen urged his colleagues in New York, Pennsylvania, and Maryland to dissuade northern Indians from attacking his Catawba allies, inciting the Creeks, and threatening whites in the Carolina piedmont. The governor's insight was well considered. It was not uncommon for Iroquois warriors to head south via the Susquehanna River and persuade Delaware and Shawnee men to join forays against the Catawbas.[32]

The vastness of southern Appalachia offered space for Native groups that settled or camped there on a seasonal or short-term basis. The area was still relatively removed from white settlers. Glimpses of Nottawega movements appear here and there in colonial records. In April 1752, headman Asaquah of the "Nittawiga Nation" addressed Governor Glen on behalf of about sixty men of allied bands then at Keowee. One of his co-petitioners claimed to be from Conestoga in the Susquehanna Valley. Asaquah stated that his people passed through South Carolina's white settlements solely as necessary to fight their Catawba enemies. They meant no harm to the English even if they sometimes killed their cattle for meat because the warriors were far from home. Needless to say, this reasoning did little to satisfy white settlers. The Nottawega letter is itself an enigma, a document handed by Cherokees to a young white man, unwitnessed by colonial traders and without Native signature marks.[33]

Dislocations in the Indian world intersected in intricate ways with violence across Native-colonial frontiers. Questions arise without

166 *Cherokees, Native Peoples, and Empires, 1730–1762*

simple answers. Did Nottawega men strike at South Carolina whites in consequence of being forced off their land in Pennsylvania or interior Maryland and Virginia? That is probable, though we cannot always know what prompted violence in specific instances. Consider, for example, the situation of two Shawnee men who peacefully entered the piedmont home of Isaac and Mary Cloud one evening in early May 1751. Fluent in Shawnee, Isaac conversed amiably with the guests; they shared dinner and smoked pipes until all went to bed late that night. As the cock crowed the next morning, the Shawnee men shot dead both Isaac Cloud and a young white man and then killed the couple's two children. Mary Cloud survived only by feigning death after being struck by a tomahawk. The killers plundered the house and hurried off. Glen and council received word that many "distressed" settler families had fled southward to find security.[34]

Indian motives are unclear in the Cloud murders, a notable but unusual episode at the time. Native hostility to white settlers is more explicable when Cherokees or other Indians killed settlers' livestock, which served as ready symbols of colonial intrusions into Indian hunting grounds. Captain James Francis by the Saluda had his crops uprooted by Cherokees. He found two calves shot dead with arrows. The tongue of one calf was cut out, while the other animal lost only the tongue's "backstrap." Other whites reported Indians who shot their hogs and cows, stripped off cow tongues and tails, and stole horses. One farmer lost a bull to Nottawega men who helped themselves only to the dead animal's tongue and horns—items that had talismanic power and ornamental use.[35]

Some slaveholders felt threatened, though there was no general panic of a Black uprising among piedmont whites. Edmund Gray, a well-to-do landholder, complained in May 1751 that a "half-Breed fellow" of the "Cherokee Nation" had persuaded six Black men in his household to flee to freedom in Indian country. Three of the six escapees returned, perhaps out of fear, while the others headed onward. The "half-Breed" man, a devil-may-care fellow by the name of Andrew White, was fluent in English while thoroughly Cherokee by loyalty. Unabashedly violent, he bragged that he had recently killed a white storekeeper by the Oconee River in Creek country. In this episode, White and several northern Indian confederates fought a handful of Chickasaws, while colonials were ancillary targets. Posing as a fearless warrior, Andrew White threatened to plant his ax in the head of any whites who came to grab him at Glen's command. This talk came from an individual

Confronting Colonialism and the Creek Nation

who had no obvious attachment to any single Cherokee community and was quite unlike headmen who resorted to pleasantries and obfuscation to mollify an English governor's concerns. Though a marked man, White remained free because Cherokees would not surrender him to colonials.[36]

Growing familiarity between Indians and colonials often bred contempt, undoubtedly beyond what is occasionally revealed in the documentary record. One anonymous English trader reported that a "half breed [Cherokee] wench named Peggy" had attended a "Ball Play" near Keowee when no whites were present. Peggy heard Nottawega men urge Cherokees to kill all the white traders, take their goods, and then come to live among northern Indian friends. The anonymous colonial informant picked up additional news while traveling in Overhill country. By his account, it appeared that the Shawnees were calling on the Cherokees to unite with the Creeks and other Indians in a war to "Cut off all the White People." Then the Indians "would have Hoggs and Cattle & other things Enough of their own and would Live well."[37]

In all probability, the idea of entirely cutting off the whites was a release of anger and not an actual war plan. When four Shawnee men harassed Ludovick Grant at his Great Tellico home and storehouse in May 1748, two Cherokee women, who lived in a town fifteen miles distant, were on the scene wishing to trade. Grant believed that the women helped to save his life by their very presence. In his mind, the Shawnees dared not hurt him because whatever they did would be reported by the women to Tellico's elders, as indeed proved the case. Women's intervention in this instance, as in many others, had the purpose of averting violence that might harm their own community and even others in the vicinity.[38]

Most Cherokee towns did not want a break with the English. There were nevertheless pockets of discontent all over the Cherokee map by 1750. Trading grievances were acutely felt in particular towns where hunters recoiled from indebtedness and felt cheated or deprived of a just price. This problem, hardly new, was exacerbated by growing rum sales to Indian men who were prone to violent outbursts when drunk. Escalating Cherokee conflict with the Creeks heightened insecurity.[39]

The year 1751 saw suspicions burst into panic across Cherokee and Carolina frontier communities. Interestingly, a Cherokee "Ball Play" was once more a charged venue. Just after the game, young braves unloosed pent-up emotions. Trader Abraham Smith, who happened to be in the vicinity, overheard Indians "laughing Extravagantly" at reports

Cherokees, Native Peoples, and Empires, 1730–1762

of "the last dying words" of colonials, one badly wounded and the other shot dead, by a small band of Cherokees and Nottawegas in the past year. The dying man had cried: "O how; O Lord, have mercy upon us"—a heartfelt English prayer but somehow risible to Cherokee youths steeled to hardihood. Stunned by this event and other frightening reports, veteran trader James Maxwell was convinced he had to flee Cherokee country or be killed. Hearsay had it that Nottawega men, if not Cherokees themselves, were intent on killing him and other Anglo traders. The crisis seemed real. After all, several of the traders' Cherokee wives and female companions urged the men to flee to safety. Taking no chances, Maxwell left Middle Town Joree for Keowee and then hurriedly departed for Augusta, Georgia, in the company of seventeen whites and two Blacks.[40]

Panic and Resolution

It took several months for what Gregory Dowd has called "the panic of 1751" to peak and gradually unwind in Cherokee country and the bordering South Carolina piedmont. Rumors of violence and cross-border warfare gathered momentum over several years. Lower Town Cherokees were agitated about colonial intrusions that spread across their hunting grounds and appeared headed toward their villages. As the piedmont's settler population increased, white men steadily filtered into Native territory. Anthony Dean, a licensed trader at Great Tellico, attributed "a great deal of the mischief" in Cherokee territory to whites—a situation he remarked was not surprising "when every horse Stealer here can Screen himself from Justice" by scampering into Indian country. Robert Goudy, a veteran trader fearful of a Cherokee uprising, declared he was leaving the business because of the "bad management among the White People" in Indian territory, "where every one does as he thinks proper and without Controul." Unlicensed colonial traffickers sold mainly rum, which inflamed Cherokee tempers as much as ever. Some Indians remarked that they could eliminate their debts by shooting colonial traders. There was no reason to pay dead men. This refrain was sounded far and wide in Indian country even if it was seldom acted on, apart from extreme crises such as the Yamasee uprising.[41]

Colonial settlers' nerves were on edge. They could not easily protect their dispersed homesteads from Indian raiders who slaughtered livestock, plundered barns, and sometimes threatened their lives.

Theft was, of course, a double-edged sword. In early 1751, a few white men stole three hundred deerskins and some tobacco pipes that Tugaloo hunters stored at a wooded campsite. After a lengthy investigation, Captain James Francis had a warrant served on two colonial men who shared the same house in Ninety-Six. When a district officer arrived at the dwelling, the householders threatened to blow out his brains. There the matter ended, much to Cherokee vexation. A subsequent raid by Indian assailants on Francis's homestead may have been payback.[42]

The rumors feeding colonial-Cherokee tensions were bred of mistrust that had not yet hardened into pervasive racialized hate. The great fear of Cherokees in 1751 arose from rumors that South Carolina was going to send an army to crush them and the Nottawegas. This false report, which by the spring was spreading like wildfire, originated from a colonial trader's hired man of loose tongue and uncertain motives. Chickasaw chief Squirrel King churned the rumor mill, passing word that Creek warriors were ready to join the English and destroy the Cherokees. The message was a vintage scare tactic. Squirrel King, whose Savannah Valley people had faced Cherokee attacks for several years, wished to throw off the enemy. He knew quite well that Cherokees dreaded the Muscogees above all else.[43] Overhill Cherokees received yet more alarming news. Reports spread that the governors of New York and South Carolina were scheming to turn the Nottawegas against the Cherokees. This was false, too, but in the charged atmosphere the claim appeared credible.[44]

In several communities, Cherokees unleashed anger as if purging themselves of poison. Towns of the Tuckasegee Valley, an area in the Great Smokies remote from white settlers, were at the center of the disturbances. In one village, Native men and women robbed trader Bernard Hughes's storehouse, tore items to pieces, and divided the deerskins, horses, and back saddles among themselves. In another episode, a Cherokee man shot and wounded trader Daniel Murphy. It is unclear if Hughes and Murphy were targeted for specific reasons or were objects of Native resentment toward wayward forces—a shortage of munitions, the stranglehold of debt, the thirst for liquor, and the feeling that Creeks, other Indian enemies, and the "white people" were out to get them. These episodes triggered scattershot rumors that passed to the South Carolina piedmont and eventually to Charles Town. Some colonials believed that the Cherokees had killed four white traders. Actually, only Murphy was shot, not lethally, but this information remained unknown for weeks. Many white traders fled Cherokee country in fear for their lives. Others stayed, serving as translators and couriers for Indian headmen who wished to restore trade and avoid any punitive action by Charles Town.[45]

Crisis accelerated collaborative action in Cherokee towns. Headmen of several communities gathered to formulate talks—essentially policy statements—to colonial interpreters for transmission to Governor Glen. At Great Tellico, "old Cesar," an elder who knew English, assisted in the proceedings. (He was almost certainly the same man who was at the forefront of Cherokee–South Carolina relations during the 1710s.) Because very few Cherokees were fluent in English, experienced traders such as Anthony Dean, Cornelius Dougherty, Robert Bunning, and others had a vital intermediary role. Head Warrior Raven of Hiwassee, once again a proponent of conciliation, summoned the voices of many communities. He sent his son and five warriors to Konontroy, Stecoe, and Kituwah—the towns of the Tuckasegee Valley that had lashed out at the Anglo traders. The situation required diplomatic finesse, especially since Kituwah was considered the mother town of all Cherokees.[46]

That only three towns were implicated in the most glaring anti-English violence facilitated diplomacy. While the Raven met with English traders by the Hiwassee, headmen of ten Cherokee communities gathered at Joree in Middle Cherokee territory, where most inhabitants moved to quiet fears and resume customary trade. The Joree meeting, in which Tuckasegee cooperated, sent word to Charles Town that all was in order. Apologies were soon forthcoming from the convulsed Cherokee towns. Tuckasegee's head warrior regretted that "his brother," trader James Maxwell, "has run away." The warrior had not forgotten trader Maxwell "but holds fast his love to him." As for his people, "they Mourn for Goods," and hoped that "His Father" Glen would not stop traders from bringing ammunition to his town. The Cherokees' [Indian] enemies were "very many upon them from the Southward and Northward." To admit dependency on friends was honesty, not weakness. Raven said, "My Eyes loves to see White People for what is it we can do for our Selves." The warrior of Notoly added a universal peace talk: "The White People and them [the Cherokees] lives upon one Earth, and hopes our heart is as one to each other."[47]

The Raven of Hiwassee was determined to avoid a clash with South Carolina over retributive justice. He forwarded a conciliatory follow-up message to Glen as soon as he learned that the wounded white

Confronting Colonialism and the Creek Nation   171

trader had not been killed; there was therefore no cause for the Cherokees to kill one of their own as recompense. As for the stolen goods, Raven believed the three culpable towns should admit fault or else have no resident traders, whether white men, Indian, or "half breed" agents. Villagers would then learn what it was like to have "weary legs" to carry goods over a considerable distance.[48]

In missives to Glen, Cherokees described the violent outbursts against colonial traders as bouts of madness induced by fear of invasion. The people of Stecoe, Konontroy, and Kituwah were sorry for behaving as if they had been "Rum drinking when their Blood was hot." From a Cherokee perspective, it made sense to palliate a governor whose decisions affected their sustenance. Good talks could prevent a rupture with the English. If not acting as a wholly unified nation, Cherokees collaborated politically across village and even regional lines to safeguard their general welfare, mitigate ill consequences, and set things right as they believed necessary. The Middle Town deputies at Joree said that they acted with the approval of the Overhill region. Whether that was literally true was beside the point. A Native talk based on broad consensus had greater weight in Charles Town than words passed by a few villages. While the Raven of Hiwassee acted as a foremost mediator in Cherokee country, he was aided by others of like mind. Johnny of Great Tellico sent a conciliatory talk to Glen not only for his community but also in the name of the Lower Towns. He explained that his own Overhill region required additional consultation before it could speak as one. Johnny was doubtless anxious about Chota, the heart of Shawnee and French maneuvers in the area and a potential tinderbox.[49]

Glen was at his best in crisis management in 1751, a sharp contrast to his failure with the Choctaws. The governor was steady, restraining the provincial assembly as it weighed harsh measures against the Cherokees. Being a step ahead of the game, Glen opted for a political resolution before Cherokee peace messages reached Charles Town from the Hiwassee Valley and Joree. He opposed calls for an armed invasion of Cherokee country. A South Carolina legislative committee estimated that an offensive would require 150 royal troops, 650 white militiamen, 100 Catawba, and 60 lower Chickasaw warriors, as well as forty other "neighboring Indians." Glen shot back that the plan was unnecessary and foolhardy. There was room for negotiation. Besides, it was absurd to imagine that a makeshift army could advance through a steep and narrow mountain pass above the Lower Towns where "ten men can defend against a thousand." The governor's position was strengthened because the lower house of the assembly, unlike the council, had serious doubts about the cost and efficacy of invasion.[50]

While holding fast against a military solution, the governor finally assented to the assembly's demands for a trade embargo. On June 15, he sent orders for all Carolina traders to withdraw from Cherokee country and insisted that the three obstreperous Tuckasegee Valley towns each deliver two men to account for communal misdeeds at Charles Town. He also insisted that two Lower Towns—Keowee and Oustenali— surrender men who had either killed or shot at Englishmen. The tone of Glen's messages was as important as his demands. In letters he addressed closely allied Indian headmen as "Friends and Brothers." As might be expected, the most respectful messages went to cooperative towns, and the sternest to troublesome ones. "Valiant Raven of the Hywassee and his Beloved Men of the Valley," Glen declared, "can never have anything to apprehend from us, but may promise yourselves the greatest Security." Through further exchanges of this kind, the path was clear for Cherokees to meet with the governor in Charles Town in November 1751. While Glen verbally insisted that the Cherokees offer "Satisfaction" for serious wrongs, he deferred any demands for surrendering "the Guilty" and rejected the council's advice on limiting the number of headmen invited to the capital.[51]

In mid-November, twenty-two Cherokee headmen, joined by 126 male companions along with twelve women from eighteen towns, arrived in Charles Town. The conference was a deliberative exchange that lasted two weeks. Three points are significant. First, Cherokee headmen cited unusual circumstances and misunderstandings for any harm done to the English. Second, the Cherokee stance toward northern Indians remained ambivalent, voicing opposition to pro-French groups along with friendship for "Norward Indians" who attacked the Cowetas (Lower Creeks). Third, Cherokee leaders spoke for their particular towns while advancing common interests. Mutual well-being was a foremost principle of Cherokee peoplehood, which came to life once again during crisis management with the English.[52]

Glen turned the Charles Town conference to advantage by fashioning a treaty between his province and the Cherokees. The governor pledged a new law regulating the Indian trade in a stricter, more equitable manner. Only licensed traders were to traffic in Cherokee country for particular assigned towns. Colonial traffickers were not to extend credit to Indians beyond a limited amount. Rum was to be excluded

Confronting Colonialism and the Creek Nation

from the trade altogether. These provisions were enacted into law within a few days. The provincial government continued to prohibit traders from hiring any Indians or Blacks (free or slave) as assistants or factors. The restatement of old prescripts suggests a weakness in enforcing laws already on the books.[53]

As was customary, the Cherokees were offered rewards for the capture and return of runaway Blacks in their land. Two other treaty provisions merit attention. First, Cherokees were not to sell skins or leather to any individuals in colonial settlements. Second, Cherokees were not to hunt "lower down . . . than the Place called the dividing Waters," the boundary defined in 1747 by tributary streams flowing into the Savannah and Saluda Rivers. In short, the treaty aimed at limiting contact between Cherokees and white settlers. Colonials did not want Indians passing through or near their settlements. Such travel was permitted only for attendance at official conferences as a government necessity.[54]

Glen kept to his continental aims in framing the treaty. With the French in mind, the governor asked the Cherokees to give their "utmost Assistance" in erecting British forts in their country. The proposal won hearty approval. Keowee and Tugaloo favored a garrison in their respective communities. Skiagusta of Keowee offered a telling criticism. If a fort had been built in the Lower Towns as previously pledged, their inhabitants would not have been "cut off" by the Creeks the previous spring. Scalioskie of Great Tellico put forward his region's case for a garrison. Unlike Keowee and Tugaloo, the Upper Towns faced the French directly west of the mountains. The Cherokees were ready for British forts; they waited for Glen to act. The governor was more than willing but had yet to secure funding from either his assembly or the imperial government.[55]

The accord of November 1751 was one of innumerable attempts to rectify deep-seated problems in colonial-Native trade. Its nominal restrictions had limited efficacy when it came to halting rum sales or preventing Anglo traffickers from extending credit beyond lawful limits. Did Glen expect Cherokee hunters to sell only "dressed" or cleaned deer pelts when Indians had become content to sell raw skins to traders over decades? The governor was certainly emphatic on this point. He had a colonial trader publicly cut off a deerskin's ears, hooves, and snout as an example to Cherokee observers. The main deal, the resumption of trade, went ahead. Glen concurred with a Cherokee plea that ill will of the past be forgotten. In this respect, he absorbed an Indian cultural

Cherokees, Native Peoples, and Empires, 1730–1762

understanding of peacemaking. Keowee's Skiagusta envisioned a favorable outcome from the conference's opening: "I hope that all is past will now be forgotten. The Sun is Now down, the morrow is a new day and I hope all will be forgotten."[56]

Despite the success of the Charles Town conference, not all went smoothly. Chota retained its freedom of maneuver by not sending deputies to the gathering. Cherokees clamored about their needs, to Glen's annoyance, during the distribution of presents at the conference's end. After Native deputies received arms and munitions, Raven asked for twenty-five more guns for his Valley Towns alone. Other Cherokees raised a cry for fifty-eight additional guns. Glen replied that he would give no more since he had already distributed 113 such weapons to the various Cherokee visitors. While Cherokees displayed unity on major issues, towns and regions still competed among one another for preferment.[57]

Glen's hand was strengthened in Native diplomacy by a new British policy—the shipment of Indian "presents" at royal cost from England to South Carolina and Georgia. Both colonies benefited from this windfall in 1749–1751, and South Carolina did so again in 1753. For example, one substantial cargo arrived at Charles Town in 1750 with a large assortment of cloth, metalware, beads, pipes, mirrors, and wearing apparel beside the essentials of war and hunting—300 guns, 50 of which had "ornamented Stocks," 3,500 lbs. of gunpowder, 6,000 lbs. of bullets, and 4,000 flints. The dispatch of Indian presents at British imperial expense was a response to customary French largesse of this kind. In the competition for Indigenous allies, Britain was not to be outdone. Ample supplies enhanced Glen's leverage in Native diplomacy, if not assuring his success. Cherokees, Creeks, and other Indigenous nations had expectations of suitable recompense for their goodwill and services.[58]

War with the Creeks

Nearly all Cherokee regions had a similar interest in patching up difficulties with South Carolina, especially on the trading front. The same could not be said of Cherokee relations with the Creeks. Cherokee towns differed among themselves about the feasibility of peace with the Muscogees. The Creeks were themselves not of one mind regarding the "mountain" people, that is, the Cherokees. Creek and Cherokee regions had distinct geopolitical perspectives that complicated the negotiation of a general peace. Moreover, truces had a limited lifespan when even small bouts of intertribal violence sparked cycles of blood vengeance. The difficulty of ending hostilities was all the greater when the scale of bloodletting passed from minor clashes to outright war.

There was little secret about the trigger of intensified Cherokee-Creek conflict in the years 1745–1753. The Muscogees responded virulently to northern Indian strikes initiated from Cherokee territory, just as they had resisted Chickasaw attacks coming from the same quarter two decades earlier. In 1747, Colonel George Pawley posed the issue to Cherokee headmen at Tanasee: "I suppose they [the Creeks] are angry with you for suffering their Enemies to rest with you and for your furnishing them with provisions." In early 1749, James Glen considered a Cherokee-Creek peace essential to South Carolina's strategic interests. He encouraged both nations to end fighting, recurrent for about three years, so that Britain would have the opportunity to strengthen its position in the continental interior.[59]

Creek-Cherokee diplomacy, so far as it is revealed in colonial records, followed a similar political and social geography over decades. In the 1720s and 1740s, the most noteworthy peace talks involved Upper Creeks and the more westerly Cherokees, especially towns like Great Tellico and several communities to the south. Geographic and economic forces came into play. Upper Creek (Abeika) towns—Okfuskee, Okchai, and others—were accustomed to sharing hunting grounds with Cherokees above the Coosa River. Much like Cherokees, the Abeikas displayed an openness to peace partly to get on Glen's good side and thereby assure the flow of presents and the best possible trade terms.[60]

The obstacles to successful peace talks were still formidable after intermittent clashes over decades. The safety of emissaries was not a sure thing. In the spring of 1749, Okfuskee villagers were elated to see three of their deputies return from a visit to Cherokee towns of the Hiwassee Valley. Quite as promising, the trio brought five Cherokee deputies with them. The occasion was important to nearly all Upper Creek towns, even those that might be skeptical that peace would result. Through the services of a colonial trader, Muscogee headmen sent Glen a written talk attesting to their hope in the diplomatic track. Upper Creek leaders were careful to express a caveat. They favored peace, provided that the Cherokees "drive away or kill all the Notawagees and other Northern Indians from among them." Peter Chartier of the Shawnees, now currying favor with Glen, sent a similar warning to Charles Town.[61]

176   *Cherokees, Native Peoples, and Empires, 1730–1762*

Portrait of James Glen. *Dalhousie Estates, U.K.*

As Creek-Cherokee dialogue continued, colonial interpreters assisted as couriers in exchange. Anglo traders translated Creek headmen's talks into English and sent the messages to their colleagues in Cherokee country for retranslation to Native leaders there; the same process operated from Cherokees to Creeks. This indirect method of communication suggests lingering mistrust between rival Indigenous camps. The transmission of gifts, vital to Native diplomacy, was comparatively simple. Okfuskee's chief sent a conk shell, a ritual ornament, to the Cherokee Valley towns. Also given were corn and watermelon seeds as signs of mutual sustenance. Cherokees responded by inviting Creek friends to share some of their harvest. Raven of Hiwassee sent word that he had treated one of Okfuskee's young men, an adopted war captive, as a son. Kindness begat kindness. Little Tellico was pleased that one of its beloved men, currently a Muscogee prisoner, would be released. The freed man was instructed to find his kin in their hunting grounds in one moon's time and to signal his presence by firing a gunshot into the air![62]

Cherokee women had a significant role in their people's quest for a Creek peace. Little Tellico's "beloved Women" sent white beads to the Okfuskee chief with an accompanying peace message: "The women think of [the] time to come [when] they be out in the Woods, where . . . they be in no danger of themselves nor their Children, no more [than] when the Sun Shines upon them." Interestingly, Cherokee men requested colonial traders to relay the women's words and gifts, sent on behalf of several communities. As spokesman for eight towns, the Raven explained that Cherokee women were sending a white flag to Okfuskee's chief to show "that his heart is Streight." By this gesture, the warrior-chief linked his male strength with female kindness. Cherokee towns were extraordinarily disposed to give voice to women's sense of things in peace negotiation. The meaning was both literal and profoundly symbolic of female life-giving.[63]

Boundary issues entered into Cherokee-Creek diplomacy. When headmen of seven Overhill Cherokee towns sent a peace talk by Anglo traders during the summer of 1749, they advised Creeks, Chickasaws, and Alabama Shawnees to hunt that coming winter at the forks of the Coosawattee River, but no further north. A mutually satisfactory hunting boundary was a way of avoiding conflict. If the agreement held, there could be no mistake about which groups were responsible if the Cherokees were attacked above the Coosawattee. In that event, the likely culprits would be "French Indians" and not the southerly groups that had entered the truce.[64]

The porousness of borders was a main sticking point in negotiations. The Cherokees practically admitted that they had little, if any control over northern Indian war parties that came into their territory and then journeyed south to attack the Creeks. Overhill headmen conceded little on this issue, stating only that they would not allow northern Indians to pass directly through their towns or to receive food and drink on their way further south. By the headmen's own words, the Senecas and other raiders knew "Several ways of going thro' the Woods" in Cherokee country to make war. On a positive note, Overhill leaders, thankful for Creek gifts of corn and pea seeds to plant, conveyed their wish that Muscogee men would join them for harvest at the Green Corn dance.[65] Much would have to fall neatly into place for that happy event to occur.

Glen was determined to mediate Cherokee-Creek negotiations in 1749. Unfortunately, he stumbled badly by reaching for an imperial diplomatic coup, perhaps to counterbalance his mounting failure with the Choctaws. Though Creek headmen were open to parley with the Cherokees under English auspices, they strongly preferred that the talks be held at Fort Moore, a piedmont Savannah River outpost, and not Charles Town in the sickly summer season, which many Indians had long dreaded. On this point Cherokees and Creeks were in agreement. However, the governor still scheduled the conference, in which the Catawbas also participated, for his capital seat in late summer.[66]

On the surface, the gathering of 1749 was impressive. In all, seventy Cherokee men and three women were in attendance by early September, while over thirty Creek men joined them, accompanied by two women and several children. The two principal delegations were not in balance, however. Cherokee deputies came from all major regions, with a substantial representation of headmen—Raven of Hiwassee, Ostenaco and priest-chief Connecorte of Chota, and Ammouiscossitte of Great Tellico. By contrast, the Creek emissaries were overwhelmingly of the Abeikas and Tallapoosas, with only a few men arriving from Chattahoochee towns. Malatchi of Coweta, by far the most prestigious Lower Town chief, did not attend and headed instead to Savannah to represent his people's interests before Georgia officials. As the Charles Town gathering began, Glen received a written talk from Chigelly, now an elderly Coweta beloved man whose words still carried weight. Contending that Malatchi favored peace, he accused the Cherokees of making trouble by attacks on Abeika towns. Coweta's leaders would obviously take a good deal of persuasion before accepting a truce with the Cherokees.[67]

Colonial records offer little hint at the words that passed between the Cherokees, Creeks, and Catawbas. The South Carolina council simply noted that all parties agreed to peace. Glen and the council then went on to distribute gifts and honors to the Native delegations. The proceedings give the definite impression that Cherokees and

Confronting Colonialism and the Creek Nation

Creeks came primarily to Charles Town to shore up their relations with South Carolina, notably in trade and supply. Many Native deputies doubtless favored a respite from hostilities with tribal adversaries, but that outcome was far from assured.[68]

Glen's diplomacy dealt an unwitting blow to Native attendees by exposing them to the low country at the very time that disease posed the greatest danger to life. A good many Cherokee visitors fell sick and died on Charles Town's outskirts or succumbed as they struggled to reach home. The Creeks were greatly upset by similar losses. They roundly believed that the English were trying to kill them, just as the French had warned. The Catawbas were hardest hit by disease, losing at least fifteen headmen besides others who fell to northern Indian attack on their way home. Glen lamented the death of Cherokees who were stout English friends—Yellow Bird and his wife, both of Keowee, as well as "half Breed" Johnny of Tanasee.[69]

The talks in Glen's capital scarcely brought even a fig leaf of genuine Cherokee-Creek peace since certain parties in each Indigenous nation had little if any inkling of a truce. The Abeikas generally desired détente, but not Acorn Whistler of Little Okfuskee, who led an armed band, stoked by the French, which raided Cherokee towns in the same summer that Native delegations headed to Charles Town. This information came to Glen from Peter Chartier, Shawnee leader at the Alabama, who was uncharacteristically ready to do the English a favor if he could draw the Carolina trade to his economically strapped people.[70]

Unlike most Abeikas, Creek Towns of the Chattahoochee were ready, if provoked, to escalate their running battle with the Cherokees. A trigger came in the fall of 1749 when Cherokee raiders struck Cussita, killing two women and capturing four other persons. (The two murdered women were actually Chickasaws who lived at Cussita.) The Cussitas retaliated by killing two Cherokee men and capturing another, whom they burned alive. Vengeance ran hot. By early 1750, a band of Cherokees and their northern Indian allies killed or captured seven of Cussita's most respected warriors out on a hunt. Two Lower Creek men were meanwhile killed near their home, and a woman and two children were carried off.[71]

Violent outbursts led to conflagration. In April 1750, Malatchi of Coweta led more than four hundred Creek warriors against the Lower Cherokees. This unusually large force dealt punishing blows, killing thirty to forty Cherokees and capturing at least seven prisoners who were ritually tortured to death. The Creeks set fire to two enemy towns, destroying Echoe and burning much of sizable Estatoe, where some women, children, and elderly men survived by taking cover in a palisaded townhouse. Others fled north to the Middle and Overhill Cherokee Towns. Creek leaders believed the attacks thoroughly justified. In talks with English authorities in Georgia and South Carolina, Malatchi recalled the Tugaloo killings of 1716 when Cherokee hosts cut down a dozen Creek peace emissaries. His people's first motivation lay in recent events, but the past was not forgotten.[72]

The Creek invasion exposed Cherokee vulnerability on several fronts. The battered towns were struck by a powerful enemy, while receiving virtually no aid from Middle Cherokee and Hiwassee communities, let alone the Overhills further northwest. Here is a stunning instance of disparate Cherokee locales being either unable or unwilling to unify against a foe that concentrated its might by attacking along the Blue Ridge's eastern foothills. The Creeks themselves were not of one mind in war. Upper Creek Towns largely held back from the major assault on the Cherokees, honoring their peace pledge to Glen without yielding the right of future retaliation.[73]

After the Cherokee Lower Towns were smashed, it is not surprising that the stronger Overhill villages took the lead in cautiously renewing talks with Upper Creek headmen. When the moment seemed right, Cherokee deputies set out toward the Coosa during the early summer of 1750. Great Tellico's emissaries included two men and three women—another sign of female involvement in peace diplomacy. The Cherokee visitors were accompanied by nine Shawnee men and a Chickasaw man who paved the way as mediators. Fifteen Upper Creek headmen went ahead to greet the weary Cherokee travelers who partook in ceremonial exchange of white feathers, tobacco, and beads. Chief Enostanakee, the "Gun Merchant" of Okchai, as he was called by the English, was particularly hospitable, naming a Cherokee visitor an honorary "king" of his town. The common Native custom of elevating an outsider as chieftain was a powerful way of forging kinship across adversarial bounds. An Indian interpreter of "the Cherokee Tongue," likely a Creek man, aided the proceedings, as observed by Carolina trader William Sludders. Interestingly, Sludders heard Creek men say that "they want no writing in their way of making Peace for it is a thing they cannot understand."[74] This was a common refrain, showing that many Indians, for all their reliance on written messaging with the English, had limited faith in its use.

Confronting Colonialism and the Creek Nation

Although Natives pursued peace talks in their own fashion, they could not ignore colonial influence. Gun Merchant weighed Glen's threat that there could be a trade embargo if his people rejected a Cherokee peace. Other circumstances came into play. Upper Creeks desired calm on the Cherokee front since they were in a bloody conflict with the Choctaws. Creek men meanwhile desired to hunt freely toward Cherokee country for reasons that had little to do with war. Muscogee youths were presumably eager to cavort with Cherokee women after winter hunting instead of rushing home. In a message to Glen, Gun Merchant explained that the Upper Creeks, Shawnees, and Chickasaws had all agreed "to be at Peace and Live like Brothers with the Upper Cherokees," and when they met at hunting "to eat and drink together like Brothers and not to think of anything that has past [*sic*] between us in our former differences." Purposeful forgetting was just as important to peacemaking as remembrance. The talks concluded amicably despite word that a prominent Okfuskee man had recently been killed either by a Nottawega or Cherokee warrior. Ambiguity about the killing helped prevent an immediate blowup.[75]

Once a truce was reached, the terms of retribution changed. As Gun Merchant informed Glen, he would demand "Satisfaction" of the Cherokees if they subsequently harmed persons in his nation. The peace was unfortunately short-lived. The Creek offensive of 1750 took many Cherokee lives. Retaliatory forays bred counterattacks, leading to renewed Cherokee-Creek hostilities in 1751–1752. The Raven of Hiwassee was stung when "Southward" Indians, meaning the Creeks, repeatedly attacked his town, killing his brother among others in 1752. In a message to Glen, he confessed to thinking of "nothing but War." His anger brought a plea for munitions. The Southwards would continue to "kill his People like Dogs" unless the Cherokees had the means to fight.[76] There was no separation of Cherokee-Creek conflict from the ups and downs of relations with the English.

Cherokee deputies in Charles Town in November 1751 did not presume safe passage back to their hills and mountains. Muscogee attacks were feared, which helps explain the Cherokee clamor for English guns. Before departing Charles Town, the Raven told Glen of his ominous dream: "The Enemie was in the Path." The governor himself warned Cherokee headmen that "some Creeks are lying on the Path to waylay you, most probably to Cut off some of your Strag[g]lers."

182   *Cherokees, Native Peoples, and Empires, 1730–1762*

An outbreak of fighting soon occurred, which rapidly escalated. Three Coweta warriors shot and scalped a Cherokee courier who had joined colonial traders on the western path from Charles Town. Bigger troubles lay ahead. By early 1752, a regional Cherokee-Creek truce had broken down. Cherokees killed eleven Okfuskee men on the path to Georgia, while in turn absorbing considerably greater losses.[77]

The course of fighting was partly determined by numbers and the concentration of force. The Creeks had a substantial advantage on both counts, numbering 3,500 fighting men on a fairly level terrain; the Cherokees had perhaps 2,000 strung across both sides of the Appalachians.[78] Neither side brought its full potential into battle but tended to form multiple war parties with local and regional roots. Two principal Lower Cherokee headmen, Skiagusta of Keowee and the Good Warrior of Estatoe, sent a plaintive message to Glen, practically begging him to send ammunition and "to make a Peace between our Enemies and us." Both leaders feared having to move their towns to safer ground, which was much "against our Will." They had already lost thirty-three people and expected "every Night . . . to be killed before the morning." Skiagusta and the Good Warrior explained that their Muscogee enemies could turn to the French and Spaniards if not supplied by the English. The Cherokees had no such option. The "Broad Path" to Carolina, declared the chiefs, "is sprinkled with the Blood of our People."[79]

Tragically, more blood was shed before the Cherokees and Creeks reached a truce through Glen's mediation, combined with their own efforts, in 1753–1754. One notorious outburst of violence came when twelve Cherokee men came to Charles Town in March 1752 to plead for guns and ammunition—just when a Creek delegation arrived for unscheduled talks with Glen. The governor urged peace all around, and a brief respite followed. Some Creek men smoked and drank with the Cherokees. But all came undone when the Cherokee men headed home on the afternoon of April 1. Closely tracking the Cherokees, the Lower Creek men unloosed a barrage of gunfire on the unprepared travelers just a few miles from the city. Four Cherokees were killed and scalped, another captured, and several others wounded. Only three managed to make their way back to Charles Town.[80]

Glen was outraged by the wanton violence against his direct orders. Soon afterward, he told the Creeks still in town that what had occurred "was not only perfidious to the Cherokees, but very outrageous

Confronting Colonialism and the Creek Nation

and injurious to us, and which happened at our very doors." Killings committed against the Cherokees on Carolina soil would need to be punished just like crimes against the king's white subjects. Glen told the assembly any other course would render Carolinians "cheap and Contemptible in the Eyes of all Indians." Satisfaction was demanded, but South Carolina had no realistic prospect of imposing its will by force. The governor declared that the Creeks must see that justice was done and the malefactors openly punished in their own country. To carry this message to the Muscogees, he appointed agent Thomas Bosomworth, who worked through his wife, Mary, a sophisticated Muscogee woman of Creek-British parentage who was fluent in English and her Native tongue.[81]

Glen said only the guilty should suffer the consequences. But who was guilty? Lower Creek men had killed the Cherokees, yet none of them answered for the murders. After an intricate bout of politicking, Malatchi and Chigelly worked out a backdoor deal with other headmen that deflected responsibility from their Chattahoochee neighborhood. Acorn Whistler of Little Okfuskee was fingered as the mastermind who instigated the slayings even though he had been recovering from a drunken stupor in Charles Town when the murders were committed. Cast as fall guy, he had few friends to protect him. His own nephew executed him in August 1752. The nephew was then killed at Malatchi's request to appease Upper Creeks who believed Acorn Whistler wrongly put to death. Malatchi had triumphed. He avoided a trade embargo by offering "satisfaction" and enhanced his standing as a negotiator with the British. Glen gained, too, by accepting the Coweta chief's explanation. In June 1753, Malatchi pledged to pursue peace with the Cherokees at the governor's behest. That fact was far more important to Glen than imposing British customs of retributive justice, which would have required the guilty party alone, not Indian surrogates, to answer for murder. The governor's first aim was to put a stop to intertribal warfare that compromised British imperial interests.[82]

Coda: Attakullakulla and Chota

In 1752, after more than eight years in office, Glen believed he had a good grasp of the Cherokees. But there was a real deficiency in his knowledge relative to Chota, where priest-chief Connecorte hosted

Shawnees, consulted with "French Indians," and encouraged negotiations with Williamsburg in 1751 because he had little faith in Charles Town. Glen was livid when he learned that Attakullakulla, then living at Chota, led an Overhill Cherokee delegation to meet with Virginia's government that August. Mindful of South Carolina's prerogatives in Indian affairs, Glen dispatched a sour letter to Thomas Lee, president of the Virginia council, in which he warned that Attakullakulla, the so-called "Little Carpenter" to the English, was a dangerous character—the "only Advocate" of the French among his people and "the principal Instigator . . . of all Mischief" current among the Cherokees.[83]

Nearly all that Glen initially learned of Attakullakulla came from testimony by Robert Goudy, a trader who resided in Overhill country for several years before heading south to Ninety-Six and then Charles Town during the panic of 1751. Appearing before the governor and council, Goudy offered intriguing bits of information, some of which rings true. He knew, for example, that Attakullakulla was among the Cherokees who had visited England in 1730. By Goudy's reckoning, Attakullakulla was taken prisoner by "French Indians" about ten or eleven years later, brought to Canada as a captive, and later freed. Little Carpenter returned to Chota about 1748, just when Chartier and his Shawnee friends were welcomed there. From what Goudy said, Attakullakulla "did everything in his power to give his Countrymen bad impressions of the English, and a high opinion of the French." Attakullakulla had since left the area but come back to the Overhill Towns about March 1751 and raised a war party to fight the Creeks. His "Gang" did not do battle, however, but returned north after finding that Lower Cherokees had already gone out against the enemy.[84]

Goudy's testimony hinted at facts the English had not yet absorbed. Attakullakulla was no fake but a genuine Cherokee emissary. His politics were shaped by conflicts in the Native world, not simply by Anglo-French contention. True, he might have received a French governor's commission and met Chartier, but his loyalty was centered in Overhill country. In 1751, Attakullakulla saw the Creeks as his people's foremost enemy. He would get aid in Williamsburg if Charles Town did not provide sufficient gunpowder and ball. Samuel Benn, trader at Tanasee, personally witnessed Attakullakulla's fiery animus against the Creeks. Desperate for munitions, Little Carpenter had barged into

Confronting Colonialism and the Creek Nation

Benn's house, grabbed him by the waist, and cried out that "you white People have brought no Ammunition but it goes to the Creeks and Catawbas." The frightened trader gave his uninvited guest something of what was demanded.[85] Such stories, magnified in the telling, marked Little Carpenter as an English foe. The reality would prove far different, as James Glen would discover during his first face-to-face encounter with Attakullakulla in Charles Town in July 1753.

There were limits to what British observers could discern of Cherokees by their Native names. In Cherokee speech, "Attakullakulla" means "Leaning-wood," suggesting a thin figure who stands without any obvious physical support. In reality, Attakullakulla had a warrior's pride besides his sharp intellect and wit. He was a pillar at his political height—and no mere "leaning wood" or "little carpenter" for that matter.[86]

7

Tempests of the French and Indian War

The last thing Cherokee leaders had on their minds in 1753 was being pulled into a war between the British and French. They were still debating peace with the Creeks. The battle-scarred Lower Cherokee Towns badly wanted a truce, while Chota was cool to it. This discrepancy was evident during the Cherokee negotiations with Governor Glen and council in Charles Town during the summer of 1753. The conference was a sizable affair. In attendance were seven leading headmen, three of lesser standing, and thirty other men besides four Cherokee women.[1]

Attakullakulla took center stage, verbally jousting with Glen in the council chamber just a few days after the two men met for the first time. On the morning of July 4, Attakullakulla recalled his youthful visit to England when he heard the "Great King George" promise that the Cherokees would have ammunition to fight their enemies. Did the governor, he asked, have the king's orders "to make peace" between the Cherokees and Creeks? By this uncanny question, Attakullakulla invoked a magisterial power above Charles Town. Glen shot back: "What I say is the Great King's Talk. You are not to mind any body Else." Attakullakulla next requested the governor's permission to travel to England and speak with the king. When Glen declined, the Cherokee leader said he could reach England from places other than Charles Town. This was a tête-à-tête between two prideful men. Attakullakulla was perhaps forty-five years old and entering his political prime, while Glen was fifty-two and in his tenth year as governor of Charles Town.[2]

Attakullakulla was savvy, deflecting Glen's questions about his French ties, and pausing to take a pipe from his pocket and offer it to the governor as a present from Chota's priest-chief Connecorte. After a tobacco smoke, Attakullakulla resumed the negotiation, explaining that his people could not agree to a Creek peace before consulting Connecorte, whom one headman declared was "Governor of his Towns," just as Glen was of "Your People here."[3]

Glen was as persistent as Attakullakulla in negotiation. He could not let the occasion slip knowing that the French were busily fortifying the Ohio country. Glen appealed to Keowee's Skiagusta for permission to build a fort in Lower Cherokee country. There was little difficulty here. Skiagusta approved and thanked the governor for his help in quieting the Muscogees. His people had hunted freely the last winter during a tentative truce. Glen was eager to move ahead after years of delay. At his urging, the South Carolina assembly had at last allocated £3,000 for constructing a fort near Keowee. Once the Union Jack was planted there, the governor would next aim for the Tennessee—five hundred miles from his capital.[4]

The Charles Town conference of 1753 showed once more that Cherokee diplomacy had strong local and regional underpinnings. Chota continued to value its Shawnee friends who helped to quiet hostilities between Cherokees and French-allied tribes to the north. Attakullakulla told Glen that his people would not agree to a Creek peace unless the English released six Shawnee men captured in the Carolina piedmont. Glen initially declined but decided a month later that two of the Shawnee prisoners should be freed and sent by sea to Philadelphia. His gesture was a measured compromise, a courtesy to Connecorte when Anglo-French war appeared imminent.[5]

Chota's tough talk bothered Skiagusta, who publicly chided Attakullakulla and his comrade "Long Jack" of Tanasee for behaving like "Boys" and talking "madly" to Glen before coming to their senses. The Keowee headman said he had been a warrior long before them and voiced his readiness for battle despite his old age. While Cherokee headmen seldom criticized one another before a colonial governor, Skiagusta was taking no chances given his desire for an English fort by Keowee.[6]

As customary, Cherokees gladly accepted English presents before leaving Charles Town. Glen dispatched the same favors to Connecorte as to the departing headmen, who each received a scarlet suit of clothes, a gun, saddle, and bridle. The entire assemblage brought home ample munitions besides paint, metalware, hatchets, knives, and mirrors. They gained a Union Jack as a display of loyalty, while the strategic

188   *Cherokees, Native Peoples, and Empires, 1730–1762*

Overhill Towns received "a Drum & Colours" at their request. Skiagusta merited a horse for his special goodwill. Horses were becoming important to Cherokees as well as a mark of distinction. Each Cherokee woman in attendance garnered cloth and ribbons, a pair of ear bobs, "a gilt Leather trunk, and a quart Decanter." The British "empire of goods" tugged ever more strongly at Indian country, pulling in women as much as men. The royal dispensation of presents raised Native consumer expectations to a degree not easily met through private trade alone.[7]

Before the Charles Town conference closed, Ostenaco, now head warrior of Tomotley and a prestigious leader, rose in the council chamber, handed Glen his English commission, and received it back with the governor's commendation. Attakullakulla followed by explaining that he had lost his former English commission, and almost his life, too, when made a prisoner by "Northern Indians" from Canada. He now told Glen of his true desire: "If I get a Commission we shall be alive together." The translation is awkward here, but the meaning is clear. Attakullakulla regarded the commission, which he received from Glen, as a bond between giver and recipient. He saw the value of cultivating Carolina, while not foreclosing options elsewhere. During the Charles Town talks, Attakullakulla deftly interpreted the King's "paper" or treaty of 1730, which to the Cherokees said that "the Governor of Carolina was to supply us with all Kinds of Goods but if he did not, we might have them in Virginia, that you both were . . . under the Great King George." While Glen was not about to yield South Carolina's primacy in southern Indian relations, he welcomed Attakullakulla's visit and said as much. Cherokee friendship was crucial to the governor's plans.[8]

Glen took understandable pride in mediating a Cherokee-Creek peace, which held firm once both Native societies renewed direct talks with one another. As the stronger party, the Creeks did not agree until their basic demands were met. In late July 1753, Okfuskee's Red Coat king dictated a letter to Glen in which he stated conditions for a peace. First, Cherokee headmen would need to come to his town to show their goodwill within three moons. Second, the visiting chiefs should bring two "Northern French Indian" slaves they held. The Creeks intended to burn both prisoners at the stake, thereby allaying their pain from past enemy strikes. Red Coat king was politic, no longer blaming Cherokees for killing his son, but instead holding other attackers responsible. A few months later, Cherokee deputies brought their "Peace

Tempests of the French and Indian War   189

Talk" to Okfuskee and pledged to prevent Northern Indian forays into Creek territory. A genuine halt to Cherokee-Creek hostilities was in sight. To solidify the peace, both nations honored a headman of their former adversary as a chief among their own people. This common Indigenous practice helped to ward off, or lessen, the chance of future conflict. The result was far more important than historians have previously realized. Once reaching peace with the Creeks, Cherokees had opportunities of their own choosing to assist the British in warfare to the north.[9]

The Cherokee-Creek peace coincided with the outbreak of fighting between Virginia militia and French troops in "the Ohio country," triggering the French and Indian War in North America (1754–1760). The conflict's initial phase culminated in young George Washington's surrender of Fort Necessity on July 4, 1754, to a superior force of 600 French troops, including Canadian militiamen and 100 Indian allies. The French thereby preserved their position at the Forks of the Ohio, where newly constructed Fort Duquesne threatened to arrest British colonial expansion and throw English-Indian alliances into disarray.[10] At the time of Washington's defeat, there was no sign that the imperial war would bring the British and Cherokees into closer alliance, only to eventuate in a collapse of trust and bitter fighting between the two sides that exploded in 1760–1761. That remarkable turnabout shook the Cherokee world in ways unprecedented since the arrival of English colonials in North America.

Forts and Control

In October 1753, James Glen was all ready for fort-building when he arrived at Keowee with sixty British troops and fifty colonial workmen. The moment was pathbreaking from Charles Town's perspective—and novel to the Cherokees. No colonial governor had previously set foot in Cherokee country. Glen had to request Cherokee consent for his plan once again. Old Skiagusta, who had given the go-ahead, had died since meeting the governor in Charles Town. Wawhatchee, his successor as head warrior, was not so keen on a British military presence in his neighborhood. Fortunately for Glen, the English had a strong ally in the Raven of Hiwassee, who traveled over 100 miles to lobby local headmen in favor of the fort. Glen secured approval after pledging to respect Cherokee headmen's graves, marked by "great heaps of Stones" on hills overlooking Keowee. Native tradition held strong.[11]

190 *Cherokees, Native Peoples, and Empires, 1730–1762*

Glen dispensed gifts to Cherokee participants once agreement was reached. The occasion was momentous. Cherokees were allowing British soldiers to live on their land for the first time. The new fort, named Prince George in honor of the heir to the throne, stood on the eastern side of the Keowee River, across from Keowee Town, "Mulberry Grove Place" to Cherokees. The stream flowing freely from the highlands above Keowee was now a natural divide between Cherokees and English soldiers.[12]

Fort Prince George was of no immediate help to Cherokees far to the northwest who felt the sting of Anglo-French conflict. In the fight with Virginia, the French were aided by Canada and Great Lakes warriors, some of whom were quite as interested in striking Indigenous enemies as the English. During the summer of 1754, far northern raiders killed two Cherokee women in a cornfield outside Chota. A "beloved Woman" was later slain while in a canoe on a nearby river. Cherokee fighters captured one enemy warrior—an "Over the Lake Indian" from Canada. Tortured at the stake, the prisoner boasted of an "Army of white and red men" coming to avenge him. In another assault, twelve French-allied Indians moved up the Hiwassee River, where they killed a Cherokee man, grabbed a Natchez woman villager, and killed her when pursued.[13]

These killings did not suddenly push Cherokees into the English camp, but the attacks certainly strengthened those headmen who favored a British protective arm. Cherokee bands struck a few French riverboats on the Mississippi in both 1753 and 1754. By 1755 Attakullakulla was moving in a decidedly pro-English direction; Ostenaco had similar leanings. What was unclear in the war's early stages was whether these headmen would look to Virginia rather than South Carolina as their most useful British ally.[14]

Glen was anxious about the first flames of war. While a British patriot, he could not abide the idea that his province would play second fiddle to Virginia. In 1754, he put off Lieutenant Governor Robert Dinwiddie, Virginia's chief magistrate, by discouraging Cherokee and Catawba assistance to the Old Dominion's war effort. Overhill Cherokees were themselves reluctant to provide aid until Dinwiddie furnished arms. Glen lost no chance to remind London of South Carolina's mastery in Indian affairs while deriding Virginia's inexperience and incapacity.[15]

In the event of a full-scale war with France, Glen believed Britain should establish a fort in the Overhill region, enabling royal troops to

Tempests of the French and Indian War   191

proceed deep into the continental interior. Most astoundingly, he proposed to negotiate with the Cherokees "for an actual Surrender of their whole Country" to George II. By this fanciful scheme, which Glen recommended to the king's government in August 1754, the Cherokees would "enter into a Solemn agreement to hold their Lands of His Majesty as Head and pay an Annual Tribute of a few Deer Skins for his Protection, and as an acknowledgement of him as their Superior & Lord." The governor even advised a new transatlantic voyage by Native headmen "to do Homage to His Majesty." Cherokee vassalage under British sovereignty had become as irresistible to the quixotic Glen as it had been for visionary neophyte Alexander Cuming. The governor moved breathlessly from the here and now to the future, promoting trans-Appalachian fort-building for the present while extolling "the benefit that would accrue to Great Britain by Peopling and Settling the [western] Country." Ironically, Glen learned much of what he knew about that vast region from Cherokee men who told him of "large extensive Plains and Savannahs, swarming with Deer and Buffalo." At his request, Native men sketched river courses—the Ohio, Wabash, Tennessee, and Mississippi—drawn on paper and with chalk on a floor. Glen enthused over the breadth and precision of Cherokee geographic knowledge. The Cherokee drawings, he wrote, "approach to our best [European] maps."[16]

Glen failed to win over the British ministry by his frenzied pleading and petty squabbling with Virginia. In early 1755, the Board of Trade decided that a steadier, less contentious chief magistrate was required at Charles Town. The new governor, William Henry Lyttelton, was interrupted in his ocean crossing when the French captured his ship at sea. Once released from gentleman's confinement in France, he made his way to England, sailed once more, and finally arrived in Charles Town on June 1, 1756.[17] Glen quickened his diplomatic pace in the interim, being ever more determined to achieve something great after learning that he was to be removed from office.

Overhill Cherokees understood quite well that English South Carolina strongly desired their support against the French. Glen had himself broached the construction of British forts to headmen as early as 1746. Chota, Tanasee, Great Tellico, and other communities deliberated on the potential advantages and drawbacks of the governor's plan on numerous occasions. The Cherokee situation had changed appreciably in just a short time in 1753–1754. Though the peace with the Creeks held, Upper Cherokees faced a spate of attacks by pro-French northern Indians. Anglo-French hostilities had a profoundly unsettling impact on Native peoples in much of eastern North America.

The need for security was the foremost consideration for Cherokees at the beginning of 1755. Overhill Cherokees took the diplomatic lead in English negotiations because of their military weight and relative proximity to the turbulent Ohio country. In May, Attakullakulla headed a delegation of thirty-three men, accompanied by a single woman, that made the long trek to Charles Town at Glen's invitation. By dint of intelligence and verbal ability, the man known to the English as Little Carpenter was the spokesman for priest-chief Connecorte ("Old Hop") who did not himself make the journey. The talks were amiable, if also a testing ground over two days. Glen desired a general conference where the entire Cherokee nation was to be represented. In response, Attakullakulla stated Connecorte's preference for a meeting at Keowee. Glen proposed a site in the piedmont, and the decision was left open for the moment. At a turn in the discussion, Attakullakulla remarked that Cherokee deputies presently in Charles Town could not stay long because their villages were endangered by "French Indians." Glen was perplexed. If the threat were so grave, why had a group of forty pro-French Indians, as he was informed by a colonial trader, lately visited Chota? Attakullakulla dodged the question, vaguely describing the northern visitors as Nottawegas and denying that they were among the Indian nations that had joined the French.[18]

Since the days of Long Warrior in the 1720s, Cherokees had deliberately obscured Charles Town's view of northern Indian nations, especially rival tribes that might be courted when necessary. Connecorte himself had Shawnee friends who kept in contact with French-allied Indians in the Ohio country, the Great Lakes region, and Canada. French sources tell us of Shawnee men who married Cherokee and Chickasaw women, resided in their host societies, and broadened their interethnic clout. Connecorte prized his Shawnee connections, not least because such friends might persuade their Indian allies to lay off Chota.[19]

Attakullakulla knew just how to question English intentions without the least hint of rudeness. While thanking Glen for furthering a Cherokee-Creek peace, Attakullakulla relayed a recent Creek talk warning the Cherokees to beware of the British fort by Keowee, which it was said had been built to deceive and destroy his people. The next day, Glen countered with a history lesson, reminding Cherokees that the French had devastated the Natchez and would have done the same

Tempests of the French and Indian War

to the Chickasaws were it not for English aid and supplies. The English, supreme in trade, would soon teach the French a lesson in battle. King George had sent "his Great Ships of War" and many of his warriors to help "the People of Virginia to drive away the French." Though Glen did not mention specifics, he knew that General Edward Braddock's regulars were on the march from Virginia and Maryland toward the Forks of the Ohio.[20]

With Cherokee complaisance, Glen meanwhile got his wish for a large conference in the piedmont. In late June 1755, over five hundred Cherokee men arrived at the Saluda River to meet with the governor, who was accompanied by an entourage of colonial gentry, soldiers, and traders. This was by no means an entirely male affair. In his official report, Glen noted the presence of "many" Cherokee women at the conference. The occasion was ceremonious and grand; the governor himself described the proceedings at length. Before formal speeches on July 2, Cherokee headmen delivered "many Strings and Belts of Wampum" to Glen "to put him in Mind of their requests and to confirm what they said." Connecorte sat in one chair as Glen took another close by him. Cherokee elders sat on branches placed on the ground near the two leaders, while warriors settled around the nearby trees. Holding a bow and arrows in hand, Attakullakulla rose to speak for Chota and, by inference, for all Cherokees. A Cherokee boy stood by his side to absorb the talk for future generations. Attakullakulla made no specific reference to a British fort in Overhill country. His words and gestures were eloquently metaphoric on the necessity for strong English bonds.[21]

Attakullakulla spoke of "the Great King George" as "common Father" of Cherokees and English. He then opened a small leather bag, took a handful of soil from it, and laid "some Earth" at the governor's feet. Here was a token, in Glen's telling, that the Cherokees "gave all their lands to the King of Great Britain," acknowledging him to be "the Owner of all their Lands and Waters." Attakullakulla next offered Glen a bit of parched corn flour to symbolize the produce of the Cherokee earth. Handing over the bow and arrows, he confessed that the weapons were all the Cherokees could make by themselves and that they required English arms and ammunition. The Cherokees would fight for "their Lands," those they gave to the king, as long as any one of them still lived.[22] The negotiation played out just days before Braddock's army was mauled by French and Indian forces near the Monongahela.

194   *Cherokees, Native Peoples, and Empires, 1730–1762*

More than 900 British soldiers and Anglo-American militiamen were killed or wounded of the nearly 1,400 engaged in the battle. Braddock was mortally wounded and buried on the path, while his army retreated pell-mell to Philadelphia. We can only speculate how Glen's parley with Attakullakulla would have gone if the British disaster had occurred beforehand and the news had passed to Cherokees.[23]

There is scant written evidence of the Saluda proceedings, except what Glen penned for colonial newspapers and, much later, for British officials. Peeved by his pending replacement as governor, he did not send a report on the conference to the Board of Trade until April 1756—nearly ten months after the gathering took place. In his letter to London, Glen heralded the meeting, and the apparent Cherokee cession of land made there, as a personal diplomatic coup: "I was so happy as to succeed far beyond my Expectations, and I shall ever esteem that the happiest Period of my Life, for I have had the honour thereby to add sixteen or eighteen thousand People to the number of His Majesty's Subjects, and Forty million Acres of Land to his Territories." If not for the Saluda meeting, Glen averred, the Cherokees "would have abandoned the English upon the news of General Braddock's defeat," and the Creeks, too, would "have turned to the French," compounding the "heavy blow to the British Interest in America." These were words of a man hungering for ministerial appreciation and seeking vindication after twelve years' service at Charles Town.[24]

As Glen had it, the Saluda conference amounted to a formal treaty—or did it? In truth, Cherokees guided negotiations by words implied though not expressly stated in the governor's written rendition. If Cherokees symbolically gave their lands to the king, it was not a *surrender* but recognition of kingly power that strengthened their own capacity to defend their soil. Their earth was also their father's, the Great King George's—as long as the English acted as "Brothers." From a Cherokee perspective, Attakullakulla and his fellow headmen *treated* with Glen, and in the process conveyed understandings not captured in the governor's formal "treaty." The text Glen sent to England stated that the agreement "is signed in the Woods . . . at a place called Saluda." Curiously, there is no other proof of this. The governor's official report does not include Cherokee signatures.[25] A treaty document with Indian marks preoccupied Glen far more than Cherokees, who judged words by what they heard, instilled in heart and memory, and passed by word of mouth.

Tempests of the French and Indian War

Cherokee Entry into an Imperial War

The French-Indian triumph over Braddock emboldened the Ohio country's Shawnees and Delawares, who had thus far assumed a relatively minor role in the war, to attack colonial settlements from Pennsylvania to Virginia, wreaking terrible havoc. Warriors of Canada and the Great Lakes joined the assaults. Scores of colonial farm folk were killed; women as well as men were suddenly cut down. There were child victims, too, even if the young were more likely to be seized than killed. Captives saw family members slain and mutilated before their eyes. Ohio Indians spread terror with the intent of keeping whites far away, avenging past wrongs, and preserving what they had as a people. Hundreds of colonials fled eastward to find shelter. Frontiersmen put their own families' safety before all else, refusing militia duty if it took them away from home.[26]

Cherokees had their own concerns with the war's furious escalation. They were deeply fearful of the French–northern Indian alliance that was already taking a toll on their communities. The first substantive Cherokee aid to the British war effort came through Virginia's influence. Acting as Lieutenant Governor Dinwiddie's unofficial agent, trader Richard Pearis enlisted Overhill fighters in the fall of 1755 by pledging to cancel the debts the Cherokees owed him. Head Warrior Ostenaco grabbed at the deal. An astute leader who carefully weighed communal interests, Ostenaco was an old hand at sizing up colonials and considering how they might be swayed to answer Cherokee needs. To the English, he was commonly known as "Judd's Friend"—a reference to his having proverbially rescued an obscure Briton named Judd some years earlier.[27]

In February 1756, Ostenaco led eighty Cherokee men who joined 230 Virginia rangers under Major Andrew Lewis on an expedition targeting Shawnees near the Upper Ohio. While the Cherokees held up well on the long march from Maryland's Fort Frederick, colonials buckled under cold, hunger, and the travail of crossing creeks swollen by winter rains. Weakened by deserting soldiers, Lewis was forced to retreat short of his objective. The remaining militiamen and Cherokees survived on horseflesh on their return trek. Despite the setback, Cherokee leaders did not foreclose future collaboration with Virginia. Ostenaco leaned on the English when his own community was menaced by pro-French Indians. English friendship made sense if it came with respect and proper recompense.[28]

Overhill Cherokees negotiated with both South Carolina and Virginia to see which colony would rise to the occasion of building a fort on their Native ground. In December 1755, Attakullakulla arrived in Charles Town with a large delegation of ten to twelve leading headmen, 120 other men, and an unspecified number of women. Glen initially chided the Cherokees for visiting without his prior consent but then warmed to their message with its anti-French punch. Attakullakulla declared he was "sent by all the Headmen of the Overhill Towns" to know what help could be expected "from their Elder Brothers [the English] and at what time." Lest there be delay, he added that Shawnee visitors had passed a war belt from a northern Indian group—"Nantas"—revealing a plot to kill all white traders in Cherokee country. ("Nanta" or "Nuntaweas" was a common Cherokee name for northern Indians, such as the Ottawas of Canada and the Great Lakes.) Attakullakulla conjured frightening scenarios intended to spur the British to action. The French were said to be allied with Shawnees, Miamis, and Delawares with the intent of stripping the Iroquois and Cherokees of their lands. Conspiratorial phantoms flittered eerily in wartime, their shadows obscuring what English colonials might comprehend when peering toward Indian country.[29]

Cherokee geographic understandings far surpassed what could be seen from Fort Prince George in late 1755, let alone Charles Town. When Glen asked visiting Cherokees for military intelligence, Great Warrior Willanawa of Toqua borrowed pen and inkwell, took some paper, and sketched a series of rivers, identifying the site where the French were said to be building a fort on a river near the confluence of the Tennessee and Ohio Rivers. (Unfortunately, there is no extant copy of Willanawa's map.) While Frenchmen were scouting the area, they did not begin to construct a garrison along the Ohio, just above its confluence with the Tennessee, until the spring of 1757. As for a British Overhill fort, Willanawa assured Glen that his people would share their corn with an English work crew, at least through the coming summer despite the drought and limited harvest of the previous year. He was pleased to offer the use of the Cherokees' horses, which were "fat and running in the Woods." While desiring an English garrison, Willanawa said he would be "ashamed" to ask for himself because "he was a Warriour" and "not afraid to die," but that the fort was needed "for the Women and Children."[30] On this level, Cherokee and British men understood each other quite well.

Glen's personal eccentricities and imperial ambitions should not obscure his genuine concern for Cherokees and considerable knowledge

Tempests of the French and Indian War

of their ways. Before dispensing gifts to Cherokee visitors in December 1755, he advised Wawhatchee, Keowee's head warrior, to make sure that the Lower Towns aided Tuckasegee Valley villages to the north in case the latter were attacked. Wartime cooperation between Cherokee regions could not be taken for granted. Wawhatchee pledged to help and voiced approval of a British fort "for the Overhill people"—a distinct Cherokee group from his own. He was glad that Fort Prince George's soldiers had behaved like "Brothers" since the garrison's opening two years before. Glen was at pains to appear fair. Just days before, he had told Indian deputies that his government would show no "Partiality" because Cherokees "Differed in Colour from the White." In his judgment, the Cherokees merited an equal share of royal protection since they had transferred all their lands to King George. Indian headmen listened discreetly and took in the governor's message that their people would be "as Powerful and as flourishing a nation as ever."[31]

While this latest Charles Town conference was still ongoing, Glen pulled Attakullakulla aside for a private talk in which he said that South Carolina would begin construction of an Overhill fort in April—just four months off. Glen's trust in Attakullakulla came with a hitch. The governor wanted the Cherokees to surrender French army deserters living in their territory, especially "French John," a trader and an enemy agent allegedly responsible for robbing and murdering Englishmen. Attakullakulla was guarded, offering help only after saying he would consult Connecorte on the matter. He did not reveal that John, a Canadian and former Cherokee captive, had a special bond with Chota's priest-chief, who happened to be his old master.[32]

The idea that Connecorte was Cherokee "emperor" was commonplace in Williamsburg as much as Charles Town. Lobbying energetically for Cherokee military support, Dinwiddie sent a courteous letter to the priest-chief in late 1755 in which he proposed a meeting of Virginia officials with Cherokee headmen at Broad River in the North Carolina piedmont. The Cherokees took up the offer since it was to their advantage to be courted by two British governors and not only one. In mid-March 1756, twelve headmen, traveling without the elderly Connecorte, arrived at the appointed place. Oconostota, Chota's great warrior, was present along with Attakullakulla, other Overhill chiefs, and at least two Lower Town leaders.[33]

Before conferencing with the Cherokee men, Virginia commissioners Peter Randolph and William Byrd conferred with Catawba representa-

198   *Cherokees, Native Peoples, and Empires, 1730–1762*

tives who lived in the vicinity. Being a small nation, the Catawbas pledged forty warriors to aid the English war effort by the Ohio. Cherokee deputies responded carefully to Virginia's request for five hundred fighters. Spokesman once more, Attakullakulla explained that Connecorte, "our Governour," could not himself be present since he was too "old and infirm" to cross the mountains. Cherokee deputies offered four hundred warriors to assist the English but only after Virginia completed a fort in Overhill country for "the protection of our Wives and Children." Such a contingent arrangement was astute. Virginia would need to make good before the Cherokees committed to their part of the bargain. Attakullakulla played to the occasion by criticizing Glen for not fulfilling his own promise of fort-building. Randolph and Byrd acceded to the main Cherokee terms. Headmen then shared toasts with the Virginians, drinking to His Majesty's health and the royal family. Randolph and Byrd exclaimed: "Success to the Cherokee Nation," while the Native deputies hailed "their Brethren the English."[34]

Dinwiddie eagerly grasped the challenge of fort-building in Overhill country while South Carolina dithered. On April 24, 1756, the governor authorized Major Andrew Lewis to enlist sixty militiamen, hire artisans, procure provisions, and proceed "with all possible Expedition" to Chota for fort construction. Dinwiddie assured Cherokees by letter that he was of good heart. Cherokee youths at the Indian College of William and Mary—a separate small school for Indian boys— were well treated. A few months later, Dinwiddie wrote apologetically to Connecorte, explaining that the boys had left the school of their own accord because they "did not like Confinement ... [and] could not be reconciled to their Books."[35]

Lewis and his party reached Chota on June 28, 1756, several weeks later than Dinwiddie hoped. The delay is not surprising since the Virginians had to gather necessities and round up cattle for a mobile food supply during the long trek down the Shenandoah Valley and a traverse along highland rivers and streams to Overhill country. Lewis was most fortunate to have Ostenaco as guide for the five-hundred-mile journey. Well received at Chota by Connecorte and Attakullakulla, Lewis put his men to building a log fort that was 105 feet long on each side. After the work was completed in a month's time, the major was nonplussed when Cherokees hemmed and hawed rather than supplying warriors to accompany his party back to Virginia. When Lewis left Chota, he was accompanied by seven Cherokee men and three women—and not the several hundred men he expected! Not a single

Tempests of the French and Indian War   199

Virginia militiaman remained at the vacated post, which fell into disrepair. It never occurred to Lewis that Cherokees might not be impressed by the makeshift fort. Native men were not about to hurry off with his small militia party when villagers were in harvest season and looking ahead to the winter hunt.[36]

Knowing of Virginia's supposed head start, Glen played catch-up with all his assets. Unlike Virginia, South Carolina had well-established trading routes through Cherokee country that were a springboard for fort-building. Once British soldiers manned Fort Prince George at Keowee in 1753, there was a base from which troops could head further northwest and still be supplied from Charles Town.[37] A nagging problem delayed Glen. While he had imperial approval for the Overhill fort, South Carolina assemblymen were reluctant to advance money for the project before royal reimbursement was in hand. On April 9, 1756, Glen admonished legislators to see the big picture and move quickly ahead. In an emotional appeal six days later, the governor called on assemblymen to keep alive "the Fire that they [the Cherokees] have kindled with the English." Referring to the present Easter, Glen struck a religious chord. An Overhill fort would be "a work of peace and love" for Carolinians and Cherokees. The alternative was terrible to contemplate. If the garrison did not rise, Carolinas's "back settlements . . . must become a Field of Blood." Glen would personally supervise the work across the mountains as soon as he could get there. The funds at his disposal would suffice for the time being.[38]

Anxious about his pending replacement, Glen audaciously headed northwest on May 22, 1756, with a motley party composed of ninety British troops under Captain Raymond Demere, accompanied by two hundred colonial militia and workmen. On June 8, Glen was well up the piedmont at Ninety-Six when he received Governor William Henry Lyttelton's express letter, requiring his return to Charles Town. South Carolina's new executive, whose ship had docked at Charles Town a few days before, showed that he was in charge, sending his own message to "emperor" Connecorte on the fort-building mission. Glen dutifully returned in his coach to the city. It was now left to others to realize his vision. Demere and company—apart from the militiamen dismissed from service—marched on with thirty wagons of supplies for Fort Prince George, which they reached on June 19. The captain was impressed that Wawhatchee and three other Keowee chiefs greeted him "with the greatest civility."[39]

200   *Cherokees, Native Peoples, and Empires, 1730–1762*

Keowee and four nearby towns put on a good show for the British the day after Demere arrived. Three hundred Cherokee men approached Fort Prince George in fine order. As Demere described the scene, young men led the way at a slow pace, singing while holding aloft eagle tails and rattles. Youths on each flank played Indigenous flutes. "Chief men and their Councilors" were followed by a drummer, while one man in the throng held aloft a large sycamore bow, and another carried a long stick with a "White Ragg" at the end—this last clearly a peace symbol balancing the token of war. Nearly all males had well-painted faces. Many men were bedecked "with large belts of Wampum round their Necks and Silver hanging to their Breasts and round their Arms." Demere did not comment on Cherokee women as participants in the procession; it does not seem that females entered the fort during the initial talks. A few days later, women were quite apparent. As festivities resumed, they danced for the English and offered the captain an abundance of corn cakes. Individual women came forward with food-bearing baskets and furnished peas and squashes for Demere and his men.[40]

The women's gifts expressed Cherokee feelings that all had gone well when the headmen talked with Demere. Voicing his people's collective memory, Wawhatchee recalled the Cherokee visit to London in 1730 and his people's bonds with their "Father King George." The headmen and the young warriors delighted when "great Guns" at Fort Prince George's four corners were fired as they had requested. Cherokees hoped that the new governor, "their Brother," would send them British colors and a drum. Native men volunteered to guide Lyttelton to Overhill country if he liked.[41] Not all was good cheer. Wawhatchee conveyed some sobering news. The Cowetas continued to warn that English friendliness was a mask hiding dark schemes of destroying the Cherokees and enslaving their women and children. The French has supposedly offered to supply goods "at no Expence" to Keowee and other Lower Towns. Wawhatchee obviously did not wish the English to take Cherokee support for granted. For the moment Demere was not concerned. He was smitten by Cherokee generosity and the many smiles that greeted his talk.[42]

Lyttelton won his council's approval to build a garrison at a different Overhill locale than Virginia's, which was yet to be completed—and finally proved a dud. There was no political obstacle to South Carolina's plan. Overhill Cherokees were not averse to having two forts

Tempests of the French and Indian War

rather than one to safeguard passages to the north and northwest.[43] On July 13, 1756, Attakullakulla and two Chota chiefs arrived at Keowee and asked Demere to send up troops. An advance party of twenty soldiers marched northwest ten days later. While pleased by this token of English resolve, Attakullakulla was temperamental, variously charming, moody, and stormy with Demere, who yielded to his plea for a keg of rum to revel at night with his Keowee friends. The headman showed up quite drunk at Fort Prince George the next morning and made a swipe with a bottle as if he aimed to strike Demere in the head. Once rebuked, Attakullakulla apologized profusely, blamed it all on the rum, and professed friendship. Demere responded amiably but was convinced that Attakullakulla "had a great deal of Deceit in him" and should not be trusted even if sober.[44]

Attakullakulla is an example of innumerable Indian men who became hooked on strong liquor over time. How could it be otherwise when rum was a standard item in colonial-Native exchange over decades? It did not matter that Glen had seen to the passage of a law prohibiting liquor sales in the Indian trade in 1751. That measure was no more honored than similar South Carolina directives dating back to 1707. Indian men expected to receive rum in trade and by gift. They knew of liquor's deleterious effects but often found its power irresistible. Strong drink transported individuals to a psychic and spiritual realm free of ordinary constraints. Like other Indian men, Cherokees commonly disavowed responsibility for misdeeds committed under rum's power.[45]

Examining Attakullakulla's conduct more closely, we see a man beset by pressures, feeling obliged to be a British friend while serving as Connecorte's intermediary and spokesman. Attakullakulla's remarks to Demere expressed grievances and doubts. There was anger at unfair trade, a caustic put-down of the captain as "a little Boy" instead of "a very great Warriour," and disgust with Virginians who expected Cherokee warriors to fly to their aid when that colony was incapable of erecting more than a log enclosure, a poor substitute for a genuine fort. Attakullakulla mulled Dinwiddie's complaint about Cherokee fighters who seized or killed colonial livestock on their return from Virginia in 1755. Little Carpenter wondered what might go wrong if a great number of warriors traversed the Shenandoah Valley.[46]

Attakullakulla's misgivings were modest compared to Major Lewis's feelings of betrayal after his failed mission to Overhill country. In his view, the Cherokees had not only refused to supply warriors but were actually conspiring with Creeks, Chickasaws, and Choctaws to "rush

Cherokees, Native Peoples, and Empires, 1730–1762

upon" all English in their territory "and kill them like a parcel of fowls." The major's fears were overheated, though he was understandably concerned about rumors coursing among Native groups. While at Chota, Lewis heard from colonial traders that Attakullakulla had received messages from far northern Indians, Shawnees, and the French at the Alabama fort. "French John" traveled with a Cherokee "Wench" fluent in the Shawnee language. Then there was "great Elk," a "Nuntewe" man who had long lived among the Cherokees and served as a conduit to the north and Canada. More trouble loomed at Great Tellico, the most populous Overhill Town, which sent envoys for talks with the French and their Native allies at Alabama. Writing alarmingly to Dinwiddie, Lewis believed the Upper Cherokees could be brought to heel only by sending several hundred soldiers "to Strike Terror to them, and force a Compliance & Submission." Neither Dinwiddie nor Lyttelton, who received a copy of this same message, accepted Lewis's admonition. The governors remained convinced that a Cherokee-British alliance could be solidified to counter French influence.[47]

Lyttelton relied greatly on Demere for intelligence in Cherokee country. A veteran officer, Demere was meticulous and forthright. After three months at Keowee, he faced a tougher assignment once taking command at the British camp in Overhill country in October 1756. There he viewed preliminary work on Fort Loudoun, perched along the Little Tennessee River, tributary of the great Tennessee a few miles to the north. Chota was only five miles south of the new garrison, which from its inception depended on Native goodwill. While not as conspiratorially minded as Lewis, Demere believed that little could be counted on. Cherokee friendship would essentially need to be purchased by gifts. In a telling letter of November 18, Demere opined that "Indians are a Com[m]odity that are to be bought and sold, and the French will bid very high for them." The British would have to go one better, for "Indians are but Indians and are but very little to be depended on; the highest Bidder carries them off." Demere was not entirely cynical, though. He believed that diplomatic finesse was still an essential tool for the English to retain Cherokee friends.[48]

Diplomacy, Localism, and Women's Agency

Like their French counterparts, British and Anglo-American officers rejected the idea that Indian allies could possibly be friends if they "treated" independently with imperial enemies. Many Cherokees,

Tempests of the French and Indian War

The Little Tennessee Valley, 1757, by Chester Martin, 1973. *Fort Loudoun Association, Vonore, Tennessee.*

wanting a more open political space, pushed back against confinement as much as their restless youth at Williamsburg's Indian college. They had to be on their guard lest Virginia, South Carolina, and King George's soldiers fall short as trustworthy and strong allies. Besides, they could not ignore messages from other quarters, Indian and French, that offered some security. To many Cherokees, Anglo-French and Native warfare hung in the balance. The French had definite advantages over the English in the breadth of their Native alliances even while the British appeared the only colonial power capable of satisfying Cherokee material needs.

Cherokee leaders kept the British in the dark on numerous occasions, only to burst forth with revelations at timely moments. When Demere conferred with Connecorte and other Indian headmen by the Tennessee in late October 1756, the priest-chief talked freely, but abruptly stopped and asked the interpreter to put away pen and ink as soon as Attakullakulla came into view and was about to join the parley. Adding to the mystery, Connecorte described himself as a "Rogue" who "cannot keep a Secret, for when he sees a White Man his Heart beats and his Flesh trembles to think of what is to happen." These rather cryptic words soon became clear. The priest-chief was afraid the English were proceeding too slowly with fort-building and exposing themselves to harm; the Cherokees, too, stood in danger, not being sufficiently supplied even though they merited help as King George's "children." Connecorte believed "his Life is not more than an Inch long, and he knows not how soon a Bullet may kill him."[49] Here was talk intended to put the English to the test—would they be stalwart friends upon whom the Cherokees could count when invasion threatened?

Connecorte's messages moved within a gray zone between revelation and obfuscation, playing up his power and implying that the English would have to work to gain his support. He purposefully disclosed his range of diplomatic contacts, telling Demere that his town had sent a talk and wampum to pro-French Nuntaweas [Nuntaways], a vaguely described group that lived to the north. The belt, clearly one of peace, was one that Chota had received from the Nuntaways in the past. He went so far as to say that "his Town belongs to the Nuntuways and the Nuntuways belong to him." Even in translation, these words convey a powerful sense of kinship.[50]

Demere was rightly concerned about this talk, which suggested Chota's bonds with Indian "Brothers" who "lived among the French."

Tempests of the French and Indian War

Connecorte's discourse to Captain John Stuart a few weeks later scarcely set Demere at ease. In the priest-chief's telling, a Shawnee man had recently come to Chota, carrying pieces of barbecued English flesh to be eaten, much as unnamed northern nations had already feasted on. Connecorte said that he had refused to take the English scalps and flesh and reprimanded the Shawnee bearers. How were the British to read this story? Should they respect Connecorte for confiding in them or rather wonder why he told them at all? The wily priest-chief offered to send warriors to aid Virginia the next spring—a half-year ahead. Demere remained cool under the circumstances. Writing Lyttelton, he crisply summed up the situation: "Old Hop is very Serious in his Talks with me; therefore we must not pinch the Cause. The Purse must be loose and open on this Occasion."[51] Demere believed the priest-chief might still capture and deliver Frenchmen for a good price in deerskins. The captain had his eye on Antoine de Lantagnac, a French agent with a colorful past. An officer, Lantagnac had deserted his Alabama post in 1745 and lived as a trader in Cherokee country for years before returning to his former station about the time of Braddock's defeat. Once back in France's service, he cultivated Shawnee and Creek contacts and worked to subvert English influence in Cherokee country. Lantagnac was fluent in Cherokee and had a Native wife at Great Tellico and a child by her. His friend, "French John," had a liaison with a Cherokee woman who was fluent in Shawnee. The British had cause to be wary of such individuals.[52]

While Connecorte kept the English second-guessing, a small group of Cherokee headmen pursued an openly pro-French course. During the fall of 1756, Great Tellico's head warrior, Mankiller (Outacite), led two dozen men of his neighborhood to Fort Toulouse (the Alabama post), where the visitors conversed with a slew of Indian peoples besides the French. *Outacite* was an honorific in Cherokee culture since it connoted a warrior of high distinction.[53]

At first glance, Mankiller's anti-English stance appears surprising, even a dramatic reversal from the past. After all, Great Tellico's warriors had spearheaded attacks on the French by the Ohio and Wabash Rivers, and as far as the Mississippi, from the 1710s to 1740s. In actuality, the shift in political outlook was not so sudden. Bruised by war, Tellico was among several Cherokee towns that sought peace with the French and their Indian allies through Shawnee mediation during the mid- to late 1740s. Tellico's regional rivalry with Chota added to its headmen's growing unease with the English. South Carolina and Virginia looked to Chota as a virtual Cherokee national capital whose leaders had to be courted at all cost. Great Tellico felt slighted by comparison. By 1755, Mankiller and his brother Kenoteta aired their town's unhappiness with the absence of a resident English trader. In actuality, the pro-French movement in Tellico had far from universal support in the town, but this fact was not known to anxious Britons in the neighborhood. The British feared that Tellico's courtship with Shawnees and other pro-French Indians might well spread across Cherokee country.[54]

Shawnee influence was very much alive in the broad sweep of territory from the French Alabama post to the Ohio country and Illinois. Indian peoples absorbed Shawnee talks of ousting the British from the continent or pinning them well east of the Appalachians. Those who heard the message responded in various ways. Some Natives brought the talk to heart and envisioned a reclaimed world. Others harbored doubts or voiced opposition. Few were indifferent. The stakes were high. As one French officer observed in 1757, the Shawnees were waging *guerre à outrance* (war to the extreme) and doing their utmost to persuade others to follow their path. The marquis de Vaudreuil, elevated to Governor-General of New France in 1755, heartily supported Indian guerrilla warfare.[55]

Cherokee-Shawnee contacts evolved over decades and quickened during crisis. Women were critical to these bonds. Oxinaa, a Cherokee woman fluent in Shawnee, was a conduit of information between Tellico and the Alabama post in the fall of 1756. Soon thereafter, she accompanied five Tellico men and several Shawnees on a mission that took the group to Mobile and then to New Orleans for talks with Louis Bouillart de Kerlérec, Louisiana's governor. While outwardly favoring the French, Oxinaa was independent-minded and something of a double agent who shared sensitive information with the English. In fact, she offered news of the Louisiana venture to Captain Demere not long after her return to Overhill country. By her account, Kerlérec grasped a "Warr Hattchett" and handed it to a Shawnee man and then to a Cherokee. The French governor promised great presents to Cherokee visitors if their nation rose against the English. Small details added to Oxinaa's credibility. She recounted that the Cherokees were eight days out of sight of land when they sailed on a three-masted French ship from Mobile to New Orleans.[56]

Oxinaa was not alone in informing Demere of political maneuvers in Overhill country. Even before she reached New Orleans, a good

Tempests of the French and Indian War   207

number of Tellico residents decided to thwart their townsmen who were taking a pro-French slant. The Mankiller, who did not himself travel as far as New Orleans, was a leader in search of a following rather than a headman with unimpeachable clout. His risky political venture was prone to defection, not unlike a war party that set out without sure communal backing. "Leaks" about Mankiller's activities originated with Cherokees, who accompanied him to the French Alabama fort and talked broadly when back in their home villages. In little time, several Cherokee men informed Demere of what was afoot, shaping their accounts to gain credit with the English. Tomotley's "Old Warrior" told of Lantagnac's scheme to supply the Cherokees with loads of goods once Tellico sent horses his way. Significantly, Old Warrior did not badmouth Great Tellico itself. The "Tellico People," he said, "may be called Rogues yet the English shall find them as True as any Indians in the Nation."[57] Internal Cherokee disagreements were kept in bounds for the good of all Overhill communities. Demere and his lieutenants were pleased to have Indian informants, though confused by conflicting stories and alarmed by supposed Cherokee plotting with pro-French Shawnees, Choctaws, and Creeks.

Cherokee men talked with Demere in quite formal settings, with a colonial trader-interpreter present. Native women were especially discreet in relaying sensitive information, doubtless because they were wary of kindling communal dissension. Nancy Butler, the Cherokee wife of a colonial trader, offers a fascinating example of womanly political engagement. Adept at navigating ethnic boundaries, she was a semi-official purchasing agent, entrusted by Demere with buying Indian corn to feed troops at Fort Loudoun. While at the garrison on December 12, 1756, Butler shared some arresting intelligence with Demere that came to her from Chota's "Old War Woman" who made it her business to shape opinion beyond her household. Pledging Nancy Butler to secrecy, the War Woman told of pro-French scheming she had overheard in a lengthy conversation between Tellico's Mankiller and Connecorte himself. Her account spoke of French John and most strikingly of Mankiller's plan to acquire munitions from "some People from the southward."[58]

A week later, Butler talked again with Demere, who said that Nancy spoke "good English." Her information jibed with stories that Cherokee men had recently engaged in backdoor plotting. The French, Shawnees, and Choctaws were said to be about to invade the Cherokee homeland and drive out the English. (Nancy Butler's alarmist information had the

208   *Cherokees, Native Peoples, and Empires, 1730–1762*

Creeks rather than Choctaws as the likely attackers.) Butler had her ear close to the ground. Besides speaking to women, she made it her business to overhear headmen's conversations. In her telling, Kenoteta, the Mankiller's brother, had reportedly turned against him and now declared his willingness to die with the English. Nancy captured part of the story by eavesdropping, and other details came from a high-ranking Cherokee woman with yet other female sources. One woman in this behind-the-scenes network gleaned information by proximity to her own brother, who happened to be one of Mankiller's companions. The man threatened to kill his sister if she told of his pro-French designs. The flow of womanly talk nevertheless continued, all but unstoppable. Acutely sensitive to their own people's interests, women voiced fears that the Cherokees would be left poor and vulnerable if the "White People" (the English) were pushed out of Overhill country. Nancy Butler and the "Emperor" Ammouiscossitte's wife both cried in public view or in conference, making their concerns seem all the more genuine to Demere. In Nancy Butler's telling, Connecorte himself wondered what might follow if the English were driven from the Tennessee by the French and allied Indians. "Must we throw away our White Men at last?" was his supposed question.[59] The precise spirit in which he uttered this sentiment is unknowable.

"Old Hop" might be emperor to the English, but headmen such as Ostenaco and Attakullakulla charted their own course with considerable freedom. This was a strength of Cherokee community, which gave space for autonomy within social circles in which formal respect but not unanimity was expected. Ostenaco told Demere of his displeasure that Connecorte had sent a sensitive message to the French and Creeks without consulting him and other warriors. Attakullakulla felt insulted when Captain John Stuart asked him if he would follow Connecorte's orders. He answered that he was "a Man and a Warrior"—and not a boy—and in fact, "the Head Man of this Nation."[60] Wartime tensions exacerbated internal discord among Overhill leaders. Matters were in flux in other Cherokee regions, too. The Raven of Hiwassee, by far the strongest English friend in his valley, died toward the close of 1756. His son soon pledged friendship to the English but does not seem to have assumed his father's course.[61]

Absorbed in local and regional concerns, the Cherokee people as a nation are only intermittently evident during the early stages of the French and Indian War. A general sense of peoplehood appears here and there. Citing the threat of a French and Indian invasion, Ostenaco

Tempests of the French and Indian War   209

spoke of rallying Cherokees by "send[ing] Runners off immediately all over the Nation." He meanwhile vowed to remain in "hearing" of Fort Loudoun, in his native land, which he would defend alongside his English "Brothers" to the death. Ostenaco hoped his words would "go as swift as an Arrow out of a Bow" to "the Governors of Carolina & Virginia" as if those men were the Cherokees' "Neighbours." Inferentially, he would wait until his home territory was secure before assisting another English campaign in the Ohio country.[62]

The Native concern for security was a desideratum in confused times. The eastern Chickasaws, living by the Savannah River, offer a telling example of a small Native group that took a pro-English stance during the French and Indian War to win credit with British authorities and safeguard their land from white settler encroachments. In 1758, the Chickasaws showed their allegiance by attacking pro-French Shawnees in the Alabama country. The mighty Creeks meanwhile had internal disputes concerning the Anglo-French war. The town of Okchai in Upper Creek country personified this rift. The town's chief, Gun Merchant (Enostanakee), a skilled diplomatist, favored English ties on optimal trade terms. The Mortar, Okchai's proud head warrior, distrusted the English and kept alert to Shawnee and French overtures.[63] Both leaders pushed distinct agendas without coming to blows.

Mankiller of Tellico, who cultivated friends at Okchai, was an active source of French propaganda meant to stoke Cherokee fears of English domination. As Ostenaco reported to Demere, the French commandant at Alabama told Cherokee visitors that "the Carolina People" had conjurors who would send up sickness and death to Indian country. Once English soldiers were planted by a Cherokee town, they would "beat and abuse their Warriors, and debauch their Women." Was it not true that the English had "brought up a number of handcuf[f]s and Irons for their Feet," besides bringing large guns for foul purposes? Ostenaco and Attakullakulla did not believe these tales but wanted reassurance that such bad things were untrue. While asking Captain Demere to have Governor Lyttelton's newly arrived missive translated, they relayed Connecorte's barb that the written paper came from "the Place of Lies," that is to say, Charles Town. Attakullakulla and Ostenaco may not have concurred with Connecorte but they deliberately reported what he said.[64] This was sophisticated diplomacy in which doubts were artfully aired so that a British officer might grasp the importance of allaying Cherokee concerns.

210   *Cherokees, Native Peoples, and Empires, 1730–1762*

Mankiller's Struggle

Cherokee headmen cared deeply about their own town's stance relative to nearby communities. To be alienated from town or regional consensus was a dreaded condition. Leaders who felt isolated were prone to emotional travail expressed in words, dance, and other physical acts. Mankiller of Tellico felt compelled to do an about-face within weeks after returning to Overhill country from Alabama. The weight of communal opinion against him and his pro-French stance was simply too strong for him to bear alone.

On January 5, 1757, Mankiller heeded kin, neighbors, and Cherokee worthies by entering Fort Loudoun alone to meet with Captain Demere. The warrior was painted all black, signifying his grim countenance and downcast, deathly look as cold as the frigid air. Demere took him by the hand and patiently heard his plaint. Mankiller felt ashamed because he carried the full weight of a wrongheaded political move for which none of his fellows would accept the least responsibility. "I am hated and disliked," he confessed, "by every Body in the Nation, which has made me so uneasy that I did not know what to do with myself. I was like a lost Man. . . ." Demere brought comfort by hosting a dinner for Mankiller and as many as 150 other Cherokee men. Mankiller and six stout comrades stayed overnight at the fort. While the repentant warrior pleaded for presents, Demere gave few, and then only after his guest begged and pledged good conduct. The English upper hand was paternalistically disciplinary, a lesson for Mankiller to bear.[65]

A catharsis occurred five days later when Lieutenant Robert Wall, acting as Demere's deputy, visited Great Tellico in the company of British traders. A reconciliatory mood was set. All thoughts of French alliance were gone. Cherokee men hoisted the Union Jack atop their townhouse early on the morning of January 11. That afternoon, Wall addressed nearly three hundred Cherokees within the council house in which headmen sat in a circle about him. Once the lieutenant concluded his talk, Mankiller gave him a peace string of white wampum and a large buckskin, the latter being a gift from the Great Warrior of nearby Tuskegee. Now that good feelings were restored, the Cherokee assemblage was overjoyed at Wall's presents, even though the lieutenant said they amounted to "not the Value of a Pair of Boots per Man."[66]

As night fell, Mankiller and a group of warriors and young men danced before the British visitors. Freed of nightmarish thoughts, the warrior left the council house and returned alone after some minutes

Tempests of the French and Indian War   211

to the entrance, whooping to welcoming yells or shouts. To a drum's steady beat, Mankiller reentered almost naked, "painted in Streaks of White all over his Face and Body." More than fifty warriors and youths followed him in the same unclothed and decorated manner, dancing about a large fire before all of the men joined a ritual dance that continued for several hours. After a "Masquerade" that Wall found impossible to describe, young and older women sequentially entered and danced in their own group. When the lieutenant grew tired in the wee hours, Mankiller ordered all dancing to stop. Silence reigned. An unnamed Tellico warrior then stood to speak at length of the Cherokees' goodwill. All bad thoughts were forgotten, and all hearts were "straight toward the English."[67]

Mankiller's dance was a rite of outcry, a release of hurtful emotions that exhibited his individual plight and his restoration to village, kin, and clan by the spiritual power of communal song and dance. Lieutenant Wall's amazement at the "Masquerade" is understandable. This was no European masked ball. Cherokee masks embedded supernatural forces. Carved from wood and often adorned with animal fur and paint, masks had phantasmagoric qualities, displaying a man's nose as phallus or taking the form of a wasp nest, an animal's features, or a human head crowned by a coiled rattlesnake. Masking accentuated role-play, transforming the individual masker and giving him or her the power to ward off evil and summon strength for occasions such as war, hunting, and courtship.[68]

Ceremony brought a healing unity to Great Tellico and assuaged British suspicions, at least for the time being. At a brief follow-up conference with Demere, Mankiller again aired soothing words. "His Thoughts" had been "very bad for the English," but "the Great Man above" and the captain's talks "had changed his Heart." Acknowledgment of God and the king were now jointly entering Cherokee speech with similar intent. Great and higher powers would see that justice was done. Mankiller told Demere that Tellico had no reliable trade. The town's former trader, Robert Goudy, marketed goods at Ninety-Six to white settlers who came north to sell wares to Cherokees without extending credit. Much as always, it was irregular and exploitative trade, and not exchange itself, that aroused Cherokee anger.[69]

Demere knew this quite well; his letters to Lyttelton evinced contempt for most traders, whom he called "a Sett of Villains." Naturally, the captain played up British strength when dealing with Cherokees. In late January 1757, he reprised an old message in a meeting with

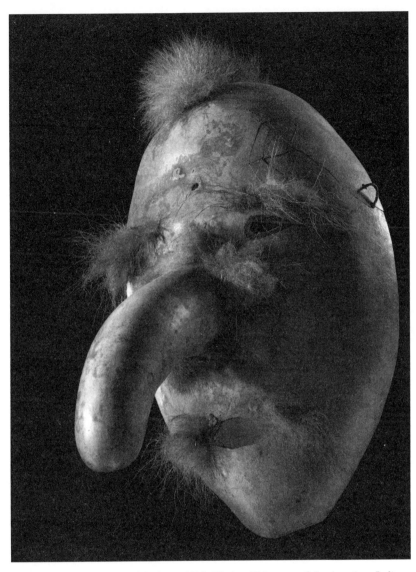

Cherokee Booger Dance Mask, ca. 1910. *National Museum of the American Indian, Smithsonian.*

Connecorte and other Overhill headmen. The English alone could supply the Cherokees. The Choctaws were "naked" through their dependence on the French. And what of Shawnees running about "naked" like "a Gang of Wolves"? The captain concluded his talk with an appeal for Cherokee engagement against the French and their Indian allies. "Nothing," he declaimed, "is more valuable amongst brave Men and Warriours than Trophies of War." There would be recompense. He

Tempests of the French and Indian War

offered thirty pounds of leather for each French or enemy Indian scalp brought to him. A few weeks later, forty warriors from two Overhill Towns—Chilhowee and Tallassee—went out to war. There was still no uniform Cherokee military commitment to the British, as Demere and other officers desired. Most communities held back, lest they be exposed when their warriors trekked far from home. Not coincidentally, the largest Cherokee contingent that assisted the British in 1757 came from the Lower Towns, which were then the least vulnerable to northern enemies.[70]

Lyttelton and Attakullakulla

William Henry Lyttelton graciously welcomed Attakullakulla and seventy Cherokee men and several women to Charles Town in January 1757. For the governor, the occasion was critical. He had his first opportunity to meet Attakullakulla, foremost Cherokee spokesman and pro-English headman. Attakullakulla was no stranger to Charles Town. He was now in the South Carolina capital for the third time in four years, no small testimony to his extraordinary stamina, a strength quite common among his people. Besides these journeys, he met with British and colonial officers in the piedmont on three occasions during this same period. Covering several thousand miles on horse and foot, Attakullakulla adjusted to particular settings, personalities, and geopolitical circumstances. This was the case when he shook hands with Governor Lyttelton, a well-connected man within the English aristocracy and an individual with "epicurean tastes" and considerable political ability, in one historian's judgment.[71]

As discussions began, Lyttelton fulsomely praised Attakullakulla. Flattery seemed in order. The governor's pitch was for at least two hundred Upper Cherokee fighters to join the British war effort on the Ohio front in a few months. Attakullakulla was in fine diplomatic form, voicing his people's brotherly love for the English but evading commitment on raising a substantial body of warriors. Six lengthy meetings were held in the government house over an eighteen-day period. While Carolina councilors and Cherokee headmen looked on and listened, Lyttelton and Attakullakulla went one-on-one in talks that were mostly respectful but sometimes feisty, especially when Little Carpenter was annoyed by the governor's superior air. Willanawa was the only other Cherokee headman who spoke formally in conference during the marathon negotiation—on a day when Attakullakulla was indisposed.[72]

214   *Cherokees, Native Peoples, and Empires, 1730–1762*

The conference dragged on because Lyttelton would not yield his main point. It was incumbent on the Cherokees, "the Great King's Children," to fight alongside their English brethren in war. Attakullakulla agreed in principle, while voicing a litany of his people's wants and needs. Chota's villagers were unhappy with trader John Elliott, who refused credit to Cherokee men before hunting was done and skins brought in. The Great King had promised "fine Cloath[e]s," but Attakullakulla said he was essentially "naked." Tired of coming to Charles Town "to hear Lies," he expected nothing but "truth" for "the time to come." The Great King had told him long ago that his people should go to Virginia for goods if Carolina's governor did not adequately furnish them. Attakullakulla had a wonderful habit of interpreting the king's words as suited Cherokee purposes.[73]

Lyttelton had his own seemingly unassailable arguments. King George's navy had already captured "above a thousand of the French Ships," including those assigned to transport goods to Indian country. If the Cherokees permitted French inroads, they would provoke "the Wrath of the Great King" and lose all benefits. The governor extolled the British Overhill fort, now under construction, as his prime selling point. The garrison was "a place for the English and Cherokees to live together as Brothers and in times of danger to assist one another and to protect and secure the Women and Children from the Enemy." Blacksmiths at the fort would mend guns and tools. "The White Women who will live there," declared Lyttelton, "will instruct the Red Women to make all such things as are necessary for them and [they] will live together as one." The governor touted British women as helpers to Cherokee females. Perhaps he was thinking of sewing skills, though he did not elaborate. His foremost goal was to quash French propaganda—loose talk that an English fort would ensnare the Cherokees and spread disease among them.[74]

Attakullakulla listened patiently and responded in time, usually waiting a night to consult with other Cherokees before answering at length. At the conference's opening, he took the stance of distinguished messenger, formally speaking for Connecorte, and passing the priest-chief's gift of a pipe to Lyttelton for a smoke all around. Attakullakulla remarked that the governor, his "Brother," lived in a white house, as did Connecorte at Chota and King George in England. Of course, white was the color of peace and friendship. Attakullakulla had a "bright Talk to deliver," adding that he would give a string of wampum to attest to truth just as the "White People write Letters." He did not

Tempests of the French and Indian War   215

shirk from war; he loved "to Spill the Blood of Enemies." He had immediately gone to fight the French and their Indian allies whenever they cut down his people or English traders. He would not rest while his feet could carry him. There were still dangers close to home that could not be ignored. The French warned of Shawnees, Choctaws, and Creeks warring on Cherokees if the latter did not break with the English. Fortunately, "all the White People, from Georgia to New York, love their Brothers of Chottee [Chota]." Attakullakulla knew his English colonial geography. As for the French, they live "on our left hand, as we return home" from Charles Town. Here was a critical point. Chota and neighboring towns were most eager to fight the French and Indians to the west by the Tennessee, the Ohio, and in the Illinois country. War to the east, from the upper Potomac to the Forks of the Ohio—the center of British operations—was inferentially less inviting to Overhill men.[75]

Biding his time, Attakullakulla took eight days to respond to Lyttelton's words of "White Women" helping "Red Women." This showed remarkable self-restraint. He was peeved by any idea that Cherokee women could be considered less capable than English ones. When addressing the issue, Attakullakulla began gently before assuming a sharper tone. Cherokee women, he remarked, had asked him to convey their thoughts to the governor. They were happy to see "their Sisters the White Women" accompany soldiers to the new Overhill garrison. The Cherokee women's only worry was that the fort was not well positioned for their protection. By stating female concerns, of course, Attakullakulla was tactfully airing his own misgivings. He knew that Captain Demere, commanding in the vicinity, was displeased with the engineer's choice of a downslope for construction. Attakullakulla then spoke of why all men should care about women's welfare: "White Men as well as the Red were born of Women." He put a tough question to the governor. Since Cherokee men regarded it "Customary . . . to admit the Women into their Councils," he "desired himself to know if that was not the Custom of the White People also." Surely, Attakullakulla knew English political practice from previous conferences. His needling of Lyttelton on women's role carried a deliberate message. Cherokee women, bearing significant responsibilities, were to be respected. The broader point was that the English should not dictate matters but act as partners in alliance.[76]

Curiously, Attakullakulla's talk moved quite abruptly from his people's gender customs to a serious political rift in Overhill country. In

Cherokees, Native Peoples, and Empires, 1730–1762

his telling, Great Tellico remained strongly pro-French and was not to be trusted. The Mankiller cleaved to a Shawnee wampum belt, which he "Binds about his Heart," and held a Shawnee hatchet "to Strike the White People." Attakullakulla declared his determination to war on the Shawnees and the French. He added that the English should not worry about the Creeks because the latter favored his stance. In his view, it would be best for the English to stop trade with Tellico until he assured the governor that all was right there. Attakullakulla's critique is a sharp instance of Cherokee factionalism, reflecting not simply his anxiety about French-Shawnee ties but also his ambition to be the foremost English friend in Overhill country. While Lyttelton appreciated Attakullakulla's advice, he did not sanction Tellico but waited for more intelligence from that quarter.[77]

Attakullakulla was a far more accomplished and independent diplomatist in 1757 than he had been in his first meeting with Glen nearly four years earlier. He was not so much in unison with Connecorte as might appear from his politesse in Charles Town. He voiced disdain for the Shawnees while Connecorte rather favored them. He was pleased with Lyttelton's pledge of rewards for French and enemy Indian scalps. Willanawa liked the idea, too, while implying that such generous payments might divert Cherokees from their duty of capturing Blacks who had absconded from white households. On hearing this talk, Lyttelton immediately offered Cherokees a larger sum for the return of Black runaways. British wartime needs required complaisance. Attakullakulla chimed in by criticizing Anglo traders for selling Indians "such Cloth as the Negroes are Cloathed with." The idea of Blacks as lesser social beings, as treated by whites, was part of Cherokee consciousness.[78]

The Charles Town talks ended amicably, though without resolving the question of whether the Upper Towns would send any sizable force to "the Back Parts of Virginia," as Lyttelton had insisted. The governor asked Attakullakulla to use his influence with Lower Cherokee Towns to stop the men there from raiding colonial farmsteads, stealing horses, and killing cattle. Attakullakulla was agreeable but could hardly control matters in a region where Cherokees fumed over settler intrusions.[79]

Attakullakulla fixed his attention on his Overland homeland above all. He repeatedly told Lyttelton that the Upper Towns required more military hardware than other Cherokee regions because they

Tempests of the French and Indian War

were most exposed to Shawnee and French attack. He also contended that the Upper Towns had seldom received any help in defense from Cherokees to their southeast. The Lower Towns would have doubtless replied, had their headmen been within earshot, that they had borne the full brunt of Creek attack only five years before with little aid from the Overhill people. Local bias was part of the Cherokee world.[80]

Attakullakulla hinted to Lyttelton of Cherokee men fighting the French enemy in their own manner. The Overhills would likely go to war in small groups or "Gangs, seven nine or ten in a Gang." ("Gang" was the colonial interpreter's term for a modest war party.) Viewing the grander scene, Attakullakulla told the governor that he had not given up on visiting the English king once more before he died. He wished that young Cherokee men would accompany him so that the next generation would know "their Father." Cherokees had a claim on England, and Attakullakulla wanted Lyttelton to know it. The governor discouraged the idea of any transatlantic Cherokee voyage. He did not wish to lose Attakullakulla's help in wartime.[81]

Gains and Shortfalls of Alliance

Robert Dinwiddie was as disillusioned as any royal governor in British North America by the time he sailed from Virginia to England in January 1758. He had held the chief magistrate's seat at Williamsburg for seven years. Unable to raise a numerous militia for offensive operations, he complained of undisciplined colonials who were unwilling to assume the burdens of war. True, there were brave officers such as Washington, but others fell short of the mark. Frontiersmen showed a readiness to fight, though they were dispersed and not readily organized or supplied. In February 1756, Dinwiddie put the matter bluntly to the Board of Trade: "I never was among People that have so little regard to their own safety...." The governor observed a lack of "martial Spirit" among freeholders insistent on "their Privileges" and absorbed in private pursuits.[82]

Virginia's travails in war made Cherokee support all the more vital. Despite Major Lewis's failure to enlist Cherokee warriors in 1756, Dinwiddie persisted in appeals for southern Indian warriors. By the next spring and summer, his pledges of gifts and friendship brought some 400 Native warriors, including 250 Cherokees to the upper Shenandoah Valley and Potomac for forays in the Ohio theater. The results were decidedly mixed. One sizable Cherokee band of 128 men,

Cherokees, Native Peoples, and Empires, 1730–1762

drawn mainly from the Lower Towns under Wawhatchee, caused havoc as it trekked northward in March 1757, pillaging North Carolina and Virginia farmsteads and killing a Chickasaw warrior who had chided warriors for their misconduct. In one gruesome episode, two Cherokee men purportedly raped a young Virginia girl and, in Colonel Clement Read's words, "tore her in a manner too indecent to mention." A responsible officer, Read strove to pacify the Cherokees after the spate of plundering. He wanted to see the warriors head north to fight the French, assuring headmen that presents would be forthcoming from Colonel George Washington when they reached Winchester in the upper Shenandoah. Wawhatchee's band was inflamed by Virginia's slowness to provide gifts, unintentionally delayed in distribution. Cherokee fighters openly stated that the French made good on promises but "the Great Men of Virginia were Liars." The reputation of head warriors was at stake. As one Cherokee chief told a Virginia captain, he did not want his own men to think him foolish for raising their hopes of English wartime rewards.[83]

British authorities despised wanton Indian violence, but they did not allow relatively minor disturbances to derail strategic objectives. Crown officials could not do without Cherokee support. Dinwiddie cautioned Colonel Read to bring "those People [the Cherokees] to a Sense of their Errors and illegal Behaviour, in a mild Manner if possible."[84] After reaching Fort Frederick on the Potomac, Wawhatchee dictated a written message to Governor Horatio Sharpe of Maryland, sending along white beads, symbolizing friendship for the English, and black ones, expressing his men's desire to make war on "the French Shawanese." The Cherokee headman's intent was to procure recompense for service from as many provincial governments as possible. Wawhatchee and his warriors trekked to the Ohio country, where they killed four Indian foes and captured two others. On returning to the Maryland fort, the Cherokees were offered a modest amount of goods and money for the delivery of enemy prisoners and scalps. Less than pleased, Wawhatchee objected to surrendering the captives and "the Hair" of the slain. It would not do for warriors to return home "naked," meaning without the scalps as signs of bravery. Maryland officials relented by supplying the Cherokees with £200 worth of additional goods besides the £100 previously promised. While Wawhatchee looked on, another warrior handed over the scalps as a friendly reply to Governor Sharpe's letter praising the Cherokees for all they had done.[85]

Tempests of the French and Indian War

Cultural clashes frequently ruffled British-Cherokee relations. While admitting the Cherokees were of "good service" as fighters, Dinwiddie thought them "avaricious and Greedy"—a judgment the governor also made regarding the Catawbas. Washington was of a similar view, admiring Native warriors' superior "cunning and craft" in woodlands fighting and their capacity to endure "indefatigable sufferings."[86] He bemoaned the lack of a unified British command structure over Indian affairs, which led officers to pledge gifts that they did not have in hand. Writing Dinwiddie in late May 1757, the twenty-five-year-old Washington generalized from his experience: "An Indian will never forget a promise made to him: *They* are naturally Suspicious; and if they meet with delays, or disappointment, in their expectations, will scarcely ever be reconciled. For which reason, nothing ought to be *promised* but what is *performed*." One week later, Washington admonished a Virginia sergeant that Wawhatchee's Cherokees be decently supplied on their route home. They might be given "a little rum mixed with water" at nighttime if they behaved "in a mild discreet manner." Cherokees were to be told that the treat came by the militia officer's influence on the "white people," that is, householders along the path.[87] British authority was to be reinforced in small matters that served a larger purpose.

Cherokees had a sense of fair wartime exchange that exasperated colonials who expected Indians to be grateful for what they received. With budgets strained, provincial legislators were reluctant to add to swollen tax burdens. Haggling arose once more when Wawhatchee prepared to return home with his core band of forty-six men and one woman in June 1757. (One wonders about all the work that this lone female had to do along the way!) Camped in the Shenandoah Valley, Wawhatchee groused when told by Washington that Virginia had no more presents to give. The crisis ebbed somewhat when Edmund Atkin, the newly appointed royal superintendent of southern Indian affairs, arrived to offer gifts in King George's name.[88]

Before journeying home, Wawhatchee told Atkin that he was willing to bring more warriors in the future, but only if gifts were provided prior to the men's departure from their towns. Anything else, he maintained, would violate previous pledges made by Virginia in conference. While appreciative when recompensed, several Cherokees hinted that their men would strip every farm on the way home if they felt deprived. In essence, Wawhatchee conceived of a military alliance with the English Crown and its military arm, but not with colonials along the path—white people who appeared no different from the South Carolina settlers

220　　　　　*Cherokees, Native Peoples, and Empires, 1730–1762*

edging into Lower Cherokee lands. Significantly, he was pleased when Atkin brought word that Sir William Johnson, royal superintendent of northern Indian affairs, was encouraging peace between the Iroquois and southern Indian nations. Atkin presented a wampum belt from the Six Nations as tangible proof.[89]

Cherokee apprehensions waxed and waned amid the confusion besetting southern Indian country. Little held steady on the political front. In March 1757, just two months after Mankiller's disavowal of his Alabama jaunt, a French flag flew above Great Tellico's townhouse. When a British trader demanded that the flag be burned, the inhabitants replied that the white banner was a peace symbol to other Indian nations and not truly pro-French.[90] Tellico's explanation was clever and not implausible since France's royal flag was white, a symbol of purity. Cherokees were not of one mind on the encroaching European conflict. While some Tellico headmen wanted a French pact, other Overhill warriors attacked and killed Frenchmen by the Ohio and Tennessee.[91]

English fears of French-Cherokee collusion were magnified because of all that was unknown. British officers at Fort Loudoun could not see the limits of French power as exerted from the Lower Mississippi Valley. When Governor Kerlérec met with Tellico men at New Orleans, he stipulated that an alliance depended not only on the entire Cherokee nation but also on approval by Governor-General Vaudreuil in Canada, and the additional consent of France's northern Native allies. A French-Cherokee accord was as yet more talk than substance.[92]

The most critical battles of the French and Indian War in 1755–1757 occurred by the Monongahela and along the Lake George–Lake Champlain corridor between New York and Canada. Acadia (Nova Scotia) was also the scene of battle, along with the British deportation of the "neutral French" who tried to stay out of the conflict but were branded treasonous. Nearly one thousand Acadians were transported to Charles Town just in 1755.[93]

Nothing comparable to the war above the Ohio transpired between the Tennessee and the Gulf Coast, and yet the region seethed with unrest, intrigue, and clashes between Native groups. Choctaw attacks on the Chickasaws continued unabated. Tensions rose when a Cherokee war party killed three western Chickasaws and grabbed eighty deerskins from the slain men in 1756. An escalation was averted by English diplomacy, aided by a timely colonial shipment of munitions to the Chickasaws. Indian hunters became feistier and more jealous of competitors when threatened by economic duress, food shortages,

Tempests of the French and Indian War　　　　　221

and wartime disruptions in the deerskin trade. Not all was in tumult. Creek-Cherokee relations remained peaceful, while the Muscogees focused on restraining Georgia's expansion and gaining bountiful British presents as the price for neutrality in Anglo-French warfare. The Upper Creeks, wary about choosing between European combatants, rejected South Carolina's overture to establish a garrison in their country in 1756. The Muscogees had refused several times in the past and did so again.[94]

Cherokees viewed Indigenous geography as broadly as ever. Given the tumultuous continental scene, they embraced opportunities for peace talks with the Six Nations under English auspices. In July 1757, Sir William Johnson welcomed Cherokee emissaries, who came to meet Iroquois deputies at his compound by the Mohawk River. Indigenous customs of negotiation came to the fore. Iroquois headmen performed a condolence ceremony, ritually wiping away the tears of Cherokee guests, their traditional foes. Though not admitting a need for consolation, the Cherokees extended their hand in friendship, offering a wampum belt to soothe the bruised feelings of the past. They proudly announced their intent to head to the Ohio, fully confident that their "Brethren" of the Six Nations would soon hear of Cherokee war honors won against the French and their Indian allies. Following Johnson's mediation, Edmund Atkin forwarded a declaration of Iroquois friendship to Ostenaco for delivery to Connecorte, the "Governour of the Whole Nation of the Cherokee Indians." A large wampum belt accompanied the letter. Atkin's aim was unmistakable. The Cherokees would surely be more likely to assist the imperial war effort if assured of an Iroquois peace, and therefore more secure about their home front when journeying to the Ohio country.[95]

British colonial newspapers enthusiastically reported Cherokee and Catawba sorties against the French and their Native allies in 1757 along the Potomac's southern branches, today's central Pennsylvania, and even to the walls of Fort Duquesne. Although these strikes demoralized foes, they did not signal a full-throated Cherokee commitment to support the English in war. Cherokee choices to enter the conflict, or to stay outside it, elude any single formula. Diverse interests were at stake, whether expressed by women who cultivated English goodwill or by men who competed for regional leadership, headed to battle, and tested various diplomatic possibilities.[96]

Numerous episodes show a gap between Native and imperial priorities. After British soldiers killed three Shawnee warriors near Fort

Loudoun in June 1757, Cherokee men of Great Tellico and nearby Chatuga complained that the "White People" had dirtied and bloodied "the path," making it likely that the Shawnees would retaliate against their communities. Demere appeased the discontented individuals by giving them gunpowder and bullets besides pledging that traders would supply them with new guns. Munitions were the grease of alliance over decades, all the more so when the English were obliged to satisfy Cherokee fighters.[97]

The fate of "French John," Connecorte's friend, shows a Cherokee wariness of fully committing to the English. While Cherokee warriors might badmouth John, they put off British demands to surrender him for a healthy payoff. Attakullakulla, who was stoutly pro-English, held the line, too, explaining that Connecorte looked upon John as "his own Child." This episode was a replay of the Cherokees' past refusal to turn over supposed enemy agents, whether Christian Priber, Peter Chartier, or visiting French deputies. To yield might please the English but at the expense of betraying Native customs and stirring internal dissent. Demere's frustration over French John led him to storm privately about "Savages" who observed "no Law nor Subjection amongst them. . . . The very lowest of them thinks himself as great and high as any of the Rest, every one of them must be courted for their Friendship . . . and made much of."[98] A Cherokee-English test of wills arose on matters large and small within an uncertain alliance.

During the summer of 1757, Attakullakulla's brother and thirteen other Cherokee fighters returned from Ohio-Tennessee warfare and brought a young French officer's scalp with them. Attakullakulla played this occasion to the hilt, asking Demere to reward each of the warriors with a gun besides other presents. The captain initially refused but agreed after Attakullakulla said the men would not go to war unless encouraged.[99] This was a negotiation on a par with economic exchange. Just as deerskins brought goods, a Frenchman's scalp was a matter of value. Demere's consent to Attakullakulla's terms shows which party had the upper hand in bargaining at the time. Cherokee warriors brought this same approach to their greatly expanded involvement in the Anglo-French war in 1758. The results were disastrous for an alliance that could not stand under the weight of heightened expectations.

Tempests of the French and Indian War

8

Prelude to the British-Cherokee War

British officials had great expectations of enlisting Cherokee fighters for Brigadier-General John Forbes's campaign of 1758, aimed at taking Fort Duquesne at the Forks of the Ohio. Stationed in Philadelphia that April, the general looked forward to collaborating with Native warriors. He was less optimistic of obtaining British colonial assistance since provincial assemblies dragged their heels at raising troops, provisions, and wagons. Forbes wrote in mock humor to the Earl of Loudoun, outgoing commander-in-chief, that "necessity will turn me a Cherokee, and don't be surprised if I Take F[ort] du Quesne at the head of them, and them only."[1]

Forbes's quip is ironic given the problems that would ensue between Cherokees and the British army. On paper all looked bright in a muster roll of April 21, 1758, which showed that there were nearly 230 Cherokee men encamped near the British fort at Winchester, Virginia. More than 360 others had tracked and episodically skirmished with the French and their Native allies during the previous six months. In little more than two years, perhaps one-fourth of Cherokee men of fighting age had seen service in aid of King George. But that fact was unavailing to the ongoing British military effort. Scores of Cherokees on the Ohio front were fatigued, restless, and resolved to return home, while General Forbes was not yet close to beginning his westward expedition. Many Native fighters felt shortchanged by what they considered insufficient British gifts for their sacrifices. Others simply desired to be in their towns for the summer's Green Corn Festival and the next hunting season.[2]

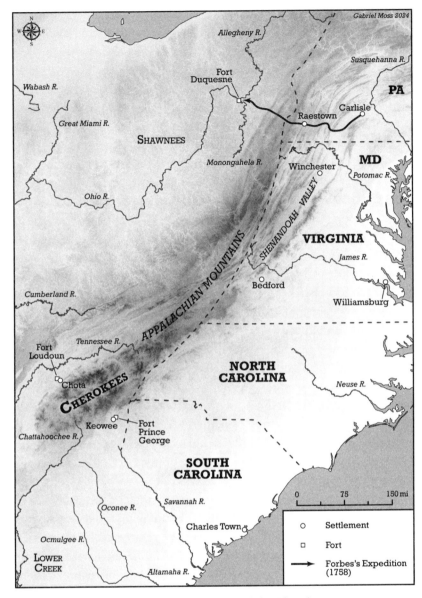

Forbes's Expedition, the Shenandoah Valley, and the Cherokees

As the situation played out, there was a large homeward movement of Cherokee warriors from the Pennsylvania-Ohio theater through the spring and summer of 1758. The departure did not, however, mark an end to the Cherokee war effort, which continued in scouting, intelligence gathering, and guerrilla raiding as far west as Fort Duquesne's

Prelude to the British-Cherokee War   225

outskirts. What seems remarkable is that any Cherokees remained in the British camp after the bloody encounters between homeward-bound warriors and frontier settlers in Virginia's Shenandoah Valley. The first serious clash erupted in May 1758. Angered by the Indian plunder of livestock and property, colonists resorted to arms, shooting down and scalping three Cherokee men in one clash. In a still deadlier engagement, militiamen killed sixteen or seventeen Cherokees. One white man was apparently killed in the fighting and another wounded.[3]

Evidence of the clashes is rather spotty, though several points seem clear. Native looting of Virginia farms during the spring of 1758 was a repeat of what had occurred the previous year, pushing colonials to the breaking point and triggering the killing of Cherokees out of fear, a thirst for revenge, and a growing hatred of Indians. Indigenous perspectives were radically different. Cherokee dissatisfaction with British recompense for military service was a continual irritant, inciting warriors to seize what they regarded as their due from ordinary settlers. Things were becoming unhinged, and motives blurred within both the Native and colonial camps.[4]

The Virginia-Cherokee bloodletting of May 1758 was tragic, a foreboding of racialized violence, if not a headlong rush to outright war. At least a few Virginians tried to avert violent clashes and resolved to fight only after their plea for the return of stolen horses was rejected. By one account, colonials called on Indian men to cooperate as "brothers," but it is doubtful that Cherokees understood.[5] Worse was to come. As Cherokee fighters trekked home via the Shenandoah in August and September, they were attacked by whites who were on the lookout for Indians. Militiamen shot dead four Cherokees in one ambush and then scalped the slain with the intent of collecting bounties under the pretense that their grisly trophies were taken from enemy Shawnees. Colonial vigilantes killed thirteen Cherokees and wounded others in subsequent confrontations. Most of the victims were men of the Lower Towns and Hiwassee Valley. This time, many Cherokees openly cried for war on Virginia, which had become a field of death where they were wantonly targeted and murdered. Hostilities were averted only through negotiations between Cherokee leaders and Governor William Henry Lyttelton of South Carolina, who mediated on Virginia's behalf.[6]

The first spate of settler-Cherokee clashes in Virginia showed an alliance under strain, if not broken. In July 1758, Keowee headmen invoked the long-standing ideal of brotherhood in a talk forwarded to

226   *Cherokees, Native Peoples, and Empires, 1730–1762*

Lyttelton. Their people had gone to war on behalf of English brethren but while on the path home found that those "we thought to be our Brothers" instead "proved our Enemies." This was strong talk, an emotive release by which headmen aired grievances without foreclosing further negotiation.[7] The powerful Overhill Towns weighed in, voicing their desire for an amicable resolution to both Charles Town and Williamsburg. Connecorte, his nephew Standing Turkey, Attakullakulla, and Willanawa expressed shame at how Cherokee "young fellows" had acted in Virginia. The chiefs, few of whose men were victimized in the clashes, hoped that "the path will still be open" and the disturbances forgotten by both sides. "What has happened seems as if it was done by People in their Sleep who dreamt a bad Dream, but were now wakened out of it."[8]

Chota's peace overture was a bid for time, a gesture of palliation to quiet matters for the present, and an assertion of Overhill authority in Cherokee country. Significantly, the talk was given after the violence of the spring but before the Virginians' premeditated killings of Cherokee men in late summer. These murders were not forgotten by communities struck by nightmarish losses, too haunting to be swept away by daylight. In the spring of 1759, a few Cherokee war parties from one of the affected towns swooped down on North Carolina farmsteads by the Yadkin and Catawba Rivers. More than twenty whites were killed and scalped; roughly half of the slain were women and children. The victims were cut down in revenge for what had occurred in Virginia even though they had no personal connection to the previous year's Shenandoah violence.[9]

The killings by the Yadkin radically altered the political situation. Lyttelton felt duty bound to punish lethal attacks on the king's subjects. His position admitted no compromise. If the Cherokees wished for continued trade and peace, they must surrender the killers of whites for retributive justice and execution. Cherokees saw things differently, believing they had already suffered enough at English hands in Virginia. Moreover, their sense of communal loyalty precluded bowing to an ultimatum. By the fall of 1759, Lyttelton pushed toward a military solution, torpedoing negotiations with Cherokee leaders at Charles Town, raising troops to enforce his will, and later reducing Native men to hostages at Fort Prince George, cheek and jowl by Keowee. Cherokee revulsion at the governor's hostage-taking ignited an explosive conflict in which smoldering Native resentment at British colonialism burst into conflagration.

Prelude to the British-Cherokee War

Attakullakulla's Quests

British officials viewed Attakullakulla as a veritable white knight, a steadfast ally who could be relied on more than any other leader to rekindle Cherokee support for the imperial war effort in 1758. He had proven himself by spurring raids against the French near the lower Tennessee and Ohio over several years. To Edmund Atkin, royal superintendent of southern Indian affairs, Attakullakulla was "the second Man in the Overhill Towns," that is, of a rank just below priest-chief Connecorte. Atkin counted on Attakullakulla to expedite the British war effort in collaboration with Colonel William Byrd of Virginia, who ventured to Charles Town in March 1758 to raise supplies and then headed to Keowee to launch his recruiting drive for Cherokee fighters. In actuality, Atkin's assessment of "Little Carpenter" was simplistic. There was no official "second man" of the Cherokees, though several historians have misleadingly identified Attakullakulla by that title.[10]

On March 30, Byrd by chance encountered Attakullakulla, accompanied by seventy-four Cherokee men and eight women, headed east in the Carolina piedmont toward Charles Town. Excited by what seemed good luck, the colonel asked Attakullakulla and his party to travel west with him to Keowee for enlistment. Less than enthused, Attakullakulla said that he could not turn back since he needed to show Governor Lyttelton what Cherokees had accomplished against the French by the Tennessee. He carried two enemy scalps as proof, a sign that the Cherokees merited arms for their service. When Byrd pressed his case, Attakullakulla gave some ground, agreeing that over fifty of his fellows travel with the colonel to Keowee.[11]

Little did Byrd know, but his Cherokee entourage had no intention of journeying to Virginia and the war front. After being fitted out with clothing, knives, and paint, the men headed home to Overhill country. Seven women, whom the colonel satisfied with "trifles," went with them. Compounding Byrd's difficulty, he found Attakullakulla slow to return from Charles Town and content to wait for weeks at Keowee to receive a wagonload of presents, courtesy of Lyttelton. "The Carpenter," wrote the colonel, was no more than "a little savage," but his aid was essential. Byrd put on a different face in public than private, showing outward respect while masking inward contempt toward "savages." Drawn to Cherokee women, he confessed his inability to "break" them of their habit "of anointing themselves with Bear Grease,

Cherokees, Native Peoples, and Empires, 1730–1762

& depriving themselves of the greatest Ornament of Nature." When Byrd finally headed north in early May 1758, he was joined by a mere fifty-seven warriors, not the hundreds he had expected.[12]

Attakullakulla knew what he was about. His patience paid off. When he left Keowee in early June, he brought back guns and munitions aplenty to his native ground. As politic as ever, Attakullakulla sent a translated dispatch to Lyttelton promising that his people would gladly fulfill their pledge to King George, just as promised long ago in England. The French, he said, "have spilt a great deal of my [English] Brothers blood & I have taken up the Hatchet & my People [as well] to have Satisfaction." Retribution in a common fight was a duty among kin, while bloodshed between them was dangerous. Attakullakulla blamed Lower Cherokee men, and not the Overhills, for the violence in Virginia. Interestingly, he made a distinctive mark, which might be interpreted as a warrior's curved bow, on the copy of his talk to Lyttelton. He stated his eagerness to head north now that gunpowder, bullets, and arms had arrived at Fort Prince George for Cherokee use.[13]

While Attakullakulla was no simple "peace chief" and took pride in being a warrior, his prestige among his people came from his diplomatic skill far more than his exploits in war. His influence in Overhill country was less powerful than British officials presumed. George Turner, supply agent, learned as much after reaching Fort Loudoun on June 12, 1758, and encountering a holdup in a pending Cherokee march to Virginia. Eight days later, Great Warrior Oconostota brought sobering news to the British garrison. Warriors could not go on the mission without first hearing from their shamans. The next evening, Cherokee men gathered at Connecorte's house spoke of "bad Omens." Many warriors who ventured north, it was foretold, would die of disease after two moons' time, and the survivors would struggle to return home alive. With regret, Attakullakulla told Turner that the Cherokees "could not recruit their People as the Whites did, who were [numerous] like the Leaves of the Trees."[14]

The Shenandoah killings undoubtedly cast a pall on the British recruiting drive. The thought of trekking north via Virginia was fodder for Cherokee nightmares. Overhill men worried, too, about going to war in the hot summer and the danger of disease. After the expedition was aborted, Attakullakulla put the best face on events, telling Turner that he would bring three hundred fighters to aid the British that autumn. He chided the agent for not offering wampum belts as a show of

Prelude to the British-Cherokee War   229

good faith. Turner regarded the advice as "a poor dirty Evasion," no more than an excuse for the failure to deliver warriors. What Turner did not discern is that Connecorte carried more weight than Attakullakulla at Chota. The priest-chief was not keen on Attakullakulla's growing commitment to the English. As early as October 1756, Connecorte told Captain Raymond Demere that Great Warrior Oconostota and his brother were the only men in the nation to be trusted after his death.[15]

Chota and surrounding communities generally held back from the English war drive of 1758. Once the corn harvest was over, Attakullakulla led sixty warriors northward, reaching Forbes's camp at Raestown, about 100 miles east of Fort Duquesne, on October 13, 1758. While impressed by Cherokee fighters, the general had no patience whatsoever for Attakullakulla, whom he privately scorned "as consummate a Dog" as any southern Indian chief for "his most avaricious demands" for presents. Forbes's contempt was exacerbated by his deteriorating health, campaign pressures, and prejudice. Ironically, the general displayed far greater diplomatic skill in accommodating former Indian foes such as the Delawares than in befriending Attakullakulla, a heartfelt English ally.[16]

Forbes's rift with the Cherokee leader deepened over the next month, just as the British army, with colonials and Native allies, made a final push toward Fort Duquesne. By November 19, Attakullakulla and about ten of his companions pulled out of the campaign. Aghast, Forbes ordered his officers to compel the departing Cherokees to surrender the guns, ammunition, and horses they had received. The general's anger at Attakullakulla remained hot even after the French abandoned Fort Duquesne on the twenty-third, setting fire to the garrison and allowing the victorious British to take possession the next day. On the twenty-sixth, Forbes dispatched a withering letter to Lyttelton, urging him not only to ruin Attakullakulla's reputation "in the eye of his own nation" but also to treat him "with the utmost infamy and Contempt if he presumes to go into So. Carolina."[17]

Attakullakulla's recovery from Forbes's censure is a remarkable instance of diplomatic acumen and perseverance. His efforts required patience, strategic understanding, and the physical capacity to travel hundreds of miles in journeys from the Ohio theater to Williamsburg, a return visit to Overhill country, followed by a parley with Lyttelton in Charles Town, and a trek to his home west of the Appalachians—all this within four months for a man around the age of fifty. Attakullakulla was determined to ease tensions from the slaughter of Cherokee warriors in the Shenandoah. Personal vindication was also on the line. Forbes's censure shamed him, undercutting his position among his own people. He was said to feel that "his arms had been taken from him; that he was like a child & no man." Manliness was imperative for Attakullakulla, a warrior whose slight frame belied his powerful intellect and stamina.[18]

Attakullakulla had reasonable success in talks with Lieutenant Governor Francis Fauquier in Williamsburg in January 1759. Accompanied by fourteen Cherokee men, he explained that he went north not so much to aid Forbes but to "heal all Wounds" between his people and Virginia. He cagily invoked Connecorte's approval of his negotiation, knowing that Chota's priest-chief had a favorable reputation at Williamsburg. When talks resumed the next day, Fauquier admonished Attakullakulla for not doing justly by Forbes, but then smoothed the path by pledging the flow of trade goods to the Cherokees. The conference ended with some satisfaction on both sides. Attakullakulla was thankful for Fauquier's advice to be on his guard and to take back routes on his way southward. As the Cherokee leader and his party neared Catawba territory, they were followed by white men who intended to kill them. Fortunately, the group safely reached Overhill country.[19]

Attakullakulla's next venture took him to Charles Town, with a stop at Keowee where he nudged Lower Town headmen to enter a peace with Virginia. Their villages, having suffered losses in the Shenandoah, were restive. Ensign Lachlan Mackintosh, who observed the scene, naively reported that the Cherokees accepted Attakullakulla's admonition that Indians who killed "White People" should suffer death as a consequence.[20] In reality, the proposition was yet to be tested.

Attakullakulla showed his mettle when he conferred with Lyttelton in Charles Town in April 1759. Well prepared for the governor's sharp questions, the Cherokee leader forthrightly refuted Forbes's charge of desertion. "Great Warrior" Forbes, he averred, "has told things that are false of me." Attakullakulla explained that he had left the war front only after learning from Shawnee contacts that the French had decided to abandon Fort Duquesne. It was therefore pointless for him to stay longer when his foremost responsibility was to head for Virginia and repair the Cherokee position at Williamsburg. This was no ordinary alibi but a measured and plausible account. Lyttelton had little

Prelude to the British-Cherokee War 231

choice except to "forgive" Attakullakulla for what was "amiss" in his conduct toward Forbes. The governor again needed to accommodate his strongest Cherokee ally.[21]

Before the meeting with Lyttelton concluded, Attakullakulla spoke poignantly of why he hewed close to the English: "My Love for my own People and their Young ones has always determined me to do every thing in my Power to prevent their falling-out with the white People, having told them [the Cherokees] they would thereby be destroyed." It was a stunningly realistic insight shaped by a lifetime's experience. The "Old Warriours" who were now dead had "loved their Brothers the English," and Attakullakulla would do likewise, though he could not control what came after his death. A few days later, Lyttelton gave Attakullakulla a string of wampum in response to the Cherokee leader's similar gift. Tellingly, the governor's string had white beads, except for three black ones, which Lyttelton pledged to remove when Attakullakulla next visited Charles Town, provided the latter lived up to his promise of opposing the French at every opportunity.[22] The governor's trust was less than complete.

Settico's Attack

Neither Attakullakulla nor Lyttelton anticipated what happened next. Head warrior Moytoy of Settico led Cherokee war parties that spread destruction on the North Carolina frontier in late April 1759. Two to three small bands, numbering perhaps twenty-five men each, killed more than twenty whites, including at least eight children, in two days of raids on isolated and virtually defenseless farmsteads. Nearby Catawba men, friends to Carolina, helped bury the dead while other Catawbas pursued the killers. Moytoy did not hide what he had done—far from it. Settico had suffered several dead in the Shenandoah killings, now seven months past. The wounds still haunted. Before returning to his town in Overhill country, Moytoy visited several Lower Cherokee villages, including Conasatchee, where he displayed nineteen scalps to Wawhatchee in a bid for support. Wawhatchee tactfully stated his disapproval of the killings to Lieutenant Richard Coytmore. What the headman actually felt is less certain.[23]

Why did Settico warriors unloose their fury on whites who lived far from the Shenandoah and had done no ostensible wrong to them? In effect, the slain were surrogate victims, individuals who appeared to the Settico killers as kin to Virginia's whites. What is highly speculative

232   *Cherokees, Native Peoples, and Empires, 1730–1762*

is the idea, broached by some historians, that the Carolina settlers were targeted primarily because some were German and therefore associated with culpable "Dutchmen" of Virginia who had taken Cherokee lives. In fact, Captain Robert Wade, at the head of settlers with mostly British surnames, was as responsible as any man for the previous summer's Shenandoah killings.[24] Settico warriors likely struck where they did because the North Carolina homesteads were comparatively easy targets. Cherokee talk of "Dutchmen" appears in only a few instances relative to the killings. It is even possible that Moytoy spread word of the "Dutch" for political reasons. English Carolinians might be less concerned about what happened to Germans than their own kind. If that thinking surfaced in some Cherokee quarters, it was badly mistaken. Colonials simply focused on the fact of "whites" being slaughtered.[25]

Is it possible that Moytoy launched a deadly attack in order to undermine Attakullakulla's peace diplomacy in Charles Town? There is no definite proof of such a motive, though it cannot be ruled out. Captain Paul Demere, who replaced his brother Raymond as Fort Loudoun's commandant in 1757, was keen at gauging Cherokee opinion through information culled from Native sources and colonial traders. In May 1759, he received intelligence of fifteen white scalps recently brought by Overhill warriors from the North Carolina frontier. At least twelve of the scalps were carried by Moytoy and his followers. Before heading out on his deadly raid, Moytoy had met at Chota's townhouse with the Mortar ("Wolf Warrior" by clan name), the most influential Upper Creek head warrior who was a decided foe of English colonialism. Connecorte had himself welcomed the Mortar's visit. While there is no "smoking gun" connecting Connecorte to the Settico raiders, Moytoy may have felt that Chota's priest-chief gave him some space to deal a blow.[26]

On May 22, 1759, Lyttelton forwarded a strong rebuke to Connecorte and Attakullakulla, expressing his disgust with Settico men who had killed and scalped "white people, Subjects of the Great King George; so the path is now fouler than ever, & stinks with their blood." All had shockingly occurred, wrote Lyttelton, "while you, the Little Carpenter, and I were eating like brothers out of the same Dish" at Charles Town. Knowing that Attakullakulla was strongly in the peace camp, Lyttelton put the onus on "Old Hop" (Connecorte), "as Emperor of the Nation," to consult with "Headmen & Warriors, & to give me Satisfaction." The governor's meaning was obvious. The Cherokee killers

Prelude to the British-Cherokee War

of colonial settlers would have to be brought to justice and suffer execution.[27]

Cherokee country was a diverse social nexus with competing views on the crisis. Many towns and their headmen distanced themselves from the Settico raids. On May 16, 1759, deputies of thirteen communities, centered in the Middle Towns, sent a formal message to Lyttelton in which they repudiated "Disrespectfull" talk toward "White men" that was "much Practiced in Other Parts of the Nation." The headmen complained that discontented villages such as Settico were unduly secretive, acting as as if they were "a different People" than their Middle Town kin. Cherokee obligations to one another in crisis depended on mutual consultation beyond town and region. Not wishing to be held accountable for others' misdeeds, Middle Town leaders messaged Lyttelton of their desire to move beyond the deaths suffered in Virginia, so those events "shall be utterly Buried in Obscurity and never no more thought on." Round O, head warrior of Stecoe who had served beside the English in the war, led the way for this group by sending his British medal along with white beads to Charles Town. By this gesture, he evinced his trust that Lyttelton would recognize his sincerity and give back the medal in time.[28]

Round O and his fellow headmen heralded their attachment to "our Father the Great King George," whose "Blood was like ours." In reality, many Cherokees and colonials were feeling more and more threatened by one another, and hardly like "brothers." Here we may recall Connecorte's derision of common "white people" "as Swine Herds or Hog Cleaners." In effect, the priest chief counted solely on colonial leaders, "the great beloved men," to uphold alliance. If South Carolina's governor turned enemy, Cherokee ties to the English would be gravely weakened. Once informed of Lyttelton's demands for satisfaction in June 1759, Connecorte delayed his response to Captain Paul Demere for some nine days and then spoke only in platitudes. His silence on the main issue, the delivery of the Cherokee killers or their scalps, spoke volumes.[29]

With Connecorte holding his ground, Demere probed Cherokee opinion through confidential talks with Attakullakulla. Sagely reading the landscape, Attakullakulla warned that delivering the killers would only "make bad Worse." Cherokee kin ties had to be considered. Great Warrior Oconostota of Chota was kinsman to Moytoy, Settico's war leader, and would not countenance retribution. Attakullakulla asked Demere to understand his own position, "That he was but one Man &

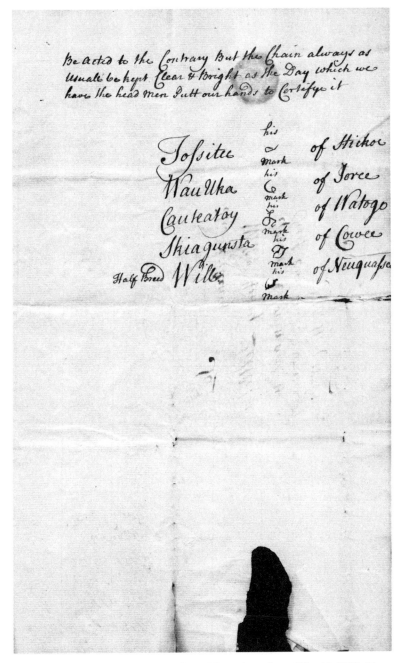

Cherokee Chiefs to Governor William Henry Lyttelton, May 16, 1759. Five Middle Town headmen appealed for peace in this letter, which includes their signatures or marks. *William L. Clements Library, University of Michigan.*

Prelude to the British-Cherokee War

Could not do what he wished" but would work to restore calm. Attakullakulla was as good as his word, visiting Settico, interceding with town elders, and retrieving eight white scalps from the village so that Demere could see to their burial. Not all remnants of the dead were recoverable. Dogs had reportedly torn five scalps to shreds. Attakullakulla told Lyttelton of Settico's sorrow for spilling blood and the town's desire to make amends by fighting the French. This message was dead well before arrival. Lyttelton had already decided to set an example. Cherokees would not be allowed to murder the king's subjects without consequence. The governor cut off the flow of trade goods to Settico and ordered its resident British trader to remove from the village. Singling out one Cherokee town for punishment, the governor still somehow believed Connecorte could be nudged to compliance.[30]

Frontier commandants were diplomatic intermediaries, and their conduct reflected on British authority with Cherokees on an almost daily basis. Paul Demere held his ground without taking undue risks at his isolated post in Overhill country. Lieutenant Richard Coytmore, a headstrong and brash officer, took a far more aggressive stance as Lyttelton's point man when he replaced Ensign Mackintosh as Fort Prince George's commander in April 1759.[31] Coytmore did not hesitate to intrude into hidden corners of the Cherokee world. In late June, he was tantalized by Jemmy, shaman of Estatoe, who confided in him while visiting the British fort. Of Cherokee-English parentage, Jemmy appeared eager to reconnoiter French maneuvers to the north. Coytmore was further intrigued because the shaman was brother to Seroweh, Estatoe's "Young Warrior," a Cherokee militant and a major force in his neighborhood.[32]

Within days of this encounter, Coytmore received information that "five Young Fellows" of Estatoe had carried three white scalps and lodged them in Jemmy's house. Without revealing what he had learned, Coytmore visited Jemmy at his home, nine miles from the fort, before returning to quarters. The next evening, he set out again, hoping to learn more of Estatoe's role in recent violence. Arriving by morning with a junior officer and an interpreter, the Englishmen met alone with Jemmy's Cherokee wife while her husband was out hunting. A frank discussion followed. Admitting that the scalps had been delivered to her, the woman of the house unhesitatingly called them a pleasing gift, satisfaction for a kinsman's death at the hands of whites. Her statement was a succinct reflection on what Cherokees regarded as legitimate retribution. While reluctant to hand over the scalps, she hinted that she

Cherokees, Native Peoples, and Empires, 1730–1762

might surrender them for a reward. War trophies were important and were to be yielded only for a price. Jemmy's wife then looked for the three scalps and, not finding them, assumed they had been taken by Seroweh, "the Young Warrior," when he passed by her place. Young Warrior was "the Head of All," she added. Coytmore left Estatoe in the middle of the night, and brought back only one "white Sculp," which he thought "an old one," to be laid to rest.[33]

Coytmore had learned that Estatoe was a place to be watched. How deeply he probed into the town's background is unclear. We know that Virginia men had disarmed and gunned down three Estatoe men the previous summer, a murderous act that Seroweh and his friends were determined to avenge. Desperate to bring Cherokees to order, Coytmore met with Lower Town headmen at Keowee. He got nowhere when he declared that it was now "the time to show if ever they intended to give Satisfaction."[34] While most Cherokees did not want war, they would not surrender warriors who had killed whites.

Rebuffed at Keowee, Coytmore depended a good deal on Cherokee women for intelligence. In late July 1759, a woman of Conasatchee ("Sugar Town" to the English), a village close by Keowee, tearfully told Coytmore of Cherokee designs to launch a preemptive strike against the English and of Creek intentions to support the Cherokees in war. Formerly a white man's wife, she said "her heart was heavy to think what was soon to happen" since plotting was rife "throughout the Nation" from Chota to Keowee. Her stark message, a product of fear and rumor, misleadingly cast nearly all Cherokee leaders as "Rogues" unalterably bent on war. But how was Coytmore to know the actual state of affairs? He was bound to pay heed to a woman who begged him not to speak openly of her words lest she be killed by her own people.[35]

Coytmore became even more suspicious when he received intelligence at Fort Prince George from yet another Cherokee woman. In this case, the informant was Buffalo Skin ("Oxinaa" to her people), who two years before had relayed intelligence to the English on Great Tellico's flirtation with the French. Shrewd and capable, Buffalo Skin made it her business to be in the know about backdoor political movements that could upset the Cherokee world. In the late spring of 1759, she accompanied a small group of Cherokee men who set out with the Mortar en route to the latter's village of Okchai, where French traders handed out rum and shirts to the formidable Creek chief and his visitors. The travelers' next stop was the Alabama fort, where the French

Prelude to the British-Cherokee War   237

dispensed more gifts and urged the Cherokees to break with the English entirely. The Cherokee group headed back to their country with a wampum belt, courtesy of the Mortar, intended for Connecorte. The belt had white beads on each side to signify routes to the French while a middle row of black beads represented the English at Fort Loudoun. The upshot was clear. Connecorte, and possibly Great Warrior Oconostota, were open to an alliance with New Orleans and Mobile, provided the French could furnish supplies.[36]

Buffalo Skin likely warned Lieutenant Coytmore of the apparent plot for the same reason she had previously divulged French-Creek-Shawnee connections to Captain Raymond Demere. She believed her people's well-being was best served through an English alliance. When Coytmore dispatched this intelligence to Lyttelton, he reported that a slew of Cherokees towns, though not the whole, were conspiring against the English. Keowee was a trouble spot right next door to his garrison, while Chota threatened Fort Loudoun. The danger seemed about to explode, at least as far as the anxious lieutenant was concerned.

Trigger Points and Diplomatic Deadlock

Historians typically distinguish between trigger points of war and deeper, more underlying causes. The escalating conflict between British South Carolina and the Cherokees in the fall of 1759 is no exception. What many Cherokees believed they owed the English was not at all the same as what Lyttelton expected of them. In brief, there was cultural asymmetry about the foundation of justice and law. Cherokees overwhelmingly defied South Carolina's insistence that they surrender their warriors for slaying whites, especially after the Indian men's kin had been cut down by Virginia settlers. There was some "give" to the Cherokee position—as we shall see—but not what satisfied Lyttelton's understanding of his high office and its duties. The governor believed himself fair to Natives, whom he saw as subordinate nations under royal protection. In early 1758, he pledged to punish whites who killed Natives, though he was unable to visit justice in the case of four scalped Estatoe Cherokees (three men and one woman) quite probably murdered by white vagabonds on the South Carolina frontier the previous autumn. Estatoe men retaliated by killing two white men on the way north to Virginia. This was a sign of things to come.[37]

Unlike small-scale tit for tat, Settico's fearsome attacks of April 1759 that took twenty settler lives were too egregious for Lyttelton to bypass. The governor's position grew tougher after Cherokee militants killed at least four South Carolina frontier settlers, including a woman and child, that August. (Another woman and child were scalped but somehow survived.) Late that month, Lyttelton ordered a complete halt to the trade in arms and ammunition to the Cherokees and procured pledges of support from Lieutenant Governor Fauquier of Virginia and Governor Henry Ellis of Georgia. While both governors doubted Lyttelton's confrontational approach, they finally deferred to the South Carolina executive's insistence on setting the terms of satisfaction within his jurisdiction.[38]

Fauquier had a most ironic role. Just one week before agreeing to Lyttelton's embargo, he had agreed to a truce with two Lower Cherokee deputies, Yellow Bird and an unnamed warrior, who came to Williamsburg for direct talks. Shaking hands with the Native men after an initial demurral, Fauquier decided to take up the peace offering by accepting a white wampum string and removing a black bead from one of its ends. This was a time for mutual forgetting. Tragically, Fauquier's overture lost force with South Carolina's rejectionism.[39]

Lyttelton's arms cutoff incensed the Cherokees. In early September, Wawhatchee came to Fort Prince George and asked Coytmore for a supply of gunpowder. The lieutenant refused, saying no more could be given since Cherokee "young Men" had already "fired it away at the White People." Wawhatchee retorted that his people could get gunpowder from other places to shoot all the more. Other Lower Town headmen told Coytmore of their desire for peace but declined to bring eight white scalps to the fort so long as the lieutenant withheld ammunition. In this tug of war, the return of human remains had become a measure of satisfaction as much as the delivery of munitions. Had the scalps been surrendered in this instance, Coytmore intended to burn them, disposing of remnants he no longer thought appropriate for burial. Cherokees had their own understanding of what was at stake. With the breakdown of trust, Indians would not help the English cover the dead, and the white people's souls would know no rest.[40]

Besides the nagging business of munitions, how critical were colonial encroachments on Indian lands in the movement toward a South Carolina–Cherokee war? The answer is not clear-cut because Cherokees in certain regions were far more affected than others by intrusive

Prelude to the British-Cherokee War

white settlement. Geography mattered greatly. Lower Cherokees, living closest to South Carolina, were alarmed at the press of white settlers into their eastern hunting grounds within fifty miles of their towns. In March 1758, the region's Native leaders spoke of the "white People" who "incroach too nigh upon out Lands and kill all our Deer so that we cannot find Meat to eat." It seemed only a matter of time before the threat grew to the point of peril. For Middle and Upper Towns far from colonial settlements, this danger was less immediate.[41]

Overhill Cherokees were increasingly wary of Fort Loudoun and the military threat it might pose if reinforced. On September 13, Captain Demere informed Lyttelton that all had been "peaceable" in his neighborhood until Cherokees heard "the Ammunition was stopped, & then they grew very uneasy." The embargo magnified Cherokee suspicions. The French and their Creek friends appeared right to warn of a coming storm. The English would first deprive the Cherokees of munitions and then attack and destroy them. It mattered not that there was no such conspiracy. Charles Town's deeds spoke otherwise. Was that city not "the Place of Lies," as Connecorte had remarked?[42]

Angered by apparent English betrayal, warriors struck here and there, slaying a soldier who strayed outside Fort Loudoun and killing two colonial traders in Overhill country within a ten-day period. There was no general Indian war cry, but this scarcely comforted the English who received word that Cherokee men brought the victims' scalps to the Alabama fort for a supply of French ammunition. Ominously, the Cherokees would not allow any traffic to enter or leave Fort Loudoun, whose 130 soldiers, weakened by scanty provisions, were cut off from Fort Prince George, with its ninety men being closely watched by warriors commanding nearby hillsides and "lurking" or "skulking" about the garrison as officers reported. The British military presence was hanging by a thread.[43]

Cherokee outrage at the English waxed hottest in several Lower Towns, where whites pushed into Native hunting grounds and unscrupulous traders bilked Indian men in promiscuous rum sales. Virginia killings of the past year still rankled. Lower Town militants bid actively for Muscogee support, though with limited headway. Conversing with Lieutenant White Outerbridge in early September 1759, Creek headman Ishempoaphi said that "the Cherokees especially the Lower [towns] are very Jealous and very much afraid of white people." Where fear was great, so too was the potential for violence. Young Cherokee

240   *Cherokees, Native Peoples, and Empires, 1730–1762*

warriors openly taunted Lieutenant Coytmore, a man whom they despised, about scalps they had taken. Seroweh of Estatoe was the most brazen, heading a group that bragged of killing whites as easily as "Fowls."[44]

Acts of humanity did not gain the attention that killings stirred. About the time Seroweh tormented Coytmore, a black-painted Creek warrior encountered two German settlers looking for their cattle in the woods well south of Cherokee territory. He warned them to return home if they wished to save their lives. The grateful men invited the warrior to come with them, but the latter declined since he did not wish to be seen with whites. Interestingly, the Native man, who talked "a little English," was part of a small Creek band that collaborated in Cherokee raids on white households. Catawba men, meanwhile, displayed their friendship for the English by informing settlers of rumored Creek and Cherokee attacks. Colonial fears grew apace, often beyond the degree of actual danger.[45]

As violence continued, white traders took to their heels rather than risk becoming the next target. A bevy of traders flocked to Fort Prince George or fled even further southeast. White flight from Cherokee country was not a new phenomenon, as the panic of 1751 demonstrated. Eight years later, the situation was even more grave. Many Cherokees were upset at killings of whites, which chased away friends along with malefactors. The absence of traders meant a dearth of goods. As much as Indians despised exploitative trade, they were aghast when left high and dry without the British manufactures on which they relied for the hunt, raiment, and sustenance. In September, Middle Town Cherokee men shepherded their resident traders to Fort Prince George as a goodwill gesture signifying their desire to keep the path open.[46]

That same month, Oconostota and Ostenaco sought to defuse tensions by heading a party of eighteen Cherokee men that sheltered three British traders on the path from Overhill country to Fort Prince George. The Cherokees also came for a quite practical reason—to obtain ammunition. Just one day after arrival, Oconostota and Ostenaco requested a supply from Captain John Stuart, the interim ranking British officer. In light of Lyttelton's orders, the captain firmly declined but kept open a lifeline by advising the headmen, who were visibly upset at the refusal, to visit Charles Town for formal talks, which the governor had suggested by a missive that had not yet reached the Overhill men. After consulting for two days, Oconostota and companions accepted the invitation despite warnings from Stuart that they

Prelude to the British-Cherokee War

241

would be expected to give satisfaction for the murders of whites committed by Cherokees. The headmen still hoped for an understanding. Several Lower Town leaders took the same diplomatic route to Charles Town and were followed by a contingent from the Middle Towns and Hiwassee Valley.[47]

Most Cherokee representatives desired an open-ended negotiation that would bear fruit in renewed trade and harmony. The deputies included men of a militant bent such as Wawhatchee, along with Tistoe of Keowee and others who counseled reconciliation throughout the crisis. Ostenaco, formerly a stout British ally in war, appeared uneasy and doubtful of peace. He accompanied Oconostota a short way toward Charles Town before heading home. Only a few Cherokee leaders, notably Moytoy of Settico and Seroweh of Estatoe, were outside the negotiating circle because of their notoriety for heading lethal attacks on whites. At the other end of the political spectrum, Attakullakulla, the foremost "dove," could not make it to Charles Town because he was just returning to Overhill country after leading a warrior band once more to fight the French by the lower Tennessee. Increasingly distrusted by his people for being too soft toward the English, he took a temporary leave from the heart of controversy. It would not be until December, and after a serious deterioration in affairs, that Attakullakulla threw himself back into the diplomatic maelstrom.[48]

The Cherokee deputies to Charles Town could not know that Lyttelton was moving toward war while the headmen departed Fort Prince George for the low country. On October 4, the governor informed the provincial council of his resolve to be at the head of an army that would march into Cherokee country. Two days later, the council approved his call for an emergency militia draft to repel invasion and guard against "Insurrection and Rebellion," these last threats ever present in a slave society. On the eleventh, the Commons House issued a cautionary note. While weighing military measures, the assemblymen advised Lyttelton *not* to declare war on the Cherokees until he was certain that a negotiated settlement was out of reach. Anxious about the expense of war and its uncertain outcome, the House believed a precipitous declaration "at this Time, will be attended with the greatest Evils & Calamities, & be productive of the most dangerous, & even fatal Consequences" to South Carolina and neighboring provinces. Dissatisfied with the assembly's fastidious budgeting, Lyttelton exercised his prerogative by adjourning the Commons House. The Cherokee delegates were then only a few

242   *Cherokees, Native Peoples, and Empires, 1730–1762*

days' journey from Charles Town. In all, there were thirty-seven men, thirteen women, and five children on the way. There would be a diplomatic reckoning.[49]

Lyttelton was dutiful to a fault. He had no doubt of the right course when His Majesty's authority was at stake. After the Cherokee deputies entered the council chamber on October 18, 1759, the governor was coldly unwelcoming, telling Oconostota and company that they were "permitted" to visit only if they desired peace. Surprised that Lyttelton had no formal "Talk," the Great Warrior requested a delay until the next day. For the moment, Oconostota explained, he had only his "naked hand to shew" and not the usual "tokens of Friendship" to express "the sincerity of my Talk, and to knit it strong."[50]

The conference's second day brought revelations but no resolution between the contending parties. Oconostota declared once more that his words were those of Connecorte, the respected priest-chief who merited trust. There were "Good Talks" at Chota and only a few nearby "bad Towns." Oconostota had come to clear away "some Blood spilt" in the path. All should remember that "the Great King over the Great Water talks good and desires that all matters shall be straight between the white People & the Indians." Royal authority was invoked again as a protective and unifying principle. Cherokee peacemaking ultimately depended on mutual and purposeful forgetting and beginning anew. Oconostota, a powerfully built man, likened the day to a cloudy morning: "I am willing to make Clear Weather once more, and to bury the Hatchets of my Young People, and to put weights upon them never to be taken up again."[51]

A conference was a time to air grievances that might oblige the other party to admit wrongs and to lessen the sacrifices the other would need to make. Tistoe complained of Lieutenant Coytmore, who "gets drunk" and "goes to our Houses & draws our women from us . . . and has to do with our women at his own pleasure." Was the accusation one of rape, as some historians have suggested? The precise facts are elusive, while the tenor of the complaint admits little doubt. By Tistoe's words, Coytmore's misdeeds were not only his willfull sexual exploitation of Cherokee women but his disrespect for Indian men. The captain "paints himself and says that he is a Warrior, but [that] we are not Warriors." Tistoe's feeling of being unmanned and mocked as a warrior are undeniable. Clearing the air was actually part of his quest for peace. He recounted how he "loved" a former garrison commander who had pleased his Cherokee "Brethren" by firing one of the fort's cannons

Prelude to the British-Cherokee War   243

to announce the governor's message from Charles Town. Coytmore severed the chain of friendship. His alleged beating of Cherokee men, besides sexual license with women, provoked Native outrage.[52]

Tistoe's words failed to sway the governor. When meeting again with the Cherokees, Lyttelton announced his determination to lead an army into Cherokee country. "Satisfaction" would be taken by force unless his demand for surrender was met. Rebuking the Cherokee assemblage for the killings, Lyttelton evinced distrust for Oconostota, whom he denied was deputed by Connecorte to speak for his people. There was no breathing space for talk. The Cherokee deputies said not a word as they left the council chamber. All was clouded over and dark. The governor did not divulge his plan, which he discussed with the provincial council, of requiring the Cherokees to surrender Indian of-fenders similar in number to the twenty whites killed in both Carolinas and two more persons scalped but not dead.[53]

Lyttelton had a Machiavellian streak, however high-minded he was in principle. In his final word to the visiting Cherokees on October 22, he told Oconostota and the assemblage that the entire group "shall return in Safety to your own Country." As a guarantee, he pledged that he would accompany the Cherokees with his soldiers on the north-western main path to safeguard them from any vengeful white settlers. Their lives might be "in Danger" should they "go out of the High Road, and straggle into by paths."[54]

The governor departed Charles Town on October 26, soon gathering a few hundred militia, regulars, and volunteers, alongside his charges: fifty-five Cherokee men, women, and children. There were no signs of foul play early on the march. Four days into the journey and about eighty miles from Charles Town, Lyttelton and company were met by another Cherokee party of forty-nine persons, led by head warrior Round O of Stecoe. Oconostota's people and Round O's embraced, overjoyed to see one another. The governor himself welcomed Round O, a strong advocate of peace who purposefully came south to further a negotiated settlement. But all was not right. On consecutive nights, November 5 and 6, a few Cherokee men in Round O's party escaped and quickly made their way to their homeland. From this point on, Lyttelton barely hid the fact that the Cherokees were hostages. Though not shackled, Indians were closely guarded, separated in two groups, and enclosed by solders at night. Lyttelton's troops swelled to one thousand by the time he reached the piedmont and perhaps 1,300 as he pushed from Ninety-Six toward Keowee and Fort Prince George.

Cherokees, Native Peoples, and Empires, 1730–1762

Though sapped by illness and desertion, the governor's force was by far the most numerous colonial army that had ever entered Cherokee territory—and the first English army carrying an ultimatum in its collective scabbard.[55]

Lyttelton seems to have convinced himself that he had the upper hand in the crisis. Surely the Cherokees would finally relent under pressure, and without a full-scale war. Before setting out on his march, he reviewed the strategic situation. The governor's sources told him that the Creeks would remain neutral rather than side with the Cherokees. The Catawbas and the Savannah River Chickasaws were well disposed to the English. Nothing could be taken for granted, however. One day after the Cherokee conference ended, Lyttelton wrote Governor Arthur Dobbs of North Carolina, explaining the situation and requesting military assistance. He did the same with greater urgency to Williamsburg, hoping that Fauquier would summon his militia to box in the Cherokees east of Fort Loudoun. Most important, he sent word to Major-General Jeffrey Amherst, who was then absorbed in the conquest of French Canada. Without yet asking for regular troops, Lyttelton wished Amherst to be prepared for that eventuality.[56]

Lyttelton and his advance guard entered Fort Prince George on December 9, nearly six weeks out of Charles Town. At least four Cherokee escapees from the forced march spread word well before then that soldiers were holding their people as slaves and were now on the way to destroy all. Indian runners carried red-painted tomahawks throughout the nation. And yet there was no armed clash and no Cherokee attack as Lyttelton's force made its way from Twelve-Mile Creek on its last dozen miles to the fort where the governor intended to dictate a peace. Cherokees of the Lower Towns, the region immediately invaded, were of differing minds. While a number of young warriors hungered to assault the British, elders tended to favor a wait-and-see approach, leaving room for negotiation. There was yet another cautionary factor. Smallpox was then beginning to take a toll in Keowee Town, separated by just a few hundred yards and a river from Fort Prince George. As soon as Lyttelton was apprised of smallpox's spread, he posted guards so that Keowee residents would be kept apart from his troops.[57]

When Attakullakulla first heard of Lyttelton's march, he did not hurry south to negotiate with the English but consulted with headmen of various towns. He proceeded carefully and apparently with cause. Connecorte threatened to kill him if he steered his people to attack

Prelude to the British-Cherokee War   245

the French. At least this is what Attakullakulla told officers Demere and Stuart. Little Carpenter's break with Chota's priest-chief, his former mentor, is a dramatic sign of his rising ambition and desire to secure English favor at virtually any price. Attakullakulla even told the officers that he desired Lyttelton's appointment as Cherokee "Emperor." Whether Attakullakulla expressed this same idea to his own people, beyond perhaps a select few, is doubtful. Connecorte was a fearsome presence, and much honored, as long as he breathed. The elderly priest-chief was physically weak and close to death, but his growing distrust of the English carried weight. Cherokees were daily opting for war with the "white people." Connecorte died about one month after Attakullakulla vainly appealed for English appointment as foremost Cherokee leader. Kanagatucko (Standing Turkey) succeeded the great Connecorte, his deceased elder, as Chota's priest-chief.[58]

A Fig Leaf of Peace and the Onset of War

Lyttelton had managed to bring a makeshift army to Fort Prince George but struggled with maintaining his force in Cherokee territory. Within a few days, a good number of his sick and exhausted militiamen began to desert. The governor anxiously awaited Attakullakulla's arrival so that a deal might be struck, seemingly on English terms. While releasing all female hostages and some men, Lyttelton kept twenty-eight Cherokee males within the fort as a bargaining chip. Significantly, the captives who remained under guard were the more influential men among those initially held. On December 19, Attakullakulla came to the fort, carrying an English flag and bringing a French prisoner with him. Lyttelton made a token goodwill gesture by removing three black beads from Attakullakulla's wampum string—the same belt that Little Carpenter had received on his last visit to Charles Town. The next morning, talks began in earnest. Attakullakulla entered the garrison with several headmen, including his friend Willanawa and two deputies who spoke for Connecorte. Oconostota and Round O joined the parley after being released by Lyttelton, perhaps at Attakullakulla's confidential request. Negotiations could hardly proceed while two foremost Cherokee leaders were being kept as prisoners after being offered the governor's safe passage.[59]

Attakullakulla spoke as if his words could bring peace. Good feelings had to be restored and many lies "on both sides" cast away. Attakullakulla told Lyttelton that Great King George "has desired that we should both walk in the light . . . that unity and friendship should be between us." One of Connecorte's deputies spoke, too, of the governor standing for the king as if the English monarch were himself present. Oconostota and Round O listened in silence.[60]

Lyttelton gave no ground. There would be peace, he declared, only if the Cherokees offered "satisfaction" for the murder of whites by surrendering at least twenty-four "guilty" men to him to be "put to death" or "disposed of" as the governor pleased. If not, there would be a devastating war in which Virginia and North Carolina, "brothers" to South Carolina, would join against the Cherokees. Lyttelton dwelt on the imperial war's course. The British had defeated the French from the Great Lakes to the Ohio, and captured "their chief city," Quebec. Shawnees and Delawares had laid down the war hatchet for the peace pipe. The Choctaws, longtime French allies, were now seeking British trade. Lyttelton claimed to favor peace, but his ultimatum presented Cherokees with a nightmarish scene: "Your men will be destroyed, and your women and children will perish for want and nakedness." The governor insisted that Cherokee deputies give their definitive reply the next day.[61]

Attakullakulla put all his considerable skill toward preventing a catastrophe. After talking to the Cherokee hostages, he consulted privately with Lyttelton, won further time for diplomacy, and secured the release of Tistoe of Keowee and Estatoe's head warrior. Attakullakulla now had two Lower Town headmen to help him in their own neighborhood. His plan was to appease Lyttelton as far as in his power, which required local Cherokee consent. Through urgent diplomacy, he and his two companions gained custody of two Conasatchee men responsible for killing colonists. The offenders, handed over to the British, were effectively consigned to death by their community for the greater purpose of averting a destructive war.[62]

Over the next several days, Attakullakulla attempted to gain Estatoe's consent for the surrender of another three men. But the town refused. Attakullakulla could do no more to appease the English. Lyttelton was himself stymied. Some of his militiamen had contracted smallpox, and most of the remainder were on the verge of deserting *en masse*. The governor had no means to wage war as threatened. His last stab at salvaging a failed campaign was a face-saving treaty by which the Cherokees would acquiesce on paper to his demands before he departed for Charles Town with British troops and his remnant provincial force.[63]

Prelude to the British-Cherokee War   247

The treaty, drafted by Lyttelton, was presented to a small group of Cherokee leaders who must have wondered if they would be seized and imprisoned unless they gave some hint of consent. With two Indian offenders in hand, the governor now required that twenty-two Cherokee men responsible for killing whites be handed over as soon as possible. For each perpetrator brought in, a Cherokee hostage would be released and "set at liberty." Until then, hostages were to be held in custody for the treaty's "due Performance." All culpable men, once delivered to British hands, were "to be put to Death." There were additional requirements, but the surrender of the presumed killers mattered most. Only if the Cherokees fulfilled all obligations would they regain English trade. Lyttelton inscribed the names of six Native leaders, including Attakullakulla, Oconostota, and Round O, as treaty signatories "for ourselves & for our Nation." Cherokee men were present at the treaty's reading, but their consent was dubious. If verbally given, it was no more than a formality to forestall an immediate clash and to keep open some chance of further negotiation.[64]

Lyttelton was heralded by the citizenry when he arrived back in Charles Town on January 7, 1760. The next day, ships and harbor forts fired celebratory blasts as if the governor had won a great triumph in the field. He accepted praise from his council and a congratulatory address from the Presbyterian clergy. Lyttelton thanked the ministers but did not gloat. All he had gained from his failed military expedition was a piece of paper that supposedly obliged the Cherokees to his peace terms. In fact, no accord existed.[65]

Unrest in Cherokee country mounted while Lyttelton and company were on the path to Charles Town. Incomprehension mixed with anger over the English holding of hostages at Fort Prince George. Delivering white beads to Lieutenant Coytmore in good faith, Tistoe said that the hostages' kin were "very uneasy" at their relatives' treatment. Middle Town men were among the prisoners even though it was well known that those communities had not engaged in anti-English violence. Round O said he did not understand "the contents of the Paper," that is, the treaty he had been persuaded to mark. Two of his sons were hostages in the fort, and he was desperate to retrieve them. Before heading to Overhill country, Oconostota stopped by Estatoe to advise inhabitants not to surrender any killers of whites until he conversed with Connecorte, who was then near death but whose views still counted. Revulsion over the hostage situation was bringing Cherokees together. Nearly all regarded imprisonment as tantamount to enslavement.[66]

Violence was not long in escalating. Killings of white traders burst forth in several areas, a release of individual and communal anger rather than a broad national plan of attack. In January 1760, John Kelly, a trader in the Hiwassee Valley, was killed and his body hacked to pieces. One Hiwassee head warrior whose son was a hostage at Fort Prince George was said to have called on his men to kill all whites. The atmosphere about Fort Loudoun was at a razor's edge. Captain Demere found not a single white man who would risk carrying a letter to Charles Town. He finally entrusted his dispatch to Abraham, an enslaved Black man with undoubted skill as a courier in Cherokee country. Abraham managed to reach Charles Town and, even more re-markably, skirted danger and arrived back at Fort Loudoun that spring. Demere promised Abraham his freedom—a pledge fulfilled by the South Carolina assembly in 1761.[67]

The hostage crisis gave impetus to Cherokee militants. None was more daring than Seroweh, who attempted to capture Fort Prince George by subterfuge in January 1760. His plan was to persuade Lieu-tenant Coytmore to allow him and as many as seventy followers into the garrison for ostensible negotiation. Coytmore refused entry to any of the party until the men placed their guns two miles from the garrison. He had reason to be wary. British sentinels spotted Cherokee warriors ringing the hills about the fort. After further bargaining, Seroweh was finally admitted but with only twelve companions. He talked of handing over three or four men who had murdered whites, but his true intent was to probe for attack. Two Cherokee hostages made their escape during the confusion of Seroweh's comings and goings.[68]

Seroweh was clever at his business. In Coytmore's words, he "talked and behaved to all outward Appearance in a friendly Manner." Unable to seize the British post, Young Warrior's comrades chose an easier target by slaying John Elliott, a leading Anglo trader, and eleven other white traffickers residing within a short distance of the fort. The attackers, who struck during a driving rainstorm, helped themselves to a storehouse of booty, twenty to thirty kegs of rum, and 120 head of cattle. A day or two later, Seroweh was spotted on horseback carrying a white man's scalp, said to be Elliott's, according to a Cherokee woman who saw the rider by her house. Another warrior wore the slain trad-er's boots and silver spurs while mounted on a horse with Elliott's

Prelude to the British-Cherokee War

saddle and bridle. This was visceral payback, parading the wealth of a deceased trader whom Cherokees demeaned for shortchanging them.[69] One doubts, however, if trade grievances would have incited the brutal mass killing had it not been for British hostage-taking that tore at Cherokee community.

While Lower Town warriors exacted revenge, some headmen were loath to yield their status as potential peacemakers. A few days after the traders were cut down, Tistoe hoisted a British flag atop his house in Keowee and sent word to Coytmore not to blame him for the massacre. The head warrior of Middle Town Nequassee ventured to Fort Prince George, where he pleaded with Coytmore to release his village's hostages. Headmen were keenest at gaining the freedom of prisoners from their own town and region. They refrained from insisting on the immediate release of all hostages, perhaps because they believed any such plea unlikely of success and not nearly so important as winning back their highly cherished neighbors and kin. Coytmore was sympathetic to Nequassee's plea but could do nothing without Lyttelton's approval.[70]

Revenge and retaliation were not under central command in Cherokee communities, and killings did not foreclose negotiation from a Native perspective. Seroweh, who admitted his role in the massacre of traders, marched with his companions with "Colours flying, and Drum beating" in sight of Fort Prince George just a few days afterward. Unlike moderate Tistoe, his display had no Union Jack. Cherokees cooperated on the hostage issue even when they differed on the resort to violence. After the killings at Elliott's place, Seroweh relied on Tistoe to carry a white wampum string and a message telling Coytmore of his willingness to call off his men if the lieutenant freed four hostages—those of his town and vicinity. There was no deal.[71]

One of Seroweh's band was so reckless and drunk that he was nabbed by sentries after coming close by the fort. Confined with other Cherokees, he boasted of killing four white men near Elliott's house and berated the hostages for being "afraid" and "like Women" for not rushing the soldiers and making their escape.[72] His insult was commonplace warrior talk, a cliché that should not obscure women's active, risk-taking role during crisis.

The hostage crisis of 1760 elicited varied female responses. In several instances, women felt a need to aid white men, especially those to whom they were connected by affection and interest. One Cherokee woman vainly warned white traders at Keowee of Seroweh's planned attack on Elliott's camp two days before it occurred. Trader James

250   *Cherokees, Native Peoples, and Empires, 1730–1762*

Atwood was saved by a Cherokee woman who came to him in the middle of the night and warned him to flee when he was about to be targeted by Middle Town warriors. Henry Lucas, another trader, faced danger as a courier between Charles Town and Fort Prince George. Shot at by Cherokee men, he hid in a corn house, a woman's traditional preserve, for three days before gaining the fort. While Lucas was in the hideout, his Cherokee mistress came to feed him each midnight. The Keowee River ran high in a rainy January, making hazardous any crossing by ford from the Cherokee side of the stream to Fort Prince George. Traders Cornelius Dougherty and James Welsh narrowly averted danger outside the garrison when approached by three young Cherokee women, who methodically stepped backward toward a narrow ford as if luring them into Indian territory. Warned by a sentinel on the fort's ramparts, the men made an about-face when two Indian warriors with guns crept toward them at a distance. In this instance, youthful Cherokees of both sexes were plotting to ensnare their foes.[73]

Because women participated in Cherokee town councils and observed their men's movements beyond villages, they had considerable knowledge of wartime targets. They were able to approach garrisons in relative safety when the gates were closed to Native men. In late January 1760, one young Cherokee woman arrived at Fort Ninety-Six, a stronghold in that district, to tell trader Aaron Price, clearly a friend, that as many as six hundred Lower and Middle Town warriors were ready to launch an immediate assault on whites across the piedmont. Her information was accurate about Cherokee intentions, though not quite on the timing of attacks, which came in waves rather than one great surge over the next month. On February 1, several women stood by the Keowee River and shouted news of hostile warrior movements to the British in Fort Prince George. Round O soon came into view and drove the women away, "chiding them for telling anything." The next day, another woman came by the fort and told of Cherokee men seizing traders' cattle and horses and shooting those animals they could not catch. Round O angrily yelled at her. Tistoe's wife offered her own warning of warriors stalking the fort just out of view. These women acted in an apparently sincere manner, making it nearly impossible for the English to know if they acted of their own accord or colluded with their men to spread ominous news.[74]

One unnamed Estatoe woman took a great risk by traveling to Fort Prince George and visiting Coytmore while smallpox raged in the vicinity. Speaking to the Cherokee hostages, she talked of Seroweh's

Prelude to the British-Cherokee War   251

foiled plan of seizing the garrison and his role in the war party that killed Elliott and his fellow traders. The Estatoe woman was brave, entering the fort with Coytmore's permission on January 20 and spending some time with the hostages, perhaps to see how they were holding up under enormous strain. Struck by smallpox, she was led outside the gates on February 1 by Round O, who also contracted the disease. The sick woman struggled to walk but soon collapsed and died on the fort's parade ground. Round O himself succumbed a few weeks later without again seeing his two imprisoned sons.[75] Like much else that happened during the hostage crisis, the Estatoe woman's fate leaves unanswered questions. Where did she stay while at the fort several days? According to Coytmore's account, the hostages wanted the sick woman sent away lest she infect them. Did the British lieutenant himself abandon her when she was dying and no longer needed?

Fort Prince George was becoming a death house for Cherokee hostages and soldiers alike. On the evening of February 8, an imprisoned warrior of Stecoe died of smallpox. Hostages' cries were heard beyond the walls. The Cherokee death wail pierced the air at Keowee three times about midnight. From the fort's parapets, soldiers saw a large fire lit in the town plaza where Cherokees chanted the entire night. On the twelfth, an Indian woman came to the garrison and told the English that a white man's scalp had just been brought into Conasatchee. Warriors were gathering there while many Middle Town fighters had set out to attack white settlements.[76] This warning, adding to what other women had already said, was surely calculated to alarm the English about all that was mounting against them. The officers in redcoats might finally get the message and decide to release their hostages and negotiate peace. Cherokee women maneuvered on a diplomatic front outside formal Native-colonial conferences. It was precisely when official negotiations were in disarray that women's influence was most keenly exerted.

With Connecorte's death in January 1760, Great Warrior Oconostota was unquestionably the most formidable headman in the mother town of Chota. As a war leader, he acted deliberately, channeling his deep sense of betrayal after personally witnessing how Lyttelton broke his pledge of safe passage to Cherokee men before imprisoning them. Since the English had used subterfuge, the Great Warrior would show his skill at stratagem. In February, Oconostota, along with Attakullakulla and other Overhill men, headed to Fort Prince George, ostensibly to see if there was any last space for negotiation.

One imagines the Great Warrior wanted Attakullakulla with him to display his own quest for peace. All knew that Little Carpenter was desperate for reconciliation with the English. On February 14, the two leaders, along with another warrior and two white traders, approached the Keowee River's banks near the British garrison. Walking with a white interpreter to the fort's parade ground, Oconostota forwarded letters dictated by Overhill headmen calling for the hostages' release. Lieutenant Coytmore answered that he had to abide by the governor's treaty requiring Cherokees to deliver the killers of whites in exchange for freeing any Native hostages. Oconostota heatedly denied any such agreement and went back to share the glum news with Attakullakulla. One white trader in Oconostota's party soon entered the fort and brought word of Cherokee warriors, who had killed many whites, including women and children, and taken colonials as prisoners and "slaves." Overhill men were immersed in the fighting and had just brought in two white youths' scalps to Keowee.[77] Oconostota wanted the English to feel fear.

On the morning of February 16, two Keowee women came to the riverside, where they chatted with trader Cornelius Dougherty. The women were not there by happenstance. Oconostota soon came by and talked with Dougherty. The Great Warrior, who carried a bridle, requested a horse and a white man as escort so that he could travel safely to Charles Town for talks with Lyttelton. Deciding to converse with Oconostota, Coytmore left the fort and came to the riverbank with Ensign John Bell and an interpreter. The lieutenant offered Oconostota an escort but no horse. The Great Warrior suddenly hoisted and swung the bridle above his head, turned his back, and walked off. As if on cue, hidden Cherokee gunmen fired away, hitting Coytmore and lightly wounding the ensign and interpreter. Shot in the chest, Coytmore was somehow carried to the fort by trader Ambrose Davies. He died about twelve days later. By all appearance, the Cherokee women's talk with Dougherty was the first lure in Oconostota's plan to ensnare the lieutenant and kill him if at all possible. Attakullakulla, humiliated by the violence, retired to his native ground.[78]

Enraged when Coytmore was dragged bleeding into the garrison, the soldiers immediately fixed bayonets and swore to kill the Cherokee hostages. Ensign Alexander Miln, now the commanding officer, attempted to restrain them, at least by his account, and ordered the prisoners, about fifteen in number, to be put in irons and tied up. A bloody scene followed. British soldiers entered the garrison house, where the

Prelude to the British-Cherokee War   253

hostages were under guard and, taking matters into their own hands, shot down and killed all the prisoners. Miln claimed that the hostages resisted by tomahawk and knife before the troops "laid them all lifeless," a rather tame description of the massacre. British musket blasts unquestionably aroused the Cherokees outside the fort. Something horrific had occurred. Warriors' shouts filled the air, calling on the hostages to "fight Strong and we will relieve you." Through the night, Cherokee men kept up continual gunfire at the British fort. There was little letup over the next week. Cherokees could only imagine the worst of the hostages' fate.[79]

Escalation and British Invasion

Lyttelton's hostage-taking unloosed Cherokee anger at white settlers, spurring a rapid succession of killings across the piedmont. On February 1, 1760, about a hundred Cherokee warriors on horseback attacked a group of settlers who had abandoned their homes by the Long Canes and were heading toward shelter in Fort Augusta, Georgia. In the assault, more than twenty whites were killed, including some women and children, while nearly as many were captured. Days later, child survivors, some of whom were wounded, were seen wandering aimlessly in the woods near the site. The Cherokees lost some men in the fight to colonists who scurried to load and fire their guns. In the next few days, Cherokee warrior bands killed nearly thirty whites in two assaults by the Saluda River. Two hundred settlers hurriedly fled the area, with those who remained in some doubt that they could long survive. Cherokees killed Blacks, too, whom Indian fighters saw as appendages of white society. At Fort Ninety-Six, settlers beat off an attack by 250 Cherokees in early March. The bodies of several slain Cherokees were dragged into the garrison for degradation. As Captain James Francis wrote Lyttelton, "we have now the Pleasure . . . to fatten our Dogs with their Carcas[s]es, and to display their Scalps, neatly ornamented on the top of our Bastions." By that time, the South Carolina assembly had voted £25 to each militiaman who brought in a Cherokee scalp, provided an officer certified the authenticity of the torn flesh.[80] This was indeed a savage war.

Cherokee warriors were fearsome in attack, spreading havoc far and wide in the piedmont, though they did not kill in a wholly indiscriminate manner. Many Native fighters took white prisoners, mostly women and children, who not only signified Cherokee power but could be

254   *Cherokees, Native Peoples, and Empires, 1730–1762*

bargaining chips in negotiations with English officials. Reports put the number of white captives in Cherokee country at "about a Hundred" by late March 1760. Trader Robert Scott, a captive at Nequassee, witnessed Cherokee villagers burn one male prisoner to death at the stake when the victim's wife and five small children were held in that town. One boy in the family was slain during the capture itself. Cherokee towns distributed prisoners among several households in order to lessen the burden of maintaining them. Warriors brought up horses, cattle, and hogs from the piedmont whenever they could.[81]

Cherokee communities were strained in war as their ammunition ran low. Some headmen counseled a pause to fighting in order to test negotiation. In mid-March, Cherokees halted firing on Fort Prince George for more than two weeks. On the fourteenth, Keowee's townhouse flew a white flag, a sign that headmen wanted a respite from Fort Prince George's guns, which had compelled the inhabitants to move to Conasatchee. Eight days later, a Keowee woman came to the fort in the morning with a white flag and a peace message from Tistoe. Later that same day, she returned with Tistoe's offer to escort all British soldiers south to the white settlements, where they could find ample food. Something else was at issue. The female messenger begged both morning and afternoon to have a view of the hostages. Her words were inquisitive and bold, raising Ensign Miln's doubts of Tistoe's intent. The woman said that the Cherokees were holding six "big [white] Women Prisoners" at Conasatchee and five white girls and some boys at Estatoe. A few days later, another Cherokee woman arrived at the fort to spread word that Middle and Overhill warriors had set out to attack white settlements. Oconostota had himself "declared War . . . throughout the Nation."[82] Words of prowess counterbalanced peace messages in Cherokee diplomacy, with women serving as frequent couriers during the hostage crisis.

Tistoe continued his quest for breakthrough and resolution despite getting nowhere with his offer to shepherd soldiers out of the fort. While knowing that something terrible had occurred to the hostages, he was apparently unsure about their fate six weeks after they had been put to death. His feelings were shared by others. Nequassee's head warrior, who displayed goodwill by releasing captive Robert Scott, told Miln that "it was dreadful to think of their Brethren shut up in the Fort" and asked to see them at a distance even if he was not allowed to speak to them. The ensign demurred and called on the Cherokees to halt their "scalping Gangs." As for the hostages, they "could not be seen."[83]

Prelude to the British-Cherokee War

On April 1, 1760, Colonel Archibald Montgomery's force of 1,300 British troops put into Charles Town harbor from New York. General Amherst had decided to answer South Carolina's pleas for imperial aid. Lyttelton was then in his last days in Charles Town, readying to return to England before assuming the prestigious governor's post of Jamaica. The crisis he had built into a war was left to others. By Amherst's orders, Montgomery was to employ his soldiers for the protection of Carolina's frontiers and "the punishment of those Barbarian [Cherokee] Savages for their Inhuman Acts of Cruelty." The general voiced confidence that Montgomery's detachment "is every way Sufficient to March against and Overcome any Indians. I flatter Myself that Business will soon be Over."[84] Indeed, Amherst wanted a short campaign so that Colonel Montgomery and his troops could return north as soon as possible to secure British mastery in Canada. Amherst did not foresee that it would take more than a single offensive to conclude war with the Cherokees, and that peace, when it finally came, would not bring about the abasement of "savages," who though ravaged by invasion and disease retained their pride and independence.

256 *Cherokees, Native Peoples, and Empires, 1730–1762*

9

Carnage and Peace Diplomacy

In early June 1760, Colonel Archibald Montgomery's army faced scant opposition as its long train moved up steep and rocky country near Lower Cherokee towns by the headwaters of the Broad and Saluda Rivers. The British force was formidable, consisting of 1,300 regulars, mainly Scottish Highlanders with other veteran Scots battalions, assisted by over 300 South Carolina provincials besides forty to fifty Catawba scouts. Fired on by Cherokee warriors near Little Keowee, regulars stormed the hamlet on the morning of June 2, bayoneted men, and captured women and children. Montgomery applauded his troops while admitting that some Native women and children "could not be saved" and were among the dead. Most fighters in the Cherokee war party quickly fled.[1]

Montgomery's army continued on the march to Estatoe—the prime British target because of that town's forward role in the previous year's violence. The great majority of Estatoe's inhabitants hurriedly abandoned their homes before the army's forceful entry. Over the next twenty-four hours, the British burned four towns to the ground—Estatoe, Qualatchee, Conasatchee, and Toxaway. Keowee was largely deserted by its inhabitants before the British invasion. Sixty to eighty Cherokees were killed, some of whom were consumed by fire. Soldiers captured thirty-five women and children and brought them to Fort Prince George. Only two Cherokee men were brought in alive, a sign that males of fighting age were unlikely to be spared if caught. This was not warfare as waged between large armies on European battlefields. One British officer asked rhetorically, "What honour or glory can be acquired in an Indian war?"[2]

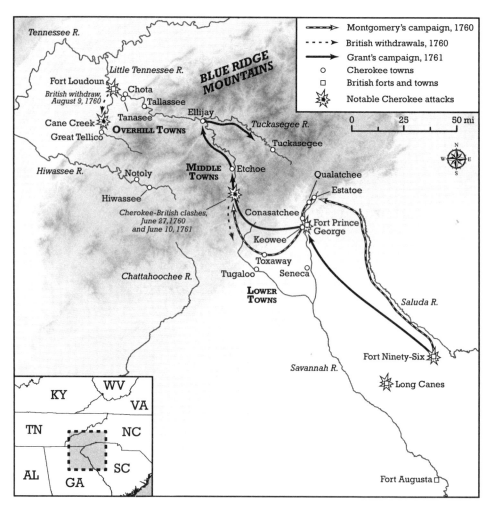

The British-Cherokee War, 1760–1761

Colonel Montgomery described Cherokee towns, now destroyed, as "more considerable than could be imagined ... and well provided with every Necessary of Life." Major James Grant, second in command, admitted that he "could not help pitying them [the Cherokees] a little; their Villages were agreeably situated their houses neatly built and well provided, for they were in the greatest abundance of every thing," and had "every where astonishing magazines of corn, which were all consumed in the flames." (Only the cornfields and planting grounds beyond the town centers were left untouched.) Estatoe and Conasatchee, the two largest of the four ravaged towns, had about two hundred houses each. The homes, open to plunder by soldiers before being set ablaze, yielded coins, a handful of silver watches, and stores of clothing, wampum, guns, and ammunition. In Conasatchee, the British found the remains of a white male captive, put to death earlier that day. Cherokees spared some white prisoners, including a woman left at Estatoe.[3]

Montgomery and Grant were not brutal men despite the devastation wrought by their army. In a report to South Carolina's Lieutenant Governor William Bull, Grant hoped that "the whole nation" of the Cherokees would "readily come into terms" after receiving "a correction . . . that has been pretty severe." Montgomery had simply executed General Amherst's instructions requiring troops to chastise the Cherokees by "destroying their Towns, and Cutting up their Settlements." Amherst's contempt for Indians was unmistakable, though not the sole influence on his decision-making. "Punishment" was to be harsh without delaying Montgomery's return to New York as soon as feasible.[4]

Montgomery was keen to open peace negotiations when he returned to Fort Prince George after his troops had destroyed the four towns. He did not understand how deeply the Cherokees were estranged by British betrayals and how difficult it would be to win back the least trust. While his army was still on its march northwest in the piedmont, a crisis erupted at Fort Prince George. On May 7, Ensign Alexander Miln, the fort's unsteady junior commander, ordered soldiers to seize Tistoe and eight other Cherokee emissaries who were dining, drinking, and smoking with him at his own invitation outside the garrison. In a crude version of former Governor Lyttelton's hostage-taking, the ensign vowed to hold the arrested men as prisoners until the Cherokees delivered their own white captives to him.[5]

Less than pleased by Miln's highhanded conduct, Montgomery decided to release the confined Cherokee men at the fort, though not all at once. Among the first freed were Tistoe and Estatoe's Old Warrior, whom the colonel tasked with important missions. The Estatoe Warrior was to visit the Lower Towns and attempt to gain the release of white captives. Tistoe had the still greater responsibility of conveying Montgomery's negotiating terms to Middle and Overhill Cherokee villages and reporting back to him within ten days. The colonel proposed peace talks, provided Attakullakulla came to parley with him and the Cherokees offered food to beleaguered Fort Loudoun, the lone British bastion in Overhill country. If these conditions were not soon met, however, Montgomery threatened to reduce the Overhill Towns

Carnage and Peace Diplomacy

to ashes. Confidentially, neither Montgomery nor Grant believed it possible to lead an army over the mountains, but that judgment counted little at the time. The British threat infuriated Cherokees already shocked and angered at the destruction of the Lower Towns.[6]

Time passed without the Cherokees bending to imperial demands. The Lower Towns were not about to deliver white prisoners. Tistoe kept to the north for the while, not returning to Montgomery's camp at Fort Prince George, a place where Cherokees had met enslavement and death. The colonel extended his deadline to await an answer. None came. Attakullakulla did not head south since he lacked the communal authority to negotiate with the enemy. Overhill men taunted him as "the white people's friend" and even threatened his life. By all reports, Oconostota intended to overpower Fort Loudoun, already under siege. In early June, warriors about the fort threatened to kill any Cherokee woman attempting to enter the British post. Just four years before, James Glen had conceived of the fort as "a work of peace and love." The garrison was now on the brink, besieged by the same Cherokees Glen had imagined as loyal and willing allies.[7]

Foiled on the negotiating front, Montgomery determined to carry war to the Middle Towns. Setting out on June 24, troops strained to negotiate steep ascents with numerous defiles, narrow and sinuous mountain passes through densely forested terrain. The rear guard had four hundred packhorses besides cattle in tow. Three days later, a large body of Cherokee warriors, perhaps as many as 600 in number and hidden in thick brush, surprised the British and colonial advance guard as it approached a muddy river flanked by hilly and steep ground. In a fierce fight, the British were hit by heavy fire, but eventually forced the Cherokees to give way. As the fighting raged, Cherokee warriors yelled to steel their courage, while the Scotsmen "returned the cheer," as one soldier recalled, "with three whirra's and three waves of our bonnets and hats." Seroweh, the famed militant, and Tistoe, of more moderate disposition, were battle leaders for their people. The British paid heavily, losing twenty men dead and another sixty wounded. The Cherokee dead numbered perhaps fifty. Before retreating, Cherokee fighters dug three large holes and placed some forty of their dead in a standing position, a sign of the warriors' unshakable and undying pride. Hours after the engagement, the British entered Etchoe, mother town of the Middle Cherokee region, stayed there two days, and hauled off what corn they could. Montgomery's offensive by no means marked a Cherokee defeat in a strategic sense. Indeed, the Cherokees felt unbowed.

260   *Cherokees, Native Peoples, and Empires, 1730–1762*

Averse to a prolonged campaign and unwilling to risk more losses, Montgomery resolved that his army had shown its mettle and that it was time to return to Fort Prince George and then Charles Town for an outward voyage to New York.[8]

South Carolina's leaders, aghast at the colonel's decision to end the campaign, pleaded with Montgomery to remain in the province or at least delay his embarkation until receiving Amherst's approval. Lieutenant Governor Bull, son and namesake of a previous Carolina chief magistrate, put the case in a supplicatory letter to the colonel. South Carolina did not alone have the means to defend the king's subjects against immediate danger. The Creeks were on the verge of war and appeared ready to join the Cherokees, who would boast of their "imaginary Triumphs" over His Majesty's troops "to all the Neighbouring Indians." The French at Mobile and New Orleans would surely exploit the situation for an assault on South Carolina. Bull's arguments did not prevail on Montgomery, who shipped out with the great portion of his troops in August, leaving only four companies of regulars to aid in frontier defense.[9]

The Cherokees were certainly relieved to see Montgomery's force retreat. Overhill warriors tightened the noose around Fort Loudoun that summer. On August 6, 1760, Demere and his officers arrived at a painful decision. The garrison could no longer hold out. Sickened by a diet of horseflesh, the men had practically no food remaining except some hogs and beans that Cherokee women had stealthily brought them. Captain John Stuart was soon on his way to Chota to meet with Oconostota and other headmen to negotiate what the British hoped would prove honorable terms of surrender for some 160 soldiers and forty colonial workmen, women, and children.[10]

Soon after Stuart's arrival at Chota, an agreement was put to writing in the style of European articles of capitulation. The accord required Fort Loudoun's surrender, with safe passage of soldiers and civilians under Cherokee escort south to Fort Prince George. These terms had no meaning whatsoever to warriors who felt impelled to strike the English enemy. On August 10, British troops and colonials were about to begin their third day's retreat from the fort when they were attacked by several hundred Cherokee fighters in a field near Cane Creek. A massacre ensued but not total slaughter. Twenty-three British privates were slain along with three white women. Warriors killed three officers in the initial onslaught, inflicting a horrific death on Captain Demere, who was shot twice then scalped alive and made to

Carnage and Peace Diplomacy

"dance about" bareheaded before his arms and legs were cut off. John Stuart of South Carolina was the sole officer who escaped the killing site alive. Captured by one warrior, he was purchased within a few weeks by Attakullakulla, who led him to safety as a free man.[11]

British respect for Attakullakulla rose to new heights but brought no reprieve to his people. Through the winter of 1760–1761, the Cherokees suffered terribly from food shortages and lack of clothing caused by limited hunts and a trade cutoff in war. Worse was to come. Amherst was determined to compel the Cherokees to bow to British power after the fall of Fort Loudoun and the lethal assault on those who had surrendered. By June 1761, James Grant, now a lieutenant colonel, led another British invasion of Cherokee country, which proved more terrible than the first. Grant's force wrought destruction once it penetrated to the Middle Towns. The British record speaks of numbers—fifteen towns set aflame and their bountiful cornfields burned and destroyed.[12] The question arose whether Cherokees could bring any strength to negotiation after the catastrophe, especially when they could not count on Creek support in war, as many of them expected.

A Creek-Cherokee Alliance?

In the summer of 1759, rumors passed from Indian country to British officers that the Upper Creeks, encouraged by the French, were in league with Cherokee militants. Edmund Atkin, royal superintendent of Indian Affairs, probed for answers in a conference with Billy Germany, head warrior of Okfuskee. A "half Breed" by Atkin's reckoning, Billy was one of a newly emerging group of Muscogee headmen born of British traders and Native women. Interestingly, he was uncomfortable speaking English. His father, James Germany, served as his interpreter with Atkin. Billy disclosed that two Cherokee men had passed a war talk to the Creeks of Coweta: "That now the Red People were all at Peace. . . . And they desired they would continue so, and forget all past Grudges; & join together as one, & go against the English." The Cherokee men signaled their bellicose spirit by a war belt, which they first received from pro-French Indians and then shared with the Mortar and other Creeks as far south as Coweta. The belt had the arresting image of three headless men daubed with blood-red splotches. Cherokee militants thereby bid for widespread Native support in their own struggle with the British. Significantly, their venture arose at a time of rising tensions and violence but before the onset of major hostilities provoked

262   *Cherokees, Native Peoples, and Empires, 1730–1762*

by Lyttleton's hostage-taking. Cherokee militancy was still limited in extent, and the Creeks were not of a single mind on the Mortar's scheming. Billy Germany's revelations to Atkin show that the Muscogees and allied groups feared the loss of English trade should their people go to war with South Carolina and Georgia.[13]

To Atkin, the Mortar's pro-French maneuvers were an immediate threat to the British southern colonies. Creek alienation from the English could easily spread to other Native peoples, especially when Carolina's relations with the Cherokees moved toward the brink. Atkin's approach was Machiavellian, subtly fanning doubts about the Mortar in Creek country while relying on conferences with headmen to convey a message of English strength and French perfidy. In September 1759, the superintendent imagined he was on the verge of triumph at a gathering with Creek leaders at Tuckabatchee. But he badly misjudged the situation. His anti-French harangue infuriated one head warrior who interrupted the proceedings by striking Atkin on the head with a pipe hatchet, wounding but not killing the superintendent, who, rather astonishingly, continued his talk the next day.[14]

For all his eccentricity and maladroitness, Atkin had insight into Native fears and desires. The superintendent scorned "Charles Town Politicians" as "Seaside Theorists" who believed that boasting of British military success in the Ohio country and Canada would impress the Creeks and deepen their dependence. Atkin found that the Muscogees took such war news "with profound Silence." He then elaborated: "They [the Creeks] have an Opinion, that sooner or later they shall lose their Freedom, & become Subject to one of the European Powers. And they would keep that Day as far off as possible. Wherefore the greater our Success is, the more they are inclined in their Hearts to assist & prop up the tottering French; not so much out of Compassion or real Love to them, as out of a True Regard to themselves, & their own Independency."[15]

The British bargaining position in Creek country received a boost once Colonel Montgomery's troops docked at Charles Town on April 1, 1760, and prepared to invade Cherokee territory. A few weeks later, Governor Henry Ellis of Georgia enthusiastically informed William Pitt of a small Creek war party that had just arrived in Savannah with three Cherokee scalps. The visitors sang of their triumph to the salute of cannon fire. Ellis praised the Creeks before his provincial council, observing that their warriors were "the first of their Nation who had spilt Cherokee Blood" in the conflict. While pleased

Carnage and Peace Diplomacy

263

by the governor's gifts of silver gorgets and bracelets, the Creek visitors put off his suggestion that they undertake another mission. Ellis haughtily concluded that gaining Creek assistance against the Cherokees was of great importance, but that "nothing is to be effected with the Savages without distributing considerable presents." Although the governor reckoned that £5,000 expended for that purpose might save "ten times that Sum," the imperial government did not move on his recommendation as it gave priority to consolidating British control of Canada, Fort Pitt and the Great Lakes.[16]

As matters unfolded, the English gained few Creek recruits in 1760 despite the inducement of scalp bounties. Ellis was rightly worried about the Upper Creeks, especially the Abeikas, whose towns stood north of the French Alabama fort. The Mortar continued to hover, moving freely between the French garrison and his camp near Cherokee country. A Cherokee war party, joined by the Mortar's brother, brought two English prisoners and several white scalps through Abeika territory to the Alabama fort in the early spring of 1760.[17] That May, a terrible outburst occurred when young Abeika warriors killed five Anglo traders, six of their white assistants, and one Black man, a slave to a storekeeper. The murders stoked a flight of colonial traffickers from Creek country. What ignited the violence is not entirely clear. Muscogee anger with traders overpricing was a combustible element. The assailants' outburst was a display of manhood, a sign of discontent with cautious elders and of apparent empathy for beset Cherokees.[18]

While the Mortar was not directly involved in the killings, his fiery anti-English talk inflamed young admirers. The Mortar likened whites to "fowls . . . crawling about" that were ready for the knife or hatchet. He boasted that "Cherokee women knocked the white people down with junks [or trifles]." By his telling, Montgomery's army had been defeated, and "even the old Cherokee women with their corn pestles, knocked many of the soldiers on the head as they stooped to cool their mouths with water out of the runs." Mortar's talk was a visionary war cry. It made the rounds even before British troops clashed with the Cherokees at Etchoe and then withdrew to the south. And the talk was widely believed. Prior to Montgomery's march into the Middle Towns, Attakullakulla told Paul Demere that the Creeks had sent a painted hatchet into Cherokee country as a token of their readiness to fight the English, too.[19]

The war message was overstated. Unlike the Mortar, most Upper Creek leaders strived to defuse tensions after the deadly rampage in their towns. The Gun Merchant of Okchai took the lead for headmen who were interested in reaching an accord to reduce the price of English wares. After the slaying of Anglo traders, Gun Merchant sent a conciliatory message to Governor Ellis in which he attributed the bloodshed to "a few young Fellows" who had acted without consulting "the Headmen of the Nation." This explanation was a diplomatic half-truth, downplaying the degree of animus toward the English. Ellis asked the Abeikas to put the killers to death but backed off when realizing that the Creeks would not yield. Okfuskee, the heart of the uprising, did its part to restore peaceable English relations. That summer, Handsome Fellow, the town's militant leader, brought in a Cherokee scalp to Augusta to make amends for his past conduct.[20] Creek-English bonds were on the mend when Cherokee war fury reached a fever pitch during the summer of 1760. Many Cherokee fighters believed they would gain widespread Muscogee support in their struggle against the British; they were to be bitterly disappointed. However much he tried, the Mortar could not carry the day.[21]

Cane Creek and Its Aftermath

Captain John Stuart was in the thick of the killing field by Cane Creek when Cherokee warriors took their revenge on surrendered British soldiers in retreat on August 10, 1760. Caught by a surprise attack at daybreak, he told his men to stand their ground with their muskets and pistols, which they still held as part of the surrender terms. Soldiers were thrown into confusion as they saw warriors creeping in the tall grass, shouting the "war-whoop," and running at them at full pace. Stuart witnessed horrors even if he could not know how many Britons and colonials were struck down by gunshot, arrow, club, and tomahawk. There was a bevy of soldiers taken prisoner as he was. Nearly all women and children in the British camp fell captive too. British soldiers knew quite well the likely fate of male captives in Native hands. The prisoners' lives were not their own. The Cherokees took some of their captives, including Stuart, to Fort Loudoun. A great many others, if surviving their initial ordeal, were brought to Native villages.[22]

We do not know why warrior Onatoy took Stuart prisoner at Cane Creek rather than killing him. The captor certainly had cause for blood revenge. He was brother to Round O, the headman whose two sons were imprisoned at Fort Prince George and who himself died of

Carnage and Peace Diplomacy   265

smallpox during the hostage crisis. Onatoy perhaps desired honor for bringing off an officer and becoming his master. But this is speculation. Cherokees in Overhill country were familiar with Stuart, whom they nicknamed "Bushyhead" for his thick reddish hair. A native Scotsman, he had emigrated to South Carolina at age nineteen in 1737 and had become a merchant before gaining a captain's commission in South Carolina provincial forces in 1756.[23]

Stuart credited his life to Attakullakulla, "who generously offered all he had in the world to preserve his Friend." The captain had cause to be grateful. Attakullakulla opposed Cherokee militancy and took no part in the attack on Cane Creek. Soon after the battle, Attakullakulla purchased Stuart from Onatoy but did not yet dare carry the captain to safety. Oconostota had his own plans for Stuart. Within a few weeks, the Great Warrior summoned the captain to Chota and demanded his service for a Cherokee advance on Fort Prince George. Stuart was to be a gunner in charge of captured British cannon hauled south to blast the garrison. Desperate to escape, he passed word to Attakullakulla, who quickly determined on rescue. Under the pretense of hunting, Attakullakulla shepherded Stuart, his servant, an escaped soldier, and an elderly white man far east of Chota in early September 1760. Little Carpenter was assisted along the route by his brother and wife, at least two other Cherokee women, and eventually three warriors. Trader William Shorey joined the trek for his own safety and served as interpreter. After a six-day journey of 130 miles, the group reached the Holston River, where they encountered Major Andrew Lewis of the Virginia militia. Lewis accompanied Attakullakulla, Stuart, and friends over the next week to Colonel William Byrd's camp 120 miles to the northeast. Ironically, Byrd was the same officer who felt little but contempt for Attakullakulla when the latter failed to raise a large body of Cherokee men for the British Ohio campaign of 1758.[24]

Oconostota and Ostenaco weighed matters carefully after Fort Loudoun's fall and the Cane Creek assault. Along with priest-chief Standing Turkey (Kanagatucko), they had approved of the attack on the defeated British soldiers. Oconostota did not himself participate in the killings, but he was in the vicinity. Ostenaco's role is shrouded in myth. In late October 1760, two months after the assault, a report circulated that Ostenaco had saved British lives during the slaughter by going "round the field, ordering and calling the Indians to desist" and thereby "prevent the massacre from becoming almost general." The story may seem apocryphal since it spread after Cherokee leaders made peace overtures and wished to allay English anger. One cannot be so sure, however. Cherokee warriors were in a position to kill a great many more British soldiers than were finally cut down, scalped, and mangled at Cane Creek. Perhaps there was some advice given by Ostenaco, himself a decent man, that the killings be limited so that the chance for peace would not be foreclosed. Ostenaco's apparent call for restraint was corroborated by an English trader who claimed to have spoken to John Stuart about what had transpired at Cane Creek. We should recall that Ostenaco was stoutly pro-English at the onset of the French and Indian War; it took Lyttelton's betrayal and the hostage crisis to push him to militancy.[25]

Cherokees differed among themselves on the value of negotiating peace with the English after Cane Creek. Much blood had been shed, and there was little reason for Cherokees to consider that hostilities would soon cease. Oconostota, with the support of priest-chief Standing Turkey, was contemplating a strike on Fort Prince George. As previously stated, both Cherokee leaders wished to enlist John Stuart, then still a captive, to be one of the white men manning the cannon for the assault. The plan was shelved not simply by Stuart's escape but also by the sheer difficulty of hauling cannon from Forth Loudoun far southward over steep terrain. The Cherokees were not sure how to proceed on the war front. Consultation was necessary before any major offensive was launched. In Charles Town, Lieutenant Governor Bull meanwhile stewed over Colonel Montgomery's pending departure for New York when news came of Fort Loudoun's fall and the resulting massacre. Distraught at recent events, Bull decided on a conciliatory message to the Cherokees, proposing peace talks at Charles Town and a possible prisoner exchange. This was an attempt at cooling the temperature and playing for time to strengthen provincial defense, request Virginia's support, and, most important, plead with His Majesty's government to raise another imperial invasion force.[26]

Oconostota and Ostenaco, the two most prestigious warrior-diplomats in Overhill country, responded warily to Bull's proposal. Consulting numerous headmen and towns, they sent a written talk to Charles Town via a white courier, Charles McLemore, an unlicensed trader scarcely trusted by colonial authorities. To assure the message's delivery, Corn Tassel of Toqua and the Wolf of Keowee accompanied McLemore to South Carolina's capital. Both Oconostota and Ostenaco favored a halt to hostilities but rejected talks in Charles Town—a place not to be trusted.[27] While leading headmen spoke for their people, individual

Carnage and Peace Diplomacy

Cherokees and particular communities advanced negotiations in their own manner. Prior to the Cane Creek killings, Rachel Hatton and John Downing, both of Cherokee-Anglo heritage, passed word to Fort Prince George of Native villages willing to talk peace provided that the English restore trade and pledge not to destroy the corn crop "now standing." Hatton and Downing spoke for Cherokees of the Lower and Middle Towns that had either experienced invasion or feared being similarly victimized. Rachel Hatton was likely the daughter of English trader William Hatton's Cherokee mistress or wife. She carried on the work of cross-cultural amity that her mother's generation had once pursued.[28]

Communication across ethnic lines in wartime passed through a fog of rumor and speculation. According to one report, both Oconostota and Ostenaco addressed a meeting at Middle Town Nequassee attended by no less than 2,000 Cherokees—including 1,400 warriors—about three weeks after the surrender of Fort Loudoun. A gathering on this scale implies considerable consultation between regions and the participation of women as well as men. Oconostota and other headmen weighed a letter just received from Colonel William Byrd, stationed at his militia camp on the northeastern margins of Cherokee country about twenty miles from the Great Kanawha River. Byrd's missive offered the prospect of negotiation with the threat of invasion unless the Cherokees immediately halted violence and released English prisoners. The Virginian's postscript was a blustery ultimatum: "If you refuse my offer now, my Guns shall talk of War, not Peace."[29]

While Oconostota expressed his desire for peace, he proceeded cautiously. Venturing near Keowee on October 1, he declined Ensign Miln's invitation to visit him in Fort Prince George, where he feared being imprisoned in the same place that his brethren had suffered and died. He instead sent a courteous talk, explaining that he was headed on a peace mission to Estatoe, where he intended to persuade the Seed, a militant warrior of Settico, to bury the hatchet as others had done. Oconostota saw little good in a negotiation with Bull in Charles Town. His last visit to the city for talks with Lyttelton had been a nightmare. Besides, he needed to return to Chota to pay heed to Byrd's Virginians. Ostenaco's brief written talk informed Charles Town of what his people expected for making peace—the resumption of English supply and trade, which South Carolina's government was unwilling to approve until the Cherokees' release of prisoners and a formal treaty-making process in Charles Town. Ostenaco, as wary as Oconostota of

268   *Cherokees, Native Peoples, and Empires, 1730–1762*

going to the city, hoped that the lieutenant governor would "send some of his warriors nigher hand to talk."[30]

Cherokee peace gestures continued in piecemeal fashion as individuals and localities weighed their interests. On September 25, 1760, "old Cesar" of Chatuga delivered two captive British soldiers to Fort Prince George. A Middle Town headman had already brought in an English soldier who paid a £60 ransom for his freedom. A trickle of captives was released outside any overarching Cherokee policy. Unlike Oconostota, Attakullakulla worked to free as many British soldiers as possible. In early November, he was joined by over thirty Cherokee men, who delivered ten British soldiers to Byrd's camp and returned with an ample store of presents. Individual Cherokees and their kin benefited, though peace was not at hand; Indian prisoners were still in British confinement.[31]

Cherokee women once more assumed their own way of peacemaking, sharing intelligence with British officers about Native militants and their French supporters who threatened an expanding conflict. In November 1760, Ensign Miln identified one prominent female informant as "Nancy," quite possibly Nancy Butler, the same woman who passed intelligence to the British four years earlier on Tellico's flirtation with the French. Her specialty was gleaning information from other women on events beyond her purview. Based on these conversations, she reported on French agent Lantagnac's current stay in Overhill country. Some Cherokees did business with Fort Prince George simply to help their families. On November 17, Miln gladly received bear meat and a little corn from "several [Indian] wenches." That evening, "half-breed Tom" arrived with "two sides of a steer" for the garrison's use. On the twenty-fifth, a Hiwassee man came with two or three women to deliver corn.[32]

Lantagnac sustained French influence in Cherokee country through the flow of goods and arms from Fort Massiac, an outpost by the confluence of the Ohio and Tennessee. His most ardent Cherokee ally was Seroweh, the Young Warrior of Estatoe, who came north to visit his friend and vow loyalty. Lantagnac greeted Seroweh with a fiery gesture, driving a red-stained hatchet into a log and calling on any warrior to take up the weapon for the French. Seroweh pulled out the hatchet and, joined by others, danced for continued war against the English. When Seroweh returned south, he hosted a band of Creek fighters and kept a close watch on Fort Prince George. The Young Warrior's maneuvers did not go unnoticed. At least three Cherokee women spied

Carnage and Peace Diplomacy

on him and reported back to Miln. One of the female informants was captured by Seroweh's comrades, though she easily escaped her drowsy guards when the latter slumbered at night. She was fortunate. Seroweh had threatened to whip her and cut off her hair. Intelligence gathering was an intricate affair at this level. The female spy was mistress of Anglo trader James Welsh; she had a son by him who Seroweh considered to be part of his family. In brief, the Young Warrior found it difficult to discipline a Cherokee woman within his own social circle.[33]

Small-scale diplomacy and espionage were constant, while bigger players weighed broad policy moves. In this last arena, Oconostota chose a radically different path than Attakullakulla's peace track. Returning to Chota in October 1760 from Fort Prince George's outskirts, the Great Warrior again considered negotiation with Colonel Byrd but passed on the Virginian's overture, which held out a stark choice between Cherokee submission or else continued war. Byrd said he would "not leave one Indian alive, one town standing, one grain of corn" untouched if the Cherokees harmed any of their white prisoners. The colonel expounded on English supremacy and France's defeat from the Ohio to Canada. Cherokees should ask themselves of their people's fate once the French were driven from the south: "Then what will become of you? Who will supply you with goods to keep yourselves and your families warm? Who will let you have ammunition to kill deer; or knives, or salt, or any necessaries of life?" Byrd believed his logic unassailable but he proved to be wrong. Oconostota would not come to the Virginian's camp to bow. There was still no truce even if Attakullakulla probably gave Byrd the impression that one was in the offing.[34]

Oconostota was not rash. He refused to pick up Lantagnac's red hatchet at Chota when Seroweh did so. While not giving away his hand, Oconostota decided to test a French option. Perhaps Lantagnac and friends could supply more gunpowder and other necessities. We do not know Oconostota's exact course in November 1760; he probably made his way via the Tennessee and Ohio to the Mississippi and New Orleans. That winter, Governor Kerlérec of Louisiana was visited by an unnamed Cherokee chief, whom he called "the great chief of that nation." Oconostota was the distinguished guest. Reports reached Charles Town in early February 1761 that Oconostota had recently returned to Chota with goods and ammunition from French territory. The Great Warrior, meanwhile, kept up his Creek contacts. Oconostota was said to have declared: "What nation or what people am I afraid of? I do not regard all the forces the great King George can send against me

270   *Cherokees, Native Peoples, and Empires, 1730–1762*

among those mountains." This pronouncement, like so much evidence from Indian country, comes to us secondhand. The Great Warrior's meaning is clear, whatever his precise words. He was not about to make peace with the English until trust was restored. Oconostota went to the French out of desperate need, not fondness. He had led sorties against the French about the lower Ohio just a few years before but accepted Kerlérec's commission as "great medal Chief" in February 1761 when necessity beckoned.[35]

Writing to Paris, Kerlérec took credit for timely wartime aid to the Cherokees. Besides providing material assistance for the siege of Fort Loudoun, his government encouraged Alabama and Lower Creek chiefs to spur the Cherokees to action. French Louisiana's economic weakness, however, compromised any sustained aid to the Cherokees. Politics intruded as well. In March 1761, Kerlérec reported that Cherokee leaders had asked him to provide gunners to operate the cannon

Commission Granted by Louis de Kelérec, Governor of Louisiana to Oconostota (Okana-Stoté), February 2, 1761. *National Archives at College Park.*

Carnage and Peace Diplomacy   271

and mortars taken at Fort Loudoun. The governor deferred any commitment, explaining to Paris that caution was warranted when Franco-British peace talks were ongoing in Europe. French Louisiana would not take undue risks for the sake of the Cherokees. Kerlérec had his hands full with restive Choctaw and Alabama allies that France lacked the capacity to supply during the war with Britain.[36]

Oconostota and Attakullakulla

In all likelihood, Oconostota turned to the French partly to distance himself from Attakullakulla, who fashioned provisional peace terms with Byrd in September 1760. The document spelled out a prisoner exchange, the cessation of hostilities, and the return of Fort Loudoun to the English. A key stipulation required the Cherokees to surrender "Such Offenders" as Byrd demanded by the full moon in October. Writing to London, Lieutenant Governor Bull doubted that Byrd's punitive terms would do much good, especially because the Virginian's frontier militia was already scheduled to disband. As the lieutenant governor saw things, provincial weakness was likely to inflame Cherokee resistance and stir the Creeks to join in war against the English.[37]

Byrd's treaty terms envisioned a revolution in Cherokee politics—a peace in which the English appointed Attakullakulla as "Governor" of the Cherokees. Bull concurred on this important issue. As publicized in Charles Town, Little Carpenter's position was raised to grand heights: "That Attakull-Kulla shall be declared and acknowledged Emperor and head of the whole Cherokee nation." As in the months before Connecorte's death, Attakullakulla clearly desired an exceptional English honor, with attendant power. The questions arise: How did he understand English terms such as "governor" and "emperor"? Did he aspire to rule or rather to assure his place as top Cherokee negotiator with the English? The second explanation appears the more plausible. Attakullakulla was too intelligent to believe that he could wield the same power as an English provincial governor, let alone a king, among his people. To exercise authority in that way was wholly contrary to Cherokee political tradition. True, Charles Town and Williamsburg had acknowledged previous Cherokee "emperors" such as Connecorte and Moytoy of Tellico, but these men did not owe their authority to any colonial designation. Their prestige came from within Cherokee society. Attakullakulla's aspirations appear inseparable from his belief that he was uniquely qualified to bring peace and to save his people from ruin. In fact, Byrd wrote that Attakullakulla wanted Bull to call him "King of the Cherokees, and give him a Fire Crown as he Calls it, on his bringing about a peace to our Satisfaction."[38]

One doubts that Attakullakulla shared his desire for English appointment as "emperor" with Oconostota. Chota had not yielded to peace entreaties and still welcomed Lantagnac. In December 1760, Attakullakulla considered killing Lantagnac and companions but was warned by Chota men that they would put to death English prisoners if the French were harmed. This standoff reveals a serious divide in Overhill country. Attakullakulla backed off, scoffing at the few presents that Lantagnac brought his Cherokee supporters.[39]

Cherokee society was sustained by a broad respect for personal autonomy and an aversion to internal strife. Attakullakulla and Oconostota were at political odds during the crisis but managed to keep their differences in bounds. This fact is remarkable considering Attakullakulla's pro-English leanings as opposed to Oconostota's war leadership and willingness to consider a French alliance. If Attakullakulla had openly thrust himself forward as emperor of fellow Cherokees, he might have pushed communal tolerance to the breaking point. He was smart enough to play his hand carefully and not to overreach.

Oconostota's loss of trust in English South Carolina was glaring. In October 1760, he demurred on Lieutenant Governor Bull's offer to bring British captives to Ninety-Six for a general prisoner exchange. The Great Warrior had other priorities, namely shoring up his position at Chota and testing a French option. There was another factor at work. British captives were owned by individual Cherokees who had captured them or acquired them by purchase or transfer. They were not in Oconostota's gift. The Great Warrior was keenly attuned to communal opinion.[40]

A Second British Invasion

Attakullakulla's bid to end hostilities had little chance in the fall of 1760. Wiliam Bull put out peace feelers but did not see the war ending soon. While eager for Virginia's military assistance, the lieutenant governor was convinced that only imperial troops could compel Cher-

Carnage and Peace Diplomacy

okee submission. He was elated to receive news in mid-October that British forces had achieved the surrender of French Canada. At last, he could make his adulatory plea to Major-General Amherst, the conquering hero. Bull hoped that Amherst would combine operations against the Cherokees with the seizure of Mobile or New Orleans, but the general could not oblige on that massive scale. Stationed in New York City by late November, Amherst decided to send 1,200 troops to Charles Town under the command of Colonel James Grant, a veteran of the prior Cherokee campaign in June 1760. In Amherst's view it was crucial that British superiority be shown as an example to all Indians. The slaughter of the king's troops after Fort Loudoun's surrender could not go unpunished. Despite the hazards of mountainous Cherokee country, Amherst believed that British troops could prevail by "destroying" Indian "Towns & Settlements . . . the loss of which must of necessity make them fly to us and reduce them to that Dependance, which and only which, can secure Tranquility & a lasting peace to the Province."[41]

Lieutenant Colonel Grant, whose troops put into Charles Town in January 1761, has been portrayed as something of a peacenik by historians, and not without cause. He expressed sympathy for Cherokees while serving as the right-hand man to Montgomery during the previous year's offensive. Once arriving in South Carolina as the top-ranking commander, he gave little credence to colonial talk of recent Cherokee "Cruelties & Barbarity's." Expanding on this theme to Amherst, he believed that in such matters, "there are Faults on both sides, & if both Parties were heard I fancy the Indians have been the worst used." Grant was very close to the mark in one judgment: "I believe that the greatest part of them [the Cherokees] are sorry for what has been done & would be glad to make Peace, if they knew how to bring it about." As John Oliphant has persuasively written, the Cherokee desire for "a reasonably dignified peace" was an overwhelming preference.[42]

The political obstacles to such a settlement were formidable. South Carolina's government expected Grant's army to strike a blow so that the Cherokees would be thoroughly cowed. Grant was himself under Amherst's orders to defer in peace negotiations to southern provincial governors. Moreover, Amherst did not buy Grant's assessment that the Cherokees wished to make amends. If Indians "now feign a repentance," he wrote, it was only because they feared "Chastisement," which the general believed necessary for the safety of His Majesty's "Southern American Colonies." In January 1761, Amherst formulated a two-tiered assault. South Carolina's militia would aid Grant's northward advance into the Lower Cherokee towns, while Virginia and North Carolina troops would head west to strike at Overhill country. Within two months, it became obvious that Virginia lacked the military strength and political will to perform this role, leaving Grant's regulars with the burden of carrying the offensive without aid from the north.[43]

Could the Cherokees satisfy colonial demands before their towns felt the brunt of British regulars? There was little Cherokee hesitancy on the delivery of British and colonial prisoners, which gathered speed in April 1761, aided by the South Carolina assembly's payment to Natives for the delivery of captives to Fort Prince George. At the time, sixty-seven captives were recently admitted into the fort, and another twenty-five soon expected. Bull estimated that the Cherokees still held about a hundred prisoners. Attakullakulla was hopeful. In early March, he gladly accepted Bull's request to come to Fort Prince George for talks with Captain Lachlan Mackintosh, who now commanded there instead of Ensign Miln. Cherokees took Mackintosh's appointment as a favorable sign since they respected him and loathed Miln. Bull regarded the talks as a holding action, a stratagem to feel out Cherokee opinion and, above all, to quicken the release of Britons before Grant's campaign was underway.[44]

Attakullakulla spoke for Tistoe, Ostenaco, and other headmen who strongly favored a peace based on reciprocity. His transcribed talk, dispatched to Charles Town, was a vintage Cherokee peace entreaty, calling for a mutual forgetting and reminding Bull that the Cherokees had suffered losses as well as dealt blows. It was the young warriors, Attakullakulla declared, that had "begun this War that knew nothing of the Danger & were fools." Handing a string of white wampum to Mackintosh, he appealed for all to remember "our Great Father, the King over the Great Waters" who "has heard of our being in Darkness, & no doubt, will be pleased to See us all in the Light Again." Knowing that Bull was a native of South Carolina, Attakullakulla believed him "a good Man, for he was born on the same Land with ourselves." While Cherokees still held English captives, they had released a good number without yet receiving a single Native prisoner in return. The Cherokees, in want and "Naked," longed that traders "may be let to come Among us." The strength of Cherokee peace sentiment is evident in the large retinue that accompanied Attakullakulla to Fort Prince George. At the Cherokee camp, there were five hundred warriors,

Carnage and Peace Diplomacy

headmen, and women. The Cherokee leader asked for clothing for the group and received a good amount. Mackintosh distributed the items with the help of Attakullakulla's female companion. Women looked after communal needs.[45]

Bull thanked Attakullakulla by letter, showing a hint of mercy. Tistoe and his people would not be molested once they resettled by Keowee. There could be no peace, however, until Cherokees entirely ceased hostilities. Bull urged Cherokees "who are for peace" to "separate from those who are still mad for War." This was the type of demand that Cherokees could scarcely contemplate. Persuasion, not coercion, was the Native way of reaching a common understanding among themselves. At Attakullakulla's urging, Seroweh reconsidered his prowar stance. In April 1761, he sent his own peace talk to Fort Prince George. He recalled his sadness while standing by the Keowee River, knowing that it was not safe for him, a notorious manslayer, to join Attakullakulla and friends as they crossed the stream and entered the fort to speak to "my Brother" Mackintosh. Seroweh disputed his reputation as a great "Rogue" even if "white and red People" blamed him for all wrongdoing. He wanted it known that Middle Town Cherokees, not his war band, had recently taken two white scalps. Seroweh did not deny responsibility for war: "'Tis true I was the beginning of the Mischief, but it was owing to bad talks, and ill usage my People and I got several times at the Fort before we began, which made my Young people mad."[46] This was a Cherokee talk, like so many others, interpreted in colloquial English and still resonant with a Native voice and sensibility.

Neither Attakullakulla nor Grant finally had the capacity to forestall a British march into Cherokee country. In a message of May 22, Attakullakulla pleaded with the colonel to be merciful, just as he hoped the Great King would be, "and not have our whole Nation destroyed." He admitted the presence of "a great many Rogues" in his nation and even hoped that some of them would be put to death and the English satisfied on that score. That outcome was not in Attakullakulla's power to dictate, however. He knew that "some of the red People," namely Cherokee fighters, were determined to "disturb" and contest Grant's march. As active as ever when emergency loomed, Attakullakulla journeyed back and forth between Overhill country and Fort Prince George, where he had a cordial meeting with Grant, but to little effect.[47]

Grant somehow believed that peace could be reached with minimal bloodshed. He advised Attakullakulla, whom he sincerely respected, that Cherokees would not be harmed if they took shelter in their homes and did not resist his army. If found in the woods or mountains, however, they would be treated as enemies. In Grant's imagined route to peace, Cherokees would submit to British authority once his troops entered their towns. In the next step, compliant Indians would put "some" of their most notoriously guilty to death within the English camp. For all his goodwill toward Indians, Grant could not escape Amherst's orders to exact punishment and to respect Bull's prerogative in negotiations. While the colonel would have his say on the diplomatic front, his moderating influence was most keenly felt in the wake of his military offensive. Bull's draft "peace" plan, still unknown to Indians, would compel Cherokees to identify and kill two notorious militants in each of four regions before any halt to the war. If the killings were done outside British view, the scalps of the executed were to be shown to the English as proof.[48]

Grant's sense of decency and duty were at odds. He badly wanted Bull to offer less punitive terms and to discard any attempt at South Carolina's territorial aggrandizement at Cherokee expense. He still told Attakullakulla that the Cherokees "must give strong Proofs of their Repentance" to show "that their hearts are good." As a necessary first step, they should immediately release all British prisoners, formerly of Fort Loudoun, whom Grant believed were attacked and captured "in a treacherous manner" by Cherokees at the Cane Creek killing site. Grant keenly felt the loss of slain army comrades and a need to vindicate their sacrifice. The colonel would give a hearing to Oconostota only if the latter came to him together with Attakullakulla. In that case, both men "must keep [to] the Path, carry a white Flag, & call out Amherst" as a password. This bizarre formula had no chance of winning Oconostota's consent.[49]

Grant's army dwarfed Montgomery's force of the previous year. Setting out from Fort Prince George on June 7, 1761, the colonel had 2,600 men under his command—1,400 British soldiers, 1,000 provincials, and two other notable elements—eighty-one Blacks, most of whom were enslaved laborers, and fifty-seven Native warriors, mainly Eastern Chickasaws and Catawbas, along with Mohawks and New England Algonquian men who had come to Charles Town on British transports. The Native contingents nursed old enmities toward Cherokees and had a keen desire for war spoils.[50]

From a purely tactical view, Montgomery and Grant puzzled over the Cherokee response to their successive invasions. Why did the Cherokees not mass warriors along mountainous defiles and passes to

Carnage and Peace Diplomacy

stop the British advance before soldiers progressed far on the march? Reviewing his campaign, Montgomery remarked: "So difficult and Strong Country I never saw; Passes innumerable, which would make the march of a body of Troops almost impracticable, if the People who are in possession of the Country had the Spirit to Defend it; I am convinced two hundred men properly Conducted might make the passage of two Thousand a very difficult matter." Grant's comments were similar a year later, when his army negotiated steep heights and precipitous descents on scant trails, forcing men to clamber in "an Indian file," one at a time through narrow passes along cliffsides. In the aftermath of the campaign, Grant wrote Amherst with great relief: "We have been lucky . . . the Country We have been in, is Impenetrable, if it was Defended by a very few Men of any Degree of Spirit, they might Kill & Wound a Number of Men Every day, without running the smallest Risk, and it would be next to Impossible to Guard such a Line of Packhorses, if the Inhabitants deserved the name of an Enemy." Grant confronted the greatest risk when Cherokee warriors deliberately assaulted his army's rear convoy in the campaign's single battle.[51]

It was not for want of courage that Cherokees chose when and where to fight. Their way of war reflected intense local loyalties and the absence of central command over a unified force. The Overhill Towns, which boasted a reputation for having the nation's best fighters, would not send warriors to defend the Lower Towns against Montgomery's army in 1760 any more than make a stand there against Creek invasion eight years before. Cherokees waged their strongest resistance to the British in 1760 and 1761 just below Etchoe, the southernmost Middle Town rather than confront the enemy in the mountainous country below. We do not know the precise number of warriors involved in these sharp engagements. If there were truly above six hundred warriors as estimated against Montgomery's relatively small army, it may seem puzzling why the Cherokees did not halt the British well before Etchoe. In all likelihood, the Cherokees needed time to consult across regions and to prepare for an auspicious and opportune time to strike the enemy, whose path was certainly tracked on its three-week march from the Lower Towns to the major battle site. A year later, the Cherokee capacity to attack Grant's powerful force was much reduced by privation, war weariness, and shortages of gunpowder.[52]

The Cherokee approach to war was radically different from that of the professional British army. As much as Cherokees loved their villages and life-sustaining crops, they chose to withdraw with their women and children rather than contest every inch of ground when threatened with a catastrophic death toll. They had an enormous, though not inexhaustible, ability to endure hardship and to rebuild when they needed to do so. A few old Cherokees men and women did not flee. They remained in villages and were killed by Catawbas, Mohawks, and other Native fighters. Chickasaws, too, joined the fight and earned Grant's respect as reliable allies.[53]

The British under Grant's command went about destroying abandoned Cherokee towns. Desolation reigned where there had been vital life. At Nequassee, where the Long Warrior of Tanasee once addressed a large parley, only the village townhouse stood as an army hospital after troops had done their dirty work. As Grant himself recorded, his soldiers were sent in groups "to burn the scattered Houses & to pull up Beans, Pease, & Corn, & demolish every Eatable thing in the Country." The Tuckasegee towns met the same fate as the Middle Towns by the Little Tennessee River. Kituwah, the cherished Cherokee mother town, was among fifteen ravaged communities. As measured by numbers, hardly in themselves expressive of the scale of human suffering, the British force burned and tore down 800 Cherokee dwellings, eviscerated 1,500 acres of corn and other crops, and compelled as many as 5,000 persons to seek refuge with sister communities to the north and west.[54]

Grant did not test the Overhills in their own country but regathered troops in the Middle Towns before heading south to Fort Prince George. For all that was destroyed by the army, some South Carolinians were upset with the colonel for not laying waste the Hiwassee Valley communities and killing a greater number of Cherokees. Provincial officers bristled at the colonel's manner of command and apparent put-downs of colonists. Before Grant departed Charles Town in December 1761, he fought a duel with Thomas Middleton, scion of a wealthy planter family, who had fumed while in army service. Fortunately for Middleton, who missed his shot, Grant seems to have purposefully fired above his opponent's head. Both men emerged physically unscathed but with raw feelings. The clashing perspectives of empire and colony were in full view.[55]

Negotiation on Several Fronts

Peace negotiations were a complex affair in the aftermath of Grant's offensive. On the imperial-colonial side, Grant and Bull gradually moved toward common ground despite testy, at times even icy, per-

Carnage and Peace Diplomacy

sonal relations. Virginia entered the diplomatic scene, too, during the late summer and fall of 1761. Attakullakulla, the most active Cherokee peace negotiator, was beset by difficulties—and none greater than that of representing a divided people. South Carolina made his task all the harder by insisting that the Cherokees surrender a number of men who were culpable of killing white colonials. This demand, a carryover of Lyttelton's policy, was aimed at compelling Cherokees to assume the burden of war guilt and admit subordination to British authority.

In Cherokee custom, as exemplified by Attakullakulla, it was no shame to admit weakness or fault when striving for a desperately needed peace. Accompanied by supporters, Attakullakulla appealed to Grant's humanity while meeting him near Fort Prince George in August 1761. The colonel's army had burnt and destroyed, and it could continue that course unless peace came. "The white People," Attakullakulla explained, "are too many for them [the Cherokees] . . . but hopes Col. Grant will take Pity on them and spare them." Attakullakulla believed that Great Warrior Grant had a good heart. Grant would take "pity," which in Cherokee usage connoted empathy and shared feeling, not simply sorrowful condescension.[56]

Attakullakulla paid respect to Cherokee local allegiances by offering wampum strings or beads to Grant on behalf of particular warriors and towns. Gifts had a spiritual power to speak. Chota sent its wampum, declared Attakullakulla, so "that all the Warriors may hear and all things may be straight." Oconostota, while not present, was said to give beads "in token that his heart is straight, and he has no bad thoughts." Settico, a militant town, sent beads to say that its people had listened to the French, but now "their Ears were open and they would only listen to the English." Attakullakulla gave beads for "the Middle Settlements people" who had sought refuge with the Overhills. The refugees, he said, "are Dying Naked and Starving," and were thankfully pitied by the Overhills, who gave them some food. Compassion was a genuine force in Cherokee society. Attakullakulla pitied "his people when he thinks what will come of them after his death." Perhaps a mighty British commander would feel as he did. Attakullakulla told Grant that he had saved Captain Stuart and "as many of the Fort Loudoun people as he could." His visit to England long ago was in his heart. The great King George "looked on the Cherokees and the English as one people."[57] Attakullakulla's words slid past harsh realities. After all, he presumed to speak for Cherokee leaders and communities that had decidedly mixed or hostile attitudes toward the

280   *Cherokees, Native Peoples, and Empires, 1730–1762*

English. He imagined a Cherokee nation that acted in a unified spirit to restore peace. This was his hope but not yet a reality.

For all his soft and beguiling talk, Attakullakulla kept to a hard line on one critical issue. He opposed South Carolina's demand that at least several Cherokee offenders be surrendered for execution. Grant again played diplomatic mediator by advising Attakullakulla to agree to surrender four Cherokee militants rather than Bull's required eight—provided the Cherokees kill the culprits within twelve nights and bring the scalps to the British camp as proof of execution. The colonel recognized, much as Bull did, that warriors were not about to kill their own in British view. This English concession, if it may be so deemed, was of no meaning to Cherokees who could not fathom paying blood price for English satisfaction amid a devastating war. After a night of deliberation, Attakullakulla told Grant that he had "looked all about" but could not find any offending men "for they are all grown better; but if any of them grow bad again they shall be killed."[58]

Little Carpenter's answer was shrewd and effective. Perhaps he had won Grant over before their formal talks began, but the record is silent on this score. After sounding out Attakullakulla, Grant wrote a deft letter to Bull, suggesting that the lieutenant governor remove the surrender article, demanding the execution of alleged murderers, from his draft treaty. The colonel's advice finally had a positive impact in Charles Town. Bull faced political reality by persuading the hardline South Carolina assembly to drop that demand on September 17, only days before negotiations commenced with Attakullakulla and companions in Charles Town. Outstanding issues remained, but a peace settlement was in sight. On the twenty-second, Attakullakulla put his mark to treaty terms signed by Bull and sealed the next day. The accord required that headmen of four principal Cherokee regions, "the Upper, the Valley, the Middle and Lower Settlements," come to Charles Town within one month to confirm the agreement and to arrange terms for renewed trade. Bull insisted on additional Cherokee assent because he wished to ensure the delivery of the remaining white prisoners and to assure Native acquiescence in a cession of piedmont lands as stipulated by treaty.[59]

Grant's political input was sage once again. Before the treaty was put to writing, the colonel convinced Bull to discard a proposed article that would have named Attakullakulla as Cherokee "Emperor." Attuned to Cherokee ways, Grant understood that an English appointment would lower Attakullakulla's standing, "Ruin his Interest with the

Carnage and Peace Diplomacy

[Cherokee] Nation," and be of dubious worth in "a Country where there is no Coercive Power." Bull tactfully backed off the idea, telling the South Carolina assembly that he did not wish to provoke opposition by Attakullakulla's "Rivals," namely Kanagatucko and Ostenaco. Attakullakulla was disappointed that he did not gain the honor but chose not to make a public fuss about it. In Grant's view, "the Carpenter" was determined "to save his Nation from Destruction, & to become the leading Man in it."[60]

That the Cherokee deputies reached a tentative peace with South Carolina in late September 1761 did not mark war's end. For one, Bull still expected Cherokee ratification of his treaty. For another, the situation was uncertain on the Virginia front where seven hundred militiamen moved toward Cherokee country under Colonel William Byrd during the summer of 1761. After Byrd resigned his commission in August, Colonel Adam Stephen led the Virginians to the Great Island of the Holston River, 130 miles east of Chota. Overhill Cherokees suddenly faced a renewed Virginia threat when they did not yet know the outcome of Attakullakulla's bid for peace at Charles Town.[61]

In a feeling-out process, priest-chief Kanagatucko of Chota forwarded a friendly message and a peace pipe to the Virginians in September 1761. There was sorrow, not abject apology in his words: "I am very Sorry for the War that has been between us & our Elder Brother [the English]. . . . We have had a great deal of Mischief done on Both Sides, but not let it be thought on." Kanagatucko further explained that his people were building a "Strong House" where any warriors who harmed whites would be kept "until the English fetch them, & do with them as they think proper." By this clever allusion, the priest-chief aired his commitment to surrender future malefactors, even though it is highly doubtful he had a jail in mind for Chota.[62]

Stephen's reply was courteous but tough and laden with demands. Cherokees should send a principal headman with at least one white prisoner to the Virginia camp as proof of their desire for peace. The colonel asked for a written copy of any treaty that Governor Bull entered into with Attakullakulla and friends. He also wanted to meet with the priest-chief before a peace was arranged in Williamsburg. An ultimatum abruptly followed. Failing Cherokee cooperation, Stephen warned Kanagatucko that he had Amherst's orders to "do you all possible mischief." The Virginia colonel's message to Oconostota was still harsher. Unless Stephen's conditions were met, he would "proceed against your

Towns & destroy your Nation." The threat was bluff, as the Virginians lacked the strength to invade, but how could Cherokees know?[63]

The labyrinth of negotiation in the autumn of 1761 was a maze in time and space. Colonials set deadlines for treaty conferences, Indian compliance, and ratification, while Cherokees maneuvered within and around these limits. Bull expected Attakullakulla to travel to Overhill country, recruit a Cherokee delegation, and return to Charles Town in little more than one month to confirm the peace accord of September 22, 1761. The governor was anxious because he knew that Grant was determined to depart South Carolina with his troops before year's end, leaving the province with no effective military cover. Similarly, Stephen wanted Kanagatucko to hurry to his Holston River camp before winter set in and his militia disbanded. Unlike Attakullakulla's unstinting long-distance diplomacy, Kanagatucko was in no hurry to reach Stephen's camp. With an entourage of four hundred Cherokees, including women and children, he arrived at the Holston on November 17, about five weeks after receiving the colonel's threatening missive. While en route, he shrewdly sent messengers ahead, letting Stephen know that his party had to hunt for food along the way. Kanagatucko wanted the war's end, but without Cherokee submission.[64]

On November 20, the priest-chief, joined by Ostenaco and three other headmen, put their marks to a peace accord with Captain Stephen. All had received news via Attakullakulla and his couriers of Bull's preliminary treaty with the Cherokees. Overhill headmen approved Virginia's proposition to cease hostilities, with the proviso that Cherokees agree to surrender or execute their own men who would henceforth be culpable of the "murder" of whites. Negotiation was not hindered by this colonial demand put to writing. For the time being, Cherokees cared most about proceeding to peace so that they could resume the exchange of deerskins for English goods. One month after the truce was made, Cherokee headmen sent a wampum belt to Williamsburg as a mark of "Truth and Friendship," while Native women offered a gift of small white beads. Female involvement in Cherokee peacemaking was deliberate and purposeful.[65]

Oconostota was not yet persuaded of English goodwill. Though desirous of peace, he deliberately avoided treaty-making formalities with either Virginia or South Carolina. His message for Stephen and the Virginians was succinct: "I think it very troublesome the War has

Carnage and Peace Diplomacy

lasted so long, but now it is all over with us & I hope it is the same with you . . . for all of my people want peace, and you may believe this, as I am no Child, & will stand to what I now say, forever & never will forget it."[66] Frustrated that Oconostota would not come begging, Stephen answered with his threat of invasion. Oconostota chose not to reply, and negotiation went ahead without him.

Kanagatucko was himself uncertain of Virginia's motives. While accepting Stephen's treaty terms, he asked the colonel to send an officer to Chota to show English sincerity. Stephen was dubious, but he assented once Lieutenant Henry Timberlake volunteered for the mission. Accompanied by interpreter John MacCormack and a sergeant, Timberlake was befriended by the Slave-Catcher of Tanasee, who invited the Virginian to his hunting camp for a dinner of dried venison, hominy, and boiled corn. Ostenaco befriended Timberlake in his village of Tomotley and took him under his wing. While visiting Chota, the lieutenant listened as Ostenaco confirmed the peace with Virginia: "The bloody tommahawke, so long lifted against our brethren the English, must now be buried deep, deep in the ground, never to be raised again."[67]

Ostenaco's friendship with Timberlake grew under duress. An English peace did not end Cherokee troubles. Overhill Towns were beset by northern Indian raiders. After a few months, Ostenaco finally accompanied Timberlake, friends, and the released prisoners to Williamsburg. Arriving in Virginia's capital in March 1762, Ostenaco and his entourage of seventy Cherokees were welcomed by Governor Fauquier. Writing to the Board of Trade, the governor described Ostenaco as "a Man of great Influence," and more trustworthy than Attakullakulla, "tho' he has not his parts nor such Command of Words." Ostenaco took advantage of the visit by obtaining Fauquier's permission to travel to England to meet the Great King. He would do so with two other Cherokee men, accompanied by Timberlake and a colonial interpreter who unfortunately died in the passage to Britain.[68]

Granted a royal audience at St. James Palace, Ostenaco and companions conversed congenially with the young George III for an hour and a half. We cannot know precisely what was said, any more than fathom the great bellowing sound Ostenaco uttered, which Timberlake likened to a "solemn dirge," at the end of his first ocean crossing as he headed by small boat to Plymouth's harbor. Ostenaco's song and painted visage astonished the hundreds of English onlookers who mobbed the landing place. The chief had traversed the ocean's figurative depths in one moon's time to a strange new earthly realm. Once his

Cherokees, Native Peoples, and Empires, 1730–1762

mission across the great water was accomplished, he would no longer have to bear Attakullakulla's words that the latter was the only Cherokee man living who had seen the English monarch.[69]

Timberlake marveled at Cherokee headmen's ability to disagree among themselves without coming to blows. As he remarked on the rivalry between Ostenaco and Attakullakulla: "Here is a lesson to Europe; two Indian chiefs, whom we call barbarians, rivals of power, heads of two opposite factions, warm in opposing one another, as their interests continually clash; yet these have no farther animosity, no family quarrels or

Ostenaco or "Outacite, Chief of the Cherokees." Engraving, London, 1762. *National Portrait Gallery, Smithsonian Institution.*

Carnage and Peace Diplomacy

resentment." Ostenaco's own brother openly inclined toward Attakul-lakulla's camp, and without being shunned by kin. Timberlake may have rhapsodically overstated his case, but he was right on a basic point—the importance that Cherokees and many other Native American peoples attached to avoiding internecine violence.[70]

Overhill Cherokees had a preponderant, though not the only say in negotiations with British and colonial officials. Tistoe of Keowee had an imprint on the final Cherokee peace accord with South Carolina. In October 1761, he resettled with two hundred men, women, and children near his old town with Grant's encouragement. Along with headman Wolf, Tistoe sent a joyful letter to Captain Mackintosh, re-spected as an "Eldest Brother" for his decency in command. Tistoe's message, transcribed in English, is poignant for its theme of home-coming after enduring the hostage crisis and seeing Keowee aban-doned after being seized by British troops. During the war, Tistoe, who had felt "Lost" when "over the Hills," had now "come down to hunt on my own Land." His people "Danced all Night for Joy of coming home again." Tistoe's peace talk was in a similar vein to At-takullakulla's: "I am Sorry to See our Town [Keowee] Empty; but it was our own faults, & I hope all bad Talks are now over, & the white people & we shall Settle in our Towns as before."[71]

Once at home, Tistoe sent a piece of soil ["Earth"] to Bull to remind him of the Saluda River meeting of 1755 when Attakullakulla gave a pouch of soil to former Governor Glen. Tistoe's gesture had a similar meaning of living in peace if not precisely on the same ground. He was determined to preserve Lower Town hunting lands between Long Canes Creek and Tugaloo—an area that whites had thrust into prior to 1760. Tistoe declared that if his people were secure in their rights, they would share some hunting territory—what he called "the middle Ground"—with white settlers. There was a mythic quality to Tistoe's linking of past and present. He remembered when the "old people" who has visited England had said that "we [Cherokees and English] were all one people, & that [what] the one had, the other had."[72] The ideal was worthy, if sadly a far cry from reality.

Gifts mattered, as always, in negotiation. Tistoe gave a "beloved Pipe" to Mackintosh, to be passed to Colonel Grant, "the dreadful Warrior," and then sent to Bull for the taste and smell of the talk. Tistoe knew Grant to be sympathetic and needed his help. A problem loomed. The pending peace accord included a large cession of Lower Chero-kee hunting grounds to South Carolina. Grant himself, believing the

286   *Cherokees, Native Peoples, and Empires, 1730–1762*

provision unwise and likely to reignite fighting, lobbied Bull to reduce the extent of Cherokee land loss. The treaty was finally revised when Attakullakulla and other headmen finalized negotiations with Bull in December 1761. South Carolina still gained territory at Cherokee expense, but not so much as previously stipulated. Curiously, Grant was not an enemy of the Cherokees for all the destruction that his troops wrought. He saw them as a worthy people even if "Savage" in government, a word connoting "primitive" in this vein—not brutal or degraded.[73]

Grant and most of his troops had left Charles Town for New York by the time the formal peace treaty was signed on December 18. What did the provisions mean? On paper, there was a strict rule for cases in which a Cherokee killed an Englishman: "Any Indian who murders any of His Majesty's Subjects shall be immediately put to death by the Cherokees as soon as the murder and murderer are known in the Cherokee Nation and that the Head or Scalp of the Murderer be brought to the Commander of the next English Fort."[74] This was something of a face-saving gesture on South Carolina's part. In 1759, Cherokees had refused to surrender or execute accused killers. They remained unyielding through two British invasions. One-sided treaty provisions did not sit well with Native peoples. They knew that English colonials did not punish *their* malefactors for killing Indians. The issue of retributive violence only grew hotter as conflict intensified between "white people" and "the red" on Native ground during the next twenty years.

The Charles Town treaty of 1761 did not quickly resolve tensions over the exchange of war prisoners. South Carolina's insistence on an immediate delivery of colonial captives, including Blacks, was carried out in a far slower and less complete fashion than Charles Town desired. Provincial assemblymen were eager for the delivery not only of their human "chattel" but also of horses and cattle. This last demand was largely unavailing. Famished Cherokees had slaughtered and eaten cattle and resorted to horseflesh in wartime. As Attakullakulla tactfully explained, missing livestock had perished or "gone into the woods." Some white prisoners and Blacks remained in Cherokee country to hunt and serve their Indian masters during the winter of 1761. The captives were dependents in particular households, and their treatment consequently varied. Lower Town Cherokees finally pressured the Overhills to give way on prisoner exchange so that they could regain their own captives held in South Carolina.

Carnage and Peace Diplomacy

When released, Cherokee prisoners faced hostile white settlers on their homeward path. Two hundred whites had been killed in the war. Colonial animosity toward Indians grew exponentially and would tragically be passed to future generations. The Cherokee war dead may have numbered from 1,500 to 2,000, although we do not know the full loss, which was enormous. Fifteen to twenty percent or even more of the Cherokee people perished within little more than two years. Want and disease claimed the most victims in wartime's hell.[75]

British invasions of Cherokee country epitomized the type of destruction that would be carried out in Indian country by the Continental Army and state militias during the American Revolutionary War. Military commanders utilized whatever means necessary to crush "savages" in campaigns conducted under the justification of reprisal and pacification. The Cherokees, as will be seen, experienced more than their share of scorched-earth militia offensives in brutal warfare with American settlers from 1776 to 1794.

Attakullakulla, Peace Negotiator

Attakullakulla was an astute negotiator. One of his great strengths was to keep anger and inner rage under control, though his fiery emotions occasionally came to the surface. When traveling south in November 1761 for what seemed to be final peace negotiations, he was startled to hear from two Cherokee women that Grant, who had taken camp at Ninety-Six, was allegedly planning to seize him and his party at a "Strong House," put the confined men and women in different compartments, and then "drive us to Charles Town like a parcel of Sheep." Attakullakulla confronted Captain Lachlan Mackintosh with these accusations at a tense meeting. Mackintosh denounced the rumors as false, as indeed they were. Attakullakulla's alarm is revealing. Colonel Grant might express sympathy, but he was still "the Corn Puller," as Cherokees called him, whose troops had burned towns and destroyed crops. If Cherokee women were kept isolated in a "Strong House," their men could not prevent British officers and soldiers from sexually forcing themselves upon Indian females. Such abuses were common in the buildup to war and were not forgotten. Physically exhausted and with his tongue unloosed by rum drinking, Attakullakulla fumed at Carolina's "lies" about promising him horses and provisions for his most recent trek to Overhill country. He needed flour and beef for his party. He asked Mackintosh what he would receive for two white prisoners, one Black woman, and two horses that he brought with him for release. He would bring no more captives without receiving something in return.[76]

The day after this outburst, Attakullakulla returned to the fort and expressed sorrow for his "bad Talk," superficially motivated by disappointment that Grant was not present to greet him with a pipe and white wing, as promised. His demands reflected not only need but thirst for reciprocity and respect. Mackintosh provided Attakullakulla and his sizable party with an ample amount of flour, beef, and pork for yet another journey to Charles Town.[77]

Attakullakulla finally entered the South Carolina council chamber on the morning of December 14 ready to negotiate a true peace. There were eight headmen with him, including Oconostota's brother Ketagusta ("the Prince" of Chota), Ostenaco's brother of Stecoe, and Onatoy of Toqua (the warrior who captured Stuart at Cane Creek). In each case, the men were carefully identified to inform the English that the delegation was sufficiently distinguished to speak for all Cherokees. There was one representative from the Middle Towns and two from the Lower Towns besides six Overhill men. Attakullakulla was disappointed that Governor Bull was sick and not in attendance for the ritual accord. As on previous occasions, Cherokees wanted a good and faithful interpreter. Veteran James Beamor fulfilled this essential role. The treaty terms were reviewed carefully by the Native delegation, which asked questions on points requiring clarification. After three days of consideration, Attakullakulla and fellow headmen approved the accord for their nation. A Cherokee consensus emerged through interregional consultation without which a broad peace was not attainable.[78]

To Cherokees, the atmosphere and ceremony of peace mattered at least as much as treaty conditions. As Attakullakulla explained, "we make use of Feathers in place of paper" in concluding a peace. He gave feathers for Lieutenant Governor Bull, though the latter was not present, as a sign that the "Blood [that] was spilt in the Path . . . is now wiped away." The Cherokee peace pipe was smoked by all councilors and headmen. Attakullakulla then gave an eagle tail for his nation and wampum strings for eleven towns, including Chota. Oconostota's brother delivered wampum in the Great Warrior's name, a clever way of bringing a foremost Cherokee leader symbolically into the peace process even if he did not desire to be in Charles Town. Large matters were at stake, and Attakullakulla laid aside his prior demand of payment for the future

Carnage and Peace Diplomacy

release of white prisoners. With Bull's consent, the Cherokees gained the freedom of two of their three prisoners held in Charles Town. Most important, the Cherokee delegation spoke for their people as a nation. Ketagusta stated that he represented the "Council of the Headmen of the Cherokees," just as South Carolina's "beloved Men here" were "Council to the Governor." The ideal of Cherokee unity came to life through a spirit of collaboration among headmen whose communities actually encompassed a range of perspectives on present and future.[79]

To treat with mutual understanding was even more vital to Cherokees than a written treaty's peace articles. Attakullakulla was no simple appeaser of an imperial power. His perseverance and patience and ability to stand above the fray helped the Cherokees to gain peace with a modicum of honor, and also with the hope of recovery after devastation. He was not an unblemished hero or a magician-diplomat. His diligence counted greatly. Attakullakulla raised the banner of mutual forgetting, a cultural ideal of peacemaking that was far more Native than European. His words were at once mythic and politic:

> I have always been in favour with the English, and have suffered great Hardships in going about continually, often starved and naked, in order to convince my people of their Error in falling out with the English; they are now convinced of their Folly, and hope the Governor & his beloved Men ... will not remember what is past, seeing that it has been so ordered by the Great Man above and as the white people have more knowledge than we, of the affairs above, we hope and desire to live in Peace & Friendship with them.

The "Great Man above" was the idea of a supreme god that Cherokees understood in their own way—a unifying force between themselves and the white people. Mutual respect was inseparable from peace between nations. Ketagusta, a peace chief, known to the English as "the Prince of Chota," exulted in the large white flag that Colonel Grant had given him for his community. In return, he declared, "the Nation have sent the greatest present they can, namely an Eagle's Tail, through which they hope light will ever shine between the English and them, whom they now regard as their own people."[80] Cherokee generosity of spirit endured after a destructive and bitter war. It would soon be tested by a British peace settlement replete with promise but bereft of permanence or stability.

290   *Cherokees, Native Peoples, and Empires, 1730–1762*

III

Upheavals and the Will to Live

1762–1795

10

The Politics of Alliance and Survival

The Cherokees were as battered by warfare as any populous Native people in eastern North America from 1755 through 1761. No other Indigenous nation experienced such a startling turn of affairs, pushed from English alliance to bitter antagonism and beset by harrowing invasions that left uprooted survivors on the brink of starvation. Cherokee peace accords with South Carolina and Virginia, which became operative by early 1762, brought little quiet. Geopolitical instability across half a continent afforded no such luxury. Even while facing an onrush of colonial hunters and settlers, Cherokees contended with a slew of attacks by Indian foes from their north and west. Given this threat, Cherokee headmen called on British imperial authorities for double diplomatic duty—to mediate peace with their Native adversaries and to establish firm and lasting boundaries with colonials.

Cherokee diplomacy in the period 1762–1775 sometimes seems an exercise in supplication. Headmen repeatedly pleaded for fair English dealing and directed many of their talks to John Stuart, royal superintendent of Indian affairs in the vast southern region. Stuart, the former captain saved by Attakullakulla, had a daunting task by any measure. His jurisdiction encompassed Native frontiers with Virginia, the Carolinas, and Georgia besides taking in East and West Florida—new British colonies won by victory over Spain and France in the Seven Years' War.[1]

Stuart obtained the superintendent's station with the support of General Amherst, who admired the captain's judgment and fortitude. Unlike Amherst, whose words and deeds seethed with contempt for Indians, Stuart had some sympathy for Native peoples even though he did not manage affairs on that basis. His strategy took shape in a British imperium wary of lingering French influence, Spanish designs, and pan-Indian unity that threatened Crown interests. Stuart was a highly competent officer even if he could not match William Johnson, superintendent of northern Indian affairs, in panache and political finesse. While traveling extensively on diplomatic business, he relied on surrogates for detailed regional information. Alexander Cameron, Stuart's deputy to the Cherokees, brought dedication and insight to his position. He was comfortable enough with Cherokees to tell them of his Scottish heritage. They affectionately called him "Brother Scotchie." Cameron and Stuart, both native Highlanders, had the trying duty of mediating between Cherokees and colonials, not least the Scots and Scots-Irish, who had a well-merited reputation for pushing aggressively into Native lands.[2]

The Overhill Cherokees, hitherto at some remove from white settlement, keenly felt the accelerating pace of colonialism in the aftermath of the Seven Years' War. While shielded by mountains from distant South Carolina, Overhill Towns lacked similar protection relative to Virginia and North Carolina, whose soaring white frontier populations hungered for more land. Mountains towered at the "back" of these provinces, but colonial hunters readily journeyed through corridors in the highlands via the Holston, Clinch, and Powell Rivers. Daniel Boone, the most renowned of the "long hunters," roamed the area while venturing to and from Kentucky during the 1760s. The threat faced by Native peoples came from colonial magnates and land speculators, not simply from humble white frontier folk who by 1770 had taken up residence in the Watauga and Nolichucky valleys near the heart of Overhill Cherokee country. Since the 1740s, Virginia's governors were especially lavish in offering land grants, totaling many hundreds of thousands of acres beyond the Appalachians, to well-connected men. With French defeat in war, provincial grandees looked to make good on bulging land claims well beyond the Proclamation Line of 1763, the British monarch's attempt to protect Native rights and establish frontier stability in the face of turmoil.[3]

Cherokee headmen adopted a nuanced, if largely defensive approach toward British colonialism from 1762 to 1775. While asserting their rights, they made substantial land cessions to provincial governments with the goal of establishing enforceable limits east of the mountains. The principal Cherokee negotiators were largely the same men who assumed leadership during the British War: Oconostota, Ostenaco,

Attakullakulla, Willanawa, Tistoe, along with Ketagusta (the "Prince" of Chota), who became a major figure by that conflict's end. The elders' most trying task was somehow to accommodate colonial territorial demands without alienating their young men who buckled under appeasement. The land question was not the only Cherokee concern. Quite as testy was the negotiation of "satisfaction" in cases when whites murdered Cherokees or vice versa. Cherokees retained their own sense of what was right in such cases. Their leaders advised colonial authorities to restrain white settlers or else risk retaliatory strikes by young warriors. Headmen negotiated slippery diplomatic ground by frank talk about what they could control and what lay beyond their power.[4]

The story of white settler expansion into Native territories occupies such a central place in the overarching historical narrative that other significant developments can too easily be shunted from view. Cherokees could not afford to focus their sole attention on the "Virginians"—a name used generically, and often caustically by southern Indians when referring to white frontier settlers during the 1760s and beyond. Like other Indigenous peoples, the Cherokees were part of a turbulent Native American world with its own conflicts, watchful diplomacy, and possibilities of alliance or enmity. This was a geopolitical landscape in rapid motion. The "French and Indian War," as it came to be called by English colonials, did not have a definite or sudden conclusion from an Indigenous perspective. Native peoples struggled with not only the consequences of British military victory over the French but also the highly unsettled conditions among themselves.

The Cherokees and Pontiac's War

When Ostenaco was making his way from Overhill country to Williamsburg in March 1762, he passed Cherokee towns whose inhabitants were crying over their war dead. The attackers belonged to a group of "northern Indians." Cherokees did not sit by passively while suffering losses. In one foray to the Ohio River, warriors attacked a Shawnee camp in the dead of a freezing night and brought four enemy scalps to Ostenaco and his band. Three of the scalps were Shawnee; the fourth was a Frenchman's. Later that year, Colonel Henry Bouquet, British commander at Fort Pitt, reported that "frequent Parties" of Iroquois warriors passed southward to attack the Cherokees. The Iroquois had become "very troublesome" since British officers, acting

The Politics of Alliance and Survival

under General Amherst's orders, had reduced gifts of gunpowder and ball to warriors to a bare trickle.[5]

These events, as random as they may seem, were signs of impending upheaval in Indian country. With triumph over France, commander-in-chief Amherst felt little need to placate Native sensitivities. By the fall of 1761, he ordered a severe cutback in presents, especially of munitions and liquor, to Indians. What Amherst saw as a wasteful practice was a necessity to Native men, who viewed such gifts as a badge of respect and alliance. The British military presence at the Forks of the Ohio, Niagara, and Detroit stirred Indian anger. Shawnees and Delawares grumbled about growing white settlement about Fort Pitt. The Overhill Cherokees had no such immediate worries since the British decided not to regarrison Fort Loudoun, which fell to ruins after Demere's surrender and war's carnage.[6]

Imperial France was in the process of withdrawal from North America, but the facts on the ground told another story. French traders operated widely. French officers were still in command at forts in the Illinois country. Some Indian groups envisioned a French revival, while others harbored doubts. France's Indigenous allies recoiled on learning that their "father," Louis XV, had surrendered their lands east of the Mississippi to the British. By another treaty arranged in Paris, the French king transferred New Orleans and Louisiana's western portions to his nephew, the Spanish monarch. In a world far from European palaces, a militant Nativist message spread far and wide: red people had to take control by their own strength. Prophets such as Neolin of the Delawares preached cultural and spiritual renewal, sounding the call to drive out the English. This teaching was at the heart of Pontiac's War, a Native revolt against British colonialism that raged hotly about the Great Lakes, the Ohio Valley, and the frontiers of Pennsylvania, Maryland, and Virginia. The conflict, which spiked in 1763–1764, left scars and wounds of far longer duration.[7]

Stunned by a wave of unexpected Native attacks, British authorities hurried to reassure southern Indian nations and prevent them from joining northern militants. The result was the Augusta Congress of November 1763, a momentous gathering in Georgia where British bigwigs met with deputies of the Chickasaws, Choctaws, Creeks, Cherokees, and Catawbas. The conference was sponsored by superintendent John Stuart in coordination with the governors of Virginia, the Carolinas, and Georgia. Native emissaries shaped the proceedings as much as the British, who dared not alienate them.[8]

296   *Upheavals and the Will to Live, 1762–1795*

The Congress's importance was obvious by the sheer number of Indians who came to the gathering, partly to partake of food and drink in the king's gift. By the end of October that year, 300 Cherokee men, women, and children had arrived at Fort Augusta. In Stuart's summation, 846 Indians "of all Ages and Sexes" were present at the conference. Fifteen Cherokee men represented their people in deliberations. These deputies included Attakullakulla, Ostenaco, Ketagusta of Chota, Seroweh, Tistoe, and Willanawa. Great Warrior Oconostota chose not to attend, probably a sign of his continuing displeasure with the British.[9]

Ostenaco arrived at Augusta with an outwardly optimistic view, having returned from a voyage to England the previous year with tales of the king's grandeur and other wonders. Speaking to Governor Thomas Boone of South Carolina in November 1762, Ostenaco remarked that "the Number of Warriors and people being all of one Colour" in London "far exceeded what we thought possible." Population was strength, and Ostenaco looked ahead for recovery: "Our Women are breeding Children Night and Day to increase our people." This hopeful sign did not foreclose trouble. Ostenaco admitted that some of his people harbored resentment of the British after their kin had been killed in the recent war. He therefore promised Boone that he would douse any "bad word" that Cherokees might say of the English. To strengthen his talk, the chief declared his good heart: "I speak not with two Tongues, & am ashamed of those who do." Ostenaco was a man of feeling and sagacity, more flesh and blood than may appear in Joshua Reynolds's portrait of him painted in the artist's London studio. While conversing with Boone, Ostenaco deliberately looked above the governor's seat to the portrait of George III on the wall. The "Great King," declared Ostenaco, was present to witness and hear. His protection was surely needed.[10]

Royal governors at Augusta understood quite well that colonial territorial ambitions were at odds with the king's mandates for safeguarding Native lands. Given the risks of an openly expansionist position, the governors played their hand coolly. Speaking on their behalf, Stuart told Native deputies that all met "at the command of the great King George, who under God, the master and giver of breath, is your and our common father and protector." The superintendent affirmed royal "assurances" given in regard to Native lands. He and the governors respected these pledges, "which we now from our own hearts confirm."[11]

The Politics of Alliance and Survival

Portrait of Scyacust Ukah (Ostenaco) by Joshua Reynolds (1762). *Gilcrease Museum, Tulsa, Oklahoma.*

Attakullakulla took little comfort from Stuart's glib promise. With a strong entourage at his back, he talked boldly of Native rights, asserting that Cherokee lands must not be settled by whites south of the New River on the Virginia frontier, well to the east of the Overhill heartland. Renewed trade and the guarantee of hunting grounds were paramount concerns. Ketagusta presented a string with three knots to symbolize points along the path of peace. The two end knots linked Chota to Charles Town, while the middle knot represented Fort Prince George by Keowee. "The king George," Ketagusta announced, "has sent a good talk, the path shall always be kept straight to hear good talks."[12]

Stuart and the governors carefully addressed Attakullakulla's concerns. Outstanding issues would be resolved to Cherokee satisfaction. As proof, Stuart gave the Cherokee delegation a copy of the king's instructions of July 1763 to his American governors. The paper was read aloud in translation. Much to Cherokee satisfaction, the royal order announced the king's respect for American Indian territories. It was His Majesty's "Determined Resolution to support them [the Indians] in their just Rights, and inviolably to observe our Engagements with them."[13]

Cherokee delegates absorbed British promises at Augusta with great seriousness. They brought up these pledges time and again as evidence of their people's rights. What they learned at Augusta anticipated the royal proclamation of October 7, 1763, which prohibited colonial land grants or settlement west of the Appalachians without the king's prior permission. Native peoples, living under His Majesty's "Protection," were recognized as rightful possessors of their lands, "reserved to them ... as their Hunting Grounds" within the king's dominions, wherever Indian land had not actually been "ceded to" or "purchased" by the Crown. This statement was broader in scope than is commonly described in textbooks. "Reserved" lands included territories both east and west of the Appalachians.

The imperial map was not set in stone, however, since the Proclamation of 1763 authorized purchases of Native territories east of the Appalachians on certain conditions. Lawful purchases were to be executed by provincial governors, acting with royal assent, at a "Publick meeting or Assembly" of Indians if the latter "should be inclined to dispose of the said Lands."[14] The treaty-making guidelines were immediately relevant. A large portion of Cherokee lands and most Creek territory lay east of the mountains.

While the king's governors consorted, Native delegations at Augusta sought common ground. Attakullakulla announced his intent of being heard by all the "red people" at the conference. While accusing the Creeks of recently killing two Cherokees, he tactfully underplayed the attack because it was supposedly not ordered by Muscogee beloved men. Attakullakulla observed that his people had no ill will toward "the Southward Indians," meaning the Creeks, but that the "Northward Indians are troublesome." Cherokees continued to put a premium on peace to their south while beset by northern foes. Speaking confidentially to Stuart, Cherokee men voiced no love for Creeks, who had urged them to war against the English two years earlier, only

The Politics of Alliance and Survival   299

to leave them hanging during Grant's invasion. For the present, however, Cherokees expressed a desire to attack the Ottawas—British foes in Pontiac's War. This was cagey Cherokee diplomacy and music to Stuart's ears.[15]

From the outbreak of Pontiac's War, British strategy hinged on divide and rule. General Thomas Gage, who replaced Amherst as commander-in-chief of His Majesty's North American forces in December 1763, readily adopted this approach. Informed of southern affairs, he trusted that superintendent Stuart would exploit "the visible Jealousy, which now subsists between the Creeks and Cherokees." The Mortar of the Creeks bothered the British more than any single figure. Writing to Stuart, Gage suggested that it might be possible to "prevail upon some bold Cherokee to knock [the Mortar] on the Head."[16] No simple solution was forthcoming, however.

In the face of the great Indian uprising, Gage was determined that his troops occupy French outposts in the Illinois country as soon as possible. The task was daunting no matter the transfer of territories stipulated by the Treaty of Paris. Desperate for Native allies, British officials called on the Cherokees for assistance. Gage put special value on Overhill fighters given their intimate knowledge of the Ohio and Tennessee watersheds.[17] Cherokee headmen responded cautiously. Their people were still recovering from the damages wrought by British invasion. Then, too, Cherokees were reluctant to aid until properly supplied. The defense of their home ground came first. In February 1764, Oconostota informed Stuart that he would join Attakullakulla in three nights to "go against the white people's Enemys to the Northward." He meanwhile sent some warriors south to protect white traders journeying to Augusta lest the latter be set upon by the Creeks who, in Oconostota's words, "are another people from us" and not to be trusted.[18]

Overhill fighters went north in small numbers during the spring and summer of 1764. Writing to London, Gage expressed some unease at resultant French casualties. The *habitants* of Illinois were now British subjects and officially under royal protection. By the general's explanation, Cherokee fighters killed four individuals who "looked like French men" traveling by canoe on the Ohio—a route used by Illinois traders to convey munitions to the Shawnees and Delawares in exchange for skins. By inference, the British ministry could brush aside the episode as an incident of war, especially since it did not involve an attack on a colonial settlement.[19]

Upheavals and the Will to Live, 1762–1795

Cherokees fought as they pleased. When autumn came, they took to deer hunting rather than accede to English initiatives to continue raids to the north. One exception was Ostenaco, whose warriors seized enemy craft on the Ohio and toasted King George's health with the brandy on board. Two French captives, fortunate to be spared, gladly shared in the toast, too! The South Carolina assembly voted a reward to the Cherokee fighters "equal to the Profit they might have made by Hunting," with a double share of £15 sterling going to Ostenaco himself.[20]

Pontiac's War ebbed by late 1764. While punished by English arms, Ohio tribes were unbowed. Shawnees, Delawares, Mingoes, and others demanded British respect in return for ending hostilities and exchanging war captives. Illinois Indians, among the last nations to make peace, were alarmed by rumors of English plotting to uproot them and give their land to Cherokee foes. The news was false but still felt in Indian country when French commandants yielded their mid-Mississippi posts to British officers in 1765.[21]

Cherokee conflicts with Native peoples during the 1760s had a strikingly similar geography with the warfare of fifty years past. The Iroquois remained archenemies, as did Illinois and Wabash tribes. The Shawnees, former Cherokee friends during Connecorte's heyday (circa 1746–1755), were frequent foes once more. This last turnabout may appear puzzling unless we recall the bloodletting of the French and Indian War. Cherokees aided the British early in the war, taking up the hatchet against the Shawnees, who struck back in time. Cherokee vulnerability bred assault from various quarters. In early 1765, reports reached Charles Town that Mississippi Valley warriors, most likely of Illinois, had killed fourteen Cherokees, nine of whom were women and children. A few months later, a Delaware and Shawnee war party of thirty fighters surprised a Cherokee hunting camp, killed one man, and captured two young men, three boys, and two women. The Cherokees soon countered. Seroweh led fifty fighters who tracked the enemy, huddled outside the Delaware-Shawnee camp on a freezing night, and attacked the next day. Besides killing four, the Cherokees freed nearly all their prisoners and hauled off guns, tomahawks, and wampum belts. One Cherokee man was killed in the clash while three others were wounded. Cherokees took pride in the enemy's defeat. Chota celebrated the news with the blast of old British cannon.[22]

The end of Pontiac's War brought no peace to the Cherokees. In May 1766, Ketagusta of Chota told agent Alexander Cameron that

The Politics of Alliance and Survival

northern enemies had attacked his people in greater number and more frequently than ever remembered. The chief wished to know if the assailants were egged on by any Englishmen. It was clear, he said, that the enemy "trade with the English, and from them get their Hatchets, which are very sharp, and have been lifted up against white as well as red Men in our Nation." Cherokee suppositions were close to the mark. Superintendent William Johnson informed Stuart in 1765 that all Iroquois nations, save the Mohawks, were engaged in long-distance attacks on the Cherokees. Johnson actually believed the forays useful, so long as they did not hurt "our Southern Colonies," since the Iroquois attacks provided an outlet for "turbulent Spirits" that might otherwise upset his district. He was not sanguine about mediating peace between the Six Nations and the Cherokees.[23] Attacks had various motives besides revenge. Raiders commonly replenished their own depleted ranks by adopting children and females seized from enemy tribes. Few captives were safe, however, as they could be enslaved or sold off at a whim.

It is often guesswork to identify the northern intruders into Cherokee territory. Fighting commonly had a dramatic character. One Cherokee man escaped death by a northern raider when the latter's gun misfired. As the two combatants wrestled, the Cherokee warrior was getting the worst of it until he called on a nearby young woman, herself Cherokee, who promptly tied the adversary "Neck and Heel" and delivered him for judgment and ritual execution. Life and death depended on split-second decisions in chance encounters. Trader Jack Welsh and his Cherokee daughter and granddaughter were headed to Tugaloo when accosted by six northern warriors, said to be Shawnees. Sensing danger after shaking hands with the men, Welsh yelled to his daughter to escape on horseback. She gave her horse the whip and rode off even though wounded by enemy gunshots. Her small daughter and Welsh were clubbed to death. Later that year, northern raiders struck Lower Town Cherokees again, killing three men, a woman, three boys, and a girl, this time near Fort Prince George.[24]

In 1766, Tistoe of Keowee and Seed of Settico led a war party that fought two engagements with an unnamed enemy group, with losses sustained by both sides. Wounded by musket fire, Seed told fellow Cherokees that he would die in six nights. After six days of marching, the warrior felt near death. He told his comrades that "he was a man, and Warrior; that he did not die like a Woman, in Bed, that he died in War." Asking not to be buried and "smothered" in the ground, he made a final request: "Tye me up with Vines to a pretty high tree, where the enemy cannot find my Scalp, but I can see them when they are going to war against you, and if I can do no more, I shall bring you Intelligence." These are the warrior's words as told by Tistoe and comrades to Alexander Cameron. The Seed's talk seems very real, even if given a literary air by Cameron.[25]

The Cherokees suffered severely in warfare with Native enemies no matter the outcome of particular fights. At a minimum, 200 Cherokees were maimed or killed from 1763 through 1768 in these conflicts. For a people of no more than 9,000 persons in 1760, these losses sapped communal strength and morale. In August 1766, the Cherokees pleaded with Stuart to mediate peace with the Illinois tribes, just as the superintendent's intercession was desired for an accommodation with the Six Nations. The Cherokees were meanwhile plagued by epidemics. Headmen sent word to Stuart that "Sickness" was more dreadful than at any other time with the exception of smallpox outbreaks. The "Cries of Women and Children" over the loss of loved ones pierced the day. Disease and intertribal war depleted the Cherokees while they were dealing with an unprecedented surge of colonials into their hunting grounds and still other dangers that undercut the very idea that they had the king's protection.[26]

"To Kill a Savage"

Thomas Gage was a military man, and as such he had the task of suppressing Nativist uprisings posing a threat to British power. On replacing Amherst, he believed it essential for His Majesty's forces to carry on "an active and vigorous War against the Savages, till their Distresses shall oblige them to sue for Peace." The outcome should bring stability, "a solid Peace" founded on "Equity and Moderation" and reinforced by "the sense the Barbarians will retain of our Power to chastise Them." Not unusual for his time, Gage believed in an imperial order within law. This does not mean that ruthless measures were out of line during an emergency. Gage approved Amherst's notorious idea, executed independently by subordinates, of distributing smallpox-infested blankets to Delaware Indians at Fort Pitt. There were nevertheless public norms. Gage was disgusted when a group of Pennsylvania frontier settlers, "the Paxton Boys," avenged Indian attacks in December 1763 by deliberately murdering six innocent Conestoga Indians and then breaking into Lancaster's workhouse and slaying fourteen more

The Politics of Alliance and Survival

Conestogas sheltered there. Gage dispatched troops to Philadelphia to forestall another massacre when a mob of frontiersmen marched toward the city.[27]

In May 1765, the Paxton fever passed to frontier Augusta County, Virginia, where more than twenty settler vigilantes ambushed ten Cherokee men on their way to the Ohio country, shooting five dead and wounding at least two others. The murders, horrific by any standard, were a flagrant subversion of law. The ambushed Cherokees had come north with the aim of fighting Ohio Indian foes. They had permission for their journey from Colonel Andrew Lewis, whose Virginia militia had collaborated with Ostenaco during the French and Indian War. Lewis, who was not without prejudice against Indians, described the murderers as "Villainous bloody minded Rascals" who had attacked "in the most treacherous manner" even as they knew that the Cherokees were allies and wore special colors as visible proof. In Williamsburg, Lieutenant Governor Francis Fauquier proclaimed rewards for the apprehension of the Augusta ringleaders, though without effect. When a single white perpetrator was jailed in Staunton, one hundred armed settlers marched into town and cheered on comrades who smashed the prison door and freed the prisoner. The self-styled "Augusta Boys" derided Colonel Lewis by issuing their own proclamation with a mock reward of £1,000 for his arrest. Asserting their loyalty to the king, the group claimed to have cut down "known Enemies," that is, Delawares and Shawnees disguised as Cherokee "friends." The proclamation's anonymous authors expressed not the least compunction for the Cherokee deaths, a sign of hate toward all Indians.[28]

The British Board of Trade was disturbed by Fauquier's report on frontier vigilantism. Commenting on the Augusta Boys' proclamation, the Board observed that the individuals who penned it "have adopted an Opinion . . . that the killing a Savage is an Action, for which no Man ought to suffer." Anarchic colonial violence was dangerous. It could trigger a war with the Cherokees, who would retaliate given "the vindictive Disposition, which is the particular Character and Spirit of all Savages, but more particularly of this Tribe." The Board's members denounced a "barbarity" inflicted on Cherokees almost in the same breath as they decried the Indians' allegedly savage character. In their judgment, frontier order hinged on respect for royal authority. Pennsylvania and Virginia settlers should be forthwith required to vacate lands by the Ohio River that they had "usurped" from the Indians. The king's proclamation must be obeyed. Although squatters in the area

304 *Upheavals and the Will to Live, 1762–1795*

moved off in late 1766 when warned by the British military, many frontier families returned by the next spring. Gage believed it futile to make another attempt at enforcement.[29]

For the Augusta Boys to get away with the murder of blameless Cherokees was heinous. Just after the murders, Lewis composed a letter to his "Brothers," the "Chiefs" of "the Over Hill Towns," in which he attributed the killings to "very bad" young men. Two of the killers were said to be locked up in "the Strong House" or jail. He would know no peace until all the guilty were taken and "suffer death for the bloody Crime." One doubts that Lewis believed such an outcome possible. His true purpose was to assuage Cherokee anger and forestall retaliation. Fauquier sent his own apologetic letter to Overhill country, vowing that the offenders would be judged "exactly as if they killed white men!" The exclamation mark was in the governor's own hand.[30]

Cherokee pain ran deep. Overhill Towns and others debated what should be done. True to form, Attakullakulla decided on yet another peace-saving mission to Virginia. Tellingly, he was accompanied by just one other Cherokee man and Scots trader-interpreter John Watts on the long and dangerous journey to Williamsburg. Eleven other Cherokee men went part of the way, being understandably anxious about entering the Shenandoah Valley. In July 1765, Attakullakulla had a private audience with Fauquier before meeting with the governor and council eight days later. In the public session, "the Carpenter" handed Fauquier a string of white beads while delivering black beads from Oconostota who thereby spoke for a great part of the nation—those who felt that Virginia had done nothing to "wipe the blood clean."[31]

Fauquier offered condolences, denounced the murderers, and granted Attakullakulla's request for two horses, a rifle, a pair of pistols, and some guns for his return journey. Attakullakulla asked for the governor's assistance in mediating peace between the Cherokees and "northern Indians." He also requested permission to voyage across the sea and see the king. If justice could not be had in Virginia, then it must be sought in London. Attakullakulla persisted in his desire for another royal visit, which he voiced on at least three occasions between 1763 and 1766, only to be put off by royal governors.[32]

As for the Cherokee peace quest with northern foes, Fauquier could do little except request Sir William Johnson's mediation. A more immediate danger loomed soon after Attakullakulla's departure from Williamsburg. The Virginia council mulled news that forty Augusta County men were conspiring to waylay and kill the Cherokee

The Politics of Alliance and Survival

leader. While the council declined to send a militia escort, it sent word that Attakullakulla should alter his route for his own safety. As resourceful as ever, he arrived home without harm.[33]

Attakullakulla's peace path did not satisfy all Cherokees. A year after the Augusta murders, several Cherokee men exacted vengeance by killing an Anglo trader and his aides on their way to Virginia. John Stuart handled the crisis carefully to avoid a greater blowup. Deliberately obfuscating, he informed Fauquier that northern Indians, and probably not Cherokees, were responsible for the murders. Stuart kept mum on how he had already chided Cherokees for the killings. The superintendent employed Native customs to drive home his point. Working through Cameron, he sent Cherokee headmen a string of white beads overshadowed by seventeen black ones. The black beads represented two sets of victims—the Cherokee dead gunned down in Virginia and whites killed in retaliatory attacks. The message was that the innocent on both sides should not die for the foul deeds of others. Stuart had inside sources, namely Attakullakulla's wife, who told a British ensign that Cherokees had indeed killed the white traders. She fingered White Owl, an Overhill warrior whose men sang "the Death Whoop" when passing by Chota after the killings. Here was yet another woman who did not want rash warriors to propel her people into a spiral of deadly conflict. Oconostota praised Stuart for his deft crisis management: "My Warriours and Young men joyns [*sic*] me in holding you fast within our Arms." An accord between beloved men kept violence in check.[34]

Cherokees and the Six Nations

The imperial policy of divide and rule, which reigned supreme during Pontiac's War, meant that Cherokees were hard pressed to gain British mediation of their conflict with the Iroquois confederacy. The Earl of Shelburne, who became secretary of state for American affairs in 1766, took a different tack by admonishing colonial officials to avoid "spiriting up one Tribe to cut the Throats of another." After Pontiac's War, Shelburne wished to establish an equitable Indian policy that would bind Native peoples more strongly to the Crown. Both Johnson and Stuart received Whitehall's instructions to mediate the conflict between the Cherokees and "Northern Indians." Gage also came on board.[35] At Stuart's suggestion, Cherokee deputies shipped on a brig from Charles Town to New York City and then traveled up the Hudson for negotiations

306   *Upheavals and the Will to Live, 1762–1795*

with the Six Nations in the Mohawk Valley. Prior to the voyage, Chota's leaders sent two wampum belts as a peace offering, via Gage and Johnson, to the Iroquois. The Cherokees also dispatched an Illinois tribesman's scalp and headdress so that Gage would realize the danger they faced from Indian intruders who, in Ostenaco's words, took the lives of both "White and Red People." As previously seen, signals of strength frequently accompanied peace messages.[36]

After ten days at sea, an impressive Cherokee delegation docked at Manhattan on December 11. At the head were Oconostota, Ketagusta, Attakullakulla, Tistoe, and the Raven of Tugaloo accompanied by several other men. The next day, the voyagers paid their respects to Gage before heading to the theater in the evening. Cherokees invariably enjoyed play-acting with its vivid gestures and dramatic backdrops even if they did not understand the actors' words. In this case the show was *Richard III* "with a Pantomi[m]e Entertainment." A party of Mohawks happened to be in the city at the same time, and three of their chiefs smoked the peace pipe with Cherokee headmen before both Native groups boarded the same sloop for Albany. By late December, the Cherokee visitors, with interpreter John Watts, hurtled in sledges across snow-packed ground toward Johnson Hall, Sir William's residence.[37]

The Cherokees quickly went to meet Johnson in his spacious home warmed by a blazing fire in the main hearth. Cherokee visitors handed the calumet to Sir William before the pipe was passed among all, including colonials and Mohawks. Oconostota stood and displayed the wampum belt of Chota, representing the deputies' authority to speak for all their people. The Cherokees then took to their lodgings in the depth of winter for what proved an extraordinarily long wait until negotiations began. Two months passed before the arrival of deputies from all Six Nations, their Canadian brethren, and allies of the St. Lawrence. The Cherokees may have felt a little overwhelmed, being perhaps a dozen men while the Iroquois and related delegations numbered 760—chiefs and warriors with an unspecified number of women and children. On March 2, 1768, Johnson invited Cherokee guests to his house to meet the recently arrived Iroquois emissaries. A wondrous scene ensued. As Attakullakulla entered Johnson Hall, he saw and embraced Taghtaghquisera, the chief of the Caughnawaga Mohawks who had personally adopted him as a "brother" during his Canadian captivity of the 1740s. Both men were joyful. Attakullakulla invited his Caughnawaga brother to his lodge, and Sir William supplied both men with pipes, tobacco, body paint, and liquor for their

The Politics of Alliance and Survival

merriment. This was an extraordinary moment, a sign of Native American ability to transcend ethnic hostility through respect, affection, and a profound identification with "the other" born of shared experience.[38]

The conference began on a nearly opposite feeling than that exhibited in Johnson Hall. The Iroquois mood was glum in the wake of the recent murder of ten Indians, including six women and children, by Frederick Stump, a Pennsylvania German settler, by the Susquehanna River over a two-day period. The Iroquois were directly affected; two Seneca men and their wives were among the dead. The killing spree was barbarous, a fiendish outburst of violence after Stump had drunk heavily with some of the victims in his house. The murderer was protected by his colonial neighbors from any judicial proceeding. "To kill a Savage," as the Lords Commissioners of Trade had observed, was no crime to many white frontiersmen.[39]

In comparison with the bitter feelings aroused by the murders, the Cherokee meeting with the Six Nations and allies proceeded amicably. Oconostota understood the pain inflicted on the Senecas. When offering gifts, he told a Seneca chief to hold fast to the Cherokee wampum belt "for our Father the Great Spirit above knows that it comes from our hearts." It was time to bury the hatchet "so deep that it can never arise to hurt us, for our heads our Flesh and Blood being alike it were a pity we should kill one another." Cherokee belts were given to each of the Six Nations and to the Caughnawagas. Oconostota announced that Chota had received a Caughnawaga belt twenty years before and had carefully preserved it. The Caughnawagas were fearsome long-distance raiders, which is precisely why Cherokees had pursued peace with them when Connecorte held sway at Chota. Similar overtures were made by Tanasee's Long Warrior during the 1720s.[40]

While royal governors periodically mediated Cherokee-Iroquois peace talks, it was ultimately up to Native peoples to exchange gifts and convey consoling words to one another toward a cessation of hostilities. Oconostota symbolically included women, quintessential Cherokee peacemakers, in his conciliatory talk to the Six Nations. He presented the Iroquois with "a Belt from our Women to yours, and we know that they will hear us for it is they who undergo the pains of Childbirth and produce Men, Surely therefore they must feel Mothers pains for those killed in War." Cherokee headmen's recognition of women was extraordinary and reached beyond what was commonplace for many Native peoples. The Great Warrior gave a belt on behalf of Cherokee boys,

308   *Upheavals and the Will to Live, 1762–1795*

who until they arrived at manhood should be free to hunt birds and rabbits without fear. He invited the Six Nations and the Caughnawagas to send some of their people to "open the Path between your Towns and Chotte [Chota] . . . so that we may be at peace."[41]

The Iroquois replied with far less enthusiasm than Oconostota's warm appeal. To the Six Nations, the Cherokees were "Younger Brothers" who should be admonished even if gingerly welcomed. While giving belts, spokesman Ganaghquiesn of the Oneidas remarked that the Cherokees had neither cleared the road of all "rubbish" nor yet taken the "Axe" out of Iroquois heads. It took some nudging by Johnson before the Six Nations declared the Cherokees to be of the same flesh and blood as themselves.[42] The sharpest Iroquois criticisms were reserved for English officials who failed to enforce laws against white men who foisted rum bottles on Indians, defrauded them of lands, and even murdered their people. Why should Native headmen restrain their warriors under such conditions? Johnson offered gifts to relieve Iroquois grief, while emphasizing that one drunken murderer such as Stump should not be allowed to destroy peace. The superintendent reminded the Iroquois of past colonial deaths at Indian hands. There should be patience in mourning—time to wait until grass covered the Native victims' graves.[43]

The peace conference, which lasted five days, allowed Cherokees and Iroquois to talk among themselves entirely out of Anglo earshot. While old adversaries, both peoples faced common problems of rapid colonial intrusion into their territories, trade grievances, and vulnerability in the face of lawless whites. Cherokees voiced dissatisfaction over yielding too much land to North Carolina by a recent treaty. Iroquois spokesmen told Johnson that they did not want to be treated like Cherokees since "the line [that] was run in their Country . . . has surrounded them so that they cannot Stir." For the Cherokees, the business of running protective "lines" was less important than seeing that boundary agreements were enforced. Lines that were crossed were no longer lines.[44]

Land and Boundaries

Since English authorities often brought up Indian treaty obligations, Cherokee spokesmen invoked what they heard and remembered from conferences such as the Augusta Congress of November 1763. Nearly three years later, Cherokee headmen recalled that four southern

The Politics of Alliance and Survival

309

governors were present at Augusta "when the Great King's Proclamation relative to his red Children was read to us, and we were promised quiet possession of our Lands."[45] This is but one example among countless others of how Native American leaders asserted their own sense of justice in dealings with imperial authorities.

The Cherokees' pursuit of secure boundaries is palpable in talk and action. Knowing the impossibility of keeping white settlers out of their once-capacious eastern hunting grounds, they were willing to make concessions for the sake of stable and lasting agreements. John Stuart, meanwhile, had the delicate task of mediating between Indigenous nations and provincial governments on boundary issues. Lacking the authority to impose his will on colonials or Indians, he depended on royal governors to follow his lead as negotiations proceeded province by province. Deputy Cameron managed talks with the Cherokees in 1765–1766, securing a cession of Native land to South Carolina, while giving assurance that the new piedmont boundary line would be honored. From a Cherokee perspective, this was a measured retreat, unwelcome but seemingly unavoidable and made with the hope of strengthened royal protection. Significantly, the accord was signed or marked by six headmen, including Ostenaco and Ketagusta of the Overhills along with Lower Town leaders Tistoe and Seroweh, the latter a mature man and no longer the hell-bent youthful militant. Overhill chiefs consented because they wished to bolster their leverage with Stuart and safeguard their land from white hunters who were already coming into their territory. Settlers would surely follow—and they did.[46]

While heartened by the South Carolina treaty, Stuart knew it would mean little unless followed by a Cherokee boundary agreement with North Carolina whose white population had shot upward in its extensive piedmont counties. William Tryon, North Carolina's royal governor, warmed to the idea, eager as he was for stable colonial-Indian relations when his province was internally rent by political dissension. In May 1767, Tryon traveled with an entourage of fifty men more than 300 miles from his tidewater seat at Brunswick to meet with Cherokee deputies in the piedmont. (The initial gathering took place near present-day Greenville, South Carolina, an area that had then but a smattering of whites.) Ostenaco served as principal Cherokee spokesman, acting once more in concert with Tistoe, Seroweh, and three other Lower Town chiefs who cherished their hunting grounds east of the Blue Ridge—the same land claimed by North Carolina.[47]

310   *Upheavals and the Will to Live, 1762–1795*

The negotiations began on a friendly footing on June 1, with Tryon offering smoothing generalities and Cherokees listening intently before replying formally the next day. Invoking "the Man above" as Witness, Ostenaco said he spoke for "all our Nation." Indeed, he gave special emphasis to this point because more than twenty years of dealing with colonials had taught him that the English expected Cherokee unanimity or at a least broad consensus if a treaty were to gain legitimacy and force. While admitting that "few of my People" were present at the deliberations, Ostenaco declared: "All the Towns in the Cherokee Nation are as one." Whether his statement was literally true is debatable, but there is little doubt of the Cherokees gaining a more definite sense of nationhood through negotiation and travails with colonials. In the spirit of reciprocity, Ostenaco expected uniformity on the English side, as pledged in the king's name at Augusta, so that an agreement with North Carolina would not be contradicted by Virginia or other provinces. Ostenaco, who had seen the Great King George in London, remembered: "His Majesty told me when I was there [in London], and I have since heard that he desires a Line may be run between us, & that neither shall encroach on the other."[48]

Cherokee deputies were well prepared for their meeting with Tryon. Several months before, they knew of the English boundary proposal, which John Stuart sent by letter to Cameron for public airing. The Cherokees were asked to accept a new border that closely hugged the Proclamation Line from North Carolina's southern border to Virginia. In effect, the proposal required a Cherokee cession of expansive hunting grounds east of the new "dividing Line," as Tryon called it, which at its northern terminus eked about twenty miles west of the royal Appalachian boundary, still not precisely marked. For Stuart and Tryon, a successful Cherokee negotiation was a means to enhance frontier stability and still give ample space for colonial growth.[49]

For Ostenaco and friends, the situation was entirely different. It required painful Cherokee sacrifice with little guarantee beyond reassuring words. As Ostenaco said, it would be up to "Brother" Tryon, together with "Father Stuart," to control the "Rogues" among their own people who might stomp across treaty lines. Acting by what he believed "fair and right," Ostenaco again invoked the tradition of reciprocal exchange. The Cherokees had a claim on the king for all they gave for the sake of peace. What the British thought of as an Indian cession was actually a gift. Ostenaco's words speak for themselves: "I am now come to

The Politics of Alliance and Survival

run it [the line], and the Land that is on this [eastern] side I won't love, I give it to the white People. The price the white People give for Land when they buy is very small, they give a Shirt a Match Coat and the like, which soon wear out, but Land lasts always."[50]

Ostenaco said his people were "naked" and wondered where the governor's gifts were. Tryon indicated that the presents were in the provincial town of Salisbury, where the Cherokees could retrieve the goods, valued at the modest sum of £175 in North Carolina currency. On June 4, the governor traveled with his party and the Cherokees to the southern point of the new line, designated by an elm tree beside a riverbank. Crossing the river and establishing evening camp, colonials and Cherokees joined in festive dining and drinking in honor of George III's birthday. Tryon, honored as "Great Wolf" by Cherokees, frolicked with them in a mock "War Dance." Two days later, the governor was on his way back to Brunswick, while his boundary commissioners and Cherokees went about marking the line. The commissioners had surveyors' equipment but did not know the land. Cherokees guided and observed closely lest they be cheated.[51]

Over the next week, the boundary team progressed fifty miles until reaching a summit at the Blue Ridge's eastern face. The commissioners named the heights "Tryon Mountain" in the governor's honor. The Cherokees told colonial officers that if they climbed to the summit, which rises to an elevation of 3,200 feet above the piedmont, they would "discover the Hills from whence the Western Waters took their Run." Native men then described the impracticality of continuing further north over the Blue Ridge to Chiswell's Mines, the point on John Stuart's ideal map where North Carolina gave way to Virginia. For Cherokees, the permanent border should be that formed by nature—"the great Chain of Mountains"—the Appalachians. On June 13, 1767, six Cherokee headmen placed their marks on the North Carolina boundary treaty. Alexander Cameron signed the accord along with three colonial commissioners.[52]

By proclamation of July 1767, Tryon affirmed Native possession west of the "Partition Line," ordered all intruders to remove from Indian lands, and declared that violators would forfeit "the protection of this Government." One year later, Stuart confirmed the North Carolina line with Cherokee headmen by a follow-up treaty held at Hard Labour, South Carolina. A general agreement remained elusive, however. Virginia's government balked at the new line because its leading men wanted even more of Native land than Stuart had implicitly licensed. Many Cherokees, as will be seen, were profoundly upset at all that had been lost.[53] Tryon could scarcely control white hunters and settlers who crossed the line with scant regard for proclamations. Ironically, his policy of bestowing county offices on fee-grabbing favorites caused a storm among piedmont settlers, leading some of the disaffected to seek new homes west of the mountains. This is not to argue that North Carolina's Regulator Movement—the embodiment of popular protest—alone impelled the province's far western settlement before the American Revolution, but it contributed to the migratory swell and the breach of the Appalachians.[54]

Virginia's colonial elite railed at Stuart's treaty-making because of long-standing territorial ambitions to lands bounded by the Ohio and Holston and Tennessee Rivers, especially the Tennessee's lower portion, which approached the Mississippi.[55] Private stakeholders believed that the Proclamation Line, in Washington's well-known phrase, was but a "temporary expedient" and would ultimately be superseded by Crown adjustments to colonial advantage. Ambitious men in several colonies lobbied the king's ministers at Whitehall to bend to their arguments. Why should settlement be precluded, they argued, from territories that would flourish and add to the empire's wealth and power? Benjamin Franklin, a staunch advocate of western settlement and the establishment of new interior provinces, was among the more noteworthy figures making that case to high-ranking British officials.[56]

William Johnson had a still greater impact. Negotiating with the Six Nations at Fort Stanwix in November 1768, he managed a cunning westerly adjustment of the Proclamation Line by offering a large stash of goods to the Iroquois for ceding a huge swath of lands encompassing much of the Ohio Valley and beyond. The Fort Stanwix treaty was based on a fiction. Johnson deliberately ignored that nearly the entire region, ceded on paper to the Crown, was outside of Iroquois control and instead the homeland of the Shawnees, Delawares, and numerous Ohio Indians. The Cherokees' western hunting grounds were also threatened.[57]

Johnson's coup was welcomed by his cronies, but a wake-up call to rival speculators, notably Virginia's Dr. Thomas Walker and confidant Andrew Lewis, who feared losing out unless they secured the Old Dominion's stake in the Fort Stanwix cession and coveted Ohio-Tennessee Valley lands. Walker, principal of the Loyal Company, had procured a vaguely defined Virginia council grant of 800,000 acres in 1749, entitling him and associates to locate lands west and north of the Old

The Politics of Alliance and Survival

Dominion's border with North Carolina. Lewis, whose Greenbrier Company vaunted trans-Appalachian claims, was the same gentleman who denounced the Augusta Boys as villainous murderers of Cherokees. Distasteful of frontier ruffians, he preferred Indian land sales by treaty, negotiated by legerdemain if necessary to pave the Old Dominion's path toward the Mississippi. Many other gentlemen took a similar view.[58]

After seeing Johnson at work in the Mohawk Valley, Walker and Lewis moved hurriedly, embarking from Virginia to Charles Town in December 1768 in a bid to sway Stuart to approve their scheme of land engrossment and settlement. Stopping in North Carolina on the way, they persuaded Ostenaco and Seroweh, who were visiting Governor Tryon, to join the final leg of the voyage along with two Cherokee woman and an interpreter. Once in Charles Town, the two headmen conversed with Walker and Lewis in the company of John Stuart. Just as the Virginians wished, Ostenaco and Seroweh apparently agreed that white settlers currently living by the Holston River, a crucial artery in Overhill country, be permitted to remain even though they lived west of the Appalachians. One imagines that some douceur was employed to gain this fig leaf of Native approval. Walker and Lewis wanted the Holston as a wedge for something far grander, a secure title to lands sweeping from the Ohio and Cumberland Rivers, and portions of the Tennessee River watershed, reaching toward the Mississippi. They shared this conception with Stuart but not with Ostenaco and Seroweh.[59]

Walker and Lewis would have been grateful for Stuart's endorsement, though they could not have been surprised that the superintendent, a diligent Crown servant, opposed their most far-flung designs. His answer was compromise, or more accurately a papering over of clashing colonial and Native interests. Someone had to give, and it was the Cherokees, whom Stuart asked to accept a Virginia borderline that was considerably further west than what he had previously pledged. The new boundary would run from the Holston River, prime Overhill Cherokee hunting ground (in present-day eastern Tennessee) to the Great Kanawha River, which flows north through today's West Virginia before meeting the Ohio. His Majesty's license was requisite, and here Stuart was fortunate. Secretary of State Hillsborough approved the newly suggested line, though the decision was not known in the colonies for some months. Stuart meanwhile opened negotiations with the Cherokees since their consent was necessary by royal mandate.[60]

In early 1769, Cherokees were stunned to receive Stuart's word by letter requesting that they part with Holston and Kanawha lands, west of the mountains, to secure the livelihood of their "Virginia brethren" currently squatting there. The superintendent mentioned Ostenaco's approval of the deal in Charles Town. This news doubtless embarrassed the Cherokee leader. The Holston Valley, now in question, was one of the foremost routes used by North Carolina and Virginia settlers as a gateway to Cherokee territory. In March 1769, Overhill headmen gathered to put their case to Cameron. Speaking for the whole, Oconostota complained that some governors had forgotten what was said at the "great Congress" at Augusta. He had no trust in Virginians who would pretend not to know what former Governor Fauquier, recently deceased, had promised at that conference. Not ruling out a land sale, Oconostota said his people would only accept a deal if they gained sufficient goods and protection: "we want to keep the Virginians at as great a distance as possible, as they are generally bad Men & Love to Steal Horses & Hunt for deer." The Virginians would need to pay well, so that the headmen "may not be ashamed for what we do for our People." After all, "what are a few goods" compared to "good Land [that] will last for ever"?[61]

Colonial intrusions into Cherokee lands continued while the boundary question was in negotiation. In July 1769 five Overhill headmen, including Oconostota, Attakullakulla, and Ostenaco, spoke of an intolerable situation. Their people could not even hunt by the Holston, "for the whole Nation is full of [white] Hunters and the Guns Rattling every way, and Horse Paths on the River both up and down [and] we are Sure they have Settled the Land a great Way on this Side of the Line." The headmen warned of a possible violent eruption since "the Virginia people will not listen to any body but do as they please for they Steal our Deer and Land." Cherokee "Young fellows" were said to be "very angry to see their Hunting Grounds taken from them."[62] Those lands were vital to the Cherokee hunter's sense of being a man whose skills provided for his people.

The Cherokees had geographic priorities. They cared far more about the Great Kanawha's southern rim than that river's northerly banks, which were prime Shawnee hunting grounds. The Holston mattered enormously for physical and spiritual sustenance. The Great (Long) Island of the Holston (at today's Kingsport, Tennessee) had been a Cherokee sacred place and a site for peace talks with other Native peoples for generations. In 1766, Cherokees rejected the proposal

The Politics of Alliance and Survival   315

of a Virginia trader to establish a storehouse on the Great Island. Oconostota adamantly opposed the idea and suggested that a trading warehouse be established well eastward.[63]

In 1770, Stuart addressed a root cause of Native discontent for which there appeared only makeshift and temporary solutions. Writing to Baron de Botetourt, successor to Fauquier as Virginia's governor, the superintendent explained that the Cherokees could never accept Williamsburg's most extreme boundary demand, which by Stuart's estimate would meet the Tennessee River only sixty miles from Overhill Cherokee towns and within a short distance of the Chickasaws, too. Both Native peoples would thereby be "cut off . . . from their most Valuable Hunting Grounds, it being a Fact well known, that they always Hunt at the distance of One or two Hundred Miles from their Villages for an Obvious Reason, the Scarcity of deer near the dwellings of a Nation of Hunters."[64]

Treaty boundary lines were thin reeds against surging colonial expansion. If the Cherokees were some 9,000 persons living in villages clustered within hunting lands of 40,000 square miles, how could they prevent white settlers moving into what colonials viewed as unoccupied lands? By 1770, the number of hunters and settlers living "beyond" the boundary line and in Cherokee territories was several hundred, but what if it should increase over time to thousands? Stuart's duty required him to prevent such a situation from developing in the first place. The superintendent had two cards to play with Virginia. The first was to invoke royal authority. The second was to raise the fear of provoking a pan-Nativist union at war with British colonialism. As Stuart warned Botetourt, Virginia's overreach would spark "the Jealousies and Apprehensions of every Tribe on the Continent," threatening "a General Rupture, & Coalition of, all the Tribes."[65]

Stuart's warning was well timed. While prominent Cherokee headmen negotiated a testy Virginia boundary settlement in 1770–1771, Shawnees welcomed Native emissaries of the Ohio and Great Lakes to collaborate against the British. Cherokees and Creeks frequented these meetings, too, which centered at a great council house on the Scioto River north of the Ohio. Colonials were not the only object of scorn. Ohio Indians vented disgust with the Six Nations over the Fort Stanwix treaty and shared news of the sellout with the Cherokees. In October, General Gage reported that the Shawnees had persuaded "all the Western Tribes over the Lakes, & about Lake Michigan as well as the Ouabache" to make peace with the Cherokees. The Shawnee plan was then "to form a Confederacy of all the Western & Southern [Indian] Nations." What was good news for Cherokees in this instance was precisely what Gage most feared.[66]

British officials were adept at using their diplomatic leverage to forestall a pan-Nativist union. Kept in the know by John Stuart, William Johnson got word in 1769 that the Cherokees sorely desired English and Iroquois mediation to achieve a halt to lethal northern and western Indian attacks. Johnson was quite ready to assist Stuart's efforts on this score. The Cherokees had their own security at heart. As previously seen, Cherokee headmen visited the Mohawk Valley in 1768 for peace negotiations with the Six Nations and their Canadian Indian allies. On the return home, Attakullakulla was accompanied by Iroquois guests who were hosted at Chota. Good talks had a positive momentum. In July 1770, six Cherokee deputies arrived in the Mohawk Valley to confer with the Six Nations. Unfortunately, the visitors' names are unrecorded in the conference proceedings. Playing bigwig, Johnson won a pledge by Iroquois chiefs to restrain their Illinois "cousins" from attacking the Cherokees. The superintendent meanwhile furthered his personal interest by assuring his Cherokee guests that the Fort Stanwix cession, which he had engineered, did not extend so far south as to threaten their people's lands. The Cherokees could not rest on these words. Whatever was gained through Johnson's pull, they counted most on John Stuart to tame Virginia's enormous territorial ambitions.[67]

Lochaber and Its Aftermath

In October 1770, Stuart's role as mediator was put to the test at a major conference with Cherokee deputies and Virginia representatives, headed by Colonel John Donelson. The setting was Lochaber, Alexander Cameron's plantation in South Carolina's Long Canes district, a quiet spot in what had recently been an embattled and bloodied frontier zone. When the conference began on October 18, about 1,000 Cherokee men, women, and children had planted themselves on the grounds. The number is astonishing; above 10 percent of the entire Cherokee nation was present. Some had traveled from relatively nearby Lower Towns while others had journeyed several hundred miles to partake of food and drink, courtesy of superintendent Stuart, and to await gifts at

The Politics of Alliance and Survival   317

the conference's end. Large Native attendance at such conferences was hardly novel, but it now bordered on extremity, an unmistakable sign of Cherokee dependency on colonials.[68]

The negotiations resulted in an agreement weighted toward Virginia's interests, if not to the extent that the Old Dominion desired. Stuart framed a treaty under intense colonial pressure, doing what he could to restrain Virginia's grasp west of the Proclamation Line. The Cherokees gave up cherished lands, while barely preserving what mattered most to them. The new line's southwestern terminus was to be marked only six miles east of the Great Island of the Holston. Speaking for his nation, Oconostota aired his sadness in the midst of the talks: "I pity the white people but they do not pity me." Ironically, the Cherokee cession, purportedly situated within "the dominion of Virginia," was officially made to George III, the Indians' supposed benefactor.[69]

Lochaber marked a Cherokee retreat, a strategic withdrawal intended to maintain peace with the hope of securing a modicum of protection and steadier trade. Oconostota and Attakullakulla were the only two Cherokee headmen who spoke at length at the formal treaty sessions. Oconostota warned of an impending generational divide, remarking that "young [Cherokee] fellows are gone out to Hunt, & know nothing of this, and will say why should these Old men give away the Land without our knowledge." He complained of a Captain Guess of Virginia, who "comes into our Grounds & Hunts with Fifty Men, & kills our deer and when we tell him of it, he threatens to Shoot us down." Oconostota's gift of a two-headed pipe to Stuart was a symbolic closing to his talk. Each pipe head, "looking to the other," would allow the superintendent to see his Cherokee "Children" as he smoked from afar.[70]

Oconostota spoke of an unpalatable reality in a dignified, somber way. Attakullakulla rose to poetic heights, articulating a world founded on supernal justice. He talked of the Being "above" who "made this land" and "gave it to the Indians to Live upon," while "the white people's Land is beyond the great Water." Attakullakulla's vision was not one of evicting colonials but preserving his people's way of life rooted in an ancient past. While wishing to live peaceably with "white brethren," he had come to believe in multiple cosmic creations manifest in the human world. As Attakullakulla said, "There are Three Great Beings above, one who has Charge of the White, one of the Red, & one of the Black people." Similar ideas had circulated among Delawares in the Susquehanna Valley since the 1750s and passed to other Native peoples. Attakullakulla likely absorbed the teaching firsthand since he had traveled about the upper Ohio Valley over many years. Why did he state it at Lochaber? While his motives are not obvious, it is noteworthy that Attakullakulla did not mention the current King George at the conference. He simply stated that "there was a very good King over the Great Water" when he was there. Attakullakulla's words were poignant, an implicit admission that the English king was distant and all but absent. "The Great Being above" could alone order things so that "no Injustice" was done. Attakullakulla assumed a supreme cosmic force for good despite all that appeared wrong. He could not fathom why the white people were now practically at the Cherokees' door. Surely, they were acting outside the law, without Stuart's approval or the assent of Virginia's governor.[71]

Cherokee discontent was rife after the Lochaber treaty. Five months later, Oconostota and other headmen called Cameron to Chota for a candid talk. Speaking for all, the Great Warrior talked of walking back the treaty because his "young People" were disturbed by the enormous land cession. Oconostota wanted to return the wampum beads that he had received from the British at Lochaber as a sign of accord. Cameron would have none of it. He opposed any departure from the treaty, refused to take back the beads, and went so far as to warn the Cherokees that noncompliance with the cession would be looked upon as an act of war. "Scotchie" knew that Stuart had no desire to bargain again with Virginia about a boundary line, which, however onerous for the Cherokees, had struck Williamsburg as insufficient for colonial expansion. An uneasy status quo held. Oconostota once more told "Eldest Brother" Cameron of his nation's "young men" who "have an equal right to the land" as their elders. The Great Warrior was careful not to sacrifice his standing among his people by doing the Virginians' business of marking the new boundary line.[72]

Cherokee restiveness prompted conferencing with similarly troubled Indian nations out of English earshot. In addition to journeys to Ohio country, Cherokees welcomed Shawnee, Delaware, Mingos, and "Nantoogas" (Nottawegas) to Chota. Unlike the Cherokee-Iroquois peace brokered by Johnson, these bonds were forged by Natives alone. Cameron was anxious. Informing Stuart of events, he reported that no white person had been present at the Chota gathering and that "Half breeds were even turned out of the Town House" where talks were held. Oconostota adroitly kept Scotchie in the dark. If King George's men worried about pan-Indian stirrings, they might be more apt to assuage

The Politics of Alliance and Survival

Cherokee concerns. Cameron deliberately got drunk with Oconostaota one night "in order to sift him to the bottom," but admitted to being "not . . . the wiser for it" the next day.[73]

For all Cameron's empathy with Cherokees, there were limits to his tolerance. As a British agent, he found Oconostota's standing as "a great politician" to be an obstacle to deciphering Cherokee diplomacy. Cameron cultivated friendships with Willanawa and Ostenaco as he strained for cooperative sources. While knowing some Cherokee vocabulary, he was not fluent and invariably called on a colonial interpreter when necessary. Unburdening himself to Stuart, Cameron opined that Cherokees "will never unanimously consent to Strike us, unless they compelled by a Superior force of Indians; but Damn them, they are blood thirsty, and must have blood somewhere; their young men at this juncture long more for it, than a pregnant woman for that she loves." In fact, Oconostota did not want a war with white settlers. Overhill Cherokees had other foes to fight. Before northern Indian visitors left Chota, Cherokee men gave them ten western Indian scalps, in all likelihood those of Illinois war victims.[74]

Unlike Oconostota, Attakullakulla was long past taking a tough position toward the "white people" and sticking to it. In May 1771, "the Carpenter" and a few Overhill friends teamed with Donelson and Cameron in marking the new Virginia-Cherokee treaty line through rugged, hilly country. Tiring of the trek and open to bribery, Attakullakulla proposed a boundary change in favor of the Virginians. Donelson pledged £500 to Attakullakulla as recompense. Instead of the Great Kanawha River as the border, Attakullakulla approved an easier natural boundary—the Louisa River (today's Kentucky River), to the southwest. The Virginians gladly accepted. Donelson reckoned that Virginia thereby procured an additional ten million acres above the initial Lochaber cession! The Old Dominion's governors cooed at territorial gains quite as much as the gentry. Assuming the governorship in 1771, John Murray, the Earl of Dunmore, mastered the art of hewing to London's official line on Indian policy while pushing an expansionist agenda.[75]

Perhaps Attakullakulla thought that Overhill headmen would acquiesce in his deal if they shared in his payoff. If so, he badly miscalculated. Three years later, he was still asking Donelson for money that Virginia's government declined to pay. The matter was no secret. In 1774, Oconostota told Cameron that there "was but One [Cherokee] Man that Sold the Land" in a bargain with Donelson—and that man "did it without Acquainting us about it, and that Man is dead." The "dead" man was Attakullakulla, who walked the earth but in near isolation from his people.[76]

Under the Proclamation of 1763, Native peoples were not obliged to sell or transfer land except by consent and under royal auspices. By choice and necessity, Cherokees nevertheless came to offer land to particular colonials. About 1768, Cameron received a gift of land by the Saluda River courtesy of Seroweh, Tistoe, and the Wolf of Keowee. The tract, twelve miles square and on the Indian side of the Cherokee–South Carolina boundary, was situated along a prime trading path. Learning of the deal two years later, Stuart upbraided Cameron for accepting the land without his imprimatur and express royal permission. If his deputy could receive such a favor, what was to prevent other colonials from bribing Indians to yield acreage? Cameron responded with a lengthy justification, explaining that Seroweh intended the land for Cameron's son born of Scotchie's Cherokee mistress. Seroweh was the boy's grandfather. According to Cameron's account, which seems credible even if self-interested, Cherokees viewed the child "as one of their own" and hoped that he "would be brought up in the manner of a white Man" with learning that might be of service to his Native kin. Stuart acquiesced. He could do little else after Cameron produced Oconostota's written talk extolling how the boy would "resemble both Red & white Men & live amongst us when his Father is dead." There was nothing illegal, the superintendent reasoned, if Cameron held the land in trust for his son, a Cherokee himself.[77]

The Cherokee temptation to cede land for immediate gain went far beyond the gift to Cameron. In early 1771, senior Overhill headmen decided to yield a large tract of land to a group of merchants operating out of Augusta, Georgia. The traders initiated the negotiation by offering presents and the cancellation of current Cherokee debts. Cameron regarded the agreement as problematic not only for violating the royal proclamation but because the cession was situated on the west side of the Savannah River—an area in which the Creeks had a stronger interest than the Cherokees. He did not flinch at upbraiding the headmen for signing papers they could not understand and without any supervising official, like himself, who had their interests "at heart" and could protect them from fraud. Unless such practices were halted, he warned, the Cherokees might "shortly be dispossessed" of all they had.[78]

The Politics of Alliance and Survival

The matter did not rest. Ostenaco, Oconostota, Ketagusta, and other headmen soon met with "Scotchie" to make their case. Turning Cameron's argument on its head, Ostenaco contended that his people were entirely justified in making the sale since the land belonged to them, while the "Great man above" had given lands to "the white people" on the other side of "the great water." Moreover, the bargain was done "with the unanimous consent of our warriors, and young people." Ostenaco explained that the Cherokees had no other means to pay their debts since they had to fight enemies over a long span and had little time to hunt. Rather than violating the king's wishes, he said everything had been done according to the Augusta Congress, which in his view provided that his people should "give some of our Lands to our Brethren the English," and having done so, "made their boundary very high," as formidable as the mountains. Cherokees clearly felt a great debt burden. When consenting to the land deal, they insisted that the traders burn their account books. The debts would exist no more if there was no paper record that traders used to calculate what was due.[79]

Native peoples paid a price for desperately needed short-term gains in an environment where their options were narrowed by reduced hunting lands, an unremitting need for goods and liquor, and a deerskin trade that put them badly in debt. While the Creeks initially opposed the Cherokee land cession west of the Savannah, they reconsidered the matter with the encouragement of James Wright, governor of Georgia, who contended that they, too, would benefit by relinquishing land for the remission of debts. In June 1773, Wright negotiated a treaty at Augusta by which Creek headmen, acting jointly with the Cherokees, ceded 2.1 million acres west of the Savannah River. The lands included not only what the Cherokees had already parted with but an enormous area of indisputably Creek territory to the south.[80]

As part of this "New Purchase," Georgia agreed to pay off Creek trading debts through funds raised from the sale of ceded land to speculators and settlers. Many Creeks, especially in the Lower Towns, were angered over what had been lost. Violence burst forth from pent-up frustration over years. In December 1773, a Creek war band killed a Georgia settler family; other lethal attacks occurred a month later. Retaliation followed. Okfsukee chief Mad Turkey, who was visiting Augusta, was murdered by a white man who escaped without consequence. Georgia and bordering Creek country were in turmoil. Cherokees stayed out of the maelstrom. Physically closest to Creek

322   *Upheavals and the Will to Live, 1762–1795*

country, Lower Cherokee spokesmen sent messages to the Cowetas, lecturing them not to attack colonial traders. If the Creeks wished to fight, they should "go where the White people live" and not come "near our Towns." Headman Chinisto of Conasatchee sent another talk to Coweta on behalf of Cherokee women, "as they are the Mother of us all and ought to be heard." His rendering of the women's talk had a personal voice: "I shall stay at Home and mind my Fire while my young Men are killing meat for my little ones. We go to bed and rise in peace, and we desire to Continue so."[81] The ideal of woman-peacemaker was repeatedly summoned in Cherokee culture, and sometimes self-servingly by men.

The road toward a Creek-Georgia "peace" in 1774 was bloody. Hurt by a colonial trade embargo, Lower Creek headmen consented to execute three Indian killers of whites as satisfaction to the English. Upper Creeks did the same to two of their own. These self-inflicted deaths, unprecedented in scope for the Muscogees and allies, occurred against a backdrop of intense pressure. The Creeks could not afford to lose access to munitions when they were at war with the Choctaws. That conflict, which began about 1765, seemed a godsend to the British, who, with rare exceptions, stoked the flames or at a minimum declined to mediate an end to the intertribal conflict, which persisted for a decade. Creek leaders who favored peace made little headway against those headmen and young warriors who exacted retaliation against the Choctaws and invited reprisals. In 1774, the Mortar, an adversary whom Stuart respected for "his Sensible & Manly Love to his Country," met his demise when leading a Creek war band to procure munitions at New Orleans. He was struck down by Choctaw fighters near the Alabama River.[82]

Violence and the Collapse of Authority

The Cherokees had no occasion for rest while the seaboard British colonies cried "slavery" over the Tea Act. In May 1773, two Cherokee youths were helping to mark the new Georgia-Cherokee boundary line when they took a little rest and came to a white family's home to ask for some milk. Being alone, the hospitable woman of the house gave them some food and drink. Her son, Hezekiah Collins, was of a different mood. Coming home and seeing the Cherokees, he readied his rifle, shot one Indian guest to death, and clubbed the other with his gun before finishing his bloody work with an ax. Both victims were about

The Politics of Alliance and Survival   323

twenty years old. Collins's father then helped his son throw the bodies in a river. Young Collins was briefly detained by Georgia authorities but soon escaped. Governor Wright's call for his arrest was as feckless as nearly all official attempts to bring white murderers of Indians to justice. Two Lower Cherokee headmen, meanwhile, sent word to Cameron that their people would not seek revenge for the murders. One even stated that "Poor [white] People" of the area "may be afraid of our People when they see them." The desire for peace, which was overwhelming among vulnerable Cherokee communities, did not mean that those towns restrained their young warriors from doing what they thought necessary. Lower and Middle Town headmen admitted that three of their men had recently joined the Creeks in killing whites. There were virtually no British troops in the area that could help to restore order. The crown had withdrawn Fort Prince George's soldiers in 1768 as a cost-saving measure.[83]

A still greater crisis ensued after Colonel William Russell and Daniel Boone, with several families and thirty men, set out from Virginia toward the Ohio River in October 1773 to reconnoiter lands then expected to become part of a new British interior province. The large party established several camps as it negotiated the Cumberland Gap. At daybreak one morning, Shawnee warriors surprised the lead group, killing Henry Russell and James Boone, sons of the two frontier leaders, along with three other whites and a Black man. The bodies of several victims were badly mangled and shot with arrows. The killers placed a war club near the bodies—an open display of warrior prowess. From reports, it became clear that two Cherokee fighters participated with Shawnees in the attack. When questioned by Cameron, Oconostota laid blame on the Delawares instead of the Shawnees who were then mending ties with the Cherokees.[84]

The slaying of young Russell and Boone bred retaliatory violence. Isaac Crabtree, the sole white survivor of the attack, burned with revenge and found his moment in 1774 when spotting three Cherokee men peacefully attending a colonial horse race near the Watauga River. After sizing up the potential victims, Crabtree and his companions shot dead and scalped a Cherokee man named Will who was described by Cameron as "an Active resolute good Man & very friendly to the White People." Governor Dunmore issued a reward for the murderer's arrest, but Crabtree escaped justice by fleeing into Kentucky.[85]

White settlers were not of a single mind about Indians despite widespread colonial animosity toward "red" men. A short time before

324   *Upheavals and the Will to Live, 1762–1795*

the Watauga bloodshed, several frontiersmen cared for Ostenaco's son-in-law when they found him in the woods after his canoe overturned in a river. (A white companion drowned in the accident.) Befriended by whites, Ostenaco's son-in-law went to attend the same Watauga horse race where Crabtree stalked. When a white mob went for the kill, other colonists brought Indians to safety. One Cherokee man and his wife were saved; Ostenaco's son-in-law fled that same night. Of course, such kindness was too late to save Will, who refused to run before he was gunned down. Headman Chinisto, kin of Will, ached to avenge the death but was persuaded to stay his hand by a Cherokee man who escaped the murder scene with the help of white settlers. Reviewing these events, Cameron contended that "if the Indians committed Half the Irregularities the Virginians did since the Conclusion of [the] last War, they would have been at War with them long ere now."[86]

Changes in the landscape were ongoing. As white settlement grew in Cherokee country, colonials followed a timeworn practice of adopting Native place names. By doing so, they identified with their new environs in the act of taking possession. This was true of settlers by the Watauga River, which flows north into the Holston in what is now East Tennessee. The Nolichucky River was another nearby white settlement zone. Few settlers knew that "Nolichucky" was a corruption of the Cherokee Nanatlugunyi, "Spruce Tree Place." Bargaining across ethnic bounds sprung up in this frontier environment. Settlers by the Watauga and Nolichucky sometimes paid "rent" to Cherokee headmen to live on the land for indefinite periods. These arrangements by no means appeased other Cherokees who dreaded losing their ancestral soil.[87]

During the summer and fall of 1774, Oconostota weighed the consequences of wrongs suffered by his people, besides harm inflicted by them. Cameron, his most trusted colonial friend, strongly advised him not to strike at white settlers after Will's death. Scotchie meanwhile urged the Cherokees to offer satisfaction for "the Death of Young Russell." Oconostota objected that he did not think that suggestion fair because of recent Cherokee lives lost to whites. Before year's end, however, Oconostota and other headmen gave way by having one Cherokee man put to death for complicity in the Russell affair. The slain man's comrade escaped to Chickasaw country, doubtless with his people's allowance. For a time, John Stuart worried that the "principal" Cherokee chiefs were "falling into Contempt" among their people by

The Politics of Alliance and Survival

failing to assert their authority. From another perspective, the elders' decision to appease the English by executing the accused warrior probably widened the divide between senior headmen and young warriors who were ready to make common cause with Shawnee militants and their "Western" tribal allies.[88]

White frontiersmen were meanwhile going their own way with little respect for the king's law. Arthur Campbell, a tough frontier leader of Fincastle County, Virginia, is a prime example. While denouncing the Watauga racetrack murder as "detestable" in a letter to Cameron, he warned that Cherokee "Reprisals" might result in "a bloody & destructive War which might not End but in the total Extinction of the Cherokee Nation, and the desolation of many hundreds of his Majesty's good Subjects." The threat was seemingly meant to forestall violence, but it had a searing tone that spoke otherwise. Angered by the killing of young Russell and companions, Campbell wrote of settlers' growing frustrations. Superintendent Stuart seemed to care little "when any of our People is robbed or murdered by the Indians." Some whites even suspected Cameron of instigating Cherokee attacks. Campbell observed that the Cumberland Gap, which he admitted lay within Cherokee territory, "is the common and indeed almost the only accessible way, for this Country['s] People to travel to the Ohio, and the Lands between that, and the Waters of the Cherokee [Tennessee] River," which he believed lawfully open to settlement.[89]

Campbell's view was the epitome of British-American colonialism, expanding on settler rights in the broadest possible construction. It was scarcely in tune with British imperial policy, which finally nixed the idea of a new British colony west of the mountains. In March 1773, the earl of Dartmouth, secretary of state, warned of chaos ensuing from the "dangerous Spirit of unlicensed Emigration into the Interior parts of America." The British imperium was losing control in the continental interior for many reasons, including cost-cutting and allowing individual provinces to regulate the Indian trade, which fostered uncontrolled competition to the detriment of Native peoples. There was also military pullback, symbolized when troops withdrew from Fort Pitt in 1771. The resultant vacuum set the stage for Virginia's conflict with Ohio Indians in 1774—"Lord Dunmore's War"—which presaged the struggle for Kentucky during the American Revolutionary War.[90]

Campbell put Cameron on notice that frontiersmen would not heed obstructive royal officials. That was indeed the case, if not part of a colonial master plan. In 1774, land speculator Richard Henderson of

North Carolina bypassed the king's authority altogether by pursuing an enormous purchase of Cherokee lands through Attakullakulla. Early the next year, Governor Josiah Martin of North Carolina issued a proclamation nullifying Henderson's private bargaining with Indians. In March, Dunmore personally wrote Attakullakulla and other chiefs to warn against entering into any agreement or land sale with Henderson. The king's governors and "duly authorized" officers could alone safeguard their "Brothers the Cherokees." Dunmore predicted endless contention if "very wicked men" such as Henderson made "private arrangements" to grasp Cherokee land. The probable outcome was chaos and war—circumstances that could "prove fatal to the whole Indian Race in the End." Dunmore's inflated prose, while expressing genuine concerns, was written with London in mind as much as the Cherokees. He was the faithful royal servant admonishing Cherokees to depend on the king's "Fatherly love and Care" or risk losing his protection.[91]

Weeks before Attakullakulla received Dunmore's message, he determined on a land cession to Henderson for a large payout in trade goods craved for sustenance. The result was the notorious treaty of Sycamore Shoals, negotiated by the Watauga River in March 1775. Oconostota initially approved the deal but soon tried to step back. The purported sale encompassed huge swaths of Native lands in what is now Kentucky and central Tennessee. The generational divide within the Cherokees widened as if an unbridgeable ravine.[92]

Attakullakulla was no coward. In 1773, he led a party of thirty men to fight Illinois tribes. He was then nearing seventy years old. Prior to setting out for war, Attakullakulla set aside a wampum string for his old friend, John Stuart, in case he died in combat. The gift was intended to remind the superintendent of Attakullakulla's two children. It was useful to have powerful British friends. Attakullakulla survived the clash with the Illinois, a type of warfare he had known since young manhood.[93] The idea of fighting the "white people," with all their numbers and strength, was another matter. Attakullakulla had come to believe that such a battle was a losing and destructive proposition for his people. One year later, his son Dragging Canoe would be the foremost Cherokee war leader against the Americans who were themselves engaged in their own struggle for independence from Britain. Cherokee survival hung in the balance.

The Politics of Alliance and Survival

11

Cherokees and the American Revolution

When Cherokees today speak of their history, they take pride in Dragging Canoe, their boldest war leader of the American Revolutionary era. According to legend, he was so strong as a boy that he could carry a canoe. He grew to be six feet tall, muscular, and physically imposing. Curiously, he scarcely appears in the colonial record before 1774, when Alexander Cameron, alias "Scotchie," offered a pithy description: "The Dragging Canoe is the only Young Warriour of Note now over the Hills." What Cameron meant by "young" is an open question. Some historians believe that Dragging Canoe was above forty years old at the time. Whatever his precise age, he had sufficient experience to guide young warriors and a bold spirit and firm countenance that earned respect.[1]

Dragging Canoe was a son of Attakullakulla. Though a Cherokee boy was not of his father's blood and not strictly kin, one cannot help but imagine that Dragging Canoe forged his identity by taking a deliberately different course than Attakullakulla, the most decidedly pro-English advocate among his people from the French and Indian War to the dawn of the American Revolution. In the wake of the British-Cherokee war, in which Dragging Canoe most probably fought, he came to live at Mialoquo, a village on the Great Island on the Little Tennessee River only a mile south of where Fort Loudoun stood. According to Cherokee tradition, Mialoquo was founded by former inhabitants of Kituwah, the Cherokees' beloved mother town destroyed by the redcoats in 1761. To Cherokees, connectedness to place was cherished and not something to be lightly given up.[2]

Dragging Canoe enters history most strikingly at the Sycamore Shoals conference held alongside the Watauga River in March 1775—a gathering of 1,000 to 1,200 Cherokees that came to the site at the invitation of Richard Henderson and his Transylvania Company associates. The principal speculators in attendance, encouraged by previous meetings with Attakullakulla, had expectations of gaining title to immense Native territories. Dragging Canoe was disgusted by Henderson's swollen ambitions. At one point in the talks, he walked out "in a passion" when Henderson threatened to withhold any goods from the Cherokees if his terms were not met. Other Cherokee men joined the walkout.[3]

Dragging Canoe was ready to listen to Henderson, up to a point. While apparently willing to part with lands northeast of the Kentucky River, he warned against any surrender of his people's core hunting grounds and living space to the south. One Virginia man recalled Dragging Canoe issuing a stern warning about lands "below" the Kentucky: "It was the bloody Ground, and would be dark, and difficult to settle it." Other Cherokee men said much the same, knowing that Shawnee warriors were combating Daniel Boone's small Kentucky settlement— itself supported and financed by Henderson, who was outwardly brash but inwardly desperate for Cherokee complaisance to buttress his company's incipient and precarious empire-building.[4]

The scene at Sycamore Shoals was a virtual riot of wheeling and dealing, carousing, and bargaining that consumed four days. Besides Henderson and friends, several hundred white men were on hand to make money by selling food and drink in addition to seeking a piece of Cherokee ground. The gathering had a helter-skelter air, quite unlike the orderly negotiations John Stuart favored. In fact, no British official was present at Henderson's land grab. Superintendent Stuart was at his Charles Town residence, where he was closely watched by American Whigs distrustful of royal officialdom. Alexander Cameron was at his Lochaber estate in the piedmont. Wary of Henderson's intrigues, Scotchie decided to set out for Overhill country but turned back when he realized that he could do nothing to stop Cherokees from going to the Watauga. His own interpreter, Joseph Vann, skedaddled to Sycamore Shoals to serve at Henderson's parley for a price.[5] British authority was on the verge of collapse in the Cherokee homeland. This situation was a godsend to sophisticated colonial gentlemen who yearned for riches of an entirely different order than an ordinary

Cherokees and the American Revolution

white family's homestead. Henderson was himself a former North Carolina judge and a politically conservative man until casting westward for the big haul with plans to sell parcels of the company's lands to settler-adventurers.[6]

Cherokees were in abundance at Sycamore Shoals but without a consensus among themselves. While Dragging Canoe stoutly rejected a land cession, a great deal of confusion prevailed in the Cherokee camp by the Watauga. One colonial observer found a group of chiefs "almost all Drunk" when Henderson's cooked-up deeds were completed. Only three headmen were said to mark the papers—Attakullakulla, the Raven of Chota, along with Oconostota, who had immediate misgivings. Oconostota's wife doubtless had something to do with his second thoughts since she openly complained of the proposed cession of Watauga River lands. The morning after the drunken bout, Oconostota and fellow headmen were entirely sober, drawing maps on the ground and contending that their people had not given away the Watauga but had only permitted white settlers to pass along riverbank paths in journeys to the west.[7]

Few Cherokees grasped, let alone accepted Henderson's conception of his full heist—the idea of acquiring up to twenty million acres of land in exchange for £10,000 worth of trade goods. The Transylvania Company's claimed purchase extended from the Cumberland River to the Ohio, encompassing much of what is present-day Kentucky, north-central Tennessee, with strategically situated river valleys and corridors in eastern Tennessee and southwestern Virginia. In reality, the windfall was moot because of staunch Native opposition and also a legal challenge by Virginia, soon to be an independent state, which rejected the Transylvania syndicate's pretensions to western land within its own purported domain.[8]

The Sycamore Shoals "treaty," as it is sometimes called, involved a plethora of face-to-face dealings and bargains between colonials and Cherokees. Many white settlers operated outside of Henderson's purview, seeking to rent or purchase coveted lands on which they resided, aspired to live, or wished to travel through with security. Headmen sometimes agreed to colonists' propositions at a price—a practice that undermined Native traditions of communal consent and made a mockery of British policy. As recently as July 1774, Cameron had warned Cherokee leaders "against granting, renting, or anywise bargaining with the White People for Land." And yet his advice was not heeded. Cherokees could not easily bypass all dealings with whites when many hundreds

330   *Upheavals and the Will to Live, 1762–1795*

of Indians suffered from the diminished deerskin trade and the inconstant supply of British presents.[9]

The impact of Sycamore Shoals was felt long after the conference ended. The gathering exposed fissures that widened into chasms during the American Revolutionary War. The most obvious fault line was between white settlers and Cherokees desperate to hold their ground. Cherokees were divided among themselves. Many of their young men, especially in Overhill country, were disgusted by appeasement and ready to take on "the Virginians"—the name southern Indians gave to nearly all white Americans who intruded into their lands. (The name was not a compliment when most Indians spoke.) But a substantial number in the Cherokee nation did not want a war with the "white people" that could bring hardship and disaster. In the months after Sycamore Shoals, Cherokees felt the rift between Great Britain and its colonies. They knew that Scotchie was at odds with other white men who scarcely praised the king but rather spoke of things gone wrong that must be put right. Cameron admonished Lower Town chiefs to stay true to the Great King George, but his own position during the summer of 1775 was hardly secure.[10]

Native peoples had difficult choices to make when considering whether to align with Britain, remain neutral, or even side with the Americans as strife intensified. For the Cherokees the tipping point toward war came in 1776, when the British supplied them with munitions. Buoyed by Shawnee and northern Indian support, Dragging Canoe was then ready to lead warriors against "the Virginians." His offensive fell far short of driving out white settlers from Native land. Instead, it brought a furious counterblast by Southern state militias that nearly broke the Cherokee world. The crisis was not only one of physical survival but whether Cherokees could retain a sense of common peoplehood when divided over fundamental issues of continuing warfare or negotiating peace with any hope of dignity.

The militia invasions of 1776 were more devastating to Cherokees than the destruction wrought by British troops in 1760–1761. Considering the carnage in burned towns and the hundreds of Native deaths, it is astonishing that Dragging Canoe and his supporters did not give up the war when so many Cherokees were consumed by the challenge of daily sustenance. Dragging Canoe's stalwarts and their families moved south to establish new villages by Chickamauga Creek along the Tennessee River's southeastern margins. Thousands of other Cherokees, including hundreds who had shunned war, either rebuilt former

Cherokees and the American Revolution

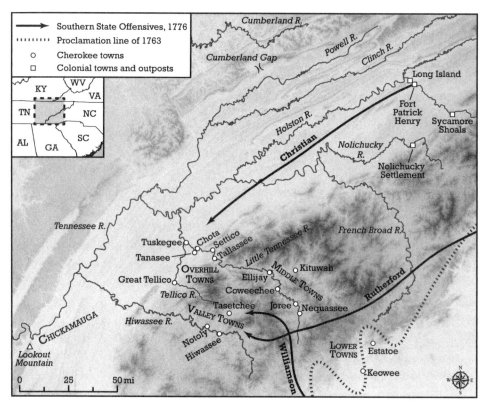

Southern State Invasions and Cherokee Country, 1776

communities or formed villages elsewhere within their people's ancestral lands. The geography of dispersion amounted to a reordering of communal bonds, which were stretched but did not break. The migration to Chickamauga Creek and environs was a revolution in its own right, no less radical in its implications than the American colonial struggle for independence.[11]

Cherokee diplomatic initiatives during the Revolutionary War assumed varied trajectories that reflected diverse and contrasting communal perspectives. Militants hewed to the British and strengthened their ties with Crown officials who labored just as assiduously to keep the Chickamaugas and others on their side. While fighting raged, headmen such as Oconostota and Utsidsata (Corn Tassel) tested negotiations with American authorities. The peace advocates pursued the politics of preservation. They were willing to consider necessary, though painful, territorial concessions toward security, sustenance, and survival. Cherokee women were part of this effort, and none more famously than Nancy Ward (Nan-ye-hi), a remarkable example of female adaptability and perseverance in the face of adversity. The American Revolutionary War was not only a period of great suffering and loss in Cherokee society but one of hardihood and resolve, whether represented by Dragging Canoe, Corn Tassel, or Nan-ye-hi in their different ways.[12]

The British and Cherokees

The spring of 1775 was a time of crisis for royal officers and white Loyalist subjects in the Southern colonies. In Charles Town, Patriot militia companies drilled almost daily after receiving news of the fighting at Lexington and Concord. Tories suffered continual harassment. John Stuart, falsely suspected of stirring Indians to murder American frontier settlers, faced the wrath of South Carolina and Georgia Whigs who pored over his correspondence. The Georgia men spotted a smoking gun in one letter in which the superintendent urged deputy Cameron to encourage the Cherokees "to act in defence of His Majesty and Government, if found necessary." In truth, Stuart strongly desired to gain Native support in the crisis but had as yet done little that way. Fearing arrest in late June 1775, he set sail from Savannah to St. Augustine in British East Florida—a safe Tory haven with a royal garrison.[13]

British possession of the Floridas—a result of imperial victory in the Seven Years' War—was critical to Stuart's evolving plan of channeling munitions to the Cherokees for their own defense, with attendant obligations to the Crown. Because routes were blocked through South Carolina and Georgia, the superintendent looked to alternatives via Pensacola and Mobile in West Florida. In the fall of 1775, he received the go-ahead when General Gage, commanding at Boston, authorized him to arm Indians to "distress" the "rebellious" colonies. Stuart appointed his brother Henry to be his point man in West Florida for the delivery of gunpowder and ball to the Cherokees and Creeks. British policy toward southern Indians underwent a radical change from the prewar era when royal officers exploited distrust between rival Indigenous nations to forestall any hostile pan-Indian union. Divide and rule was no longer warranted. The king's forces required a united Native front to defeat the American revolutionaries.[14]

While John Stuart was safely ensconced in Florida, Cameron had his hands full in staving off Whigs who sought to arrest or even kill

Cherokees and the American Revolution   333

him. South Carolina's revolutionary council had cause to worry about Scotchie, who was rumored to promise gunpowder to Lower Town Cherokees. In July 1775, William Henry Drayton, a leading South Carolina Whig, made a pitch for Lower Cherokee support, accusing Cameron of being a man of "two Tongues."[15] Over the next two months, the political heat intensified. Worried that some Native chiefs might sell him out, Cameron reminded headmen of his defense of Cherokee land rights. Though Scotchie politicked ably, he could not remain safely in the area. In September, Drayton conveyed his "request" that Cameron remove from the Cherokee Nation and preferably depart by sea for St. Augustine or Pensacola. Disdaining the order, Scotchie traveled to his old residence at Toqua in Overhill country, where Dragging Canoe was surely glad to see him. British and Cherokee interests steadily converged.[16]

In December, Dragging Canoe was in Mobile to secure a critical English supply line from the Gulf. Henry Stuart, then at Pensacola, went to meet the Cherokee leader, who distinguished himself from the "Old" chiefs who had yielded to Henderson. Unlike cautious elders, he had "a great many Young fellows that would support him" and "were determined to have their land" from "the White People." Dragging Canoe soon returned northward, while Stuart transferred a large stockpile of munitions from Pensacola to Mobile for northern shipment by horse load. On the long journey north, Stuart's convoy was aided by Chickasaw headman James Colbert, son of a Scots trader and Native woman, who was as staunchly pro-British as the Chickasaws among whom he lived.[17]

After a trek of some three months, Henry Stuart joined Dragging Canoe and eighty Cherokees waiting for him at the Tennessee River in April 1776. As Stuart and the Cherokee men headed east, they encountered whites traveling west to the Mississippi and the Natchez district, an area of growing Anglo settlement in West Florida. Stuart knew that Peter Chester, West Florida's royal governor, aspired to attract American Loyalist immigrants by offering them free Mississippi land grants. Henry Stuart took an interest in the colonization scheme, which might be broadened to encourage white settlers living in Cherokee territory to take up land by Natchez. If frontier whites emigrated far southwest, Cherokees would have no need to wage a risky war for their homeland. Stuart's idea may appear a pipe dream, but it was seriously entertained at the time.[18]

Cameron welcomed Henry Stuart to Toqua on April 24, 1776. Within several days, the two British agents sized up the situation. As Stuart later reported to his brother, "nothing was talked of but War" in Overhill Cherokee country. Warriors had recently brought in one white scalp to Mialoquo, Dragging Canoe's town. Stuart told the Cherokees in conference that he had ammunition for their use; Colbert was slated to deliver more gunpowder and ball through Chickasaw territory. The Cherokees were told that the king's "Obstinate Children" (the Americans) had threatened their brother "Scotchie." While Dragging Canoe's Cherokees ultimately made the decision for war, their British friends played a significant part in the drama.[19]

Henry Stuart's account of events in the spring and summer of 1776 is an invaluable historical source, if one that should be read with some healthy skepticism since it was written retrospectively, that is, after Dragging Canoe and his adherents had gone on the offensive in July 1776 and been repulsed. It was more than a month later, on August 25, that Henry Stuart recounted the ups and downs of the previous nine months in a lengthy letter to his brother, the superintendent. Henry was then safe in British Pensacola, but the Cherokee situation was rapidly deteriorating in the face of the American militia invasion. The last thing Henry Stuart wanted was for his brother to be blamed by his superiors for goading Indians to launch attacks that provoked a deadly rebel counterassault.[20]

Concerned about political fallout, Stuart wrote that Dragging Canoe himself decided for war despite British advice to the contrary. By this account, Stuart and Cameron explicitly told the Cherokees that "their Father [the King] was willing to support them with Ammunition while they paid Regard to our Talks. But that we did not yet think it time for them to go out unless they were Certain that there was an Army coming against them." Moreover, Stuart claimed that he personally had Dragging Canoe "acknowledge himself before all the Chiefs [as] the sole Cause of the War." This last flourish from Stuart's pen presents a neat scenario for British official purposes, though it is puzzling to historians, who may well question whether Tsi-yugunsini (Dragging Canoe) offered any such admission before his people.[21] Stuart's account is a masterpiece of its kind because it has arresting details, many of which appear credible. Dragging Canoe was disappointed when Stuart left Cherokee country on the eve of war. Brotherly kinship meant common sacrifice, the willingness to fight and die together. Unlike Stuart, Cameron stayed

Cherokees and the American Revolution

on and would raise the sword in coming months, though not in the first rush to war in Overhill country. He and Dragging Canoe came to feel like "blood brothers." Their bond was the subject of Cherokee storytellers into the early twentieth century.[22]

Diplomatic Stalemate and War

U.S. historians of the nineteenth and early twentieth centuries almost universally attributed the Cherokees' decision for war in 1776 to British machinations and munitions. That viewpoint was vintage colonial American; it tied the white frontiersmen's fight against the Cherokees to the broader American Revolution. What could be wrong about smashing the Indians who happened to be on the British side and were therefore foes of freedom? That this perspective originated during the Revolution should not surprise us. Supporters of the "Glorious Cause" felt victimized by British perfidy. In the well-known words of the Declaration of Independence, the crimes of "the present King of Great Britain" were manifold. Among numerous acts of tyranny, he "has endeavoured to bring on the inhabitants of our frontiers, the merciless Indian Savages, whose known rule of warfare, is an undistinguished destruction of all ages, sexes, and conditions."[23]

Thomas Jefferson's words echoed widespread American beliefs, which gained urgency on news of impending hostilities between Cherokees and white frontier inhabitants, a good number of whom regarded themselves as Virginians. In June 1776, news passed from the Tennessee frontier to Williamsburg and Philadelphia that provided fodder for Jefferson's charge. Weeks earlier, Henry Stuart had written a letter, purportedly in his own hand, which carried an ominous warning to white settlers of Watauga and Nolichucky. A British army was about to march from the Gulf Coast to Cherokee country and be reinforced along the way by five hundred warriors from each of the Creek and Chickasaw nations. The letter put the matter bluntly. The only way for white settlers to save themselves from "inevitable ruin" was for each family head "immediately to subscribe a written paper, acknowledging their allegiance to his majesty king George, and that they are ready and willing, whenever called upon, to appear in arms in defence of the British rights in America." Stuart's letter was quite probably a forgery, and likely written by an anonymous American frontiersman, but this was unclear at the time. If the writer was a settler, his ruse certainly achieved its purpose. Major Anthony Bledsoe of the local militia dispatched the letter to his superior for transmission to Williamsburg—just as he had forwarded previous correspondence in which Cameron and Stuart warned white settlers to move off Cherokee land or face peril. The forgery fed into a broad flow of information and rumor that heightened American Whig suspicions of British plotting in Cherokee country.[24]

Henry Stuart and Cameron were not reckless firebrands. While determined to strengthen British-Cherokee bonds, they aimed to do so without precipitating an uncontrollable war for which the Crown could be held responsible. Their first solution was to persuade white settlers in Cherokee country to vacate their homes peacefully while there was still time. On May 7, 1776, the two British agents aired their proposal in a public letter to "the Inhabitants of Watauga and Nonatluchky [Nolichucky]." Writing of discontented young Cherokee men, Stuart and Cameron warned of the danger the settlers faced "from a Mercyless & enraged [Indian] Enemy" that would never accept colonial land claims west of existing treaty lines. Nor did the settlers have the least hope of being supported "by Government or the Laws of your Country." The sole answer was movement "to a Country more favourable to industrious White people." Stuart and Cameron gave assurances of safe passage to West Florida where colonists could obtain bona fide land grants. The offer came with an ominous threat. The Cherokees expected the settlers to "remove in twenty days."[25] One assumes that Cameron and Stuart collaborated with Dragging Canoe and other chiefs on the ultimatum, but we cannot know for certain.

John Carter, a prominent Watauga settler, responded to Stuart and Cameron in a politic way. Referring to the Cherokees as "Brothers," he voiced a willingness to yield land back to them if they should insist on it by direct talks. Carter was inwardly confident. He had successfully dealt with Attakullakulla and other pliant headmen and would bargain again to confirm purchases and extend leases. Watauga colonists had no intention of suddenly packing their bags and leaving their farmsteads. Playing for time, Carter sagely asked for "a longer Respite" so that his people could decide on their best course. With no small irony, he thanked Stuart and Cameron for their timely warning, "so Laudable that it Certainly must be handed down to posterity after we shall be no more."[26]

Stuart and Cameron continued to press emigration in follow-up letters of May 23 to Carter and other white settlers. Surely the Watauga and Nolichucky settlers would get the message. There was no hope,

Cherokees and the American Revolution

declared the agents, of assuring "the safety of any persons that may be hardy enough to remain in the Land after the time Limited." Cherokee "young fellows" were determined to have their land. This last statement was certainly true.[27]

It was during this diplomatic standoff that Stuart's forged letter, carried by an unknown man, reached the home of Charles Robertson, a prominent Watauga settler. The missive only strengthened the settlers' resolve not to yield. While playing for time to build their arsenal, the Whig majority solidified its hold on the frontier district by arresting Tories or summoning them to account for their conduct. In the opposing camp, Cameron and Stuart welcomed fifteen white men in their neighborhood who willingly took the oath of allegiance to the king.[28]

Native diplomacy took on its own life during the crisis. Cherokees did not regard the twenty-day limit as a fixed deadline, as Cameron and Stuart had let on. While matters hung in the balance, Overhill headmen and villagers welcomed fifteen Native emissaries—Mohawk, Ottawa, Shawnee, and Delaware men who boasted of a healthy munition flow from French traders and talked further of their battle against the Americans, which was waged with the support of "all the Northern Tribes." From that day on, wrote Henry Stuart, "every Young Fellow's face in the Overhill Towns appeared Blackened & nothing was now talked of but War." Villagers set about preparing spears, clubs, and scalping knives.[29]

After an initial meeting with northern Indians, the Cherokees invited the visiting deputies to a conference at Chota some ten days later. Stuart's account offers a close view. In preparation for the gathering, the townhouse's flagstaff and portions of its walls were painted red and black. A Mohawk deputy presented a large belt of white and purple wampum to Dragging Canoe. An Ottawa leader gave a "white Belt," flecked with purple beads, signifying a desire for lasting friendship "with all their Red Brethren." A Shawnee war belt commanded attention. It was nine feet long, six inches wide, and strung with purple wampum and vermilion thread. Along with this magnificent gift came a powerful oration. The Shawnee man declared that his nation, formerly "a great people," was "reduced to a handful . . . [and] the Red people who were once masters of the whole Country hardly possessed ground enough to Stand on." Colonial forts and settlements threatened Native lives. It was "better to die like Men than to dwindle away by inches." The "Great Being who governs every thing" favored them.

338   *Upheavals and the Will to Live, 1762–1795*

Now was time for action. It was up to the Cherokees to decide whether they would take up the hatchet the Shawnees gave them six years ago. A Cherokee warrior of Chilhowee rose, took the great wampum belt from Dragging Canoe, and sung the war song as the northern visitors joined the chant.[30]

Inspired by visiting militants, Cherokees debated about when to attack. Some young men wanted to move quickly ahead before white frontiersmen strengthened their position. Trader Isaac Thomas, a courier between Henry Stuart and the American settlers, meanwhile returned to the Cherokees with a sobering letter from colonial leaders. The message began courteously enough, addressed to senior headmen Oconostota, Ostenaco, and Attakullakulla. While hoping for peace with their Cherokee "Brethren," the Whig committeemen warned the chiefs of "bad Counsel from some white Men who live amongst you"—an obvious reference to Cameron, Stuart, and friends. The committee emphatically told the Cherokees that the settlers they represented were not "Rebels to the great King your Father." The idea of the king as a protector of Indians was not lost on anxious colonists who masked their strong feelings for American independence.[31]

While settler leaders were cautious about criticizing royal authority, they did not hesitate to send an ultimatum to the Cherokees. The committee demanded that tribal elders find and execute warriors who had killed two young white men traveling on "the very path that Col. Henderson purchased" for "a valuable Consideration." The route to the Cumberland Gap and Kentucky was at stake. To whites, there could be no tolerance for "hotheaded" Indians attacking "Innocent Travelers or helpless families." If such acts occurred, the Cherokees would feel "the Vengeance of the Virginians and the neighbouring Colonies, who will march Armies into your Country to the destruction and perhaps utter extirpation of the Cherokee Nation." There was, however, still time to avoid war and "brighten the Chain, to wipe the blood out of the path and shake the hand of Friendship." Moving abruptly from bloodcurdling threat to diplomatic nicety, the committee exhorted the Cherokees to "send some of your Old men" for peace talks at the Great Island of the Holston River.[32]

The old men did not go. Attakullakulla and Oconostota sat dejected in councils. Dragging Canoe and militants held sway. Cherokees were angered rather than intimidated by the Virginian threat. Their people had declined to bow before previous warnings of destruction. Governor Lyttelton had brandished the sword when offering his futile

Cherokees and the American Revolution

peace terms after taking Native hostages. Colonels Montgomery and Grant had later sent ultimatums to Cherokee country in advance of invasion. There were certain red lines, points of pride and honor, to Cherokee men. White settlers had violated treaty lines and taken over cherished Native hunting grounds. There would be little land left if Henderson and his followers were not stopped from colonizing an immense area.

Besides posing a growing threat to the Native way of life, Virginia and North Carolina had little to offer Indians in a positive sense because both colonies had little Cherokee trade. In April 1776, Overhill headman Doublehead told North Carolina commissioners frankly that he was embarrassed to return to his country with so little from them when "the people from Pensacola"—the British—offered so much. Supply was critical. Many Creeks chose neutrality in the early stages of the American Revolutionary War because of their ties to trader George Galphin, who lent his considerable political skills to Congress.[33]

Cherokees were far from being uniformly militant. Some Hiwassee Valley and Middle Town headmen inclined toward peace because their regions were relatively unaffected by white settlement compared to either the Overhill or Lower Cherokee towns. The Overhill region was the heart of Cherokee resistance to the "Virginians," but opinion was mixed even there. Stuart wrote of opposition to Dragging Canoe in Toqua and Chota. Cherokee customs of individual and local autonomy meant that the nation was not fully behind any single course. Dragging Canoe had a good measure of respect for white friends, too. Though he wanted traders to remain in Overhill country, he did not prevent them from finding safer ground as war approached.[34]

A Failed Offensive and Deadly Counterattack

The first major Cherokee offensive against American settlements of the Tennessee frontier was furious but short-lived. On July 19, 1776, 600 to 700 Cherokee warriors advanced on colonial stockades by the Watauga and Holston Rivers, while smaller parties went out to attack colonial farmsteads. The next day, Dragging Canoe's fighters, no more than 200 men, were repelled by militia in a sharp engagement by the Holston. Thirteen warriors were killed, others wounded, and the ground was soaked with blood. Dragging Canoe himself suffered a leg wound from rifle fire. The frontier militia suffered no deaths and had only four men wounded. On July 21, about one hundred Cherokees attacked and laid siege to Fort Caswell on the Watauga, where 150 to 200 white men, women, and children were holing up with enslaved Blacks. The Cherokee fighters withdrew after two to three weeks when Virginia reinforcements neared.[35]

It is unknown if Dragging Canoe's initial war plan was influenced by British tactical advice. Cameron certainly did not want indiscriminate guerrilla raiding. If there was to be a war, it should be one to retake the Watauga and Nolichucky lands, while avoiding the killing of women and children. The first Cherokee strikes were aimed mainly at American colonial stockades, with some attacks on outlying settlements. Eighteen-year-old James Moore was captured, brought to a Cherokee town, and ritually burned at the stake.[36]

Many warriors opted for guerrilla fighting after the initial repulse. Dragging Canoe and other chiefs led war parties into the Holston, Powell, and Clinch Valleys. Hundreds of ordinary whites fled east and crowded into stations with other frontier residents. According to colonists' recollections, which passed into family lore, Cherokee fighters took eighteen white scalps in these forays. White militia struck back when they crossed the enemy's path. After one fight, Virginia militiamen carried eleven Cherokee scalps on a pole and hung the trophies above their fort's gates. The Virginians acted just as South Carolina settlers at Fort Ninety-Six in 1760 when Cherokee scalps were strung high as an emblem of martial pride and contempt for the "savage" foe. White frontiersmen tracked, reconnoitered, and killed as if they were themselves Indians.[37]

Overhill country witnessed notable clashes between Cherokees and white settlers during the summer of 1776, but it was not the only scene of frontier conflict. Cherokee warriors targeted settlers of the South Carolina piedmont in late June—more than two weeks before fighting occurred to the north. On June 29, Cherokee men Terrapin and Glass peaceably entered settler David Shettroe's house by the Keowee River but then took him captive along with an elderly white man. Other Cherokees abducted about ten colonial men, women, and children in the vicinity. In all, warriors killed more than forty persons in settler households by the Catawba River and nearby piedmont areas by the end of July. Women and children were among the scalped and mangled. Lower Town Cherokee fighters, who collaborated with Overhill militants, acted for similar reasons as Dragging Canoe's supporters, who were disgusted by settler intrusions and their own feckless village

Cherokees and the American Revolution

elders. The piedmont killings stirred immediate calls for revenge among whites in both Carolinas.[38]

To American Whigs, the outbreak of fighting in Cherokee country signaled a possible conflagration across a broad interior front where Indians, if well supplied by the Crown, might well gain the upper hand. Though frontier vulnerability worried many in Congress, General Charles Lee, commanding the American troops at Charles Town, had a different view. He knew that the powerful Creeks had not yet made a decisive turn to support the British. Lee saw the Cherokees as a prime target under the circumstances. So, too, did the South Carolina authorities with whom he closely consulted. On July 7, 1776, Lee penned a biting letter to the North Carolina Council of Safety:

> As it is now certain that a capital and favourite plan laid down by his most excellent and clement Majesty George the Third, is to lay waste the Provinces . . . and mix Men, Women & Children in one common carnage by the hands of Indians. . . . We can now with the greatest justice strike a blow which is necessary to intimidate the numerous tribes of Indians from falling into the measures of the Tyrant, and as these Cherokees are not esteemed the most formidable Warriors, we can probably do it without much risk or loss.

Lee proposed that North Carolina raise a "a body of Rifle Men" to "act in conjunction with the South Caroliners against the lower [Cherokee] Nation, whilst the Virginians march against the upper." Similarly, he urged Edmund Pendleton, president of the Virginia convention, to send militiamen "to crush" the Cherokees before the "Evil" of Indian uprisings "arises to any dangerous height."[39] Lee's idea was taken up enthusiastically by the new state authorities. The white population in the southern interior had shot up by the thousands since the French and Indian War. This fact added considerable strength to the Americans despite Whig-Tory tensions brewing in the Carolina backcountry.[40]

American Whigs had a running start in turning against the Cherokees because of prior mobilization for battle with the mother country. South Carolina's militia, with aid from North Carolina and Virginia, repelled the British army's amphibious approach toward Charles Town in late June. The American victory enabled the Southern states to shift military resources from the seaboard to the interior. For the ensuing invasion of Cherokee country, Virginia and the Carolinas raised over six thousand

342   *Upheavals and the Will to Live, 1762–1795*

men, and Georgia contributed a few hundred. The American military buildup of 1776 against the Cherokees was among the largest generated in the Southern states during the entire Revolutionary War.[41]

The Lower Cherokee Towns were at a terrible disadvantage relative to the invaders. The Native villages had a little above 350 men, perhaps one-half of their strength circa 1720. In late July, 200 Georgia militiamen marched up the Savannah River and laid waste to Tugaloo. The village's destruction was a sign of a world turned upside down. In 1716, Tugaloo had taken the lead in forging an alliance with South Carolina against the Creeks. Sixty years later, Georgia's militia thrust was followed by Colonel Andrew Williamson's formidable South Carolina force that burned Cherokee Lower Towns to the ground after the great portion of residents had fled. Keowee, Conasatchee, and Toxaway met that same gruesome fate. At Qualatchee, militiamen fed on Cherokee peaches and roasted corn while the village was, as one soldier wrote, "committed . . . to the flames." When the Carolinians moved west, they engaged in a sharp firefight with perhaps 200 Cherokees. The militia held its ground. After the battle, sixteen dead Cherokee fighters were scalped where they lay. With 1,000 men under his command by August 15, Williamson marched on the Middle and Valley Towns with the intent of spreading "Desolation" there.[42]

South Carolina's militia continued its deadly work after ascending seemingly impassable heights and entering the Hiwassee Valley and the Little Tennessee River's banks below the Great Smoky Mountains. Williamson's army was bloodied, though not stopped, by a sizable Cherokee attack as the militia passed through a ravine, "the Black Hole," not far from the site where the British regulars met their stiffest resistance during Grant's invasion of 1761. By September 9, South Carolina's troops were reinforced by Brigadier-General Griffith Rutherford's 2,300 North Carolina militiamen. Catawba scouts aided the invaders, following the same course as in the British-Cherokee war. To the north, Colonel William Christian of Virginia set out for Overhill country with 1,800 troops, along with several hundred white frontiersmen. The combined American forces burned and laid waste to more than fifty Cherokee towns or villages from August through October 1776. The militia of the two Carolinas outdid all others in the onslaught. Invasion broadened Cherokee regional resistance, though without uniformity across a shattered landscape.[43]

Wherever the Americans struck, they put cornfields to the torch. Officers and ordinary men commented on the Cherokees' well-ordered

Cherokees and the American Revolution

villages and plentiful harvests before all was destroyed. One South Carolina soldier described Little Tellico as a "brave plentiful town," while Tomasee had "curious buildings, great apple trees, and whitemanlike improvements." No "improvements" remained after the militia finished its work. This same Carolina soldier was somehow surprised that "heathen" Indians had a habit of "lurking by creeks and thickets" and attacking when they caught foes unaware. One militiaman was shot dead while gathering potatoes.[44]

The Cherokees suffered above three hundred dead in the American invasions of 1776. While men were most numerous among the dead, women and children were victims too. One Cherokee woman was killed with barely an afterthought by South Carolina militia. Another woman was killed and scalped by North Carolina men at Ellijay, "Green Verdant Place" in Cherokee speech. One militiaman murdered an infant in revenge for his own kin slain by Cherokees. Two North Carolina soldiers each intentionally killed a Cherokee man, one a prisoner and the other an elderly noncombatant, in retaliation for relatives who had been killed in past Indian attacks. We cannot know the number of Cherokee women and children killed in assaults. Scores died from flight and privation after their villages were consumed.[45]

War, Resettlement, and Living Space

On October 14, 1776, Colonel William Christian weighed Cherokee peace overtures just after his vanguard forded the Broad River (today's French Broad) and marched deep into Cherokee territory with little opposition. The Virginians were astonished, as nearly all invaders were, by Cherokee fields of corn and potatoes amounting to thousands of bushels. Christian, a humane man for his place and time, was inclined to spare Chota, a prestigious community that appeared ready for peace. He did not wish to burn other villages without first holding talks with the Raven, Oconostota, and Attakullakulla. He deliberately singled out Mialoquo, Dragging Canoe's town, which was destroyed before any parley.[46]

Cherokees invariably chose flight when a vastly superior enemy approached their villages. Some burned their own dwellings and corn to deprive the enemy of vengeful satisfaction. Overhill villagers either escaped overland or hurried by canoe down the Tennessee. As much as Cherokees loved their towns, men accompanied women and children to safety whenever possible. The people's survival came first. Some women found their own way. Virginia troops came upon an old Cherokee woman with two young children in the woods who had been without fire and had subsisted on nothing but berries for six days and nights. The soldiers helped the survivors. A few Cherokee women aided the invaders when communal survival was on the line. One elderly woman of the Hiwassee Valley told Colonel Williamson, after her village had been destroyed, that the Overhills were the cause of the trouble and that her people were ready for peace. Guiding South Carolina troops during their offensive, she was rewarded with a horse by Williamson at the campaign's end.[47]

William Christian could not fathom the reasons that Cherokees had gone to war. He blamed all on Cameron and Stuart's "Bribing" along with Dragging Canoe's domineering ways. The Virginia colonel conferred with Attakullakulla and Oconostota at Chota, perhaps in separate meetings. Christian insisted that peace could come only if the Cherokees surrendered Cameron and brought in Dragging Canoe or his scalp. No deal was forthcoming. The Virginians then destroyed four Overhill villages but left Chota standing—a sign of respect to Oconostota who told Christian that his town was the only honest one in the nation.[48]

The Southern states' campaign against the Cherokees had a fiercely retaliatory character besides the goal of dissuading Indians from taking the British side in war. A "savage" foe was ravaged and plundered, with no distinction made between militant towns as opposed to those where many residents desired peace and were ready for compromise if offered. Virtually all villages, with their inhabitants, were uprooted. If Chief Justice William Henry Drayton of South Carolina had had his way, the Cherokees would have been "extirpated," their lands forfeited, prisoners enslaved—with the nation's "removal beyond the mountains." While many in the Carolinas and Virginia shared such thoughts, the offensives were not geared for several reasons to achieve what Drayton imagined. First, Cherokee fighters dealt serious blows to the invaders, especially to South Carolina's troops. Second, militiamen had only so much staying power when it came to trekking through steep and mountainous terrain. Southern states had badly damaged the Cherokee but in the short term could do no more. Their next step was to see if they could detach the peacefully inclined from the militant and perhaps even persuade the latter to negotiate on American terms.[49]

Dragging Canoe had no intention of giving up the struggle. After learning of what had happened in his homeland, he passed word to

Cherokees and the American Revolution

Cameron and John Stuart that his "Thought and Heart is for War as long as King George has one Enemy in this Country." As Dragging Canoe understood things, there would soon be a supreme test of strength. "The Virginia Warrior" (Colonel Christian) was challenging John Stuart and friends, "White & Red," to compete at "a Ball Play next Spring when Grass is plenty." The British would wager all their goods and the Virginians all their "Land Negroes and Stock," and "whoever wins let them take all." Dragging Canoe had a sixth sense of what was at stake in the war beyond Indian country. The outcome of battle lay ahead.[50]

Attakullakulla was devoted to his people despite all his concessions of the past. While Overhill fighters were at war, Attakullakulla guided Henry Stuart on a long journey to the Gulf Coast during the summer of 1776. Arriving at Pensacola in late August, Little Carpenter pleaded for supplies from his old friend John Stuart and returned to Chota in time to participate in the parley with Christian. He had traveled more than 1,000 miles in three months—and this at age seventy or so. Attakullakulla did not betray Dragging Canoe or his whereabouts.[51]

Dragging Canoe's path during the American invasion of 1776 is not fully known. He traveled southwest while the Virginians were in his homeland before returning north. His journey was a reconnaissance—prelude to the migration and resettlement of five hundred Cherokees at Chickamauga Creek by the next spring. Well south of the Overhill heartland, the Chickamauga's branches flow into the Tennessee River, where Lookout Mountain rises dramatically just to the west. Most Cherokee refugees by the Chickamauga were from Overhill country. They felt the power of Dragging Canoe's message along with the fear of remaining in a ravaged land vulnerable to invasion. Not all Chickamaugas were young militants. Ostenaco and Willanawa, who had struggled for peace with "the white people" over years, now joined the movement south. A rising star at Chickamauga was Kunoskeskie, known to whites as John Watts, the son of a Cherokee woman by a colonial trader-interpreter.[52]

Dragging Canoe had strategic reasons for selecting Chickamauga as a safe place before new villages arose there. John McDonald, a Scots Loyalist trader with ties to Cameron, made his home by the creek, which was within easy reach of Coosa River's headwaters and Upper Creek country where potential friends might be found. By distance, Chickamauga is five hundred miles north of Pensacola, hardly making

British supply a swift business, though less onerous than routes from the Gulf to Overhill country.[53]

One should not minimize the difficulties besetting Cherokees in the aftermath of the American militia's campaign of destruction. While the Upper Creeks were not hostile to Dragging Canoe's movement, they held back from offering military support. In fact, the Cherokees' harrowing defeat shocked many Creeks and made them more cautious until they saw evidence of British strength. By the end of January 1777, two hundred Cherokee men, women, and children had fled all the way to Pensacola for succor. John Stuart described the refugees as "entirely naked and destitute." Chickamauga villagers had little to sustain them apart from hardihood in the first several months in their new homes. In July 1777, Cameron observed that "the Canoe" and fellow warriors were eager to fight again "as soon as they can get a little Corn to eat." The time of the Green Corn and its ripeness that summer could not come fast enough.[54]

Over time, the Chickamauga towns became a new Cherokee core region. Just as noteworthy, Cherokee recovery from invasion appeared in areas of vibrant village life over centuries. The Hiwassee Valley remained vital. Cherokees rebuilt at Settico, Chilhowee, and many other venues. What is not easily imagined is how the British invasions of 1760–1761, followed by the still greater damage inflicted by the Americans, forever altered the Cherokee world. The old Lower Towns east of the Blue Ridge, which had been a core Native region for countless generations, were reduced to a handful. The once-populous Middle Towns were depleted but hung on here and there. With hunting grounds greatly diminished, Cherokee women assumed even greater responsibilities as prime horticulturists and gatherers of nuts, berries, and other forest edibles. Female adaptability and strength were vital to renewal in a physical and spiritual sense—the preparation of new hearths to preserve bedrock traditions and kin networks. This capacity, little seen in the documentary record, was tested time and again when war hovered over years.[55]

British Calculations

Cameron was no bystander to war. While Dragging Canoe readied to attack the Watauga settlers in July 1776, Scotchie headed southeast, attempting to hold the line below the Blue Ridge with a dozen white

Cherokees and the American Revolution

Loyalists and perhaps 150 Cherokee fighters. Finding the enemy too numerous, Cameron withdrew northwest to Tugaloo and then to Toqua. Whig militiamen burned his beloved Lochaber home and stripped his landholdings, taking "Negroes . . . and a good Stock of Cattle and horses."[56] Cameron described the Cherokees as badly divided among themselves and angered by the lack of Creek assistance in war. Some Cherokees even wished to kill Cameron for their plight, ridiculing him for boasting of British victory at Charles Town when defeat was the outcome. Scotchie still had Cherokee friends. Sometime in the fall of 1776, he headed to Florida and lived to fight on.[57]

Cameron joined John Stuart in Pensacola when Cherokee refugees straggled into the port. With the past year's disaster, both men believed that Native warriors required direct British guidance or white Loyalist leadership to be effective on the war front. Stuart was especially skeptical of Indian guerrilla raiding. As he advised George Germain, His Majesty's principal war strategist, "Indians by themselves will never perform any thing great but [by] co-operating with [British] Troops conducted by able Leaders." Moreover, "a scalping War" itself would fall "indiscriminately upon the innocent defenceless and guilty" in white settlements and prove "ineffectual against an Enemy who had a collected force." Cameron took a bolder course and ached to lead Cherokees and white Loyalists in battle himself.[58]

In the war's early stages, British influence, exerted from Florida, was more effective in nearby than distant regions. Supported by Loyalist rangers and some British regulars, Seminoles and Lower Creeks eagerly took the fight to Georgia in early 1777 and held their own in the ensuing year. By contrast, the Cherokees could not stand against an overwhelming American militia offensive when they had virtually no allied Indian support and scant prospect of British military assistance.[59]

Cameron was determined to strengthen the Cherokees at Chickamauga. Meeting there with Dragging Canoe in the summer of 1777, he heard directly of the Native need for supplies. Scotchie lobbied John Stuart to send more gunpowder and ball than what had thus far arrived. Cameron understood that material aid was all-important if the Cherokees, presently courted by Virginia, were to stand with Britain and "refuse to take the Rebels by the Hand." Stuart, a realist to the core, concurred. "Indians," he wrote, "are different from regulars, we court their assistance, we do not command it."[60]

Upheavals and the Will to Live, 1762–1795

War, Treaty-Making, and Recovery

Hundreds, even thousands of Cherokees felt an overwhelming impulse to hit back at frontier whites. Perhaps an equal number, who had somehow survived invasion, desired peace simply to live and recoup. We can see both tendencies at work in the early months of 1777. In February, Cherokee warriors killed a white family living by the Holston River. The next month, an unnamed Cherokee woman traveled as courier on a mission from the Overhill Towns to Virginia's Fort Patrick Henry on the Holston. At the fort, she met Colonel Nathaniel Gist, formerly a trader in Cherokee country, who gave her Governor Henry's letters offering to discuss peace with her people. The female courier returned safely and delivered the message, which resulted in a Cherokee visit to Williamsburg.[61]

Who was the trusted woman bearing such important letters? Though we cannot know for certain, the most likely candidate is Nan-ye-hi (Nancy Ward), a woman of the Cherokee Wolf Clan who became legendary in her own lifetime. In Cherokee lore, Nan-ye-hi is remembered for taking up her slain husband's gun after he was felled in a battle with the Creeks in the 1750s. With bravery and confidence, she shot down the enemy and inspired Cherokee warriors to triumph.[62] Nan-ye-hi, a mother who had a young daughter named Ka'ati, was honored as war woman and then as *Ghighau*, "Supreme Beloved Woman" of Chota. A few years later, she married Bryant Ward, a South Carolina trader, and had a daughter, Betsy, by him. Bryant Ward left Nancy for South Carolina by the outbreak of the British-Cherokee war in 1760. She continued among her people. Perhaps she was one of the Cherokee women who gained raiment or some benefit for her household by offering food to besieged British soldiers at Fort Loudoun. Nan-ye-hi was a niece to two prestigious headmen, Attakullakulla and Willanawa, and close to Oconostota.[63]

Nan-ye-hi used her power to heal, a quality associated with the Wolf clan, during the bloodshed of July 1776. Most famously, she saved the life of Lydia Bean, a colonial woman and mother who was captured during Dragging Canoe's offensive and brought to a Cherokee town for ritual execution. In Tennessee folkloric memory, Nancy Ward came to the rescue just as the fire brands were lit about Mrs. Bean. Nan-ye-hi cut the rope that bound the captive to the stake and sheltered her in her own home. The two women became friends.[64]

Cherokees and the American Revolution 349

Peace advocates Oconostota and Attakullakulla respected Nan-ye-hi and probably considered her an ideal courier to the Virginia frontier. A capable woman was an apt choice when Cherokee men worried about traveling through hostile territory in wartime. The Cherokee peace camp was encouraged on the courier's return. Within a few weeks, eighty-five Cherokee men, accompanied by some women, traveled to the Holston fort to learn of Virginia's terms. The men were gratified by the prospect of peace but declined an American alliance since they "could not fight against their Father, King George." Their declared preference was for neutrality in the war between Britain and its former colonies, just as they had told Colonel Christian the previous fall. Attakullakulla, who was among the group, informed British officers that Dragging Canoe was adamantly opposed to negotiating with the Americans. Native women seconded this intelligence. They were confident the great war leader would not bow.[65]

In May 1777, forty Cherokee men and women arrived in Williamsburg as a follow-up to the preliminary talks at the Holston. Oconostota, Attakullakulla, and Woyi (the Pigeon) were among the chiefs in the delegation. After meeting with Patrick Henry, the Cherokee assemblage performed a dance for colonial spectators in front of the governor's palace. Colonial onlookers could hardly imagine what the Cherokees had suffered at the hands of the Virginia militia the previous summer. The Cherokee women's presence reinforced the message that peace was intended and whites need not fear Indian visitors.[66]

Diplomacy proceeded step by step. The Williamsburg meeting led to a conference between Upper Cherokee headmen and Virginia and North Carolina commissioners. The talks, held on Long (Great) Island of the Holston in July 1777, witnessed the sunset of senior Cherokee leaders. Attakullakulla was present but reserved, no longer a spokesman. Oconostota deferred to others because of age, while reserving the right to speak. The Raven of Chota, himself quite old, served as one of two leading Cherokee spokesmen. The other was Utsidsata—Corn Tassel—then entering his political prime, and commonly called "Old Tassel" by whites. Though the Cherokees were in a tenuous bargaining position because of extreme poverty, they contended strenuously for their rights and yielded only so much land as necessary to affirm peace, secure provisions, and further trade.[67]

Corn Tassel curried favor with Colonel William Christian, Virginia's chief negotiator, by sharing intelligence regarding northern Indians who vowed to strike American settlements from Kentucky to the Forks of the Ohio. According to Tassel, Nottawegas (presumably Iroquois) had received a strong talk at a "great Town," rumored to be Quebec. The British there were said to have scolded their Indian visitors: "will you be always fools? Will you never learn sense? Don't you know that there is a line fixed between you and the white people, that if they set their foot over it you might cut if off?" Tassel's story, artfully told, was relevant to his people's situation. If Christian listened carefully, he might infer that the Virginians should not push the Cherokees too hard lest they be driven into the arms of northern Native militants.[68]

Both Corn Tassel and Raven found it less trying to bargain with Virginia than North Carolina. While Christian pressed for a land cession to clear passage through the Cumberland Gap, he was not insensitive to Native concerns. The Cherokees, as he openly stated, were "a Great Nation" that had every right to be heard. Thorny issues emerged with North Carolina since that state, with Virginia's acquiescence, claimed jurisdiction over the Cherokees' Watauga and Nolichucky lands. Cherokee revulsion against white settlement there had triggered the war as much as any other cause. North Carolina's commissioners were not about to give up what their state possessed by military might. They offered peace only if the Cherokees accepted a new boundary line some thirty miles west of the old. Taken aback, Corn Tassel could not understand why North Carolina men, his "elder Brothers," asked for "so much land near me" when it "spoils our hunting ground. . . . Your stocks are tame and marked, but ours . . . are wild." Without any compromise in store, Raven finally asked North Carolina's deputies to show "pity" for his people by offering compensation for the land, though he would not demand it. The headman's pride and call for "pity" were of a piece. Tassel himself sounded words that had become pained and sorrowful: "The land I give up, will ever hold good . . . and when we are all dead and gone it will continue to produce." The land "will afford bread to those yet unborn, when goods will be rotten and gone."[69]

When the Virginia boundary treaty was read in conference, Raven and Corn Tassel did not contest the Cumberland Gap pathway but rejected any idea that their people had given up their sacred Long Island—the very conference ground on which they spoke. Cherokees took special protective measures, offering the island in custody to Colonel Gist, their "friend and Brother," who had formerly lived among them and was present at the talks. Tassel's eloquent words on the issue are part of the treaty record: "We will not dispose of this Island but we reserve it to hold our Great Talks on. Even the grass is for

Cherokees and the American Revolution   351

our creatures and the wood to kindle our beloved fire with." This was heartfelt diplomacy aimed at preserving the sacred in dangerous environs. For the time being, the Cherokees' plea kept Long Island of the Holston in their domain, however tenuously.[70]

Irked by North Carolina's territorial demands, Corn Tassel requested that his words be conveyed to a higher authority, namely "the Great Warrior of America"—George Washington. Christian tried to turn the idea to U.S. advantage by urging the Cherokees to send some of their "young warriors" to the general's camp so that "they could see the riches and Grandeur of our Army and Country" and even learn "the white peoples art of War." Tassel, himself an elder who had been a warrior in his youth, was cool to the idea. Though wishing to cultivate Washington's friendship, he cautiously avoided any act that might bring his Cherokees back into the war between the Americans and the British. Neutrality was the consensus among the Cherokees for whom he spoke. As negotiations neared a close, Tassel voiced displeasure at past deceptions by Colonel Richard Henderson, a man who had told "many lies." Henderson's duplicity at Sycamore Shoals was fresh in mind even if the colonel was not himself present at the Holston conference. Tassel signed North Carolina's treaty document only after eliciting words of good faith from state commissioners.[71]

The Cherokee treaties with Virginia and North Carolina were mainly the work of Overhill headmen. A small group of deputies from the devastated Lower and Valley Towns meanwhile reached a diplomatic settlement with South Carolina and Georgia that involved a substantial Native land cession in exchange for pledges of renewed trade and peace. Colonel Andrew Williamson, head of the South Carolina delegation, insisted that the ceded lands had been gained by "conquest" in the recent war. All Southern state treaties with Cherokees reiterated colonial verbiage obligating Indians to return enslaved Blacks, whether captives or runaways, for compensatory payment.[72]

It would be misleading to view the Cherokee treaties with Southern states simply as a Native sellout in the aftermath of defeat. The Cherokee impulse for peace and recovery in 1777 is as noteworthy as rising Chickamauga militancy and the refusal of Dragging Canoe and other headmen to enter negotiations with the Americans. The Cherokees were a people in crisis. The choices before them were not only between the "white" feather of peace and the "red" stick of war. Not all in the peace camp were necessarily of the same mind. Peace entreaties, accompanied by land cessions, were a safety net for hundreds of war

352   *Upheavals and the Will to Live, 1762–1795*

victims. For others, they were a temporary expedient, a truce before conditions were right for renewed attack.[73]

No Escape from War

The Chickamaugas and other militants received a great boost when the British invaded the Georgia sea islands in December 1778 and captured Savannah the next month. Pro-British Creeks moved to the fore of their nation. By the spring, royal agents equipped Native allies for a strike on the Georgia and South Carolina frontiers. The fighters included 200 to 300 Chickamaugas and other Cherokees. The results were hardly successful from a Cherokee perspective. As warriors trekked east, Chickamauga villages were struck from the rear by American frontiersmen navigating by boat and canoe down the Holston to the Tennessee. Elderly Ostenaco, who guarded the Chickamauga towns with a small retinue, had no choice but to flee. Tuwekee, a head warrior, feared the attackers would "destroy the Women and Children."[74]

Colonel Evan Shelby of Virginia, who headed the offensive into Chickamauga, reported that his men burned eleven towns, destroyed twenty thousand bushels of corn, and seized a great number of horses and cattle. These losses, wrote Cameron, "reduced" the Cherokees "to the utmost distress." The Virginia offensive was a preemptive blow, intended by Patrick Henry to prevent the Chickamaugas from heading northwest to undercut George Rogers Clark's militia in the Illinois country. After Shelby's onslaught, Cameron worried that Virginia officers might sway the Chickamaugas to return to their old towns on condition of wartime neutrality. Oconostota wished to mediate peace talks while Dragging Canoe kept to his hard line. Most Cherokees might have grasped at neutrality if they could be assured of American goodwill, a halt to inordinate land engrossment, and some measure of supply and trade. Neither Virginia nor North Carolina had the will or means to carry out these conditions.[75]

John Stuart, superintendent of southern Indian affairs for fifteen years, died in Pensacola on March 21, 1779. His duties were provisionally assumed by Cameron and Colonel Thomas Brown, an intrepid Loyalist who had shown his mettle by fighting alongside Lower Creeks and Seminoles against Georgia Whigs. Scotchie was of the same mind. In August, he joined 305 Cherokees and forty-five white Loyalists in yet another offensive aimed at South Carolina and Georgia. Informed of what was afoot, Colonel Andrew Williamson raised 705

Cherokees and the American Revolution   353

South Carolina cavalrymen to do battle. He was aided by sixteen Cherokee scouts of Lower Town Seneca—a village that mended relations with the Americans for its own protection. The upshot was a dramatic confrontation once the opposing forces came within three miles of one another. The pro-British Cherokees, mostly Chickamaugas, deliberated on whether they should fight or fall back. Fearing that Williamson had as many as twelve hundred men, they opted for withdrawal. A few chiefs went to parley with Williamson, who countered with an ultimatum: Indians could have peace if they delivered Cameron to his hands. If not, the Carolina army would destroy Cherokee towns.[76]

American Whigs had wanted Cameron dead or alive for the past three years. His Cherokee friends once more refused to surrender him. As Cameron later remarked, Williamson "was as good as his word." His militia marched into seven or eight towns and burned and ravaged all, destroying thousands of bushels of corn just as the Green Corn festival neared. The towns put to flames, probably those by the Savannah River's headwaters, are unnamed in Cameron's report and Williamson's correspondence. Their inhabitants bore the brunt of the Chickamauga advance and sudden retreat.[77]

Only weeks after escaping Williamson's clutches, Cameron went about gaining Cherokee approval for another foray. Scotchie was not solely concerned with the Cherokees' welfare. He valued Native attacks as a way of diverting rebel militiamen and securing the British position in Savannah and environs. For a time, Cameron took up quarters at the Coosawattee River amid hunting grounds shared by Cherokees and Creeks. Pan-Indian sentiment remained alive. Cameron delighted at a Wabash warrior's visit to the Coosawattee, where a Chickamauga chief, perhaps Dragging Canoe, honored the visitor as "one of our own flesh & Blood." The northern speaker was resolute, urging that all should "hold fast" to "the Great King our Father" and "join with His White Warriors" to strike "the Virginians."[78]

In late 1779, Cameron was jolted on receiving news that His Majesty's government had transferred him to a new post—principal agent to the Chickasaws and Choctaws. In a disconsolate letter to Germain, he described the Cherokees as "much dejected since they have been told that I have no more to do with them." His personal disappointment went deeper. He would no longer be with a people with whom he lived and had "had the management and Cultivating of . . . from the Year 1764." The Cherokees were as faithful as any Indians to the king, "altho'

354   *Upheavals and the Will to Live, 1762–1795*

they suffered more from the Rebels than any of the Nations." And they "were more Tractable and Civilised than their Brethren," in his view. Cameron assumed his new duties, while proudly stating all he had done to win Cherokee fighters for the king: "I have the vanity to think that they should follow me to any part on the Continent provided I should support them."[79]

Scotchie saw the Cherokees as a free people whose loyalty to Britain was conditional on respect and ample supply. Much to his regret, he found that General John Campbell, commanding at Pensacola, was a man "who does not understand any thing of Indians" and failed to grasp "that Indians have a Right" to presents beyond the time they were called "upon Actual Service." All this spelled trouble for the British once Spain entered the war as an ally of France in 1779 and captured Mobile in May 1780. Despite Creek, Choctaw, and Chickasaw willingness to defend Pensacola, Campbell was unable to summon Native warriors *en masse* when most needed. Lacking naval support, he surrendered Pensacola after a mammoth Spanish siege, aided by the French, in May 1781.[80] The loss of the Gulf ports compromised the British position among southern Native nations months before Yorktown. Cherokees could hardly foresee this train of events.

Turmoil and Turning Points

British commanders in the southern theater were unable to sustain any durable union between the disparate ethnicities—Loyalists, Blacks, and the Native peoples—that looked to the king for succor. Thousands of the region's Blacks escaped slavery by fleeing to the king's troops but were often commandeered by royal officers for military labor or personal gain. Black men, when given the chance, proved more than willing to fight as pioneers and dragoons. Only a small portion of Black escapees, however, were equipped by the British for battle.[81]

White Loyalists, who had their own stake in slavery, were repeatedly exposed to Whig vengeance when the British army marched from one area to another across the vast southern terrain. In a daring maneuver, American "over-mountain men"—Nolichucky and Watauga settlers—trekked far east to join patriot forces that overwhelmed Patrick Ferguson's Loyalist militia at King's Mountain on October 7, 1780. In the heat of the fight, western partisans sounded the "warwhoop," Indian style, as they clambered up wooded hillsides to gun

Cherokees and the American Revolution

down the enemy. This was cultural appropriation with full-throated confidence.[82]

Charles, Lord Cornwallis, who assumed command of British forces in the southern theater in late May 1780, had a negative view of Indian warriors, whom he saw as inordinately expensive to supply and of limited value in campaigns. He worried, too, about warriors who might indiscriminately kill settlers of all political persuasions. Initially confident of success with his regulars alone, Cornwallis ordered Colonel Brown, who replaced John Stuart as superintendent for southern Indian affairs, to discourage Creek and Cherokee attacks on the South Carolina and Georgia frontiers. Anxious about wartime costs, Cornwallis approved annual presents for Cherokees but believed it unnecessary to lend special aid to those Natives whose houses had been destroyed by American militia. "The Rebuilding an Indian Hut," he remarked, "is no very expensive Affair." The general did not quite grasp the flip side of his commentary. In the teeth of war, the Native capacity to rebuild simple dwelling structures was a strength.[83]

While Cornwallis disdained Indians, he heartily endorsed their employ against American "Back-Mountain men" after the slaughter at King's Mountain. Brown was enthusiastic. With timely Cherokee support, he held off a rebel attack on Fort Augusta in September 1780, though was himself wounded in the battle. By December, he was urging a major Native offensive against American Tennessee settlements and claiming to have the go-ahead from chiefs representing 2,500 Cherokee men and 500 Upper Creeks. His count was a vast exaggeration, wishful thinking about unifying disparate Cherokees besides obtaining ample Creek support. Knowing precisely the correct words for the British paper trail, Brown reassured Cornwallis that Native fighters would be directed by white commissaries, who would prevent the Indians' frequent "wanton outrages to which their savage ferocity might hurry them." The Cherokees would wage a just war against "the plunderers & banditti, who have taken forcible possession of their hunting grounds" by the Watauga and Holston and to the Cumberland and Kentucky. In actuality, few white Loyalists were present to act as Brown idealized. Busy with supply at Augusta, he did not join Cherokees to the north.[84]

Cherokee militants gladly took to guerrilla warfare, if far short of the numbers Brown envisioned. The element of surprise all but vanished, however, after warriors killed a few white traders in Overhill country toward the close of 1780. Indian fighters in the vicinity talked openly about coming battle, and Cherokee women made it their

356   *Upheavals and the Will to Live, 1762–1795*

business to be in the know. Nan-ye-hi came to the fore and took great risks to undermine Native militants. In this instance, she passed word to traders Isaac Thomas and Ellis Harlan of an impending Cherokee attack on the Watauga and Nolichucky settlements. Harlan was married to Nan-ye-hi's daughter Ka'ati. The traders quickly told militia officers to prepare for war.[85]

Nan-ye-hi had family that bridged the Cherokee-colonial divide. Her battle was for the preservation of kin and community. Other women were of a similar disposition. In early December, five Anglo traders escaped from danger after receiving advance warning, as one survivor stated, from "some Indian friends and the assistance of Nancy Ward with other Indian Women." Nan-ye-hi did not act alone, contrary to the romanticized stories told by the Tennessee settlers' descendants. That several Native men cooperated with women to aid white traders indicates an undercurrent of Cherokee discontent with any upsurge of bloodshed in their neighborhood.[86]

While some Cherokees shunned war, others moved back and forth between accommodationist and militant stances. The Raven of Chota, who put his mark on Henderson's land swindle of 1775, was a war chief the next year, a peace negotiator in 1777, and once again a war leader three years later. Steadiness could not be had when the Virginians violated trust. In 1780, Raven told one white trader "that he was done with the Big Knife [the Americans] and would now only listen to his Father over the Great Water." Many Cherokees counted on a Nativist union with British backing from the Great Lakes to the Gulf. Cherokee couriers conferenced with Hurons, Wyandots, and other Native deputies at British-occupied Detroit. In April 1780, a Huron chief at Detroit passed an Iroquois war belt to Cherokee deputies, who pledged to share it with southern nations.[87]

The Raven had not joined the migration to Chickamauga but had similar thoughts to Dragging Canoe. Cherokees were greatly disturbed by a new white settlement springing up by the Cumberland River in 1780 well to the west of their towns. James Robertson, the settlement's leader, was a well-known "Big Knife" who had lived at Watauga before heading to "French Lick," the future Nashville, on the Cumberland. The Cherokee plan to strike Watauga and Nolichucky whites was part of a design to reclaim wide-ranging lands taken by the Americans. Not all Cherokees agreed that war was the right choice. The Big Knives were likely to destroy all in their path if they gained the upper hand. Elderly Oconostota clearly held that view.[88]

Cherokees and the American Revolution   357

Major Joseph Martin, Virginia's agent to the Cherokees, had an interest in stopping a war at his doorstep. While he had a white wife and family in Virginia, he was also spouse to Nan-ye-hi's daughter Betsy and lived with her at their residence on Long Island of the Holston. On December 12, Martin sent messages to Chota warning Cherokees not to go on the attack, but to no avail. Warriors had already launched lethal raids on outlying frontier settlements. A response came quickly. Colonel John Sevier, recently back from the Battle of King's Mountain, assembled three hundred Watauga militia for an offensive. Within the next four days, Sevier's force crossed the French Broad River and clashed with seventy Cherokee fighters. Thirteen Cherokees were killed, while the militia suffered not a single loss.[89]

Sevier fell back to await Colonel Arthur Campbell's four hundred troops that arrived on December 22. Once the militiamen gathered strength, the main body marched on Chota. Cherokee warriors, situated on hills below the town, decided not to give battle. Being outnumbered and outgunned, they chose withdrawal. Many Cherokees, presumably older men and women with children, fled west. The refugees included those who did not want war and felt at odds with "the Chickamogga People."[90]

On December 24, the militia entered Chota and feasted deep into the night on Cherokee stores of corn, hogs, and poultry. There was also beef, with cattle provided by Nan-ye-hi, a resourceful woman who made the most of her family bond with commissary Martin. The militia's festive hours were brief. On Christmas Day, a Virginia detachment of sixty men went north to attack and burn Chilhowee. They were stopped from full-scale destruction by "a superior [Cherokee] force." It took two additional militia detachments of a combined three hundred men to complete Chilhowee's burning over the next two days.[91]

While Chilhowee was being destroyed, Nan-ye-hi, "the famous Indian Woman," as Campbell described her to Governor Thomas Jefferson, came to the main militia camp about Chota. According to Campbell, she offered "various intelligence, and made an overture in behalf of some of the Chiefs for Peace." Nan-ye-hi delivered a message from headmen who were themselves reluctant to meet with white frontiersmen, perhaps out of fear of being earmarked as weaklings by militants. It seemed safer for a woman linked to the "white people" to be mediator. There is no record of the actual words exchanged between Nan-ye-hi and Campbell. What specific "intelligence" she divulged is unknown.[92]

Nan-ye-hi's mission to restrain the Americans was brave but fruitless. Sevier, Campbell, and comrades were determined to wreak havoc, bury the Cherokee-British connection, and foreclose future resistance. Campbell targeted not only what he labeled "the vindictive part of the [Cherokee] nation" but resolved "to distress the whole, as much as possible." On December 28, the militia burned Chota, Settico, and Little Tuskegee. Within the next few days, Campbell's corps marched west, seizing a great deal of Cherokee corn, horses, cattle, and swine. Seven more "principal Towns" were burned to the ground by militia units. Overhill Cherokee country and areas to the south were ravaged. The Native inhabitants were stripped of food and shelter in the teeth of winter. In all, Campbell estimated the destruction of "upwards of One thousand Houses, and not less than fifty thousand Bushels of Corn, and large quantities of other kinds of Provisions." The militia stopped short of Chickamauga country. Campbell and Sevier could push their men just so much in the depth of winter. They had ravaged and plundered enough and wanted to get home alive.[93]

Before Virginia men burned Chota, Campbell had come upon and seized what he called "the Archives of the [Cherokee] nation" from Oconostota's "Baggage" left behind when the chief fled. In a report to Jefferson, the colonel contended that the stash of letters and commissions showed that Oconostota's Cherokees were playing a "double game," pretending peace but plotting for war over years. In fact, the documents, which cover the years 1763–1778, tell a very different and fascinating story. Oconostota had a certificate of honorary membership from the St. Andrews Club of Charles Town, where he had dined with John Stuart in 1773. The Great Warrior was his own man during the terrible war to come. In 1777, he declined to join the migration to Chickamauga, though admonished to do so by David Taitt, Stuart's deputy. He did not follow Stuart's advice to foreclose negotiations with the Virginians but instead received Governor Patrick Henry's invitation and went to see him in Williamsburg. Oconostota kept a copy of the Virginia-Cherokee peace treaty of 1777 just as he had King George's directive of 1763 ordering royal governors to protect Indians "in their just rights and possessions." The archive attests to Oconostota's sagacity by keeping important written records—a precedent dating back to the Cherokee London treaty of 1730. The documents could be used as proof to show pledges made by the British and, later, by the Americans. Of course, Oconostota did not rely on

Cherokees and the American Revolution   359

what was written on paper alone. Words read aloud in Cherokee council became part of a collective memory with meanings superseding any text.[94]

Coda: 1781 and a Look Beyond

Thomas Jefferson was desperate as Virginia's governor in early 1781. The British had invaded his state, pushing up the Potomac, the James, and other rivers. Since the previous fall, Jefferson had been hoping for a peace with the Cherokees. A truce on that front might free Virginia's far western riflemen to come to the aid of the beleaguered east. On February 28, Jefferson wrote Arthur Campbell a congratulatory letter regarding his recent victory over the Cherokees, while urging him to employ his favorable situation "for the purpose of bringing about peace." Jefferson urged that Nancy Ward, who "seems rather to have taken refuge with you," ought to be respected in "her inclination," whichever course she chose. Virginia owed Nan-ye-hi fair treatment at the very least after all she had done to avert war and save lives. To say that few Native women ever gained such respect from American leaders would be an understatement.[95]

Jefferson's desire for peace went unfulfilled despite interest on the Cherokee side. Scolacutta ("Hanging Maw"), a prominent Overhill chief who had lived at Chickamauga for several years, was appalled by warfare that left his people digging for roots in the woods to feed themselves. He appealed to Virginia agent Joseph Martin by sending two Cherokee men with a white flag to the Long Island. The envoys were murdered by militiamen before they could reach the island, which Raven had described as the place where "we have the white seats of justice, and the beloved fire."[96]

Cherokee peace advocates badly desired negotiating space but had little room to escape punitive American attacks in response to warrior raids. In March, John Sevier led another expedition, burned at least six towns by the Tuckasegee River, killed thirty Cherokees, and seized two hundred horses. Campbell pinpointed British-held Augusta, Georgia, as the lifeline of Cherokee-Chickamauga militancy. As he informed Jefferson, there were "several hundred of the Indian Women and Children being now subsisted in that State by the British." In fact, many of the women and children were refugees who found shelter in the Chickamauga towns. Cherokee men flocked southward, too. Campbell's apparent triumph was not complete. The

360   *Upheavals and the Will to Live, 1762–1795*

devastation of towns and food stores threatened Cherokees with famine but did little to lessen Chickamauga fighting capacity.[97]

War-weary Upper Cherokees were eager to grasp peace negotiations when offered by Virginia and North Carolina in the spring of 1781. Informal talks got underway at Long Island of the Holston at least two months before a conference finally began there on July 26. Several Cherokee groups, consisting mainly of women and children, came by canoe to Long Island. Martin requested corn, meat, and money to support the arrivals. The women's first duty was to keep their children alive. About six hundred Cherokee women, children, and men were present at the conference's opening.[98]

On the American side, representatives included moderates such as Martin and Christian, who desired a peace accord, along with the hawkish Campbell and Sevier who saw little point in negotiating before the Chickamauga towns were destroyed. On July 28, 1781, an unnamed Cherokee woman, almost certainly Nan-ye-hi, spoke openly before all. She first chastised the Americans: "You came . . . and settled on our land and took it . . . by main force." The treaty of the Holston four years past was "broken," and a new peace was needed for all time. Nan-ye-hi's appeal summoned the ideal of shared kinship: "You know that women are always looked upon as nothing, but we are your mothers. You are our sons. Our cry is all for peace. Let it continue for we are your mothers. This peace must last forever. Let your women's sons be ours, and let our sons be yours. Let your women hear our words."[99]

Nan-ye-hi's talk was unprecedented. One can search several thousand pages of conference records dating back to the early 1700s and not come once upon an instance of a Cherokee woman speaking in formal negotiations between her people's headmen and colonial officials, whether British or French, Virginian, Carolinian, or Georgian. Nan-ye-hi's forwardness built on the past, even as it entered new ground. Cherokee women had served over decades as couriers, go-betweens, and messengers behind the scenes. Their encounters, liaisons, friendships, and commercial exchanges with colonial traders, and later with British soldiers, gave them intimate knowledge of "the white people." Beyond influencing male decision-making, Cherokee women acted autonomously on numerous occasions, supporting war or peace agendas as they believed right for kin and community. Nan-ye-hi's talk at Holston, heard in formal conference, was a sign of Cherokee women going a step beyond by assuming a direct role in the all-important realm of treaty conferencing with powerful foes.

Cherokees and the American Revolution

Headmen required women's open assistance to try to soften the "Virginians" and bring them to reason. A woman's empathetic plea might prove of greater power in dire circumstances than a gun or tomahawk.

The highly unusual character of Nan-ye-hi's declaration is shown by the one other talk given by Cherokee women at the Holston conference. In this instance, five Cherokee female elders, aided by Scolacutta's wife, whispered a talk, which Scolacutta conveyed aloud to the American commissioners. Their words, too, spoke of woman's primal importance as mothers and unifiers:

> We the women of the Cherokee nation now speak to you. We are mothers, and have many sons, some of them warriors and beloved men. We call you also our sons. We have a right to call you so, because you are sons, and all descended from the same woman at first. We say you are our sons, because by women, you were brought forth into this world, nursed, suckled, and raised up to be men before you reached your present greatness. You are our sons. Why should there be any difference amongst us? We live on the same land with you, and our people are mixed with white blood: one third of our [people are] mixed with white blood.

While the portion of Cherokees with Anglo "blood" was below one-third during this period, children of mixed ancestry were growing in number and influence. The Cherokee women's argument was emotive and even predictive of change.[100]

The Virginia and Carolina men at the conference gave every appearance of understanding the women's words. William Christian thought carefully before answering. When he did so, it was in a spirit of empathy, leavened by advice:

> Mothers: We have listened well to your talk. . . . No man can hear it without being moved by it. Such words and thoughts show the world that human nature is the same everywhere. Our women shall hear your words. . . . We are all descendants of the same woman. We will not quarrel with you because you are our mothers. We will not meddle with your People if they will be still and quiet at home and let us live in peace.[101]

This last point was the rub. Cherokee men, being the sons of strong women, could not simply stay at home when their people were being threatened by white settlers in the act of swallowing up their land with no end in sight. However eloquent the women's words, those words could not produce peace. Sevier, Campbell, and their fellows believed that Native resistance had to be crushed. The Chickamaugas were defiant. A terrible era of war lay ahead long after Cornwallis's surrender at Yorktown. Dragging Canoe remained paramount, though his friend Scotchie was gone. Alexander Cameron, who had first arrived in Georgia as a British soldier in 1738, died of illness at Savannah on December 27, 1781.[102]

The American Revolutionary War cannot be understood apart from convulsions in Indian country any more than its history would make sense apart from the myriad struggles between Whigs and Tories, Black quests for freedom, and decisive American victories such as Bunker Hill and Trenton, Bennington and Saratoga, King's Mountain and Yorktown. There was no simple end to the war for the Cherokees and other Native peoples. The British-U.S. peace treaty of 1783 gave way to new chapters of destructive warfare and creative peace diplomacy in Cherokee country.

Cherokees and the American Revolution

12

Bloodshed and Quests for Peace

The shock of British defeat in war was felt by Native peoples from the Gulf Coast to the Great Lakes. In November 1783, Chickamauga chief Little Turkey (Kahanetah) shared his feelings of betrayal to Colonel Thomas Brown, royal superintendent of southern Indian affairs. When a "thick Cloud darkened the Land," his people "raised the Hatchet against the Virginians who in shedding the Blood of our [English] friends opened our veins." Now word came "that the English have smoked the Pipe of Peace with their Enemies" and given away Cherokee lands "at a Rum Drinking." It seemed like madness had descended. Kahanetah and fellow leaders wished to believe otherwise: "We know the English are Men and that they will Die rather than forsake their friends."[1]

Upper Creek chiefs told Brown much the same thing in a meeting at Tallassee. They had heard that the English had "sent a white wing with a Peace Talk to their Enemies." To save their own land, the British had allegedly given away Creek lands to American and Spanish foes. Incredulity reigned at Tallassee. The story must be "a Virginia Lie." But it was true. By peace negotiations held in Paris, the British king recognized American independence and ceded to the United States all Crown territories from the Great Lakes as far south as Florida. As for the two "Floridas," King George surrendered both East and West Florida to the Spanish monarch. The treaties made no mention of Native land rights.[2]

U.S. independence was attained at a great cost, not only in patriot sacrifices but in the price paid by others. The Revolutionary War meant "independence lost" for America's Native peoples, in Kathleen DuVal's powerful phrase, though as she observes this outcome would not become apparent until the early nineteenth century, as the balance of power swung heavily in favor of the United States. Along that tortuous path, much blood was spilt.[3]

For Cherokees, the American Revolutionary War brought convulsive change. The sudden rise of the Chickamauga towns and the evisceration of old villages east of the Blue Ridge brought a profound transformation, accentuating differences between Cherokees inclined either to diplomatic accommodation or militant resistance to white settlement. There were unmistakable differences in political outlook between Cherokee regions, though these variations should not be considered fixed polarities. While Upper Cherokee communities of the old Overhill region had notable peace advocates, their young men frequently raided white settlements. The same might be said of the Hiwassee Valley Cherokees. To the southwest, the Chickamauga towns were strongly prone to militancy but not averse to negotiating with the Americans when feasible, especially after British imperial withdrawal and the entry of Congress into Indian diplomacy. The Cherokees' capacity to maintain comity across factional divides was vital to their endurance as a people. In a chaotic era, this was no small accomplishment.[4]

Indian peoples were compelled to rethink diplomacy in the wake of the American Revolution. Native leaders had considerable difficulty in finding consistent and reliable negotiators on the U.S. side. Through most of the 1780s, federal authority in the trans-Appalachian west was negligible. State and territorial governments had competing agendas and little control over frontier citizens who took the law into their own hands. Power brokers such as Arthur Campbell, John Sevier, James Robertson, and others pursued agendas of land engrossment and fashioned their own regional diplomacy. In 1785, Sevier and his followers founded the State of Franklin, a breakaway region of far western North Carolina, which was aggressively expansionist vis-à-vis Indian country. Franklin's brief and shaky period of proto-independence was one sign of American frontier restlessness and ambition that heightened Native militancy and undermined Cherokee quests for compromise.[5]

A remarkable feature of the Cherokee situation is how diplomacy and warfare developed simultaneously on various fronts. Alliance-building with other Native peoples, especially the Creeks and Shawnees, bolstered resistance to American expansion. Cherokee diplomacy

Bloodshed and Quests for Peace

with American states and the federal union meanwhile evolved as a life-preserving strategy. The Cherokees' determination to fight was critical, but so too was their concurrent ability to adapt by seeking cessations of violence and creating opportunities, however tenuous, for peaceful interchange. The white wing of peace vied with the red hatchet of war— forces in uneasy tension rather than simple balance.

Population and Power

White settlement was slowed but not arrested in trans-Appalachian regions where Native peoples battled to stave off colonial intrusions. Through the 1780s, the number of settlers in what is now eastern Tennessee—the heart of Upper Cherokee country—climbed from 7,000 to about 30,000, including enslaved Blacks. Far to the west, the Cumberland River's white settlement, miniscule in 1779, grew to about 7,000 persons by 1790 and to nearly 12,000 in 1795. By the time Tennessee became a state in 1796, Blacks accounted for roughly 20 percent of the population in the Cumberland region and nearby areas. Demographic change altered the human landscape in a remarkably short period.[6]

Kentucky furnishes an even more striking example. White settlers in the "district," as it was called by its parent state Virginia, struggled against a wave of Native attacks through the Revolutionary War. By one estimate, there were only 8,000 settlers in Kentucky in 1782. Five years later, the settler population had shot up to 50,000 and stood at 73,000 in 1790 when enslaved Blacks comprised one-fourth of the whole. "Violence, chaos, and uncertainty," as Patrick Griffin writes, shaped the broader scene since there was little letup to conflict between Natives and white settlers in the Ohio Valley.[7]

The entire Cherokee population, including the Chickamaugas, numbered 8,000 to 10,000 persons for much of the 1780s. The Chickamaugas had greater power than the numbers alone can suggest because of their wide-ranging, multiethnic character through bonds with Creeks, Shawnees, Delawares, and Britons. In 1791, Alexander McGillivray, the notable leader of Creek-Scots heritage, told a white visitor that the Creeks had 5,000 to 6,000 gunmen, "exclusive of the Seminolies." Though not acting as a single force, Creek fighters added appreciably to Chickamauga strength.[8] This had been the case since the Chickamaugas and various Creek groups allied with the British during the American Revolutionary War.

366   *Upheavals and the Will to Live, 1762–1795*

The Cumberland

James Robertson, Cumberland pioneer, was accustomed to picking up stakes and heading west. Born in Virginia to a humble Scots-Irish family in 1742, he moved with kin to the North Carolina piedmont in early youth and made his way to the Watauga settlement in Overhill country by 1771. A rising leader in Watauga, he served as a militia captain in battle with Dragging Canoe's fighters in July 1776 and joined Virginia's offensive into Cherokee country that autumn. Ambitious and shrewd, Robertson had little formal education but knew how to build relationships that promised riches greater than farming. Even before the war, he cultivated the friendship of Richard Henderson, whose machinations at Sycamore Shoals brought the Cumberland's watershed within his Transylvania Company's claims. Gentlemen speculators like Henderson had a need for trailblazers such as Daniel Boone, Robertson, and others to put settlers on colonial ground and thereby turn paper landholdings into profit. Pioneer leaders had their own stake in pressing into Indian country, a dangerous, if potentially profitable business.[9]

In early 1779, Robertson had Henderson's backing when heading a small exploratory party into Kentucky and then on a long southwest path to French Lick on the Cumberland River. Impressed by the country, he drummed up support for the area's colonization on his return. Robertson, now a bigwig at Watauga, was an old hand at sizing up opportunities and dangers. His scouting party had found rich soil by the Cumberland where there was but a handful of white traders and settlers. The chance to break new ground had a strong appeal, but the landscape was not empty. Cherokee hunters had taken note of Robertson's trek. The distance between Watauga and French Lick was more than 300 miles—and with virtually no intervening white settlements along the way. Robertson's prospective colonial site lay within hunting grounds vital to Cherokees, Chickasaws, Creeks, and Shawnees.[10]

Cherokee fears of losing more land to whites had assumed a nightmarish quality since the Southern state invasions of 1776 and territorial cessions made the following year by peace-inclined headmen who wished to hold onto what they could. Corn Tassel was a prominent headman of the moderate camp in Overhill country. Distancing himself from the Chickamauga movement, he was among a good portion of Cherokees who, seeking a chance to rebuild, vowed neutrality in the

Bloodshed and Quests for Peace

ongoing war between American colonials and Britain. His hope was security, but the realities spoke otherwise.

Corn Tassel was put on the spot in late September 1779. Given his desire to maintain peace, he and like-minded Overhill leaders agreed to a new round of talks with Virginia and North Carolina commissioners at Long Island of the Holston. The mere presence of Richard Henderson, North Carolina's chief deputy, was enough to stir Cherokee apprehensions. The commissioners spoke of their intent to mark a "dividing line" or boundary between Virginia and North Carolina to an indefinite western point. The Native deputies were suspicious of what the white men had in view. The "dividing line" in the hands of Henderson and friends could become another mark drawn on paper at Cherokee expense.[11]

Knowing of James Robertson's recent western trek, Corn Tassel had "Cumberland River"—or its equivalent in Cherokee speech—much on his mind. While state commissioners denied any intent of seeking a Cherokee land cession, Corn Tassel was not put off by smooth-talking white gentlemen. His words admitted no doubt: "My Land reaches to Cumberland river." A "cut off" of "our hunting grounds," he declared, would "bring us to nothing." "Cut off" was the same phrase (as translated into English) that Cherokees used to describe striking a foe to death. To sever a people from its land was akin to killing them.[12]

Henderson replied, but not in a manner that Cherokees approved. The conference record omits his speech, only indicating that headmen "did not seem to like" his talk. Virginia deputies Thomas Walker and Daniel Smith took a softer, more paternalistic approach, telling Cherokees not to fear the boundary survey, while advising Indian men to improve their people's condition: "we recommend it to you to live as we do and only hunt for meat and skins to make you moccasons," and to "raise corn and Cattle horses and hogs and sell them to cloath your wives and Children which you will find much surer and easier than your present manner of life." Left unstated was the obvious. Native men who gave up long-range hunting would need comparatively little land and presumably be less likely to contest American expansion. Walker himself had been a consummate western land speculator since the 1740s.[13]

The commissioners' suggestion on adopting new customs elicited silence. Cherokee headmen saw no point in answering. Their way of life was their own as much as the land on which they hunted. They could not possibly grasp the American settler perspective that territory was vacant in the absence of Native villages and growing fields. The breadth of land between Chota and the Cumberland's westerly banks was 170 to 200 miles, largely forested and a veritable wilderness to white newcomers. To Cherokee hunters, it was familiar ground that spoke to them through all its spirit force. The people needed space, as did the animals with whom their lives were intertwined, and whose meat and peltry were food, raiment, and more beyond the deerskin trade that had withered with war and deprivation.

While the boundary commissioners trekked west in the fall of 1779, Robertson was back in the Watauga-Holston area and about to lead a small party of colonials overland to French Lick and vicinity. Working in tandem with Robertson, Colonel John Donelson of Virginia had a still more onerous task. His plan was to reach the settlement site with some two hundred men, women, and children—and for the entire assemblage to voyage in river craft well down the Tennessee before deciding on a best course to the Cumberland. His group endured great hardship because of an exceptionally cold winter that delayed the flotilla's launch on icy waters and slowed its hazardous movement amid shoals for two to three months. It was not until early March 1780 that the boats finally navigated from the Holston to the Tennessee.[14]

Adding to the drama, Donelson's flotilla had to brave turbulent waters running through Chickamauga territory—and this during wartime. All was deceptively calm when the voyagers put ashore on their fourth day on the Tennessee and camped overnight at a vacant Native village. At relaunch the next morning, all hell broke loose. Chickamauga warriors, with bodies painted red and black, pursued by canoe. The race was one of life and death. Colonial boats plunged ahead with the Tennessee's current. Chickamauga fighters chased along riverbanks and fired downward at colonial voyagers. One straggling vessel, in which smallpox had struck, was easy prey. Warriors seized the boat and killed or captured all twenty-eight persons aboard. Native gunmen kept up their fire as the convoy entered the river canyon's "Whirl" and "Suck" of wildly churning water. Boats were tossed about like driftwood. Several voyagers drowned, succumbed to enemy bullets, or were taken captive. But the great majority survived. The Chickamauga attack was both a deadly warning and a rejoinder to recent militia invasions, notably the destruction of Chickamauga villages by Evan Shelby's force the previous spring.[15]

When the convoy came in view of Muscle Shoals, Donelson and company looked for signs that Robertson was expected to place there,

Bloodshed and Quests for Peace   369

indicating whether or not the settlers were safe to trek by land to French Lick. Finding no mark or note, the voyagers continued down the Tennessee and braved the roaring rapids of Muscle Shoals before quieter waters resumed on the river's northern upswing to the Ohio. By then, some exhausted families, leery of venturing deep into Indian country on the Cumberland, steered their boats to Illinois or descended the Mississippi to Natchez. It was not until April 24, 1780, that Donelson's weary party put into Robertson's new settlement of Nashborough, to be called Nashville within a few years. The travelers gladly bedded down in log cabins, built for their use on bluffs above the Cumberland.[16]

Settlers were pleased that Colonel Henderson was in the neighborhood during the last leg of their journey on the Cumberland. After all, they pitched on land that they believed his Transylvania Company had legitimately purchased from the Cherokees in 1775. The colonel was elated when his boundary survey showed that Nashborough and vicinity fell within the jurisdiction of North Carolina, where he had ample political pull. Henderson was a gentleman who displayed noblesse oblige when it served his interest. While organizing government for the Cumberland, he did not insist that colonists pay right away for acreage. He would take his gains in due time when North Carolina legislators bought him out in 1783, just as Virginia had already done when vacating his Transylvania claims in that state. Cherokees did not mourn when they learned of Henderson's death a few years later.[17]

Many of the Cumberland settlers journeyed west less than ten years after building their first homes by the Watauga, Nolichucky, and other valleys in what became eastern Tennessee. The colonists' impulse to relocate, find more fertile land, and escape debts and taxes signaled an extraordinary restlessness. Long-distance migration was often a way for settlers to break free of old restraints. The right of freemen to form a new government, where none appeared adequate to the security of their persons and property, had deep roots in the colonial era. The American Revolution revived this ideal time and again, especially in western regions where settlers were far removed from established provincial or state authorities. Assisted by Henderson, Nashborough's founders adopted a body of formative laws—the Cumberland Compact of 1780—similar to the Watauga Association spearheaded by Robertson only eight years before.[18]

The migration of Dragging Canoe and friends from ancestral villages to Chickamauga was a Native equivalent to new state formation, though without formal government structure. Native independence, achieved in environs ripe for war, was the warriors' answer to being confined and at the mercy of the "Virginians." The Chickamaugas accepted white Loyalists into their ethnically diverse ranks. Voluntary association was the foundation of numerous, often clashing struggles for freedom embedded in the American Revolutionary era.

Robertson was a strong colonial leader, though it is not obvious that he informed fellow colonial adventurers of the danger of settling the Cumberland. The newcomers were probably aware there might be Native attacks, but nothing like the violence they encountered. In the first eighteen months of Cumberland settlement (1780–1781), sixty-five to seventy settlers were killed by Indians. This number is staggering when one considers that only 300 to 500 colonials were then in the area. Many residents were vulnerable because they lived in dispersed homesteads and weakly palisaded stations. We do not know the ethnic identity of warriors in many instances. By all evidence, it seems that Chickamauga fighters, allied with Creeks, were responsible for most attacks, while Delawares, Shawnees, and Chickasaws also participated in raids. For many Natives, the land was not only hunting ground but a corridor for travel and collaboration between Indian peoples north and south of the Ohio. Having suffered American invasions and inroads, warriors struck with little distinction as to white or black, young or old. Most Indian attacks were sudden guerrilla strikes, but this was not always the case. Determined to extinguish a colonial threat to the west, several hundred Chickamaugas assaulted Nashborough in April 1781. The attack was repelled after a hot exchange of gunfire. The settlers held on, aided by the dogs they unleashed against their foe.[19]

Joseph Martin and the Cherokee Peace Camp

It may seem improbable that a budding Virginia land speculator could be a friend to Indians. The case of Joseph Martin, an ambitious frontiersman and foremost American liaison to the Cherokees from 1777 to the early 1790s, certainly raises that possibility. Born near Charlottesville in 1740, Martin was an adventurer before his twentieth year. He joined long hunts into Cherokee country and staked land claims in Powell's Valley, just east of the Cumberland Gap, under the sponsorship of Thomas Walker in 1770, and of Richard Henderson five years later. Though some white families settled by his frontier station, they soon left rather than stand against Dragging Canoe's

Bloodshed and Quests for Peace   371

warriors. Martin did not plant roots there. As he acquired wealth, he established a plantation in southwestern Virginia. He also served as the head of a scouting company in Virginia's war against the Shawnees in 1774.[20]

Martin was not unlike Daniel Boone in character. While fighting Indians, he did not become an Indian hater. In 1776, Martin served as a captain in Virginia's invasion of Overhill country and came to Chota with Colonel William Christian's troops. After scouting in the vicinity for a few months, Martin returned to Chota and developed an intimate relationship with Betsy, Nan-ye-hi's daughter, and soon came to live with her at Long Island of the Holston. It is a safe assumption that the relationship met Nan-ye-hi's approval and encouragement. In time, Betsy had a daughter and son by the Virginian, an imposing figure at six feet in height and above 200 pounds. (Cherokees proverbially nick-named him "Tall.") Martin was not one to be tied down. While enamored of Betsy, he had an Anglo-American wife in Virginia, who bore him seven children before her death in 1782. He subsequently remarried in Virginia and added considerably to his progeny there.[21]

By the summer of 1777, Martin secured appointment as Virginia's agent to the Cherokees. He opened a storehouse at Long Island for managing the state's business and assumed responsibility as a diplomatic intermediary. In May 1779, Martin received a visit by chiefs Raven and Scolacutta, who desired peace with Virginia and hoped the state would supply their towns with ammunition and goods. Raven, who had been a partisan of Dragging Canoe in 1776, claimed that he had always refused "bad Talks" from Chickamauga towns. Scolacutta joined the migration to Chickamauga, but now had returned north. While conversing with the two chiefs, Martin took encouragement from an anonymous Chickamauga headman who vowed an attachment to "our Brothers in Chotey." The old Overhill towns remained beloved by many Cherokees who had to flee from there in wartime.[22]

Scolacutta's visit to Martin marks a friendship between the two men that lasted into the 1790s. In British and American records, Scolacutta is nearly always identified as "Hanging-Maw"—a reflection of his girth. The moniker was not an insult, however indelicate it seems today. Scolacutta thought it wise to have an influential Virginia friend once he decided that the Chickamaugas had chosen a mistaken course. Interestingly, he had in the recent past been a militant himself. In one foray of 1776 into Kentucky, he and a few Shawnee companions seized Daniel Boone's daughter, Jemima, and two other white girls, before the captives were rescued. According to Boone lore, Scolacutta was kind to Jemima. If so, he acted in keeping with all that is known of him.[23]

From his station at Long Island, Martin distinguished between the "old towns" of the Upper Cherokees, which he strove to win over to the American side, as compared with the southerly Chickamaugas in league with the British. In late 1780, Cherokee fighters of several regions attacked white settlements from the Watauga to Powell's Valley near the Cumberland Gap. British agents stirred Chickamaugas to join the offensive, but the result was a scattershot thrust from the south. As we have seen, Colonels Arthur Campbell and John Sevier's militiamen crushed resistance by burning fifteen Overhill and Hiwassee Valley towns.[24]

Martin, promoted to major, was a man with interests across the settler-Native divide. While leading militia forays against Naïve militants in 1781–1782, he encouraged a prisoner exchange with the Chickamaugas toward a broader Cherokee peace. By contrast, Governor Alexander Martin of North Carolina took a harsher line, vowing that the Chickamaugas would have peace only if removing to ancestral towns to the north, ceding land along the French Broad River, returning prisoners and escaped Blacks, and surrendering Tories and British agents. No negotiation followed from this diktat, which was issued after state militia readied for war with the Chickamaugas. In the offensive, Sevier's militia burned eight or nine Indian villages but again failed to achieve the objective of subduing the Chickamauga movement.[25]

North Carolina now surpassed Virginia in its hunger for Cherokee lands. The reason can be seen on the map. A great portion of Cherokee country lay directly west of North Carolina and therefore within territories claimed under the state's old royal charter. In April 1783, the state legislature engaged in a notorious land grab, enlarging its western domain by limiting Cherokee bounds to portions of what is today's eastern Tennessee. While no less expansionist, Virginia had its hands full with keeping a hold in Kentucky, especially after Shawnee, Delaware, and other Native fighters defeated the militia at Blue Licks just south of the Ohio in August 1782.[26]

With the coming of peace between the United States and Britain, Martin's position changed. While still representing Virginia, he had more political leeway to expand his ambitions beyond that state. He saw no contradiction in safeguarding Cherokee rights within a limited compass and advising influential patrons such as Patrick Henry on

Bloodshed and Quests for Peace

potential windfalls in Indian country.[27] Now a militia colonel besides an experienced hand at Indian relations, Martin was not averse to speculating far afield for private gain and concealing his machinations from Benjamin Harrison, Virginia's governor, who had instructed him in early 1783 to work with John Donelson toward negotiating formal peace agreements with the Cherokees, Chickasaws, and Creeks. Along with Donelson, Martin plotted a more ambitious agenda. Going beyond Harrison's narrowly defined charge, both men grasped the opportunity to become associates in a syndicate, the Bend of the Tennessee Company, headed by William Blount of North Carolina, the most voracious western land speculator of the 1780s and 1790s. In line with Blount's plans, Martin and Donelson aspired to induce Cherokee and Chickasaw headmen to sell their people's rights to the Tennessee River's Great Bend, including Muscle Shoals, an ideal venue for U.S. entrepreneurs eager to develop a profitable trade in a region of rich and still uncolonized lands.[28]

With Blount's patronage, Martin gained appointment as North Carolina's agent to the Cherokees in June 1783. (This fact did not preclude duties under Virginia.) In his new station, he had license to achieve a boundary treaty with "Friendly" Cherokee towns and even negotiate with the Chickamaugas whom North Carolina's government still wished to see remove north to their old towns and be under closer state watch. Blount, himself master at bribery, was confident about persuading the North Carolina legislature to approve whatever Native land cession Martin and Donelson could swing. The company's plan was modified within months when surveyors found that the Tennessee's Great Bend fell within Georgia's western territorial claims, necessitating politicking in that state. This obstacle was piddling, however, compared to obtaining Native acquiescence. For all Martin's savvy, he and Donelson failed to procure a cession of the Great Bend and Muscle Shoals from Native leaders, whether Cherokees or Chickasaws.[29]

All of this complicates the issue of Martin's relationship with the Cherokees, whom he befriended with mixed personal and pecuniary motives, especially when it came to lobbying for the Great Bend. True, he had a genuine rapport with Oconostota who relied on Martin and wife Besty to care for him in his last year as his health failed. Feeling the end was near about 1783, the great chief actually gifted his beloved Chota to Martin so the town would be safeguarded after his death. Responding to Oconostota's plea, Martin replied that while Virginia would supply Chota, that village would not alone be favored: "I look

374 *Upheavals and the Will to Live, 1762–1795*

on all the old [Cherokee] towns, and I love them all who are friends to the United States." When Oconostota died, Martin carved a coffin from a canoe for the chief's burial. Remarkably, archeologists in 1969 found the remains, which were subsequently reburied.[30]

While Martin felt a deep bond with Oconostota, his personal devotion did not guarantee Cherokee security in any broad sense. At the Revolutionary War's end, Martin's diplomatic charge was to secure a peace with southern Indian nations, not least for the purpose of weaning them from lingering British influence. This aim hardly jibed with the Blount syndicate's attempts to corner the Great Bend, which aroused Native vigilance and resistance. One of the great foes of the United States in the southern region was Alexander McGillivray, a principal Creek chief whose father was a well-heeled Scots Indian trader and whose mother was of the Koasati (Coushatta) tribe. From his home at Little Tallassee, Alexander became a power broker through his intelligence, British Loyalist connections, and his commitment to defend Native peoples against the upstart American states. Schooled in Charles Town before the Revolutionary War, he was highly fluent in English and conversant with colonial society. This was an unusual talent for a Native American leader of his era, perhaps surpassed only by Joseph Brant (Thayendanegea) of the Mohawks.[31]

Confusion in the States

McGillivray of the Creeks was bitter about British defeat in the war, though he was comforted in 1784 by the weakness of the United States. As he reported to Irish-born Arturo O'Neill, Spanish commandant of Pensacola, "the back Inhabitants of Georgia & Carolina are in arms to oppose the Tax Collectors, the whole Continent is in confusion [and] before long I expect to hear that the three Kings [British, Spanish, and French] must Settle the matter by dividing America between them." McGillivray's judgment was a bit facile, if not at all far-fetched when he penned this sarcastic barb. That same year, Joseph Martin heard from British traders that Indian men were much taken with the idea that "the Americans had no King & were nothing of themselves & was now like a man that was Lost & wandering about in the woods."[32]

The American Union under the Articles of Confederation was something like the proverbial lost and wandering man relative to the west and Native affairs. The problem lay in a Congress that was hamstrung

Bloodshed and Quests for Peace   375

by states that jealously guarded their sovereignty. The Southern states were notoriously slow to cede their western territorial claims to the Union. A big step forward came in 1783 when Virginia yielded its claims above the Ohio, with a few exceptions, while retaining jurisdiction in Kentucky. North Carolina went back and forth on western issues, tossed hither and yon by rival speculative interests. In early 1784, the state legislature approved a cession to the federal government of its trans-Appalachian territorial claims, only to rescind the act later that year. The situation became still more complex when a group of discontented settlers in the Watauga, Nolichucky, and French Broad Valleys seceded from North Carolina and declared an independent State of Franklin in December 1784. The Franklin movement, while sensitive to poor whites' economic problems, favored a tough and aggressively expansionist policy toward the Cherokees and other Indians. John Sevier, elected governor of Franklin in March 1785, had recently partnered with Blount but now competed with him for pathways to Muscle Shoals and the Great Bend or "the Bent," as it was called in frontier speech.[33]

Blount and Sevier were both ardent expansionists, though they differed in method. An eastern gentleman, Blount specialized in backdoor intrigues that had the veneer of legality, whether it came to amassing land titles or achieving cessions of Native territory, which in his view should ideally be purchased from leading headmen and authorized by the relevant state or federal authorities. Sevier, a frontier militia colonel, had no problem with this model but carried things to the edge. His government did not shy from imposing its will on Cherokees by intimidation and the threat of force.

The State of Franklin had its own propaganda arm, boosted by Arthur Campbell of bordering Virginia, who espoused the new government's admission to the Union and forwarded favorable notices on that subject for circulation in eastern newspapers. One notice of May 1785, written in Campbell's style, put an optimistic gloss on Franklin's relations with the Cherokees, who were soon to be "incorporated" as "useful citizens." This same article condescendingly described those Indians as "poor creatures . . . more desirous of peace than ever, since the commencement of the late war; and indeed well they may, for we have them in our power." David Campbell, a Franklin officeholder, confided to his older brother Arthur that some white settlers in his district favored "immediately attempting the utter Extirpation of the Indians; but I am decidedly against the measure, as being in our Situation, totally

376   *Upheavals and the Will to Live, 1762–1795*

impracticable & at all events evidently unjust." Detestation of Indians in white settlement districts ran deep. It was an open question whether such hatred could be contained by seemingly respectable white frontier leaders. This was the brutal reality.[34]

Arthur Campbell wholeheartedly backed western citizens' quest for their own self-governance. Writing James Madison in 1785, he made a case for the admission of three new western states: Kentucky; "Frankland," as Franklin's adherents sometimes called it; and his own region in Virginia's southwest—to be called Washington. With a view toward the Spanish realm, Campbell argued that "Kentucky and Frankland, would circulate eastwardly some of the riches of Mexico, and keep the Spaniards, [and] the Southern and Western Indians in awe." That the Castilian monarch officially closed the lower Mississippi to U.S. traffic in 1784 seemed a temporary barrier to western Americans eager to exchange their agricultural produce for Mexican silver at New Orleans.[35]

The American use of vital waterways from the Tennessee and Cumberland to the Gulf depended quite as much on the Native peoples as on the Spanish. This is why Sevier held a conference in July 1785 with Chickasaw headmen in his tiny capital town of Jonesboro. The Native delegation, headed by Piomingo (Mountain Leader), was assisted by one Cherokee man who was Chickasaw by adoption. After Piomingo spoke of expanding trade, Kiateh, his Cherokee ally, said that the Chickamaugas approved his mission to "keep quietness" with "the white people." Sevier spoke warmly to the Native assemblage and gave them a few presents. His immediate aim was for the Chickasaws to safeguard his state's commerce on the Tennessee from Chickamauga and Creek attack.[36]

Political disarray in the trans-Appalachian west greatly concerned Congress, which feared that unconstrained speculative land fever and settler adventurism could ignite clashes with Native nations and place the United States on a collision course with the British in Canada and Spain in the Floridas and Louisiana. The establishment of Franklin was only one of several trouble spots. Kentucky had its own separatist faction that was disgusted by Virginia's tight-fisted government that failed to defend the region against Indian attack. In early 1785, Georgia unilaterally declared the Natchez region, under dispute between Spain and the United States, to be within its jurisdiction. Although Georgia's machinations failed to dislodge the Spanish, Congress worried about that state's illicit and roguish ambitions. In 1786, Congress's prestige

Bloodshed and Quests for Peace

plummeted to a nadir in the south and west when foreign secretary John Jay proposed a treaty by which the United States would yield navigation on the Mississippi for twenty-five to thirty years in exchange for commercial privileges in peninsular Spain. The prospective treaty was shelved after months of heated debate that heightened sectional tensions and threatened the Union's dissolution.[37]

The federal government's movement to direct Indian policy in the mid-1780s was bound to be messy because of the shaky and uncertain balance between national and state authorities. There was also the question of enforcing boundary lines in the event of treaties negotiated with Indigenous nations. The United States had just a smattering of troops in the Ohio Valley by 1786 and virtually none in the vast southern region. It was a nearly impossible task for a Congress with limited resources to establish order in lands that were part of a vast Indian country, even if falling within the bounds of the United States. White frontier districts petitioned insistently for government protection against Indian attack. Native peoples, meanwhile, demanded justice and respect. Many in Congress believed there was no alternative except to effect treaties with Indian nations based on clearly defined boundaries and pledges of amity and trade. This general formula appeared essential to stave off British and Spanish attempts to draw Native peoples into alliances that might reduce the United States to a nullity, all but negating American sovereignty in trans-Appalachia.

Cherokee perspectives were of course radically different from what is sketched above. For those Native communities that welcomed American diplomatic initiatives, the main issue was to secure land rights in a lasting and not on a provisional basis. There was also an expectation of trade and supply, needed more than ever before given the diminution of the deerskin and fur trade. Reciprocity and respect were paramount. Cherokees in the old Overhill region, the Hiwassee Valley, and areas to the east were in a different geopolitical position than the Chickamauga towns, which had veteran British Loyalist traders in their midst and viable connections to the powerful Creeks and to Shawnees above and below the Ohio. All Cherokees knew quite well that the Creeks were holding their own against the Georgians. Shawnees, Miamis, and a host of northern Native peoples ravaged Kentucky and Ohio Valley settlements whose militia retaliated in kind. Even in this bloody arena, some Shawnee communities favored a negotiated peace with the American Big Knives if that could be achieved with dignity.[38]

This was the question that confronted Corn Tassel and other Cherokee peace advocates.

A small number of Cherokees felt long-distance migration was the only way to escape conflict with white settlers and to live more secure lives. They were not alone. In August 1784, Francisco Cruzat, Spanish commandant at St. Louis, welcomed 260 Indians of several nations to his post. The visitors included Iroquois, Cherokees, Shawnees, Chickasaws, Choctaws, and Abenakis. Complaining bitterly of the Americans, the Native deputies asked that the Spanish allow them to settle west of the Mississippi. Considering their desire to shore up defense against the United States, the Spanish willingly obliged. By the mid-1790s, several hundred Shawnees and Delawares lived in villages ranging from the area west of St. Louis to locales in what are now southeastern Missouri and neighboring Arkansas. Small bands of Cherokees trekked to that region, settling by the St. Francis River and further south along the White River in the mid- to late 1780s. These western Indian emigrants faced new challenges as they had to stand their ground in clashes with the Quapaws (Arkansas Indians) and Osage. The first Cherokee pioneers could hardly foretell how their small numbers would swell from 1800 to 1820 as their eastern kin sought to escape impoverishment, the pressure of cultural change, and the threat of dispossession by the United States.[39]

The Path to Hopewell

In the spring of 1785, Cherokees were pleased to learn that the American Congress had decided to arrange a treaty with them. The information came from Joseph Martin, one of several commissioners chosen under federal authority to negotiate outstanding issues with southern Indian nations. By early June, Martin and two colleagues—Andrew Pickens of South Carolina and Benjamin Hawkins of North Carolina— were in Charles Town to prepare for a meeting with Cherokee and Chickasaw delegates by the Keowee River. The commissioners desired to treat with the Creeks as well, though Alexander McGillivray, having no trust in the United States, tactfully declined Pickens's offer of negotiation. Later that year, McGillivray wrote Spanish commandant O'Neill that the sole means of keeping the Americans "within due bounds" was to build a "formidable Indian Confederacy" in alliance with Spain, just as Native peoples were in league with the British ensconced at Detroit, Niagara, and other "posts on the Lakes."[40]

Bloodshed and Quests for Peace   379

Unlike McGillivray, Corn Tassel had no real possibility of testing a Spanish option from Upper Cherokee country. Counting on Martin, he headed a Cherokee delegation that journeyed to the Keowee River in the fall of 1785 to meet with American commissioners under the aegis of Congress. The talks took place at Hopewell, the estate of General Pickens, who lived a stone's throw from the site of Seneca, one of many Cherokee villages in the area abandoned since South Carolina's invasion of 1776. Pickens had himself led forces in the assault and now did business in the Indian trade. Cherokees generally respected him as an honorable warrior and a fair man. The American commissioners met first with Cherokee representatives followed by negotiations with Choctaw and Chickasaw delegations.[41]

U.S. ideas of lawful authority over Indian territories had a direct bearing on the Hopewell negotiations. Congress asserted the American confederation's rights to all land ceded by Great Britain in the Treaty of Paris. Southern Indian peoples were officially deemed "aggressors" who had committed "barbarities" in the American War of Independence and therefore had no grounds to object to whatever boundaries or limits were imposed on them. In practice, however, Congress favored a moderate course in the southern theater, "neither to yield nor require too much; to accommodate the Indians as far as the publick good will admit, and to avoid the hazards of a war" at great expense. The southern U.S. commissioners took a modulated tone in negotiation, far more politic than their counterparts who dealt with Native peoples above the Ohio.[42]

To be sure, the Hopewell commissioners were not unduly soft. As talks got underway, they delivered a preliminary lecture in which the Cherokees were instructed that they were living within the territories of the United States. But the commissioners also talked of fair treatment. Their purpose was "to remove, as far as may be, all causes of future contention and quarrels."[43]

Since we know that the Hopewell treaty failed to protect the Cherokees, it is all too easy to dismiss the talks as window dressing. The conference record is still important for allowing us to hear Cherokee voices from diverse elements of the nation. Besides thirty-six male chiefs present at negotiations, there were nine hundred Cherokee men, women, and children on the treaty grounds. This was a major gathering of a people not only in need of goods but of hope. At least three Chickamauga headmen participated. They wished to know what the Americans were offering. A good many Cherokee deputies came from

380   *Upheavals and the Will to Live, 1762–1795*

towns that had been rebuilt after being destroyed in war on at least two occasions: Nequassee, Hiwassee, Ellijay, Great Tellico and Little Tellico, Cowee, and Chilhowee. Their people did not give up.[44]

Nan-ye-hi spoke at the conference on a single occasion. In a forceful and poignant way, she gave her talk not only for herself but for "the young warriors" in her town of Chota. Her words, accompanied by the gift of pipe and tobacco to U.S. commissioners, aired a past refrain and also spoke to future generations: "I am fond of hearing that there is a peace, and I hope that you have now taken us by the hand in real friendship. . . . I look on you and the red people as my children. . . . I am old, but I hope to yet bear children, who will grow up and people our nation, as we are now to be under the protection of Congress, and shall have no more disturbance." The commissioners listened but did not officially reply. While not unfeeling men, perhaps they did not want to appear as swayed by emotion in deliberations.[45]

Corn Tassel did not make his common request for "pity" at the conference. He projected a strong voice before an assembly of distinguished headmen. Lines had to be drawn. Tassel recalled with great precision the treaty bounds that his people had accepted with Virginia's commissioners at the Holston in 1777. He believed that accord to be a fair guidepost. Virginia and North Carolina settlers had repeatedly tramped over the lines into Cherokee territory, including the precious ground at the confluence of the Holston and French Broad Rivers, gateway to the Tennessee. Tassel responded scornfully when the commissioners presented one of the late Richard Henderson's deeds. If Henderson were still alive, declared Corn Tassel, "I should have the pleasure of telling him he was a liar." He did not believe that Oconostota had signed Henderson's paper. The "rogue" Henderson must have secretly and illicitly placed the mark there.[46]

Tassel and other headmen outlined a map of the river valleys they believed were rightfully their people's. The Cumberland and Tennessee watersheds were at the heart. The headmen knew how urgent it was to fix limits before all was lost. When drafting a treaty, the commissioners specified "hunting grounds" for the Cherokees "within the limits of the United States." While cutting into ancestral Cherokee lands in the western Cumberland watershed about Nashville, the commissioners offered reasonable terms considering that they lacked the authority to annul any state's pending territorial claims. The treaty's fifth article was the boldest attempt yet made by the federal government to protect southern Indian lands. All white persons, living in

Bloodshed and Quests for Peace

Cherokee territory south and west of the new treaty line were to leave the region within six months or else forfeit government protection. The same rule applied to non-Natives settling beyond the boundary after the treaty took hold. The Cherokees were explicitly entitled by treaty to "punish" any such person "as they please." An exception was made for American citizens already living in the thickly colonized area between the French Broad and Holston Rivers. Just as headmen had done on past occasions, Tassel agreed to this concession for what seemed the greater good. He still could not help but wonder about the oddity of bending the rule: "Are Congress, who conquered the King of Great Britain, unable to remove those people?"[47]

Cherokees cited models of past diplomacy as examples for the present. Headman Nowota of Chickamauga recalled how "Captain" Cameron had once been a friend and now believed that the American commissioners would fill that same role. Chescoenwhee wished to be a friend of "the thirteen United States" so long as the latter saw to "justice." Fair treatment was at the heart of things.[48]

Within a few months of the Hopewell Treaty, the threat against the Cherokees was magnified, not lessened, given the failure of enforcement. Besides an absence of federal troops, Congress did not have the means to impose a treaty on the states responsible for its execution. William Blount, an observer at Hopewell, quickly protested the Cherokee treaty in the name of North Carolina. He could not accept any agreement that diminished the state's enormous military reserve above the Cumberland. Above all, the treaty recognized Cherokee lands over a broader compass of territory than allotted by North Carolina's legislature. Blount was irritated by unfinished private business, unmentioned in his formal protest. The Great Bend seemed to be slipping from his grasp. The State of Franklin, negotiating with Georgia authorities behind the scenes, was seeking to absorb the Bend and Muscle Shoals for its own enrichment.[49]

Chickamauga-Creek Connections

Joseph Martin, who had numerous sources in Indian country, described the Chickamauga region in 1785 as "the Middle-Grounds" between the Upper Cherokees and the Creeks. Tory traders lived there, along with "disorderly whites" who remained at large and "are daily urging the Indians to steal horses from the frontiers of Virginia and North Carolina, which they send to the Floridas." Two white men, perhaps

382   *Upheavals and the Will to Live, 1762–1795*

traders, had just come to Martin's residence and told him of being captured by Creeks and earmarked for ritual execution before making their escape. One of the Indian captors, who spoke good English, boasted that his group had recently taken four white scalps in the Cumberland settlements and seized a Black slave boy there. The marauders planned to snare whites on the Kentucky Road, the main path for settlers traveling from the Cumberland Gap north to settlement districts. Curiously, the two white escapees came across some friendly Chickamauga men who helped them on their way to Upper Cherokee country and the Holston.[50]

This single story, which had myriad variations, reminds us that small war parties did not necessarily follow any general command even if many frontier whites believed that Alexander McGillivray controlled all Creek guerrilla strikes. The object of individual raiders was not necessarily some grand strategy but rather visiting terror on whites to keep them at bay and concurrently gaining war honors, taking captives, and plundering. Widespread exchange networks, often reaching across Native-colonial bounds, proliferated in the barter and sale of stolen horses, goods, and enslaved Blacks.[51]

Joseph Martin made it his business to open a correspondence with John McDonald, a Scots trader who had lived at Chickamauga Creek from the days prior to the American Revolution and was said to speak Cherokee as fluently as any white man in memory. McDonald was a factor for the merchant House of Panton, Leslie and Company, the Tory firm that won Spanish license by 1785 for a virtual monopoly of the Indian import-export trade from St. Augustine to Pensacola. William Panton, a hard-driving man who established his headquarters at Pensacola that year, had a close relationship with McGillivray, who depended on the firm's goods, supplemented by Spanish munitions, to build his prestige as a Creek beloved man.[52] McDonald was himself coy in relaying information to Martin. His intelligence was of a kind meant to make a foe beware. Vastly exaggerating Spanish military might, he wrote that Madrid had as many as 5,000 to 6,000 troops in upriver Mississippi posts and a similar number to spare at New Orleans, Mobile, and Pensacola. There were also American prisoners at New Orleans, apparently arrested for illicitly trading in Spain's royal dominions. In a politic, if idiosyncratic valedictory, McDonald assured Martin: "and believe me Sir, I shall never turn Spaniard."[53]

McDonald passed intelligence on American expansionist maneuvers to Alexander McGillivray who successfully requested more munitions

Bloodshed and Quests for Peace

from the Spanish. In 1786–1787, McGillivray urged the Creeks to take to the offensive. Abner Hammond, a Georgia trader with Creek informants, reported that McGillivray had told his people "Either to go against the settlements of Cumberland or fall on the frontiers of Georgia." Joseph Martin conveyed similar intelligence on Chickamauga and Creek forays. The reports were on the mark.[54]

If McGillivray was not quite the potentate he appeared to be, his influence should by no means be discounted. In May 1786, he proudly informed Governor Esteban Miró of Louisiana that his warriors had not only "cleared" Georgia settlers from the Oconee River to the east but had destroyed building materials that colonials had readied at Muscle Shoals. Creek fighters ravaged and destroyed "plantations & out places," that is, dwellings large and small along the Cumberland and killed several inhabitants—a fact McGillivray justified by citing the settlers' "extreme hated and rancor to Indians."[55] In fact, the attackers were Chickamaugas and not simply Creeks. Colonel Anthony Bledsoe, a leading Cumberland settler, admitted his bafflement in May 1786 when it came to identifying the Native fighters who had killed seven white men and wounded six others in just two months. Though not fully certain "by what hand we suffer," the colonel assumed the killings were "in part by the Cherokees and . . . [in] part by the Creeks." One informant of Cherokee-Anglo parentage told Bledsoe that the Creeks would continue attacks so long as whites were intent on "Settling the Bent of [the] Tennessee."[56]

There is an additional factor to consider, namely McGillivray's strategic compass. The Creek leader was both Native and British in this sense. He thought about his people's land as an Indigenous whole that encompassed towns and hunting grounds. He meanwhile conceived of the continental balance of power in a European manner. It was not enough to defend one's people or to enlist allies for that end. Native peoples were certainly adept on that score, though they often found it difficult to enlist distant tribes in a sustained campaign. Indian men had to hunt as well as to defend their towns. McGillivray intended to surmount these limitations. His continental map said that the Creeks were in danger of encirclement by Americans and consequentially vulnerable to subordination if they became dependent on U.S. traders. Panton and Leslie were therefore as vital to Creek security as Spanish support. As McGillivray read the map, trade ruled Indian alliance; it was an inescapable force.

For McGillivray, it was not sufficient to unify southern Native nations in an ad hoc, short-term manner. He wanted a durable confederation far stronger than what then existed. One nation's defection could bring the fall of all. He strongly distrusted the Chickasaws, especially those who harkened to pro-American chief Piomingo. At the Hopewell conference in early 1786, federal commissioners made some headway with the Chickasaws, who permitted them, at least on paper, to establish a trading house at Bear Creek just west of Muscle Shoals. Whether this could be achieved was doubtful. Georgia agent William Davenport cultivated Chickasaw friendship but was treading on dangerous ground. Not hiding their distrust, several Chickasaws told Davenport that the Americans "only Pretends to be their friends to get their land from them." McGillivray and the Creeks closely watched Davenport over the next year.[57]

While Cumberland settlers often fell victim to Indian attack during the settlement's beginning (1780–1781), there was a dramatic decline in such deaths over the next four years. Not a single settler is reported to have been killed in 1784 and 1785 when the Creeks were preoccupied with Georgia following British imperial withdrawal. The number of victims then shot up to 13 in 1786 and then climbed startlingly to 45 in 1787. In 1788, 24 persons fell victim, and 18 the next year. The historian's challenge is to make sense of the killings as a window into a shared American past—colonial and Native—intertwined and not comprehensible in isolation from one another. Creeks, Chickamaugas, and many of their Cherokee kin were alarmed by the American push for Muscle Shoals and the growth in the Cumberland's settler population. Whites were growing fast enough to appear as a threat, but their absolute number—about seven thousand in 1790—was small, dispersed, and open to attack.[58]

Cumberland's settlers were beset. Besides the searing toll in lives, other problems loomed. Settlers did not have safe navigation to the Ohio and Mississippi, and even if they had, Spanish officials allowed little American traffic on the great river below Natchez. Cumberland's whites were dependent on pathways of communication and trade with their counterparts in Kentucky and eastern Tennessee. It was precisely in these areas that the Chickamaugas attacked with a vengeance, absorbed not only in retaining their hunting lands but in horse-stealing and plunder. While not nomadic, they were nearly as skilled as Comanches in predatory raiding over considerable distances.[59] In certain cases, attack routes went both ways. During early 1786, a handful of white

Bloodshed and Quests for Peace

Kentuckians stealthily approached a Chickamauga town whose raiders had supposedly stolen their horses. The intruders killed four Indian men but suffered three dead themselves. Chickamaugas retaliated by murdering a white man and his wife and child on the path between Kentucky and the Cumberland. The assault party was headed by Nentooyah ("Bloody Fellow"), a chief and brother of one of the slain Chickamauga men. Cumberland's settlers barely held on. There was much talk that the settlements would "break up" under pressure, but the settlers' stubborn spirit prevailed. They held their ground.[60]

The Chickamaugas drew strength through bonds with northern Indian groups. There was nothing new about such alliance-building, but it gained increased urgency with the unmistakable and rapidly growing American threat. Wyandot visitors of the Ohio/Great Lakes region brought the war hatchet to Chickamauga towns in the fall of 1785. Shawnee militants had frequent contacts with the Chickamaugas, and the latter had men living in the Ohio country. Moluntha, head of the Shawnee peace faction, advised American officers in 1786 of his inability to restrain Mingo and Cherokee warriors in the area. Within a year, Kentucky militia attacked a village of "Chickamoggies" near the Scioto in Ohio.[61]

Native militancy came at a great cost, often paid by Indians who had no connection to the killing of white settlers. One example will suffice here. In July 1786, two Overhill Cherokee youths visited a nearby colonial settlement, played with two young white men, and then shot them dead. In response, Colonel Alexander Outlaw of Franklin gathered 250 militiamen and rode toward Coyatee, the town where the alleged killers lived. After futilely demanding the culprits' surrender, the militia entered Coyatee, killed four Native men, and burned the village to the ground. Within days, Outlaw and the other officers summoned Upper Cherokee headmen to a meeting where they lambasted the assemblage, which included Corn Tassel and his ally Scolacutta. The Upper Town leaders were stunned, as they had had nothing to do with the killings.[62]

Tassel was highly disturbed by the charge that his people were complicit in the deaths of Colonels John Donelson and William Christian in Kentucky the previous spring. Donelson had died of a gunshot wound in uncertain circumstances while traveling from Kentucky to the Cumberland. Christian was killed by Indian gunmen, possibly Chickamaugas, while on a military expedition in Ohio. Corn Tassel declared that Christian was a "brother" whom he loved and who loved him in kind. What counted was mutual respect, not the fact that the dead man had once led an invasion of Cherokee territory. Corn Tassel remembered Christian's decency at conferences when the colonel acknowledged the Cherokees as a great people and responded respectfully to Nan-ye-hi's plea for peace.[63]

Christian was mannerly in negotiation, so unlike the Franklin commanders, who peremptorily demanded that Corn Tassel and Scolacutta cede Cherokee land about the Tennessee and Holston or else face war. Both headmen marked a spurious Franklin treaty-deed placed before them under duress. There was no accord. Corn Tassel did not give up on diplomacy even after Kentucky militiamen, patrolling near the Cumberland, killed seven Cherokee hunters. The Kentuckians said they had shot in error, mistaking unoffending Cherokees for Chickamauga marauders. Forty Upper Town warriors went out to seek revenge. Arthur Campbell, an old foe, sent an apologetic letter to Tassel in which he said that Virginia wanted no quarrel with "friendly Cherokees." He clearly believed it foolish to antagonize all Cherokees and push them into the Chickamauga camp.[64]

With Joseph Martin's encouragement, Corn Tassel forwarded a candid talk to Governor Edmund Randolph at Richmond. The chief wished good news from Congress, which he hoped would remove white settlers who had planted themselves on Cherokee land and within areas recognized as Cherokee by the Hopewell treaty. To strengthen his case, Tassel shared some valuable intelligence with Randolph. His report was stunning. Frenchmen at Muscle Shoals were currently plotting with Spaniards and Englishmen against the Americans, while Creeks and northern Indians were purportedly planning strikes on white settlements the next spring. Tassel added that he had refused Indian militants' talks and would not harken to Spanish overtures until he heard first from Congress.[65]

Corn Tassel was not the sole Native leader who gave "state's evidence" to gain credit with the Americans and, in effect, to save his people. Piomingo, the prominent Chickasaw chief, did so under less pressured circumstances. By the spring of 1787, Piomingo sent word to Anthony Bledsoe of Cumberland concerning French and Spanish traders conspiring with the Chickamaugas along the Tennessee. The merchants' suspected sale of munitions to Indians greatly bothered Kentucky and Cumberland settlers. Piomingo's warning spurred action. That June, two Chickasaw warriors guided Colonel James Robertson's force of 130 men from the Cumberland toward the target zone—a site on the

Bloodshed and Quests for Peace

Tennessee's south bank just to the east of Muscle Shoals that the settlers barely knew. The Chickamauga town of "Coldwater" came into view after a trying river passage in which men maneuvered by boat or made their way on horseback along narrow, twisting trails, fording as necessary. The attack was daringly ruthless. The Chickamaugas and their Creek allies were caught by surprise. The invaders killed about twenty Chickamaugas, mostly men by what is known. They also shot dead three Frenchmen and a white woman fleeing by boat. Other French traders were captured, and a great store of goods was seized. Writing Governor Richard Caswell of North Carolina, Robertson reported proudly of the expedition, observing that the dead woman had been killed by accident. He had not lost a single man in the assault and was grateful for Chickasaw assistance. It would be most worthwhile, he wrote, to supply that nation with trade goods at Chickasaw Bluffs on the Mississippi. Robertson kept his eye on the great river as a future prize.[66]

The Great Compass

There is a tale in Tennessee folklore of John Peyton, his two brothers, and three other young white men eating and lounging around a winter campfire after a long day of surveying by the Cumberland in 1786. Hearing their dogs hiss and horses snort, they imagined that nearby wolves had smelled their pungent dinner. Instead, a group of Cherokees appeared, loosed gunfire that wounded four of the six companions, and stole their horses. Somehow, the entire surveying team managed to scamper home on foot across seventy miles of snowy ground to Bledsoe's Station. The wounded youths recovered. In a year's time, John Peyton sent a note with an offer to the Cherokee headman suspected of the attack. The Cherokees could keep the seized horses, guns, and saddlebags on condition that the chief return Peyton's chain and compass. The headman's reply went something like this: "You, John Peyton, ran away like a coward . . . and as for your *land-stealer* [the compass], I have broken that against a tree!"[67]

While the story seems apocryphal, the detail about the compass is telling. What the settlers saw as a useful instrument Cherokees and other Natives feared as a "land stealer," a spirit with dark power to rob them of their ground. The compass needle's movement amid the clash of nations and cultures had both limited and larger purposes. It might pinpoint a small piece of earth or take in far broader horizons. The battle for the Cumberland was bound to the struggle for Kentucky and the Ohio, the U.S.-Spanish rivalry over the Mississippi, Piomingo's budding quarrel with McGillivray, and scenarios where the men of Franklin cooked up plans of wresting Muscle Shoals from Native peoples. Peyton had his compass proverbially stolen in the same year that John Jay lost strategic view of the Lower Mississippi Valley. Crazily, there were linkages between all the above, together with all the killing and bloodshed over a great compass.

History has been called an "exact imagining"—not an empirical science, perhaps, but requiring an essential evidentiary foundation that is then raised by imaginative insights. For example, we know how Corn Tassel's words were transcribed in English. The far more difficult task is to conceive what he truly thought and intended at crucial instances. He certainly believed his people required a protector against aggressive colonialism. Good-willed American "beloved men" surely had some power over their people. Tassel conversed and shared a great deal with Joseph Martin, who cared about Chota through his bond with Betsy and Nan-ye-hi. While self-interested, Martin came to oppose the State of Franklin's hell-bent expansionism. Tassel gave his trust in turn. The chief also respected Benjamin Hawkins and Andrew Pickens, who spoke in the name of the great Congress. He had not given up on Virginia's governors. High and mighty friends seemingly had the power to rein in ordinary whites who were all too ready to kill or drive off Indians.[68]

It is little wonder that Tassel was badly disappointed in the spring of 1787 when Governor Randolph upbraided him by letter for Cherokee violence against whites. Just weeks before, Tassel had shared information with the governor about all manner of threats posed by the English, French, and Spaniards as well as a hostile Indian alliance. Replying to Randolph's criticism, the chief took issue with each allegation. No white woman had been burned alive in Chickamauga. Nor had Cherokees killed any whites in that fashion since the 1777 peace treaty forged with Virginia during the past war. The governor had spoken in his letter of carrying "the Tomahawk and fire" into the Cherokee towns unless Corn Tassel and his people surrendered Native men who were henceforth guilty of robbing or killing whites. "It seems," answered Tassel, "that you was fond of Believing Lies and Looking over Truth. . . . It is well known you have Taken almost all our Country from us without our consent. That Don't seem to satisfy my Elder Brother, but he talks of fire and sword." Corn Tassel let Randolph know that the governor's letters had not even followed the proper form of addressing Cherokee

Bloodshed and Quests for Peace

headmen. Randolph's talk was not sealed as customary and had the barest salutation and also lacked date or place information written at the top. Hoping for better, Tassel wanted to live in peace with his "Elder Brother of Virginia." The Cherokee chief's sentiments were conveyed through an unnamed amanuensis—by all signs his friend Joseph Martin, whose writing style was uncannily similar to the frank talk of Tassel's message.[69]

Martin was active, gauging the lay of the land over a broad front. He had sufficient respect among Cherokees to be welcomed to Chickamauga towns in June 1787. Doubtless he had an advance invitation, perhaps through the auspices of John Watts (Kunoskeskie), who happened to be Corn Tassel's nephew—the son of the chief's sister by John Watts Sr., a Scots trader among the Cherokees who had died before the Revolutionary War. On a rare visit to Chickamauga country in 1787, Martin attempted to fathom a world little known to whites. Early on, he attended a conference at Ustanali near the Coosawattee. The site was at the heart of customary hunting grounds shared by Cherokees and Creeks over generations despite warfare between those peoples. At Ustanali's townhouse, Cherokees exchanged beads with a Shawnee headman. Also present were deputies of the Creeks and the "Nont[u] ees and Nottowagoes" of the Great Lakes. The latter were members of northern Native nations that Cherokees invariably described by generic names. Martin learned of a planned meeting of numerous "Tribes" to be held at the Creek town of Tuckabatchee.[70]

While there were diehard Chickamauga leaders, others were open to negotiation. A few Chickamauga headmen responded positively to Martin's conciliatory overtures. In a talk forwarded to Randolph, headman Tuskegetchee said that he loved war, but was now for peace and had come to live in a town between Chickamauga and Chota, a mid-region locale signifying Cherokee unity. Admittedly, Tuskegetchee might seem to have a special reason to please. He was kin to Martin by being brother to Nan-ye-hi, mother of the Virginian's Cherokee wife. Tuskegetchee's talk has a realistic air. If the "Virginians" had greater fear of the Cherokees, they would not be so cavalier about taking their land. It was the Creeks, he said, "that does the greatest mischief ... because they are strong and willing to fight."[71]

In September 1787, there was a moment of brightness at Chota. Alexander Dromgoole, Virginia trader, arrived from Philadelphia with a trove of silver gifts, courtesy of Benjamin Franklin, president of the Pennsylvania council. There were two medals and gorgets apiece for

Corn Tassel and Scolacutta. Also presented were silver gifts for the beloved woman Katteuha, who received a hair clip or pin, two pairs of "bobs" or earrings, and a silver medallion bearing Franklin's likeness. Katteuha gained Franklin's attention by sending a written peace talk to Philadelphia, thanking the famous man for his own friendly message to her people. Significantly, Katteuha offered the letter on behalf of all Cherokee women, and not herself alone. The letter was endorsed by Corn Tassel and Scolacutta—a sign of collaboration between men and women in conciliatory messaging to American authorities.[72]

Katteuha's message came with a gift of tobacco and a wish for reciprocity. She had filled the pipes of Cherokee beloved men; she now did the same for Philadelphia's beloved men, whom she addressed as a mother: "I have Taken the privilege to Speak to you as my own Children, & the same as if you had sucked my Breast—and I am in hopes you have a beloved woman amongst you who will help to put her Children Right if they do wrong, as I shall do the same." The "great men" have promised "to Keep the path clear & straight." Mothers would be sure to pass the lesson on to their children. All must consider why Katteuha spoke: "woman is the Mother of All—and that woman does not pull Children out of Trees or Stumps nor out of old Logs, but out of their Bodies, so that they [the people] ought to mind what a woman says." These powerful words, conveyed to Philadelphia by Dromgoole, were translated by Moses Price and Tom Ben, both sons of Cherokee women by Anglo fathers. They were part of a new American world, strife-torn with innumerable, often contradictory pronouncements and pursuits of human betterment that seldom rose to Katteuha's ideal.[73]

Connections between "white" and "Native" worlds were proliferating in diverse Cherokee regions and in varying ways. For example, Moses Price lived at Chickamauga for the most part, but that did not itself make him a militant firebrand. In September 1787, the same month that he served as translator at Chota, he informed Dromgoole of prime intelligence—Creek warriors had killed Georgian William Davenport and three other Americans attempting to build a trading store in Chickasaw country. Quite aware of Davenport's activities, McGillivray targeted him for drawing Chickasaws into the U.S. camp. McGillivray was by no means desirous of continuous war. In April 1788, he let Robertson and Bledsoe know that his warriors had recently hit the Cumberland settlements in retaliation for Creeks being killed in the Coldwater attack. Having settled the score, he was

Bloodshed and Quests for Peace

ready to call a truce with the Cumberland, but not with Georgia until that state was brought to heel.[74]

A Terrible Reckoning

Despite Corn Tassel's tireless efforts, Cherokee country was wracked by crisis. The Franklin people and other whites continued to plant themselves over treaty lines that had been previously negotiated in good faith and largely at Cherokee expense. Tassel had no control over young Cherokee men who took to war out of deep frustration but whose exploits brought unremitting retaliation. Chickamauga warriors did not halt attacks even if some of their headmen considered peace. The influence of Dragging Canoe, wielded out of the view of whites, stoked the fires. The Chickamaugas did not possess a monopoly on Cherokee militancy, but their example counted mightily. They were more secure than the Upper Cherokee towns and far better stocked through Spanish connections, their own plentiful harvests, and a deerskin commerce through a host of traders.[75]

The Chickamaugas would have been compromised if bordering Creek towns fell prey to Franklin's expansionist goals in conjunction with Georgia. In the fall of 1787, Sevier plotted to raise fifteen hundred volunteers to aid Georgia in an offensive against the Creeks, provided that his officers and soldiers were guaranteed lands in the Tennessee's Great Bend. The plan fell through, however, partly because of rifts among Franklin's settlers about their state's separation from North Carolina. Georgia's government, meanwhile, had second thoughts about backing the scheme as Franklin's woes deepened. "The Franks," as staunch Franklinites called themselves, would return to North Carolina's jurisdiction by the close of 1788 but without yielding ambitions on Indian country. The larger problem was an American frontier population that was loath to respect the rights of Native friends, let alone foes.[76]

Joseph Martin could only do so much as mediator between white settlers and Cherokees. In March 1787, he warned Edmund Randolph that "the Pretended State of Franklyn" had opened a land office for the sale and settlement of Indian lands between the French Broad and Tennessee Rivers—an area that North Carolina's legislature had reserved for the Cherokees, who now feared the loss of their "Beloved" Chota itself and "several of their Principal Corn fields." Martin met face to face with leading settlers and showed them a state proclamation

392   *Upheavals and the Will to Live, 1762–1795*

ordering whites off the land. "Their Reply," wrote Martin, "was that they had Knowledge Enough to Govern themselves." None of the settlers budged.[77]

With the Cherokee peace camp's influence diminished, warriors aggressively fought the advance of white settlement. By March 1788, Martin reported that "the white people on Holston was in great confusion." Over the winter, Cherokees killed a man, captured his wife and four children, and headed downriver in canoes. A few months later, warriors came into the same locale, wounded one white man, and took off with about a hundred horses. Cherokee raids reached into the Powell and Clinch Valleys, where southwestern Virginia and Tennessee meet today. In one instance, a Native war party raided a settler house, scalped a young man, and rode off with fifteen horses after killing cattle and calves. That spring, lethal violence and captive-taking continued to mount. A white woman and two men were killed in separate episodes. Settlers widely believed that the Cherokees were playing "Double Games," committing wanton violence under the "colour" that whites would attribute it all to the Creeks.[78]

Fear gripped many Cherokee towns, where most inhabitants wanted none of the violence. While at Chota, Martin saw that some Upper Cherokees had moved out to seek shelter in Chickamauga territory. He urged villagers to "stay in their towns and plant their corn," adding that they would not be harmed. Corn was planted in the spring of 1788, but there was no safety. One morning, a party of white men, acting "without any provocation," as Martin wrote, attacked a Cherokee town and killed an old woman and wounded two children. For a few days, Chota's men put Martin under watch, along with his aide, Joseph Sevier (son of John Sevier). Scolacutta suspected that Martin had lulled the Cherokees into a false sense of trust, only to prepare the day for their destruction. His presumption was not correct, even if understandable given the perilous conditions. After seeking a truce in fighting, Martin gathered his possessions, including several enslaved Blacks, and departed Cherokee country for a respite at his Virginia home. While Martin's story of being confined at Chota is not easily corroborated, his account of a deteriorating frontier situation was all too true.[79]

In mid-May, bloodshed spiked. A band of Cherokee warriors surprised the Kirk family household and massacred all eleven persons in the homestead on the Little River. The home was about twelve miles southwest of White's Fort (today's Knoxville) in Cherokee territory. John Kirk Jr., a son of the householder, was away at the time of the

Bloodshed and Quests for Peace   393

murders. He lost his mother and six sisters and brothers, cut down in a single blow. He vowed revenge. His moment came after John Sevier, no longer Franklin's governor, raised 150 volunteers for an offensive into Upper Cherokee towns. Martin attempted in vain to convince Sevier to halt his operation. On the militia's approach in early June, chiefs Oskuah (Abram) of Chilhowee and Corn Tassel went out to meet Sevier and told him of their people's peaceful intentions. It was for naught. Sevier rode west with his men and burned Kiewah, a Hiwassee Valley town. His men killed at least nine villagers before riding off.[80]

Returning to the Little Tennessee Valley, Sevier ordered a detachment to Chilhowee. Major James Hubbard, commanding the volunteers, requested Corn Tassel to join him for negotiation. Tassel made his way from Chota to Chilhowee and crossed the river to meet Hubbard at a house under a flag of truce. Oskuah, his son, and another Cherokee chief and his brother were also present. Disdaining the Cherokees, Hubbard handed a tomahawk to his guest, John Kirk Jr., of the slain settler family, and said: "Take your vengeance." Corn Tassel bowed his head with resignation. Kirk murdered Corn Tassel and the other Cherokee men. Kirk knew he could act with impunity. John Sevier was about a quarter of a mile away at the time. Sevier soon entered the cabin and saw the bodies and blood all about. Though expressing disgust at the murders, his actual motives are less obvious. Sevier had allowed Hubbard, a known Indian hater, to be in charge at the scene.[81]

In this violent era, the murder of Corn Tassel, Oskuah, and friends was not unique. In September 1777, Virginia soldiers at Fort Randolph on the Ohio slaughtered five Shawnee prisoners, including peace chief Cornstalk, in reprisal for an attack committed by other Indians. In 1786, Shawnee chief Moluntha, an honorable peace advocate, raised the American flag and attempted a peaceful talk with the Kentucky militiamen who entered his largely abandoned town. All came to a sudden end when the chief was confronted by Captain Hugh McGary, who bitterly decried the Shawnees' triumph over his comrades at Blue Licks four years earlier. McGary tomahawked Moluntha to death.[82]

These killings were acts of raw hate, not policy. They arose in a vengeful climate that reduced "savage" enemies to less-than-human standing, erased distinctions between Indian militants and peace advocates, and placed all beyond the pale. In the case of Moluntha and Corn Tassel, the attackers deliberately struck with the hatchet or tomahawk—itself a Native weapon. There was an apparent lesson. Whites would not flinch from being as fearsome and merciless as any Indian warrior in

394   *Upheavals and the Will to Live, 1762–1795*

the commission of violence. "Tribe" stood against "tribe" and, in this case, without a middle ground of dialogue, let alone peace talk.

Not all white Americans accepted this brutal state. Joseph Martin deplored the murders at Chilhowee. And he did so not simply on moral grounds but for the pragmatic reason of avoiding anarchic violence that would be as harmful to whites as Cherokees. In the aftermath of the murders, Martin encouraged Cherokee headmen, including John Watts (Kunoskeskie), to send peace talks to Andrew Pickens of South Carolina.[83]

Watts's involvement in this round of diplomacy is notable. He had a profound interest. As previously noted, the slain Corn Tassel was his maternal uncle. Deeply attached to his Cherokee heritage, Watts joined Dragging Canoe's movement to Chickamauga about 1777 while maintaining his ties to friends in the Upper Towns. He was already a significant warrior-diplomat by the time the Tassel was cut down. He supported Scolacutta's talk, which spoke highly of Martin for standing by his Cherokee brothers at Chota and interceding so that John Sevier's men would not destroy the beloved town. Since Corn Tassel and friends were murdered, Scolacutta and other Upper Town people had gone southwest for safety. How could they accept the white people's recent call to return to their towns? The whites had said it was "against the law of Nations to hurt any One who carried a white flag." And yet, as Scolacutta remarked, Sevier's men had hoisted a white flag at Chilhowee and then murdered under that banner. Scolacutta feared that those same people wanted "to drive us off our Lands." He still hoped that Pickens would "see justice done us," and "to hear a good Talk."[84]

Scolacutta's plea was likely transcribed by Martin or an unnamed trader-interpreter he trusted. The reference to "the law of nations" spoke of Cherokee rights in a new language that may have derived from Martin or Watts, or perhaps both men in conversation. Pickens responded with assurances of goodwill. He would protect Cherokees who had journeyed into his neighborhood for safety. Most notably, he joined with twelve other justices of Abbeville County, South Carolina, who directed a public letter to the settlers of the Nolichucky, French Broad, and Holston Valleys. The letter, widely publicized in American newspapers, condemned the massacre at Chilhowee, the murder of peaceful Hiwassee River villagers, and other "outrages" and "cruel & unprovoked injuries" committed on the Cherokees. The address had an air of benevolent condescension: "It is unworthy of American Valor,"

Bloodshed and Quests for Peace

the authors declared, "to kill & plunder a few naked and unarmed Savages, who wish for nothing but to possess their Lands & kill their Venison in peace." In the main, the Abbeville County letter was a work of decency and moderation. The justices termed the Cherokees "a free & independent Nation to whom the protection of the United States has been granted for their freedom & possessions by the most Solemn Treaties." When Native men came to treat under a white flag, they were acting "with the Character of Ambassadors, a Character held sacred by the Law of Nations."[85]

The high notes of enlightenment were balanced by "policy" and pragmatism. The letter recounted the time when the Revolutionary War was its "darkest season" for Americans. A substantial portion of Cherokees had then decided on peace and friendship with the United States at a time when "a great part" of their own Nation—the Chickamaugas—was united with the British. Pickens and friends portrayed a clear-cut divide between two parts of the Cherokee Nation—the Upper and Lower, the friendly and the hostile. It was a simplistic and even misleading view but one that was presently practical. Harm would come to Americans by alienating well-disposed Cherokees. Chaotic violence, caused by "bad men," could shatter the prospect of a peace settlement between "the Creeks & Georgians," the most deeply rooted settler-Indian conflict in the south.[86]

According to the Abbeville County justices, who lived in a piedmont zone that had been at the forefront of Cherokee-colonial violence just a generation earlier, frontier settlers should police themselves and above all act with "the Virtuous & considerate part of the Community," and prevent "the undeserving . . . from involving their Country in Calamities to gratify their own base & unworthy passions." This was a worthy republican vision, if disconnected from the terrible realities of frontier conflict and bloodshed. Who would control the licentious or violent, those who would act as "bad men" no matter if white or red? Corn Tassel wrestled with this same question, speaking truth so long as he had breath. He could do no more.

396   *Upheavals and the Will to Live, 1762–1795*

13

An Unbroken People

Alexander McGillivray, Creek leader and beloved man, was a skilled publicist who passed news to U.S. dignitaries and newspapers to advance his aims at opportune times. In July 1788, he forwarded a message, drafted at his request by an American intermediary, to Governor George Handley of Georgia, the state his people had fought over some years. McGillivray's report cagily signaled his hope for peace with the United States. To prove his goodwill, he offered revealing information on a recent Native conference at Tuckabatchee, just a few miles from his home, where Creek headmen met with Cherokee, Choctaw, and Chickasaw deputies. According to the report, Chickamauga chief Little Turkey (Kahanetah) aired "a virulent talk from the Northward Indians," urging all southern tribes to "strike [the white people] hard." McGillivray purportedly objected and belittled the Cherokees as "a broken people, scattered, and divided amongst themselves." The Creeks, he pronounced, were "the only nation that could assist" the Cherokees, and not "the Northwards" (Indians) being "far off."[1]

McGillivray's revelation was timely. He was then being courted by American commissioners Andrew Pickens and George Mathews, whose charge was to bring the Creek leader to the negotiating table. McGillivray was interested, if not willing to show his hand too quickly. He had various factors to weigh, notably whether the Spanish would resume the Creeks' supply of arms, which had been curtailed because of Madrid's fear of war with the United States. By the summer's close, McGillivray again broadcast his pan-Indian loyalties. In a letter published in South Carolina, he denounced John Sevier as a "barbarian" for engineering Corn Tassel's murder and "meditating another expedition for . . . the total extirpation of the Cherokees." McGillivray's message was double-edged, castigating frontier vigilantism without discarding the idea of détente with the United States. The Creek leader knew that a new American Constitution was being debated by the states, and he pondered whether a revamped federal system would at last respect Indians and "restore to us our just rights."[2]

What should we make of McGillivray's remark that the Cherokees were a "broken people," "scattered" and "divided" and therefore reliant on Creeks rather than northern Native allies? McGillivray was not wholly off the mark. The Cherokees were geographically disparate, even more so than the Creeks. The Upper Cherokee Towns of the old "Overhill" region were much weakened in the face of white settler incursions and militia strikes. Chota, a formerly dominant town, by the mid-1780s was reduced to a village of perhaps thirty houses, a hamlet compared to its five hundred residents a generation earlier. Chota was 25 miles east of White's Fort, established in 1786, and soon to be called Knoxville, a strategic site by the confluence of the French Broad and Holston Rivers, founts of the Tennessee. This ground was for centuries a Cherokee heartland, but it was no longer secure.[3]

Cherokee population shifted strongly to the south and southwest during this period. Dragging Canoe's migration of 1777 to Chickamauga Creek, ninety miles southwest of Chota, was only the beginning of this process. Over the next decade, five towns stood at the northern apex of Chickamauga militancy. In Anglo-American parlance, these communities were Nickjack, Running Water, Long Island (of the Tennessee River), Crow town, and Lookout Mountain Town. (This last village was 15 miles south of the summit, rather than on the mountain itself.) Other towns sprouted farther south on an east-west plane of 200 miles across what is today northern Alabama and Georgia. The Cherokee aim was to gain physical distance and a measure of safety from whites and not simply to further war-making.[4]

John Watts (Kunoskeskie) became a leader at Willstown, 40 miles southwest of Lookout Mountain. There he joined Will Webber, known to whites as "Red-Headed Will" for traits inherited from an Anglo-American father. Traders of the broad Chickamauga region came in different hues. Tory men were present, as were their children born of Cherokee mothers. Couriers, informants, and spies of various ethnicities filtered in and out again. This Cherokee environment was not so much "broken" as multifaceted. The Cherokees might be small in total population, but they had far-reaching connections beyond their towns

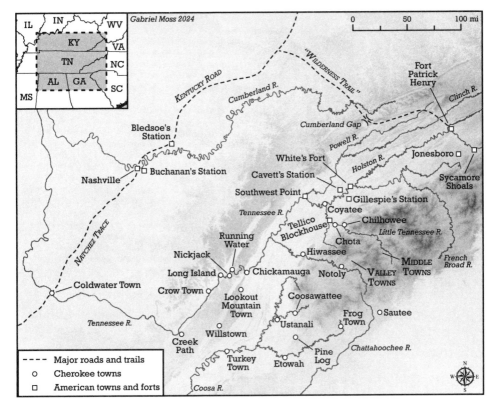

Cherokee Migrations and the Chickamauga Region, 1777–1795

and a growing diversity within them, which not only perplexed American officials but infuriated white frontier inhabitants, who were often hard pressed to identify Indian assailants, let alone distinguish between "red" friends and foes.

Cherokee voices can be heard in scores of transcribed talks or messages forwarded to leading American authorities. This was a diplomacy not only of personal conferencing but also of communication over considerable distance—a practice Cherokee leaders honed over decades in their give-and-take with British and colonial officialdom. Their aim was to preserve the people and their land, and they attempted mightily to do so by diplomatic initiatives and not war alone. That said, it is important to acknowledge that Native warriors were often brutally unsparing toward settler families whose urge for retribution rose with repeated assaults. White vigilantism was itself a deadly force triggering Native fears of annihilation. So, too, were militia offensives that employed scorched-earth tactics, killing innocents and destroying survivors' means of subsistence.[5] This should not be forgotten.

General Arthur St. Clair, governor of the U.S. Northwest Territory above the Ohio, was disturbed by reports in the summer of 1788 that "the People of Franklin"—John Sevier's followers—had invaded Cherokee territory and forced Native residents to disperse. Writing to Secretary of War Henry Knox, St. Clair predicted that northern Indians would blame the United States for the violence and "will despise us, as having no control over our own People."[6]

St. Clair's concerns reflect the interconnectedness of Native territories from the Gulf Coast to Canada. The Chickamaugas, who had allies in Creek country, also operated in conjunction with the Shawnees, other Ohio Indians, and their British backers at Detroit. If Anglo-American frontiersmen wantonly killed Cherokees—as had occurred in the murder of Corn Tassel—the repercussions would be felt far to the north. Henry Knox was attuned to these issues because of the breadth of correspondence reaching him at New York—then home to Congress. One of his important southern sources was North Carolina brigadier-general Joseph Martin, troubleshooter par excellence, acting in this instance as federal agent to the Cherokees.[7]

Viewing the broad political scene, Knox was elated by the prospect of shelving the Articles of Confederation and building a stronger federal union. In late July 1788, he wrote Washington with great relief that New York State had ratified the Constitution. Eleven states had now approved the new constitutional order, making it a near certainty that the system would come into effect the following year. A New England man and a Federalist, Knox focused on gaining Native acquiescence to ample land cessions in the Northwest Territory, the sole trans-Appalachian region then under direct congressional authority. He put a premium on quiet to the south. Forwarding Martin's reports to Congress, Knox offered a biting critique of North Carolina's white frontiersmen, who "have frequently committed the most unprovoked and direct outrages against the Cherokee Indians"—an indication of the settlers' "avaricious desire" for "fertile lands," especially around the "ancient town of Chota." Not holding North Carolina wholly blameworthy, Knox lambasted the "violent claims" of inhabitants within "the district styled the state of Franklin" that violated the U.S.-Cherokee Hopewell treaty of 1785, thereby undercutting "principles of good

400   *Upheavals and the Will to Live, 1762–1795*

faith, sound policy and every respect which a nation, owes to its own reputation and dignity."[8]

How did Cherokees confront the crisis that troubled Knox? While warriors in various communities intensified attacks on whites, a good many headmen strove for accommodation. The Black Dog, a chief in the Hiwassee Valley region, was strongly inclined that way. His town, Notoly, was under the threat of an American arms embargo after one of the village's warriors killed an itinerant white trader in an isolated incident the previous year. Responsible for a small and vulnerable community, Black Dog promised commissioner Pickens that the perpetrator would be slain by his people. This decision found support beyond Notoly itself.[9]

In late June, Cherokees of several towns sent a peace talk to Pickens after a gathering at Ustanali, a "beloved" council center by the Coosawattee River (in today's Georgia). Either at the meeting or just afterward, Scolacutta, the well-known peace-seeking headman, forged a common message with John Watts, at least as expressed in written documents addressed to Pickens and forwarded by Joseph Martin to Knox. The two headmen asked Pickens to prevent John Sevier from entering the neighborhood "to spoil the Towns here," as he had done in the Overhill villages. In reality, Watts was not convinced of American assurances after his uncle Corn Tassel was cut down. Little Turkey, a prestigious leader said to favor an American peace, was quite open to British overtures and close to Creek militants. The Cherokee written talks certainly aired Native concerns, though in words chosen by Martin, who presented himself as the sole federal agent capable of restoring order. It is curious that Scolacutta's message praised "General Martin," now a North Carolina brigadier, as "our greatest friend" who had forestalled white vigilante attacks on Cherokees three times within twenty-five days. This was not fiction, but possibly overstatement.[10]

Joseph Martin's letters to Knox during the late spring and summer of 1788 were scarcely optimistic on the peace front. Sevier's men had spread panic by killing about twenty Cherokees along the Hiwassee River even before the Tassel's murder. Responding to anarchic violence, some Cherokees fled the "old" Upper Towns for fear of settler attack. On one occasion, thirty armed white men came into a seemingly abandoned Cherokee village to pick fruit from an orchard and were set upon by Indians, who killed seventeen of the intruders, with a number "massacred in a most barbarous manner—their privates cut off

An Unbroken People

and put in their mouths &c—near the place the old Corn Tassel . . . was killed." Martin's report—regarding casualties if not mutilations—is corroborated by a newspaper piece that lists the names of sixteen white men and four others wounded during the reprisal attack. Martin did not identify the responsible Indians, who quite possibly were Cherokees of the vicinity and not the more distant Chickamaugas. Pickens wrote with some certainty that a group of white men had murdered eight Cherokee women who had fled south from the mountains and "hid out, to get some beans" and sustenance for their children. Atrocity and fear stalked the land.[11]

Politically astute and occasionally downright Machiavellian, Martin earned Knox's trust by praising Cherokee peace advocates and condemning Sevier and friends as prime culprits in the settler community. Martin concurrently nudged Knox toward his views by painting an overly simplistic picture of "good" versus "hostile" Cherokee regions. By this reading, Upper Cherokee headmen were overwhelmingly for peace. Their towns would readily fall into line. The situation was entirely different with the Chickamaugas, whom Martin now regarded as an irredeemable threat for siding with Britain during the Revolution, harboring Tory traders, and "murdering and robbing our frontiers for ten years past." The danger was all the greater because Chickamauga "banditti" had recently consorted with Creek militants and killed white boat passengers headed down the Tennessee.[12]

In August, Martin wrote Knox that he was preparing a military offensive against the Chickamaugas in order to bring "a permanent peace" with the Cherokees, "the greatest part" of whom would presumably approve his operation. Acting in his capacity as a North Carolina brigadier-general, he moved decisively to command, bypassing Sevier who was out of commission as the State of Franklin internally collapsed. One North Carolina officer apprised Martin of what was at stake: "Your conduct at this crisis will consummate your character in this country." There were settlers who "say you are an Indian's friend . . . while your friends assert the contrary." Skeptics thought that Brigadier Martin could not manage a campaign because of his bond with his Cherokee wife Betsy and her kin and friends. Martin badly wanted to prove otherwise, sending a neat paper trail to Knox as proof of his authority to raise as many as a thousand men to subdue the Chickamaugas.[13]

One may wonder why Martin dared to mount an offensive considering Knox's desire to calm the waters with the Cherokees and prevent an escalation in Creek country. An answer lies in two factors—first,

402   *Upheavals and the Will to Live, 1762–1795*

Martin's desire to present Knox with a fait accompli—a victory the secretary could embrace if the outcome strengthened the moderate Indian camp. The second factor is the sheer distance in space and time between the trans-Appalachian frontier and eastern venues. Knox happened to be traveling from New York City to Boston and his Maine landholdings when Martin plotted his offensive. The secretary of war had no knowledge of the campaign before it was launched.[14]

Martin and his fellow officers raised a considerable force, if not quite the number they had hoped. The brigadier's troops were perhaps five hundred when they neared Lookout Mountain on a September evening and crossed to the Tennessee's south bank the next morning. Chickamauga fighters were well prepared. Militiamen trudged up steep ground in single file, only to be shot down by smartly positioned warriors on the heights. Martin's force neared panic when three captains were killed. Some men in the ranks murmured "Blue Licks"—chilling words that recalled the disaster that befell the Kentucky militia in Indian country a half-dozen years before. Martin tried to rally his troops but was compelled to retreat. Chickamauga warriors had triumphed. A host of chiefs was said to be at the scene, including Dragging Canoe, Watts, Bloody Fellow, Little Turkey, and the Glass.[15] Martin's defeat was an enormous boost in prestige for the Chickamaugas.

In retrospect, we can see that it was but six years between the surge of Chickamauga power in 1788 to the ebb tide of September 1794 when two militant towns—Nickjack and Running Water—were destroyed by Southwest territorial militia and Kentucky forces. Two months later, deputies of the Cherokee nation entered a peace accord with the United States. When war's end was reached, the decision came through consensus, with Upper and Lower Towns laying aside differences for mutual welfare. Peace allowed space for life. It was no simple defeat despite the devastation wrought by invasion.

The interval between the Chickamaugas' military triumph and their defeat was tumultuous. It witnessed the birth of the first U.S. national government under the Constitution, Washington's presidency, and an accelerating federal push for authority over the trans-Appalachian west. The Cherokees and other Native groups found themselves enmeshed in imperial rivalries cutting across their homelands. Great Britain and Spain strived to check U.S. expansionism by alliance with Indigenous peoples that viewed the Americans as their greatest threat. Despite Washington's acumen, his administration overrated its capacity to subordinate Indians to its will. Moreover, the United States did not speak with one

An Unbroken People   403

voice. Private stakeholders involved in land speculation, settlement projects, and mercantile pursuits swayed frontier developments to their emolument and power. It was not at all clear in the 1790s whether the federal government could prevent anarchic and unauthorized forays into Native and Spanish territories.[16]

Cherokees themselves took many pathways during the years 1788–1794, often moving between militancy and accommodation toward whites. John Watts, who became the foremost Chickamauga war leader after Dragging Canoe's death in 1792, was a politically savvy man who operated by consultation, testing negotiations but ready to fight as necessary. Along with the Cherokee struggle over land and sovereignty, there was a human drama that commands our attention. Leaders in opposing camps—Indigenous and white American—often knew one another by face-to-face encounters. Notwithstanding violence and bloodshed, there were occasions when Cherokees and whites met in friendly or peaceful exchange. War's terrors meanwhile created rough parallels across ethnic divides. In white settlement zones and in Cherokee country, debates ensued about how to get on with life amid fear and danger. In the aftermath of Native attacks, settlers conversed about summoning volunteers or the militia. Women, children, and old men huddled in overcrowded and noisome frontier stations. Cherokees faced their own choices of how to defend or attack, and how to protect their women and children. It was dangerous for Indian men to go hunting or to pass by white settlements for peaceful purposes. Cherokee women were at risk when leaving their towns for food gathering let alone escaping or sheltering during militia attacks. Besides a great deal of fighting, there came revealing moments when white Americans and Natives exchanged written messages with each other. In several cases, the messages vented anger and frustration, telling us about the rawness of human emotion in battle zones. There is no mistaking the war of words and deeds in which life and death were at stake.

Warfare and Words

Buoyed by victory over Martin's militia, Watts and company went on the offensive. On October 17, 1788, three hundred Indian fighters attacked Gillespie's Station, a small settlement about ten miles southwest of White's Fort (Knoxville). Cherokee and Creek warriors easily overwhelmed the stockade and killed an unknown number of defenders and noncombatants. One contemporary report counts the dead at between twenty-seven and thirty, and mostly women and children.[17]

Before departing the station, four Chickamauga leaders left a sharply written note addressed to John Sevier, Joseph Martin, and "the inhabitants of the New State" (Franklin). Said to be the words of Bloody Fellow, the letter was probably composed by Watts who turned the usual American moral code on its head: "The Bloody Fellow's talk is, that he is here now upon his own ground. He is not like you are, for you kill women and children, and he does not." It was only by "accident" that white women and children were slain by Cherokee fighters at the station, which was attacked because whites had refused to surrender and depart unharmed. The war had begun when the headman (Corn Tassel), who was "your friend," was beguiled and slain. A warning followed. White settlers on Cherokee land were given thirty days to move off or face the consequences. The chiefs claimed to have five thousand men at their command—a vast exaggeration, if one that could not be dismissed so easily.[18] Watts felt especially embittered that Martin had led an army against his people. After all, the brigadier was someone who had befriended Corn Tassel and taken Chota's interests to heart over the years.

Martin's offensive—and the payback at Gillespie's Station—did not rule out diplomacy. In November 1788, Cherokee headmen, meeting again at Ustanali, dispatched a conciliatory message to Richard Winn of South Carolina, federal superintendent for Indian affairs in the southern district. The chiefs included Little Turkey, Dragging Canoe, Glass, and Richard Justice of the Chickamauga towns and Scolacutta of the Upper Cherokees. Their words, put to writing, lauded a recent congressional proclamation affirming the Hopewell Treaty, especially its section denying government protection to U.S. citizens living on lands within prescribed Cherokee territories.[19] Cherokees, eager to get white settlers off their land, preferred that Congress carry out the responsibility so that war would be unnecessary.

The congressional proclamation followed Knox's lead by criticizing "disorderly Persons" lawlessly moving onto Cherokee hunting grounds and committing "unprovoked outrages." Congress did not press the matter beyond a scolding, conceding that it did not intend to compromise "the Territorial Claims of the State of North-Carolina." When North Carolina finally ceded its far western territorial claims to Congress in December 1789, the state legislature deliberately included

An Unbroken People

provisions that gave broad legal protection to citizens' claims that already intruded into Cherokee lands.[20]

Congressional deference to North Carolina in legalistic fine print probably escaped Cherokee attention. There was little doubt, however, of the hatred generated by violence. On the same day that Gillespie's Station was attacked, John Kirk Jr., calling himself "Captain of the Bloody Rangers," addressed a public letter to John Watts that circulated in newspapers from Georgia to New Hampshire. Refuting accusations against Sevier for killing Corn Tassel and his companions, Kirk took responsibility for the terrible deed himself. He then told why. For months before the slayings, his mother had welcomed Cherokees, "little and big, women and children" to the family home, fed them and treated the guests with kindness. When all was peaceful, a group of Cherokees, led by "Slim Tom" and Settico town "fellows," came into the house and, in Kirk's words, "murdered my mother, brothers, and sisters, in cold blood, when the children was just before playful about them as friends." It was the "bloody tomahawk," wielded by Cherokees "smiling" at their victims, that began the war. Kirk added that he had taken "ample satisfaction, and can now make peace, except with Slim Tom," who remained untouched by vengeance. Kirk's story discloses the shock of violence visited on a white family that had a false sense of security from the outwardly friendly encounters with Cherokees whose fury against settlers rushed suddenly to the surface.[21]

It is highly probable that John Sevier, nicknamed "Nolichucky" or "Chucky Jack" by friends, had a hand in writing Kirk's letter. After all, the message to Watts began by clearing Sevier of the Tassel's murder. The letter's heading identified the writer as "young Kirk, the noted Indian killer," a title Sevier had the infamous distinction of claiming as much as any American frontiersman. Here one thinks back to "Tuscarora Jack" (John Barnwell) of the early 1700s and ahead to "Old Hickory" (Andrew Jackson). As early as 1793, Jackson asked rhetorically: "Why do we attempt to Treat with Savage Tribe[s] that will neither adhere to Treaties, nor the law of Nations."[22]

Sevier recouped prestige in his frontier neighborhood after the Chickamauga defeat of Martin's militia. While Sevier irked North Carolina officials by championing the Franklin separatist movement, by November 1788 he had regained that state's good graces. Early the next year, he headed a militia force that targeted a Cherokee-Creek encampment by Flint Creek at the edge of the Appalachians. In this scantily documented episode, Sevier was a mythmaker who courted fame by

406   *Upheavals and the Will to Live, 1762–1795*

penning a newspaper piece on his exploits. Undeterred by snow and biting cold, his cavalry and riflemen took command of the battleground and then rushed for the kill with sword and tomahawk. His victory was complete and sanguinary: "death presented itself on all sides in shocking scenes." Sevier claimed that his militia buried 145 Indians killed in the fighting. The casualty count is unprovable as there is no other contemporary account of a battle on such a scale. Sevier's losses were six dead and sixteen wounded. General McCarter, one of his commanders, took a Cherokee tomahawk blow just as he was "taking off the scalp of an Indian." Sevier was at once shocked by bloody clashes while he reveled in triumph. McCarter's men were "the bloody rangers"—the same phrase "young Kirk" used for his fighting unit.[23]

Joseph Brown's Tale

Sevier's battle story has an overheated, even sadistic character where vengeance rules. There is quite as much to be learned of colonial-Native conflict from the experience of Joseph Brown, a boy captive seized by Chickamauga warriors in an attack on his family's crowded keelboat headed down the Tennessee toward the Cumberland settlements in May 1788. The boat was no tiny vessel. It was seven feet wide and fifty feet in length, and shielded by high side barriers with portholes for shooting, and a mounted swivel gun. Many years later, Joseph Brown recalled how all seemed peaceful when four Chickamauga canoes, each with about ten men and a white flag, approached the family's boat on the Tennessee. John Vann, son of a Cherokee woman by a British man, was in one of the canoes and told whites of his interest in trade. Chickamauga men soon boarded the boat, which continued downriver, only to be met by other canoes whose warriors rushed on board to plunder and commit mayhem. Young Brown witnessed his father being cut down and his body thrown into the river. Cherokees seized and brought ashore two of Brown's brothers, aged nineteen and twenty-one, and five other white men. All seven were soon shot dead or otherwise killed. Creek men, who joined the assault, grabbed Brown's mother, and four of his siblings, all under ten years of age, though two of these captives, both girls, were claimed by Cherokees, who took them into custody at Nickjack. Four Blacks were also taken captive. Several months later, Joseph Martin reported that the Blacks were purchased by French traders near Muscle Shoals and taken toward Detroit.[24]

An Unbroken People 407

A pattern is apparent here, unique in its particulars but following a common sequence. Indians killed white men of fighting age after capture. A colonial mother, her little children, and enslaved Blacks were meanwhile taken into captivity. But what of Joseph Brown, who seemed to fall in between, not a small boy though not yet a man? A debate ensued among Cherokees at Nickjack about his fate. Though Brown could not understand a word of what was said, he picked up something from Indian gestures and learned more from a sympathetic Irishman who lived by Chickamauga Creek and was married to a Cherokee woman of French background. Herself a former captive, she deflected Nickjack warriors from immediately killing Brown. Another Nickjack woman wanted Brown dead since he was on the verge of manhood, when he would doubtless become a dangerous foe. She ran a dull knife over the captive boy's scalp and cut off a piece of his hair. Headman Cotteotoy, who talked of killing Brown, finally agreed that the decision of life or death belonged to warrior Kiatchatalla, the actual captor. Chief Breath, the most prestigious town leader, then entered the scene and chose to raise Brown as a Cherokee boy. Captor Kiatchatalla became Brown's adopted brother. The youth took off his pants and other clothes and was given a small shirt, a loincloth, and leggings. His hair was cut so that only a small patch remained at the top; his ears were "bored" for earrings and his face dabbed with paint.[25]

Brown's adoption brought him into a strange world in which he could not tell the difference between a Cherokee or Creek. One young Cherokee warrior, returning from a raid far to the north, beat him with a stick in anger over the death of his companions in firefights with white settlers. After the thrashing, Chief Breath gave Brown a knife to protect himself. Brown's Cherokee family scrupulously cared for him during illness. In old age, he recalled being bled, induced to vomit, and otherwise nursed in Indian fashion. He also remembered the words of a Cherokee man who said that whites would not be content until they had driven his entire people entirely off their ancestral land.[26]

Brown owed his life partly to John Sevier, who had taken a number of Cherokee women and children captive for a prisoner exchange. It was through Sevier's exchange of two Cherokee prisoners, one of whom was chief Little Turkey's daughter, that Brown was released in 1789. Once freed, Brown lived in South Carolina for a brief period before moving to the Cumberland settlements, where he became a post rider traversing the dangerous ground between Nashville and other settlements. In 1794, Brown served as a lead scout in a critical offensive, guiding the militia toward Nickjack, his former Chickamauga home. The elderly Cherokee woman who culled Brown's scalp was prescient. The boy would grow to be man and, if still alive, would be a warrior for the white people.[27]

Above and Below the Ohio

The advent of the Washington administration in 1789 was a hopeful moment for the Cherokees, who sorely desired a strong American "brother" or "father" who would protect them. They were encouraged from what they heard of Henry Knox, Washington's secretary of war, who continued to be a prime architect of Indian policy as he had been under Congress. Knox appeared to be a good man whose messages expressed a desire for peace and justice.[28] In fact, his approach to Native affairs, much like Washington's, had a moralistic element anchored in cultural transformation transcending equity. Knox favored a long-term plan of "civilization" and "progress" among Indians centered on instilling Anglo-American customs of individual land ownership in concert with Christian missionary influence. Such a program would ideally benefit Native men who gave up the hunt for the plow while concurrently aiding federal treaty purchases of Indian lands and well-regulated white settlement.[29]

The Washington administration's high-minded and ostensibly benevolent principles jarred with reality. Knox underestimated the depth of Native opposition to territorial concessions in the Ohio country. Refusing U.S. demands to cede ground above the Ohio, Indian militants attacked American river traffic and raided frequently into Kentucky. Thwarted diplomatically, the United States fared even worse on the military front. Two armies—Josiah Harmar's by the Maumee in October 1790 and Arthur St. Clair's near the Wabash in November 1791—suffered humiliating defeats. St. Clair's debacle was astonishing in magnitude, with 630 soldiers killed and more than 280 wounded out of a force of 1,400 men. The victors were a formidable coalition of 1,000 warriors of Shawnees, Delawares, Miamis, Ottawas, Ojibwas, Potawatomis, Iroquois, and Wyandots with some Creek and Chickamuaga fighters.[30]

The Chickamaugas and Creeks exulted in American defeats. In fact, southern Native militants went on the offensive in 1792–1793 in

An Unbroken People   409

no small part because they believed that the United States could be beaten and held back. One turning point came when McGillivray's détente with the United States, signaled by the Treaty of New York of 1790, aroused internal Creek opposition and challenges to his leadership. A second came when Francisco Luis Héctor, barón de Carondelet, assumed the Spanish governorship of Louisiana in the final days of 1791 and took a far more aggressive stance in stirring Native militancy than did his predecessor, Esteban Miró. Chickamauga chiefs were Carondelet's partners at the height of their conflict with the Americans in 1792–1794.

War took on a terrible momentum of its own. Creek warriors drove the conflict against the Cumberland settlements in tandem with Chickamaugas and other Cherokees who never accepted the loss of those hunting grounds. To the east, the Holston and other river valleys remained embattled. Native fighters attacked where whites were at their most vulnerable, either in isolated homesteads or in travel on trails and roads. The human toll in dead, wounded, and captured was horrific. In late 1789, Cumberland settlers dispatched a petition to Washington pleading for military assistance. They counted fifty-eight inhabitants that "had been barbarously murdered" by "our merciless and Savage Enemies" since the beginning of 1788. The national government's incapacity to offer military protection in the region over the next seven years tragically exacerbated white violence and hatred of Indians.[31]

Anxious for a letup in Indian attack, Colonel James Robertson of Nashville hankered for Spanish goodwill at New Orleans. At his recommendation, the Cumberland region was now called "the Mero district" in honor of Louisiana governor Esteban Miró. Robertson, who had lost a brother and then a young son to Indian attack, thought beyond his own family interest. Following the example of James Wilkinson of Kentucky, the colonel corresponded with Miró in early 1789 to open the New Orleans market to western American settlers. Robertson understood quid pro quo. He assured Miró that there was no frontier plot afoot to invade Louisiana. The governor replied amicably and offered assurances on the trade front. Through McGillivray, Miró would do what he could to discourage Creek attacks on Cumberland, though he admitted that the Cherokees were beyond his influence. It was safer for Miró to promise what might be honored rather than overstate Spanish control over a vast Native world.[32]

Federal Authority and the Southwest Territory

William Blount, eastern gentleman and land speculator, felt blessed in June 1790 when Washington commissioned him to be the first governor of the newly established Southwest Territory, formally the Territory South of the River Ohio. Blount had lobbied strenuously through friends for the office, which gave him oversight of a region in which he possessed many thousands of acres in land entries, certificates, and warrants. In a double coup, Blount secured appointment as superintendent

William Blount. *The Miriam and Ira D. Wallach Division of Art, Prints and Photographs, New York Public Library Digital Collections.*

An Unbroken People 411

of Indian affairs in the Southern District and became regional kingpin in negotiations with the Cherokees and Chickasaws. Colin Calloway aptly likens Blount's appointment to the fox made "to guard the chicken coop." Washington was himself in a political tight spot. He wanted a Federalist at the helm in the Southwest Territory—and Blount fit the bill since he had represented North Carolina at the Federal Convention of 1787, signed the new Constitution, and supported its ratification.[33]

"The Territory south of the Ohio" was a general description of the area under Blount's purview. The Southwest Territory did not include Kentucky, a district that fell under Virginia's governance before it entered the Union as a new state in 1792. Blount's jurisdiction reached from Kentucky's southern border to Georgia's northern limits, which extended as far west as the Mississippi. Georgia still held fast to what it claimed by royal charter and the U.S.-British peace treaty of 1783.[34]

What did all this mean for the Cherokees and Chickasaws, whose sense of land was wholly different from U.S. prescriptions for the "southwest," which to them was neither south nor west? Native leaders knew that Blount, once taking up quarters by the Holston and Watauga in October 1790, was President Washington's chief man for negotiation over land, trade, and the resolution of disputes. The next summer, the governor established a more permanent residence at White's Fort, which he named Knoxville in honor of the secretary of war. The Cherokees understood something of American federalism with its various levels of authority, not so different to them than the distinction between a British colonial governor and the king. Blount was not a supreme chief but answered to superiors to whom Indians appealed on important occasions.[35]

Cherokees were not slow to tell Blount of their concerns over illicit white settlement. In January 1791, a group of headmen, unnamed in the record, dispatched a written talk in which they complained that "the Georgians" were attempting to sell Native land by Muscle Shoals. This was indeed the case—and the Shoals was a small, if critical venue in a huge speculative scheme. In December 1789, the Georgia legislature granted 35 million acres of the state's far western land claims to three private land companies (the Virginia, Tennessee, and South Carolina Yazoo Companies) on the condition that the associates pay the state for the allotted acreage within a two-year period. Zachariah Cox, the prime mover of the Tennessee Company, viewed the Shoals as the key to his association's fortunes. The Washington administration rightly

412   *Upheavals and the Will to Live, 1762–1795*

saw the Yazoo companies as a serious threat to national authority. If unopposed, private investors, empowered by a single state, could breach existing treaty lines and likely trigger war with Indian nations and the Spanish by the Mississippi. On August 26, 1790, the president issued a proclamation that affirmed national sovereignty, advising citizens that they were prohibited by law from trading with Indian nations without federal license or purchasing Native lands guaranteed by the United States through treaty.[36]

Cox and associates did not give up simply because of Washington's proclamation. They reconnoitered Muscle Shoals in 1791 but were dissuaded by the threat of Cherokee and Creek attack from putting their plans into operation. Many frontiersmen admired Cox's pluck even if they stayed aloof from his project. When a Southwest territorial judge brought charges against Cox and a few friends, a Knoxville grand jury returned no bill. William Blount played his hand carefully, doing little to discourage Cox while informing Washington's administration that he had no tolerance for lawless adventurism. This was precisely the message Washington and Knox wanted to hear.[37]

Blount was anxious that all go according to plan as he prepared for his first major Cherokee conference, held by the Holston in June 1791. Some Cherokees worried about coming to the treaty grounds lest they be assailed by white settlers along the way. One militia scouting party had recently fired at Cherokee hunters and killed at least one Native man. Blount's conference went ahead only after James Robertson, whom the governor had recently promoted to a general's rank, personally assured Cherokee leaders that the territorial militia had fired in mistake.[38]

The Holston parley was a large affair, indicating that many Cherokees wanted to see if Blount meant well. Forty headmen of both the Upper and Lower Towns attended. Twelve hundred Cherokees were on the treaty grounds, following the practice of mass gatherings at conferences, with the expectation of presents. The atmosphere was enlivened by a Cherokee eagle tail dance, though there was tension below the surface. In the Cherokee telling, Blount attempted to purchase the Muscle Shoals but was refused. The governor secured one of his most important goals—a land cession south of the French Broad River, an area greatly prized by Cherokees and already being settled by whites. Blount was a skilled hand at deception. While sending the treaty text to Knox, the governor withheld the record of Cherokee speeches at the conference, including the chiefs' message calling for mutual

An Unbroken People

respect: "Do the white people look on us as the Buffaloe and other wild beasts in the woods, and that they have a right to take our property at their pleasure? Though we are red we think we were made by the same power, and certainly we think we have as much right to enjoy our property as any other human being that inhabit[s] the earth."[39]

Taking the long view, we can see the Holston treaty as a mix of incompatible, even contradictory elements. Like the Hopewell treaty of 1785, the new accord defined the Cherokees as "under the protection of the United States, and [of] no other nation." In theory, the Cherokees were a subordinate nation while also a people with lawful possession of lands within specified boundaries and the discretionary power of punishing white intruders who "shall forfeit the protection of the United States." The treaty included several provisions for the adjudication of Indian-settler violence. Most whites and Indians regarded these paper guarantees as worthless.[40]

Blount's Holston treaty borrowed directly from the Treaty of New York of August 1790, which formally ended hostilities between the Creeks and the United States. Knox negotiated the accord with McGillivray, with twenty-three Creek headmen signaling their approval. In return for a land cession along the Oconee River, the Creeks obtained a federal annuity of $1,500. The annual stipend was itself a novel procedure, a way of extending U.S. influence beyond a brief period. The Holston accord allotted a $1,000 annuity to the Cherokees, later raised to $1,500 by the Senate at the request of a Cherokee delegation that visited Philadelphia in January 1792 and demanded not a penny less than the Creeks. Blount's treaty virtually copied word for word the language of social improvement Knox employed, urging Native men to become "Herdsmen and cultivators"—and mandating the federal government to furnish them with "useful implements of husbandry." These annuities were only a fraction of U.S. expenditures used to pacify, dominate, and control Indian nations during the 1790s.[41]

Neither the Creek nor the Cherokee treaties of 1790 and 1791, respectively, brought peace. McGillivray gained little for his people through secret treaty provisions by which he obtained the rank of U.S. brigadier-general and an annual stipend of $1,200. One week after signing the treaty, McGillivray took an oath of allegiance to the United States. This was a gambit that did not pay long-term dividends. Georgia's expansionist push was continual; the Creeks remained in conflict with American settlers. In May 1792, McGillivray renewed his Spanish alliance, with Carondelet all but dictating terms to him. No longer the

414   *Upheavals and the Will to Live, 1762–1795*

force he had once been, McGillivray had a little less than one year to live at the time. The strains of leadership, drinking, and loose living took their toll.[42]

The Holston treaty papered over yawning gaps between Cherokee needs and U.S. interests. The treaty might say that the American republic should alone regulate Cherokee commerce, but the Chickamaugas maintained vibrant exchange with traders working through William Panton at Pensacola. The treaty afforded the United States "the free and unmolested use" of a road between eastern Tennessee and Nashville and unimpeded navigation on the Tennessee River. Chickamaugas hardly regarded the Tennessee or pathways through their territory as open to Americans no matter what a written treaty mandated.[43] This point was obvious well before Blount's Holston treaty. In March 1790, a Cherokee-Shawnee band of forty warriors attacked U.S. Major John Doughty's reconnaissance party as it navigated from the Ohio up the Tennessee for prospective talks with the Chickasaws at Bear Creek west of Muscle Shoals. Lulling Doughty by feigned friendship, Native fighters fired on American rivercraft, killing five privates and wounding six others among fifteen men. Doughty reversed course, thwarted in his mission to establish a U.S. military post near the Shoals.[44]

Despite Knox's anger at Doughty's repulse, he retained his belief that Cherokee relations could be stabilized through prudent management. In January 1791, the secretary of war was pleased at an unanticipated visit by six Cherokee men for talks in Philadelphia. The guests included Jean Dougherty, a woman of Cherokee-British parentage who served as one of two interpreters. The delegation's principal spokesman was Bloody Fellow, a prestigious Chickamauga warrior-chief who was adroit with words as well as weapons. His name, one of several he had, recalled the time he killed a Cherokee man who had betrayed the chief's brother for a British payoff before the Revolutionary War.[45]

Bloody Fellow told Knox of Cherokee discontent. Blount had used the Holston treaty conference to bid for Native land, including Muscle Shoals. In Bloody Fellow's words, the goods offered for the land were too paltry even to buy "a breech clout" for each man of his nation. He repeated a truth that his fellow headmen had told the Americans long before. Cherokees could not sell Muscle Shoals since the area belonged to "four nations," not only themselves but the Chickasaws and the Creeks—and an unnamed fourth.[46]

An Unbroken People

The Cherokee visitors left Philadelphia with assurances of goodwill, an increased annuity, and wagonloads of presents. Bloody Fellow received an unusually large silver medal engraved with Washington's likeness next to his own. Knox was overly optimistic about the Cherokees, thinking that they might be induced to furnish fighters to aid the United States against "hostile Indians" above the Ohio. This was a chimera.[47] Little came of Knox's effort to recruit John Sevier and Tennessee militiamen for Arthur St. Clair's expedition of 1791 intended to force Ohio Indians into submission. Sevier resigned his command because of illness, and many of his two hundred men deserted well before the climactic battle. Those who went home were fortunate compared to their comrades who were killed or wounded in St. Clair's defeat.[48]

A British Alliance—South and North?

As the United States battled fecklessly, British agents encouraged Chickamauga bonds with northern tribes. One royal officer by Ohio's Miami River sent gifts to Dragging Canoe, adding a message that the king, "Your Great Father," would fulfill all promises to "his Indian Children." Dragging Canoe's brother delivered the presents, which included a feathered hat, metal armbands, and a silver gorget. On the way home from Ohio, the courier brought a captive white boy, evidently purchased from northern Indians. War's prizes were tangible, evident in enemy prisoners, scalps, captured horses, and other booty.[49]

For most Chickamaugas, the war that had begun with Dragging Canoe's initial attack on the white people by the Holston in 1776 was still ongoing. English friends about the Great Lakes remained active. Spanish garrisons had displaced the British along the Gulf Coast, but that circumstance might change. Moreover, the "English" (who were often Scotsmen) lived in Indian country. Many of them had Cherokee wives and children, a good number of whom were now of age. John McDonald, who befriended the Chickamaugas during the Revolution, was married to Anne Shorey, herself of Cherokee-Scots parentage. After the war, he became an agent for William Panton, whose firm dominated Florida's Indian commerce and extended its reach well above the Gulf under Spanish license.[50]

While trading through Panton and company, Creeks and Chickamaugas were not wedded to any single trading house. Many Natives complained that Panton's prices for goods were too high. They were

416   *Upheavals and the Will to Live, 1762–1795*

ready to deal with other Britons, especially if they brought sorely needed military muscle to the table. In the spring of 1789, the charismatic William Augustus Bowles, a former Tory soldier, visited Lower Creek country with big plans in mind, nothing less than to oust Panton and Leslie from Florida's Indian trade and to take on the Spanish in due time. Stationed in Florida during the Revolutionary War, the teenage Bowles absconded from his unit and lived among the Creeks by the Chattahoochee River before returning to his station at Pensacola in a futile defense against Spanish siege in 1781. These experiences stayed with him when he emigrated to the Bahamas after the war, tried his hand at stage acting and portraiture, and aspired for greater things under the patronage of the Earl of Dunmore, royal governor of the islands. While not officially endorsing Bowles's endeavors, Dunmore and his merchant friends schemed to exploit Spain's tenuous position in Florida and gain a share of the Indian trade.[51]

Bowles was twenty-six years of age in 1789 when he joined a large gathering of Creek and Cherokee headmen at Coweta. Fluent in Muscogee speech and familiar with Native customs, he made the most of the occasion. According to his record, twenty Creek leaders and thirteen Cherokees, predominantly of the Chickamauga region, attended the conference. The Cherokees were an impressive group, including honorary Coweta chief Little Turkey, Scolacutta, Dragging Canoe, Bloody Fellow, and Unakata ("White Man Killer," brother of John Watts). Bowles listed all but one of the headmen by their Native names, not Anglo monikers, indicating his close attention to Cherokee identity and pronunciation. McGillivray himself reported to Spanish officials that "the whole Chiefs of the Cherokee Nation" attended a large conference where they supposedly claimed Creek "protection." This gloss was a bit misleading since the Chickamaugas were open to alliance, not subordination.[52]

There was a blurred line between Bowles as self-promoter and champion of Native rights. At Coweta, he drafted two petitions addressed to George III—one on behalf of the Cherokees and the other for the Creeks. In each declaration, chiefs and warriors appealed to George III as "Father," stated grievances against the Americans, and called on the king to help his loyal Indian friends with supplies and munitions. In both petitions, Native leaders referred to Bowles as "the Beloved Warrior," an honorific he did not mind either accepting or bestowing on himself.[53]

An Unbroken People   417

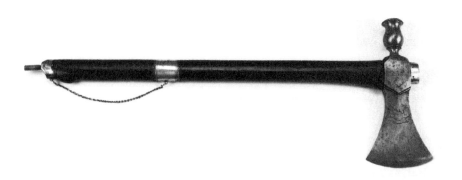

Pipe tomahawk ("Bowles" engraved on head). *National Museum of the American Indian, Smithsonian.*

One imagines Bowles appearing at Coweta in a scarlet British military coat, a symbol of his intent to forge a new English alliance with the Creeks and Cherokees, especially the Chickamaugas. He was no doubt mum about the fact that he was a retired officer—a former ensign of junior rank. The key point is that three Cherokee men and two Creeks agreed to voyage with Bowles to England. To call it an arduous excursion would be an understatement. The passage took eighteen months from Florida to the Bahamas and then to Canada for talks with Governor-General, Earl of Dorchester at Quebec before London was finally reached in October 1790. Two of the three Cherokee voyagers were notable, if not principal individuals. One was Moses Price (Wosseo), a man of mixed Cherokee-British ancestry who was politically shrewd besides being literate in English. Another companion was Richard Justice (Uwenahi), shaman of Lookout Mountain Town in the Chickamauga heartland.[54]

Bowles dominated his diplomatic entourage in London, wearing his own version of Native headdress and garb, penning a lengthy memorial to George III, and sending a similar address to Lord Grenville, the king's foreign minister with whom he conversed. It is not easy to discern what Bowles's Native companions derived from their stay in the great metropolis besides taking in sights, being hosted at dinners, viewing stage plays and attending opera at Covent Garden. Previous Cherokee transatlantic voyagers had enjoyed similar entertainment in England since the young Attakullakulla's stay of 1730. Bowles's diplomatic gambit, publicized in London newspapers, was known to his fellow travelers well before all reached England. His hope was that England and Spain would soon be at war and that Britain would call on American Indians for assistance. He said little in public at the time about taking on the United States.[55]

In an appeal to Grenville, Bowles wrote, with no small exaggeration, that the Creeks and Cherokees were a "united nation" capable of fielding twenty thousand warriors ready to take on the conquest of the Floridas and New Orleans—and even support Hispano-American revolution in Mexico! While skeptical of Bowles's pronouncements, Grenville did not wish to discourage an adventurous man who might be of service if tensions with Spain, then on the wane, were to heat up again, or should Indian assistance be needed against the United States. His Majesty's government would allow the Creeks and Cherokees to traffic in British Caribbean ports, "should they [the two Indian nations] find themselves in a situation to avail themselves of this indulgence." The permission meant little for the present because there were no merchant vessels yet under Bowles's control and certainly none with Spanish license to trade in Florida.[56]

Bowles lied prodigiously, but there was some basis for his tall tales, especially in turbulent continental zones where instability reigned in Native lands and bordering U.S. and Spanish environs. The Chickamaugas, if only part of the Cherokee people, were close to the Creeks, though not entirely in unison with them. When Bowles and his Native friends returned to the Gulf Coast in the fall of 1791, the Cherokee men soon went north to their home ground. Early the next year, Henry Knox judged it necessary to counteract Bowles's influence by offering silver medals to the Cherokee headmen then visiting Philadelphia. He requested similar favors for Chickamauga chief Little Turkey and other headmen who were not present. Knox had little inkling that Little Turkey could not be bought off.[57] The larger question was whether the Chickamaugas and other Cherokees could rely on some combination of Native allies—Creeks and Shawnees—besides building on British or Spanish connections to stave off the Americans.

An Unbroken People

A Scalp Dance at Lookout Mountain Town

Richard "Dick" Justice, Cherokee shaman, might seem to have an Anglo name, but the matter was not so simple. He was "Dikkeh" in Cherokee and was known as "Dick" to whites. He apparently adopted the surname "Justice" as an expression of what his people should hold onto and what was right. Dikkeh led a scalp dance at Lookout Mountain town in Chickamauga country on the night of February 26, 1792. Along with Chief Glass, the two men gnashed and tore at a white man's scalp with their hands and teeth and then shared the scalp with warriors. All danced in a circle while a singer rhythmically beat a drum. The dancers took turns, chanting and singing of their exploits while the drumming paused. In a traditional scalp dance, a Cherokee man held an eagle feather wand in the left hand and the scalp in the right. The eagle feather, a symbol of peace, balanced the scalp as war trophy.[58]

Major David Craig, who had arrived at Lookout Mountain Town one day before the dance, learned of the ceremony through his companion, agent-interpreter John McKee. The white man's scalp was the "hair" of a traveler killed on the path between Kentucky and the Cumberland settlements. Two other scalps, those of a white woman and her daughter, were also part of the ritual dance, though these remains were not gnawed or handled roughly. A warrior gained honor by displaying a man's scalp in a way that would have been demeaning in treating a woman's or girl's—not a "kill" over which to boast.[59]

While repelled at the "ferocity" of the scalp dance, Craig commended Justice and Glass for their personal courtesies and care of American visitors. The major attributed his hosts' attention to the Cherokees' special respect to "public messengers." During his stay about Lookout Mountain town, Craig conversed freely with Price, whom the major described as "a sensible half breed, who can read and write." Price remarked that Shawnees had roused Chickamauga fighters to aid them since St. Clair's defeat. The message confirmed what Craig gleaned from other Native men and white traders, namely that the Chickamaugas and Creeks were not about to stop their attacks on the Cumberland settlements. The reason was a geographic truth as unshakable as if a geometric axiom. The Cumberland was a corridor for Creeks and Chickamaugas on their way to their Ohio Native allies, while northern nations such as the Shawnees used the same path to strengthen their southeastern connections. The Native lifeline had the very opposite meaning for white settlers.[60]

Craig was taken aback by Price's assertive political talk, which indicated that the Chickamauga towns did not accept the British-U.S. peace treaty of 1783, let alone subsequent treaties, as having any bearing on their territorial rights. Price cleverly framed his message so that the Americans would fear the Cherokees. He deliberately spoke of Bowles as a "very great man" who could procure English soldiers and arms for the Cherokees, besides opening a Florida "free port" for Native supply. When Craig visited Dick Justice's home, he was flabbergasted by a painting showing Bowles in a standing pose, flanked by a Cherokee chief on each side. The painting bore the title: "General Bowles, commander-in-chief of the Creek and Cherokee nations." The American officer was dumfounded. He had regarded Justice as "heretofore one of the warmest friends of the United States" in Chickamauga territory.[61] To Justice and Price, Bowles gave hope of British support for Indian nations in common cause from Florida to the Great Lakes.

Craig reported all he witnessed and heard to Blount in Knoxville. Events moved ahead at a dizzying pace. Dragging Canoe had died quite recently, and it appeared that John Watts was to be named head warrior in his place. Other changes were afoot, though not yet known in Cherokee country. In January 1792, Bowles appeared master of the Florida Gulf Coast with considerable Creek-Seminole support and personal prestige that rocketed above rival McGillivray. Spanish officials, who considered Bowles a reckless "adventurer," were seemingly helpless to contain him. A month later, the erstwhile kingpin made a costly error by accepting an invitation to negotiate with Governor Carondelet in New Orleans. Carondelet had Bowles arrested, sized him up in negotiation, and then shipped him to Havana. Bowles's next stop was prison in Spain. Seven years passed before the adventurer once more returned to Florida, roiling the Creek-Seminole world. Bowles's influence remained alive in Cherokee country for a time after Carondelet nabbed him. In 1793, his associate George Welbank worked tirelessly to strengthen ties between Creeks, Chickamaugas, and the northern Indian confederation. Little Turkey was at the heart of this alliance. His written talk, sent by courier to the British by Lake Erie was for "the English our fathers" to supply arms and ammunition as soon as possible.[62] It was Bowles the British Loyalist who appealed to the

An Unbroken People

Chickamaugas, who respected English power but would collaborate with the Spanish as necessary.

The Height of Conflict

Unlike the more cautious Miró, Carondelet saw the Cherokees as central to his plans of establishing a defensive barrier against the Americans far above the Gulf Coast. In a lengthy missive of February 1792 to conde de Floridablanca, the king's first minister, he contended for unifying all four major southern Indian nations—Cherokees, Creeks, Chickasaws, and Choctaws—in a "defensive confederation" under Spanish imperial protection. As long as Madrid nodded, Carondelet was determined to supply arms, gunpowder, and ball in abundance to headmen on condition that the latter not give the appearance of being the aggressors in war. The governor drew confidence from St. Clair's defeat. He initially learned of the American reverse by a letter dispatched to New Orleans by James Wilkinson, U.S. general in Ohio and secret agent on the Spanish royal payroll.[63]

The Cherokees were courted simultaneously by the Americans and the Spanish. For all Blount's land lust, he ideally favored the acquisition of Cherokee hunting grounds by treaty and not war. At the beginning of 1792, he adopted a cautious approach because Washington and Knox were adamantly against a southern Indian conflagration. By Knox's instructions of August 1791, Blount was to call out no more than two militia companies at any one time for "the defensive protection of the frontiers." Congress was obliged to compensate the militia for pay and rations only if territorial officers adhered to regulations. Blount was later instructed that troops were to range within limits and not to cross over "the Indian Boundary," in effect precluding operations against the Chickamauga towns. With Washington's backing, Knox held fast to his position even after learning of a major Chickamauga-Creek offensive. He took the occasion to remind Blount that Congress alone had the power to declare war.[64]

Blount was caught off guard by rising Chickamauga militancy in early 1792. In his view, the Shawnees and Creeks appeared to be the main source of disturbances rather than Cherokees. He predicted that Watts would decline the position of first warrior in the wake of Dragging Canoe's death. The governor was wrong. Watts, who was adept at hoodwinking American officials at opportune times, was in union with the Chickamaugas even if he resided for a time in the Upper Towns, a

422   *Upheavals and the Will to Live, 1762–1795*

point Blount misread. Dick Justice was adroit in his own manner, keeping various paths open. He sent a conciliatory message to the governor little more than a week after leading the scalp dance.[65]

In mid-May, Blount wrote McGillivray for help in preventing mounting Creek attacks on the Cumberland, where Indian raiders had recently killed several white men and boys, a woman and her three children, besides taking female and child captives and stealing many horses. Believing McGillivray might still be assuaged, the governor wondered if "the disorders of the Creeks have flowed from the villainy of Mr. Bowles." Blount did not yet know that Bowles was a Spanish prisoner, and McGillivray had decided to repair his Spanish ties. There would be no pause in Creek assaults on the Cumberland.[66]

While sending peace feelers to McGillivray, Blount readied for talks with influential Cherokee and Chickamauga headmen at Coyatee in the Upper Towns in late May. The occasion attracted two thousand Cherokees—nearly one-fifth of the entire nation—to the conference grounds for the distribution of the first federal annuity of trade goods, received with gladness by Bloody Fellow (now known as Iskagua) and John Watts.[67] The conference's most dramatic moment occurred when Glass and other Chickamauga chiefs, joined by young warriors, arrived in "great parade," as Blount described the scene. The men were "painted Black with White Flour sprinkled over it as evidence of their having quit War and resolved on peace." Bloody Fellow, Watts, and the other headmen led the new arrivals to Blount's quarters where there was "erected the Standard of the United States . . . on a high poll [sic] like a liberty Poll." Lower Town warriors fired a celebratory volley that was returned in like fashion by Upper Town men "to the great Joy of both parties." Blount's sense that the Lower Town participants had decided on peace was premature. The sprinkling of white flour on black body paint may have signaled an indeterminate state in which war or peace hung in the balance. Cherokees rejoiced on meeting their kin and friends who resided apart from one another. Their sense of peoplehood endured despite distinct regional affiliations and differing views on resistance to the Americans. Chiefs Breath, Scolacutta, and Watts announced that their people's common negotiating stance toward the United States would be decided at a council held in twenty-eight nights' time—one moon ahead—at Ustanali. Scolacutta emphasized that it was vital for all principal headmen to attend. Here we see the genesis of a Cherokee national council. Though not a government with coercive power, the council had a more formal standing

An Unbroken People 423

than previous interregional gatherings of Cherokee chiefs, whether of Oconostota's day or further in the past.[68]

Backdoor machinations were commonplace in testy political environs in which a multitude of actors vied for influence. About May 1792, William Panton journeyed from his Pensacola residence to confer with John McDonald in the Lower Towns. It was time for Panton to shore up his Cherokee connections now that his archfoe Bowles was imprisoned. Moreover, U.S. commercial inroads were spreading into southern Indian country. Panton charged McDonald with convincing the Cherokees that their best interests lay with the Spanish by the Gulf. It was not an easy sell. "A large majority" of Cherokees, McDonald later wrote Panton, were wary "that the Spaniards and Americans might be confederated with the purpose to ensnare them." McDonald might not have been so concerned. The Chickamaugas' distrust and hatred of Americans finally overcame their doubts about Spaniards.[69]

In August 1792, Watts and a few companions, including his honorary Creek uncle Talotiskee, visited Governor Arturo O'Neill and Panton in Pensacola. Watts and company returned with packhorses laden with munitions and with promises of more arms, powder, and lead to come. By the fall, this business was quite well known in Knoxville. Blount's agent James Carey was a valuable source.[70] General James Robertson called on trader Richard Finnelson, himself of Anglo-Cherokee parentage, to spy on Spanish maneuvers with Native militants. At Robertson's behest, merchant André Fagot of Illinois provided passage to Finnelson on a river voyage to New Orleans in June 1792 and introduced him to Carondelet, who was blind to the spies about him. In little time, Finnelson and trader Jacques Deraque were in Pensacola, where they learned more of Spanish funneling of arms to Native allies.[71]

Spies Finnelson and Deraque proceeded far north from the Gulf Coast. Their most telling revelations came at Willstown in Chickamauga territory, where they heard Watts advocate war in a large council. Bloody Fellow openly challenged Watts, reminding the assembly of the goods he had gained for the Cherokees by his visit to Philadelphia. Pointing to his American silver medal and fine scarlet coat, he gestured to the U.S. banner standing in the plaza: "Look at that flag; don't you see the stars in it? They are not towns, they are nations; there are thirteen of them. These are people who are very strong, and are the same as one man; and if you know when you are well, you had better stay at home and mind your women and children."

If his people decided for war, he might well "go over the mountains and live in peace." The idea of separating from what seemed an errant, weak, or wayward community was in keeping with Cherokee tradition. Dragging Canoe had famously led a separatist movement to renew battle against the Americans. Now Bloody Fellow questioned if that battle should continue.[72]

Watts's view prevailed, though his was not a power of command. Others spoke for war, including White Owl's son, who had visited the British at Detroit. So, too, did the Shawnee Warrior who had lived for years with thirty of his compatriots at Running Water town. After fiery talks, 400 to 500 warriors left the town square for a brief time and returned in battle pose. Stripped to black-painted flaps, they danced about the flag of the United States while carrying guns and hatchets. Men fired shots through the flag until Bloody Fellow warned them to stop. A war dance resumed in the townhouse that night and lasted until dawn. The decision for a major offensive was taken with great seriousness and made through consultations and rituals over several days. At one point, a group of men left off war preparations to release tensions in whisky-drinking. Finnelson and Deraque, meanwhile, left the Chickamaugas in due time. One Cherokee woman warned Finnelson that, as warriors were plotting to kill him and his companion, they had best be off. This lone woman may have reflected common female doubts about war, though we cannot know for sure.[73]

By September 1792, the Lower Town Cherokees and their Creek allies had decided for war. Deception was therefore in order. A few weeks before the coming offensive, Watts, Little Turkey, and Glass sent deceptive peace messages to Blount at Knoxville. Young Cherokees John Walker and John Fields gave similar professions as a cover to stout militancy. What lay beneath the surface of Cherokee courtesy was often unknown to whites and even surprised Blount's interpreter and spy, James Carey, once a youthful white captive whom Little Turkey had raised as if his own child.[74]

Bloody Fellow was guarded, informing Blount that Cherokee negotiations with the Spanish "neighbors" should not be taken as a sign of enmity toward the Americans. He meanwhile complained of white settlers who were "daily encroaching, and building houses on our lands." By written reply, Blount denied the charge of expanded settlement since the Holston treaty of the previous year. In essence, the war crisis was not brought on by a few additional settler houses but by the Native urge to strike blows that would prevent whites from swallowing up

An Unbroken People   425

their lands, eviscerating their way of life, and blocking intercourse between northern and southern tribes.[75]

Blount had multiple sources about the intended offensive. In early September, Red Bird of the Upper Towns visited Major Craig and told of Watts's journey to Pensacola and the impending conflagration. Thirty Creek fighters had already crossed the Tennessee on their way north. Red Bird wanted Craig to know that Upper Town headmen were doing what they could to persuade the Lower Towns to hold back. His caution arose from genuine fear, namely that whites would blame all Cherokees for war and unleash violence against the Upper Towns while their corn ripened. Similar deadly reprisals had occurred on numerous past occasions. Red Bird's diplomacy was quintessential Cherokee localism, the commitment to protect the community above all else. Ironically, Red Bird was known as a staunch foe of the whites and was even suspected by settlers of joining the massacre of the Kirk family in 1788.[76]

Watts was a head warrior but not a general in the sense of being the top man in a unified command structure. He harkened to many voices, including Shawnee and Creek, when his body of three hundred warriors moved on the Cumberland in late September. Though he favored an attack on Nashville, he was persuaded by fellow chiefs to concentrate his force first against a smaller target—Buchanan's Station just a few miles to the southeast. Some accounts lay the decision on Talotiskee, the Creek-Chickamauga war leader, while others identify Kiatchatalla of Nickjack as a critical voice. The ensuing battle of September 30, furiously fought, was a serious Native setback. Both Talotiskee and Kiatchatalla were slain. The roughly fifteen defenders, expert riflemen, forced an Indian retreat within thirty feet of the fort. Several white women grabbed guns and fired at the enemy too. Watts was badly wounded, shot through both thighs, but managed to leave the bloody ground safely with his comrades' aid.[77]

Hours later, Joseph Brown, former boy captive, stood outside the walls of Buchanan's Station. While a few miles away during the battle, Brown arrived to gain a firsthand view as soon as he could. There he saw the lifeless body of Kiatchatalla, his former master and adopted brother who had captured him on the Tennessee and allowed him to live. Though not marking war's end, Buchanan's Station was a sign of military imbalance. Unable to take a small post with a superior force, Native warriors could not surmount the limitations of guerrilla warfare against growing settler communities. Only so much could be achieved by attacking farmsteads and waylaying white travelers on frontier roads or waterways. The Cumberland settlements, while hit repeatedly, were not going away despite severe losses in dead, wounded, and captured. The number of dead in Native attacks on the Cumberland's settlers, including women, children, and Blacks, climbed from 21 in 1791 to 50 the next year and remained at high levels—65 in 1793 and 50 in 1794.[78]

Bloody Fellow did not apparently join the attack on Buchanan's Station but instead headed a Cherokee delegation that met with Carondelet in New Orleans in November 1792. His companions included Chiefs Breath, Tsali (Charlie), and John Taylor, accompanied by the peripatetic Moses Price. This journey was a new quest for aid at New Orleans, not unlike Oconostota's visit to that city in 1760–1761. Carondelet was quite impressed by Bloody Fellow, whom he believed an individual "of superior intelligence for an Indian [*salvaje*]." The governor pledged to supply the Cherokees and Creeks with ample munitions, so long as all was done confidentially (*bajo mano*) and with tacit royal consent. Spain would be positioned to strengthen Indian resistance and, if the occasion arose, to mediate a favorable peace between a Native confederation and the United States. All served the larger imperial purpose of keeping the Anglo-Americans from knocking at Mexico's portals.[79]

Compared to Carondelet's grand scheme, Blount's diplomacy was a constant jumble, sending agents to Cherokee country, absorbing informants' accounts, and heeding Knox's insistent peace policy by discountenancing white frontiersmen who resorted to vigilante violence against Indians. The territorial citizenry's disgust with the federal government was at a breaking point. Philadelphia seemed deaf to the westerners' entreaties on the life-and-death matter of Indian conflict. In September 1792, William Cocke, retired militia general, published a scathing piece in the *Knoxville Gazette* in which he contended for warfare against all Cherokees, with no distinction between the supposedly peaceful Upper Towns and the Chickamaugas. It was senseless in this view to think peace could be purchased or to credit the professions of Little Turkey, "Hanging Maw" (Scolacutta), or indeed any "savages." Cocke's words drew a sharp public rebuttal from an anonymous author, likely Joseph Martin, who repudiated the idea that "all the Indians must be killed, because some of them are bad men and go to war."[80]

An Unbroken People   427

Blount was quite aware that Cocke spoke for a growing majority of white frontier citizens. On January 28, 1793, the governor issued a proclamation warning "disorderly, ill disposed persons" not to enter Upper Cherokee towns with the intent to kill or destroy. White vigilantism nevertheless reared its head in response to a rash of Creek and Chickamauga attacks. In May, three white men killed John Morris, a Chickasaw man, and wounded Morris's brother and a Cherokee companion—all within 600 paces of Blount's home. The assailants, who were never prosecuted, were perhaps ignorant that Morris was the governor's guest and an ally in Chickasaw battles with the Creeks. The killers saw only an Indian target. Blount arranged Morris's burial with full military honors and accompanied the dead man's brother at the cemetery. The governor consulted with Scolacutta, his most trusted Indian friend, so that there would be no revenge taken for the murder.[81]

Despite a plethora of sources, Blount was uncertain if the Lower Towns, or the Cherokees as a whole, were to continue the battle or opt for peace in the early months of 1793. On February 6, he held amicable talks with Watts, Scolacutta, Doublehead, and other Cherokees at Henry's Station by the French Broad River. A Cherokee woman, Susanna Spears, served as interpreter, another sign of female engagement in diplomacy. In line with Knox's instructions, the governor requested that a Cherokee delegation visit Philadelphia for peace talks. Speaking for the assembly, Watts was noncommittal, attributing Indian attacks on the Cumberland settlements to Creek warriors and underplaying Creek-Chickamauga collusion. In early April, trader David Gilliland told Blount that two parties of Creek warriors, each of thirteen to twenty fighters, had come into Lookout Mountain Town. Their prizes were five scalps (three of whites and two of blacks), along with an elderly Black man as captive and eight horses, one of which was a white trader's "roan race horse." Cherokee warriors had themselves brought in a few scalps and three horses just a few days before. Much to Gilliland's surprise, he was treated well by two Chickamauga chiefs, including the redoubtable Doublehead, a foremost militant. In fact, Gilliland said that Doublehead and headman Pumpkin Boy were "best friends" who saved him from death at the hands of other villagers.[82]

One imagines Blount, the shrewd governor and land speculator, taking advantage of the Cherokees, but the latter certainly had a subtle way of understating or concealing their people's animus toward white settlers. At yet another meeting with headmen in April 1793, Blount was astonished that he could learn little from the "jocular"

428   *Upheavals and the Will to Live, 1762–1795*

Watts over two days, even with much time given to eating, cavorting, and whiskey drinking. Watts once again deferred an answer on a Cherokee journey to Philadelphia, which his Chickamauga entourage disdained. Many Lower Town men doubted anything positive would come of such a trip when so much was pending—the delivery of munitions from Pensacola and the outcome of U.S. conflict with northern Indian nations.[83]

Blount's informants told him that the Chickamaugas were in union with Muscogee and Shawnee militants, but he preferred to believe that the Creeks were the heart of the problem. Alexander McGillivray had died in February 1793, leaving no clear successor on the diplomatic front. That June, Blount headed for Philadelphia to persuade Washington and Knox that the United States should war on the Creeks. His own backyard, meanwhile, seethed. Within one week of Blount's departure, forty mounted militiamen under Captain John Beard went on a murder spree. Frustrated by a failure to nab Creek warriors, the troops rode into Coyatee, a peaceable Cherokee town by the Tennessee River, and went on a rampage, murdering seven Native men, one woman, and a white man, besides wounding five other villagers. The dead included chiefs Tsali and Scantie, individuals noted for their friendship to whites. Among the wounded were Scolacutta and his wife and son as well as Betsy, daughter of Nancy Ward. Scolacutta happened to be hosting a group of whites and Cherokees in his house at the time. Two white visitors at Scolacutta's home believed the perpetrators were as much incensed at the whites as the Indians in the home. Friendship across the ethnic divide was itself verboten. The murderers were not indicted, let alone tried.[84]

Daniel Smith, serving as acting territorial governor, was appalled by Beard's action for its "inhuman[e]" and "detestable" vengeance. As he wrote Knox: "There are many, too many individuals of this Country whose conduct is so violent that they have no just claims to the benefits of Government," in contrast to the "great numbers of meritorious citizens who ought instantly to have it." Smith resorted to the time-worn practice of writing a polite letter, addressed to Scolacutta and other Cherokee chiefs, urging them not to revenge a "horrid and unmanly" act but to await satisfaction from the "great father," in this case President Washington.[85]

To Scolacutta, the massacre bespoke the failure of white leadership. In a written talk, the chief lectured Smith that his word was no good: "You are no head-man, no warrior. . . . I think you are afraid of these

An Unbroken People   429

bad men," meaning the killers who had spilled blood, and "make fun of you." A true leader was expected to restrain those who would do wrong. American chiefs supposedly had greater command over their people than a Cherokee headman had over young warriors. They were obliged by law and treaty to punish malefactors. But the truth was otherwise. Whites were themselves edgy because of a feared Native retaliatory assault. Years of fighting had not brought security. James Ore, a militia commander who repudiated Beard's attack, ruefully concluded: "I think we shall hav[e] a Bloodey War."[86]

The militia assault on Coyatee unquestionably ignited Cherokee anger, though the Chickamaugas and their allies deferred a major offensive until further deliberations. As was commonplace for years, Piomingo of the pro-American Chickasaws relayed information to Robertson of Creek forays against the Cumberland. The chief's way of protecting his people was to offer services for U.S. munitions and trade. Piomingo was well aware of the American appetite for Native land. As the leader of a small people, itself divided by factions, he played a delicate and risky game of hewing close to the Americans without alienating the Spanish. In July 1793, he sent a message to Robertson to be watchful because "there are very bad talks from the Cherokees," who were carrying "scalps and war instruments."[87]

When Cherokees next mounted a major offensive, Chickamauga warriors were again the core striking force. The fighters deliberately targeted Cavett's Station, a tiny settlement just eight miles from Knoxville, and on land Cherokees believed was rightfully theirs. The assault of above six hundred warriors overwhelmed the station early in the morning on September 25, 1793, after a nighttime march from the Tennessee. Twelve of thirteen inhabitants were immediately killed. The victims were three men and nine women and children. A lone boy was taken captive by a Creek man but slain soon thereafter. The most notable warriors at the massacre site were Doublehead, John Watts, James Vann, and Captain Benge. Like Watts, Vann and Benge were sons of Cherokee mothers and British men. The red-haired Benge spoke fluent English but was as adamant a Chickamauga warrior as any man. He was a latter-day Andrew White, one of the first "mixed-blood" Cherokee militants who was at his peak circa 1750.[88]

Acting Governor Smith informed Knox that the attackers of Cavett's Station were "not less than a thousand." In truth, the number of warriors was sizable but probably not quite so great. He wrote just two days after the massacre, and it made sense for him to estimate on the high side in a bid for federal military assistance, which had thus far been minimal. Before Blount returned to Knoxville in early October, Smith called on John Sevier to lead an offensive against the Chickamaugas. Sevier was not a force to be stopped, no matter that his militia had Knox's standing orders not to conduct such an invasion across the "Indian boundary." At the head of more than six hundred men, the veteran general resorted to form. His troops burned Ustanali, which had been abandoned by its inhabitants, before the militia marched on to seize and destroy villages on the Coosa and Etowah Rivers that had budded well south of the Tennessee in what is today's northern Georgia. Three hundred head of cattle and five hundred hogs were slaughtered simply to destroy the Cherokee food supply. One wounded militiaman deliberately murdered an Indian woman and her child. Cherokee fighters offered some resistance at a few locales but were compelled to retreat. Creek towns to the south were neither prepared nor inclined to defend Cherokees living near their northern hunting grounds.[89]

Creeks were as prone as the Chickamaugas to raiding the Cumberland settlements and Kentucky. Multifarious Native loyalties did not, however, produce a durable interregional alliance. During the summer of 1793, a group of prominent Upper Creek leaders contacted American agent James Seagrove with an urgent message for Knox. Fearful of a loss of control and a descent into chaos, the headmen declared their willingness to cooperate with the United States against militant towns in their own nation. At that same time, Blount and General Andrew Pickens lobbied in Philadelphia for a U.S. offensive against the Creeks but received a negative response from Washington and Knox, who kept to their strategic priority of gaining ascendancy above the Ohio. The president and secretary of war had the good sense to avoid military overcommitment and an escalation of conflict on the combustible Georgia-Creek frontier.[90]

There were strengths and weaknesses to Chickamauga-Creek collaboration, which involved Creek Towns of the Coosa, Tallapoosa, and Alabama more than the Lower Towns of the Chattahoochee. The strengths were enhanced fighting prowess along with space for Cherokees to shelter far from whites. The weakness was that Creek war parties, ranging as far north as Kentucky, inevitably generated a white frontier backlash in which the Chickamaugas were implicated. Ultimately, the Chickamauga and allied towns could not alternatively turn on and shut the spigot of war while escaping counterattack.

An Unbroken People

Sevier's assault below the Tennessee was a turning point, showing that white frontiersmen would not be stopped from taking the fight below the federal treaty line, notwithstanding Knox's orders. On September 13, 1794, Colonel William Whitley's 150 Kentuckians and Major James Ore's 400 Southwest militiamen invaded and destroyed Nickjack and Running Water—the foremost Chickamauga villages along the Tennessee River and a nexus with Creek and Shawnee militants. General James Robertson, who had long contemplated the offensive, was the architect who put the plan in motion with Governor Blount's tacit consent. Blount was initially careful to avoid political responsibility for the campaign, which violated Knox's instructions, though he might not have been so punctilious had he detected the shift in mood that took place in Philadelphia after Anthony Wayne's victory in early July over the northern Indian coalition at Fallen Timbers. Knox was pleased with the southern militia expedition's success so long as it furthered peace and stability in U.S.-Cherokee relations.[91]

Details of the attacks come from the recollections of white militiamen fifty years or more after the events. One Cherokee woman at Nickjack loosened her clothes and jumped into the Tennessee while the firing was ongoing. Fortunately, she was able to swim to her escape. General James White recalled a frightened Cherokee woman who crossed the river at Nickjack by canoe with her child. Halfway across, she threw the child into the river and leapt after it. She repeatedly dove to escape gunshots and reached the other side; the child drowned. While some Chickamauga men hurriedly fled to safety, others fired on the militia to keep them in check so that their women and children had a chance to flee. Writing after the engagement, Colonel Whitley reported that his men had routed a "degenerate" enemy and killed "not less than 70 of that merciless Banditti" in a single day without losing a man. The Chickamaugas as a people yet endured the destruction.[92]

Chickamauga defeats hastened the end of open warfare between the Cherokees and the United States. Battle scars were not the sole force that led to Cherokee withdrawal from concerted warfare against "the white people." Spanish support for Indian resistance lessened dramatically by 1795 because of Madrid's European engagements and movement toward rapprochement with the American republic. The Creeks were themselves rent by deep discord that intensified after McGillivray's death. A nasty Creek-Chickasaw conflict undercut peace and stability. The Cherokees had to distance themselves from disorders in

432   *Upheavals and the Will to Live, 1762–1795*

neighboring Indian societies even while grappling with the Americans. The challenge was arduous and continual.[93]

Four months before the destruction of Nickjack and Running Water, Washington and Knox signaled that the Cherokees must bow to American authority to have peace. The occasion was a lecture the president gave a Cherokee delegation, headed by Doublehead, which arrived in Philadelphia by ship from Charleston in June 1794. With the outcome of Wayne's campaign still uncertain, Knox bid for quiet by pledging to increase the Cherokee annuity from $1,500 to $5,000. Compliance was expected in turn. In his address to the chiefs, Washington insisted that the Cherokees, whom he called "My Children," had no choice but to accept the boundaries indicated in Blount's Holston treaty of 1791. The president was willing to "Bury deep and forever the red Hatchet of War," though without further negotiation. The headmen should pay heed:

> You must restrain your bad young Men from stealing of horses and murdering our frontier people. Unless you have force sufficient for this purpose peace will never be established. The frontier people will not suffer their property to be stolen, much less will they suffer their friends to be murdered, without seeking satisfaction. We shall endeavor to order the White young Men and prevent their doing you any injury.

Washington said that there were more than ten thousand Americans "seated" by the Cumberland, "and they cannot be removed." A boundary "must be marked so that no disputes shall happen or any white people cross over it." This last pledge would scarcely be fulfilled during the remainder of Washington's presidency, let alone decades thereafter.[94]

Disparate Paths to War's End

The Cherokees made a decision for peace with the United States in the weeks prior to a conference held with American officials at Tellico Blockhouse, a newly built fort along the Little Tennessee River, in early November 1794. It was a consensus many towns already favored, while others joined for lack of an alternative after severe militia blows to the Lower Towns. Significantly, peace came by a general accord and not by a formally written treaty with any Native land cession.

An Unbroken People

For some Cherokee leaders, the decision for peace was too long in coming. Scolacutta was the most prominent representative of this viewpoint. For others, such as John Watts, the road to peace was torturous, an enormous strain to yield the battle with dignity intact. Many diehard militants had fallen in conflict well before the peace conference at Tellico Blockhouse. One example is Captain Benge, who raided into Powell's Valley and was killed by militia in April 1794. While calling the dead man "an artful, atrocious villain," a Richmond newspaper observed that Benge, who spoke English, had told his last white prisoners that they could expect to be released at a "general peace." The "villain" was not without mercy.[95]

A plainspoken man, James Robertson laid out what he considered unassailable facts in a letter to Watts just one week after the smashing of Nickjack and Running Water towns. The militia officers who led the attack under his orders had found letters and objects that belonged to whites slain by Indian warriors on the Kentucky Road. Robertson also alluded to a Chickamauga attack a few months before on a boat carrying white passengers and enslaved Blacks on the Tennessee River. (Newspaper accounts tell us that all the whites were killed, including six men, three women, and three or four children, while all twenty-two Blacks were captured.) Now that the two Chickamauga towns were destroyed, Robertson was willing to move past the river killings and conclude peace if the Cherokees ceased hostilities and stopped the Creeks from passing through their territory en route to attack. A prisoner exchange and negotiations were possible if Watts came with a white flag to concede to terms. If not, Robertson advised that General Benjamin Logan of Kentucky might well come south to retrieve a Black woman and her three children, said to be "his negroes," captured by the Chickamaugas. This was a threat even if largely bluff. Logan was reckoned to arrive with troops.[96]

Having admonished Watts that the government would not accept a "half-way peace," Robertson cited the peaceful tenor of certain Chickamauga towns as a reason why the militia had not destroyed them like Nickjack and Running Water. The general praised Watts and another chief of Willstown for recently giving "good talks." Dick Justice, "head" of Lookout Mountain Town, "is known to be a good man." One wonders whether Justice, the former friend of Bowles, had made any rapid about-face or was renewing peace talks for personal interest and communal preservation.[97]

434   *Upheavals and the Will to Live, 1762–1795*

Robertson's letter, strongly supported by Blount, led to talks on November 7–8, 1794, at Tellico Blockhouse in which Watts and Scolacutta served as spokesmen for their people. Besides American officers and troops, 400 Cherokee warriors were in attendance. There were also many women and children outside the blockhouse. James Davidson, Cherokee headman of the "Valley Towns," was alone said to bring 450 of "his people" to Tellico. The mood in many Cherokee communities before the conference must have been tense. Women could not help but worry. Would their young men continue at war? Would the white people ever allow them to live in peace and without dread? In one talk at Tellico, Watts explained why he had not yet delivered prisoners, including the captured Blacks, as Robertson had demanded. Rather than go himself to Nashville under a flag, he suggested that he had first entrusted the role to a Cherokee woman, but she "was pursued by some bad white people, and obliged to quit her horse," and save herself by hiding in the cane. Considering her troubling experience, he had delayed a visit to the general, whom he called "a good man." This story, incomplete as it is, offers a glimpse of a Cherokee woman's readiness to undertake a peace mission at great personal risk.[98]

Courtesy was as important as ever to fruitful diplomatic exchanges. Blount showed his respect for Watts by calling him "Colonel Watts" during the talks. Watts delivered a string of white beads to the governor. He admitted the difficulty of the moment. He had thought beforehand of what he would say with tears in his eyes. Running Water and Nickjack were destroyed. He had talked to both towns of peace in the nights before the militia attacked. Many villagers of Running Water had accepted what he said and wished him to negotiate the return of their prisoners. He now acted with the cooperation of Glass and Bloody Fellow, both of whom supported his course. Watts deferred to Scolacutta who he recognized as "the head of the Nation," sitting at his side.[99]

Scolacutta, honored elder, assumed his role with dignity, balancing criticism of the Lower Towns for having brought "Destruction" on themselves, while offering "to make peace for them." He was outspoken on his charge: "I am the Headman of my Nation as Governor Blount is of the white people." The Lower Towns were not his "People" when they sheltered thieves and killers, but he cared about them and was peacemaker on their behalf. Watts backed up Scolacutta by saying Upper Town men had done right by tracking and

An Unbroken People

435

killing two Creek marauders and seizing another in their vicinity. The captured warrior, who had murdered a white man, was brusquely turned over to the U.S. authorities and then tried and executed. Watts displayed Cherokee unity on the peace front by recounting the episode, which Scolacutta said he had set in motion.[100]

Scolacutta's talk had an overriding theme of self-protection and communal survival. Just the previous spring, he heard that people in various parts of his own nation wanted him dead for talking peace with John McKee, Blount's agent. The alleged plot would involve Cherokees killing whites in Scolacutta's vicinity, deliberately provoking settlers to slay him and friends in reprisal. The Lower Towns' violent course had already incited white men to wound and nearly kill him—a clear reference to all he suffered in Beard's murderous raid. Scolacutta's hope for his people to live in peace was the reason he approved the building of Tellico Blockhouse on Cherokee land. It should be a safe fort, a place of peace where "the White & Red People" would meet in friendship. Scolacutta was looking ahead to a better time—one for communal recovery and life.[101]

Watts joined in the customary smoking of the peace pipe with Blount, Scolacutta, and other chiefs and American officers. The accord was a mutual goodwill pledge, not a formal written treaty, and it was made possible because Blount asked for no land cession when peace was on the line. The governor asked Watts if he would like to know the details of Wayne's "victory over the Northern Indians." The Cherokee headman said there was no need; he already had heard from his own people who were in the battle. His pride held strong. There was a time for speaking, and other times when few words were best.[102]

There was no immediate cessation of violence after the Tellico Blockhouse accord. Some Cherokees had scores to settle against whites from the recent past. On November 10, 1794, several Cherokee men joined a band of Creek warriors who brought terror to the home of Colonel Joseph Sevier, brother of John Sevier. In the attack, the colonel and his wife escaped death, but two men, one woman, and five children were murdered. The killings did not flare into war. Robertson and Blount decided to downplay the episode, attributing the violence to the Creeks alone. The governor wanted to preserve a Cherokee peace. Cherokee headmen themselves overwhelmingly wished to avoid being drawn into further conflict. They kept to what Scolacutta and Watts pledged. Virtually the entire Cherokee people did so as well.[103]

Blount had his own plans for the Cherokees. In early 1795, he wanted them to supply fighters as American allies who would range the Cumberland frontier to protect white settlements against Creek attack. Watts and Bloody Fellow put off the governor. Their people wanted a respite from war and had no desire to be Blount's auxiliaries. Nor did they want to be targeted, as had recently occurred, when Chickasaws skirmished with Creeks and the Muscogees' presumed Cherokee friends. Cherokee chiefs Little Turkey and Black Fox were pleased when General Robertson induced the Chickasaws to return Cherokee captives. The headmen recalled their talks with Robertson and Blount years earlier: "We told one another" of "hopes," that "we should see the day that we might Live to see white hairs Grow in our heads . . . we are Determined to be in peace with the U[nited] States" and "would wish to be in peace with all the world." Little Turkey wished that Chickasaw chief Piomingo, his nephew, would hear his talk. Piomingo had lived with the Cherokees in his youth when Little Turkey had adopted him.[104] Those were bonds of blood that could heal a wound. Tragically, Cherokees and other Native peoples could hardly rely on the United States in any such manner.

An Unbroken People

CONCLUSION

Washington's Farewell and Cherokee Paths

In August 1796, George Washington was only weeks away from delivering his Farewell Address to his fellow citizens when he forwarded a letter of paternal advice to the Cherokee Nation—addressed as "Beloved Cherokees" in his words. The president did not speak of bloodshed over recent years between white settlers and the Cherokees. He devoted his talk to recommendations on "how the condition of the Indian natives of the country might be improved." While admitting that little had been achieved that way "since the White people first came to America," he believed in "one path" that "Indian tribes" could take to "make life comfortable and happy."[1]

Washington's address to the Cherokees is noteworthy even if the speech was composed by two members of his cabinet. Secretary of War James McHenry wrote an ungainly first draft, which was refashioned by Timothy Pickering, secretary of state. Washington wanted his words to circulate widely. Silas Dinsmoor, federal agent to the Cherokees, was instructed to have the printed "Talk" distributed and read aloud in Native towns so that its message would be clearly absorbed.[2]

Washington's talk exemplifies the idea of Indian "improvement" that the president and former Secretary of War Henry Knox had conceived over years. Cherokees were advised that "the game with which your woods once abounded, are growing scarce." Hunting was no longer practical for subsistence or trade. Cherokee men should better themselves by using the plow to "vastly increase your crops of corn." Then, too, the land was capable of producing wheat ("which produces the best bread"), flax, and cotton. Native men could tend sheep besides raising hogs and cattle, while women learned to spin, weave, and fashion clothing for their people. A federal agent would live among the Cherokees and distribute livestock, equipment, and tools and give "all necessary information" to promote success. There would be medals and rewards "to such Cherokees as . . . shall best deserve them."[3]

Washington and the cabinet offered advice on Cherokee governance. The president's model was a simple representative system under U.S. tutelage:

> The wise men of the United States meet together once a year, to consider what would be for the good of all their people. The wise men of each separate state also meet together once or twice every year, to consult and do what is good for the people of their respective states. I have thought that a meeting of your wise men once or twice a year would be alike useful to you. Every town might send one or two of its wisest counsellors to talk together on the affairs of your nation, and to recommend to your people whatever they should think would be serviceable. The beloved agent of the United States would meet with them. He would give them information of those things which are found good for the white people, and which your situation would enable you to adopt.

Laws might be passed "for the preservation of the peace; for the protection of your lands; for the security of your persons; for your improvement in the arts of living, and for promoting your general welfare."[4] Left unstated was how Cherokees and other Native peoples could possibly defend their rights under a federal government that answered above all to expansive states and settler populations with little or no tolerance for a permanent Indian presence.

Washington's advice was tendered as if the Cherokees were a passive people fit to follow the U.S. agent's guidance rather than make their own decisions. In reality, Cherokees were accustomed to holding town councils for untold generations. Through much of the 1700s, regional or interregional meetings were called as necessary to consider war and peace and to deliberate on relations with the French, English, and an array of Native peoples. Cherokee towns sent deputies to such gatherings as they pleased. Participation was voluntary. There was no national council with authority over the whole. The thought of following a single national stance in war and peace was scarcely in Cherokee consciousness at the dawn of the eighteenth century CE. And yet a Cherokee sense of peoplehood, rooted in town and clan, was a reality through ceremonial life and the shared feeling of being human in a special way.

In the early 1700s, Cherokee relations with outsiders were shaped more by town and regional decision-making than national consensus. Certain towns entered exchange with Carolina traders and became partners in the Indian slave trade. Others followed suit, joining the deerskin trade as well. Turmoil in this "new world" was stirred by interlocking forces—the colonials' pursuit of profit, their persistent quest to secure Native allies and to subjugate "savage" foes, and the Native desire for European goods and guns for sustenance and advantage over Indigenous rivals. Cherokees were active agents in a rapidly changing southeastern continental landscape where "Old World" diseases ravaged many Native peoples but without necessarily sapping their ability to cope with challenging and threatening conditions. This was particularly true of potent Indigenous ethnicities in interior regions that rival European nations courted and dared not alienate as a whole.

Did the Cherokees become a more tightly bound nation through the need to forge a common approach to English colonialism? My answer is yes, provided we remember that this was not a linear or ineluctable process. South Carolina recognized the plurality of the Cherokee people for quite practical purposes. Colonial officials learned that Overhill Cherokees expected to be supplied in trade just as fully as the "Lower" or the "Middle" Towns. Regional communities weighed what they were owed relative to one another, just as Cherokees and Creeks measured English largesse relative to what their rivals received.

Cherokee diplomatic acumen grew over decades. In part, this was a process of learning what could be expected from the English and French. Cherokees absorbed differences between various English provinces and played to Virginia when South Carolina failed to serve their needs. They called on British mediation when they believed it necessary to resolve Creek hostilities and to restrain Iroquois attacks. The idea of treating with English officials as beloved men and "brothers" or "elder brothers" came naturally to Cherokees, who wished to bring powerful and useful strangers into their circle of kinship.

Through the eighteenth century, Cherokees preserved and even strengthened their sense of common peoplehood through diplomacy as

Conclusion

much as war. A watershed came in the mid-1720s when far-flung communities deliberated and called on the Long Warrior of Tanasee to be their foremost spokesman in negotiations that culminated in direct talks between Cherokee and Creek headmen in Charles Town. A keen diplomat, Long Warrior advanced a hallmark Cherokee policy of seeking truces on particular fronts so that his people would not be overwhelmed by enemies from all quarters. A peace with the "Southwards" (the Creeks) made sense when Cherokees faced dangers from a slew of Indigenous nations to the north and west. Though a Cherokee-Creek truce of 1727 was short-lived, Long Warrior's diplomatic approach lived on, and nowhere more so than by his refusal to bow to English demands despite the importance of Charles Town's trade.

Cherokee war and diplomacy had regional underpinnings and more general characteristics. In the early 1740s, for example, a band of Lower Town warriors enlisted in the English war against the Spanish in Florida, while Overhill fighters waged slashing guerrilla warfare on French river traffic on the Ohio and Wabash. While these attacks on the western waters rattled the French, the latter responded by arming their Native allies of the Great Lakes and St. Lawrence to wreak havoc on the Cherokees. The dénouement was a Cherokee effort to attain a French peace and a letup in northern Indian attacks. Here again, diplomacy came to the fore when continued warfare was untenable.

Cherokee diplomacy was pluralistic. Diverse initiatives originated in distinct locales. In 1747, thirteen Lower Towns made a substantial land cession to South Carolina, while other Cherokees regions were seemingly aloof. But all took note. Five years later, Connecorte of Chota commented on the large picture in a message to his "Brother" Governor James Glen:

> he looks every Day to the Rising Sun where his Brother lives close to the Great Water Side, and that when he was a little Boy the white People began to settle thick in the Country . . . till the King their Father told them [all] to live together as Brothers upon one Land, but now he [Glen] says that they [the Cherokees] are . . . debarred from it, his People being not suffered to go further than the dividing Waters commonly called the Long Canes.

Connecorte was disturbed by Glen's most recent treaty of 1751 that virtually prohibited Cherokees from hunting and traveling in piedmont settlement zones to their southeast. The priest-chief reminded

Glen that Chota kept the English king's sealed talk—the same brought back from England in 1730—stored in its town house. The king's talk, in Connecorte's words, admonished the English to "be kind and good to his People, that accordingly they were well supplyed for some Time, for which Reason they assisted the white People in the Tuskoraro War. That they are now very bare of every Thing, though their Enemies from all Parts are brisk upon them, particularly the Creeks who are well supplyed, by which it would seem as if the white People loved them better than his People."[5]

Connecorte's sense of time was metaphoric rather than strictly chronological in this instance. It did not matter that the Great King offered his protective mantle well after the Tuscarora War rather than before it. The priest-chief wanted Glen to remember the principle of reciprocal exchange—the heart of alliance. While not expecting the governor to stop supplying the Creeks, he wanted to make sure that "his people" received their rightful share considering all that they had done for the English.

Cherokee words in English translation hint at Indigenous cultural values but pose difficulties in historical interpretation. For example, what precisely did Connecorte mean by "his people"? In certain instances, he implied the Cherokees as a whole, while elsewhere his references were local, referring mainly to Chota. At one point, he mentioned "the Lower Towns People," meaning Cherokees who lived east of the Blue Ridge. As the priest-chief told Glen, he found it strange that the Lower Towns were compensated for the land cession of 1747, "but that neither he or his People living in the Mother Town of all ever got any Thing for it."[6] This declamation is telling. Connecorte's deepest loyalties were rooted in a particular place while his sense of belonging to a Cherokee nation had a broader, if more diffuse meaning. After all, he felt deprived of compensation precisely because Chota, "the Mother Town" of all Cherokees, was connected to "the Lower Towns People."

Cherokee diplomacy was not simply a matter of what came top-down or was decided by headmen in conferences with colonial and later U.S. officials. Cherokee women sustained community not only in daily tasks but by making their voices heard and taking risks in the political-social sphere, especially in crisis. By subtle politicking in 1755–1756, a network of Overhill women undermined Great Tellico's attempt to join a French-Shawnee-Creek alliance against the English. They did so because of deep concern about communal welfare and the continuance of trade at a time of upheaval. Cherokee women were

Conclusion   443

similarly assertive when their people's survival hung in the balance during the British war of 1760–1761. They sheltered white men with whom they were intimate, pressured English soldiers to release Cherokee hostages, aided warriors, and finally helped to move their people toward peace. Nancy Ward's endeavors during the American Revolutionary Era—while justifiably noteworthy—are examples of a much larger phenomenon.

Cherokee custom gave room for individuals to move from one community to another, not unlike the freedom that women had to divorce a husband and take a new one. Both Attakullakulla and Ostenaco lived at Chota for some time but subsequently moved to Tomotley, about seven miles to the northwest. Did both men, for particular reasons, wish to gain breathing room from Connecorte? That is quite possible. Voluntary separation sometimes defused tensions and allowed relationships to proceed on more level ground. Dragging Canoe's Chickamauga movement, which came in the wake of wartime devastation, was a jarring separation from ancestral villages, though it did not foreclose union between distinct regional communities at some future time.

Cherokees managed to maintain a remarkable degree of comity among one another when taking diverse and even opposing paths in periods of great travail. Oconostota tolerated Attakullakulla's pro-peace diplomacy in 1760–1761 even though the Great Warrior spurned the English and ventured to New Orleans in hope of a French alliance. Years later, the elderly Oconostota disapproved of Dragging Canoe's war and tactfully reopened negotiations with Virginia months after the punitive militia invasions of 1776. Along with other Overhill leaders, he opted for wartime neutrality rather than take up Patrick Henry's offer to aid the Americans, which would have put his own people in conflict with their Chickamauga kin. Cherokee men and women commonly put their foremost loyalty in their immediate community, as compared to nation, when survival was on the line. Nanye-hi and other Cherokee women did so when they saved the lives of white traders, including their own kin, in the wartime upheaval of 1780–1781. Nan-ye-hi was no less a Cherokee for following a particular path to safety. She spoke strongly for her people as a whole at treaty conferences with American representatives in 1781 and 1785, hoping for peace and permanency for Cherokees in their homeland.

In 1796, the Cherokees were advised by Washington's administration to form a national council so that laws might be passed "for your improvement in the arts of living, and for promoting your general welfare." In fact, the business of "improvement" as Washington understood it was underway by that time—and in large measure because Cherokee women grasped at ways to improve their people's lot. In late November 1796, U.S. agent Benjamin Hawkins met three Native women at a village near the Etowah River, an area settled by Cherokees moving south after the Revolutionary War. Hawkins lodged at the home of one of the women, a "half-breed," in his words, who treated him hospitably despite her poverty. This unnamed woman expressed pleasure at Hawkins's message that the American government was furthering "a plan . . . for bettering the condition of the Red people." Hawkins said something about encouraging females to spin and weave. The Cherokee woman answered that she "had once made as much cotton as purchased a petticoat, that she would gladly make more and learn to spin it, if she had the opportunity." She also said that she had been much put out by the conflict between the "Red and White People." Her arm bore a wound inflicted by white men who had attacked a group of Cherokees as they traveled in the neighborhood. The assailants lived at Tugaloo, for generations a Cherokee mother town but now a place in Georgia.[7]

When Hawkins arrived at Pine Log town two days later, a Black woman served as his interpreter with Cherokee villagers. At another meeting in Pine Log, he relied on Sally Waters, the "half-breed wife" of a white colonel, who was herself a Cherokee speaker who knew a little English. With men out hunting, Cherokee women told Hawkins of their desire to plant cotton, learn spinning, and raise pigs and cattle. They could not grow enough corn to depend on that alone. Within the next dozen years, Cherokee women became major producers of cloth through their skillful use of U.S. government-supplied spinning wheels and looms. They were ardent supporters of betterment, though not necessarily of a grander plan of "civilization" that would supplant Cherokee culture.[8]

Scolacutta died shortly after the peace of 1794 that he had a major role in brokering with the United States. In 1801, his widow, called "Granny Maw" by whites, received two sheep for family use from Return J. Meigs, federal agent to the Cherokees, who was punctilious in paying Natives what they were due from the government. Late that year, Meigs determined that Scolacutta's widow had a just claim to two of her horses stolen by three white men who intruded into Cherokee territory near his Tellico Blockhouse headquarters. Although the

Conclusion   445

animals were unrecoverable, the widow and her son-in-law received $120 as government compensation a year later. In September 1803, the agent paid a sum to a white man for helping to recover "Granny Maw's Negro woman," who had almost certainly run away in an attempt at freedom. From these scattered records, one gleans something of an elderly Cherokee woman who survived militia invasions and white vigilante assaults and lived into a new era when individual property-holding and Black slavery had a growing place in southern Indian life.[9]

The Cherokees of the 1790s were a multifarious people, probably more so than in any previous generation since first encountering the English about the 1670s. A generation of headmen and notable figures that came of age during the 1780s and 1790s included many individuals born of Cherokee mothers and Anglo/Scottish fathers. Their names leap from the page—Walker, Taylor, Elders, Benge, Price, Shorey, Watts, and others. Cherokee genealogies became quite complex over time. Veteran trader John McDonald wed Anne Shorey, herself the daughter of Scots trader-interpreter William Shorey and Guigooie, a Cherokee woman of the Bird clan. In the mid-1780s, McDonald assisted Daniel Ross, a Scots newcomer who established himself in commerce about Lookout Mountain Town. A few years later, Ross wed Mollie, daughter of McDonald and Anne Shorey. Mollie had nine children by Daniel Ross. John Ross, one of their offspring, had skin color resembling a white youth's and still became a steadfast Cherokee leader. In 1835, he was the principal chief who strenuously opposed Andrew Jackson's treaty that imposed the cession of Cherokee land and forced removal—the Trail of Tears.[10]

The emergence of an influential Cherokee minority with European ancestry during the period 1790–1820 coincided with similar trends among the Creeks, Chickasaws, and Choctaws. Native men of "mixed" backgrounds had an outsized role in their respective nation's diplomacy vis-à-vis the United States. This fact was owing, as Theda Perdue writes, to personal advantages from "familiarity with Anglo-American customs, some knowledge of English," and "an openness to cultural change." Cherokee men with some white ancestry often had a leg up in the social order because their fathers had accumulated property in trade and their mothers benefited from inheritances in dwellings and barns. These assets were commonly turned to the acquisition of enslaved Blacks. It would be a mistake, however, to think that only so-called "mixed-bloods" owned slaves, even though they had by far the greatest share. Doublehead, a man of full Cherokee ancestry, seized or purchased Blacks during the Chickamaugas' fight against white settlers. He was adamant about holding his gains after peace was reached with the United States.[11]

A Native American elite of an entirely new kind emerged. In 1780, there is little documented evidence of Black slave ownership in Cherokee country. In 1810, there were nearly six hundred enslaved Blacks within the Cherokee nation's homeland, which then had a population of thirteen thousand Natives. The exploitation of slave labor skewed wealth distribution among Cherokees. Perhaps only 5 percent of Cherokee households had slave ownership in 1810 while 7 percent did in 1835, when the Black population was nearly 1,600. James Vann, the wealthiest Cherokee slaveowner in his lifetime, alone possessed 115 enslaved Blacks at his death in 1809. A hard-driving man with a violent streak, his plantation estate, highly unusual in its grandeur, was the product of business acumen and relentless ambition. Vann's father, himself of Scots-Cherokee parentage, was a trader-interpreter of some means who had come to own several Blacks.[12]

Slavery was generally not as harsh or regimented among Cherokees as in the Southern states. Blacks at Vann's estate intermixed with Cherokees and participated in communal ceremonies and festivals. Slavery's degrading impact should still not be minimized. Tragically, Cherokee laws regarding slavery tended toward greater severity in the 1840s after the terrible upheaval of the Trail of Tears. Taking a broad view, Cherokees had come to look upon Africans and their descendants as slaves since they first encountered English colonial society. This prejudice was not easily shaken. In an extraordinary case of 1824, the Cherokee National Council permitted Shoe Boots, a respected chief, to free three children he had by Doll, his Black wife, but ordered him to have no more children by her since she was a "slave woman" by law.[13]

The great question that the Cherokees faced at the onset of the 1800s was how they could maintain unity as a people under enormous stress. There was division between Lower Towns, oriented to the southwest, and the more easterly Upper Towns, with the latter being generally poorer and exercising less clout in treaty-making with the United States. Some Cherokee households adapted to new ways while others wanted no part of the white man's habits of plowing the land, let alone praying to the Christian God, as the Moravian and Presbyterian missionaries preached. Men struggled with depleted hunting grounds, though some found a new outlet in the raising of livestock. Cherokees

Conclusion   447

had no recourse within the state or federal judicial systems to obtain justice if their own kind were killed or murdered by whites. These episodes by no means ended with the Cherokee-U.S. peace of 1794.[14]

The Cherokee community ethic, the ideal of living in harmony (*gadugi*), was severely strained by the federal government's pressure on headmen to consent to land cessions through treaty-making. Bowing to the State of Tennessee and white citizens, U.S. commissioners extracted a large Cherokee cession in 1798, amounting to nearly one million acres—609,000 in Tennessee and 375,000 in North Carolina. Cherokee negotiators reluctantly consented on condition that they receive $5,000 in goods for their people and an increase of $1,000 in the nation's annuity.[15] Indian boundary lines, meticulously outlined in treaty after treaty, were sundered by invariable federal renegotiation over ensuing decades. All was done in the interest of burgeoning white populations that roundly despised Indians.

Given the danger of living on constricted and threatened Native ground, a growing number of Cherokees chose long-distance western migration to live more freely. As previously seen, this movement began in the mid- to late 1780s with a small Cherokee exodus to the Missouri-Arkansas area, then under Spanish sovereignty. Cherokee far western migration picked up in the next decade. In 1796, Will Webber, the founder of Willstown in the southwestern Chickamauga region, led a number of families to Arkansas. Knowing of Webber's departure, Governor John Sevier of Tennessee became anxious that westering Cherokees might side with Spain or France if war should come in the Mississippi Valley. William Blount, now a U.S. senator, meanwhile schemed for a British takeover of Louisiana lest the French gain control of the region. When his conspiracy unraveled in 1797, he was impeached and expelled from the Senate. The Louisiana Purchase greatly eased U.S. fears of a revived French empire at mid-continent, while hastening the American republic's plans for Native people to relinquish their lands east of the river for migration to the trans-Mississippi West.[16]

Cherokees had their own reasons for testing long-distance migration that had more to do with finding secure living space than imperial permutations. By 1807, perhaps 300 to 400 Cherokees lived in the area of the White and Arkansas Rivers. Western migration was an inviting safety valve to some Cherokees but painful to many others who dreaded being separated from kin and living in a reduced ancestral homeland that could more easily fall prey to the white people of the United

448   *Conclusion*

States. When Cherokee chiefs wrote President Jefferson of their opposition to trans-Mississippi relocation, they "pit[i]ed" their women since "tis by them that we are all Borne and Raised." Mothers "Love their Children to be near them as when they are in the Corne field [*sic*] they Expect to see them at me[a]l Times." This was a core belief, generation after generation.[17]

Cherokee society was vulnerable, convulsed by land cession controversies well before the emigration issue threatened to bring all into chaos. Federal annuities were a foundation of material well-being, but at what price? Cherokees were put off by the U.S. government's practice of offering private land "reserves" and other benefits—essentially bribes—to Native men who were cooperative in treaty-making. The distribution of annuity payments was also a sore point, aggravating cleavages between Cherokees, some of whom favored payment in basic goods rather than the transfer of large sums to pay off the nation's debts to traders.[18]

It is little wonder that internecine violence rose under these circumstances. In August 1807, two Cherokee men assassinated Doublehead, the former Chickamauga militant, for accepting douceurs of money and land during U.S. treaty-making. One of the killers was The Ridge (Kahnungdatlageh), who had himself adapted from youthful warring against whites to become a prosperous householder, if one whose speech was Cherokee and required an interpreter to communicate in English. A few months after Doublehead's slaying, a group of forty-six chiefs insisted in a public letter to Jefferson that they could never accept a future treaty as "Binding on Us" until "it is Received and Approved and [by] a Majority of all our Beloved Men and Warriors." In short, treaties were inadmissible if made by a small coterie of chiefs motivated by personal gain rather than for the good of "our Nation."[19]

In asserting Cherokee nationhood, the chiefs relied on a universal language of rights enshrined at the foundation of the United States. Just as the people of the United States had the authority to accept or reject a treaty through their government, so, too, did the Cherokees possess that same right "as a free people . . . to Claim for Ourselves and Our Children." Significantly, the chiefs addressed President Jefferson as their "Beloved Father," living "a long way" from them but within the same communal circle: "We consider you a father and Still hope you Guard Us as part of your Family." The chiefs acted on faith. They saw no contradiction in being a "free people" and trusting a powerful protector "to Do Us Justice." This was essentially a reformulation of what many Chero-

Conclusion
449

kees desired from the Great King George of the past.[20] The letter was collaborative, written by Cherokees who were fluent in their Native language and also literate in English.

Jefferson's idea of Cherokee relocation attempted to turn what was until then a limited western migration into a radically transformative project, ostensibly designed for Native betterment but amounting to an Indian nation's removal from homelands coveted by Georgia, Tennessee, and North Carolina. The Cherokees were internally divided over the federal proposition, which held out inducements to cooperative Indian migrants. A group of influential Lower Town leaders favored the idea, while a great number of men and women in the nation were adamantly opposed. After Meigs encouraged the pro-cession group to send a deputation to Washington, the opposing side mobilized in council and appointed its own deputies to the federal capital. In January 1809, two rival Cherokee deputations had separate meetings with Jefferson at the White House. The opponents of emigration appealed to the president by emphasizing their commitment to social betterment. In a written declaration of December 1808, they stated how far their people had "progressed in Agriculture & domestic manufactures" and by English-language schooling for children. Behind these words was a fear that Jefferson barely grasped. Many Cherokees apprehended that emigration, bound to the cession of their treasured land, would be their people's death knell.[21]

Jefferson condescendingly praised his Cherokee guests for their "anxious desires to engage in the industrious pursuits of agriculture & civilized life," but told them that they still had a long way to progress on that path. They required "fixed laws," especially for "the punishment of crimes and the protection of property." Jefferson proposed that a Cherokee council allot a "separate parcel of land" to each male "head of family" for himself and his descendants. The custom of communal landownership, which persisted in parts of the Cherokee nation, did not figure in the president's thinking any more than did the role of Native women as heads of households. Above all, Jefferson showed a decided preference for the Cherokee delegation that favored migration to Arkansas; he lent little encouragement to the deputies who voiced their desire to dwell on ancestral soil in "the bosom of the Country," where they "may become a usefull part of the great family on which the great spirit looks with equal eye."[22] The foremost Cherokee ideal was living in neighborly friendship with the United States while remaining a distinct sovereign nation.

450   *Conclusion*

The Cherokees were almost ripped apart by the emigration controversy, but allayed discord by consultation among several factions, which reached consensus at a major council held in Willstown in September 1809. The result was a strengthened union. Deputies stated that they stood for "the whole Cherokee nation" and not for either the Lower or Upper Towns, which Meigs was prepared to see politically separated from one another if that measure advanced trans-Mississippi migration. On the pressing issue of land cession and western relocation, the chiefs declared that "nothing could be done . . . without a national council and by the majority of the nation." This was not the type of compliant and subordinate Cherokee annual meeting that George Washington had recommended in 1796.[23] Cherokee leaders at Willstown moved to establish a central governing Council, operating through an executive National Committee, to reach consensus and keep order among themselves, not out of a sudden desire to replicate the American republic's political institutions.

The new National Council, which generally favored economic advance along Anglo-American lines, encountered considerable opposition within the nation, especially from poorer Cherokees who struggled with subsistence and worried about the weakening of Indigenous cultural traditions. The Ridge (Kahnungdatlageh), a proponent of progress on the National Committee, found himself physically assaulted at a Cherokee assemblage of 1811 where many attendees hungered for spiritual deliverance, not the white man's "plan of civilization." The violence erupted when The Ridge openly criticized Charley (Tsali), a Cherokee prophet, for declaring that the people must shun the ways of whites to regain the Great Spirit's favor. Visionary Nativist talks circulated for months, admonishing Cherokee men and women to perform traditional healing rites, ceremonies, and dances. Such prophecies did not necessarily counsel war but suggested that supernatural power was necessary to restore life as it should be. The Cherokees would then regain Tugaloo, their sacred town lost to the white people decades before.[24]

The prophetic upsurge gathered strength when Tecumseh, the charismatic Shawnee leader, brought his talk to the Creek town of Tuckabatchee. Thirty Cherokees were in attendance when Tecumseh called on all Native peoples to unite and prepare for war against the United States. He foretold cataclysmic events—heavenly panthers (comets) ablaze in the night sky, the earth shaken with the stomping of his foot.

Conclusion

Tecumseh's prestige grew when Cherokees soon beheld a bright comet and later felt tremors from a great earthquake centered in Missouri, which rocked their western kin. Many Native women and men in the old Cherokee country believed the earth's destruction was near. Longings for redemption pulsed amid the burdens of daily life and the passage of time.[25]

The Muscogees and their allies occupied a large space in Cherokee consciousness for generations. It mattered greatly to the Cherokees when the Creeks erupted in internecine violence and civil war in 1813. Within a few months, the rebel or dissident party attracted 2,500 fighters. Called "Red Sticks" for their red-stained war clubs, they were inspired by prophecies and rites of uncompromising meaning. A defiled land must be destroyed before a purified Native world could emerge. The Red Sticks unloosed their fury on the Creek political elite, the great portion of whom had some white ancestry. But this was not a simple racial cleavage; several Red Stick leaders were themselves of "mixed" parentage. Personal choice regarding allegiance counted, too. The Red Sticks struck ruthlessly, murdering women, capturing or killing enslaved Blacks, casting plows and looms into rivers, and slaughtering thousands of cattle, hogs, and chickens. The tensions behind the violence had built up over years.[26]

Many Cherokee headmen saw the Red Stick convulsions as a threat to communal order and their own path to amity with the United States. They accordingly steered their people to involvement in the American war against the Red Sticks. General Andrew Jackson, head of U.S. regional forces, meanwhile attracted Cherokee recruits by offering pay and bestowing officers' commissions. In early 1814, The Ridge received the title of major—the head of all Cherokee volunteers. The men were proud to be warriors once more, bonding with one another and impressing American officers with their fervor.[27]

In the war's climactic campaign, more than five hundred Cherokee fighters collaborated with Jackson's army at the Battle of Horseshoe Bend on March 27, 1814, where Red Stick forces built a stout defensive barrier at the head of a great loop in the Tallapoosa River. General John Coffee, who witnessed his Native allies in action, was astonished when several Cherokee men intrepidly swam across the Tallapoosa to capture canoes by the banks of the Red Stick encampment. Cherokees brought the canoes to their side of the river and piled into them to recross and secure yet more canoes for their attack. Cherokee fighters contributed mightily to Jackson's bloody triumph. Interestingly, at

452   *Conclusion*

least a few Cherokees took an entirely different path by fighting along-side Tecumseh in Canada that same year. These men had lived for years among Shawnees and kept to a militant stance.[28]

Jackson took maximal advantage from the Red Stick defeat. In the Treaty of Fort Jackson of August 1814, he demanded a cession of Creek lands amounting to twenty-three million acres. The Creek conferees, nearly all of whom had supported the United States during the war, had no choice but to consent. Jackson interpreted the vaguely defined cession to include two million acres of Cherokee land, and this from the people that had just helped him win a war. The Cherokees' plight was compounded by white soldiers who plundered and raised havoc as they passed to and from Native homesteads and lands.[29]

Cherokee sacrifice for the United States brought little respite from the federal government's drive to push Native peoples to cede lands east of the Mississippi and to migrate west of the great river. The hunger for Native soil was nowhere greater than in Georgia, Tennessee, and the Alabama Territory established in 1817. Under these circumstances, it is not surprising that a growing number of Cherokees decided on relocating to Arkansas under federal guarantees. About three thousand were living there by 1820. The trans-Mississippi region seethed with turmoil. Arkansas Cherokees battled the Osage over hunting grounds and territory in a deadly cycle of feuding and fighting. Diplomacy followed apace. Cherokees aligned with other Native emigrants, notably Delawares and Shawnees, against the Osage. They meanwhile lobbied federal officials for a broad western domain in satisfaction for all they had yielded in their Native country. Like most "eastern" Cherokee leaders, western chiefs sought the good graces of the U.S. by declaring their interest in Christian missionary work and education. An evolution of lifeways was ongoing that had no simple or certain outcome.[30]

A Cherokee diaspora, born under trying conditions, spawned new identities and loyalties, undercutting but not erasing a sense of common peoplehood. In 1817, the U.S. government again played different parts of the nation against one another by pledging ample lands to Arkansas Cherokees and Indian emigrants who would cede Native soil. Cherokee leaders exercised forbearance and skill while negotiating with Andrew Jackson and two other federal commissioners at Hiwassee in talks from late June into July. Jackson obtained cessions totaling above 650,000 acres, but not all he wanted. Moreover, the anti-removal eastern Cherokee majority gained strength in the treaty's

Conclusion   453

wake, in no small part because of the widespread Native belief that too much had already been conceded. Without resorting to violence, the National Council gave notice that lines were drawn. Rules of allegiance, promulgated a few months earlier, were to be enforced. Individuals who chose to "remove themselves" beyond "the limits of the Cherokee Nation," and to Arkansas, would have no right to alienate the nation's "common property." If a man chose to leave the nation and his wife remained on the land, all "improvements and labors of our people by the mother's side shall be inviolate." Maternal blood was a bond of nationhood, preserving all that might possibly be saved.[31]

Cherokee women played a vital role in the anti-removal campaign. In early 1817, they were greatly disturbed by reports that a Cherokee man murdered his wife and three children at their home by the Hiwassee River. According to a white missionary, the episode occurred after the man resolved on emigrating to Arkansas, but his wife refused to go. When the national council met at Amohee by the Hiwassee, Cherokee women had already mobilized to make their voices heard. Petitioning the council, they summoned their duty as mothers to "our beloved children and headmen" who "we raise ... on the land which we now have and God gave us to inhabit." It would be "bad" for the people to leave for an "unknown country" across the Mississippi. For children to remove would amount to "destroying" their mothers. Cherokee men should not bargain for themselves with U.S. officials but instead keep their hand off "paper talks" since "our own country" was at stake. The elderly Nan-ye-hi was present at the council to tell the "Warriors" to "take pity and listen to the talks of your sisters ... I have [a] great many grand children ... [I] wish them to do well on our land."[32] These are her last recorded words before her death.

The great portion of Cherokees who set out to Arkansas were not traitors, but instead chose new paths to preserve traditions and better their lot in what initially appeared to be safer, less threatening environs. In the process, they developed communal interests apart from the great majority of Cherokees living in the homeland. In early 1818, a coterie of Arkansas Cherokee chiefs, joined by a few eastern allies, met at Knoxville with Joseph McMinn, Tennessee governor who strongly favored Indian out-migration from his state. Through McMinn, the deputies appealed to their "Father"—President James Monroe—asking that their group be recognized as a "separate, and distinct Tribe, or Family of his Red children, who are not to be under ... any arrangement or Law ... made by the Cherokees, who

Statue of Nancy Ward (Nan-ye-hi). *Photograph courtesy of Ray Smith.*

reside east of the Mississippi." The petitioners, whose interpreter put their words into English, had their eye on the immediate goal of income and sustenance. As leaders of a distinct "Tribe," the western chiefs claimed a good share of federal annuities due to the Cherokee nation. The U.S.-Cherokee treaty of 1819 allotted one-third of the annuity to the western group—a makeshift compromise that scarcely ended wrangling over the distribution of a critical resource.[33]

Talohnteskee, head warrior of the Arkansas Cherokees, did not regard the eastern Cherokees as entirely "separate" even while he tugged for maximal economic benefits for the western migrants. In a message of February 1818 to Governor William Clark of Missouri Territory, he hoped for peace with the Osage so that his eastern kin, "our people of the Old [Cherokee] Nation," would "Come over and Settle with us." By inference, the Cherokees were one people even if they had competing regional interests and widely disparate areas of residence. The Arkansas migrants were themselves of greatly varying means. By the mid-1820s, their ranks included many modestly productive farming and hunting households as well as an affluent slave-owning elite engaged in cotton production.[34]

U.S. authorities described Arkansas as a virtual paradise for westering Indians, but these words rang hollow as white settlers and speculators poured into the area. In 1825, John Jolly, a chief of the western Cherokees, complained ruefully to Arkansas territorial governor George Izard that "the government never cared for their Treatys with us after they got our land." No areas were truly safe for Indians if within the range of U.S. ambition.[35]

Long Warrior of Tenasee, the great Cherokee headman of the 1720s, could not possibly have grasped Cherokee society of the 1820s had he somehow supernaturally reappeared from the grave. He could have scarcely understood transformative social and economic changes let alone made sense of the rifts between "eastern" and far "western" Cherokees living well west of the Mississippi. In fact, many Cherokees of the early nineteenth century were perplexed at all they witnessed in a quite brief period—from the time that Scolacutta and Watts pledged peace (1794), to Sequoyah's invention of a syllabary of the Cherokee language (1821–1822), and the first publication of a newspaper, the *Cherokee Phoenix* (1828), printed in both Sequoyan symbols and English. Then there was the first written Cherokee constitution (1827), adopted by a special convention of delegates, and the promulgation of a governmental order in the name of "the people of the Cherokee Nation." George Lowrey (Agili), one of the constitution's framers, was a Protestant convert and a principal chief who helped to translate the New Testament into the Cherokee syllabary. Known for his keen wit, Lowrey was proud of his Native heritage. His personal ornamental wear featured nose and ear pendants, besides a medal bestowed by President James Monroe.[36]

As William McLoughlin explains in *Cherokee Renascence in the New Republic*, the constitution provoked considerable opposition from full-

Portrait of George Lowrey. Unknown artist, nineteenth century. *Gilcrease Museum, Tulsa, Oklahoma.*

blooded traditionalists who spoke little if any English and were uncomfortable with cultural change and political centralization over the previous twenty-five years. The National Council struck at the customary rule of clan revenge in 1810, ruling that any accidental death should not be avenged by any "clan or tribe" in the nation. Cherokee "lighthorse patrols," effectively a police force, were first established in the late 1790s and became more formalized over time, until superseded by marshals, sheriffs, and constables in 1825. In the interim, the traditional role of town councils diminished. What had once been decided by local communities increasingly came under the jurisdiction of institutional state authority. The idea of a formal order of men passing judgment over criminal offenses and enforcing their judgments by whippings or executions was entirely foreign to Cherokee tradition. Horse-stealing and theft became a matter for police action, as some Cherokees accumulated private property on an entirely new scale and desired protection for their holdings, including enslaved Blacks. The problem of crime itself reflected the loosening of the Cherokee ethic of self-control and communal harmony. The tendency of a beleaguered people to turn against itself was apparent in increasing witchcraft accusations—a problem that wracked Cherokees despite a national law of 1827 outlawing the murder of suspected witches. Then, too, Cherokee beliefs in witchcraft were a way of asserting tradition in the face of Protestant missionary proselytizing, and perhaps a backlash against the Native conjuror's declining status over time.[37]

In Cherokee society of the early 1800s, innovation and custom often appear as opposites locked in battle. In reality, these forces sometimes worked in synergy, rather than conflict. For example, Sequoyah became renowned in the 1820s for fashioning a stunningly innovative Cherokee syllabary even though he had a strong penchant for Native tradition and had no interest in becoming a Christian. Though friendly to some missionaries, he was strongly opposed to those who declined to have Cherokee children taught to read and write in their own language rather than English.[38]

Sequoyah had a quiet dignity and pride in his people. Known to whites as George Guess, he was born in Overhill country, probably at Tuskegee in the 1770s. Like many Indians of mixed ethnic ancestry, he was raised almost entirely by his Cherokee mother, and deeply loyal to her. His discipline and self-determination in full adulthood came after periods of despondency, self-doubt, and inebriation in youth. As a young man, he also showed talents in silver-working, engraving, and blacksmithing that served him well in life. Engraving was itself a type of signifying by emblems and marks that had spiritual content in Native culture.[39]

Sequoyah's syllabary, which he brought to light about 1820, is folkloric. Interestingly, he seems to have first taught the alphabet to his daughter Ahyokah, who astonished Sequoyah's kinsman George Lowrey by her ability to sound the symbols, which were inscribed on paper that spoke as a "talking leaf." In 1821, Sequoyah journeyed to Arkansas to see the land where he was considering moving with his family. His journeying back and forth across the Mississippi reflected social and cultural connections between Cherokees east and west. Within a quite brief time, Cherokees embraced the syllabary as a "mystery" with the power of "spiritual regeneration."[40]

Sequoyah's youth spanned the time from the Chickamauga upheaval to the peace of 1794 with the United States and well into an era of accelerated adaptation and change. While generally keeping distance from whites, that personal habit did not foreclose accommodation, especially if some benefit might be gained. Serving as a volunteer for the U.S. during the Red Stick War, he gained prestige but did not become a foremost leader. In 1816, he joined a group of fifteen Cherokees who were prevailed upon by General Jackson to cede a large portion of their nation's lands south of the Tennessee River within what is today's northern Alabama. The Cherokee compensation was a ten-year annuity besides a one-time $5,000 payout. The agreement, originally rejected by the national council, was confirmed at Jackson's insistence.[41]

Cherokee earnings from treaty-making and bribery hardly quieted U.S. demands. In 1819, Sequoyah and his wife Sally removed hurriedly from Upper Cherokee country to Willstown when their home fell to the United States under the cession treaty of 1819. Left behind were Sally's spinning wheel, Sequoyah's iron plow, and some of the family's livestock. Though uprooted, Sequoyah and family rebuilt in the vicinity of kin and friends. Five years later, he and Sally, with the couple's children, migrated to Arkansas. Stability was short-lived. In the spring of 1828, Sequoyah was part of a western Cherokee delegation that traveled to Washington ostensibly to negotiate secure boundaries but was persuaded by the federal government to enter a major treaty of quite another kind. What followed was an "exchange" of territory, with Cherokees being asked to give up all in Arkansas for compensation, which included a large lump sum and lands still further west, this time granted "in perpetuity," a phrase that U.S. officials had deliberately avoided in numerous treaties that swallowed Eastern Native homelands piece by piece.[42]

Sequoyah derived some personal benefit from the treaty. He was awarded $500 by the U.S. government and a saline to the west for land he lost in Arkansas. Ironically, the money was officially given in recognition of "the great benefits he has conferred upon the Cherokee people . . . from the use of the Alphabet discovered by him." Sequoyah's name is denoted "George Guess," in the treaty, but alongside that formal signature, written by a U.S. agent, is Sequoyah's Cherokee name penned by himself in his own characters. While Sequoyah's writing is clear, it is far more difficult to gauge his motives during the

Conclusion

459

treaty negotiation, in which far more well-to-do Cherokee leaders caved to government bribery and pressure. The land cession was denounced by many Arkansas Cherokees, but it went into effect within a year. Cherokees once again remade their lives and rekindled fires in unfamiliar soil, losing all they had toiled on for years.[43]

Cherokee negotiators labored strenuously for decades to uphold their people's rights. Two men of great importance in the diplomacy of 1810s were Charles Hicks, a well-to do man of mixed ancestry, and Pathkiller, a Cherokee traditionalist. In the next decade, two stalwarts were cousins Elias Boudinot and John Ridge, both of whom came of age in the 1820s. Boudinot, born Gallegina or "Buck," was the son of headman Oowatie and Susanna Reese, herself a woman of Cherokee-Anglo parentage. John Ridge was the child of chief Ridge and Susanna Wickett, a Cherokee woman with at least one white grandfather. The boys attended a Moravian mission school at Spring Place (Conasauga), in today's northern Georgia. The parents of both youths marked them for future leadership and considered English-language instruction essential toward that end.[44]

John Ridge and Gallegina successively went on to study in their teen years at Cornwall, Connecticut's Foreign Mission School, an institution specially dedicated to the education of Native boys. (It was on the journey to Connecticut that Gallegina adopted the name "Elias Boudinot," in honor of a well-known Philadelphia benefactor.) Both youths broke with convention by falling in love and marrying young New England women of Cornwall. The marriages raised an uproar among Connecticut townsfolk anxious about the girls' unions with Indians. The couples nonetheless went ahead. Sarah Northrop, spouse of John Ridge, and Harriet Gold who wed Boudinot, were courageous in their own right and strongly committed to their adopted nation.[45]

Boudinot was stung by the Northern whites' mockery of his marriage. Was he not a well-educated Christian, precisely the type of young man that devout New England Protestant "friends" said they wished an Indian to become? As David Brown, another Cherokee attendee of Cornwall, wrote, "if white men may marry among us without offence, how can it be thought wicked for us to marry among them." Interestingly, Boudinot probably faced some Cherokee criticism, as John Ridge certainly did, for marrying outside his people. Major Ridge told a missionary that his son John's marriage had displeased "the lower class" of Cherokees who were "prejudiced against the white

460   *Conclusion*

John Ridge. Copy after Charles Bird King, ca. 1838. *National Portrait Gallery, Smithsonian Institution; gift of Betty A. and Lloyd G. Schermer.*

people." The Ridge carried weight, and the Cherokee national council took notice. Following the Ridge-Northrop marriage, the council enacted a law that entitled children born to Cherokee men by "white women," resident in the nation, to all the rights "enjoyed by the citizens descending from the Cherokee race, by the mother's side." No written law, however, could erase the traditional belief in a mother's blood as *the* life source.[46]

For all the ridicule of the marriages in the American press, the Cherokee cause for holding onto Native soil became popular among middling and upper-class citizens of the Northeastern states and even in some southeastern locales, though certainly not in Georgia. No other Native people drew such widespread sympathy among the U.S. public—a fact that speaks to stereotypical perceptions of the Cherokees as "civilized" and meriting special treatment unlike most other Indians. John Ridge himself excelled as a diplomat and writer. Boudinot was an accomplished public speaker who earned plaudits from Boston to Charleston. A fervent Christian who shunned "superstition," he adeptly employed the language of moral improvement while addressing American Protestants. If no traditionalist, Boudinot had a deep national pride. As editor of the *Cherokee Phoenix*, he took great pleasure in putting Sequoyah's symbols to use in the newspaper with articles in both English and Cherokee.[47]

John Ridge's thought ranged widely. In an essay of 1828, for example, he raised a striking question as posed by the eminent eighteenth-century jurist Emmerich de Vattel: "It is asked if a nation may lawfully take possession of part of a vast country, in which there are none found but erratic nations, incapable by the smallness of their numbers to people the whole?" While John Ridge did not dispute Vattel's contention that colonial possession could be lawful in such a case, he emphasized that the Cherokees were not "an erratic" Indian nation. And even "wandering" Indians, he remarked, had a right to "*their share*" of the land. This argument would have not occurred to Ostenaco or Attakullakulla, but they would have surely agreed with John Ridge's goal of preserving the Cherokee people.[48]

While eastern Cherokees had thus far resisted making any additional land cession to the United States since 1819, Georgia believed it had the power, and even the legal foundation, to take full sovereignty over Cherokee lands in its bounds as defined by the United States. A key point came in 1802 when the Jefferson administration finally induced Georgia to cede its far western territorial claims, extending to the Mississippi, to the Union. In return for the cession, the United States pledged "to extinguish the Indian title" to all lands within Georgia at the federal government's expense. Indian title to lands were to be acquired "as early as the same can be peaceably obtained, on reasonable terms." This agreement was the legalistic engine that Georgia used to justify its outright seizure of Cherokee lands when Jackson became president. The fact that gold was supposedly aplenty in the coveted Indian country accelerated the expansionist drive into a violent rush—a fury that trampled on John Marshall's decision of 1832 in *Worcester v. Georgia*.[49]

The forced removal of the Cherokees in 1838–1839 was imposed by Jackson's Treaty of New Echota of 1835, which the great majority of the Cherokee Nation adamantly opposed and protested. In a radical political turnabout, Major Ridge, John Ridge, and Elias Boudinot

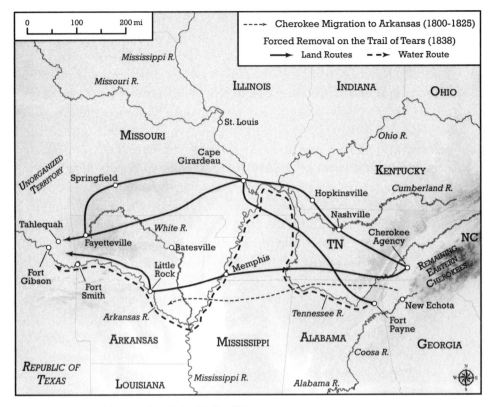

Migration, Forced Removal, and the Trail of Tears

shifted ground to support the treaty and signed it as the sole way they believed their people could secure their own western territory and be saved from destruction. Georgia's white citizens, with the active support of their state government, literally invaded Cherokee country in the early 1830s, forced Native residents from their homes, and took charge at gunpoint. What room for diplomacy remained? Perhaps it made sense to negotiate for the optimal portion of western land and the largest funds possible rather than to lose everything. Boudinot decided on this course with a passionate belief that the Cherokees would experience a Christian revival in the west. It is doubtful that Major Ridge shared that viewpoint. He is said to have remarked that marking the treaty was his "death warrant." The prediction came true when anti-treaty men, furious at what they saw as betrayal, killed Major Ridge, John Ridge, and Boudinot in "Indian Territory" (later Oklahoma), on June 22, 1839. It is of little use to think of right and wrong relative to the assassinations. By Cherokee law, individuals who signed away the

Conclusion

homeland against the national council's will were liable to punishment by death.[50]

The main story lies beyond a grim episode. The cruelty of forced removal beset the Cherokees who, by the terms of an imposed treaty, were stripped of all their lands east of the Mississippi—their heartland in Georgia and Alabama and what remained in Tennessee and North Carolina. Many other Native peoples were uprooted by the same U.S. government policy during the years 1820–1850, followed by more outrages and swindles west of the Mississippi in subsequent decades. This policy was a matter not simply of government action but of the white citizenry's demands, advanced by private financial interests and land development barons.[51] The Cherokee expulsion, which occurred under the presidency of Martin Van Buren, began in 1837 when pro-treaty Cherokees trekked westward. By May 1838, the U.S. government was resorting to harsher measures. General Winfield Scott's 3,500 soldiers rounded up Cherokees at gunpoint, often dragging entire families from homes, which were commonly plundered. Troops confined Indians in government encampments as holding places before expulsion. Hundreds died from exposure and disease in the camps. The trek, in which the dispossessed moved out in stages, became a prolonged agony of privation and death. Government mismanagement was appalling, so much so that John Ross and his council had to assume responsibility for overseeing the forced migration. Well-to-do Cherokee slaveholders, who had the help of Blacks, tended to fare better on the journey, and endure less hardship at its end, than the mass of poorer Indians. When exiles set out in the fall of 1838, they soon faced winter's blast while suffering the hardship of traveling 1,000 miles by riverboat and overland marches. Many refugees were scantily clad and without adequate food and drink. The duration was five to six months for those who survived. Of the 13,000 Cherokees who were expelled, 4,000 died, and many of the survivors struggled with starvation conditions on arrival.[52] It was a Trail of Tears (*Nunna-da-ul-tsun-yi*—"The Place Where They Cried") for a people exiled from their beloved and sacred land. Like the great majority of Native peoples, the Cherokees posed no threat to white Americans when they were uprooted. They had not been at war with the United States since 1794 and were allied with Jackson during the Red Stick War. The Cherokees had kept true to the peace that Scolacutta and Watts pledged.

Cherokee migrations, forced and unforced, were numerous in the era of the Trail of Tears. Cherokees of Texas, moving south from Arkansas during the early 1820s, experienced travails and peaceful times until a deadly reckoning. In 1839, the Republic of Texas sent troops to expel Cherokees on the dubious grounds that the group was conspiring with Mexico. After Chief Duwali refused Texas's ultimatum of compensated removal, the Cherokees gave battle along with allied Delawares, Kickapoos, and Shawnees. The Indian men were defeated and Duwali shot dead. He was eighty-three years old. The Cherokees and allies moved to safety, with most heading north of the Red River, while others remained in Texas.[53]

We should remember the 1,400 Cherokees who escaped the Trail of Tears by hiding in the Appalachian hills and insisting on their rights under North Carolina's state government, which favored removal but finally did not demand the expulsion of a small and largely poor Native population. Junaskala, a regional chief who had fought at Horseshoe Bend, remarked that he would have killed Jackson had he known what would happen to his people. Most important, The Eastern Band of Cherokee Indians have preserved a place in its homeland to this day.[54]

The tortuous history of the Cherokee Nation in Indian Territory of the 1800s is a subject unto itself, connected with a people that endured through multiple ordeals. Successive migrations and forced removals entailed enormous hardship and aggravated fissures in many Native American societies. On the political level, Cherokees were divided into mutually suspicious and often hostile camps well into the 1840s. There was considerable bitterness between kin groups that approved Jackson's treaty and those who had stood against it. Emigrants to Arkansas during the early 1800s, the self-described "Old Settlers," had distinct interests from those who came west by the Trail of Tears. Internal feuds and violence wracked Cherokees in the new Indian territory. The social divide between a slaveholding Cherokee elite and materially poorer individuals persisted over many years, as did strains between individuals modeling their conduct on Anglo-American standards as compared to more traditionally inclined families. Blacks in Cherokee society experienced their own struggle for dignity, freedom, and communal recognition over decades. Cherokee engagement in the American Civil War was itself disastrous, sundering the Nation into warring pro-Confederate and pro-Union camps little more than twenty years after the Trail of Tears.[55] In all these ways, Cherokee and Native American histories are interconnected with the broad American past.

The Trail of Tears was not a short-lived agony. Many Cherokees struggled in the new Indian territory with its arid climate and less than

Conclusion 465

fertile soils. On the spiritual level, the dispossessed encountered inward travail, the difficulty of finding connectedness and meaning in their new environs. John Silk, a Cherokee man, recounted what he had learned of his people's traditions in Oklahoma of the 1930s. He told of how a group of wise men who crossed into the new Indian land nearly a century before had laid down a deerskin on a hilltop, placed tobacco on the skin, and smoked peace pipes shortly after their arrival. They then called on God and prayed for guidance concerning the sick, impoverished, and orphaned in their village. After thunder and wind gusts, came silence. The men heard a sky voice telling them to look to the grass, trees, and plants about them to find the medicine they needed.[56]

To the present day, the great gifts of the Cherokees and many other Native American groups derive from ideals of communal harmony, spiritual connectedness to nature, and the capacity to negotiate differences among themselves. Wilma Mankiller, who became the first female principal chief of the Cherokee Nation in 1985, wrote of her people's "extraordinary ability to face down adversity and continue moving forward." There is diversity and cultural hybridity in today's Cherokee communities, in Oklahoma, the Appalachians, and many other locales. What is truly Native as compared to "white" is a common subject of debate. Cherokee identity is often a matter of personal choice, founded in cultural outlook and historical memory and not simply by blood lineage or fluency in Native language. Attachment to people and place may be both a physical and emotional reality. It may also be brought to mind and felt at a distance from places of ancestral origin. The Cherokee Keetowah Society, born before the Civil War and taking various forms since then, recalls ancient Kituwah, mother town of the Great Smokies. The ideal of *gadugi*—working for the common good and social harmony—is deeply embedded in the Cherokee past and the Cherokee present.[57]

Abbreviations

Notes

Acknowledgments

Index

Abbreviations

AC		Colonial Louisiana Records Collection, Collection 329, Acadiana Manuscripts Collection, University Libraries, University of Louisiana Lafayette, https://library.louisiana.edu/sites/library/files/Colonial_Louisiana_Records_COLL329.pdf
	13A	Series II: French Colonial Records, F: Archives des Colonies, Serie C 13a, Inventaire et Volumes 1–54, reels 473–536
AHN		Archivo Histórico Nacional, Estado, legajo 3898
ASPIA		*American State Papers, 1789–1838*, II. *Indian Affairs*, Library of Congress, http://memory.loc.gov/ammem/amlaw/lwsplink.html
ASPPL		*American State Papers, 1789–1838*, VII. *Public Lands*, Library of Congress, http://memory.loc.gov/ammem/amlaw/lwsplink.html
BIA		Bureau of Indian Affairs, RG 75, National Archives and Records Administration
CO		Records of the Colonial Office, National Archives, Kew, Great Britain
	CO 5	Board of Trade and Secretaries of State: America and West Indies, Original Correspondence, 1606–1822
	CO 5 / 4, 14–84, 94	Secretary of State. Despatches; Military Despatches; Indian Affairs

	CO 5 / 225, 229, 230, 283, 306, 310, 318	Correspondence, Original. Secretary of State
	CO 5 / 358–403	Carolina, South. Correspondence, Original. Board of Trade; Secretary of State; Entry books
	CO 5 / 412, 425–491	Carolina, South. Acts and Sessional Papers. Assembly; Council
	CO 5 / 640, 656, 695, 697	Georgia. Sessional Papers. Council, Assembly, 1759–1761
	CO 5 / 1063, 1094	New York. Correspondence, 1749–1751
	CO 5 / 1258, 1264, 1265, 1289	Correspondence, Original. Board of Trade
	CO 5 / 1330–1368	Virginia. Correspondence. Secretary of State; Board of Trade; Commissions, Instructions
	CO 5 / 1429, 1436	Virginia. Sessional Papers. Council, Assembly
CRG		*The Colonial Records of the State of Georgia*, ed. Allen D. Candler et al., 26 vols. (Atlanta: Franklin Printing Co., 1904–1916)
CSP		*Calendar of State Papers, Colonial: North America and the West Indies 1574–1739*
	vol. 31	*January 1719–February 1720*, ed. Cecil Headlam (London: Her Majesty's Stationery Office, 1933), https://www.british-history.ac.uk/cal-state-papers/colonial/america-west-indies/vol31
	vol. 41	*January 1734–June 1735*, ed. A. P. Newton (London: Her Majesty's Stationery Office, 1953), https://www.british-history.ac.uk/cal-state-papers/colonial/america-west-indies/vol41
CSRNC		*Colonial and State Records of North Carolina*, 1662–1790, 26 vols., Documenting the American South, Digital Collection, University of North Carolina, https://docsouth.unc.edu/csr/index.php/volumes

CVSP		*Calendar of Virginia State Papers*, ed. William P. Palmer, 11 vols. (Richmond: Virginia State Library, 1875–1893)
DCAR		David Center for the American Revolution, Sol Feinstone Collection of the American Revolution, Mss.B.F327, American Philosophical Society Library, Philadelphia
	Amherst Papers	War Office, Great Britain, Sir Jeffrey Amherst Papers, WO 34/47, WO 34/39
	Cornwallis Papers	Public Records Office, Great Britain, Charles Cornwallis Papers, PRO 30/11
	Forbes Papers	General John Forbes Papers, microfilm 434
	Grant Papers	James Grant Papers
	Haldimand Papers	Sir Frederick Haldimand Papers, Add. MSS. 21672
	SPG Papers	Society for the Propagation of the Gospel Papers
DRCHNY		*Documents Relative to the Colonial History of the State of New York*, ed. E. B. O'Callaghan and Berthold Fernow, 15 vols. (Albany: Weed, Parsons, and Co., 1853–1887)
DRIA		*Documents Relating to Indian Affairs*, ed. William L. McDowell, Jr., 2 vols. (Columbia: South Carolina Archives Department, 1958; South Carolina Department of Archives and History, 1970)
EAID		*Early American Indian Documents, Treaties and Laws, 1607–1789*, ed. Alden T. Vaughan, gen. ed., 20 vols. (Washington, DC: University Publications of America, 1979–2004)
EJCV		*Executive Journals of the Council of the Colony of Virginia*, ed. R. McIlwaine et al., 6 vols. (Richmond: Virginia State Library, 1926–1966)
FHS		Filson Historical Society, Louisville, KY
	Campbell Papers	Arthur Campbell Papers, MSS A C187
	Military Papers	

Abbreviations 471

FO		Foreign Office, National Archives, Kew, Great Britain
GW: Colonial		*Papers of George Washington*, Colonial Series, ed. W. W. Abbot and Dorothy Twohig, 10 vols. (Charlottesville: University of Virginia Press, 1983–1995)
GW: Confederation		*Papers of George Washington*, Confederation Series, ed. W. W. Abbot, 6 vols. (Charlottesville: University of Virginia Press, 1992–1997)
GW: Presidential		*Papers of George Washington*, Presidential Series, ed. Dorothy Twohig and others, 21 vols. (Charlottesville: University of Virginia Press, 1987–2020)
GWLC		George Washington Papers, Manuscript Division, Library of Congress
JBT		*Journals of the Board of Trade and Plantations*, 14 vols. (London: His Majesty's Stationery Office, 1920–1938)
	vol. 4	*Journals of the Board of Trade and Plantations*, vol. 4, *November 1718–December 1722* (London: His Majesty's Stationery Office, 1928), https://www.british-history.ac.uk/jrnl-trade-plantations/vol4
	vol. 6	*Journals of the Board of Trade and Plantations*, vol. 6, *January 1729–December 1734* (London: His Majesty's Stationery Office, 1928), https://www.british-history.ac.uk/jrnl-trade-plantations/vol6
	vol. 8	*Journals of the Board of Trade and Plantations*, vol. 8, *January 1742–December 1749* (London: His Majesty's Stationery Office, 1931), https://www.british-history.ac.uk/jrnl-trade-plantations/vol8
	vol. 9	*Journals of the Board of Trade and Plantations*, vol. 9, *January 1750–December 1753* (London: His Majesty's Stationery Office, 1932), https://www.british-history.ac.uk/jrnl-trade-plantations/vol9.

JCHA		*Journals of the Commons House of Assembly of South Carolina* (Columbia: Historical Commission of South Carolina, 1907–). Citations of JCHA are also found in the series CO 5, as indicated in the notes.
	JCHA 1750–1751	*The Colonial Records of South Carolina: The Journal of the Commons House of Assembly, April 23, 1750–August 31, 1751*, ed. R. Nicholas Olsberg (1974)
JCIT		*Journals of the Commissioners of the Indian Trade: September 20, 1710–August 29, 1718*, ed. W. L. McDowell (Columbia: South Carolina Archives Department, 1955)
JCSC		Journal of the Council and Upper House of Assembly of South Carolina, CO 5 /: 425–491
LVA		The Library of Virginia, Richmond, VA
	Randolph Papers	Virginia, Governor's Office, Edmund Randolph Executive Papers, 1786–1788, accession 40084, State Records Collection
MPAFD		*Mississippi Provincial Archives: French Dominion*, ed. and trans. Dunbar Rowland, Albert G. Sanders, and Patricia Galloway, 5 vols. (Jackson: Mississippi Department of History and Archives, 1927–1932; Baton Rouge: Louisiana State University Press, 1984)
NARA		National Archives and Records Administration. *See* BIA; PCC; RCIAT
PA		*Pennsylvania Archives* [First Series], ed. Samuel Hazard, 12 vols. (Philadelphia, 1852–1856)
PCC		Papers of the Continental Congress, microfilm M247, Record Group 360, National Archives and Records Administration
PCP		*Minutes of the Provincial Council of Pennsylvania, 1683–1775*, ed. Samuel Hazard, 16 vols. (Philadelphia and Harrisburg, 1850–1853)
PPC		Papeles procedentes de la isla de Cuba in the Archivo General de Indias, 1765–1821, Seville, MSS 61928, Library of Congress

Abbreviations

	legajo 197	Correspondencia Nacional y Estrangera entre los Gobernadores de Florida y varias Autoridades Estrangeras
RCIAT		Records of the Cherokee Indian Agency in Tennessee, 1801–1835, NAID 233580374, RG 64: Records the NARA (National Archives and Records Administration), https://catalog.archives.gov/id/233580374
RVA		*Revolutionary Virginia: The Road to Independence*, compiled by William J. van Schreeven, ed. Robert L. Scribner, 7 vols. (Charlottesville: University Press of Virginia, 1973–1983)
SHC		Southern Historical Collection, Wilson Library Special Collections, University of North Carolina, Chapel Hill
	Steele Papers	John Steele Papers, coll. 00689
SSC		*The Statutes at Large of South Carolina*, ed. Thomas Cooper and David J. McCord, 10 vols. (Charleston: A. S. Johnston, 1836–1841)
THNOC		The Historical New Orleans Collection, Documentos de la Louisiana, 1724–1801, Biblioteca Nacional, Madrid
	Fondo Floridas	Archivo Nacional de Cuba, Fondo Floridas
TJ		*The Papers of Thomas Jefferson*, ed. Julian P. Boyd et al., 48 vols. to date (Princeton: Princeton University Press, 1950–2025)
TP		*The Territorial Papers of the United States*, ed. Clarence Edwin Carter and John Porter Bloom, 28 vols. (Washington, DC: Government Printing Office, 1934–1975)
TSLA		Tennessee State Library and Archives, Nashville
	Sevier Papers	John Sevier Papers, 1752–1947
UGA		Hargrett Rare Book and Manuscript Library, University of Georgia Libraries; Digital Library of Georgia
	Cuyler Collection	Telamon Cuyler Collection, ms 1170

	SNAD	Southeastern Native American Documents, 1730–1842
VUSC		Vanderbilt University, Special Collections
	Robertson Papers	James Robertson Papers, MSS.0366, https://www.jstor.org/site/vanderbilt /manuscripts/jamesrobertsonpapers -29775068/
WCL		William L. Clements Library, University of Michigan
	Amherst Papers	Jeffrey Amherst Papers
	Gage Papers	Thomas Gage Papers
	Lyttelton Papers	William Henry Lyttelton Papers
WHC		*Collections of the State Historical Society Wisconsin*, ed. Lyman C. Draper and Reuben G. Thwaites, 21 vols. (Madison: State Historical Society of Wisconsin, 1855–1915)
WHS		Wisconsin Historical Society, Madison, WI
	Draper Mss.	Lyman Copeland Draper Manuscripts Collection
WJ		*The Papers of Sir William Johnson*, ed. James Sullivan et al., 14 vols. (University of the State of New York, 1921–1965)

Abbreviations

Notes

Introduction

1. A Copy of Conocotocko's [Kanagatucko's] Letter, September 1761, in Stephen to James Grant, 5 October 1761, Grant Papers, DCAR. For metaphorical speech among Indians of eastern North America, see James H. Merrell, *The Indians' New World: The Catawbas and Their Neighbors from European Contact through the Era of Removal* (New York: Norton, 1989), 148.

2. Kanagatucko's Letter, September 1761.

3. Kanagatucko's Letter, September 1761.

4. In this case, Attakullakulla ("Little Carpenter" by English name), spoke for himself and other Cherokee leaders who were not present. See "The Talk from the Little Carpenter . . ." to Ensign Lachlan Macintosh (and to be conveyed to Colonel James Grant), 12 March 1761, Grant Papers, DCAR.

5. James Adair, *The History the American Indians*, ed. Kathryn E. Holland Braund (1775; Tuscaloosa: University of Alabama Press, 2003), 65.

6. "The Talk from the Little Carpenter . . . ," 12 March 1761. For a perspective on the meaning of "white" and "red" in diplomatic contexts, see Nancy Shoemaker, *A Strange Likeness: Becoming Red and White in Eighteenth-Century North America* (New York: Oxford, 2004), 129–140; Nancy Shoemaker, "How the Indians Got to Be Red," *American Historical Review* 102 (June 1997): 625–644. For "red" as unifying symbol among Native peoples, see Gregory Evans Dowd, *A Spirited Resistance: The North American Indian Struggle for Unity, 1745–1815* (Baltimore: Johns Hopkins University Press, 1992), 44–47; Robert M. Owens, *Red Dreams, White Nightmares: Pan-Indian Alliances in the Anglo-American Mind, 1763–1815* (Norman: University of Oklahoma Press, 2015).

7. For geography, see Donald Edward Davis, *Where There Are Mountains: An Environmental History of the Southern Appalachians* (Athens: University of Georgia Press, 2000), 59–69; Tom Hatley, *The Dividing Paths: Cherokees and South Carolinians through the Revolutionary Era* (New York: Oxford University Press, 1995), 3–8, 13–14; John R. Finger, *Tennessee's Frontiers: Three Regions in Transition* (Bloomington: Indian University Press, 2001), 1–6, 19–21.

8. On white as a mythic color of peace, see James Mooney, *Myths of the Cherokee* (1900; reprint, New York: Dover, 1995), 397. On "white" and "red," see Charles Hudson, *The Southeastern Indians* (Knoxville: University of Tennessee Press, 1976), 235, 238–239. For "black" as the color of death, see Steven Peach, *Rivers of Power: Creek Political Culture in the Native South, 1750–1815* (Norman: University of Oklahoma Press, 2024), 46–49. Susan Power, *Art of the Cherokee: Prehistory to the Present* (Athens: University of Georgia Press, 2007), 60–61, 95–96. On "the language of beads," see James H. Merrell, *Into the American Woods: Negotiations on the Pennsylvania Frontier* (New York: Norton, 1999), 187–190. For the Creek beads to the Cherokees and Chickasaws, see Talk of Chigelly, 24 September 1726, in Tobias Fitch to Arthur Middleton of that same date, JCSC, CO 5/429/Pt. 1/002.

9. Creek towns were not only deemed "white" or "red," but had these dual elements within their social matrix. See Steven C. Hahn, *The Invention of the Creek Nation, 1670–1763* (Lincoln: University of Nebraska Press, 2004), 21–22; Robbie Ethridge, *Creek Country: The Creek Indians and Their World* (Chapel Hill: University of North Carolina Press, 2003), 92–94.

10. Gregory D. Smithers, "'Our Hands and Hearts Are Joined Together': Friendship, Colonialism, and the Cherokee People in Early America," *Journal of Social History* 50 (Summer 2017): 609–621, 610–611.

11. On the "performative" in Native diplomacy and intercultural encounters, see Joshua David Bellin and Laura L. Mielke, eds., *Native Acts: Indian Performance, 1603–1832* (Lincoln: University of Nebraska Press, 2011). On gifting and women's diplomatic role, see Colin G. Calloway, *Pen and Ink Witchcraft: Treaties and Treaty-Making in American Indian History* (New York: Oxford University Press, 2013), 18–35.

12. Richard White, *The Middle Ground: Indians, Empires, and Republics in the Great Lakes Region, 1650–1815* (Cambridge: Cambridge University Press, 1991), x, 52–53.

13. Edward Countryman, *Americans: A Collision of Histories* (New York: Hill and Wang, 1996), 35.

14. Christopher B. Rodning, *Center Places and Cherokee Towns: Archaeological Perspectives on Native American Architecture and Landscape in the Southern Appalachians* (Tuscaloosa: University of Alabama Press, 2015), 1–6, 32–39, 43–49, 148–151, 172–175; Alan Gallay, *The Indian Slave Trade: The Rise of the English Empire in the American South, 1670–1717* (New Haven: Yale University Press, 2002), 203–206. For broad perspectives on Native North America, see Daniel K. Richter, *Before the Revolution: America's Ancient Pasts* (Cambridge, MA: Harvard University Press, 2011); Neal Salisbury, "The Indians' Old World: Native Americans and the Coming of Europeans," *William and Mary Quarterly* 53 (July 1996): 435–458; Pekka Hämäläinen, *Indigenous Continent: The Epic Contest for North America* (New York: Liveright, 2022); Colin G. Calloway, *New Worlds for All: Indians, Europeans, and the Remaking of America*, 2nd ed. (Baltimore: Johns Hopkins University Press, 2013).

15. For an insightful recent interpretation, emphasizing the "Overhill" Cherokees, see Kristofer Ray, *Cherokee Power: Imperial and Indigenous Geopolitics in the Trans-Appalachian West* (Norman: University of Oklahoma Press, 2023). An essential work is Tyler Boulware, *Deconstructing the Cherokee Nation: Town, Region, and Nation among Eighteenth-Century Cherokees* (Gainesville: University Press of Florida, 2011), 11–24.

16. Daniel K. Richter, *Facing East from Indian Country: A Native History of Early America* (Cambridge, MA: Harvard University Press, 2001), 155. Native diplomacy, which excelled in playing-off colonial powers against one another, is emphasized in the pathbreaking work of Gary B. Nash, *Red, White, and Black: The Peoples of Early North America*, 7th ed. (1974; New York: Pearson, 2015).

17. Ellen Cushman, "'We're Taking the Genius of Sequoyah into this Century': The Cherokee Syllabary, Peoplehood, and Perseverance," *Wicazo Sa Review* 26 (Spring 2011): 67–83. For critical eras in Cherokee history, see Hatley, *Dividing Paths;* William G. McLoughlin, *Cherokee Renascence in the New Republic* (Princeton: Princeton University Press, 1986); Daniel J. Tortora, *Carolina in Crisis: Cherokees, Colonists, and Slaves in the American Southeast, 1756–1763* (Chapel Hill: University of North Carolina Press, 2015); Theda Perdue and Michael D. Green, *The Cherokee Nation and the Trail of Tears* (New York: Penguin, 2007).

18. On peace and honorary chiefdom, see Bryan C. Rindfleisch, *Brothers of Coweta: Kinship, Empire, and Revolution in the Eighteenth-Century Muscogee World* (Columbia: University of South Carolina Press, 2021), 48–58; Peach, *Rivers of Power,* 54–58. On condolence ceremony, see Daniel K. Richter, *The Ordeal of the Longhouse: The Peoples of the Iroquois League in the Era of European Colonization* (Chapel Hill: University of North Carolina Press), 40–42.

19. On one occasion, Cherokees referred to Washington as a "Greate [*sic*] & Beloved Brother." See Colin G. Calloway, *The Indian World of George Washington: The First President, the First Americans, and the Birth of the Nation* (New York: Oxford, 2018), 338. The appellation "father" or "great father" was more common in Cherokee references to Washington. See the Conclusion to this book.

20. For French-Native diplomacy, see White, *The Middle Ground;* Kathleen DuVal, "Interconnectedness and Diversity in 'French Louisiana,'" in *Powhatan's Mantle: Indians in the Colonial Southeast,* ed. Gregory A. Waselkov, Peter H. Wood, and Tom Hatley, rev. ed. (Lincoln: University of Nebraska Press, 2006), 133–162; Patricia Galloway, "'The Chief Who Is Your Father': Choctaw and French Views of the Diplomatic Relation," in Waselkov et al., *Powhatan's Mantle,* 345–370. On political processes, see Robert Berkhofer Jr., "The Political Context of a New Indian History," *Pacific Historical Review* 40, no. 3 (1971): 357–382.

21. For Ani-Yunwiya, see Mooney, *Myths of the Cherokee,* 510. For the Shawnees, see Sami Lakomäki, *Gathering Together: The Shawnee People through Diaspora and Nationhood, 1600–1870* (New Haven: Yale University Press, 2014), 230–231.

22. My definition of peoplehood draws on scholars Tom Holm, J. Diane Pearson, and Ben Chavis, who posit a "Peoplehood Matrix" composed of four closely integrated forces: "language, sacred history, religion, and land," or "place" and "territory." See Holm, Pearson, and Chavis, "Peoplehood: A Model for the Extension of Sovereignty in American Indian Studies," *Wicazo Sa Review* 18 (Spring 2003): 12–13. For a provocative study on the roots of modern nationalism, see Benedict Anderson, *Imagined Communities,* rev. ed. (London: Verso, 2006), 3–7.

23. On the custom of vengeance, see Theda Perdue, *Cherokee Women: Gender and Cultural Change, 1700–1835* (Lincoln: University of Nebraska Press, 1998), 52–53 ("crying blood," 52); Circe Sturm, *Blood Politics: Race, Culture, and Identity in the Cherokee Nation of Oklahoma* (Berkeley: University of California Press, 2002), 32–33, 40;

Notes to Pages 6–10   479

John Phillip Reid, *A Law of Blood: The Primitive Law of the Cherokee Nation* (New York: New York University Press, 1970), 75–80, 94–101.

24. The story was told by Selukuki Wohhellengh (Turtle-at-Home), Attakullakulla's son, to John Norton, a British officer of Cherokee-Scottish ancestry and an adopted Mohawk chief. See *The Journal of Major John Norton, 1816*, ed. Carl F. Klinck and James J. Talman, reissued with notes by Carl Benn (Toronto: Champlain Society, 2011), 40–41. For adopted captives as intermediaries, see Christina Snyder, *Slavery in Indian Country: The Changing Face of Captivity in Early America* (Cambridge, MA: Harvard University Press, 2010), 109–113.

25. Speech of the Cherokee "War-woman of Chota" (Nan-ye-hi), 23 November 1785, in *Early American Indian Documents: Laws and Treaties*, gen. ed. Alden T. Vaughan, vol. 18, *Revolution and Confederation*, ed. Colin G. Calloway (Frederick, MD: University Publications of America, 1994), 395.

26. There is a considerable literature on Nan-ye-hi. See Perdue, *Cherokee Women*, 54, 61–62, 100–101; Cynthia Cumfer, *Separate People, One Land: The Minds of Cherokees, Blacks, and Whites on the Tennessee Frontier* (Chapel Hill: University of North Carolina Press, 2007), 27–30, 38–39.

27. Gregory D. Smithers, *The Cherokee Diaspora: An Indigenous History of Migration, Resettlement, and Identity* (New Haven: Yale University Press, 2015), 251–260.

1. Cherokee Culture and Lifeways

1. *Tsalagi* is the proper name in Middle and Western Cherokee dialects; *Tsaragi* is the equivalent for the old Eastern or Lower dialect, which is no longer spoken. See James Mooney, *Myths of the Cherokee* (1900; reprint, New York: Dover, 1995), 15–16, 185; Russell Thornton, *The Cherokees: A Population History* (Lincoln: University of Nebraska Press, 1990), 7–8. On linguistic variations, see Tyler Boulware, *Deconstructing the Cherokee Nation: Town, Region, and Nation among Eighteenth-Century Cherokees* (Gainesville: University Press of Florida, 2011), 22–23.

2. Woodward to the Earl of Shaftesbury, 31 December 1674, in "The Shaftesbury Papers," *Collections of the South Carolina Historical Society*, vol. 5 (1897), 460. British interpreters referred to the Cherokee town of "Terrequo," also spelled "Telliquo" and commonly "Tellico." See "Colonel Chicken's Journal to the Cherokees, 1725," in *Travels in the American Colonies*, ed. Newton D. Mereness (New York: Macmillan, 1916), 111–112, 115–117, 121, 127, 134–135.

3. Theda Perdue, *Cherokee Women: Gender and Cultural Change, 1700–1835* (Lincoln: University of Nebraska Press, 1998), 13–19, 23, 29–38; Tom Hatley, "Cherokee Women Farmers Hold Their Ground," in *Powhatan's Mantle: Indians in the Colonial Southeast*, ed. Gregory A. Waselkov, Peter H. Wood, and Tom Hatley, rev. ed. (Lincoln: University of Nebraska Press, 2006), 309.

4. Donald Edward Davis, *Where There Are Mountains: An Environmental History of the Southern Appalachians* (Athens: University of Georgia Press, 2000), 12–13, 59–60; Boulware, *Deconstructing the Cherokee Nation*, 18. For geologic-geographic description, see also John R. Finger, *Tennessee's Frontiers: Three Regions in Transition* (Bloomington: Indiana University Press, 2001), 1–4; James Valentine (text by Chris Bolgiano),

480   *Notes to Pages 10–16*

Southern Appalachian Celebration: In Praise of Ancient Mountains, Old Growth Forests, and Wilderness (Chapel Hill: University of North Carolina Press, 2011).

5. John Nolt and Keith Bustos, "The Old River," in Nolt, *Imperiled: The Declining Health of the Southern Appalachian Bioregion* (Knoxville: University of Tennessee Press, 2005), 77.

6. Boulware, *Deconstructing the Cherokee Nation*, 18–19; Mooney, *Myths of the Cherokee*, 16–17.

7. John D. Loftin and Benjamin E. Frey, *People of Kituwah: The Old Ways of the Eastern Cherokees* (Oakland: University of California Press, 2024); Mooney, *Myths of the Cherokee*, 182 ("Ani-Kituhwagi"), 186, 525; Boulware, *Deconstructing the Cherokee Nation*, 23–26 ("beloved" and "ancient"); Christopher B. Rodning, *Center Places and Cherokee Towns: Archaeological Perspectives on Native American Architecture and Landscape in the Southern Appalachians* (Tuscaloosa: University of Alabama Press, 2015), 2–3, 58–59, 148–149.

8. Neal Salisbury, "The Indians' Old World: Native Americans and the Coming of Europeans," *William and Mary Quarterly* 53 (July 1996): 435–468.

9. Tom Hatley, *The Dividing Paths: Cherokees and South Carolinians through the Revolutionary Era* (New York: Oxford University Press, 1995), 13–16. For Cherokee political orientations, see David H. Corkran, *The Cherokee Frontier: Conflict and Survival, 1740–1762* (Norman: University of Oklahoma Press, 1962); Boulware, *Deconstructing the Cherokee Nation*, 19–21.

10. On the "Valley" and "Out-Towns," which the English were slow to recognize as distinct regions, see Daniel J. Tortora, *Carolina in Crisis: Cherokees, Colonists, and Slaves in the American Souheast, 1756–1763* (Chapel Hill: University of North Carolina Press, 2015), 11–13; Boulware, *Deconstructing the Cherokee Nation*, 19–27. On Unicoi, see Mooney, *Myths of the Cherokee*, 542; William Harlen Gilbert Jr., *The Eastern Cherokees* (Washington, DC: Government Printing Office, 1943), 180–181.

11. James Adair, *The History of the American Indians*, ed. Kathryn E. Holland Braund (London: Edward and Charles Dilly, 1775; Tuscaloosa: University of Alabama Press, 2003), 248. See also William Bartram, *Travels through North and South Carolina, Georgia, East and West Florida, the Cherokee Country, the extensive Country of the Muscogulges or Creek Confederacy, and the Country of the Chactaws* (London, 1792), 328–329. M. Thomas Hatley, "The Three Lives of Keowee: Loss and Recovery in Eighteenth-Century Cherokee Villages," in *Powhatan's Mantle: Indians in the Colonial Southeast*, ed. Peter H. Wood, Gregory A. Waselkov, and M. Thomas Hatley (Lincoln: University of Nebraska Press, 1989), 241–242.

12. For "going to the water," see Alan Kilpatrick, *The Night Has a Naked Soul: Witchcraft and Sorcery among the Western Cherokee* (Syracuse, NY: Syracuse University Press, 1997), 99–102.

13. Mooney, *Myths of the Cherokee*, 405–406.

14. Mooney, *Myths of the Cherokee*, 239, 302–303.

15. On the Nunnehi as well as animal myths, see Mooney, *Myths of the Cherokee*, 231, 239, 336–337, 475–476. The Nunnehi (Nunne'hi) may literally mean "the people who live anywhere"; see Sandra Muse Isaacs, *Eastern Cherokee Stories: A Living Oral Tradition and Its Cultural Continuance* (Norman: University of Oklahoma Press, 2019),

Notes to Pages 16–20

143–147. See also Dave Aftandilian, "Toward a Native Theology of Animals: Creek and Cherokee Perspectives," *CrossCurrents* 61 (June 2011): 191–207; Charles Hudson, *The Southeastern Indians* (Knoxville: University of Tennessee Press, 1976), 122–136; Rodning, *Center Places*, 70–71.

16. Perdue, *Cherokee Women*, 13–19, 23, 29–38 (quotation on 36). On the warriors' return, see *The Payne-Butrick Papers*, ed. William L. Anderson, Jane L. Brown, and Anne F. Rogers, 2 vols. (Lincoln: University of Nebraska Press, 2010), 2:23–24, 41–42, 61–62. The story of Selu, Kanati, and the two boys is discussed in Mooney, *Myths of the Cherokee*, 242–248; Isaacs, *Eastern Cherokee Stories*, 49–64.

17. Frank G. Speck and Leonard Broom, *Cherokee Dance and Song* (1951; reprint, Norman: University of Oklahoma Press, 1983); Gilbert, *Eastern Cherokees*, 259–268; Perdue, *Cherokee Women*, 26–27, 36; *Payne-Butrick Papers*, 2:150–156.

18. *The Memoirs of Lieut. Henry Timberlake* (London, 1765), 37–39. Cheulah is transliterated Tsula in Cherokee speech. See Isaacs, *Eastern Cherokee Stories*, 168–169.

19. Timberlake, *Memoirs*, 37.

20. On the seven clans, see Perdue, *Cherokee Women*, 42–44; Ken Traisman, "Native Law: Law and Order among Eighteenth-Century Cherokee, Great Plains, Central Prairie, and Woodland Indians," *American Indian Law Review* 9, no. 2 (1981): 273–287, 274 ("ethnic nation"). On clan, maternal lineage, and "mother's blood," see Circe Sturm, *Blood Politics: Race, Culture, and Identity in the Cherokee Nation of Oklahoma* (Berkeley: University of California Press, 2002), 30–34; Hudson, *Southeastern Indians*, 193.

21. On blood revenge, see John Phillip Reid, *A Law of Blood: The Primitive Law of the Cherokee Nation* (New York: New York University Press, 1970), 75–80, 94–101; Perdue, *Cherokee Women*, 49–53; Robbie Ethridge, *Creek Country: The Creek Indians and Their World* (Chapel Hill: University of North Carolina Press, 2003), 108 ("horrifying thought"); Adair, *History of the American Indians*, 329.

22. On clan sociability, see Adair, *History of the American Indians*, 77. On marriage, see Sturm, *Blood Politics*, 31.

23. On the Cherokee male ideal and communal chiding, see Fred Gearing, *Priests and Warriors: Social Structure for Cherokee Politics in the Eighteenth Century* (1962; reprint, Millwood, NY: Kraus Reprint Co., 1974), 40–45, 59–62; Reid, *A Law of Blood*, 237–245.

24. Traisman, "Native Law," 274. On conduct, see Adair, *History of the American Indians*, 416.

25. For the Ani-Kutani [Ani-Kwatani], see Mooney, *Myths of the Cherokee*, 392–393; Raymond D. Fogelson, "Who Were the Ani-Kutani? An Excursion into Cherokee Historical Thought," *Ethnohistory* 31 (1984): 255–263. See also Fogelson, "Cherokee Notions of Power," in *The Anthropology of Power: Ethnographic Studies from Asia, Oceania, and the New World*, ed. Raymond D. Fogelson and Richard N. Adams (New York: Academic Press), 185–194 (186, "animal or human").

26. Daniel S. Butrick, a Protestant missionary of 1820s and 1830s, imagined from conversations with Native men that a Cherokee "national council" and "metropolitan town," besides a supreme "high priest" and "great war chief," existed in an "ancient" past. His conception is not historically provable despite his keen and meticulous insights on Indigenous customs. See *Payne-Butrick Papers*, 1:55–56, 216–220, 243–245, 2:32–33. Butrick's idea of a centralized Native polity influenced Gilbert, *Eastern Cherokees*, 356–358; and Gearing, *Priests and Warriors*, 23–26, 39–43.

27. On incantations, variously used for healing or causing harm, see Mooney, *Myths of the Cherokee*, 277–278, 310–311, 400–401, 435, 504; Kilpatrick, *The Night Has a Naked Soul*, 13–15, 22–23, 26–28, 129; Lee Irwin, "Cherokee Healing: Myth, Dreams, and Medicine," *American Indian Quarterly* 16, no. 2 (1992): 237–257 On an uku's training and his councilors, see *Payne-Butrick Papers*, 1:231–232; Alexander Longe, "A Small Postscript on the Ways and Maners of the Nashon of Indians called Charikees" (1725), original transcript and modernized version ed. David H. Corkran, *Southern Indian Studies* 21 (October 1969): 6–49, 10–11. On the "white" and "red" orders, see Boulware, *Deconstructing the Cherokee Nation*, 12; Fogelson, "Cherokee Notions of Power," 191–192. The ideal priestly council, harkening to ancient times, is discussed in *Payne-Butrick Papers*, 2:206.

28. Timberlake, *Memoirs*, 32. On townhouses, see Rodning, *Center Places*, 41–47, 89–90, 111–115. On Cherokee mourning and burial customs, as witnessed by an English trader, see Longe, "A Small Postscript," 26–27. For the title of *uku* and the more archaic *ugutuyi*, see Gilbert, *Eastern Cherokees*, 321.

29. Timberlake, *Memoirs*, 35; Perdue, *Cherokee Women*, 26–27. Boulware maintains that households had their own particular lands within communally worked fields. See Boulware, *Deconstructing the Cherokee Nation*, 15.

30. For the Creek prohibition, see Ethridge, *Creek Country*, 104. On "war women" and "beloved women," see Perdue, *Cherokee Women*, 38–39; Timberlake, *Memoirs*, 77–78.

31. Fogelson, "Cherokee Notions of Power," 193. On women's influence in Creek society, see Steven Peach, *Rivers of Power: Creek Political Culture in the Native South, 1750–1815* (Norman: University of Oklahoma Press, 2024), 25, 30, 54–58.

32. For the exchange with the priest-chief, see Longe, "A Small Postscript," 32. See also Perdue, *Cherokee Women*, 43.

33. The "harmony ideal," a phrase of anthropologist Robert Thomas, is quoted and defined in Kilpatrick, *The Night Has a Naked Soul*, 126. The diplomacy of formal speech-making was largely, but *not* exclusively, a male art. See Nancy Shoemaker, "An Alliance between Men: Gender Metaphors in Eighteenth-Century American Indian Diplomacy East of the Mississippi," *Ethnohistory* 46 (Spring 1999): 239–263.

34. For marital customs, see Longe, "A Small Postscript," 30; Hatley, *Dividing Paths*, 8. On marriage and separation, see Perdue, *Cherokee Women*, 56–58; Hudson, *Southeastern Indians*, 200–201, 232; Adair, *History of the American Indians*, 182 ("petticoat government"). For "complementary" female and male roles, see Raymond D. Fogelson, "On the 'Petticoat Government' of the Eighteenth-Century Cherokee," in *Personality and the Cultutral Construction of Society: Papers in Honor of Melford E. Spiro*, ed. David K. Jordan and Marc J. Swartz (Tuscaloosa: University of Alabama Press, 1990), 172.

35. For chiefs' influence, see Kathryn E. Holland Braund, *Deerskins and Duffels: The Creek-Indian Trade with Anglo-America, 1685–1815*, 2nd ed. (Lincoln: University of Nebraska Press, 1993), 83–85, 107–108; Joshua Piker, *Okfuskee: A Creek Indian Town in Colonial America* (Cambridge, MA: Harvard University Press, 2004), 138–140; Greg O'Brien, *Choctaws in a Revolutionary Age, 1750–1830* (Lincoln: University of Nebraska Press, 2002), 89–90.

36. John Lawson, *A New Voyage to Carolina* (London, 1709), 184 ("*Indian* Traders"), 235 ("better to us"). For Lawson's death, see James H. Merrell, *The Indians' New World:*

Notes to Pages 25–28

483

Catawbas and Their Neighbors from European Contact through the Era of Removal (New York: Norton: 1989), 54.

37. On marriage and sexual liaisons between Native women and colonial traders, see Merrell, *The Indians' New World*, 63–65; Robert Paulett, *An Empire of Small Places: Mapping the Southeastern Anglo-Indian Trade, 1732–1765* (Athens: University of Georgia Press, 2012), 161–163. See also Theda Perdue, *"Mixed-Blood" Indians: Racial Construction in the Early South* (Athens: University of Georgia Press, 2003).

38. See the factional cleavages discussed in William G. McLoughlin, *Cherokee Renascence in the New Republic* (Princeton: Princeton University Press, 1986).

39. Robert Brightman, "Culture and Culture Theory in Native North America," in *New Perspectives on Native North America: Cultures, Histories, and Representations*, ed. Sergei A. Kan and Pauline Turner Strong (Lincoln: University of Nebraska Press, 2006), 356–357.

40. John Phillip Reid, *A Better Kind of Hatchet: Law, Trade, and Diplomacy in the Cherokee Nation during the Early Years of European Contact* (University Park: Pennsylvania State University Press, 1976), 9 (quotation), 16.

41. *Payne-Butrick Papers*, 1:44 and 345n82.

42. Mooney, *Myths of the Cherokee*, 242–248 (quotation on 247).

43. Mooney, *Myths of the Cherokee*, 244–248.

44. Mooney, *Myths of the Cherokee*, 263–264; Hudson, *Southeastern Indians*, 252, 301.

45. Longe, "A Small Postscript," 44–45. For the priest's lighting of fire, and the carrying of fire and the divination stone to war, see *Payne-Butrick Papers*, 2:115–116, 213. It is not obvious that fired clay pots were carried by Cherokee war parties throughout the 1700s.

46. On stripping naked, donning war paint, and carrying scalps, see Adair, *History of the American Indians*, 381, 383 ("with bark"); Timberlake, *Memoirs*, 56, 94. See also *Payne-Butrick Papers*, 1:252–254.

47. For the ball game, see Hudson, *Southeastern Indians*, 411–420; Raymond Fogelson, "The Cherokee Ball Game: An Ethnographer's View," *Ethnomusicology* 15 (September 1971): 327–338.

48. Mooney, *Myths of the Cherokee*, 529, 543; Hudson, *Southeastern Indians*, 325; Ethridge, *Creek Country*, 103–104 (quotation).

49. "Cherokee Council Minutes, 1795," ID 1000-189, E99.C5C53 1795 Ovrsz, Department of Special Collections, McFarlin Library, University of Tulsa, https://utulsa.as.atlas-sys.com/repositories/2/resources/735.

50. On ritual purification after blood-taking, see *Payne-Butrick Papers*, 2:41–42. On Cherokee numerology, see Mooney, *Myths of the Cherokee*, 431.

51. E. Wayne Lee, "Peace Chiefs and Blood Revenge: Patterns of Restraint in Native American Warfare, 1500–1800," *Journal of Military History* 71 (July 2007): 701–741.

52. On ritual torture and the scalp dance, see Perdue, *Cherokee Women*, 53–54; Mooney, *Myths of the Cherokee*, 375–376; Hudson, *Southeastern Indians*, 251–256.

53. Mooney, *Myths of the Cherokee*, 261 (quotation); Reid, *A Law of Blood*, 76–80; Sturm, *Blood Politics*, 32–33, 40.

54. See Floyd G. Lounsbury, "Iroquois-Cherokee Linguistic Relations," in *Symposium on Cherokee and Iroquois Culture*, ed. William N. Fenton and John Gulick, Bureau of

American Ethnology, Smithsonian Institution, Bulletin 180 (Washington, DC: Government Printing Office, 1961), 11–17.

55. For the priest-chief's story, see Longe, "A Small Postscript," 28–30.

56. Archaeologists debate the *extent* of Indian mortality triggered by Spanish expeditions. See Charles Hudson, *Knights of Spain, Warriors of the Sun: Hernando de Soto and the South's Ancient Chiefdoms* (1997; reprint, Athens: University of Georgia Press, 2018), 423–426; Robbie Ethridge, *From Chicaza to Chickasaw: The European Invasion and the Transformation of the Mississippian World, 1540–1715* (Chapel Hill: University of North Carolina Press, 2000), 64–69, 116–117; Marvin D. Jeter, "Shatter Zone Shock Waves along the Lower Mississippi Valley," in *Mapping the Mississippi Shatter Zone: The Colonial Indian Slave Trade and Regional Instability in the American South*, ed. Robbie Ethridge and Sheri M. Shuck-Hall (Lincoln: University of Nebraska Press, 2009), 367–372.

57. Karen M. Baker, Charles M. Hudson, and Robert L. Rankin, "Place Name Identification and Multilingualism in the Sixteenth-Century Southeast," *Ethnohistory* 39 (Autumn, 1992): 399–451, 407–409, 425–426. On Pardo's missions, see also Finger, *Tennessee's Frontiers*, 18–19.

58. John E. Worth, "Spanish Missions and the Persistence of Chiefly Power," in *The Transformation of the Southeastern Indians, 1540–1760*, ed. Robbie Ethridge and Charles Hudson (Jackson: University of Mississippi Press, 2002), 46–53; Patricia Galloway, "Colonial Transformations in the Mississippi Valley: Dis-integration, Alliance, Confederation, Playoff," in Ethridge and Hudson, *The Transformation of the Southeastern Indians*, 233–241.

59. On chiefdoms, see Ethridge, *From Chicaza to Chickasaw*, 12–18, 35–41, 60–64. For cycles between chiefdom and tribe, see Patricia Galloway, *Choctaw Genesis, 1500–1700* (Lincoln: University of Nebraska Press, 1995), 67–74.

60. For coalescent Native societies, see Robbie Ethridge, "Introduction: Mapping the Mississippian Shatter Zone," in Ethridge and Shuck-Hall, *Mapping the Mississippian Shatter Zone*, 37–40. See also in the same volume the essay by Sheri M. Shuck-Hall, "Alabama and Coushatta Diaspora and Coalescence in the Mississippi Shatter Zone," 251–263.

61. Steven C. Hahn, *The Invention of the Creek Nation, 1670–1763* (Lincoln: University of Nebraska Press, 2004), 16–29 (quotation on 20); Robbie Ethridge, *Creek Country*, 26–31. Christopher B. Rodning, "Reconstructing the Coalescence of Cherokee Communities in Southern Appalachia," in Ethridge and Hudson, *The Transformation of the Southeastern Indians*, 156–163.

62. For much of the eighteenth century, Creek clans were divided into moieties or halves, distinguished between those who were Muskogean and non-Muskogean speakers. See Ethridge, *Creek Country*, 93–94, 111; Claudio Saunt, *A New Order of Things: Property, Power, and the Transformation of the Creek Indians, 1733–1816* (Cambridge: Cambridge University Press, 1999), 13–14, 36; J. Leitch Wright Jr., *Creeks and Seminoles: The Destruction and Regeneration of the Muscogulge People* (Lincoln: University of Nebraska Press, 1986), 5–11.

63. Christopher B. Rodning, "Reconstructing the Coalescence of Cherokee Communities," in Ethridge and Hudson, *The Transformation of the Southeastern Indians*, 156–163; Marvin T. Smith, "Aboriginal Population Movements in the Early

Notes to Pages 34–36   485

Historic Period Interior Southeast," in Waselkov et al., *Powhatan's Mantle*, rev. ed., 43–56.

64. James Axtell, *The European and the Indian: Essays in the Ethnohistory of Colonial North America* (Oxford: Oxford University Press, 1981), 248–252; Daniel K. Richter, *Facing East from Indian Country: A Native History of Early America* (Cambridge, MA: Harvard University Press, 2001), 33–36, 59–67; Alan Taylor, *American Colonies* (New York: Penguin, 2001), 39–45, 72–74.

65. Daniel K. Richter, *The Ordeal of the Longhouse: The Peoples of the Iroquois League in the Era of European Colonization* (Chapel Hill: University of North Carolina Press, 1992), 33–38, 58–62.

66. Thornton, *The Cherokees*, 24–27. See also Ted L. Gragson and Paul V. Bolstad, "A Local Analysis of Early-Eighteenth-Century Cherokee Settlement," *Social Science History* 31 (Fall 2007): 435–468, 446.

67. Merrell, *The Indians' New World*, 139–148.

68. Galloway, *Choctaw Genesis*, 140–141 (quotation on 141).

69. Peter H. Wood, "The Changing Population of the Colonial South," in Waselkov et al., *Powhatan's Mantle*, rev. ed., 72–76, 81–87, 94–99; Merrell, *The Indians' New World*, 19–27, 95–106. On smallpox, see Paul Kelton, *Epidemics and Enslavement: Biological Catastrophe in the Native Southeast* (Lincoln: University of Nebraska Press, 2007), 145–155.

70. Jared Diamond, *Guns, Germs, and Steel: The Fate of Human Societies* (New York: Norton, 1997); Gary B. Nash, *Red, White, and Black: The Peoples of Early North America*, 4th ed. (Upper Saddle River, NJ: Prentice-Hall, 2000), 45–48, 117–127.

2. South Carolina and the Native Southeast

1. Kathryn E. Holland Braund, *Deerskins and Duffels: The Creek-Indian Trade with Anglo-America, 1685–1815*, 2nd ed. (Lincoln: University of Nebraska Press, 1993), 29–32, 122–126; Joel W. Martin, "Southeastern Indians and the English Trade in Skins and Slaves," in *The Forgotten Centuries: Indians and Europeans in the American South, 1521–1704*, ed. Charles Hudson and Carmen Chaves Tesser (Athens: University of Georgia Press, 1994), 306–313.

2. Theda Perdue: "'A Sprightly Lover Is the Most Prevailing Missionary': Intermarriage between Europeans and Indians in the Eighteenth-Century South," in *Light on the Path: The Anthropology and History of the Southeastern Indians*, ed. Thomas J. Pluckhahn and Robbie Ethridge (Tuscaloosa: University of Alabama Press, 2006), 165–178.

3. David J. Silverman, *Thundersticks: Firearms and the Violent Transformation of Native America* (Cambridge, MA: Belknap Press of Harvard University Press, 2016), 8, 24–35, 66–76, 148–149.

4. Alan Gallay, *The Indian Slave Trade: The Rise of the English Empire in the American South, 1670–1717* (New Haven: Yale University Press, 2002), 299–302; Christina Snyder, *Slavery in Indian Country: The Changing Face of Captivity in Early America* (Cambridge, MA: Harvard University Press, 2010), 53–55.

5. Gallay, *Indian Slave Trade*, 65–67, 99–100, 170–171, 299–302; Verner W. Crane, *The Southern Frontier, 1670–1732* (1956; New York: Norton, 1981), 17–21.

486

Notes to Pages 37–41

6. The charter referred to Indians as a "barbarous People." See William Stevens Powell, *The Carolina Charter of 1663: How It Came to North Carolina and Its Place in History* (Raleigh, NC: State Department of Archives and History, 1954), 23. See also Hugh T. Lefler and William S. Powell, *Colonial North Carolina: A History* (New York: Scribner's, 1973), 32–38; Robert M. Weir, *Colonial South Carolina: A History* (Columbia: University of South Carolina Press, 1997), 47–51.

7. See Stephen Adams, *The Best and Worst Country in the World: Perspectives on the Early Virginia Landscape* (Charlottesville: University Press of Virginia, 2001), 239–240.

8. Weir, *Colonial South Carolina*, 53–58, 61–64, 101–107; Converse D. Clowse, *Economic Beginnings in Colonial South Carolina, 1670–1730* (Columbia: University of South Carolina Press, 1971), 19–22, 25–30; Lefler and Powell, *Colonial North Carolina*, 42–52, 80.

9. Lefler and Powell, *Colonial North Carolina*, 47–48.

10. Gallay, *Indian Slave Trade*, 48–50, 59–68, 74–90. On French Huguenots, see Denise I. Bossy, "Godin & Co.: Charleston Merchants and the Indian Trade, 1674–1715," *South Carolina Historical Magazine* 114 (April 2013): 96–131. On the Sephardic interpreter, see John Archdale, *A New Description of that Fertile and Pleasant Province of Carolina* (London, 1707), 22–23; Barnett A. Elizas, *The Jews of South Carolina* (Philadelphia: Lippincott, 1905), 19–23.

11. Gallay, *Indian Slave Trade*, 49–52, 95–96, 206.

12. Peter H. Wood, *Black Majority: Negroes in Colonial South Carolina from 1670 through the Stono Rebellion* (New York: Norton, 1975), 14–24, 53–55, 144. The low country is poetically described in Peter A. Coclanis, *The Shadow of a Dream: Economic Life and Death in the South Carolina Low Country, 1670–1820* (New York: Oxford University Press, 1989), 27–30.

13. David J. Weber, *The Spanish Frontier in North America* (New Haven: Yale University Press, 1992), 70–75; Paul E. Hoffman, *Florida's Frontiers* (Bloomington: Indiana University Press, 2002), 51–62, 64–69, 76–77.

14. Marcel Giraud, *A History of French Louisiana*, vol. 1, *The Reign of Louis XIV, 1698–1715*, trans. Joseph C. Lambert (Baton Rouge: Louisiana State University Press, 1974), 14–15, 33–34, 45–47, 100–101. See also Guy Frégault, *Iberville, le conquérant* (Montreal: Société des Éditions Pascal, 1944), 303–306, 339.

15. Giraud, *History of French Louisiana*, 1:177–178, 199–211; Daniel H. Usner Jr., *Indians, Settlers, and Slaves in a Frontier Exchange Economy: The Lower Mississippi Valley before 1783* (Chapel Hill: University of North Carolina Press, 1992), 17–26 (population figures, 25).

16. Richard White, *The Middle Ground: Indians, Empires, and Republics in the Great Lakes Region, 1650–1815* (Cambridge: Cambridge University Press, 1991), 2. For speculation on the Virginians' western Indian hosts, identified as "Tomahitans" (and not necessarily Cherokees), see Paul Kelton, *Epidemics and Enslavement: Biological Catastrophe in the Native Southeast, 1492–1715* (Lincoln: University of Nebraska Press, 2007), 114–119.

17. Cherokee headman "Johnny" offered information on the Yamasees to Arthur Middleton, president of the South Carolina provincial council. See Council minutes, 25–26 January 1727, CO 5/387. Matthew H. Jennings, "Violence in a Shattered

Notes to Pages 43–46   487

World," in *Mapping the Mississippian Shatter Zone: The Colonial Indian Slave Trade and Regional Instability in the American South*, ed. Robbie Ethridge and Sheri M. Shuck-Hall (Lincoln: University of Nebraska Press, 2009), 280–286.

18. For Yamasee migration and slaving warfare, see Amy Turner Bushnell, "Living at Liberty: The Ungovernable Yamasees of Spanish Florida," in *The Yamasee Indians: From Florida to South Carolina*, ed. Denise I. Bossy (Lincoln: University of Nebraska Press, 2018), 34–37; John E. Worth, "Razing Florida: The Indian Slave Trade and the Devastation of Spanish Florida, 1659–1725," in Ethridge and Shuck-Hall, *Mapping*, 295–311.

19. Steven C. Hahn, *The Invention of the Creek Nation, 1670–1763* (Lincoln: University of Nebraska Press, 2004), 40–50; Robbie Ethridge, *Creek Country: The Creek Indians and Their World* (Chapel Hill: University of North Carolina Press, 2003), 33–38.

20. Robbie Ethridge, *From Chicaza to Chickasaw: The European Invasion and the Transformation of the Mississippian World, 1540–1715* (Chapel Hill: University of North Carolina Press, 2000), 167–168, 198–199; Kelton, *Epidemics and Enslavement*, 137–140.

21. For the Shawnee attack, see record of 13 January 1693, JCHA 1693, 12. For Shawnee migrations, see Stephen Warren, *The World the Shawnees Made: Migration and Violence in Early America* (Chapel Hill: University of North Carolina Press, 2014), 73–79. On southern Shawnees (Savannahs) and South Carolina magnates in wartime alliance against the Westo Indians see Eric Bowne, *The Westo Indians: Slave Traders of the Early Colonial South* (Tuscaloosa: University of Alabama Press, 2005), 95–101.

22. Record of 14 January 1693, JCHA 1693, 13. See also Sami Lakomäki, *Gathering Together: The Shawnee People through Diaspora and Nationhood* (New Haven: Yale University Press, 2014), 26–28.

23. J. H. Parry, *The Spanish Seaborne Empire* (1966; Berkeley: University of California Press, 1990), 267–270.

24. James Moore and Col. Robert Daniel to the Council of Carolina, 9 November 1702, CO 5/382. See also Council of Carolina to the Lords of Trade and Plantations, 26 November 1702, CO 5/382.

25. Steven J. Oatis, *A Colonial Complex: South Carolina's Frontiers in the Era of the Yamasee War, 1680–1730* (Lincoln: University of Nebraska Press, 2004), 47. For the Yamasee demand, see record of 28 April 1703, JCHA 1703, 75. Nairne's account is interlined in Herman Moll, "A New Map of the North Parts of America . . ." (London: Sold by H. Moll, 1720), Geography and Map Division, Library of Congress, https://www.loc.gov/item/2001624907/.

26. For duties on Indians and Blacks see the Act of 6 May 1703, SSC, 2:201–202.

27. Moore to the Lords Proprietors, 16 April 1704, CO 5/283. South Carolina's assembly approved Moore's raising of Indian allies. See records of 7 and 15 September 1703, JCHA 1703, 105–106, 121; Gallay, *Indian Slave Trade*, 137–140, 145–147, 295; Crane, *Southern Frontier*, 79–88; Hoffman, *Florida's Frontiers*, 176–181; Hahn, *Invention of the Creek Nation*, 73–83; Martin, "Indians and the English Trade in Skins and Slaves," in Hudson and Tesser, *Forgotten Centuries*, 312–313.

28. Testimony of Juan de la Cruz and Francisco de Fuentes de Galanca, 9 June 1705; Governor Zuñiga to the king, 30 March 1704, Series 1: Historical Documents, box 3, folder 66: "Documents Describing the Tragic End of the Mission Era," in Mark F. Boyd Collection, ASM9937, Special Collections, University of Miami.

29. Moore was imprecise about the number of Indians killed in his expedition and similarly vague about the slaves he took with him compared to those captured and retained by Indian allies. See Moore to the Lords Proprietors, 16 April 1704 and Moore to Governor Nathaniel Johnson, 16 April 1704, CO 5/384. See also Crane, *Southern Frontier*, 79–80; Gallay, *Indian Slave Trade*, 144–148.

30. On Moore's mining ambitions, see his letter to Edward Randolph, 1 March 1699 ("Appalatheean Mountains"); Randolph to the Earl of Bridgewater, 22 March 1699, CO 5/1258; Moore to Thomas Cutler, 27 December, 1700, CO 5/1289/015.

31. For Moore's death, see Mabel L. Webber, "The First Governor Moore and His Children," *South Carolina Historical and Genealogical Magazine* 37 (January 1936): 1–23, 4. On Nairne's expedition, see record of November 22, 1707, JCHA 1707, 48–49; Nairne to Robert Fenwick, 13 April 1708, in *Nairne's Muskhogean Journals: The 1708 Expedition to the Mississippi River*, ed. Alexander Moore (Jackson: University Press of Mississippi, 1988), 38, 51. On the Choctaw rejection see Giraud, *History of French Louisiana*, 1: 202–205.

32. Oatis, *Colonial Complex*, 53.

33. For "An Act Regulating the Indian Trade," no. 269, 19 July 1707, see SSC, 2:309–316. On uncertainty over legitimate authority in the English colonies, see Michael Kammen, *People of Paradox: An Inquiry into the Origins of American Civilization* (New York: Knopf, 1972), 31–34.

34. On Nairne's case against Johnson, see Nairne to the Earl of Sunderland, 28 July 1708, CO 5/306. For a detailed account, see Moore, *Nairne's Muskhogean Journals*, 12–19.

35. Peter H. Wood, "The Changing Population of the Colonial South: An Overview by Race and Region, 1685–1790," in *Powhatan's Mantle: Indians in the Colonial Southeast*, ed. Gregory A. Waselkov, Peter H. Wood, and Tom Hatley, rev. ed. (Lincoln: University of Nebraska Press, 2006), 95.

36. Nairne to the Earl of Sunderland, 10 July 1708, CO 5/382 / Pt. 1 / 008.

37. Nairne to the Earl of Sunderland, 10 July 1708.

38. David La Vere, *The Tuscarora War: Indians, Settlers, and the Fight for the Carolina Colonies* (Chapel Hill: University of North Carolina Press, 2013), 69–83.

39. It is not possible to know if Cherokees alone comprised the 310 Native warriors listed as within the "Charike Camp." See La Vere, *The Tuscarora War*, 93–108, 160–176; Gallay, *Indian Slave Trade*, 262–278, 283–286; Crane, *Southern Frontier*, 167. The diagram of the battle is in Joseph W. Barnwell, "The Second Tuscarora Expedition," *South Carolina Historical and Genealogical Magazine* 10 (January 1909): 38–39. For Barnwell's praise of "my brave Yamassees," see Barnwell to Governor, 4 February 1712, in "The Tuscarora Expedition: Letters of Colonel John Barnwell," *South Carolina Historical and Genealogical Magazine* 9 (January 1908): 30–36.

40. La Vere, *Tuscarora War*, 147–148, 170–176, 183. For the Board's instructions of 9 July 1712 counseling "loving" treatment of Indians, see JCIT, 31.

41. For the Chestowe massacre, see record of 4–6 May 1714, JCIT, 53–56. Wigan's name is often spelled "Wiggan" in documents, but he signed his name "Wigan." See Eleazar Wigan to Arthur Middleton, 7 October 1727, JCSC, CO 5/387/106.

42. For the Commissioners' examination of Wigan and Longe (5–6 May 1714), see JCIT, 54–56. On "old rabbit," see Samuel Cole Williams, *Early Travels in the*

Notes to Pages 49–53

489

Tennessee Country, 1540–1800 (Johnson City, TN: Watauga Press, 1928), 123n. Longe, whose name was often spelled Long by others, lived among the Cherokees from about 1714 to 1724. For his account of Cherokee customs, see Alexander Longe, "A Small Postscript on the Ways and Maners of the Nashon of Indians called Charikees" (1725), original transcript and modernized version ed. David H. Corkran, *Southern Indian Studies* 21 (October 1969): 3–49.

43. Testimony on the Chestowe massacre, record of 4–6 May 1714, JCIT, 53–57 ("French Indians," 53). The Board ordered that the Yuchi slaves be returned to their people. It also recommended, though without effect, that Longe and Wigan be prosecuted.

44. Longe's letters are mentioned, but not extant. The Board of Indian Commissioners found for Cesar's freedom. See record of 14 May 1713, JCIT, 45.

45. On the the transatlantic dimensions of South Carolina's trade, see Bossy, "Godin & Co."

46. William L. Ramsay, *The Yamasee War: A Study of Culture, Economy, and Conflict in the Colonial South* (Lincoln: University of Nebraska Press, 2008), 15–19, 23–25, 74–77, 94–97, 114–115. For Yamasee fears of enslavement, see Jane Landers, "Yamasee-African Ties in Carolina and Georgia," in Bossy, *Yamasee Indians*, 174. On disease, see Kelton, *Epidemics and Enslavement*, 182–183. On Nairne's death, see unnamed French Carolina settler's account, 8 May 1715, CO 5/387/002.

47. Larry E. Ivers, *This Torrent of Indians: War on the Southeastern Frontier, 1715–1728* (Columbia: University of South Carolina Press, 2016), 58–62, 86–99; Ramsay, *Yamasee War*, 112–125.

48. On the "universal Confederacy of Indian Nations," see "The humble Address of the General Assembly of South Carolina" to "the King's most Excellent Majestie," [May] 1715, CO 5/382 / Pt. 2 / 011. See also Ramsay, *Yamasee War*, 121–123; Oatis, *Colonial Complex*, 125–128; Hahn, *Invention of the Creek Nation*, 77–84; James H. Merrell, *The Indians' New World: Catawbas and Their Neighbors from European Contact through the Era of Removal* (Chapel Hill: University of North Carolina Press, 1989), 73–76. Robert Johnson estimated 400 colonial deaths during the Yamasee War. See Johnson to the Council of Trade and Plantations, 12 January 1720, CSP, 31:308.

49. Oatis, *Colonial Complex*, 130–132; Crane, *Southern Frontier*, 167–168; Hoffman, *Florida's Frontiers*, 183–184; Landers, "Yamasee-African Ties," 175. On French aid to the Creeks and Alabamas, see "Letter from the Assembly of Carolina to their Agents in Great Britain," 15 March 1716, CO 5/1265/015.

50. John Tate to John Duddleston, 16 September 1715, CO 5/1265/009. On the supposed 12,000 Indian foes, see a "Memorial from Several Planters and Merchants Trading to Carolina" to the Board of Trade, received 18 July 1715, CO 5/1264. For colonial complaints about the Proprietors, see "Some paragraphs of Letters from South Carolina," 30 August 1715, CO 5/1265/026. See also M. Eugene Sirmans, *Colonial South Carolina: A Political History, 1663–1763* (Chapel Hill: University of North Carolina Press, 1966), 118–131.

51. See Crane, *Southern Frontier*, 173.

52. For the "robbing" of slaves, see letter by Carolina agents Joseph Boone and Richard Beresford to the Board of Trade, received December 1716, CO 5/382/Pt.1/016. For the flight of Blacks, see Landers, "Yamasee-African Ties," 174–176.

53. On the peace overture, see Samuel Eveleigh to Joseph Boone and Richard Beresford, 19 July 1715, CO 5/1265/012. On Captain Chicken and the battle site, see Michael J. Heitzler, *The Goose Creek Bridge: Gateway to Sacred Places* (Bloomington, IN: Author House, 2012), 77–85.

54. Francis Le Jau to the Secretary of the Society, 26 September 1715, SPG Papers, Letter Books, vol. 11, DCAR. See also Crane, *Southern Frontier*, 179–180.

55. William Tredwell Bull to the Secretary, 31 October 1715, SPG, Letter Books, vol. 11, DCAR. See also "Letter from the Assembly of South Carolina to their Agents in Great Britain," 15 March 1716.

56. For the ceremonies, see Le Jau to the Secretary, 3 October 1715, SPG, Letter Books, vol. 11, DCAR. For remarks on Indian cruelty, see "The humble Address of the General Assembly of South Carolina" to "the King's most Excellent Majestie," [May] 1715, CO 5/382 / Pt. 2 / 011. The Cherokee priest-chief of Coosawattee spoke of Wigan accompanying his people who went to Charles Town. See "A Letter from Carolina and Journal of the March of the Carolinians into the Cherokee Mountains, in the Yamassee [*sic*] War, 1715–16" (hereafter "Journal of the March"), in *Year Book. 1894. City of Charleston*, ed. Langdon Cheeves (Charleston: Walker, Evans & Cogswell, 1894), Appendix, 334.

57. Crane, *Southern Frontier*, 180–181.

58. "Journal of the March," 326–330, 348, 351. Creek Indians called the brew "white" to indicate the drink's valued purgative power. See Charles Hudson, *The Southeastern Indians* (Knoxville: University of Tennessee Press, 1976), 226–229.

59. "Journal of the March," [30–31 December 1715], 330–331. Chicken's spelling, which was often phonetic, labeled the Cherokee enemies in Illinois as the "Coeakeas," that is, Cahokias. According to French sources, Kaskaskia, not Cahokia, absorbed the brunt of the assault. The Indian casualties are not clearly known. French officials wrote of ten to twelve of their countrymen being killed and six women taken as captives. See Bienville to Minister, 20 January 1716; Cadillac to Minister, 7 February 1716, AC, 13A-4.

60. "Journal of the March," [1–2 January 1716], 331–332. Chottee was a "white" or "peace" town, reverenced for its ancestral status and believed to be a fitting place for mediating disputes. See Hudson, *Southeastern Indians*, 238–239.

61. The priest-chief's talk of 3 January 1716 is in "Journal of the March," 333–334. The Cherokee courier's report is in Chicken's entry for 5 January 1716, "Journal of the March," 336.

62. "Journal of the March," [23 January 1716], 343.

63. "Journal of the March" [23–24 January 1716], 343–344.

64. Chicken also noted that the Cherokees gave one Creek captive to the English to be shot. See "Journal of the March," 343–344; Oatis, *Colonial Complex*, 189 (quotation); Tom Hatley, *The Dividing Paths: Cherokees and South Carolinians through the Revolutionary Era* (New York: Oxford University Press, 1995), 25–27; Hahn, *Invention of the Creek Nation*, 88–89.

65. Chicken learned of the massacre on 27 January 1716. See "Journal of the March," 345. For Cherokee talk of being at war with the Creeks, see Chicken's entry of 23 January 1716, "Journal of the March," 342.

66. Entry of 13 January 1725, "Journal of the March," 339.

Notes to Pages 56–60

67. The peace was furthered by the betrothal of Brims's niece to John Musgrove Jr. See Hahn, *Invention of the Creek Nation*, 103–105.

68. "Journal of the March" [31 January and 2 February 1716], 347–348.

69. New law of 30 June 1716, JCIT, 325–329. On South Carolina's testy relations with Virginia, see Oatis, *Colonial Complex*, 158. Spotswood to the Board of Trade, 16 April 1717, in *The Official Letters of Alexander Spotswood, Lieutenant-Governor of the Colony of Virginia, 1710–1722*, ed. R. A. Brock (Richmond: Virginia Historical Society, 1882), 241.

70. For restrictions on extending credit in the Cherokee trade, see Board to Theophilus Hastings, 10 July 1716 and 7 November 1716, JCIT, 86, 123. The strict public monopoly actually ended in 1719, when the Indian trade was opened to private individuals on a limited basis. See Crane, *Southern Frontier*, 198–200.

71. For the price schedule, see record of 30 April 1716, JCIT, 89.

72. For the instructions, see Commissioners to William Hatton, 17 June 1717, JCIT, 191.

73. For Chicken's comment, see "Journal of the March" [19 January 1716], 346. On the equal distribution of goods, see Commissioners to William Hatton, 17 June 1717, JCIT, 191.

74. The delivery of deerskins and slaves is in Commissioners to William Hatton, 17 June 1717, JCIT, 190–191. Typical pay for a Cherokee bearer was a coat, blanket, or other cloth. See record of 16 November 1716, JCIT, 125. For Cherokee bargaining over pack bearing, see record of 2 December 1717, JCIT, 236–237. On the use of "pack animals" in the Cherokee trade, see Instructions to William Hatton, 11 June 1718, JCIT, 291.

75. South Carolina's Commissioners of the Indian Trade were empowered by a law of 16 June 1716, JCIT, 325–329. On their orders regarding Indian slavery, see Instructions for Theophilus Hastings, 10 July 1716, JCIT, 86.

76. For the honor to Charitey-Hagey, see record of 16 November 1716, JCIT, 128. The purchase of the Frenchman is in record of 17 June 1717, JCIT, 189.

77. For Peggy's deal making, see record of 22–24 November 1716, JCIT, 127–128, 131. Peggy's Corn House is mentioned in record of 17 June 1717, JCIT, 191. On strouds and duffels (the latter a coarse but heavier woolen cloth), see Braund, *Deerskins and Duffels*, 122–123.

78. For Cesar's bargaining, see record of 23 and 26 January 1716, JCIT, 150–151, 153. The gift to the Cherokee women is in record of 30 January 1717, JCIT, 155. On Cesar's beating, see report of Wigan, 9 May 1717, JCIT, 178. For "old Captain Cesar," see Anthony Dean to Cornelis Doharty, 1 May 1751, DRIA, 1:72–73.

79. Testimony of John Sharp, 24 October 1717, JCIT, 222.

80. The rumored invasion is discussed in the Board to William Hatton, 4 October 1717, JCIT, 215. For Johnson's order, see the Board to Hatton, 19 July 1718, JCIT, 312.

81. These details come from William Hatton, agent in Cherokee country, author of an undated report [circa 1721] on the Cherokee trade. See "Some Short Remarkes on the Indian Trade in the Charrikees and in the Management thereof since the Year 1717," ed. Rena Vassar, *Ethnohistory*, 8 (Autumn 1961): 401–423 ("no more than dirt" on 408; "Damned" on 417).

82. Vassar, "Some Short Remarkes," 419.

3. "Not Like White Men"

1. Fitch's report was forwarded to Chicken by Arthur Middleton, president of the South Carolina council. See Middleton to Chicken, 29 August 1725, "Colonel Chicken's Journal to the Cherokees, 1725," in *Travels in the American Colonies*, ed. Newton D. Mereness (New York: Macmillan, 1916), 144 (hereafter "Chicken's Journal"). For Chicken's instructions, see JCHA, 29 May–1 June 1725, CO 5/428/Pt. 2/001.

2. For Chicken's meeting of 14 September 1725 with headmen of six towns, see "Chicken's Journal," 146–148. On Crow's commission, see entries of 5–21 July 1725, 101–102, 108–109.

3. For Crow's response, see "Chicken's Journal," entry of 25 September 1725, 153.

4. For "white men" and "white people," see "Chicken's Journal"; and "Captain Fitch's Journal to the Creeks, 1725," in *Travels in the American Colonies*, ed. Newton D. Mereness (New York: Macmillan, 1916) (hereafter "Fitch's Journal"). "White men" was standard in English-Cherokee discourse well before then. See Cherokee testimony, 5 May 1714, 5; and Trade commissioners to Cherokee headmen, 2 December 1717, JCIT, 236.

5. "The Tunisee Warriour's Answer to the Governour's Talk, 2 October 1727, in Wigan to Middleton, 7 October Oct 1727, CO 5/387.

6. "Chicken's Journal," entry of 21 August 1725, 127–128 ("Eldest Brothers").

7. Verner W. Crane, *The Southern Frontier, 1670–1732* (1956; reprint, New York: Norton, 1981), 60–63, 199–200, 233–234. On Nicholson's becoming royal governor after the Proprietary regime's demise, see M. Eugene Sirmans, *South Carolina: A Political History, 1663–1763* (Chapel Hill: University of North Carolina Press, 1966), 131–137.

8. Steven C. Hahn, *The Invention of the Creek Nation, 1670–1763* (Lincoln: University of Nebraska Press, 2004), 124–125.

9. On the invitation to England, see record of 2 and 10 February 1722, JCSC, CO 5/425, and 10 February 1710, JCHA, CO 5/426. For Nicholson and the Mohawk visit, see Alden T. Vaughan, *Transatlantic Encounters: American Indians in Britain, 1500–1776* (Cambridge: Cambridge University Press, 2006), 114–120.

10. For Brims's statement, "I am Old," and his reference to "Dogs," see his speech in entry for 28 September 1725, "Fitch's Journal," 194. See also Hahn, *Invention of the Creek Nation*, 10–13, 72–73, 96–108.

11. Message from the Lower House, 3 February 1722, JCSC, CO 5/425.

12. The Cherokee head warrior related the story on 2 November 1723, and the South Carolina council responded 7 November 1723, Orders in Council, CO 5/359/Pt. 1/009.

13. 8 November 1723, JCSC, CO 5/427/003. On Long Warrior as "Skiagunstee" (revered warrior), see record of 8 November 1723, Council Orders, CO 5/359/Pt. 1/009.

14. Hahn, *Invention of the Creek Nation*, 91; Joshua Piker, *Okfuskee: A Creek Indian Town in Colonial America* (Cambridge, MA: Harvard University Press, 2004), 6–10, 16, 21, 25–27; Robbie Ethridge, *Creek Country: The Creek Indians and Their World* (Chapel Hill: University of North Carolina Press, 2003), 28–30, 265n27.

Notes to Pages 68–74

15. Hahn, *Invention of the Creek Nation*, 10–11 ("bowels of the earth"), 171–173; Bill Grantham, *Creation Myths and Legends of the Creek Indians* (Gainesville: University Press of Florida, 2002), 123–130, 148–151.

16. Steven J. Oatis, *A Colonial Complex: South Carolina's Frontiers in the Era of the Yamasee War, 1680–1730* (Lincoln: University of Nebraska Press, 2004), 57 (quotation), 220–221; Bryan C. Rindfleisch, *Brothers of Coweta: Kinship, Empire, and Revolution in the Eighteenth-Century Muscogee World* (Columbia: University of South Carolina Press, 2021), 30–31.

17. On Hastings, see JCHA, May 28, 1722, CO 5 / 428. See also Oatis, *A Colonial Complex*, 269.

18. For the gifts to Tallapoosa chiefs, see JCHA, 4 October 1723, CO 5 / 427 / 007. On the trade embargo, see Crane, *Southern Frontier*, 265–266.

19. Conference with Ouletta and Creek deputies, 25 October 1723, CO 5 / 359. On interregional tensions, see the Tuckabatchee warrior's talk, reported in Captain Monger to Nicholson, 24 September 1723, CO 5 / 359.

20. Conference with Ouletta and Creek deputies, 16–19 November 1723, CO 5 / 359.

21. Deposition of Joseph Cabella, 9 October 1723, CO 5 / 359.

22. On the evasion of the embargo, see report of 4 October 1723, JCHA, CO 5 / 427. On 15 February 1724, South Carolina enacted a new Indian trade law, distinguishing between traders licensed for the Cherokees, Creeks, and other nations. See CO 5 / 412 / 006.

23. Sharp wrote from Noyowee, a town close to Tugaloo. See Sharp to Nicholson, 12 November 1724, with a list, dated 9 November, of the stolen items, in CO 5 / 329.

24. Hatton to Nicholson, 14 November 1724, CO 5 / 359 / Pt. 2 / 012.

25. Middleton to the Assembly, 27 May 1725, JCHA, CO 5 / 428 / Pt. 2 / 001.

26. See Middleton's instructions, and the council's advice to Fitch, 1 June 1725, JCHA, CO 5 / 428 / Pt. 2 / 001; and JCSC (Upper House), CO 5 / 428 / Pt. 1 / 004. For Chicken's appointment as commissioner, see Act of 17 April 1725, CO 5 / 412 / 007.

27. Entry of 5 July 1725, "Chicken's Journal," 101–102; Crow's talk, 25 September 1725, "Chicken's Journal," 153.

28. Entry of 16 July 1725, "Chicken's Journal," 105.

29. Entries of 5 and 16 July 1725, "Chicken's Journal," 101–102, 104. For Hatton's suggestion of 300 soldiers, see his letter to Nicholson, 14 November 1724, CO 5 / 359.

30. For the weakness of local "kings," see entries of 24 July and 20 August 1725, "Chicken's Journal," 110–111, 125.

31. On Great Tellico's fortifications, see entry of 25 July 1725, "Chicken's Journal," 111–112. I refer to Great Tellico and Tellico interchangeably. The town of Little Tellico is named distinctly when referenced. On Great Tellico's population, see the census of Cherokee towns, in Francis Varnod to the Secretary of the Society for the Propagation of the Gospel, Society for the Propagation of the Gospel Papers, 1 April 1724, (microfilm), DCAR.

32. Entry of 28 July 1725, "Chicken's Journal," 112–113.

33. Entry of 28 July 1725, "Chicken's Journal," 113–114. On Praise for Long Warrior, see entry of 21 September 1725, "Chicken's Journal," 152.

34. See Chicken's talks with the headmen of six Cherokee towns, 2 August 1725, "Chicken's Journal," 115–117. On Coosa's place in the Abeika or (Abhika) region, see Ethridge, *Creek Country*, 26–27, 33, 88–89.

35. Chicken questioned the Cherokee woman on August 12, 1725. See "Chicken's Journal," 120–121.

36. For Chicken's discussion with Great Tellico's Head Warrior, see entry of 2 August 1725, "Chicken's Journal," 116–117.

37. Chicken learned of the killing of the Coosa women from an English trader in Cherokee country. See entry of 2 October 1725, "Chicken's Journal," 155. See also entry of 14 September 1725, "Fitch's Journal," 190.

38. Bienville to the Council, 1 February and 3 August 1723, MPAFD, 3:343 ("barbarians"), 357 ("gnawed"). See also James R. Atkinson, *Splendid Land, Splendid People: The Chickasaw Indians to Removal* (Tuscaloosa: University of Alabama Press, 2004), 18–21, 31–33; Patricia Dillon Woods, *French-Indian Relations on the Southern Frontier, 1699–1762* (Ann Arbor: UMI Press, 1980), 47–53, 66–67. On Chickasaw migration to the Savannah River, see Edward J. Cashin, *Guardians of the Valley: Chickasaws in Colonial South Carolina and Georgia* (Columbia: University of South Carolina Press, 2009), 1–7. Chickasaw population is estimated in Peter H. Wood, "The Changing Population of the Colonial South: An Overview by Race and Region, 1685–1790," in *Powhatan's Mantle: Indians in the Colonial Southeast*, ed. Peter H. Wood, Gregory A. Waselkov, and M. Thomas Hatley (Lincoln: University of Nebraska Press, 1989), 94–95.

39. Entries of 16–21 August 1725, "Chicken's Journal," 122–126.

40. Entry of 21 August 1725, "Chicken's Journal," 127–128.

41. Entry of 2 August 1725, "Fitch's Journal," 182.

42. On the Creek complaint and Fitch's reply, see entry of 2 November 1725, "Fitch's Journal," 198–199.

43. The Okfuskee (Upper Creek) headman's answer to Fitch, 2 November 1725, "Fitch's Journal," 198. On Chicken's talks with the Savannah River Chickasaws, see entry of 30 October 1725, "Chicken's Journal," 171–172.

44. The attack on Cussita is discussed in Oatis, *A Colonial Complex*, 248–249.

45. For the appointments, see entry of 29 April 1726, JCHA, CO 5/429.

46. Fitch to Middleton, 1 August 1726, JCSC, session of 1 September 1726, CO 5/429/Pt. 1.

47. Cussita strongly favored a Cherokee peace while Coweta was opposed. See Fitch to Middleton, 1 August 1726, JCSC, CO 5/429.

48. Record of conference, 27 July 1726, in Chicken to Middleton, 10 August 1726, JCSC, session of 1 September 1726, CO 5/429. Along with this letter is the manuscript of Colonel Chicken's Journal [1726], not to be confused with his journal of 1725 printed in Mereness, *Travels*.

49. For Chicken's admonishment of traders over trampling Cherokee corn fields, see entry of 30 September 1725, "Chicken's Journal," 154–155. For his subsequent policy on trade, see Colonel Chicken's Journal [1726], 27–28 July 1726, CO 5/429 / Pt. 1 / 001.

50. Colonel Chicken's Journal [1726], 27–28 July 1726, CO 5/429 / Pt. 1 / 001. Wigan to Chicken, 3 August 1726, recorded in Colonel Chicken's Journal [1726], 27–28 July 1726. Wigan consulted with the Tanasee's "king" as well as Long Warrior,

Notes to Pages 80–86   495

two head warriors of Euphasee in the Valley region, and head warriors of Tellico, Tomotley, and Settico in Overhill country.

51. Fitch sent a record of the conference of 23 September 1726 in his letter of the next day to Middleton, JCSC, session of 8 October 1726, CO 5/429/Pt. 1/002.

52. Hahn, *Invention of the Creek Nation*, 126–138.

53. Conference of 23 September 1726 in Fitch to Middleton, 24 September 1726, JCSC, CO 5/429/Pt. 1/002. Ouletta was killed in a clash with the Yamasees in 1725 and Chipacasi died the next year after imbibing too much rum. See Hahn, *Invention of the Creek Nation*, 133–137.

54. Chigelly's talk of 24 September 1726, in which he offered the feather and beads, is recorded in Fitch to Middleton of that same day, CO 5/429/Pt. 1/002.

55. Fitch's exchange with Chigelly of 23 September 1726 on the Tugaloo killings, is enclosed in his letter to Middleton of the next day, CO 5/429/Pt. 1/002.

56. On the Tomahitans, see Paul Kelton, *Epidemics and Enslavement: Biological Catastrophe in the Native Southeast* (Lincoln: University of Nebraska Press, 2007), 118–119; Sami Lakomäki, *Gathering Together: The Shawnee People through Diaspora and Nationhood, 1600–1870* (New Haven: Yale University Press, 2014), 24, 38–39.

57. On the Seneca visit and talk, see entry of 11 August 1725, "Fitch's Journal," 188–189.

58. For Chigelly's concerns about Chickasaws, see of record, 23 September 1726, CO 5/429/Pt. 1/002. "Stinkard" towns were those whose villagers spoke a dialect perceived as awkward or impure by most principal Muscogee communities. See John Swanton, *Early History of the Creek Indians and Their Neighbors* (Washington, DC: Government Printing Office, 1922), 12–14.

59. Fitch to Middleton, 25 September 1726, JCSC, CO 5/429/Pt. 1/002. On the distinction between Creek white and red towns, see Ethbridge, *Creek Country*, 93.

60. Chicken's record of the Nacoochee talks of 25 October 1726 is enclosed in Chicken to Fitch, 26 October 1726, JCSC, 15 November 1726, CO 5/429/Pt. 1/002.

61. Chicken to Fitch, 26 October 1726, JCSC, 15 November 1726, CO 5/429/Pt. 1/003.

62. On the decision to hold the conference in Charles Town, see Middleton to Fitch, 3 September 1726, and Middleton to Chicken, 2 September 1726, JCSC (Upper House), CO 5/429/Pt. 1/001.

63. See the talk of Long Warrior as Cherokee spokesman, 25 October 1726, in Chicken to Fitch, 26 October 1726, JCSC, 15 November 1726, CO 5/429/002.

64. On Cherokee deputies' arrival in South Carolina's settlements, see sessions of 11–13 December 1726, JCSC, CO 5/429/Pt. 1/003. Hobohatchey arrived with several Abeika men in Charles Town on 10 January 1727. The number of men was unspecified, but likely small. On December 21, 1726, the Creeks were said to be on the way with six headmen and two male attendants. Fitch sent word that Chigelly would speak for all Creeks. See JCHA 1726, 46, 50. The Lower Creek delegation's arrival is recorded in "A Discourse with the Indians," Council Journal, 24 January 1727, CO 5/387/084.

65. Middleton to Colonel Drake, 25 November 1726, JCSC, Council minutes, CO 5/429/003.

66. Record of 13 December 1726, *Journal of the Commons House*, 34–35.

496   *Notes to Pages 86–91*

67. "A Discourse with the Indians," Council Journal, 26 January 1727, CO 5/387/084. On Cherokee men's dress, see Susan C. Power, *Art of the Cherokee: Prehistory to the Present* (Athens: University of Georgia Press, 2007), 42–43; Charles Hudson, *The Southeastern Indians* (Knoxville: University of Tennessee Press, 1976), 262–264, 325–326.

68. "A Discourse with the Indians," Council Journal, 26 January 1727.

69. "A Discourse with the Indians," Council Journal, 26 January 1727.

70. "A Discourse with the Indians," Council Journal, 26 January 1727.

71. "A Discourse with the Indians," Council Journal, 26 January 1727.

72. In the fall of 1727, Tugaloo men told Eleazar Wigan that Creek warriors were stalking their town and they expected to be attacked. See Wigan to Middleton, 3 October 1727, in "Sundry Letters, discourses with the Indians," CO 5/387/106. See also David H. Corkran, *The Creek Frontier, 1540–1783* (Norman: University of Oklahoma Press, 1967), 80–83, 195–208, 127–130, 150–156, 162; Hahn, *Invention of the Creek Nation*, 199, 210–211, 224–225.

73. The Cherokee headman "Johnny" answered Middleton most directly about the Yamasees. See "A Discourse with the Indians," Council Journal, 25–26 January 1727, CO 5/387/084. The record of 25 January 1727 included the Coweta warrior's refusal of northward migration.

74. "A Discourse with the Indians," Council Journal, 26 January 1727, CO 5/387/084.

75. "A Discourse with the Indians," Council Journal, 26 January 1727, CO 5/387/084.

76. Chicken to Middleton, 10 August 1726; Wigan to Chicken, 3 August 1726, both in "Colonel Chicken's Journal," in JCSC (Upper House), 1 September 1726, JCSC, CO 5/429/Pt. 1 / 001. The term Nottawega (spelled in many ways) appears commonly in Carolina records of the 1740s and 1750s, reflecting inroads that northern Indians of varied ethnicity made into Cherokee territory. See, for example, entry of 18 July 1753, DRIA, 1:423.

77. On the return of the pipe, see entry of 31 August 1727, JCSC, CO 5/429 / Pt. 2 / 002.

78. For destroyed deerskins and other evidence, see JCHA, 21 September 1727, CO 5/429/Pt. 2 /007. See also Oatis, *A Colonial Complex*, 277–278.

79. JCSC, 29 September 1727, CO 5/429 / Pt. 2 / 002. On the plan to raise Cherokee fighters, see JCHA, 25–26 August 1727 and 23 September 1727, CO 5/429 / Pt. 2 / 002.

80. On the small tribes in Palmer's expedition, see Commons House session of 3 May 1728, and for then scalp bounties, see resolve of 29 February 1728, JCHA, CO 5/430/003.

81. The Pon Pon Indians, living by Port Royal, were another group aiding Palmer's campaign. See Steven C. Hahn, "The Long Yamasee War," in *The Yamasee Indians: From Florida to South Carolina*, ed. Denise I. Bossy (Lincoln: University of Nebraska Press, 2018), 204–212.

82. Journal of Charlesworth Glover, 5 March 1728, CO 5/387/106.

83. On the Tyger King, see Report by Committee on Indian Affairs, 16 July 1728, JCSC, CO 5/430/004.

Notes to Pages 91–96

84. On the opening of trade with Upper Creek towns, see record of 12 April 1728, JCHA, CO 5/430/003. On Glover's independent action on the trade front, see his Journal, 15 April 1728, and his letter to Middleton, 17 March 1728, CO 5/387/106. See also Oatis, *A Colonial Complex*, 285–286.

85. On the pipe, see entry of 31 August 1727, JCSC, CO 5/429/Pt. 2/002. See also "The Tunisee Warriour's Answer to the Governour's Talk," 2 October 1727, in Wigan to Middleton, 7 October 1727, in "Sundry Letters, discourses with the Indians," CO 5/387/106.

86. "Talk to the Headmen," Colonel Chicken's Journal [1726], 27 July 1726, CO 5/429/Pt. 1/001.

87. Wigan to Middleton, 7 October 1727, in "Sundry Letters," CO 5/387/106.

88. For Herbert's meeting with Long Warrior, see John Herbert, *Journal of Colonel John Herbert*, ed. A. S. Salley (Columbia: printed for the Historical Commission of South Carolina, 1936), 16–17. On the Tellico foray and the message to Long Warrior, see Herbert to Middleton, 10 February 1728, in Herbert, *Journal*.

89. "The Tunisee Warriour's Answer to the Governour's Talk at a Meeting of the Head Men at Tunisee," 2 October 1727, in Wigan to Middleton, 7 October 1727, in "Sundry Letters," CO 5/387/106. The council recommended a present be sent to Great Tellico's head warrior. See Committee on Indian Affairs, 16 July 1728, JCSC, CO 5/430/004.

4. A Cherokee Voyage to London

1. For the Mohawk visit, see Alden T. Vaughan, *Transatlantic Encounters: American Indians in Britain, 1500–1776* (Cambridge: Cambridge University Press, 2006), 117–130; Eric Hinderaker, "The 'Four Indian Kings' and the Imaginative Reconstruction of the First British Empire," *William and Mary Quarterly* 53 (July 1996): 487–526. Hendrick had several Indian names. See Timothy J. Shannon, "Dressing for Success on the Mohawk Frontier: Hendrick, William Johnson, and the Indian Fashion," *William and Mary Quarterly* 53 (January 1996): 26–32.

2. For the Covenant Chain, see Daniel K. Richter, *The Ordeal of the Longhouse: The Peoples of the Iroquois League in the Era of European Colonization* (Chapel Hill: University of North Carolina Press, 1992), 134–141, 160–161, 208–212; Francis Jennings, *The Ambiguous Iroquois Empire: The Covenant Chain Confederation of Indian Nations with English Colonies from its beginnings to the Lancaster Treaty of 1744* (New York: Norton, 1984), 83–84, 165–167. For the renewal of the Chain, see Sachems to Governor Robert Hunter, 25 September 1714, DRCHNY, 5:385–386 ("good understanding and friendship" and "Devils or men").

3. Cuming's account of his journey into "the Cherrokee Mountains" is in the *Historical Register*, vol. 16, *1731* (London: H. B. Meere, 1731), 3–19. He used the spelling "Cherrokee" throughout.

4. On the political scene, see M. Eugene Sirmans, *Colonial South Carolina: A Political History, 1663–1763* (Chapel Hill: University of North Carolina Press, 1966), 157–162.

5. *Historical Register*, 16:6–8. A printed reproduction of Hunter's map is in A. S. Salley Jr., *George Hunter's Map of the Cherokee Country and the Path thereto in 1730* (Columbia, SC: State Company, 1917).

498   *Notes to Pages 96–101*

6. *Historical Register,* 16:2–6.

7. For Cuming's journey and the treaty terms, see *Historical Register,* 16:1–18.

8. For the thunderstorm and the citation of Tacitus, see *Historical Register,* 16:7, 13 ("barbarous People"). On colonialism and the "mastery" of "cultural space," see Jack P. Greene, *Imperatives, Behaviors, and identities: Essays in Early American Cultural History* (Charlottesville: University Press of Virginia, 1992), 3.

9. On Cuming and "Iron Ore," see *Historical Register,* 16:11.

10. See the recollection of Cuming's venture in "Historical Relation of Facts Delivered by Ludovick Grant, Indian Trader, to His Excellency, the Governor of South Carolina" [1756], *South Carolina Historical and Genealogical Magazine* 10 (January 1909): 54–68, 54–58. Grant may not have been at Keowee when Cuming first arrived but joined him on his tour of Appalachian Cherokee towns. See *Historical Register,* 16:3.

11. *Historical Register,* 16:10 ("Ooneekawy"); "Historical Relation of Facts," 57 ("above a night"). On Unicoi, see James Mooney, *Myths of the Cherokee* (1900; reprint, New York: Dover, 1995), 87, 542.

12. *Historical Register,* 16:2.

13. *Historical Register,* 16:11.

14. For the Nequassee meeting, see *Historical Register,* 16:3 ("Middle Settlements"), 4 ("the great Man" and "Emperor"), 11 ("assembled"), 12 ("Sovereignty" and "Declaration of Obedience").

15. For biographical notes on Cuming, see *Complete Baronetage,* vol. 4, *1665–1707,* ed. George E. Cokayne (Exeter: William Pollard and Co., 1904), 371. On Cuming's assertion of loyalty to the House of Hanover, see *Daily Journal* (London), 12 September 1730.

16. For the "crown" as Emblem," see *Historical Register,* 16:6, 13. See also "Historical Relation of Facts," 57.

17. "Answer of the Indian Chiefs of the Cherokee Nation," 9 September 1730, enclosed in Board of Trade to Newcastle, 30 September 1730, CO 5 / 4 / Pt. 2 / 014.

18. Attakullakulla assumed the name Chuconnunta during the interview. See "A Conversation between his Excellency the Governor of South Carolina and Chuconnunta a head man of the Cherokees Whose name formerly was Ouconecaw," 12 January 1756, in "Historical Relation of Facts," 65–68.

19. "A Conversation," in "Historical Relation of Facts," 65–66.

20. "A Conversation," in "Historical Relation of Facts," 66–67. For Cuming's speech at Nequassee, see *Historical Register,* 16:4.

21. "A Conversation," in "Historical Relation of Facts," 68.

22. "A Conversation," in "Historical Relation of Facts," 65 ("now alive"). This "Relation," in its original, was dispatched by Glen to the Board of Trade, 14 April 1756, CO 5 / 14 / 022. See also Tistoe to Lyttelton, 14 November 1758, JCSC, CO 5 / 476 / 001. One of six Native men who marked the British treaty is identified as "Tathtowe"—a likely reference to Tistoe. See *Historical Register,* 16:17. On the "performative" in Native diplomacy, see Stephanie Fitzgerald, "'I Wunnatuckquannum, This Is My Hand': Native Performance in Massachusett Language Deeds," in *Native Acts: Indian Performance, 1603–1832,* ed. Joshua David Bellin and Laura L. Mielke (Lincoln: University of Nebraska Press, 2011), 145–167.

23. Cuming implied that four of the Cherokee voyagers to England came from Tasetchee (Tasache), which he spelled "Tassetchie." See *Historical Register,* 16:5, 10.

Notes to Pages 102–108

Askiyvgvsta (sometimes spelled "Skaygusta" or "Skiagusta") was a head warrior's title. Cuming's "Skallelockee" ("Skalilosken" in the official British record) was a headman and perhaps chief war speaker. On the title, see *The Payne-Butrick Papers*, ed. William L. Anderson, Jane L. Brown, and Anne F. Rogers, 2 vols. (Lincoln: University of Nebraska Press, 2010), 1:220, 245–247, 2:113. Oukah Ulah was translated in the English press as "King [chief] that is to be," perhaps implying a prospective priest-chief. For this translation, see *Historical Register*, 16:5; *Daily Journal* (London), 4 August 1730. Attakullakulla's recollection is in "A Conversation," in "Historical Relation of Facts," ("pleasure"), 67.

24. For Bunning's role, see EAID, 13:142. On creation myths, see Mooney, *Myths of the Cherokee*, 239–240; Jace Weaver, *The Red Atlantic: American Indigenes and the Making of the Atlantic World, 1000–1927* (Chapel Hill: University of North Carolina Press, 2014), 13–14.

25. On the Cherokees' arrival, see *Daily Journal*, 12 June 1730. For British-Carolina connections, see Huw David, *Trade, Politics, and Revolution: South Carolina and Britain's Atlantic Commerce, 1730–1790* (Columbia: University of South Carolina Press, 2018).

26. *Historical Register*, 16:6. On the investiture on 18 June 1730, see Robert Richard Tighe and James Edward Davis, *Annals of Windsor*, vol. 2 (London: Longman, Brown, Green, Longmans, and Roberts, 1858), 517–518; *Daily Journal*, 20 June 1730.

27. *Historical Register*, 16:6. For the Cherokee experience in England, see Vaughan, *Transatlantic Encounters*, 142–148; Nancy Shoemaker, *A Strange Likeness: Becoming Red and White in Eighteenth-Century North America* (New York: Oxford University Press, 2004), 36–37, 51–52; Leonard J. Sadosky, *Revolutionary Negotiations: Indians, Empires, and Diplomats in the Founding of America* (Charlottesville: University of Virginia Press, 2009), 25.

28. *The Daily Post* (London), 24 June 1730.

29. James Adair, *The History of the American Indians*, ed. Kathryn E. Holland Braund (1775; Tuscaloosa: University of Alabama Press, 2003), 70. See also Edna Geraldine Saunders, "A Study of the Cherokee Indians' Clothing Practices and History for the Period 1654 to 1838" (M.S. thesis, New Mexico State University, 1969), 31–34.

30. Vaughan, *Transatlantic Encounters*, 144–145. White Owl appears to be holding a goblet in his right hand. For the English tendency to rank Cherokees as "King," "Prince," "General," and "Captain," see the *Daily Post*, 20 August 1730.

31. On the description of festivities, see notice of 27 July 1730 in *Fog's Weekly Journal*, 22 August 1730. The Cherokees left Windsor on 31 July 1720. See *Grub Street Journal*, 6 August 1730.

32. On the military review, see the *Daily Post*, 26 June 1730. For the Birchin Lane reception and Bunning, see *London Journal*, 15 August 1730. Concert and theatre performances are noted in the *Daily Post*, 18–19 August 1730. For the trip to Richmond, see *Daily Journal*, 20 August 1730. The archery display is reported in *London Journal*, 29 August 1730. See also Vaughan, *Transatlantic Encounters*, 143–144; Weaver, *The Red Atlantic*, 155–156.

33. J. A. Crowe to Cuming, 15 July 1730, CO 5 / 4 / Pt. 2 / 014. See also Cuming to the Board of Trade, letter received 15 September 1730, CO 5 / 4. The lodging at "an Undertaker in King street" is referenced in the *Daily Journal*, 3 August 1730.

34. For the Board of Trade and the "Lords Commissioners," see Oliver Morton Dickerson, *American Colonial Government, 1696–1765: A Study of the Board of Trade in relation to the American Colonies, Political, Industrial, Administrative* (Cleveland: Arthur H. Clark, 1912), 19, 25–26, 82, 204.

35. Board of Trade to the Duke of Newcastle, 20 August 1730, CO 5/4. This document is printed in EAID, 13:135.

36. For the Cherokee visit to Whitehall, see the *Universal Spectator and Weekly Journal* (London), 27 June 1730.

37. The treaty's wording appears in slightly different fashion in the document that the Board of Trade officially sent the Duke of Newcastle and what was inscribed in the Lords Commissioners' journal. I have chosen to quote from the version the Board sent to the duke. See "Articles of Friendship and Commerce," 7 September 1730, enclosed in the Board of Trade to Newcastle, 30 September 1730, CO 5/4/Pt. 2/014. The same is found in Board to Newcastle, 9 September 1730, CO 5/400. For the Board's record, which names seven Cherokee men in attendance (and not six, as listed in the letter of 30 September cited above), see JBT, 6:140–150.

38. "Articles of Friendship and Commerce," 7 September 1730.

39. "Articles of Friendship and Commerce," 7 September 1730.

40. The Cherokee statement about not being "enemies" is the Board of Trade record of 7 September 1730. See JBT, 6:140–150. On the weaponry, see the *Universal Spectator and Weekly Journal*, 12 September 1730.

41. James Adair wrote this account more than thirty-five years after the event from his recollection of a conversation with interpreter Eleazar Wigan. See Adair, *History of the American Indians*, 103–104; *Historical Register*, 16:13.

42. "Answer of the Indian Chiefs," 9 September 1730, enclosed in Board of Trade to Newcastle, 30 September 1730, CO 5/4/Pt. 2/014. For Scalilosken Ketagusta as speaker at the conference of 9 September, see EAID, 13:139.

43. "Answer of the Indian Chiefs," 9 September 1730. On the kisses and song, see the *Universal Spectator and Weekly Journal*, 12 September 1730.

44. See Cuming's memorial to the Board of Trade, received 15 September 1729, CO 5/361/030. On Cuming's summons by the Board of Trade and the Cherokees' assent, see the *Daily Journal*, 1 October 1730.

45. For Cuming's letter refuting the charge of Jacobitism and financial fraud, see the *Daily Journal*, 12 September 1730. For the accusatory letter, see "An Extract of a Letter from South Carolina," 12 June 1730, printed in the *Weekly News-Letter* (Boston), 30 July 1730.

46. On Cuming's publishing the treaty, see "Articles of Friendship and Commerce," 7 September 1730. For the Board's refusal to allow one Cherokee man to remain with Cuming, see Board of Trade to Cuming, 30 September 1730, CO 5/401/001. For Cuming's petition to serve the king in Cherokee country, see "The Humble Memorial of Sir Alexander Cuming, Baronet" [1731], CO 5/4/Pt. 2/014. Cuming's previous petition of 1730, requesting compensation for services, is found in the same file.

47. On Cuming's ideas of Jewish settlement, and establishing a bank in "the Cherokee Mountains," see Cuming to the Duke of Bedford, 24 May 1750, CO 5/656/065. For glimpses of Cuming's later years, see *Scottish Notes and Queries*, vol. 6 (Aberdeen: D. Wyllie and Son, 1893), 61; *Notes and Queries*, vol. 5 (London: George Bell, 1852):

Notes to Pages 113–118   501

278–279. Cuming became a pensioner of the Charterhouse in 1766. See Daniel Lyons, *The Environs of London*, vol. 4 (London, 1796), 20–21.

48. On the negotiation with Cherokees on their return trek, see *South Carolina Council Journal*, 18 December 1730, EAID, 13:141–142. On the homeward journey, see Vaughan, *Transatlantic Encounters*, 148.

49. *South Carolina Council Journal*, 18 December 1730, EAID, 13:141–142. On the London negotiation's impact, see Kristofer Ray, *Cherokee Power: Imperial and Indigenous Geopolitics in the Trans-Appalachian West* (Norman: University of Oklahoma Press, 2023), 54–55.

5. Warfare and Peace Quests across Half a Continent

1. For the alleged plot, see Council minutes, 25 April 1733, CO 5 /434/003. On Cherokee "Insolence," see Report, 17 May 1734, JCSC, Upper House of Assembly, CO 5/435/002. For Johnson's complaint about "young ungovernable fellows," see his letter to the Board of Trade, received 9 November 1734, in CSP, item 380, 41:277–295. For negotiations in November 1734, see JCHA 1734–1735, 7–8, 20 ("if some small things"). See also session of 23 November 1734, JCSC (Upper House), CO 5 /434/002.

2. Talk of 23 November 1734, as drafted by the assembly the previous day, JCHA 1734–1735, 22 ("because I have men"). For population estimates, see Converse E. Clowse, *Economic Beginnings in Colonial South Carolina, 1670–1730* (Columbia: University of South Carolina Press, 1971), 230–231, 252.

3. For the royal charter of 1732, see CRG, 1:18. See also Oglethorpe to the South Carolina assembly, 5 August 1736, JCHA 1736–1739, 146.

4. John Gardiner's Journal, in Committee report, 16 December 1736, JCHA 1736–1739, 91–92, 135–137. On the expulsions, see JCHA 1736–1739, 123–126, 141. See also John T. Juricek, *Colonial Georgia and the Creeks: Anglo-Indian Diplomacy on the Southern Frontier, 1733–1763* (Gainesville: University Press of Florida, 2010), 67.

5. Gardiner's Journal, 136–137.

6. Report of Committee, 15 December 1736, JCHA 1736–1739, 74–75. It is not clear if the South Carolina assemblymen, while stating their views, had in mind any particular authority on natural law and rights.

7. M. Eugene Sirmans, *Colonial South Carolina: A Political History, 1663–1763* (Chapel Hill: University of North Carolina Press, 1966), 188–195; Julie Anne Sweet, *Negotiating for Georgia: British-Creek Relations in the Trustee Era, 1733–1752* (Athens: University of Georgia Press, 2005), 99–105.

8. JCSC, 19 March 1737, CO 5/438/002; Broughton to the Duke of Newcastle, 6 February 1737, CO 5/388/Pt. 1 /050. On Oglethorpe's command, see Juricek, *Colonial Georgia*, 95–96.

9. On the Oglethorpe-Creek agreement of 11 August 1739, see EAID, 11:96; Juricek, *Colonial Georgia*, 109–113. See also Noeleen McIlvenna, *The Short Life of Free Georgia: Class and Race in the Colonial South* (Chapel Hill: University of North Carolina Press, 2015), 13–15, 51–52, 57–60.

10. On the colonial response to rebellion, see Bull to the Duke of Newcastle, 6 October 1739, CO 5 / Pt. 1 /069; "An Account of the Negroe Insurrection South Carolina

502   *Notes to Pages 118–125*

[1739]," CO 5/640. See also Peter H. Wood, *Black Majority: Negroes in Colonial South Carolina From 1670 through the Stono Rebellion* (New York: Norton, 1975), 310–317.

11. A thousand deaths would have represented roughly one-third of all Cherokee males of fighting age. See Paul Kelton, *Cherokee Medicine, Colonial Germs: An Indigenous Nation's Fight against Smallpox, 1518–1824* (Norman: University of Oklahoma Press, 2015), 85–86; Russell Thornton, *The Cherokees: A Population History* (Lincoln: University of Nebraska Press, 1990), 31. For Oglethorpe's conference with the Cherokees, see CRG, 5:229.

12. Thomas Eyre's Account [1739–1740], in EAID, 11:100–101; Rodney E. Baine, "General James Oglethorpe and the Expedition Against St. Augustine," *Georgia Historical Quarterly* 84 (Summer 2000): 197–229, 210–211. See also [William Stephens], "A Journal of the Proceedings in Georgia Beginning October 20, 1737," CRG, 4:553–554. On Native enlistment, see Oglethorpe to Trustees, 5 October 1739, CO 5/640.

13. Deposition of Lt. Bryan, 25 March 1741, JCHA [26 March–1 December 1741], 191 ("A strange Thing"). The capture of the Spanish post is related in the Deposition of Thomas Wright, 25 May 1741 [1740 as printed is in error], JCHA [1741], 184. I have approximated the number of men in the striking force.

14. Deposition of William Steads, 13 March 1740, JCHA [1741], 201 ("Spanish Indian"); Deposition of Capt. Richard Wright, 28 March 1740, JCHA [1741], 204–205. The attack on Fort San Diego began on May 11, with surrender the next day. See excerpt from Oglethorpe's Journal, 14 May 1740, JCHA [1741], 181–182.

15. Baine, "General James Oglethorpe," 215–229; Kenneth Coleman, *Colonial Georgia: A History* (New York: Scribner's, 1976), 66–73; Paul E. Hoffman, *Florida's Frontiers* (Bloomington: Indiana University Press, 2002), 192–193; Steven C. Hahn, *The Invention of the Creek Nation, 1670–1763* (Lincoln: University of Nebraska Press, 2004), 181–184; Sweet, *Negotiating for Georgia*, 141–148.

16. For Cherokee deaths, see "A Journal of the Proceedings in Georgia," CRG, 4:620. On Cherokee conflict with Yuchis and Creeks, see *Journal of Colonel William Stephens*, in CRG, Supplement to vol. 4, 55, 85–86 ("cut his Uncle"), 122.

17. Daniel H. Thomas, *Fort Toulouse: The French Outpost at the Alabamas on the Coosa* (Tuscaloosa: University of Alabama Press, 1989), 10–11, 18–20. Barnwell assessed the French threat along with colleague Richard Boone while in London in 1720. See Boone and Barnwell's letter to the Board of Trade, received 23 August 1720, CO 5/358/Pt. 1/004. Barnwell was the chief draftsman on Native affairs and penned a remarkable map countering French territorial claims. See William P. Cumming, *The Southeast in Early Maps*, 3rd ed., revised and enlarged by Louis De Vorsey Jr. (Chapel Hill: University of North Carolina Press, 1998), 24–25, 218–219.

18. Guillaume de L'Isle, *Carte de la Louisiane et du cours du Mississipi [i.e., Mississippi]* (Paris, 1718), LCCN 2001624908, Geography and Map Division, Library of Congress, https://www.loc.gov/item/2001624908/. See also Board of Trade to John Hyde, 22 July 1719; and Board to the governors, 13 August 1719, JBT, 4:88–103. See also Verner W. Crane, *The Southern Frontier, 1670–1732* (1956; reprint, New York: Norton, 1981), 224–225.

19. Spotswood to the Board of Trade, 1 February 1720, in *The Official Letters of Alexander Spotswood, Lieutenant-Governor of the Colony of Virginia, 1710–1722*, ed. R. A. Brock, 2 vols. (Richmond, 1882–1885), 2:329.

Notes to Pages 125–128

20. Marcel Giraud, *Histoire de la Louisiane Française*, vol. 4, *La Louisiane après le Système de Law (1721–1723)* (Paris: Presses Universitaires de France, 1974), 168–172, 278–280; Daniel H. Usner Jr., *Indians, Settlers, and Slaves in a Frontier Exchange Economy: The Lower Mississippi Valley before 1783* (Chapel Hill: University of North Carolina Press, 1992), 31–33; James Prichard, *In Search of Empire: The French in North America, 1670–1730* (Cambridge: Cambridge University Press, 2004), 40–43; Marcel Giraud, *A History of French Louisiana*, vol. 5, *The Company of the Indies, 1723–1731*, trans. Brian Pearce (Baton Rouge: Louisiana State University Press, 1991), 61–69, 366–368, 484–485; Jacob E. Lee, *Masters of the Middle Waters: Indian Nations and Colonial Ambitions along the Mississippi* (Cambridge, MA: Harvard University Press, 2019), 70–71, 76–80, 87–89.

21. George Edward Milne, *Natchez Country: Indians, Colonists, and the Landscapes of Race in French Louisiana* (Athens: University of Georgia Press, 2015), 176–182; James Taylor Carson, "Sacred Circles and Dangerous People: Native American Cosmology and the French Settlement of Louisiana," in *French Colonial Louisiana and the Atlantic World*, ed. Bradley G. Bond (Baton Rouge: Louisiana State University Press, 2005), 65–81; Usner, *Indians, Settlers, and Slaves*, 66–74.

22. Milne, *Natchez Country*, 195–197; Patricia Dillon Woods, *French-Indian Relations on the Southern Frontier, 1699–1762* (Ann Arbor: UMI Research Press, 1980), 96–102. On population, see Usner, *Indians, Settlers, and Slaves*, 41, 72–75.

23. Milne, *Natchez Country*, 204; Woods, *French-Indian Relations*, 106–107, 120–122. On Chickasaw attacks, see Bienville and Salmon to Maurepas, 20 May 1733; Bienville to Maurepas, 20 August 1735, MPAFD, 1:266–269.

24. On the change in administration, see Charles Edwards O'Neill, *Church and State in French Colonial Louisiana: Policy and Politics to 1732* (New Haven: Yale University Press, 1966), 219–233. See also Bienville to Maurepas, 26 July 1733, MPAFD, 1:210–213 ("dangerous" on 213); Michael J. Foret, "War or Peace? Louisiana, the Choctaws, and the Chickasaws, 1733–1735," *Louisiana History* 3 (Summer 1990): 273–292.

25. The Savannah conference record is in EAID, 11:36–37. For Choctaw unease with the French, see Diron d'Artaguette to Maurepas, 1 September 1734, MPAFD, 4:136. See also Richard White, *The Roots of Dependency: Subsistence, Environment and Social Change among the Choctaws, Pawnees, and Navajos* (Lincoln: University of Nebraska Press, 1983), 54–56.

26. Patricia Galloway, "Choctaw Factionalism and Civil War, 1746–1750," *Journal of Mississippi History* 44 (1982): 289–327, 303–304; Michael James Foret, "On the Marchlands of Empire: Trade, Diplomacy, and War on the Southeastern Frontier, 1733–1763" (Ph.D. diss., College of William and Mary, 1990), 141. (Red Shoe's visit was to Savannah, and not Charles Town as Foret writes.) For Bienville's disgust with the Chickasaws, see his letter to Maurepas, 14 April 1735, MPAFD, 1:256–259. For "expensive" scalps, see Artaguette to Maurepas, 24 October 1737, MPAFD, 4:144.

27. Bienville to Maurepas, 26 August 1734, MPAFD, 1:232. See also James R. Atkinson, *Splendid Land, Splendid People, The Chickasaw Indians to Removal* (Tuscaloosa: University of Alabama Press, 2004), 37–42.

28. Atkinson, *Splendid Land*, 43–58. For Bienville's force, see MPAFD, 1:316. For Bienville's post-campaign assessment, see his letter to Maurepas, 28 June 1736, MPAFD, 1: 305–307. On the battle and French casualties, see *The Memoir of Lieutenant Dumont*,

504   *Notes to Pages 128–131*

1715–1747: A Sojourner in the French Atlantic, trans. Gordon Sayre, ed. Gordon Sayre and Carla Zecher (Chapel Hill: University of North Carolina Press, 2012), 260–273.

29. Artaguette to Maurepas, 24 October 1737, MPAFD, 4:151 ("women"). On Chickasaws and migration, see Atkinson, *Splendid Land*, 41–42, 54, 63–66. On British traders, see Sayre and Zecher, *Memoir of Lieutenant Dumont*, 264–265. South Carolina's advice is in its assembly's resolve, 14 December 1737, JCSC, CO 5/438.

30. Salmon to Maurepas, 1 September 1736, AC, 13A-21; Artaguette to Maurepas, 24 October 1737, MPAFD, 4:149–151.

31. Bienville to Maurepas, 20 December 1737, AC, 13A-22. On Alibamon-Cherokee conflict, see Noyan to Maurepas, 21 February 1734, MPAFD, 4:139–140; Artaguette to Maurepas, 24 October 1737, MPAFD, 146–147.

32. Bienville to Maurepas, 5 September 1736, AC, 13A-21. Bienville initially believed that Chickasaws had joined the Cherokee attack on the French. See Bienville and Salmon to Maurepas, 1 September 1736, AC, 13A-21.

33. On the Chickasaws' "destruction," see Bienville to Maurepas, 26 August 1734, MPAFD, 1:234. For the officers' plans to enslave Chickasaw captives, see Sayre and Zecher, *Memoir of Lieutenant Dumont*, 261.

34. For Bienville's respect for the Chickasaws, see Bienville and Salmon to Maurepas, 1 September 1736, AC, 13A-21.

35. [Alexandre de Batz], "Nations Amies et Ennemies des Tchicachas." A reproduction is in MPAFD, 4:142–143.

36. For an analysis of the map, see Gregory A. Waselkov, "Indian Maps of the Colonial Southeast," in *Powhatan's Mantle: Indians in the Colonial Southeast*, ed. Gregory A. Waselkov, Peter H. Wood, and Tom Hatley, rev. ed. (Lincoln: University of Nebraska Press, 2006), 481–486.

37. Atkinson, *Splendid Land*, 65–67. On Colbert's policy, see W. J. Eccles, *The Canadian Frontier, 1534–1760*, rev. ed. (Albuquerque: University of New Mexico Press, 1983), 62–67.

38. For the estimated numbers of French and Indian warriors, see Woods, *French-Indian Relations*, 142. See also Bienville, "Journal de la Campagne des Tcicachas [Chickasaws]," in *Rapport de l'Archiviste de la Province de Québec pour 1922–1923* [Québec, 1923], 168. For a higher estimate of combatants, see Atkinson, *Splendid Land*, 67.

39. Atkinson, *Splendid Land*, 68–73; Woods, *French-Indian Relations*, 143–144. Iroquois continued to attack the Chickasaws after Bienville's peace accord. See Bienville to Maurepas, 30 April 1741, AC, 13A-26.

40. For the build-up to the Choctaw civil war, see White, *Roots of Dependency*, 55–63.

41. The Cherokee attack is discussed in Bienville to Maurepas, 18 June 1740, MPAFD, 3:736–737; Louboey to Maurepas, 23 June 1740, and Jadart de Beauchamp to Maurepas, 25 January 1741, MPAFD, 4:169, 176; Louboey to Maurepas, 29 June 1740, AC, 13A-25. On the attackers, see "Journal of Antoine Bonnefoy," in *Travels in the American Colonies*, ed. Newton D. Mereness (New York: Macmillan, 1916), 246–247.

42. Bienville to Maurepas, 30 April 1741 and Louboey to Maurepas, 18 July 1741, AC 13A-26; Beauchamp to Maurepas, 25 April 1741, MPAFD, 4:182–183; *Journal of Colonel William Stephens*, suppl. 4:81–82; Bull to the Duke of Newcastle, 20 March

Notes to Pages 131–136   505

1741, CO 5/384/035. For ammunition and other presents, see entry of 19 March 1741, JCHA [18 November 1740–26 March 1741], 529.

43. For the gifts, see record of 23 March 1738, JCHA 1736–1739, 551.

44. "Journal of Bonnefoy," 247–249. On the attack force, see Declaration of Cossot, 3 December 1742, AC, 13A-27; Bienville to Maurepas, 18 February and 18 March 1742, AC, 13A-27.

45. "Journal of Bonnefoy," 243–244.

46. "Journal of Bonnefoy," 245–246. On the captive experience, see Christina Snyder, *Slavery in Indian Country: The Changing Face of Captivity in Early America* (Cambridge, MA: Harvard University Press, 2010), 103–104.

47. "Journal of Bonnefoy," 250–251.

48. "Journal of Bonnefoy," 255.

49. For unknown reason, Bonnefoy referred to Priber as "Pierre Albert" in his journal. See "Journal of Bonnefoy," 247. Grant's recollection of Priber, was drafted on 12 January 1756, in a report to Governor James Glen. See "Historical Relation of Facts Delivered by Ludovick Grant, Indian Trader, to His Excellency the Governor of South Carolina," *South Carolina Historical and Genealogical Magazine* 10 (January 1909): 54–68, 59–60. See also Knox Mellon Jr., "Christian Priber's Cherokee 'Kingdom of Paradise,'" *Georgia Historical Quarterly* 57 (Fall 1973): 319–331; Julie Anne Sweet, "'A Very Extraordinary Type of Creature': Conflicting Contemporary Perspectives on Christian Priber," *South Carolina Historical Magazine* 118 (January 2017): 60–80.

50. Bull to the Board of Trade, 5 October 1739, CO 5/367/011; Grant, "Historical Relation of Facts," 60 ("great present"). See also Mellon, "Christian Priber's Cherokee 'Kingdom of Paradise,'" 325–326.

51. Grant, "Historical Relation of Facts," 61; Mellon, "Christian Priber's Cherokee 'Kingdom of Paradise,'" 326–328; Verner W. Crane, "A Lost Utopia of the First American Frontier," *Sewanee Review* 27, no. 1 (1909): 48–61, 60–61; Edward J. Cashin, *Lachlan McGillivray, Indian Trader: The Shaping of the Southern Colonial Frontier* (Athens: University of Georgia Press, 1992), 51–52.

52. Beauharnois to Minister, 12 October 1742, in WHC, 17:429. See also Norman W. Caldwell, "The Chickasaw Threat to French Colonial Control of the Mississippi in the 1740's," *Chronicles of Oklahoma* 16 (December 1938): 476–477.

53. For the gifts, ordered on 23 March 1738, see JCHA 1736–1739, 551. Moytoy's death is noted in Oglethorpe to the Trustees of Georgia, 3 March 1742, CRG, 23:224.

54. James H. Merrell, "'Their Very Bones Shall Fight': The Catawba-Iroquois Wars," in *Beyond the Covenant Chain: The Iroquois and Their Neighbors in Indian North America, 1600–1800*, ed. Daniel K. Richter and James H. Merrell (Syracuse, NY: Syracuse University Press, 1987), 115–126.

55. Warren R. Hofstra and Karl B. Raitz, eds., *The Great Valley Road of Virginia: Shenandoah Landscapes* (Charlottesville: University of Virginia Press, 2010); John Harstrar, *Breaking the Appalachian Barrier: Maryland as a Gateway to Ohio and the West, 1750–1850* (Jefferson, NC: McFarland, 2018), 44–47, 50–51.

56. Gooch to the Board of Trade, 20 September 1738, CO 5/1324/031 ("back of the mountains"). See also Warren R. Hofstra, *The Planting of New Virginia: Settlement and Landscape in the Shenandoah Valley* (Baltimore: Johns Hopkins University Press, 2004), 163–169.

57. Gooch to the Board of Trade, 20 September 1738, CO 5/1324/031 ("His Majesty's Government" to "the same Protection"); Gooch to the Board of Trade, 15 February 1739, CO 5/1324 ("the [white] Subjects"). For conceptions of the Covenant Chain, see Francis Jennings, *The Ambiguous Iroquois Empire: The Covenant Chain Confederation of Indian Tribes with English Colonies from its beginnings to the Lancaster Treaty of 1744* (New York: Norton, 1984), 43, 148–149, 170–171, 297–298, 368–375.

58. Clarke to the Six Nations, 10 August 1740, DRCHNY 6:175 ("all the Nations").

59. Answer Made by the Six Nations, and Clarke to the Six Nations, 12 August 1740, DRCHNY, 6:178 ("be united" and "Father").

60. For the conference, see Bull to Clarke, June 1741, DRCHNY, 6:210–211.

61. Beauharnois to the Senecas, and Address of the Sault [Iroquois] to the Onondagas, 31 July 1742, in DRCHNY, 9:1001–1003. On the Cherokee visit, see "Conrad Weiser's Report on his Journey to Onondaga," delivered 1 September 1743, PCP, 4:667 (entry of 31 July 1743); 4:668 ("to the End of the World," entry of 2 August 1743).

62. *A Treaty Held at the Town of Lancaster, By the Honourable, the Lieutenant-Governor of the Province, and the Honourable the Commissioners for the Provinces of Virginia and Maryland, With the Indians of the Six Nations* (Philadelphia: B. Franklin, 1744), 31 ("the Great God"), 35 ("Onontio," "our Brethren"). The spelling of Iroquois names follows usage in *The Lancaster Treaty of 1744 with Related Documents*, ed. James H. Merrell (Boston: Bedford/St. Martin's, 2008), xiv–xv.

63. A French record of attacks (December 1745 to August 1746) is in DRCHNY, 10:32–35. See also Richard White, *The Middle Ground: Indians, Empires, and Republics in the Great Lakes Region, 1650–1815* (Cambridge: Cambridge University Press, 1991), 198; Ian Steele, *Betrayals: Fort William Henry and the "Massacre"* (New York: Oxford University Press, 1990), 18–22; Eccles, *The Canadian Frontier*, 150–151; Colin G. Calloway, *The Western Abenakis of Vermont, 1600–1800* (Norman: University of Oklahoma Press, 1991), 143–159.

64. "Journal of Bonnefoy," 241–243, 251, 255. See also Bienville's reports to Maurepas of 27 June and 5 August 1742, AC, 13A-27.

65. Guy Frégeault, *Le Grand Marquis: Pierre de Rigaud de Vaudreuil et la Louisiane* (Montreal: FIDES, 1952), 160, 166, 177–186, 404–409; Khalil Saadani, "Gift Exchange between the French and Native Americans in Louisiana," trans. Joanne Burnett, in Bond, *French Colonial Louisiana*, 52–61.

66. Frégault, *Le Grand Marquis*, 121–130.

67. Vaudreuil to Maurepas, 18 July 1743, AC, 13A-28. For French anxieties about the Cherokees, see also Kristofer Ray, "Cherokees and Franco-British Confrontation in the Tennessee Corridor, 1730–1760," *Native South* 7 (2014): 33–67, 39–41.

68. On Shawnee diplomacy and geographic range, see Beauharnois to Maurepas, 13 October 1743, DRCHNY, 9:1097; "Mémoire sur la Louisiane 1746," AC, 13A-30; *The Edmund Atkin Report and Plan of 1755*, ed. Wilber R. Jacobs (Columbia: University of South Carolina Press, 1954), 65 ("the greatest Travellers"); Sami Lakomäki, *Gathering Together: The Shawnee People through Diaspora and Nationhood, 1600–1870* (New Haven: Yale University Press, 2014), 24.

69. On the Ohio country, see Eric Hinderaker, *Elusive Empires: Constructing Empire in the Ohio Valley, 1673–1800* (Cambridge: Cambridge University Press, 1997), 18–20, 26–31, 68–71; James H. Merrell, *Into the American Woods: Negotiators on the Pennsylvania*

Notes to Pages 140–145

Frontier (New York: Norton, 1999), 74–75, 166, 181, 221–222; Michael N. McConnell, *A Country Between: The Upper Ohio Valley and Its Peoples, 1724–1774* (Lincoln: University of Nebraska Press, 1992), 52–54.

70. On Peter (Pierre) Chartier, see White, *The Middle Ground*, 189–193; Warren, *The World the Shawnees Made: Migration and Violence in Early America* (Chapel Hill: University of North Carolina Press, 2014), 174–178, 199, 211; Lakomäki, *Gathering Together*, 62–63. On the capture of British traders, see Affidavits, 4 June 1746, JCSC, CO 5/455/001. For talk of "a general peace," see Grant to Glen, 19 March 1746, read before the council on 13 April 1746, JCSC, CO 5/455. On Shawnee migration from Canada to the Alabama, see Vaudreuil to Maurepas, 12 February 1744, MPAFD, 4:222; Vaudreuil to Maurepas, 28 December 1744, AC, 13A-28.

71. On Cherokee diplomacy, see Vaudreuil to Maurepas, 6 February 1746, AC, 13A-30. Many Shawnees wanted a "safe distance from imperial power." See Lakomäki, *Gathering Together*, 63.

72. Native visitors at Chota included Shawnees, "Nantueas" (possibly Ottawas or Weas), "Tewetuas" (Miamis), and "Yachtians" (perhaps Yankton Sioux who came to live in Illinois). See Grant, via Doharty, to Glen, March 1746. On the Shawnee presence, see Skiagusta of Keowee and Conontocheskoi of Estanli to Glen, 19 March 1746, and Bunning to Glen, 17 March 1746. (These messages are in South Carolina council minutes of 27 March 1746). See also report from Upper Towns, conveyed in letter by James Paris to Richard Kent, 20 March 1746 (read in council on 17 April 1746), JCSC, CO 5/455/001. For Illinois Indian involvement with the Sioux, see Robert Michael Morrissey, *Empire by Collaboration: Indians, Colonists, and Governments in Colonial Illinois Country* (Philadelphia: University of Pennsylvania Press, 2015), 90, 113, 116, 125.

73. For French conceptions of Cherokee towns, see Vaudreuil to Maurepas, 20 November 1746, AC, 13A-30.

74. Bull to Clarke, [n.d.] June 1741, CO 5/1094/Pt. 2. A record of the same conference, 23 May 1741, is in Bull to Clarke, June 1741, DRCHNY, 6:211.

75. See the reference to "Connocutee" in Grant, "Historical Relation of Facts," 62.

76. Alex Murdoch, "James Glen and the Indians," in *Military Governors and Imperial Frontiers, c. 1600–1800: A Study of Scotland and Empires*, ed. A. Mackillop and Steve Murdoch (Leiden: Brill, 2003), 141; Sirmans, *Colonial South Carolina*, 233–236.

77. On the Jacobite defeat, see Glen's speech, 16 September 1746, JCHA, CO 5/454/003.

78. Mémoire sur la Louisiane 1746, AC, 13A-30.

79. For Malatchi's words of 3 November 1746 during the conference of 1–3 November 1746, see JCSC, CO 5/455/001. See also Hahn, *Invention of the Creek Nation*, 206–207.

80. Galloway, "Choctaw Factionalism and Civil War"; Cashin, *Lachlan McGillivray*, 92–100; James Adair, *The History of the American Indians*, ed. Kathryn E. Holland Braund (1775; Tuscaloosa: University of Alabama Press, 2003), 5–15; Vaudreuil to Maurepas, July 18, 1743, AC, 13A-28.

81. For the Abeika response, see Journal of Beauchamp [16 September–19 October 1746], MPAFD, 4:275–276. On the Shawnee attack, see Anonymous Letter [1747], MPAFD, 4:309–310.

82. Galloway, "Choctaw Factionalism and Civil War," 316–326; Usner, *Indians, Settlers, and Slaves*, 92–96. Choctaw "rebels" fought the French into 1750 before being suppressed. See Norman W. Caldwell, "The Southern Frontier During King George's War," *Journal of Southern History* 7 (February 1941): 37–54, 54.

83. On Native disaffection with the French, see White, *The Middle Ground*, 198–202; McConnell, *A County Between*, 66–74; Morrissey, *Empire by Collaboration*, 177–179. On the Tennessee (Cherokee) and Wabash Rivers, see Vaudreuil to Maurepas, 22 March and 8 April 1747, AC, 13A-31.

84. On Glen as "Eldest Brother," see Notice of 30 April 1745 in *South-Carolina Gazette*, 6 May 1745. Ammouiscossitte's name is rendered "Oukaaouskassatte" in his talk of 29 April 1745, which is recorded in full in *South-Carolina Gazette*, 18 May 1745.

85. Talk of Skiagusta (sometimes spelled "Skiagunsta"), 29 April 1746, in *South-Carolina Gazette*, 18 May 1745.

86. Glen to the Cherokees and Catawbas, 30 April 1746, in *South-Carolina Gazette*, 6 May 1746.

87. For Glen's journey, see Charles Town notice of 26 May 1746, in *New-York Evening Post*, 30 June 1746; Glen to the Duke of Newcastle, 3 May and 29 September 1746, CO 5/388/Pt. 2.

88. Glen to the Duke of Newcastle, 29 September 1746 (all quotations in paragraph), CO 5/388/Pt. 2.

89. The treaty of cession of 12 February 1747 is in EAID, 13:198–199.

90. Pawley's journal records events of 26 February to 3 March 1747. See T. F. Brewer and J. Baillie, "The Journal of George Pawley's 1746 Agency to the Cherokee," *Journal of Cherokee Studies* 16 (1991): 2–22, 11–20 (quotation on 12). This fine article has an error in its title: Pawley's agency was in 1747, not 1746.

91. For Joly Coeur, see Vaudreuil to Maurepas, 20 November 1746, AC, 13A-30. The unnamed Cherokee interpreter with the Shawnees is mentioned in Brewer and Baillie, "Pawley's Agency," 13.

92. Black Dog's Talk, 2 March 1747, in Brewer and Baillie, "Pawley's Agency," 15 (quotations), 19.

93. Brewer and Baillie, "Pawley's Agency," 13–14, 19–20.

94. Ostenaco's message of 26 February 1747, in Brewer and Baillie, "Pawley's Agency," 19–20 (quotations).

6. Confronting Colonialism and the Creek Nation

1. Deposition of William Wrightknower, 23 March 1748, JCSC, 29 March 1748, CO 5/456/001/0-195.

2. James Beamor et al. to Glen, 13 April 1748, JCSC, 21 April 1748; John Evans to Glen, 12 April 1748 (on the pictures of the captured men), JCSC, 27 April 1748, CO 5/456/001/0-195.

3. Beamor et al. to Glen, 13 April 1748, JCSC, 21 April 1748; Andrew Duche to Glen, 5 April 1748, [letter read in council, 27 April 1748], CO 5/456/001/0-195.

4. Elizabeth Haig to Thomas Corker, 8 April 1748, and petition to Glen, 11 April 1748, JCSC, 16 April 1748, CO 5/456/001/0-195. On the fear of slave-stealing, see

Notes to Pages 149–156   509

Deposition of William Wrightknower, 23 March 1748, JCSC, 29 March 1748, CO 5/456.

5. Glen to Anthony Palmer (president of the Pennsylvania council), 9 April 1748, PCP, 5:303–304; Palmer to Glen, 1 November 1748 ("high words"), Council minutes of 18 March 1749, JCSC, CO 5/457/004.

6. For Tanaghrisson's response, see Weiser's journal, 12 September 1748, PCP, 5:352–353 (Council session, 16 October 1748). On Tanaghrisson's status, see Fred Anderson, *Crucible of War: The Seven Years' War and the Fate of Empire in British North America, 1754–1766* (New York: Vintage, 2000), 5–6, 16.

7. On Skiagusta, see Examination of Trader (Anonymous), 16 April 1748, CO 5 /456/001/0-195 (examination inserted after Duche to Glen, 10 April 1748, which describes Skiagusta as the "Old Warrior").

8. Beamor et al. to Glen, 13 April 1748, JCSC, 21 April 1748, CO 5/456/0-195; Duche to Glen, 5 April 1748 ("Spirit up" and "Leaves on the Trees"), in JCSC, 27 April 1748, CO 5/456/0-195. Anonymous note, 17 January 1750 ("behaved themselves"), JCSC, 22 May 1750, CO 5/462/006.

9. On 14 October 1743, the Commons House voted to petition the king *against* the project, JCHA 1742–1744, 480–486. See the record of the Trustees of Georgia, 15 June 1744, in CRG, 1:455–456. The Board of Trade deferred action on the proposal on 4 July 1744, JBT, 8:117–122.

10. For Glen's praise of the Catawbas, whom he estimated at 300 "Fighting Men," see his letter to the Duke of Newcastle of 3 February 1748, CO 5/389. On Catawba discontent with white settlement, see James H. Merrell, *The Indians' Old World: Catawbas and Their Neighbors from European Contact through the Era of Removal* (New York: Norton, 1989), 143–155.

11. On Chickasaw population in the Savannah Valley, see Edward J. Cashin, *Guardians of the Valley: Chickasaws in Colonial South Carolina and Georgia* (Columbia: University of South Carolina Press, 2009), 74–82.

12. For the Congarees and Ninety-Six, see Robert L. Meriwether, *The Expansion of South Carolina, 1729–1765* (Kingsport, TN: Southern Publishers, 1940), 54–58, 118–119, 125. See also Kenneth E. Lewis, "Economic Development in the South Carolina Backcountry: A View from Camden," in *The Southern Colonial Backcountry: Interdisciplinary Perspectives on Frontier Communities*, ed. David Colin Crass et al. (Knoxville: University of Tennessee Press, 1998), 87–107; Monica L. Brick, "The Changing Nature of Slavery in South Carolina," in Crass, *Southern Colonial Backcountry*, 112; M. Eugene Sirmans, *South Carolina; A Political History, 1663–1763* (Chapel Hill: University of North Carolina Press, 1966), 168–179.

13. For the allocation of slave duties, see Act of 7 June 1735, SSC, 3:409–411; Act of 14 June 1751, SSC, 3:739–742, 751; Act of 7 October 1752 SSC, 3:781–782. See also Meriwether, *Expansion of South Carolina*, 25–30.

14. Talk of Skiagusta, 29 April 1745, in the *Charles-Town Gazette*, 18 May 1745. I have estimated population counts, which should not be taken as exact, from Meriwether, *Expansion of South Carolina*, 57–58, 118–119, 147–150.

15. The treaty of cession of 12 February 1747 is in EAID, 13:198–199. While Cherokees granted some land for a colonial garrison ("Strong House") near Lower Town Chauga in 1734, the treaty was not executed. See "Deed of Gift and Bargain,"

510   *Notes to Pages 156–160*

23 November 1734, EAID, 13:159–160. For the "Strong House," see record of 22–23 November 1734, JCHA 1734–1735, 21.

16. On the Long Canes, see Tom Hatley, *The Dividing Paths: Cherokees and South Carolinians through the Revolutionary Era* (New York: Oxford University Press, 1995), 85–89; Meriwether, *Expansion of South Carolina*, 134–135.

17. James Beamor et al. to Glen, 13 April 1748, JCSC, 21 April 1748, CO 5/456; Andrew Duche to Glen, 5 April 1748, JCSC, 27 April 1748, CO 5/455. Haig delivered munitions owed to Lower Town Cherokees by the cession treaty. See record of 12 June 1747, JCHA 1746–1747, 378.

18. Elizabeth Haig to Glen, 11 April 1748, JCSC [petition read on 16 April 1748], CO 5/456/001/0-195. For the payment to Mrs. Haig, see record of 27 May 1749, JCHA 1749–1750, 229.

19. James Beamor, Andrew Duche, and William Ewan to Glen, 28 February 1748, JCSC, 29 March 1748, CO 5/456/001/0-195.

20. Glen to James Maxwell, 24 March 1748; Glen to the Headmen and Warriors of the Cherokee Nation, 24 March 1748, JCSC, CO 5/456/001/0-195.

21. Cherokee deliberations were relayed by a colonial courier who brought trader Andrew Duche's letter of April 10 to Charles Town, and gave his testimony on 16 April 1748, JCSC, CO 5/456/001/0/195. On Lower Town headmen's decision-making, see Beamor, Duche, and Ewan to Glen, 28 February 1748, JCSC, 29 March 1748, CO 5/456/001/0-195.

22. Glen to the Board of Trade, 26 July 1748, CO 5/385.

23. Glen brought up the fort issue in messages to be forwarded to headmen in the Lower Towns, Hiwassee Valley, and Overhill villages. See JCSC, 10 and 17 April 1748; and for Glen's invitation to select headmen, see his message forwarded by traders Duche, Beamor, and Ewan, JCSC, 10 and 17 April 1748, CO 5/456/001/0-195.

24. For the committee's recommendation, see JCSC, 28 June 1748, CO 5/455/006. See also Glen to Stephens, 13 June 1748, JCSC, CO 5/456/001/0-195; and Stephens to Glen, 24 June 1748, JCSC, 28 June 1748, CO 5/456/001. On the governor's prorogation, see record of 29 June 1748, JCSC, CO 5/456/001/0-195.

25. Report of the Committee of Conference for Indian Affairs, 20 June 1748, JCHA 1748.

26. On Glen's meeting with Cherokees, see JCSC, 30 July 1751, CO 5/456/001. The offer of presents for cooperative Cherokees is in JCHA 1748, 28 June 1748.

27. Talk of the Raven, in Bunning to Glen, 14 May 1751, JCSC, 5 June 1751, CO 5/464/003.

28. Glen to Messrs. Duche, Beamor, Ewan, 10 April 1748, JCSC, 21 April 1748, CO 5/456. Glen's conciliatory gesture is in his letter to Duche, Beamor, and Ewan, 11 April 1748, in session of that same day, which for unknown reason appears after council record of 4 May 1748, CO 5/456/001/0-195. See the Raven of Hiwassee to Glen and Council, 5 June 1748, in Ludovick Grant to Glen, 16 and 20 June 1748, JCSC, 18 July 1748, CO 5/456.

29. Beamor to Glen, 11 July 1748, JCSC, 12 July 1748, CO 5/456/001. The gifts are enumerated in session of 19 July 1748. Tugaloo men and "Half-Breed Johnny" of Tanasee received gifts for their loyalty to the English when visiting Charles Town. See JCSC, 25 June 1748, CO 5/455/006.

Notes to Pages 160–165

30. Talk of Connecorte, 29 April 1752, DRIA, 1:258.

31. For remarks on "strange Indians," see deposition of James Francis, May 14, 1751, DRIA, 1:63; Deposition of John Fairchild, May 18, 1750, JCSC, CO 5/462. For insightful readings of the panic, see Gregory Evans Dowd, *Groundless: Rumors, Legends, and Hoaxes on the Early American Frontier* (Baltimore: John Hopkins University Press, 2015), 81–101; Dowd, "The Panic of 1751: The Significance of Rumors on the South Carolina-Cherokee Frontier," *William and Mary Quarterly* 53 (July 1996): 527–560.

32. Glen to George Clinton, 7 July 1750, CO 5/1063. For a route of Iroquois attack, see William Bull Jr. to Glen, 12 July 1751, DRIA, 1:35.

33. Talk of the Nottawega Indians, enclosed in Stephen Crell to James Glen, 2 May 1751, DRIA, 1:47–48. For information on Nottawega groups, see Certificate of Thomas McKee, 1 September 1749, followed by Thomas Cresap's undated note, JCSC, 22 May 1750, CO 5/462.

34. Deposition of Mary Cloud [Gloud], 8 May 1751, JCSC, 11 May 1751; and John Fairchild to Glen, 10 May 1751, JCSC, 13 May 1751, CO 5/464. Most fleeing whites moved east, but some emigrated to Virginia. See examination of Capt. Alexander Rattray, 22 May 1751, JCSC, CO 5/464. See also Meriwether, *Expansion of South Carolina*, 122–123, 178.

35. James Francis to Glen, 24 July 1751, DRIA, 1:29–30; Stephen Crell to Glen, 2 May 1751, DRIA, 1:47. The shooting of hogs and cows is also related in Samuel Hollinshed to Moses Thomson, 18 December 1751, DRIA, 1:216–217. The killing of bulls and other animals is documented in Crell to Glen, 6 April 1751, JCSC, 11 April 1751, CO 4/452.

36. Edmund Gray to John Fallowfield, DRIA, 1:83. On White's boast of killing the white man, see Deposition of James Maxwell, 11 June 1751, JCSC, CO 5/464. A Creek account on Andrew White as killer is in the Journal of Thomas Bosomworth, 30 July 1752, DRIA, 1:271–272. White's Nottawega comrades may have been Senecas. See Cashin, *Guardians of the Valley*, 81–83.

37. Examination of an anonymous trader-courier, 16 April 1748 ("Wench"; "Cut off all the White People," and "Hoggs and Cattle"), letter follows immediately after Duche to Glen, 10 April 1748, CO 5/456/001/0-195.

38. Ludovick Grant to Glen, 20 June 1748, JCSC, 18 July 1748, CO 5/456/001.

39. For trading abuses, see Anthony Dean to Cornelius Doherty, 1 May 1751, DRIA, 1:73; Robert Bunning, Cornelius Doherty, James Beamor, and Ludovick Grant to Glen, 22 November 1751, DRIA, 1:150; Grant to Glen, 30 April 1752, DRIA, 1:236–237.

40. Smith's report of Native mockery is in the deposition of James Maxwell, who described his own fears and flight. See JCSC, 11 June 1751, CO 5/464/003. The story may have been passed by Andrew White, fluent in both Cherokee and English, who had joined the lethal attack at the Oconee.

41. Anthony Dean to Glen, 1 May 1751, JCSC, 5 June 1751; and Examination of Robert Goudy [Gandy], 4 June 1751, JCSC, CO 5/464. Goudy's name is spelled in various ways. For rum sales, see Deposition of David Dowey, 23 May 1751, JCSC, CO 5/464. The talk of eliminating debts by killing traders is in Examination of William Thomson, a trader who relayed information from Richard Smith, a trafficker in the Lower Towns. See record of 7 May 1751, JCSC, CO 5/464/002. See also Dowd, "The Panic of 1751."

42. For "Strange Indians, see Francis to Glen, 14 May 1751, JCSC, 23 May 1751, CO 5/464.

43. Deposition of David Dowey, 23 May 1751, JCSC, CO 5/464/002. The Chickasaw rumors as well as William Broadway's are relayed in Examination of Richard Smith, 12 July 1751, JCSC, CO 5/464/004. For white fears of Nottawega invasion, see "The white People of the Lower [Cherokee] Towns," in John Fairfield to Glen, 18 January 1751, JCSC, 1 April 1751, CO 5/464/001.

44. For conspiratorial rumor, see Tanasee headmen to Glen, 9 August 1751, JCSC, 1 September 1751, CO 5/456/005.

45. Talk of Cherokee headmen at Joree of 6 May 1751, is in Crawford, Langley, Murphy, and Dunckley to Glen, 5 June 1751; Deposition of David Dowey, 23 May 1751; Deposition of James Maxwell, 12 June 1751, JCSC, CO 5/464.

46. The Raven's actions are relayed in Dougherty to Maxwell, 28 April 1751, JCSC, 5 June 1751, CO 5/464/003.

47. The Cherokee talk at Joree of 6 May 1751 is in Crawford, Langley, Murphy, and Dunckley to Glen, JCSC, 5 June 1751, CO 5/464/003. The Notoly warrior added to the Raven's talk of 14 May 1751, enclosed in Bunning to Glen of that same date, JCSC, 5 June 1751, CO 5/464/003. See also the Raven's words, "My Eyes loves to see White People," in postscript of Cornelius Dougherty to James Maxwell (with Raven's mark), 28 April 1751, JCSC, 5 June 1751/CO 5/464.

48. Cherokee talk at Joree, 6 May 1751 ("Rum drinking"), in Crawford, Langley, Murphy, and Dunckley to Glen, JCSC, 5 June 1751, CO 5/464/003.

49. Talk of the Raven, with Johnny's talk attached, enclosed in Bunning to Glen, 14 May 1751, JCSC, 5 June 1751, CO 5/464/003.

50. For the assembly committee's estimate of necessary troops and Indian fighters, see report of 14 May 1751. In debates of 14–15 June, the Council favored armed force, but the assemblymen did not. The Commons House voted instead for a trade embargo. See JCHA 1750–1751, 447, 504–506, 517–519. For Glen's stance, see his address of 28 May 1751 ("ten men can defend"), JCSC, CO 5/464/002; and his approval of the embargo, 15 June 1751, JCSC, CO 5/464/003.

51. For the embargo, which Glen strived to undo, see his letter to the English traders in the Cherokee Nation, JCSC, 15 June 1751, CO 5/464/003. See also Glen to the Raven [Tacite the Mankiller of Hiwassee]; Glen to "the Emperor of the Cherokees," that is, Ammouiscossitte of Great Tellico; Glen to the Town of Tomasee; Glen to the Town of Tugaloo; Glen to the Headmen and Warriors of Keowee; Glen to the Headmen and Warriors of Kituwah. All messages were read in Council on June 8 and approved by that body on 15 June 1751, JCSC, CO 5/464/003. The Raven, his Talk, with the Seven Towns of the Valley, joined by Cesar of Great Tellico, 9 August 1751; and Glen to the Emperor and Headmen of the Cherokees, 26 August 1751, JCSC, CO 5/464/005. For the council's advice that only five or six headmen confer in Charles Town, see JCSC, 25 October 1751, CO 5/464/007. On "Satisfaction," see Glen to the Cherokees, 13 November 1751, DRIA, 1:156.

52. The conference record of 13–28 November 1751 is in DRIA, 1:156–159, 161–166, 175–200. Skiagusta praised "Noward" Indian attacks on the Creeks. See his talk of 15 November 1751, DRIA, 1:179.

53. For Glen's written treaty, see JCSC, 26 November 1751, CO 5/464/008; Ordinance for Regulating the Cherokee Trade, 3 December 1751, DRIA, 1:187–196, 198–200.

Notes to Pages 170–174   513

54. On the trade terms, 26 November 1751, see DRIA 1:191–194 ("dividing Waters," 192).

55. On the Cherokee issue of forts, see talks of 26–28 November 1726, DRIA, 1:191 ("utmost Assistance"), 194 ("cut off"), 195, 198.

56. For the demonstration of dressing skins and Glen's pledge to forget past problems, see Treaty conference, 26 November 1751, DRIA, 1:192, 195. Skiagusta's talk of 15 November 1751 is in JCSC, CO 5/464/008; DRIA, 1:183.

57. For the distribution of guns, see JCSC, 28 November 1751, CO 5/464; DRIA, 1:197–198.

58. In 1748, the Board of Trade approved £3,000 worth of Indian presents, to be divided equally between South Carolina and Georgia. Both provinces received their portions in 1749. See Sirmans, *Colonial South Carolina*, 275. A lengthy invoice of Indian presents, shipped from London to Charles Town in early 1751 is in JCSC, 23 March 1751, CO 5/462. For the allotment of July 1753, see JBT, 9:442–445; Memorial of Benjamin Martyn to the Board of Trade, 3 June 1754, CRG, 26:448–449.

59. Pawley to Black Dog and Cherokee headmen, 2 March 1747, T. F. Brewer and J. Baillie, "The Journal of George Pawley's 1746 Agency to the Cherokee," *Journal of Cherokee Studies* 16 (1991): 2–22, 15; on the diplomatic track, see Glen to the Council, 18 March 1749, JCSC, CO 5/457/004.

60. On Abeika connections to Charles Town, see Joshua Piker, *Okfuskee: A Creek Indian Town in Colonial America* (Cambridge, MA: Harvard University Press, 2004), 46–50.

61. On the Creek negotiating stance and threat regarding the Nottawegas, see Sludders and Devall to Glen, 2 May 1749, JCSC, 23 May 1749, CO 5/459/002; Glen to Council, 2 June 1749 JCSC, CO 5/459/003; Chartier to Glen, 20 July 1749, JCSC, 4 September 1749, CO 5/459/006.

62. Cornelius Dougherty to the Traders in the Creek Nation, with the Cherokees Answer to the Letters Sent them from the Creeks, 10 July 1749, JCSC, 4 September 1749 CO 5/459/006. The "Tasata" (Warrior) identified in this letter was the Raven, who was Hiwassee Head Warrior. See also the message of the "Headmen, Warriors, and beloved Men" of seven Upper Cherokee towns to the headmen of the Creeks, Chickasaws and Savannos [Shawnees] in Anthony Dean to the Traders in the Creek Nation, 5 July 1749, JCSC, 4 September 1749, CO 5/459.

63. Cornelius Dougherty to the Traders in the Creek Nation, with the Cherokees Answer to the Letters Sent them from the Creeks, 10 July 1749, JCSC, 4 September 1749, CO 4/459.

64. The Cherokee overture is in Anthony Dean to the Traders in the Creek Nation, 5 July 1749, JCSC, 4 September 1749, CO 5/459.

65. Cherokee overture in Anthony Dean to the Traders in the Creek Nation, 5 July 1749.

66. On the site of the talks, see William Sludders to Glen, 23 May 1749, JCSC, CO 5/459; Glen to the Board of Trade, 23 December 1749, CO 5/389.

67. On the Native attendees, see JCSC, 6 September 1749, CO 5/459. Chigelly's talk, 29 July 1749 is in Thomas Ross to Glen, 29 July 1749, JCSC, 4 September 1749, CO 5/459. See also David H. Corkran, *The Creek Frontier, 1540–1783* (Norman: University of Oklahoma Press, 1967), 127–132; Edward J. Cashin, *Lachlan McGillivray,*

Indian Trader: The Shaping of the Southern Colonial Frontier (Athens: University of Georgia Press, 1992), 115–118.

68. On the peace and bestowal of presents, see JCSC, 7 and 11 September 1749, CO 5/459.

69. Glen to the Board of Trade, 23 December 1749, CO 5/389.

70. Chartier to Glen, 20 July 1749, in JCSC, 4 September 1749, CO 5/459. See also Joshua Piker, *The Four Deaths of Acorn Whistler: Telling Stories in Colonial America* (Cambridge, MA: Harvard University Press, 2013), 22–24.

71. George Galphin to William Pinckney, [Memorandum], 18 October 1749, DRIA, 1:4; Intelligence . . . by Mr. Newness, in George Cadogan to [Glen], JCSC, 18 January 1750; and on the Nottawega and Cherokee attack, see Lachlan McGillivray to Glen, 5 April 1750, JCSC, 7 May 1750, CO 5/462.

72. The attack evidently came on 14 April 1750. See letters of Maxwell to Glen, 30 April 1750, and Patrick Brown to Glen, 20 April 1750, JCSC, 11 May 1750, CO 5/462; Galphin to William Pinckney, 3 November 1750, DRIA, 1:4. For Glen's assessment, see his letter to the Board of Trade, 15 July 1750, CO 5/385. Headmen of the Lower Creeks to Governor Glen, 25 July 1750, JCSC, 5 September 1750, CO 5/462/010. (Cherokee Lower Town Echoe is not to be confused with Middle Town Etchoe.)

73. Corkran, *Creek Frontier*, 145–147; Tyler Boulware, *Deconstructing the Cherokee Nation: Town, Region, and Nation among Eighteenth-Century Cherokees* (Gainesville: University Press of Florida, 2011), 57–60.

74. Talk of the Upper Creeks to Glen enclosed in Sludders to Glen, 11 July 1750, JCSC, 5 September 1750, CO 5/462/010. See also Piker, *Okfuskee*, 50–51.

75. The Gun Merchant was first spokesman of the Upper Creek talk, 11 July 1750, in Sludders to Glen, 20 July 1750, JCSC, 5 September 1750, CO 5/462/010. See also Corkran, *Creek Frontier*, 149–510.

76. For the Gun Merchant's talk of "Satisfaction" in future instances, see Sludders to Glen, 20 July 1750, JCSC, 5 September 1750, CO 5/462/010. See also the Raven to Glen, 31 March 1752, DRIA, 1:243.

77. Report of Patrick Brown, 6 May 1752, JCSC, CO 5/465. For the upsurge in fighting, see the Talk of the Raven of Hiwassee and the Warrior (Skiagusta) of Keowee, enclosed in John Fairchild to Glen, 23 December 1751, DRIA, 1:155–156; McGillivray to Glen, 18 December 1751, DRIA, 1:215–216; Galphin to Glen, 20 April 1752, DRIA, 1:257. See also Piker, *Four Deaths of Acorn Whistler*, 54–55, 165.

78. On Cherokee and Creek population, see James Habersham to Benjamin Martyn, 26 June and 30 July 1752, CRG, 26:400–402, 408–409. The estimate of two thousand Cherokee fighting men seems more accurate than Glen's claim of three thousand warriors—a number possibly intended to impress London with fort-building in the Appalachians. See Glen to Newcastle, 3 February 1748, CO 5/389. On Upper Creek-Choctaw conflict, see Vaudreuil to Rouillé, 10 May 1751 and 28 January 1752, MPAFD, 5:73–76, 112–113.

79. Talks of Skiagusta and the Good Warrior to Glen, 15 April and 5 May 1752, CO 5/467. The thirty-three dead were of the Lower Towns—"our People"—to the Keowee and Estatoe head warriors.

80. The onset of crisis can be followed in JCSC, 1–5 April 1752, CO 5/467. See also Piker, *Four Deaths of Acorn Whistler*, 22–24.

Notes to Pages 180–183

81. Glen to Acorn Whistler and seven more Upper Creeks, 2 April 1752 ("perfidious"); Glen's draft letter to the heads of the Upper Creek Nation, 28 April 1752, JCSC, CO 5/467/003. The idea of being rendered "cheap and Contemptible" is in Glen's speech to the Assembly, 29 April 1752, in JCSC, CO 5/467/003. Thomas Bosomworth's commission of 2 July 1751 is in DRIA, 1:267.

82. See Malatchi's talk to Glen of 2 June 1753, DRIA, 1:403–404. See also Piker, *Four Deaths of Acorn Whistler*, 167–177; Steven C. Hahn, *The Invention of the Creek Nation, 1670–1763* (Chapel Hill: University of North Carolina Press, 2004), 212–222; Corkran, *Creek Frontier*, 162–163. See also John Philip Reid, *A Law of Blood: The Primitive Law of the Cherokee Nation* (New York: New York University Press, 1970), 154–156.

83. Glen to the Governor of Virginia, Sept. 18, 1751, in EJCV, 5:355–360. Lee was presiding officer until a new royal governor arrived from England.

84. Attested by Robert Goudy, 4 June 1751, JCSC, CO 5/464/003.

85. Affidavit of Samuel Benn, 4 June 1751, JCSC, CO 5/464/003.

86. On Attakullakulla's name, see James Mooney, *Myths of the Cherokee* (1900; reprint, New York: Dover, 1995), 511.

7. Tempests of the French and Indian War

1. On the Cherokee visitors, see JCSC, 7 July 1753, CO 5/469/006. The conference proceedings are in DRIA, 1:429–454.

2. Conference, 4 July 1753, JCSC, CO 5/469/006.

3. Talk of Long Johnny ("Long Jack") who spoke of Connecorte as "Governor," and Talk of Attakullakulla at Conference, 4 July 1753, JCSC, CO 5/469/006. "Connecorte" apparently meant "Standing Turkey"—an honorable name. Anglicized versions of "Standing Turkey" vary greatly. For the spelling "Kanorcortuker," see Cynthia Cumfer, *Separate Peoples, One Land: The Minds of Cherokees, Blacks, and Whites on the Tennessee's Frontier* (Chapel Hill: University of North Carolina Press, 2007), xi.

4. Skiagusta's talk, 5 July 1753, JCSC, CO 5/469/006. For assembly appropriations, see sessions of 14–15 May 1752, JCHA 1751–1752. The funding was confirmed on 7 August 1753, JCSC, CO 5/469/007.

5. Conference, 5 July 1753, JCSC, CO 5/469/006. See also Glen to Lieutenant Governor James Hamilton of Pennsylvania, 3 October 1753, CO 5/469/009.

6. Skiagusta's talk, 7 July 1753, CO 5/469.

7. "List of presents," 7 July 1753, JCSC, CO 5/469/006. See also Joshua Piker, *Okfuskee: A Creek Indian Town in Colonial America* (Cambridge, MA: Harvard University Press, 2004), 165–169. The Native consumer economy grew after 1763 but had roots well before then. See Kathryn E. Holland Braund, *Deerskins and Duffels: The Creek-Indian Trade with Anglo-America, 1685–1815*, 2nd ed. (Lincoln: University of Nebraska Press, 1993), 121–129.

8. For Ostenaco's talk and Attakullakulla's request for a commission, see JCSC, 7 July 1753, CO 5/469/006. On Attakullakulla's recall of the treaty, see his talk, JCSC, 5 July 1753, CO 5/469/006.

9. Red Coat King to Glen, 26 July 1753, DRIA, 1:380; George Johnston to Glen, 2 December 1753, DRIA, 1:464 ("Peace Talk"); Malatchi to Glen, 12 May 1754, DRIA, 1:499. See also Piker, *Okfuskee*, 50–51, 83. On the naming of honorary chiefs of the

former enemy, see Bryan C. Rindfleisch, *Brothers of Coweta: Kinship, Empire, and Revolution in the Eighteenth-Century Muscogee World* (Columbia: University of South Carolina Press, 2021), 54–58.

10. Fred Anderson, *Crucible of War: The Seven Years' War and the Fate of British Empire in North America* (New York: Random House, 2000), 50–68; Colin G. Calloway, *The Indian World of George Washington: The First President, the First Americans, and the Birth of the Nation* (New York: Oxford University Press, 2018), 92–96.

11. Glen to the Board of Trade, 26 August 1754, CO 5/375; Talk of the Warriors and beloved Men of the Valley of Hiwassee and Tomotley, 15 April 1754, DRIA, 1:506. For the apparent burial stones at Keowee, see William Bartram, *Travels through North & South Carolina* . . . (Philadelphia: James and Johnson, 1791), 332, 348, 372.

12. M. Thomas Hatley, "The Three Lives of Keowee: Loss and Recovery in Eighteenth-Century Cherokee Villages," in *Powhatan's Mantle: Indians in the Colonial Southeast*, ed. Peter H. Wood, Gregory A. Waselkov, and M. Thomas Hatley (Lincoln: University of Nebraska Press, 1989), 241.

13. Examination of James Beamor [Beamer], [July 1754], DRIA, 1:517. For "Over the Lake" Indians, see Ludovick Grant to Glen, 22 July 1754, DRIA, 2:18–19. The pro-French warriors were an array of Abenakis, Algonquins, Hurons, Nipissings, Ottawas, and Canadian Iroquois. See Calloway, *Indian World of George Washington*, 94.

14. For the Cherokee attacks on French boats, see Glen to Sir Thomas Robinson (Secretary of State), 15 August 1754, CO 5/14 / Pt. 2 /103. For Attakullakulla's pro-English stance, see his meeting with Glen, 22 May 1755, JCSC, CO 5/471/005.

15. Glen to Dinwiddie, 1 June 1754, DRIA, 1:528–530. For Glen's concerns, see Glen to Robinson, 15 August 1754 (postscript of 26 August 1754), CO 5/14 / Pt. 2 /013. On Glen's obfuscation, see M. Eugene Sirmans, *South Carolina: A Political History, 1663–1763* (Chapel Hill: University of North Carolina Press, 1966), 297–298; David Corkran, *The Creek Frontier, 1540–1783* (Norman: University of Oklahoma Press, 1967), 52–53.

16. Glen to Robinson, 15 August 1754. Glen proposed two forts by the Ohio, one near the river's confluence with the Tennessee and the other at the Wabash. Glen also sent a letter to Overhill headmen asking them to pitch in by their own missive to England, requesting King George to build a Tennessee fort with "white Men Warriours in it, and great Guns to defend you his Children, and to protect your Country which is his own." See Glen to Upper Cherokee headmen, [1754], DRIA, 1:518–519.

17. Lyttelton to Thomas Robinson, 7 September 1755, CO 5/16 / Pt. 1 /006. For Lyttleton's arrival at Charles Town, see his letter to the Board of Trade, 3 June 1756, CO 5/375.

18. On Attakullakulla's discussions with Glen, see JCSC, 21–22 May 1755, CO 5/471/005. The intelligence on pro-French Indians, including Shawnees at Chota, is in Ludovick Grant to Glen, 29 April 1755, DRIA, 2:50–54. In this same letter, Grant wrote of northern Indians that attacked Cherokees.

19. Shawnee intermarriage with Cherokees and Chickasaws, which the French saw as a threat, was discussed by Louis de Kerlérec, Louisiana's governor, in his letter to the French ministry of 18 December 1754, AC, 13A-38. See also Kerlérec to ministry, 20 December 1754, AC, 13A-38.

20. Conference, 21–22 May 1755, JCSC, CO 5/471/005. See entry of 22 May 1755 for Glen's concern about "French Indians."

Notes to Pages 190–194

21. On the presence of 500 Cherokee men and "many" women," see enclosure, CO 5/375/025, in Glen to the Board of Trade, 14 April 1756, CO 5/375/022.

22. Enclosure, CO 5/375/025, in Glen to the Board of Trade, 14 April 1756, CO 5/375/022.

23. For Braddock's defeat, see Anderson, *Crucible of War,* 97–106, 760n17.

24. Glen to the Board of Trade, 14 April 1756, CO 5/375/022. Glen's rendition of the conference, in CO 5/375/025, differs slightly from the printed version, which states that 506 Cherokees attended the Saluda meeting. Charles-Town notice, 31 July 1755, *New-York Mercury,* 25 August 1755.

25. The written text sent to England includes a declaration that the treaty was signed by Connecorte, "Head King and the other Kings and Heads of the Cherokee Nation," and that the "Great Seal" was "affixed to it in their Presence." If any such ceremony occurred, the signature page was lost. See Enclosure, CO 3/375/025, with Glen to the Board of Trade, 14 April 1756, CO 5/375/22. Tom Hatley writes persuasively that the Cherokee gift of soil was "a symbolic gesture of alliance." See Hatley, *The Dividing Paths,* 76.

26. An excellent book on this difficult subject is Peter Silver, *Their Savage Neighbors: How Indian War Transformed Early America* (New York: Norton, 2008), 60–70. For Shawnee warfare, see Richard White, *The Middle Ground: Indians, Empires, and Republics in the Great Lakes Region, 1650–1815* (Cambridge: Cambridge University Press, 1991), 243–245; Ian Steele, *Setting All the Captives Free: Capture, Adjustment, and Recollection in Allegheny Country* (Montreal: McGill-Queen's University Press, 2013), 85–102. Matthew C. Ward, *Breaking the Backcountry: The Seven Years' War in Virginia and Pennsylvania, 1754–1765* (Pittsburgh: University of Pittsburgh Press, 2003), 60–70; R. Scott Crawford, "A Frontier of Fear: Terrorism and Social Tension along Virginia's Western Waters, 1742–1775," *West Virginia History,* new series, 2 (Fall 2008): 1–34, 1–2, 10.

27. For "Judd's Friend," see Henry Timberlake, *The Memoirs of Lieut. Henry Timberlake* (London, 1765), 72.

28. Otis K. Rice, "The Sandy Creek Expedition of 1756," *West Virginia History* 13 (1951): 5–19. Dinwiddie listed the number of Cherokees in the prospective expedition at 130 in one letter, and eighty in a second, written at a later point, and probably more accurate. See Dinwiddie to Governor Arthur Dobbs of North Carolina, 13 December 1755, *The Official Records of Robert Dinwiddie, Lieutenant-Governor of Virginia, 1751–1758,* ed. R. A. Brock, 2 vols. (Richmond: Virginia Historical Society, 1883–1884), 2:290; Dinwiddie to Henry Fox, 20 March 1756, *Records of Dinwiddie,* 2:373. The eating of horseflesh is recorded in Dinwiddie to Dobbs, 13 April 1756, *Records of Dinwiddie,* 2:382. For Cherokee dissatisfaction, see Dinwiddie to Washington, 23 April 1756, *Records of Dinwiddie,* 2:388.

29. For Attakullakulla's words, see JCSC, 6 December 1755, CO 5/471/009. Governor-General Vaudreuil of New France, had a good many Iroquois friends, especially among the Senecas. See record of 13–30 December 1756, DRCHNY, 10:499–518. See also Francis Jennings, *Empire of Fortune: Crowns, Colonies, and Tribes in the Seven Years' War in North America* (New York: Norton, 1988), 189–192.

30. Talk of Willanawa, 8 December 1755, JCSC, CO 5/471/009. For the French garrison, see Norman W. Caldwell, "Fort Massac during the French and Indian War," *Journal of the Illinois State Historical Society* 43 (Summer 1950): 102–105.

31. Glen's conversation with Wawhatchee, 10 December 1755, is in the same file as the governor's speech of 8 December 1755 ("Partiality" and "as flourishing as ever"), JCSC, CO 5/471/009.

32. Glen's meeting with Attakullakulla, 18 December 1755, JCSC, CO 5/471/009. French John's Canadian background is implied in Vaudreuil to minister, 19 April 1757, AC, 11A-101. On his former slave status, see Oxinaa (a Cherokee woman) to Demere, 8 April 1757, DRIA, 2:411–412.

33. Dinwiddie to "the Emperor Old-Hop, and the other Sachems, and Warriors, of the Great Nation of the Cherokees," 23 December 1755, in *A Treaty held with the Catawba and Cherokee Nations, at the Catawba-Town and Broad-River in the Months of February and March 1756* (Williamsburg, 1756), xiii–xiv. On the negotiations, see *A Treaty*, 10–22.

34. For Virginia's propositions of 14 March 1756 and the Cherokee response the next two days, see *A Treaty*, 10–16; the treaty of 17 March 1756, with commissioners' signatures and Cherokee marks, is found in the same document (pp. 19–22), with toasts recorded on p. 19.

35. Dinwiddie to Lewis, 24 April 1756, *Records of Dinwiddie*, 2:389–390. For the reference to the Cherokee youths, see Dinwiddie to the Sachems and Warriors, 23 April 1756, *Records of Dinwiddie*, 2:391; Dinwiddie to the Emperor Old Hop and other Sachems, 12 June 1756, *Records of Dinwiddie*, 2:446.

36. Lewis to Dinwiddie, 5 October 1756, CO 5/48/005.

37. Glen reviewed this history, with documentation, in addresses to the Commons House of Assembly, 23–30 January 1756, CO 5/472. He estimated the cost of building the fort at £7,000, of which Governor Dinwiddie had already advanced him £1,000.

38. For Glen's vision of the fort, see JCHA 1751–1752, 9 and 15 April 1756. Glen was held up for weeks by the council's refusal to authorize funds, forcing him to borrow £2,000 outside ordinary government channels. See Sirmans, *South Carolina*, 299–300, 308.

39. Lyttelton forwarded a message of 3 June 1756, via Demere to Connecorte, by the same express he dispatched to Glen, DRIA, 2:115. See also Lyttelton to the Board of Trade, 19 June 1756, CO 5/375. For the English arrival at Keowee, see Demere to Lyttelton, 23 June 1756, DRIA, 2:124 ("the greatest Civility"). For the march, see Demere to Lyttelton, 9–10 June and 15 June 1756, DRIA, 2:118–122. Lyttelton dismissed the militia en route as a cost-saving measure.

40. For Demere's reception, see Demere to Lyttelton, 23 June 1756, DRIA, 2:125–126.

41. Answer of the Chiefs of the Five Lower Towns of the of Cherokees, 20 June 1756, DRIA, 2:123–124.

42. Answer of the Chiefs, 20 June 1756, DRIA, 2:124 ("at no Expence"); Demere to Lyttelton, 23 June 1756, DRIA, 2:125.

43. Lyttelton to the Board of Trade, 19 June and 11 August 1756, CO 5/375.

44. Demere to Lyttelton, 25 July 1756, DRIA, 2:148; Lyttelton to the Board of Trade, 19 July 1756, CO 5/375. For the pledge of reimbursement, see Board of Trade to Lyttelton, 19 November 1756, CO 5/403. Through 1756, the South Carolina assembly expended £6,000 toward building Fort Prince George and Fort Loudoun without yet being reimbursed by the Crown, JCHA 1755–1757, 2 April 1757.

Notes to Pages 198–202

519

45. See Peter Mancall, *Deadly Medicine: Indians and Alcohol in Early America* (Ithaca, NY: Cornell University Press, 1995); Claudio Saunt, *A New Order of Things: Property, Power, and the Transformation of the Creek Indians,1733–1816* (Cambridge: Cambridge University Press, 1999), 145–147; Daniel K. Richter, *The Ordeal of the Longhouse: The Peoples of the Iroquois League in the Era of European Colonization* (Chapel Hill: University of North Carolina Press, 1992), 263–265.

46. For the complaint about Dinwiddie, see Demere to Lyttelton, 19 July 1756, DRIA, 2:143. For Attakullakulla's drunken bout and his criticism of Demere, see the captain's letter to Lyttelton, 21 July 1756, DRIA, 2:146–148.

47. Lewis to Dinwiddie, 11 October 1756, CO 5/48/005.

48. Demere to Lyttelton, 18 November 1756, DRIA, 2:249 (quotations). See also Demere to Lyttelton, 28 November 1756, DRIA, 2:260. Demere was critical of Fort Loudoun's placement, which was directed by military engineer William Gerard De Brahm. See Demere to Lyttelton, 13 October 1756, DRIA, 2:217–219. The fort was completed in late July 1757. See John Oliphant, *Peace and War on the Anglo-Cherokee Frontier, 1756–1763* (Baton Rouge: Louisiana State University Press, 2001), 113–116, 122–123; Daniel J. Tortora, *Carolina in Crisis: Cherokees, Colonists, and Slaves in the American Southeast, 1756–1763* (Chapel Hill: University of North Carolina Press), 36–38.

49. Old Hop (Connecorte) to Demere, 26 October 1756, in Demere to Lyttelton, 28 October 1756, DRIA, 2:236.

50. Old Hop (Connecorte) to Demere, 26 October 1756, DRIA, 2:235. Nuntawea is spelled in multiple variants in English records.

51. Old Hop to Demere, 26 October 1756, in Demere to Lyttelton, 28 October 1756, DRIA, 2:234 ("Brothers"); Old Hop to Captain John Stuart and Lieutenant Robert Wall, 15 November 1756, DRIA, 2:247. Demere to Lyttelton, 18 November 1756, DRIA, 2:251 ("Old Hop is very serious").

52. For Lantagnac's background, see his petition to Kerlérec, 1 October 1755, MPAFD, 5:161–166. On Lantagnac's Cherokee liaison, see Demere to Lyttelton, 16 October 1755, DRIA, 2:225. On French John, see Demere to Lyttelton, 15 June 1756, DRIA, 2:122; Lewis to Lyttelton, 11 September 1756, in DRIA, 2:203.

53. Demere to Lyttelton, 18 November 1756, quoted in Lyttelton to the Board of Trade, 25 December 1756, CO 5/375/030. See also DRIA, 2:249.

54. Governor Kerlérec of Louisiana saw the Shawnees as critical to prying the Cherokees from the English. See Kerlérec to Minister, 1 April 1756, AC, 13A-39. For Tellico, often called "Great Tellico," in contrast to a smaller town of that name to the south, see Boulware, *Deconstructing Cherokee Society*, 79–83. David Corkran analyzed Cherokee history of the mid-1700s through the lens of Great Tellico's rivalry with Chota. See Corkran, *The Cherokee Frontier: Conflict and Survival, 1740–1762* (Norman: University of Oklahoma Press, 1962), 16–23, 30–33, 39–47.

55. Duplessis to Minister [1757], AC, 13A-39. For Chartier's influence, see Daniel Pepper to Lyttelton, 18 November 1756, DRIA, 2:255. See also Anderson, *Crucible of War*, 150–151.

56. English records tell us that French John was fluent in Cherokee, but they give no hint of his knowledge of other Native languages. See Lewis to Dinwiddie, 11 October 1756, CO 5/48/006; Lewis to Demere, 11 September 1756, DRIA, 2:203. See also the Talk of Oxinaa to Captain Demere, 8 April 1757, DRIA, 2:410–411 ("War Hatchett").

57. Old Warrior of Tomotley to Demere, 25 November 1756. This intelligence is in the same file as Lyttelton to the Board of Trade, 25 and 31 December 1756, CO 5/386/029. Mankiller allegedly agreed to furnish Lantagnac and partner Samuel Brown with 120 horses for carrying goods to the Cherokees, with the items to be delivered within the span of two moons.

58. Intelligence from Nancy [Butler] to Demere, 12 December 1756, DRIA, 2:269. For the supply of corn by Cherokee women and its shipment by canoe to British soldiers, see Demere to Lyttelton, 6 January 1757, DRIA, 2:310.

59. Nancy Butler to Demere, 12 December 1756, DRIA, 2:269 ("must we throw away"). For a talk with multiple sources, see Butler to Demere, 20 December 1756, DRIA, 2:276 ("good English," "White People"). In this instance, Nancy Butler spoke to Demere and three other officers with interpreter Ambrose Davis at hand.

60. Ostenaco to Demere, 10 December 1756, DRIA, 2:265; Talk of Willanawa and Little Carpenter to Demere, 17 December 1756, DRIA, 2:270.

61. For the Raven's death, see Demere to Lyttelton, 27 December 1756, DRIA, 2:287–288. See also Demere to Lyttelton, 31 January 1757, DRIA, 2:326; Demere to Lyttelton, 13 June 1757, DRIA, 2:385. On Hiwassee, see Corkran, *Cherokee Frontier*, 88, 146, 171.

62. Ostenaco ["Judge's Friend"] to Demere, 13 December 1756, enclosed with Lyttelton to the Board of Trade, 31 December 1756, CO 5/386/756. (Duplicate letters were sent by Lyttelton on 25 and 31 December.) See also Ostenaco to Demere, 5 December 1756, DRIA, 2:261–262.

63. Edward Cashin, *Guardians of the Valley: Chickasaws in Colonial South Carolina and Georgia* (Columbia: University of South Carolina Press, 2009), 96–101. On Gun Merchant and the Mortar, see David Corkran, *Creek Frontier*, 15, 170–172, 180–186.

64. Intelligence from Ostenaco to Demere, 10 December 1756, DRIA, 2:265 ("Carolina People" to "for their Feet"); Talk of Willanawa and Little Carpenter to Demere, 17 December 1756, DRIA, 2:270 ("Place of Lies").

65. For Mankiller's supporters and Okchai, see Old Warrior of Tomotley to Demere, 25 November 1756, in letter of that same day by Demere to Lyttelton, in Lyttelton to Board of Trade, 25 December 1756, CO 5/386/756. Demere to Lyttelton, 6 January 1757, DRIA, 2:308–309 ("hated and disliked").

66. Report of Lieutenant Wall to Demere, 13 January 1757, in Demere to Lyttelton, 15 January 1757, DRIA, 2:313–314, 321–322 ("not the Value").

67. Wall to Demere, 13 January 1757, DRIA, 2:323.

68. Wall to Demere, 13 January 1757, DRIA, 2:323. See also Frank Gouldsmith Speck, *Cherokee Dance and Drama* (Berkeley: University of California Press, 1951), 26–30, 62–63.

69. Demere to Lyttelton, 15 January 1757, DRIA, 2:315 ("Sett of Villains"). A less dramatic rendering of his thoughts is in Mankiller of Tellico to Demere, 15 January 1757, DRIA, 2:320.

70. Demere to Lyttelton, 5 February 1757, DRIA, 2:334; Demere to Old Hop and other Cherokee Headmen, 25 January 1757, DRIA, 2:332. See also Tortora, *Carolina in Crisis*, 36.

71. On Lyttelton, see Sirmans, *South Carolina*, 308–309.

Notes to Pages 208–214

72. The governor aired his request for two hundred warriors on 1 February 1757. The transcript of the negotiation is nearly fifty pages—copied in a rather small script on long sheets. See record of 31 January–19 February 1757, South Carolina Council Journal, no. 26, 1757–1758, South Carolina Department of History and Archives.

73. Talk of Attakullakulla, 2 February 1757, Council Journal, no. 26.

74. Lyttelton's Talk, 1 February 1757, Council Journal no. 26.

75. Talk of Attakullakulla, 2 February 1757.

76. Attakullakulla's talk, 9 February 1757, Council Journal no. 26. Replying three days later, Lyttelton repeated his words about white women being willing to instruct "their Sisters the Red Women." He added rather insipidly that "White Men" brought females into "their Counsels" when the women were "good" in heart. See session of 12 February 1757, Council Journal, no. 26.

77. Attakullakulla's talk, 9 February 1757.

78. Talk of Willanawa, 12 February 1757, Council Journal no. 26; Talk of Attakullakulla, 17 February 1757, Council Journal no. 26.

79. Attakullakulla's talk, 9 February 1757.

80. Attakullakulla's critique of the Middle and Lower Towns is in Talk of Attakullakulla, 17 February 1757.

81. On Attakullakulla's desire to see the Great King, see his talk of 9 February 1757. Lyttelton replied on 17 February, Council Journal no. 26.

82. Dinwiddie to the Board of Trade, 23 February 1756, in *Records of Dinwiddie*, 2:345. For difficulties of frontier defense, see Dinwiddie to the Earl of Loudoun, 6 October 1756, *Records of Dinwiddie,*, 2:525–526; Dinwiddie to John Blair, 22 March 1757, *Records of Dinwiddie*, 2:597–598. See also Anderson, *Crucible of War*, 109, 159–160.

83. Clement Read's report is quoted in Corkran, *Cherokee Frontier*, 115–116. (Col. Read is spelled "Reed" in Corkran's book.) Read's report is dated April 5, implying that disturbances had begun some days earlier. See EJCV, 11 April 1757, 6:40. On Cherokee complaints, see George Mercer to Washington, 24 April 1757, GWLC; Edmund Atkin to George Croghan, 8 June 1757, PA, 3:175–176. On Cherokee robbing of frontier whites, see Oliphant, *Peace and War*, 41. For plundering of Moravian farms in North Carolina, see entry of 1 May 1756, "Bethabara Diary," in *Records of the Moravians in North Carolina*, vol. 1, *1751–1772*, ed. Adelaide L. Fries (Raleigh: Edwards & Broughton, 1922), 158.

84. Dinwiddie to Col. Clement Read, 15 April 1757, *Records of Dinwiddie*, 2:612.

85. D. Wolstenhome and J. Ridout to Sharpe, 25 May 1757, *Correspondence of Governor Horatio Sharpe*, 4 vols., ed. William Hand Browne (Baltimore: Maryland Historical Society, 1888–1911), 1:557–563; Sharpe to [Lord] Baltimore, 29 May 1757, in *Correspondence of Governor Horatio Sharpe*, 2:6–7. See also Wawhatchee [Wahachy] to the Governor of Maryland, 29 April 1757, with the Governor's Answer, 9 May 1757, *Boston Evening-Post*, 13 June 1757.

86. Dinwiddie to Lyttelton, 2 July 1757, *Records of Dinwiddie*, 2:673; Washington to Dinwiddie, 7 April 1756, GW: Colonial, 2:334–335. Washington, who likened Indians to "Wolves" that "prowl" and "do their mischief by Stealth," is quoted in Calloway, *The Indian World of George Washington*, 127.

87. Washington to Dinwiddie, 30 May 1757, GW: Colonial, 4:171–173; Washington to Sgt. John David Wilper, 7 June 1757, GW: Colonial, 4:186–187.

88. Atkin to Croghan, 8 June 1757, PA, 3:177–180; Dinwiddie to Lyttelton, May 26, 1757, *Records of Dinwiddie*, 2:633.

522   *Notes to Pages 214–220*

89. Atkin to Croghan, 8 June 1757, PA, 3:177–180. Mercer to Washington, 26 April 1757, GW: Colonial, 4:142–144.

90. Demere to Lyttelton, 26 March 26, 1757, DRIA, 2:349.

91. Kristofer Ray, "Cherokees and Franco-British Confrontation in the Tennessee Corridor, 1730–1760," *Native South* 7 (2014): 33–67, 48–53; Norman W. Caldwell, "Fort Massac during the French and Indian War," *Journal of the Illinois State Historical Society* 43 (Summer 1950): 100–119, 104–106. On the French flag, see Paul Lacroix, *The Eighteenth Century . . . France 1700–1789* (London: Chapman and Hall, 1876), 122.

92. For Kerlérec's assessment, see his letters to Marchault d'Arnouville, 30 January 1757, and to Peirène de Moras, 21 October 1757, MPAFD, 5:181, 189. Connecorte sent diplomatic feelers by northern Indian visitors to the Hurons and Ottawas at Detroit in 1756. See Oxinaa to Demere, 8 April 1757, DRIA, 2:410–411. Cherokee deputies, accompanied by Shawnees, may have visited Detroit in early 1757. See Vaudreuil to minister, 19 April 1757, AC, 11A-101.

93. On Acadian travails, see Tortora, *Carolina in Crisis*, 34–37, 87–88. Glen described the arriving Acadian deportees at "upwards of 980" in number. See Glen to the Board of Trade, 14 April 1756, CO 5/375/022.

94. For Choctaw-Chickasaw warfare, see James R. Atkinson, *Splendid Land, Splendid People: The Chickasaw Indians to Removal* (Tuscaloosa: University of Alabama Press, 2004), 83–85. On Cherokee-Chickasaw tensions, see Demere to Lyttelton, 11 August 1756, DRIA, 2:162; Jerome Courtonne to John Brown, 23 October 1756, DRIA, 2:292–293. On Creek-Georgia diplomacy, see John T. Juricek, *Colonial Georgia and the Creeks: Anglo-Indian Diplomacy on the Southern Frontier* (Gainesville: University Press of Florida, 2010), 212–225. On the Upper Creeks, see Corkran, *Creek Frontier*, 172–176.

95. Journal of William Johnson, 31 July 1757, DRCHNY, 7:324; Atkin to "Cannicharty [Connecorte], Governour of the Whole Nation of the Cherokee Indians," 4 August 1757, Forbes Papers, DCAR.

96. For Cherokee military engagement of 1757 and its impact, see Paul Kelton, "The British and Indian War: Cherokee Power and the Fate of Power in North America," *Willliam and Mary Quarterly* 69 (October 2012): 763–792, 766–772. For newspaper accounts, see *Pennsylvania Gazette*, 10 March 1757; *New-York Gazette*, 11 April and 4 July 1757; *Boston Evening-Post*, 1 August 1757; *New-York Mercury*, 7 November 1757. Catawba involvement is reported in the *Pennsylvania Gazette*, 7 March 1757, 7 April 1757, and 5 May 1757.

97. Demere to Lyttelton, 13 June 1757, DRIA, 2:382.

98. On Attakullakulla's response, see Demere to Lyttelton, 30 July 1757, DRIA, 2:392–393. For opposition to French John's surrender, or the capture of "Savannah Tom," see Lyttleton to Demere, 10 August 1757, DRIA, 2:397–398. Demere (or Demeré), a French Protestant by background, astutely described French John as "*un Esclave voluntaire*" to Connecorte. See Demere to Lyttelton, 10 August 1757, DRIA, 2:397.

99. Demere to Lyttelton, 30 July 1757, DRIA, 2:392–396.

8. Prelude to the British-Cherokee War

1. Forbes to Abercromby, 22 and 23 April 1758, in *Writings of General John Forbes, Relating to His Service in North America*, comp. and ed. Alfred Procter James (Menasha, WI: Collegiate Press, 1938), 69–71 ("necessity," 70).

2. "A Return of the Southern Indians, Winchester, 21 April 1758," Forbes Papers, DCAR. See also John Oliphant, *Peace and War on the Anglo-Cherokee Frontier, 1756–1763* (Baton Rouge: Louisiana State University Press, 2001), 54–59; Daniel J. Tortora, *Carolina in Crisis: Cherokees, Colonists, and Slaves in the American Southeast, 1756–1763* (Chapel Hill: University of North Carolina Press, 2015), 48–52; David H. Corkran, *The Cherokee Frontier: Conflict and Survival, 1740–1762* (Norman: University of Oklahoma Press, 1962), 149–154.

3. For Cherokee-settler clashes, see Deposition of Timothy Dalton, 9 May 1758; Pinkney Hawkins to Clement Read, 10 May 1758; Matthew Talbot to Read, 10 May 1758, all in John Blair to Washington, 24 May 1758, George Washington Papers, Series 4, General Correspondence, Mss. 44693, reel 31, GWLC, https://www.loc.gov/item/mgw442861/. See also a notice of Williamsburg, 26 May 1758, in *New-York Gazette*, 3 July 1758. On Cherokees and the British war effort, see Paul Kelton, "The British and Indian War: Cherokee Power and the Fate of Empire in North America," *Willliam and Mary Quarterly* 69 (October 2012): 763–792; Gregory Evans Dowd, "'Insidious Friends': Gift-Giving and the Cherokee-British Alliance in the Seven Years' War," in *Contact Points: American Frontiers from the Mohawk Valley to the Mississippi, 1750–1830*, ed. Andrew R. L. Cayton and Frederick J. Teute (Chapel Hill: University of North Carolina Press, 1998), 125–126, 145.

4. Oliphant, *Peace and War*, 54–56; Tortora, *Carolina in Crisis*, 48–49.

5. Deposition of Timothy Dalton, 9 May 1758; William Callaway to Washington, 15 May 1758 ("brothers"), George Washington Papers, Series 4, General Correspondence, Mss. 44693, reel 31, GWLC, https://www.loc.gov/item/mgw442844/.

6. Tom Hatley, *The Dividing Paths: Cherokees and South Carolinians through the Revolutionary Era* (New York: Oxford University Press, 1995), 100–101; Tortora, *Carolina in Crisis*, 52–54; Corkran, *Cherokee Frontier*, 157–159.

7. Talk of Tistoe and the Wolf to Lyttelton, 12 July 1758 ("thought to be our Brothers"), quoted in Oliphant, *Peace and War*, 63.

8. Talk of the Emperor Old Hop [Connecorte] and the Head Men of the Upper Cherokee Nation to Lyttelton, 26 July 1758; Talk of Tistoe, the Wolf, and Headmen of the Lower Towns to Lyttelton, 7 August 1758, JCSC, CO 5/376/007.

9. On the killings, see Oliphant, *Peace and War*, 72–73.

10. Atkin to Forbes, 20 May 1758, Forbes Papers, DCAR. On the recruitment drive, see Atkin to Cunnicahtarky (Connecorte), Governor, and to the Chiefs and Warriors of the Nation of Cherokee Indians, 24 March 1758, Forbes Papers, DCAR. While a superb historian, David H. Corkran overemphasized Attakullakulla as "the Cherokee Second Man," Corkran, *Cherokee Frontier*, 43–44.

11. Byrd to Lyttelton, 31 March 1758, in *The Correspondence of the Three William Byrds of Westover, 1684–1776*, ed. Marion Tinling, 3 vols. (Charlottesville: University Press of Virginia, 1977), 2:644.

12. Byrd to Lyttelton, 31 March 1758, in Tinling, *Correspondence*, 2:644 ("little Savage"); Byrd to Forbes, 30 April 1758, Forbes Papers, DCAR ("annointing themselves"). For Byrd's enlistment of Cherokees, see his letter to Forbes, 21 May 1758, Forbes Papers, DCAR; President and Council [Minute], 22 March 1758, in Tinling, *Correspondence*, 2:642.

13. Little Carpenter to His Brother the Governor of South Carolina, 3 June 1758, ("have spilt"), in Lyttelton to the Board of Trade, 17 August 1758, CO 5/376/007. This

letter also includes Attakullakulla's mark. See also Attakullakulla to Byrd, 27 May 1758, in Tinling, *Correspondence*, 2:656. South Carolina's appropriation was an amount up to £20,000. See Lyttelton to the Board of Trade, 7 August 1758, CO 5/376/007.

14. Turner to Lyttelton, 2 July 1758, in Lyttelton to the Board of Trade, 17 August 1758,CO 5/376/007 ("bad Omens"; "the Great Man"); Turner to Forbes, 23 June 1758, Forbes Papers, DCAR ("could not recruit"); Cherokees to Turner, 23 June 1758, Draper Mss., WHS, 4 ZZ4.

15. Turner to Lyttelton, 2 July 1758, CO 5/376/007. Men of Middle Town Joree talked of going to war against settlers who had "cut off some of their People." See the postscript to the above letter, 2 July 1758, DRIA, 2:473. For Connecorte's views, see Old Hop to Demere, 26 October 1758, in Demere to Lyttelton, 28 October 1758, DRIA, 2:234–237.

16. Atkin to Lyttelton, 4 August 1758, Lyttelton Papers, WCL; Forbes to Richard Peters, 16 October 1758, *Writings of Forbes*, 235 ("consummate a Dog"); Forbes to Abercromby, 24 October 1758, *Writings of Forbes*, 244. Ironically, the Cherokees contributed to British success in weaning the Delawares from the French. See Kelton, "The British and Indian War," 779–784.

17. Forbes to Col. James Burd, 19 November 1758, *Writings of Forbes*, 257; Forbes to Lyttelton, 26 November 1758, Lyttelton Papers, WCL; Forbes to Washington, 20 November 1758, *Writings of Forbes*, 259. For perspectives on Forbes, see Fred Anderson, *Crucible of War: The Seven Years' War and the Fate of British Empire in North America, 1754–1766* (New York: Random House, 2000), 268–269, 284; Colin G. Calloway, *The Indian World of George Washington: The First President, the First Americans, and the Birth of the Nation* (New York: Oxford University Press, 2018), 140–146.

18. Attakullakulla's feelings are reported in missionary William Richardson's diary, 5 January 1759, in Samuel Cole Williams, *Dawn of the Tennessee Valley and Tennessee History* (Johnson City, TN: Watauga Press, 1937), 216; Talk of Willanawa and Little Carpenter to Raymond Demere, 17 December 1756, DRIA, 2:270.

19. Minutes of the Council of Virginia, 19–20 January 1759, CO 5/1429/008.

20. Mackintosh to William Henry Lyttelton, 21 March 1759, Lyttelton Papers, WCL.

21. Attakullakulla faulted James Glen, former South Carolina governor, for inducing him to travel to Forbes's camp. Glen worked in Pennsylvania in 1758 as a liaison to the Cherokees. For Attakullakulla's talk and Lyttelton's reply, 17 April 1759, JCSC, CO 5/476/001.

22. Talk of Attakullakulla, 18 April 1759, JCSC ("My Love," "Old Warriours," "Lies"). The gift of beads was on 21 April 1759, CO 5/476.

23. Coytmore to Lyttelton, 8 May 1759, DRIA, 2:487; Demere to Lyttelton, 12 May 1759, Coytmore to Lyttelton, 23 May 1759, Lyttelton Papers, WCL. For the Catawbas' role, see Samuel Wyly to Lyttelton, 5 May 1759, DRIA 2:486.

24. The surnames of the slain Carolinians include Snap, Ellis, Adams, Holsey, Hannah, Rentford, and Mull, suggesting persons of varied ethnicity (Conrad Mull was a German settler). See Charles Town notice of 12 May 1759, *Pennsylvania Journal*, 28 June 1759. For Mull, see Oliphant, *Peace and War*, 72. For apparent Cherokee fear of "Dutchmen," see missionary William Richardson's information in Paul Demere to Lyttelton, 26 February 1759, Lyttelton Papers, WCL. James Adair wrongly attributed the Virginia killings of Cherokee Indians solely to German settlers. See James Adair,

Notes to Pages 229–233

525

The History of the American Indians, ed. Kathryn E. Holland Braund (1775; Tuscaloosa: University of Alabama Press, 2003), 263. On Wade's Virginia militiamen, see the account of John Echols, 12 August 1758, in Lewis Preston Summers, *History of Southwest Virginia, 1746–1786, Washington County, 1777–1870* (Richmond, VA: J. L. Hill, 1903), 63–66.

25. Moytoy told Lieutenant Coytmore that his men had taken scalps from the "Dutch" settlement. Wawhatchee corroborated this point. See Coytmore to Paul Demere, 8 May 1759, DRIA, 2:487.

26. On the number of scalps, see Demere to Lyttelton, DRIA, 2:488. For Connecorte's welcome to the Mortar, see Paul Demere to Lyttelton, 2 May 1759, Lyttelton Papers, WCL. On the Mortar's clan name of Yahatastanage ("Wolf Warrior"), see Adair, *History of the American Indians,* 519n272; David H. Corkran, *The Creek Frontier, 1540–1783* (Norman: University of Oklahoma Press, 1967), 161.

27. Lyttelton to Emperor Old Hop and Little Carpenter, 22 May 1759, CO 5 /376/012.

28. Talk of Thirteen Towns to Lyttelton, 13 May 1759, Lyttelton Papers, WCL (this letter is dated 16 May in DRIA, 2:404–405). Round O signed the talk as "Tassittee" (Head Warrior) of Stickoe (Stecoe), not to be confused with Settico.

29. Talk of Thirteen Towns to Lyttelton, 13 May 1759. Connecorte's words on "Swine Herds" are in his talk forwarded to Glen, 29 April 1752, DRIA, 1:258.

30. On the scalps see Demere to Lyttelton, 10 July 1759, CO 5 /376/012. For the embargo, see Lyttelton to Demere, 22 June 1759, Lyttelton Papers, WCL.

31. Coytmore arrived at Fort Prince George on 9 April 1759. See Coytmore to Lyttelton, 18 April 1759, Lyttelton Papers, WCL.

32. Coytmore to Lyttelton, 23 July 1759, Lyttelton Papers, WCL.

33. Coytmore to Lyttelton, 23 July 1759.

34. Coytmore to Lyttelton, 23 July 1759.

35. Coytmore to Lyttelton, 23 July 1759.

36. Buffalo Skin's account was recorded by Coytmore on 1 August 1759 and forwarded by letter of 3 August 1759 to Lyttelton, Lyttelton Papers, WCL.

37. On the murders, see James Francis to Lyttelton, 23 December 1757, DRIA, 2:425–426; Headmen of the Lower Towns and Warriors of Keowee to Lyttelton, 2 March 1758, DRIA, 2:444. Estatoe men initially blamed the Overhills for killing the white men, but later admitted their responsibility. See Warriors of Estatoe to Lyttelton, 20 March 1758, DRIA, 2:449. Lyttelton to Lower Cherokee Headmen and Warriors [1758], DRIA, 2:479–480. Lyttelton advised the appointment of resident royal agents among southern Indians to prevent conflicts and to bring white malefactors to justice. See Lyttelton to the Board of Trade, 7 August 1758, CO 5/376/007. See also Oliphant, *Peace and War,* 41–43.

38. Lyttelton proceeded in steps on the arms embargo. See JCSC, 14 August 1759, CO 5/474; Lyttelton to the Board of Trade, 1 September 1759, JCSC, CO 5/388; Lyttelton to Fauquier, 10 August 1759; Fauquier to Lyttelton, 5 September 1759; Ellis to Lyttelton, 27 August and 25 September 1759, Lyttelton Papers, WCL. The killing of the woman and child is in Coytmore to Lyttelton, 23 August 1759, Lyttelton Papers, WCL.

39. Fauquier to Lyttelton, 5 September 1759, Lyttelton Papers, WCL. Fauquier met with two Cherokee deputies on 27 August 1759. See Williamsburg notice, 30 August 1759, *Boston Gazette,* 24 September 1759.

40. Coytmore to Lyttelton, 13 September 1759, Lyttelton Papers, WCL. For cultural misunderstandings and conflict, see Dowd, "'Insidious Friends,'" 146–149.

41. Headmen of the Lower Towns and Warriors of Keowee to Lyttelton, 2 March 1758, DRIA, 2:444. For Lower Cherokee resentment at "daily Incroachments of the white people on their Lands," see Lieutenant White Outerbridge to Lyttelton, 3 September 1759, Lyttelton Papers, WCL.

42. Paul Demere to Lyttelton, 13 September 1759; Maurice Anderson to Coytmore, 12 September 1759, Lyttelton Papers, WCL. For Connecorte's words on "the place of Lies," see Demere to Lyttelton, 17 December 1756, DRIA, 2:270.

43. Anderson to Coytmore, 12 September 1759, Lyttelton Papers, WCL. Lyttelton cited 132 effective troops at Fort Loudoun and ninety-three at Fort Prince George, JCSC, 14 August 1759, CO 5/474; Coytmore to Lyttelton, 26 September 1759 ("lurking" and "skulking"); and Capt. John Stuart to Lyttelton, 26 September 1759, Lyttelton Papers, WCL; Corkran, *Cherokee Frontier,* 175; Oliphant, *Peace and War,* 95–96.

44. For these slayings and the boast about "Fowls," see Coytmore to Lyttelton, 23 August 1759, Lyttelton Papers, WCL. Two white men were killed about the Pacolet River later that month and a women and boy scalped but not slain. See Samuel Francis to Lyttelton, 23 August 1759, Lyttelton Papers, WCL Papers.

45. For the Creek warrior's help to the German men, see Stuart to Lyttelton, 2 September 1759, Lyttelton Papers, WCL.

46. For the Middle Town men, see Stuart to Lyttelton, 26 September 1759, Lyttelton Papers, WCL. On Lower Town reluctance to aid the English, see Patrick Calhoun to Lyttelton, 21 September 1759, Lyttelton Papers, WCL.

47. Oconostota had some of his followers accompany Stuart northward with a supply of flour, salt, and ammunition for Fort Loudoun. See Demere to Lyttelton, 1 October 1759, Lyttelton Papers, WCL. For the Cherokee decision to negotiate, see Stuart to Lyttelton, 6 October 1759; Coytmore to Lyttelton, 7 and 16 October 1759, Lyttelton Papers, WCL.

48. For Attakullakulla's absence and return, see Demere to Lyttelton, 1 October 1759 and 3 November 1759, Lyttelton Papers, WCL. On Ostenaco, see Demere to Lyttelton, 13 September 1759, Lyttelton Papers, WCL.

49. For Lyttelton's call for war, see 4–6 and 11 October 1759, JCSC, CO 5/474/001. For the House resolve of 11 October 1759 and Lyttleton's order of adjournment two days later, see JCHA, CO 5/473/002. On the Cherokees in Charles Town, see notice of 17 October 1759, *Maryland Gazette,* 6 December 1759.

50. Conference record, 18 October 1759, JCSC, CO 5/474/001.

51. Conference record, 19 October 1759, JCSC, CO 5/474/001.

52. Talk of Tistoe, 19 October 1759, CO 5/474/001. A Cherokee prisoner in Charles Town subsequently told Lieutenant Governor William Bull that Coytmore and Ensign John Bell were apt to beat Native men in their houses. See session of 20 June 1760, JCSC, CO 5/474/001.

53. Lyttelton's speech, 22 October 1759, CO 5/474/001.

54. Lyttelton to Cherokees, 22 October 1759, CO 5/474/001.

55. For Round O's peace overture, see Stuart to Lyttelton, 6 October 1759, Lyttelton Papers, WCL. For Lyttelton's march, see Charles Town notice, 1 November 1759, *Boston Gazette,* 10 December 1759; Charles Town notice, 10 November 1759, *Pennsylvania*

Notes to Pages 239–245

Gazette, 13 December 1759; Charles Town notice, 25 November 1759, *Boston News-Letter,* 3 January 1759; "Extract of a Letter dated Congarees," 15 November 1759, *Boston Gazette,* 7 January 1760; Charles Town notice, 8 December 1759, *Boston Evening-Post,* 21 January 1760; Charles Town notice, 21 December 1759, *New-York Mercury,* 28 January 1760.

56. Lyttelton wrote letters to the governors of Virginia, North Carolina, and Georgia on 23 October 1759. See also his letters of that day to Amherst and General John Stanwix, senior officer at Fort Pitt, all in Lyttelton Papers, WCL.

57. Charles Town notice, 21 December 1759, *New-York Mercury,* 28 January 1760; Coytmore to Lyttelton, 21 November 1759, Lyttelton Papers, WCL; Lyttelton to the Board of Trade, 10 December 1759, CO 5/386. On smallpox among the Cherokees, see Paul Kelton, *Cherokee Medicine, Colonial Germs: An Indigenous Nation's Fight Against Smallpox, 1518–1824* (Norman: University of Oklahoma Press, 2015), 115–124.

58. Attakullakulla's message on being threatened by Connecorte is in Demere to Lyttelton, 4 December 1759, Lyttelton Papers, WCL. On Attakullakulla's ambition, see Demere to Lyttelton, 7 December 1759; Stuart to Lyttelton, 7 December 1759, Lyttelton Papers, WCL. Kanagatucko may have been Connecorte's nephew. See Tortora, *Carolina in Crisis,* 97.

59. Charles Town, Notices, 1 and 22 December 1759, *Boston Evening-Post;* and 14 January 1760, *New-York Mercury,* 4 February 1760.

60. See Charles Town notice, 12 January 1760, *New-York Mercury,* 4 February 1760.

61. Charles Town notice, 12 January 1760.

62. Charles Town notice, 12 January 1760.

63. On the fear of smallpox, see Lyttelton to the Board of Trade, 29 December 1760, CO 5/376/14. On 28 December, Cherokee men delivered one more presumed killer to Fort Prince George. No hostage was released in exchange. See Charles Town notice, 12 January 1760, *New-York Mercury,* 4 February 1760.

64. A copy of the "Treaty of Peace & Friendship," 26 December 1759, is in Lyttelton to the Board of Trade, 29 December 1760, CO 5/376/14.

65. Charles Town notices, 12–14 January 1760, *New-York Gazette,* 4 February 1760. For Lyttelton's reception, see *Pennsylvania Gazette,* 14 February 1760.

66. Coytmore to Lyttelton, 7 January 1760, Lyttelton Papers, WCL. To Cherokees, wrote James Adair, hostage-taking meant treating people as "slaves." Adair, *History of the American Indians,* 267.

67. Deposition of James Atwood, 31 January 1760; Demere to Lyttelton, 26 and 30 January 1760, Lyttelton Papers, WCL. For Demere's pledge and a false report of Abraham's death, see Demere to Lyttelton, 6 June 1760, JCSC, 30 June 1760, CO 5/474. See also Tortora, *Carolina in Crisis,* 145.

68. Trader Thomas Beamer, who accompanied Seroweh in route to the fort, estimated his force at seventy men. See Examination of Thomas Beamer, 1 February 1760, JCSC, CO 5/474. Additional information is in "A Copy of a Journal kept [by Lieutenant Richard Coytmore] at Fort Prince George," in Coytmore to Lyttelton, 7 February 1760, Lyttelton Papers, WCL (hereafter "Copy of a Journal"). After Coytmore was shot on 16 February 1760, Miln continued the journal, 8–24 February 1760

(Miln may have used Coytmore's notes for entries 8–16 February). Miln wrote to Lyttelton on 28 February 1760 but did not indicate in that letter that he was enclosing the journal.

69. "Copy of a Journal," 19–20 January 1760 ("talked and behaved"). On Seroweh, see Deposition of James Atwood, 31 January 1760, Lyttelton Papers, WCL. Deposition of Thomas Beamer, 1 February 1760, JCSC, CO 5/474/100. It seems the attackers at Elliott's numbered from fifty to seventy men. See Tortora, *Carolina in Crisis*, 91–93.

70. "Copy of a Journal," 23 and 26 January 1760.

71. Seroweh's approach is recorded on 25 January 1760 and the killings in the Middle Towns on 28 January 1760, in "Copy of a Journal."

72. For the warrior's mockery of the hostages, see entry of 1 February 1760, "Copy of a Journal."

73. For the warning of Seroweh's coming attack, see entry of 17 January 1760, "Copy of a Journal"; Deposition of James Atwood, 31 January 1760, Lyttelton Papers, WCL. For the young Indian woman's warning, see Examination of Aaron Price, 2 February 1760, JCSC, CO 5/474. See also "Copy of a Journal," 6 February 1760.

74. "Copy of a Journal," entries of 23 January 1760 and 1–3 February 1760. On 3 February, Tistoe's wife told of smallpox spreading among the Cherokee Middle Towns.

75. For the Estatoe woman, see entries of 20 January and 1 February 1760, "Copy of a Journal." Round O died by 24 February. See Charles Town notice, 1 March 1760, *New-York Gazette*, 31 March 1760.

76. Five hostages died from 7–14 February 1760. See "Copy of a Journal," as continued by Miln, 8–24 February 1760, Lyttelton Papers, WCL.

77. "Copy of a Journal," 14 February 1760. A report from Augusta, sent there by Miln on 24 February 1760, stated that Oconostota swung the bridle three times over his head as the signal to fire. See Extracts of Letters from Augusta, dated Charles Town, 27 February 1760, *Pennsylvania Journal*, 3 April 1760.

78. Miln reported Coytmore's death to Lyttelton by letter of 28 February 1760. The Cherokee cry of "fight Strong" is recorded in entry of 16 February 1760, Journal of Miln. See Extracts of Letters from Augusta, dated Charles Town, 27 February 1760, in *Pennsylvania Journal*, 3 April 1760.

79. Entry of 16 February 1760 ("laid them all lifeless"), Journal of Miln. In that same entry, Miln reported that one soldier received a mortal wound by knife and tomahawk just before the troops killed all hostages. For a skeptical reading of Miln's report, see Oliphant, *Peace and War*, 111. Of twenty-two hostages held at Fort Prince George since January 1760, two had escaped and five died of smallpox. One other Cherokee man had been captured, so the total killed by British soldiers may have been sixteen.

80. On the killings near the Saluda River, see Edward Musgrove and Samuel Aubrey to Lyttelton, 6 February 1760, Lyttelton Papers, WCL. For the attack on the "Long Canes" settlers, see deposition of Patrick Calhoun, 2 February 1760, at Augusta, Georgia, *Pennsylvania Gazette*, 28 February 1760. On the surviving children, see Charles Town notice, 16 February 1760, *New-York Gazette*, 3 March 1760. The attack on Ninety-Six is described in a Charles Town notice of 15 March 1760, *Pennsylvania Gazette*, 10 April 1760; Francis to Lyttelton, 6 March 1760, DRIA, 2:504. For the scalp

Notes to Pages 250–254

bounty, see Charles Town notice, 23 February 1760, *Boston News-Letter*, 27 March 1760. See also Tortora, *Carolina in Crisis*, 104–105.

81. The town of Nequassee distributed the above-named white woman and her children among several households. See Charles Town notice, 19 April 1760, *New-York Mercury*, 19 May 1760. For "about a Hundred" white prisoners, see Charles Town notice, 9 April 1760, in *Pennsylvania Gazette*, 1 May 1760.

82. From 16 to 30 March, at least five different Native women passed information of Cherokee military activity to Fort Prince George. Two of these women conveyed news on two separate occasions. See Charles Town notice, 19 April 1760, *New-York Mercury*, 19 May 1760. For the pause in firing, see Charles Town notice, 3 May 1760, *New-York Gazette*, 26 May 1760.

83. Charles Town notice, 19 April 1760, *New-York Mercury*, 19 May 1760 ("Women Prisoners"; "declared War").

84. On Lyttelton's plea for aid, see Lyttelton to Amherst, 9 February 1760, CO 5 / 57 / Pt. 3 /006; Amherst to Montgomery, 6 March 1760 ("the punishment of"), CO 5/57 / Pt. 3 /016; Amherst to Lyttelton, 26 February 1760 ("every way Sufficient"), Lyttelton Papers, WCL.

9. Carnage and Peace Diplomacy

1. The plan to storm the hamlet was made about daybreak on 2 June 1760. See Montgomery to Amherst, 4 June 1760, CO 5/59 / Pt. 2 /021. For Montgomery's advance, see John Oliphant, *Peace and War on the Anglo-Cherokee Frontier, 1756–1763* (Baton Rouge: Louisiana State University Press, 2001), 113–116, 122–223; Daniel J. Tortora, *Carolina in Crisis: Cherokees, Colonists, and Slaves in the American Southeast, 1756–1763* (Chapel Hill: University of North Carolina Press), 120–122.

2. Montgomery to Amherst, 4 June 1760, CO 5/59; Grant to Lieutenant Governor William Bull, 4 June 1760, JCSC, 10 June 1760, CO 5/474/001. An anonymous officer questioned military "honour" in "an Indian War." See Notice from Camp near Fort Prince George, 4 June 1760, *Boston Post-Boy*, 14 July 1760. Toxaway was the other destroyed village. Qualatchee is also spelled Quaratchee. See Tortora, *Carolina in Crisis*, 122; David H. Corkran, *The Cherokee Frontier: Conflict and Survival, 1740–1762* (Norman: University of Oklahoma Press, 1962), 209.

3. On remaining white prisoners, unspecified by number, see Grant to Bull, 4 June 1760, JCSC, 10 June 1760, CO 5/474/001.

4. Grant to Bull, 4 June 1760, JCSC, 10 June 1760, CO 5/474/001; Amherst to Montgomery, 6 March 1760 ("punishment"), CO 5/57 / Pt. 3 /016.

5. Grant to Bull, 4 June 1760, JCSC, 10 June 1760, CO 5/474/001. See also Oliphant, *Peace and War*, 118–119, 144–145. Oliphant indicates that Miln's hostage taking occurred on May 7, 1760, and not on May 9 as reported in a newspaper notice. See Charles Town notice, 17 May 1760, *Boston News-Letter*, 19 June 1760.

6. On Cherokee anger at the destruction, see Demere to Montgomery, 6 June 1760, Council Journal, 30 June 1760, CO 5/474. For the commanders' views, see Montgomery to Amherst, 4 June 1760, CO 5/59; Grant to Bull, 4 June 1760, in Council Journal, 10 June 1760, CO 5/474/001.

7. Attakullakulla is quoted in Demere to Montgomery, 6 June 1760, JCSC, 30 June 1760, CO 5/474/001 ("white people's friend"). See also Tortora, *Carolina in Crisis*,

124–126. For Glen's vision of the fort, see record of 9 April 1756, JCHA 1755–1757, CO 5/472/013.

8. A detailed account of the battle, printed in the *South-Carolina Gazette* of 14 July 1760, is in Philopatrios [Christopher Gadsden], *Some Observations on the Two Campaigns against the Cherokee Indians, in 1760 and 1761* (Charles Town: Peter Timothy, 1762), 82–86. On the number of Cherokee fighters and the role of Seroweh and Tistoe, see Letter from Ninety-Six, 10 August 1760, *New-York Mercury*, 1 September 1760. See also Tortora, *Carolina in Crisis*, 126–128; Oliphant, *Peace and War*, 130–132. For the Scottish "whirra's," see Letter from Fort Prince George, 2 July 1760, *New-Hampshire Gazette* (Portsmouth), 8 August 1760. On the dead Cherokee warriors left standing, see Montgomery to Amherst, 2 July 1760, CO 5/59/Pt. 1/014.

9. Bull to Montgomery, 12 July 1760, CO 5/386/042.

10. The precise number of soldiers and civilians at Fort Loudoun's surrender is not known. An estimated two hundred persons were in the garrison at the time. Lyttelton cited 132 effective troops at Fort Loudoun, JCSC, 14 August 1759, CO 5/474/001. Stuart brought up reinforcements that autumn. The garrison, which probably included enslaved Black workers, was thinned by sickness and death before capitulation. See Tortora, *Carolina in Crisis*, 130. William Byrd later estimated the garrison at 180 men and sixty women and children. See Byrd to Capt. Abercrombie, 16 September 1760, CO 5/59/Pt. 2/043.

11. Articles of Capitulation, 17 August 1760, *New-York Gazette*, 29 September 1760. On the Cane Creek massacre, see Bull to Amherst, 19 October 1760, CO 5/60/008. Bull reported two provincial officers slain and one British ensign besides Capt. Demere. For the attack, see Charles Town notice, 6 September 1760, *Boston News-Letter*, 30 October 1760 ("dance about"); Tortora, *Carolina in Crisis*, 132–134.

12. Oliphant, *Peace and War*, 158–165.

13. On the talks with Billy Germany, see Atkin to Lyttelton, 20 August 1759, Lyttelton Papers, WCL.

14. On Atkin's diplomacy and the pipe-tomahawk attack, see Atkin to Lyttelton, 2 October and 30 November 1759, Lyttelton Papers, WCL. See also John T. Juricek, *Colonial Georgia and the Creeks: Anglo-Indian Diplomacy on the Southern Frontier, 1733–1763* (Gainesville: University Press of Florida, 2010), 251–255, 258–263; David H. Corkran, *The Creek Frontier, 1540–1783* (Norman: University of Oklahoma Press, 1967), 197–210.

15. Atkin to Lyttelton, 30 November 1759 (all quotations in paragraph are from this letter), Lyttelton Papers, WCL.

16. Ellis to Pitt, 16 April 1760 ("tedious and Expensive"), CO 5/19. Georgia Council Journal, 14 April 1760 ("spilt Cherokee Blood"). See also Georgia Council Journal, 17 April 1760. The bestowal of gifts, and the Creek men's response, are in Georgia Council Journal, 28 April 1760, CO 5/697/002.

17. Atkin to William Pitt, 27 March 1760, CO 5/84/023. See also Corkran, *Creek Frontier*, 215.

18. Examination of Jerome Courtonne, 20 June 1760, JCSC, CO 5/474/001; Charles Town notice, 5 July 1760, *Boston Evening-Post*, 28 July 1760. See also Juricek, *Colonial Georgia*, 281–285; Joshua Piker, *Okfuskee: A Creek Indian Town in Colonial America* (Cambridge, MA: Harvard University Press, 2004), 59–63; Edward J. Cashin, *Lachlan McGillivray, Indian Trader: The Shaping of the Southern Colonial Frontier* (Athens:

Notes to Pages 261–264

531

University of Georgia Press, 1992), 203–204; Robert Paulett, *An Empire of Small Places: Mapping the Southeastern Anglo-Indian Trade, 1732–1795* (Athens: University of Georgia Press, 2012), 168–169.

19. White traders passed reports on Mortar's fiery talk. See Extract of a Letter from Augusta, 24 June 1760, *Boston Evening-Post*, 25 August 1760; "An Account of the proceedings of the Army under Col. Montgomery [5–25 June 1760]," Charles Town notice, 5 July 1760, *Boston Evening-Post*, 28 July 1760. For Attakullakulla's assessment, see his talk in Demere to Montgomery, 6 June 1760, JCSC, session of 30 June 1760, CO 5 / 474 / 001.

20. Talk of Gun Merchant, 26 May 1760, conveyed by Upper Creek headmen, Georgia Council Journal, 30 June 1760, CO 5 / 697 / 002. Ellis's reply of 30 June 1760 is in this same record. For the situation in Creek country, see Juricek, *Colonial Georgia*, 285–289; Piker, *Okfuskee*, 135–138, 183–184.

21. Creeks regained Georgia trade during the fall of 1760. See Corkran, *Creek Frontier*, 219–224.

22. On Stuart's conduct at Cane Creek, see Charles Town notice, 4 October 1760, *New-London Summary*, 31 October 1760; Stuart to the Governor, [September 1760], Charles Town notice, 5 November 1760 ("war-whoop"), *Boston Evening-Post*, 22 December 1760.

23. For biographical detail, see John Richard Alden, *John Stuart and the Southern Colonial Frontier: A Study of Indian Relations, War, Trade, and Land Problems in the Southern Wilderness, 1754–1775* (1944; reprint, New York: Gordian Press, 1966), 157–164; Tortora, *Carolina in Crisis*, 78.

24. Stuart's praise of "Little Carpenter" for "generously" offering help is in his Memorial to William Pitt, 26 September 1761, Chatham Family Papers, 1747–1767, MSS 74260, from Public Records Office, National Archives, UK, series PRO 30/8, Foreign Copying Program, Library of Congress, 0413c. The precise members of the escape party vary by account, suggesting that some persons joined en route and others did not complete the entire journey. See Stuart to the Governor, [September 1760], Charles Town notice, 5 November 1760, *Boston Evening-Post*, 22 December 1760; Charles Town notice, 11 October 1760, *New-York Gazette*, 30 October 1760; Andrew Lewis to Byrd [September 1760], CO 5 / 377 / Pt. 1 / 018. Byrd noted the arrival of Attakullakulla, Stuart, and Shorey with three Cherokee warriors, two Native women, and two colonial soldiers. See Byrd to Capt. Abercrombie, 16 September 1760, CO 5 / 59 / Pt. 2 / 043.

25. For Ostenaco's reported intercession, see Charles Town notice, 22 October 1760 ("round the field"), *Boston Evening-Post*, 1 December 1760. Trader Samuel Terron attested to Ostenaco's call for restraint at Cane Creek. See JCSC, 22 October 1760, CO 5 / 477 / 001.

26. On Stuart as prospective gunner, see John Stuart to the Governor [September 1760], Charles Town notice, 5 November 1760, *Boston-Evening Post*, 22 December 1760. The South Carolina council favored peace talks concurrent with raising troops. See JCSC, 20 and 22 August, CO 5 / 477 / 001. The plea for British military aid is in Bull to Amherst, 19 October 1760, CO 5 / 60 / 008; Bull to the Board of Trade, 21 October 1760, CO 5 / 377 / Pt. 1 / 005.

27. Oconostota to commanding officer [Miln] at Fort Prince George, 29 September and 1 October 1760; Judd's Friend [Ostenaco] to Miln, 29 September 1760,

Charles Town notice, 18 October 1760, *Pennsylvania Journal*, 13 November 1760. On the Wolf and Tistoe, see JCSC, 17 October 1760, CO 5/477/001.

28. Extract of a letter from Fort Ninety-Six, 10 August 1760, *New-York Mercury*, 1 September 1760 ("now standing"). Trader William Hatton, friend of a Cherokee woman named Peggy, was active in the 1720s. See "Colonel Chicken's Journal to the Cherokees, 1725," in *Travels in the American Colonies*, ed. Newton D. Mereness (New York: Macmillan, 1916), 104.

29. For report of the Nequassee assembly, see Charles Town notice, 22 October 1760, *Boston Evening-Post*, 1 December 1760. See also Byrd to Standing-Turkey, Oconostota, and the Rest of the head Warriors of the Cherokee Nation, 16 September 1760, Charles Town notice, 18 October 1760, *Boston Post-Boy*, 17 November 1760. See also Notice from Fort Prince George, 10 October 1760, *Pennsylvania Journal*, 13 November 1760.

30. Great Warrior (Oconostota) to Miln, and Ostenaco to Miln, 29 September 1760 ("nigher hand"), *Pennsylvania Journal*, 13 November 1760.

31. Five British prisoners were freed at Fort Prince George by the time Cesar arrived. For the release of British captives at Fort Prince George, see Miln's report [October 1760], *Pennsylvania Gazette*, 13 November 1760. Oconostota's fear of being "shut up" is in his letter to Miln, 29 September 1760, in Charles Town notice, 18 October 1760, *Pennsylvania Journal*, 13 November 1760. For the ten released prisoners, see session of 12 November 1760, EJCV, 6:174.

32. For the Cherokee women, see Miln's record of 17 November 1760, Charles Town notice, 11 January 1761, *New York Mercury*, 2 March 1761.

33. For Lantagnac and Seroweh, see Miln's notice, 5 November 1760, *Pennsylvania Gazette*, 18 December 1760. This same notice offers information on Welch [or Welsh] and the female spy who escaped Seroweh's grasp. See also Miln's account of 5–28 November 1760, in a Charles Town notice, 11 January 1761, *New York Mercury*, 2 May 1761. For Welsh, see Oliphant, *Peace and War*, 184.

34. Byrd to Standing Turkey, Oconostota, and the Head Warriors of the Cherokee Nation, 18 October 1760, Charles Town notice [18 October 1760], *Boston Post-Boy*, 1 December 1760. For Byrd's understanding of a truce, see record of 12 November 1760, EJCV, 6:174.

35. On Kerlérec's and "the great chief," see Kerlérec to Minister, 12 July 1761, AC, 13A-42. For Oconostota's return, see report from Fort Prince George, 22 January 1761, Charles Town notice, 1 February 1761 ("What nation or what people"), *Pennsylvania Journal*, 5 March 1761. On Oconostoa's prior anti-French stance, see Attakullakulla to Glen [October 1755], DRIA, 2:78; R. Demere to Lyttelton, 31 January 1757, DRIA, 2:325

36. For French assistance and its limits, see Kerlérec, to Minister, 1 March 1761, AC, 13A-42; Kerlérec to Minister, 4 August 1760, AC, 13-42. See also Kristofer Ray, *Cherokee Power: Imperial and Indigenous Geopolitics in the Trans-Appalachian West* (Norman: University of Oklahoma Press, 2023), 110–113.

37. Byrd's own copy of 17 September 1760, and forwarded to Williamsburg, reads: "That the Little Carpenter shall be acknowledged governor of the Nation, and that he shall be obeyed as such." See *The Correspondence of the Three William Byrds of Westover, 1684–1776*, ed. Marion Tinling, 3 vols. (Charlottesville: University Press of Virginia,

Notes to Pages 268–272

533

1977), 2:706. Byrd's plan, identifying Attakullakulla as "Governor," along with Bull's critique of the Virginian's diplomacy, is in Bull to the Board of Trade, 21 October 1760, CO 5/377/Pt.1/005. For a printed version with the title "Emperor," see Charles Town notice, 18 October 1760, *New-York Gazette*, 17 November 1760.

38. Excerpt from Byrd to Bull, 16 September 1760 ("King of the Cherokees"), 6 October 1760, JCSC, CO 5/477/001.

39. For Chota's protection of Lantagnac, see Charles Town notice, 31 December 1760, *New-York Gazette*, 16 February 1761.

40. Letter from Fort Prince George, 11 January 1761, *New-York Mercury*, 16 February 1761. On Lantagnac's alleged maneuvers, see letters from Augusta, 24 March 1761, *New-York Gazette*, 6 April 1761.

41. Bull to Amherst, 19 October and 1 November 1761; Amherst to Bull, 27 November 1761, CO 5/60/008.

42. Oliphant, *Peace and War*, 143; Grant to Amherst, 17 January 1761, CO 5/61/Pt.1/033.

43. Amherst to Grant, 13 February 1761, CO 5/61/Pt.2/003. On the issue of diplomatic authority, see Amherst to Grant, 7 May 1761, CO 5/61/Pt.2/016. For Amherst's plan for provincial troops, see Amherst to Bull, 13 February 1761, CO 5/61/Pt.1/031.

44. For the delivery of the prisoners, see Bull to Amherst, CO 5/61/Pt.2/020. Bull reported that the Cherokees had delivered ninety prisoners by late April. See Bull to Board of Trade, 30 April 1761, CO 5/377/Pt.1/012.

45. The Talk from the Little Carpenter, Standing Turkey, Judge Friend [Ostenaco], Tistoe, Slave Catcher, the Wolf, and all the Warriours & head Men of the Middle Settlements to Mac[k]intosh, 12 March 1761, Grant Papers, DCAR. For the Cherokee group and the distribution of clothing, see Mackintosh to Grant, 15 March 1761, Grant Papers, DCAR.

46. Bull to "My Good Friend & Brother Attakullakulla," 30 March 1761, Grant Papers, DCAR; A Talk from the Young Warriour of Estatoe to Mackintosh, 1 April 1761, CO 5/61/017. Attakulluakulla's attempt to persuade Seroweh is mentioned in Mackintosh to Grant, 15 March 1761, Grant Papers, DCAR.

47. Attakullakulla [the Little Carpenter] to Grant, ca. 22 May 1761, Grant Papers, DCAR.

48. Grant to Attakullakulla, 23 May 1761; Grant to Amherst, 2 June 1761 ("guilty"), Grant Papers, DCAR. For Bull's preliminary peace articles, see his letter to Grant, 14 April 1761, Grant Papers, DCAR.

49. Grant to Attakullakulla, 23 May 1761, Grant Papers, DCAR.

50. Corkran, *Cherokee Frontier*, 246–247. A small number of Black men served in South Carolina ranger units. See Tortora, *Carolina in Crisis*, 145–146.

51. Montgomery to Amherst, 2 July 1760, CO 5/59/Pt.1/014; Grant to Amherst, 10 July 1761, CO 5/61/Pt.3/004.

52. For the battles and number of Cherokee fighters, see Tortora, *Carolina in Crisis*, 126–127, 148–151; Oliphant, *Peace and War*, 130–132, 158–161.

53. For Grant's praise of Chickasaw fighters, see his letter to Amherst, 10 July 1971, CO 5/61/Pt.3/004. On the killing of old persons by the Catawbas, see Oliphant, *Peace and War*, 162–163. For the Mohawk killing of an old woman, see Tortora, *Carolina*

in Crisis, 152; Edward J. Cashin, *Guardians of the Valley: Chickasaws in Colonial South Carolina and Georgia* (Columbia: University of South Carolina Press, 2009), 120–124.

54. Entry of June 12, 1761 ("to burn"), in [James Grant], "Journal of the March and Operations of the Troops under the Command of Lieut. Colonel Grant of the 40th Regiment upon an Expedition from Fort Prince George against the Cherokees"; "List of the Towns, in the Middle & Back Settlements in the Cherokee Nation, Burnt &c. By the Detachment under the Command of Col. Grant of the 40th Regiment, June 1761." The "Journal" and "List" are enclosed in Grant to Amherst, 12 July 1761, CO 5/61/Pt. 3/004. For the destruction in Cherokee country, see Tortora, *Carolina in Crisis*, 151–152.

55. For Grant and the South Carolina elite, see Tortora, *Carolina in Crisis*, 156–158, 167–168; Oliphant, *Peace and War*, 163–165, 169, 178, 189.

56. Attakullakulla's Talk to Colonel Grant, 29 August 1761, Grant Papers, DCAR. On "pity" in Cherokee culture, see Cynthia Cumfer, *Separate Peoples, One Land: The Mind of the Cherokees, Blacks and Whites on the Tennessee Frontier* (Chapel Hill: University of North Carolina Press, 2007), 34.

57. Attakullakulla's Talk to Colonel Grant, 29 August 1761, Grant Papers, DCAR.

58. Colonel Grant's Talk to the Cherokee Deputies, 30 August 1761; Attakullakulla's Answer to Colonel Grant's Talk, 31 August 1761, Grant Papers, DCAR.

59. Grant to Bull, 2 September 1761 ("Ruin his interest"); Bull to Grant, 11 and 19 September 1761, Grant Papers, DCAR. For the accord, see "The Terms of Peace to be granted to the Cherokee Indians," 22 September 1761, CO 5/477/001. A House committee expressed a desire to end the war but criticized Grant's expedition for being too "defensive," and not destroying as many Cherokees as possible. See Report, 18 September 1761, Journals of the General Assembly, CO 5/479/007.

60. Grant to Bull, 2 September 1761, Grant Papers, DCAR. For Bull's words on Attakullakulla's "rivals," see his message to the General Assembly, 15 September 1761, CO 5 479/007. On Attakullakulla's ambition to be "leading Man," see Grant to Amherst, 5 November 1761, Grant Papers, DCAR.

61. Corkran, *Cherokee Frontier*, 224–235; Oliphant, *Peace and War*, 170–171.

62. Kanagatucko initially received an invitation from Byrd and replied to him before Stephen took command. See letter of Kanagatucko [Connotocko], September 1761, in Stephen to Amherst, 5 October 1761, Amherst Papers, DCAR.

63. Stephen to Kanagatucko, [n.d.], and Stephen to Oconostota, [n.d.], in Stephen to Amherst, 5 October 1761, Amherst Papers, DCAR. For Fauquier's order, see Journal of the House of Burgesses, 14 January 1762, CO 5 /1436/003. Stephen's effectives, 529 men at his main camp, were supplemented by 150 North Carolina militiamen, and about thirty Tuscarora warriors. The "Return" of Stephen's force, 9 October 1761, is in Stephen to Amherst, 24 October 1761, Amherst Papers, DCAR.

64. For Kanagatucko's delay, see Stephen to Amherst, 24 October 1761, Amherst Papers, DCAR. On the Cherokee entourage, see *The Memoirs of Lieut. Henry Timberlake* (London, 1765), 10. The Virginia-Cherokee accord is reproduced in *The Memoirs of Lt. Henry Timberlake: The Story of a Soldier, An Adventurer, and Emissary to the Cherokees*, ed. Duane H. King (Cherokee, NC: Museum of the Cherokee Indian Press, 2007), xxii–xxiii. See also Corkran, *Cherokee Frontier*, 266.

Notes to Pages 279–283

65. Willanawa, Attakullakulla's kinsman, may have delivered word of the South Carolina agreement, with a documentary copy, to the Overhill towns. He made his mark on the Virginia treaty. See King, *Timberlake*, xxiii. Cherokee gifts to Virginia were recorded on 11 March 1762, EJCV, 6:209 ("Truth and Friendship"). See also Corkran, *Cherokee Frontier*, 264.

66. Letter of Oconostota, September 1761, in Adam Stephen to Amherst, 5 October 1761, Grant Papers, DCAR.

67. *Memoirs of Timberlake*, 10–16, 28–33 ("The bloody tommahawke," 33).

68. Fauquier to the Board of Trade, 1 May 1762, CO 5/1330/021; *Memoirs of Timberlake*, 104–113, 118.

69. For the royal audience, see the *Gazetteer or London Daily Advertiser*, 9 July 1762. On arrival at Plymouth and the Cherokees' longing to see the king, see *Memoirs of Timberlake*, 115 ("solemn dirge"), 117, 125–126.

70. *Memoirs of Timberlake*, 87 ("rivals").

71. A Talk from Tistoe, & the Wolf to Mackintosh, 6 November 1761, Grant Papers, DCAR. (Tistoe was speaker for both himself and the Wolf in this talk.)

72. A Talk from Tistoe, & the Wolf to Mackintosh, 6 November 1761.

73. For Grant's intercession on the land issue, see Oliphant, *Peace and War*, 180–186. Grant's view of Cherokee government as "Savage" is in his letter to Bull, 2 September 1761, Grant Papers, DCAR.

74. For "the Treaty of Peace and Friendship," see Council Journal, 16 December 1761 [with ratification on 18 December], CO 5/477/001. For the treaty of 26 November 1751, see DRIA, 1:190.

75. Talk of Attakullakulla, 17 December 1761 ("gone into the woods"), Council Journal, CO 5/477/001. Cherokees said that they had eaten horses. See Charles Town notice, 22 April 1762, *New-York Gazette*, 17 May 1762. One Cherokee man shot and killed a captive soldier and white woman rather than release them. See Talk of Attakullakulla, 26 April 1762, in Council Journal, 5 May 1762, CO 5/477/002. For casualties and prisoner exchange, see Tortora, *Carolina in Crisis*, 169, 174–175, 188; Oliphant, *Peace and War*, 190. Tortora estimates the Cherokee dead in war at one-third of the total population. For a more general estimate, see Paul Kelton, *Cherokee Medicine, Colonial Germs: An Indigenous Nation's Fight against Smallpox* (Norman: University of Oklahoma Press, 2015), 135.

76. Talk of Attakullakulla to Mackintosh, 13 November 1761 ("Strong-House," "Corn Puller," "Lies"), Grant Papers, DCAR.

77. Mackintosh to Grant, 16 November 1761, Grant Papers, DCAR.

78. Preliminary talk of Attakullakulla, 14 December 1761; Cherokees gave their consent on 18 December 1761. See Council Journal, CO 5/477/001.

79. Talk of Attakullakulla, 18 December 1761, Council Journal, CO 5/477/001.

80. Talks of Attakullakulla ("the Great Man above") and Ketagusta, 18 December 1761, Council Journal, CO 5/477/001.

10. The Politics of Alliance and Survival

1. Memorial of John Stuart to William Pitt, 26 July 1761, Chatham Family Papers, 1747–1767, MSS 74260, from Public Records Office, National Archives, UK, series PRO 30/8, Foreign Copying Program, Library of Congress, bundle 73, 0413c.

2. John Richard Alden, *John Stuart and the Southern Colonial Frontier: A Study of Indian Relations, War, Trade, and Land Problems in the Southern Wilderness, 1754–1775* (1944; reprint, New York: Gordian Press, 1966), 139–155, 159–169; J. Russell Snapp, *John Stuart and the Struggle for Empire on the Southern Frontier* (Baton Rouge: Louisiana State University Press, 1996), 55–57. For a Cherokee reference to Cameron as "our brother Scotchie," see A Talk from Oconostota, Attakullakulla, and ... the Cherokees to Stuart, 22 August 1766, CO 5/67/047. See also Colin G. Calloway, *White People, Indians, and Highlanders: Colonial Peoples and Tribal Encounters in Scotland and America* (New York: Oxford University Press, 2008), 152–153.

3. Kristofer Ray, *Middle Tennessee, 1775–1825: Progress and Popular Democracy on the Southwestern Frontier* (Knoxville: University of Tennessee Press, 2007); John R. Finger, *Tennessee's Frontiers: Three Regions in Transition* (Bloomington: Indiana University Press, 2001), 6, 43–46, 78; John Mack Faragher, *Daniel Boone: The Life and Legend of an American Frontiersman* (New York: Henry Holt, 1992), 55–58.

4. On Cherokee diplomacy, see Tom Hatley, *The Dividing Paths: Cherokees and South Carolinians through the Revolutionary Era* (New York: Oxford University Press, 1995), 158–160, 204–211, 217–218; Tyler Boulware, *Deconstructing the Cherokee Nation: Town, Region, and Nation among Eighteenth-Century Cherokees* (Gainesville: University Press of Florida, 2011), 134–151, 155–158.

5. For the Cherokee conflict with Shawnees and other "northern Indians," see *The Memoirs of Lieut. Henry Timberlake* (London, 1765), 93–96; Eric Hinderaker, *Elusive Empires: Constructing Colonialism in the Ohio Valley, 1673–1800* (Cambridge: Cambridge University Press, 1997), 148; Bouquet to Amherst, 5 October 1762, *The Papers of Colonel Henry Bouquet*, ed. Sylvester K. Stevens and Donald H. Kent, vol. 2, Series 21634 (Harrisburg: Pennsylvania Historical Commission, 1940–1943), 100.

6. Fred Anderson, *Crucible of War: The Seven Years' War and the Fate of British Empire in North America, 1754–1766* (New York: Random House, 2000), 524–525; Colin G. Calloway, *The Scratch of a Pen: 1763 and the Transformation of North America* (New York: Oxford University Press, 2006), 50, 55–56; Gregory Evans Dowd, *War under Heaven: Pontiac, the Indian Nations, and the British Empire* (Baltimore: Johns Hopkins University Press, 2002), 87–88.

7. Dowd, *War under Heaven*, 82–83, 89, 177–231, 141–146; Anderson, *Crucible of War*, 536–538; Hinderaker, *Elusive Empires*, 153–157; Richard White, *The Middle Ground: Indians, Empires, and Republics in the Great Lakes Region, 1650–1815* (Cambridge: Cambridge University Press, 1991), 286–289, 327–329, 344–348. See also P. M. Hamer, "Fort Loudoun in the Cherokee War, 1756–1761," *North Carolina Historical Review* 2 (October 1925): 442–458.

8. Alden, *John Stuart*, 181–186. For the conference record, see *Journal of the Four Southern Governors, and the Superintendent of that District, with the Five Nations of Indians, at Augusta, 1763* (Charles Town: Peter Timothy, 1764).

9. On Native attendees, see Stuart to Egremont, 5 December 1763 ("of all Ages and Sexes"), CO 5/65 / Pt. 2 /010. Stuart to Thomas Boone, Arthur Dobbs, and Francis Fauquier, 20 October 1763, in "Journal of the Congress" (manuscript), CO 5 / Pt. 3 /002. Cherokee deputies are listed in "Journal of the Congress," 22.

10. On Ostenaco's "amazing accounts" of England, see Stuart to Egremont, 5 December 1763, CO 5/65 / Pt. 2 /010. See also Talk between Thomas Boone ... and Judds Friend [Ostenaco], 3 November 1762, CO 5/390/002.

Notes to Pages 294–297

11. Stuart to Indian "Friends and brothers," 5 November 1763, "Journal of the Congress," 23–24.

12. Attakullakulla's talk, "Journal of the Congress," 31; Ketagusta's talk, "Journal of the Congress," 28.

13. Stuart's reply, "Journal of the Congress," 36. A printed copy of the royal instructions of 4 July 1763, signed by Stuart, was given to Oconostota and kept by him. The document is in PCC, roll 85, item 71, vol. 2:150. Stuart transcribed a passage of these "Instructions" on Native rights in his letter to the "Principal Warriors and the Governing beloved Headmen of the Cherokee Nation," 30 June 1763, PCC, roll 85, item 71, vol. 2:217–218.

14. George III, A Proclamation, broadside, 7 October 1763, GLC05214, Gilder Lehrman Institute of American History, https://www.gilderlehrman.org/collection/glc05214.

15. Attakullakulla's talk to the "red people," "Journal of the Congress," 29–30. On Cherokee enmity to the Ottawas, see Stuart to Egremont, 5 December 1763, CO 5/65.

16. Gage to Stuart, 7 February 1764 ("visible Jealousy"); Stuart to Gage, 11 April 1764; Gage to Stuart, 1 May 1764 ("prevail upon"), Gage Papers, WCL.

17. The Ouiatenons (Weas) were among the northern and western raiders. See Croghan to William Johnson, 5 October 1762, Amherst Papers, DCAR. For other threats to the Cherokees, see Johnson to Amherst, 25 August 1763, Amherst Papers, DCAR; Stuart to Egremont, 5 December 1763, CO 5/65.

18. On Cherokee distrust of the Creeks, see Oconostota to Stuart, 18 February 1764, and Ketagusta to Stuart [1764]. Both letters are in Stuart to Gage, 11 April 1764, Gage Papers, WCL.

19. Gage to the Earl of Halifax, 13 December 1764 ("looked like"); Gage to Stuart, 31 December 1764, Gage Papers, WCL.

20. On Ostenaco's mission and reward, see Bull to the Board of Trade, 15 March 1765, CO 5/378; Charles Town notice, 6 March 1765, *Georgia Gazette*, 28 March 1765; Charles Town notice, 9 March 1765, *Pennsylvania Gazette*, 25 April 1765.

21. On rumored British-Cherokee collusion, see Journal of George Croghan, entry of 18 July 1765, CO 5/66/041. See also Dowd, *War under Heaven*, 226.

22. For the Delaware-Shawnee attack, see Charles Town notice, 27 February 1765, *Boston Evening-Post*, 1 April 1765. Seroweh's assault is described in a Charles Town notice, 22 May 1765, *Georgia Gazette*, 13 June 1765.

23. Ketagusta's talk was given at a gathering of Cherokee headmen with Cameron and Ensign George Price at Fort Prince George, 8 May 1766, CO 5/67. See also Johnson to Stuart, 17 September 1765, CO 5/67/003 ("Turbulent Spirits"); Johnson to Fauquier, 12 September 1765, WJ, 11:932–933.

24. On the Cherokee woman's heroics and the attack on the Welsh family, see Cameron to Stuart, 10 May 1766, CO 5/67. For the deadly attack near the fort, in which one boy was captured, see Charles Town notice, 12 December 1766, *Georgia Gazette*, 7 January 1767.

25. On the Seed, see Cameron to Stuart, 10 May 1766, CO 5/67.

26. Stuart received intelligence that northern Indian had killed fifty Cherokees "within these three Months." See Stuart to Amherst, 4 October 1763, Amherst Papers, WCL. See also Alden, *John Stuart*, 222. For the Native perspective, see Cherokee

"Talks" to Stuart, 22 August and 22 September 1766 ("Cries of Women" and "Sickness"), CO 5/67/047.

27. Gage to Halifax, 9 December 1763, CO 5/83 / Pt. 1 / 004. For anti-Indian violence, see Peter Silver, *Our Savage Neighbors: How Indian War Transformed Early America* (New York: W. W. Norton, 2008), ch. 5.

28. The attack on the Cherokees occurred on May 8, 1765. See Lewis to Fauquier, 9 May 1765 ("Villainous . . . rascals") and 3 June 1765, CO 5/43/Pt.1/006. A printed copy of Fauquier's proclamation of 13 May 1765, and the Augusta Boys' proclamation ("known Enemies"), along with Lewis's letters and additional evidence, is in Fauquier to the Board of Trade, 14 June 1765, CO 5/1331/003.

29. Board of Trade to "the King's most Excellent Majesty," 27 August 1765, CO 5/1368/003; Fauquier to the Board of Trade, 14 June 1765, CO 5/43/pt.1/006. See also John Shy, *Toward Lexington: The Role of the British Army in the Coming of the American Revolution* (Princeton: Princeton University Press, 1965), 229–230.

30. Lewis to "my Brothers the Chiefs of the Cherokees of the Over Hill Towns," 8 May 1765; Fauquier to "My Dear [Cherokee] Friends and Brothers," 16 May 1765, CO 5/1331/003. Stuart wrote that "several" Cherokees wounded in the Augusta County massacre had died. See Stuart to Halifax, 14 August 1765, CO 5/66/014; Talk from the Great Warrior [Oconostota] to John Stuart, 5 March 1767, CO 5/68/005.

31. Fauquier held a private conference with Attakullakulla on July 9, 1765. Attakullakulla expressed his desire to "wipe the blood clean" in a talk before the Virginia council, 16 July 1765, EJCV, 6:276.

32. On Attakullakulla's desire to see the king, see EJCV (16 July 1765), 6:276 ("northern Indians"). For a similar request by Attakullakulla and Oconostota, see Cameron to Stuart, 10 May 1766, CO 5/67. For a previous request, made by Attakullakulla in his own name and Oconostota's, see Boone to Egremont, 24 November 1763, CO 5/390.

33. On Attakullakulla's bid for mediation and the council's advice to him, see sessions of 16 and 29 July 1765, EJCV, 6:276–278. The council feared that a colonial protective escort might clash with white frontiersmen. See enclosure in Fauquier to the Board of Trade, 7 August 1765, CO 5/1331/003.

34. Stuart to Fauquier, 11 April 1767, CO 5/68. On information from Attakullakulla's wife, see Price [to Stuart], 3 June 1766, CO 5/66/051. For the beads, see Stuart to the Cherokees, 5 February 1767 and Talk of Great Warrior Oconostota to Stuart, 5 March 1767, in Stuart to Shelburne, 1 April 1767, CO 5/68/005.

35. Shelburne to Johnson, 11 December 1766 ("spiriting up"), CO 5/225. Shelburne to Stuart, 11 December 1766, CO 5/225/004; Shelburne to Gage, 11 December 1766 ("Fomenting Wars"), CO 5/84/056. For Shelburne's views, see Jack M. Sosin, *Whitehall and the Wilderness: The Middle West in British Colonial Policy, 1760–1775* (Lincoln: University of Nebraska Press, 1961), 122–125; Snapp, *John Stuart*, 70–71, 75–76.

36. On Cherokee gifts to the Iroquois, see speeches of Ostenaco, the "Prince" of Chota, and the "King" of Chota, in Stuart to Gage, 21 July 1767, WJ, 12:337–340. The scalp was that of a "Youghtanow" Indian man (12:338). His group is placed in Illinois in John Gerar William De Brahm, "A Map of the Indian Nations in the Southern Department, 1766," Clements Library Image Bank, no. 562, William L. Clements Library, University of Michigan, https://quod.lib.umich.edu/w/wcl1ic/x-562/wcl000665.

Notes to Pages 304–307   539

37. The Raven was formerly of Nequassee, a town burned in Grant's offensive of 1761. See Charles Town notice, 1 December 1767, *New-York Journal*, 12 December 1767. For theater and the Mohawk-Cherokee encounter, see *New-York Gazette*, 17 December 1767. On the Cherokees' arrival at Johnson Hall, see WJ, 12:394–395.

38. "Journal of Indian Affairs," 2 March 1768, WJ, 12:457.

39. On the murders, see Johnson to Gage, 5 March 1768, WJ, 12:460; G. S. Rowe, "The Frederick Stump Affair, 1768, and Its Challenge to Legal Historians of Early Pennsylvania," *Pennsylvania History* 49 (October 1982): 259–288, 259–261; James H. Merrell, *Into the American Woods: Negotiators on the Pennsylvania Frontier* (New York: Norton, 1999), 302–306.

40. Oconostota's Talk, General Congress, 6 March 1768, DRCHNY, 8:42.

41. Oconostota's Talk, 6 March 1768, DRCHNY, 8:43.

42. Talk of Ganaghquiesn, 7 March 1768, DRCHNY, 8:43–44.

43. Talk of Ganaghquiesn, 7 March 1768, DRCHNY, 8:44–45; Johnson to the Congress, 9 March 1768, DRCHNY, 8:48, 50, and the reply of Thomas King (Mohawk speaker), DRCHNY, 8:51.

44. Speaker for the Six Nations to Johnson, 8 March 1768, DRCHNY, 8:47 ("the line").

45. Ketagusta and Cherokees to Cameron and Price, 8 May 1766, CO 5/67. Stuart forwarded this letter and others to the Board of Trade, 10 July 1766, CO 5/67.

46. The preliminary accord of 19 October 1765, implemented the next spring, is in CO 5/66. See also Talk from the Headmen and Warriors of the Cherokee Nation, 20 October 1765, and Cameron's certificate of survey, marked by seven headmen, 10 May 1766, CO 5/66.

47. Stuart to Tryon, 5 February 1766; Tryon to Stuart, 9 April 1766, CO 5/66. See also "A Copy of the Journals kept by the Commissioners appointed by his Excellency Governor Tryon to run the dividing Line, between the Western Frontiers of this Province, and the Cherokee Hunting Grounds," 4–19 June 1766, CO 5/310/Pt. 2/013.

48. Tryon's Talk to the Cherokees, 1 June 1767 and Judd's Friend [Ostenaco's] Talk to Tryon, 2 June 1767, CO 5/310/Pt. 2/008.

49. Tryon to the Cherokees, 1 June 1767 ("dividing Line"), CO 5/310/Pt.2/008. For the relevant geography, see Louis De Vorsey Jr., *The Indian Boundary in the Southern Colonies, 1763–1775* (Chapel Hill: University of North Carolina Press, 1966), 96–100.

50. Ostenaco's Talk to Tryon, 2 June 1767, CO 5/310/Pt. 2/008.

51. Ostenaco's Talk to Tryon, 2 June 1767. For the presents, see Tryon to John Mitchell, 2 June 1767, CSRNC, 7:466–467. On the festivities, see entry of 4 June 1767, in "A Copy of the Journals," CO 5/310/Pt. 2/013. For "Great Wolf," see "Commissioners Talk," 13 June 1767, CO 5/310/Pt. 2/014.

52. The treaty is in CO 5/310/Pt. 2/012. See also "A Copy of the Journals," CO 5/310/Pt. 2/013 ("discover the Hills" and "the great Chain of Mountains"). See also Alden, *John Stuart*, 272; De Vorsey, *Indian Boundary*, 107–108.

53. Proclamation, 16 July 1767, in Journal, North Carolina Council, CO 5/310/Pt. 2/018. A copy of the Hard Labour treaty, 14 October 1768, is in CO 5/70.

54. Kevin T. Barksdale, *The Lost State of Franklin: America's First Secession* (Lexington: University Press of Kentucky, 2009), 44–45.

55. Alden, *John Stuart*, 266, 270–273.

56. Colin G. Calloway, *The Indian World of George Washington: The First President, the First Americans, and the Birth of the Nation* (New York: Oxford University Press, 2018), 187 ("temporary expedient"). On major speculative interests, see Sosin, *Whitehall and the Wilderness*, 142–152, 176–180, 188–193, 222–229.

57. The Treaty of Fort Stanwix, 5 November 1768, DRCHNY, 8:135–137. On the treaty's consequences, see Timothy J. Shannon, *Iroquois Diplomacy on the Early American Frontier* (New York: Penguin, 2008), 167–169; Hinderaker, *Elusive Empires*, 136–139, 164–175.

58. For the grant of 12 July 1749, see EJCV, 5:296–297. See also Archibald Henderson, "Dr. Thomas Walker and the Loyal Company of Virginia," *Proceedings of the American Antiquarian Society* 41 (April 1931): 88–94, 100–109. On possible collusion between Johnson and the Virginians at Fort Stanwix, see Calloway, *Indian World of George Washington*, 189–191.

59. The Virginians bid for land as far southwest as a ridgeline between the Cumberland and Tennessee. See Walker to Stuart, 2 February 1769, forwarded with Stuart's letter to Botetourt, 19 January 1769, CO 5/1347. The Virginians' letter included a rendition of talks in Charles Town with Ostenaco and Seroweh (16 January 1769).

60. Stuart to the Head Beloved Man of Chota, Oconostota, Attakullakulla and . . . Chiefs and Warriors of the Cherokee Nation, 19 January 1769, CO 5/70/013.

61. A Talk from Oconostota and the other Headmen and Warriors of the Cherokee Nation to John Stuart, 29 March 1769, CO 5/70. The talk was a response to Stuart to the Head Beloved Man of Chota . . . , 19 January 1769.

62. Talk from the Cherokee Nation to Stuart, 29 July 1769, CO 5/70/037. John Watts served as interpreter in this instance. On male identity, see Nathan Sheidley, "Hunting and the Politics of Masculinity in Cherokee Treaty-Making, 1763–1775," in *Empire and Others: British Encounters with Indigenous Peoples, 1600–1850*, ed. Martin Daunton and Rick Halpern (Philadelphia: University of Pennsylvania Press, 1999), 167–185.

63. For Oconostota's warning, see George Price to Stuart, 3 June 1766, CO 5/66/051. For the Great Island as a sacred site, see Hatley, *The Dividing Paths*, 221–222.

64. Stuart to Botetourt, 13 January 1770, CO 5/71.

65. Stuart to Botetourt, 13 January 1770. White "squatters" in the Holston-Nolichucky River region numbered "hundreds" in 1770 but grew to 2,000 in the next five years. See Finger, *Tennessee's Frontiers*, 45 ("squatters" and "hundreds"), 53.

66. Gage to Stuart, 16 October 1770, CO 5/72 / Pt. 1 /006. On the Shawnees, see Sami Lakomäki, *Gathering Together: The Shawnee People through Diaspora and Nationhood, 1600–1870* (New Haven: Yale University Press, 2014), 98–100.

67. The Cherokee deputies are, unfortunately, unnamed in the record. For their meeting with the Six Nations and allies, 18–24 July 1770, see DRCHNY, 8:228–234; "Proceedings and Treaty . . . ," CO 5/71 / Pt. 2/017.

68. Stuart estimated the expense of presents and other costs at the Lochaber conference, held 18–20 October 1770, at above £21,116 (South Carolina currency). See Stuart to Botetourt, read in Virginia council, 12 December 1770, CO 5/1349.

69. Talk of Oconostota, 19 October 1770, in Lochaber treaty record. See "A Treaty for a Cession to his Most Sacred Majesty George the Third . . . ," 20 October 1770, CO 5/72 / Pt. 1 /006.

Notes to Pages 313–318

70. Talk of Oconostota, 20 October 1770, Lochaber treaty record.

71. Talk of Attakullakulla, 19 October 1770, CO 5/72/Pt. 1/006. For Native ideas of separate creations, see Gregory Evans Dowd, *A Spirited Resistance: The North American Indian Struggle for Unity, 1745–1815* (Baltimore: Johns Hopkins University Press, 1992), 31–33; Hinderaker, *Elusive Empires*, 152–155.

72. Oconostota's words are in Cameron to Stuart, 19 March 1771, CO 5/72/Pt.2/009. William Nelson, president of the Virginia council, was disappointed that the cession did not include Long Island of the Holston. See Nelson to Hillsborough, 15 December 1770, CO 5/1349/004.

73. Cameron to Stuart, 4 March 1771, CO 5/72/Pt. 2/009.

74. Cameron to Stuart, 4 March 1771.

75. The Little Carpenter's Talk [to John Donelson], CO 5/1350/004, enclosed in Dunmore to Hillsborough, March 1772 [no day is recorded], CO 35/1350/001. Dunmore enclosed Donelson's map of the Lochaber treaty line and the additional cession. See Alden, *John Stuart*, 285–286; De Vorsey, *Indian Boundary*, 83–92. See also Woody Holton, *Forced Founders: Indians, Debtors, and Slaves, and the Making of the American Revolution in Virginia* (Chapel Hill: University of North Carolina Press, 1999), 31–32.

76. Little Carpenter's Talk [to Donelson], CO 5/1350/004, in Dunmore to Hillsborough, March 1772, CO 5/1350/001. For Cherokee disgust with the lack of payment, see Alden, *John Stuart*, 284n2. For Attakullakulla's attempt to induce Donelson to pay, see Cameron to Stuart, 4 July 1774, CO 5/75/Pt.2/018. On the sale of land by the "dead" man, see Oconostota to Cameron, 2 March 1774, Haldimand Papers, DCAR.

77. Stuart to Cameron, 11 December 1770; Cameron to Stuart, 23 January 1771 ("as one of their own"), CO 5 / 72 /Pt. 2/009. Oconostota's approval, allegedly given in 1768, is conveyed in Stuart to Dartmouth, 8 January 1773, CO 5/74/012.

78. A Talk by Alexander Cameron at Toqua, 28 February 1771, CO 5/72 /Pt. 2 /009. This same file includes the informal deed, of dubious legality, by which the Cherokees made the gift of land.

79. Cameron to Stuart, 4 March 1771, CO 5/72/Pt. 2/009.

80. Alden, *John Stuart*, 301–305; De Vorsey, *Indian Boundary*, 163–172; see Snapp, *John Stuart*, 117–122; Kathryn E. Holland Braund, *Deerskins and Duffels: The Creek Indian Trade with Anglo-America, 1685–1815*, 2nd ed. (Lincoln: University of Nebraska Press, 2008), 150–154.

81. The Wolf of Seneca, a Lower Cherokee Town, spoke of the Creeks' obligation to fight "where the White people live." Chinisto's rendering of the women's talk follows Wolf's words. All was recorded by interpreter David McDonald, 21 February 1774, CO 5/75/Pt. 1/031. See also Cameron to Stuart, 25 February 1774, CO 5/75/Pt. 1/032.

82. Stuart to Halifax, 24 August 1765 ("Sensible and Manly"), CO 5 / 66 /014. See also Alden, *John Stuart*, 226–234, 314–315; Corkran, *Creek Frontier*, 254–258, 264–275, 285–287. On Creek-Choctaw diplomacy, see Steven Peach, *Rivers of Power: Creek Political Culture in the Native South, 1750–1815* (Norman: University of Oklahoma Press, 2024), 46–58.

83. For the murders, see Stuart to Dartmouth, 5 August 1773, CO 5/74/027. Big Sawney, who lost a kinsman by the Collins murder, spoke of poor whites "being

afraid" of Indians. See Big Sawney to Cameron, 5 July 1773, along with headman Ecuiy's words that "we have but a small Piece of ground left to hunt." See Ecuiy to Cameron, 5 July 1773, in Stuart to Dartmouth, CO 5/74/027. For the fort's abandonment, see Alden, *John Stuart*, 261.

84. For Oconostota's accusation, see Cameron to Stuart, 4 July 1774, CO 5/75/Pt. 2/018. For the Shawnee role in the murders, see Meredith Madison Brown, *Frontiersman: Daniel Boone and the Making of America* (Baton Rouge: Louisiana State University Press, 2008), 56–58. Stuart believed both Delawares and Shawnees were involved in the killings. See Stuart to Dartmouth, 2 August 1774, CO 5/75. (Some sources indicate two Blacks killed rather than one.)

85. On the Russell affair and the revenge attack leading to Will's death, see Campbell to Cameron, 20 January 1774, CO 5/75/Pt. 2/026; Cameron to Stuart, 4 July 1774, CO 5/75/Pt. 2/018 (Will is herein described as a "good Man"); Cameron to Stuart, 15 August 1774, CO 5/75/Pt. 2/028.

86. For Cameron's assessment of "Irregularities," see Cameron to Stuart, 15 August 1774, CO 5/75/Pt. 2/028. On Chinisto, see Cameron to Stuart, 4 July 1774, CO 5/75/Pt. 2/018. Chinisto lived in the Cherokee town of Watagi, well south of the colonial Watauga settlement. He is not to be confused with his contemporary, Chinisto of the Lower Towns. On Watagi, see James Mooney, *Myths of the Cherokee* (1900; reprint, New York: Dover, 1995), 546.

87. For Nolichucky's Cherokee roots, see Mooney, *Myths of the Cherokee*, 527. On the payment of "rent" to Cherokees, which Cameron opposed in principle, see Cameron to Stuart, 4 July and 15 August 1774, CO 5/75.

88. Cameron's assessment was summarized by John Stuart in a letter to the earl of Dartmouth, 15 December 1774 ("falling into Contempt" and "Western"), CO 5/229/005.

89. Campbell to Cameron, 20 January 1774, CO 5/75/Pt. 2/026.

90. Dartmouth to Stuart, 3 March 1773, CO 5/74/011. For differing interpretations of Dunmore's role in foisting the war, James Corbett, *Dunmore's New World* (Charlottesville: University of Virginia Press, 2013), 78–93; Calloway, *The Indian World of George Washington*, 208–212. On disordered Indian trade, see Snapp, *John Stuart*, 40–43, 91–105; Braund, *Deerskins and Duffels*, 111–118.

91. On "the Indian Race," see Dunmore to Attakullakulla, 23 March 1775, CO 5/1353/Pt. 1/039. For Dunmore's official stance against Henderson, see "A Proclamation," 21 March 1775, CO 5/1353/Pt. 1/038. For Josiah Martin's similar declaration, see "A Proclamation," 10 February 1775, CO 5/318/Pt. 1/014.

92. Hatley, *Dividing Paths*, 217–218; Finger, *Tennessee's Frontiers*, 56–58.

93. For Attakullakulla's war foray, see Cameron to Stuart, 11 October 1773, CO 5/75.

11. Cherokees and the American Revolution

1. Cameron to John Stuart, 18 June 1774, cited in John L. Nichols, "Alexander Cameron: British Agent among the Cherokees, 1764–1781," *South Carolina Historical Magazine* 97 (April 1996): 94–114, 104. For the legend of "blood brothers," see John P. Brown, "Eastern Cherokee Chiefs," *Chronicles of Oklahoma* 16 (March 1938): 3–35, 19.

Notes to Pages 324–328   543

2. On Dragging Canoe's character and age, see John R. Finger, *Tennessee's Frontiers* (Bloomington: Indiana University Press, 2001), 57–58. For Mialoquo, see Tyler Boulware, *Deconstructing the Cherokee Nation: Town, Region, and Nation among Eighteenth-Century Cherokees* (Gainesville: University Press of Florida, 2011), 129. Cameron to John Stuart, 18 June 1774, quoted in Nichols, "Alexander Cameron," 104 ("only Young Warriour").

3. The course of bargaining at Sycamore Shoals in not easily known. There is no written conference record, only what colonials and Cherokees remembered in retrospect. Dragging Canoe's departure was reported by several witnesses. See deposition of James Robertson [spelled Robinson in record], 16 April 1777, CVSP, 1:285–286 ("in a passion"); deposition of John Reid, 16 April 1777, CVSP, 1:284.

4. Deposition of Samuel Wilson, 15 April 1777, CVSP, 1:283 ("a bloody Ground"). On Henderson and Boone, see John Mack Faragher, *Daniel Boone: The Life and Legend of an American Frontiersman* (New York: Henry Holt, 1992), 74–76, 107–112.

5. On the conference atmosphere, see Finger, *Tennessee's Frontiers*, 50–51. On Stuart, see J. Russell Snapp, *John Stuart and the Struggle for Empire on the Southern Frontier* (Baton Rouge: Louisiana State University Press, 1996), 159–163. Cameron set out for Overhill country in March but returned to Lochaber without nearing his destination. See Cameron to Stuart, 2 March 1775, in Stuart to Dartmouth, 28 March 1775, CO 5 / 76. Vann is sometimes identified as "John Vann." See deposition of James [Robertson], 16 April 1777, CVSP, 1:286.

6. Archibald Henderson, "Richard Henderson and the Occupation of Kentucky, 1775," *Mountain Valley Historical Review* 1 (December 1914): 341–363, 343–345.

7. Deposition of John Reid, 16 April 1777, CVSP, 1:284–285. For signatures, see deposition of James Robertson, 16 April 1777 CVSP, 1:287. "Blank Printed Land Deed of the Transylvania Colony," probably 1775, undated and unsigned, in Mss. C T oversize, FHS.

8. Deposition of Charles Robertson, 3 October 1777, CVSP, 1:291–292. For the Sycamore Shoals treaty conference, see Finger, *Tennessee's Frontiers*, 50–51; Tom Hatley, *The Dividing Paths: Cherokees and South Carolina through the Revolutionary Era* (New York: Oxford University Press, 1995), 217–218; A. Henderson, "Richard Henderson and the Occupation of Kentucky," 350–353.

9. Cameron to Stuart, 4 July 1774, CO 5 / 75 / Pt. 2 / 018.

10. Nichols, "Alexander Cameron," 104–106.

11. Hatley, *Dividing Paths*, 218–228; James P. Pate, "The Chickamauga: A Forgotten Segment of Indian Resistance on the Southern Frontier" (Ph.D. diss., Mississippi State University, 1969); Tyler Boulware, *Deconstructing the Cherokee Nation: Town, Region, and Nation among Eighteenth-Century Cherokees* (Gainesville: University Press of Florida, 2011), 161–165.

12. On Chickamauga separatism and nationhood, see Jamie Myers Mize, "'To Conclude on a General Union': Masculinity, the Chickamauga, and Pan-Indian Alliances in the Revolutionary Era," *Ethnohistory* 68 (July 2021): 429–448.

13. Snapp, *John Stuart*, 159–163. On Whig scrutiny of Stuart's correspondence, see Joseph Habersham to Philotheos Chiffele, 16 June 1775, in John Drayton [and William Henry Drayton], *Memoirs of the American Revolution* (Charleston, 1821), 290 ("to act in defence").

14. John Stuart to Henry Stuart, 24 October 1775, CO 5/77/017; Gage to John Stuart, 12 September 1775, quoted in David H. Corkran, *The Creek Frontier, 1540–1783* (Norman: University of Oklahoma Press, 1967), 292; Stuart to Dartmouth, 19 January 1776, CO 5/77/010. See also Snapp, *John Stuart*, 166–175.

15. On the alleged gunpowder, see deposition of Jonathan Clark, 21 August 1775, in Drayton, *Memoirs*, 414. On Cameron having "two Tongues," see Drayton's message of 21 August 1775 to the Cherokee Nation, with rebuttal in Cameron to Drayton, 16 October 1775, enclosed in Cameron to John Stuart, 9 November 1775, CO 5/77/019; Nichols, "Alexander Cameron," 105–106; Jim Piecuch, *Three Peoples, One King: Loyalists, Indians, and Slaves in the Revolutionary South, 1775–1782* (Columbia: University of South Carolina Press, 2008), 65–66.

16. Drayton to Cameron, 26 September 1775; Cameron to Stuart, 8–9 November 1775, CO 5/77/019.

17. Dragging Canoe's remarks are recorded in Henry Stuart to John Stuart, 25 August 1776, CO 5/77/047. On Colbert, see James R. Atkinson, *Splendid Land, Splendid People: The Chickasaw Indians to Removal* (Tuscaloosa: University of Alabama Press, 2004), 93, 245n31.

18. Henry Stuart to John Stuart, 7 May 1776, CO 5/77/036; Henry Stuart to John Stuart, 25 August 1776, CO 5/77/047.

19. Henry Stuart to John Stuart, 25 August 1776, CO 5/77/047.

20. Henry Stuart to John Stuart, 25 August 1776.

21. Henry Stuart to John Stuart, 25 August 1776.

22. On the legend of "blood brothers," see Brown, "Eastern Cherokee Chiefs," 19.

23. J. G. M. Ramsey, *The Annals of Tennessee to the End of the Eighteenth Century* (Philadelphia: Lippincott, 1860), 143–149; John Haywood, *The Civil and Political History of the State of Tennessee from Its Earliest Settlement up to the Year 1796* (1823; reprint, Nashville: W. H. Haywood, 1891), 60; Williams, *Tennessee*, 24–28, 30–31.

24. See "Copy of a letter addressed to the frontier Inhabitants, by Mr. Stuart," *Virginia Gazette*, 7 June 1776. The article incorrectly identified Henry Stuart as "superintendent of Indian affairs." See also Bledsoe to William Preston, 14 and 22 May 1776, RVA, 7, Pt. 1:136–137, 233–234. The number of Creek and Chickasaw warriors was 500 each, and not 5,000 as printed on p. 118. The forged letter was reprinted in *Dunlap's Maryland Gazette* (Baltimore), 19 June 1776.

25. Henry Stuart and Alexander Cameron to the Inhabitants of Watauga "Nonatluchky" [*sic*] and others settled on this side the Boundary Line, 7 May 1776, CO 5/77.

26. Carter to Stuart and Cameron, 13 May 1776, CO 5/77. On Carter, see Finger, *Tennessee's Frontier*, 45, 53; Williams, *Tennessee*, 27–29. On the crisis, see Philip M. Hamer, "The Wataugans and the Cherokee Indians, 1776," *East Tennessee Historical Society Publications* 8 (January 1931): 108–126.

27. Henry Stuart and Cameron to John Carter and the other inhabitants of Watauga, 23 May 1776 ("young fellows"); Henry Stuart and Cameron to Aaron Penson [Pinson?] and the inhabitants of Nonatluchky, 23 May 1776 ("the safety"), CO 5/77.

28. Cameron to John Stuart, 9 July 1776, CO 5/77/046. On the intimidation of Tories, see Nadia Dean, *A Demand of Blood: The Cherokee War of 1776* (Cherokee, NC: Valley River Press, 2012), 337.

Notes to Pages 333–338

29. Henry Stuart to John Stuart, 25 August 1776, CO 5/77/047; Cameron to John Stuart, 9 July 1777, CO 5/77/046.

30. Henry Stuart to John Stuart, 25 August 1776, CO 5/77/047.

31. Committee of Fincastle [County, Virginia] to Oconostota, Judge's Friend [Ostenaco], Attakullakulla and the other chiefs and Warriors of the Cherokee Nation, [May 1776], CO 5/77/049.

32. Committee of Fincastle to Oconostota, [May 1776].

33. Henry Stuart to Edward Wilkinson, 28 June 1776, CO 5/77/041. On Double-head, see Fort Charlotte (N.C.) conference journal, 15 April 1776, *Revolution and Confederation*, ed. Colin G. Calloway, EAID, 18:209–210 ("people from Pensacola"). On Galphin, see John T. Juricek, *Endgame for Empire: British-Creek Relations in Georgia and Vicinity, 1763–1776* (Gainesville: University Press of Florida, 2015), 223–235.

34. On Valley and Middle Town sentiment, see Fort Charlotte journal, 15 April 1776, EAID, 18:209–210. For Overhill country, see Henry Stuart to John Stuart, 25 August 1776, CO 5/77/047.

35. Dean, *A Demand of Blood*, 105–110; Finger, *Tennessee's Frontiers*, 63–65; Williams, *Tennessee*, 37–47.

36. Cherokees reportedly killed several white women and abducted children before the Holston engagement. See John Page to Cornelius Harnett, 1 August 1776, CSRNC, 10:729. On Moore's death, see John P. Brown, *Old Frontiers, The Story of Cherokee Indians from Earliest Times to the Date of Their Removal to the West, 1838* (Kingsport, TN: Southern Publishers, 1938), 153; Williams, *Tennessee*, 43.

37. On Dragging Canoe's tactics, see Finger, *Tennessee's Frontiers*, 64. On the scalps at Black's Fort, Virginia, see Benjamin Sharp to John S. Williams, 25 June 1842, in *The American Pioneer*, ed. John S. Williams (Cincinnati, 1842), 1:335. On Cherokee scalp-taking, see Dean, *Demand of Blood*, 110.

38. Newspaper notices, Ninety-Six District, 30 June–1 July 1776, Augusta, 3 July 1776, in *New-York Gazette*, 9 September 1776. See also Griffith Rutherford to the North Carolina Council of Safety, CSRNC, 10:669. On the Terrapin, a Cherokee militant, and links between the Lower and Upper Towns, see Hugh Hamilton to Cameron, 4 July 1776; Henry Stuart to John Stuart, 25 August 1776, CO 5/77.

39. Lee to the Council of Safety, 7 July 1776, CSRNC, 10:669: Lee to Pendleton, 7 July 1776, PCC, roll 85, item 71, vol. 1:45–46; Cornelius Harnett to Patrick Henry, 21 July 1777, roll 85, item 71, vol. 1:47.

40. Hatley, *Dividing Paths*, 168; Calloway, *American Revolution in Indian Country*, 19.

41. Dean, *War of Blood*, 144, 187, 232–238; Hatley, *Dividing Paths*, 194–200.

42. For the burning of Lower Towns, see Charles Town notice, 14 August 1776, *Pennsylvania Packet*, 17 September 1776. For a first-hand account, see Arthur Fairies [Farris?], "Journal of an Expedition in 1776 Against the Cherokees, under the Command of Captain Peter Clinton," transcript, pp. 3–7, Pamphlet 973.3 1850 Fairies, South Carolina Historical Society, Special Collections, College of Charleston. Williamson to Griffith Rutherford, 14 August 1776, CSRNC, 10:669 ("Desolation"). The census is found in Drayton, *Memoirs*, 428.

43. Dean, *Demand of Blood*, 163 ("Black Hole"), 314–319.

44. Fairies, "Journal of an Expedition," transcript, 19, 21.

45. Fairies, "Journal of an Expedition," transcript, 6. On the killing at Ellijay, see J. G. de Roulhac Hamilton, "The Revolutionary Diary of William Lenoir," *Journal of*

Southern History 6 (May 1940): 247–259, 255. For the infant's murder, see Dean, *Demand of Blood*, 198–199.

46. Christian to Patrick Henry, 14–15 October 1776, CSRNC, 10:844–847; Christian to Henry, 23 October 1776, in "Virginia Legislative Papers: Reports of Colonels Christian and Lewis During the Cherokee Expedition, 1776," *Virginia Magazine of History and Biography* 17 (January 1909): 52–64, 61. On the Cherokee destruction of their homes, see John Stuart to Germain, 24 November 1776, CO 5/229/036.

47. Notice, *Virginia Gazette*, 15 November 1776. On the elderly woman guide, see Fairies, "Journal of an Expedition," transcript, 26.

48. Dragging Canoe's talk is conveyed in William Thompson to Cameron, 14 November 1776, CO 5/94/Pt.1/062.

49. Drayton to Francis Salvador, 24 July 1776, in *Documentary History of the American Revolution*, ed. R. W. Gibbes, 2 vols. (New York: D. Appleton, 1855–1857), 2:29. For the several Cherokee prisoners as slaves, see Dean, *Demand of Blood*, 204–205.

50. Dragging Canoe said that he rejected Attakullakulla's request to meet Christian for talks. See Thompson to Cameron, 14 November 1776, CO 5/94/Pt.1/062.

51. Attakullakulla told Christian, perhaps misleadingly, that Dragging Canoe had gone to Chickasaw country. See Thompson to Cameron, 14 November 1776, CO 5/94/Pt.1/062.

52. For Dragging Canoe's visit to Chickamauga, see Deposition of Robert Dews, 22 January 1777, CSRNC, 22:996–998. One scholar estimates that five hundred Cherokee warriors "and their families" were at Chickamauga by the spring of 1777. See Pate, "Chickamauga," 81. On Cherokee place names in the area, see James Mooney, *Myths of the Cherokee* (1900; reprint, New York: Dover, 1995), 311–314, 536–537, 544.

53. On McDonald, see Brown, *Old Frontiers*, 122–123, 163, 171.

54. Talk of Emisteseguo (Creek headman) to Cameron for John Stuart, 19 November 1776, CO 5/94/Pt.1/062. The refugees' "destitute" plight is in Stuart to Germain, 23 January 1777, CO 5/229/036. On the lack of corn, see Cameron to Stuart, 13 July 1777, CO 5/78/032.

55. Cynthia Cumfer, *Separate Peoples, One Land: The Minds of Cherokees, Blacks, and Whites on the Tennessee Frontier* (Chapel Hill: University of North Carolina Press, 2007), 10, 29; William G. McLoughlin, *Cherokee Renascence in the New Republic* (Princeton: Princeton University Press, 1986), 23–25.

56. On Lochaber's seizure and related losses, see Cameron to Stuart, 31 August 1776, CO 5/78/005; Charles Town notice, 31 July 1776, *Pennsylvania Packet*, 17 September 1776.

57. Cameron to Stuart, 23 September 1776, CO 5/78/005. For Cameron's reputed words about a successful British invasion, see George Galphin to the Creek Indians, 28 August 1776, in Stuart to Germain, 26 October 1776, CO 5/78/005. Cameron received a false report that Charles Town had fallen. See Hamilton to Cameron, 4 July 1776, CO 5/77.

58. Stuart to Germain, 23 January 1777, CO 5/229/036; Cameron to Stuart, 31 August 1776, CO 5/78/005. In this letter, Cameron wrote: "The Indians will not fight on a great time without being incorporated with some white people."

59. Piecuch, *Three Peoples*, 102–106.

60. Cameron to Stuart, 13 July 1777, CO 5/78/032; Stuart to Tonyn, 21 July 1777 ("Indians are different"), CO 5/557/055.

Notes to Pages 344–348

61. On the attack by the Holston, see Rutherford to Caswell, 1 February 1777, CSRNC, 11:372. On the woman as courier, see Charles Robertson to Caswell [?], 27 April 1777, CSRNC, 11:458.

62. Historians have described the fight in which Nan-ye-hi participated as "the Battle of Talwia" in 1755. The venue and date of the clash are not clear since Cherokees and Creeks were at peace in 1755. For the folkloric tale, see Pat Alderman, *Nancy Ward: Cherokee Chieftainess, Dragging Canoe, Cherokee-Chickamauga War Chief*, 2nd ed. (Johnson City, TN: Overmountain Press, 1978), 3.

63. On Nan-ye-hi's lineage and status, see Cynthia Cumfer, "Nan-ye-hi (Nancy Ward): Diplomatic Mother," in *Tennessee Women: Their Lives and Times*, ed. Sarah Wilkerson Freeman and Beverly Bond (Athens: University of Georgia Press, 2009), 7–9; Michelene E. Pesantubbee, "Nancy Ward: American Patriot or Cherokee Nationalist?" *American Indian Quarterly* 38 (Spring 2014): 177–206, 182 ("Supreme Beloved Woman").

64. Pesantubbee, "Nancy Ward," 178–179; Norma Tucker, "Nancy Ward, Ghighau of the Cherokees," *Georgia Historical Quarterly* 53 (June 1969): 192–200.

65. On the Cherokee visit to the fort, see Charles Robertson to Richard Caswell, 27 April 1777, CSRNC, 11:458–459 ("could not fight"). See also Henry to Caswell, 3 March 1777, CSRNC, 11:405–406.

66. The report of the attack by the Holston is in Rutherford to Caswell, 1 February 1777, CSRNC, 11:372. For the talks in Williamsburg, see Notice, *Virginia Gazette*, 30 May 1777.

67. Talks of Oconostota, 2 July 1777 and especially 15 July 1777, in Archibald Henderson, "Treaty of Long Island of Holston, July 1777," *North Carolina Historical Review* 8 (January 1931): 55–116, 62, 78 (Oconostota's talks). James Mooney gives Utsi'dsata for the Cherokee name of Corn Tassel (or "Thistle-head") in Mooney, *Myths of the Cherokee*, 529. Corn Tassel's name is also rendered Onitositah in English; see Cumfer, *Separate Peoples*, xi. On Tassel's warrior name, see Stanley W. Hoig, *The Cherokees and Their Chiefs: In the Wake of Empire* (Fayetteville: University of Arkansas Press, 1998), 278n14.

68. Talk of Corn Tassel, 10 July 1777, in Henderson, "Treaty of Long Island," 67 (quotations).

69. Talks of Corn Tassel, 17–18 July 1777, in Henderson, "Treaty of Long Island," 91 ("so much land," "Your stocks"), 102 ("some acknowledgement," "bread to those yet unborn"); Talk of Raven, 19 July 1777, in Henderson, "Treaty of Long Island," 103. On Virginia's demands, see Christian's talks, 16 and 18 July 1777, in Henderson, "Treaty of Long Island," 85–86, 95–96, 98–99.

70. Corn Tassel's words of 20 July 1777 are in Henderson, "Treaty of Long Island," 110.

71. For Corn Tassel's desire to hear "from the Great Warrior of America," see his talk of 17 July 1777 in Henderson, "Treaty of Long Island," 91. Christian's speech, 17 July 1777; Henderson, "Treaty of Long Island," 92; Corn Tassel on Henderson's "lies," 20 July 1777, Henderson, "Treaty of Long Island," 110.

72. The treaty of 20 May 1777, imposed by South Carolina and Georgia at Dewitt's Corner, S.C., is transcribed in Henderson, "Treaty of Long Island," 76 ("conquest"). For the return of escaped Blacks, see Henderson, "Treaty of Long Island," 77–78, 104, 107.

73. On Cherokee men who retained the will to fight, see Stuart to William Howe, 4 March 1777, CO 5/94/Pt.2/021.

74. Instructions to David Taitt . . . by Colonel John Stuart, 1 February 1779, CO 5/82/022; Tuwekee (the Cowee Warrior) to John Stuart, CO 5/80/045; Cameron to Germain, 10 May 1779, CO 5/230/009. On Ostenaco, "a Great Medal Chief" under Britain, see Commissioners Andrew Rainsford, John Mitchell, Robert Taitt, Alexander Macullagh, and David Holms to Germain, 26 July 1779, CO 5/230/009.

75. Henry to Richard Caswell, 8 January 1779, CSRNC, 14:243–246. For the attack, see extract of a letter from Robert Grierson to Taitt, 24 May 1779, CO/80/067; Williams, *Tennessee*, 95–96. For the Virginia peace overture, see Cameron to Germain, 18 December 1779 ("utmost distress"), CO 5/81/009. On Cherokee hunger and the lack of supplies, see Randolph C. Downes, "Cherokee-American Relations in the Upper Tennessee Valley, 1776–1791," *East Tennessee Historical Society Publications* 8 (1936): 35–53, 36–37.

76. On Stuart's death, see Cameron and Charles Stuart to Germain, 26 March 1779, CO 5/230/009. On the aborted offensive, see Cameron to General Augustine Prevost, 15 October 1779, CO 5/82/Pt. 2/015. For Brown, see Edward J. Cashin, *The King's Ranger: Thomas Brown and the American Revolution on the Southern Frontier* (Athens: University of Georgia Press, 1989).

77. A newspaper notice claimed that Williamson had burned seven towns and gained their inhabitants' "submission, without any bloodshed." See Charles Town notice, 22 September 1779, *Pennsylvania Journal*, 27 October 1779. See also Cameron to Prevost, 15 October 1779, CO 5/82/Pt. 2/015.

78. Cameron was unsure of the Creeks because of smallpox in their towns and general war fatigue. See Cameron to General Augustine Prevost, 25 October 1779, CO 5/82/Pt.2/015; "Speech of the Cherokees," 26 October 1779, Haldimand Papers, DCAR. Kissingua, a chief of Ottawa-Miami lineage, was a courier between northern tribes and the Creeks and Cherokees. See Dowd, *Spirited Resistance*, 57.

79. Cameron, who had General Henry Clinton's support, had believed himself in line to be appointed superintendent of Indian Affairs for the Southern District. See Cameron to Germain, 18 December 1779, CO 5/81/009.

80. Cameron to Germain, 30 November 1780, CO 5/82/018. See also David Narrett, *Adventurism and Empire: The Struggle for Mastery in the Louisiana-Florida Borderlands, 1762–1803* (Chapel Hill: University of North Carolina Press, 2015), 95–99.

81. For British policy and Loyalist connections to Blacks, see Piecuch, *Three Peoples*. See also Sylvia R. Frey, *Water from the Rock: Black Resistance in a Revolutionary Age* (Princeton: Princeton University Press, 1991).

82. For the "war-whoop," see Ramsey, *Annals of Tennessee*, 589. On the "overmountain men," see Williamson, *Tennessee*, 147–158. On the battle, see Isaac Shelby to Arthur Campbell, 12 October 1780, CSRNC, 15:116–117.

83. Cornwallis to Thomas Brown, 17 July 1780, Cornwallis Papers, PRO 30/11/78, DCAR; Brown to Cornwallis, 16 July 1780 ("plunderers"), Cornwallis Papers, PRO 30/11/2. For the fight at Augusta, see newspaper notice, Savannah, 23 September 1780, CO 5/82/024; Charles Shaw to Germain, 24 September 1780, CO 5/230/035.

84. Brown wrote that 140 Cherokee and Creek men and women were sick from smallpox, but "daily recovering with much nursing." See Brown to Cornwallis,

Notes to Pages 353–356

17 December 1780, Cornwallis Papers, PRO 30/11/4, DCAR; Cornwallis to Henry Clinton, 29 December 1780, in *Correspondence of Charles, First Marquis Cornwallis*, ed. Charles Ross (London: John Murray, 1859), 1:76.

85. Cumfer, "Nan-ye-hi (Nancy Ward)," 7–9; Tucker, "Nancy Ward"; Pesantubbee, "Nancy Ward."

86. Depositions of William Springstone, John Martin, Francis Budwine, and John Hawkins, 11 December 1780, CVSP, 1:447. Arthur Campbell wrote of a Cherokee woman's warning that saved the traders' lives. See Campbell to Jefferson, 5 December 1781, TJ, 15:597.

87. Major Abraham DePeyster to Thomas Brown, 5 April 1780, Cornwallis Papers, PRO 30/11/4, DCAR. For the Raven's views, see Deposition of William Springstone, 11 December 1780, CVSP, 1:446. See also Mize, "To Conclude a General Union," 435–437.

88. On Chickamauga resistance to Cumberland settlement, see Finger, *Tennessee's Frontiers*, 77–83.

89. Joseph Martin to Thomas Jefferson, 12 December 1780, TJ, 4:200–201. For Campbell's offensive, see Williams, *Tennessee*, 184–187.

90. For an account of the campaign, see Campbell to Jefferson, 15 January 1781, TJ, 4:359–363 ("Chickamogga People").

91. Campbell to Jefferson, 15 January 1781. See also Williams, *Tennessee*, 188–191.

92. The seven towns, some destroyed twice during the entire war, were Toqua, Mialoquo (Dragging Canoe's former home), and Kai-a-tee, Chatuga, Tellico, Hiwassee, and Chestowee. See Campbell to Jefferson, 15 January 1781, TJ, 4:359–363.

93. Campbell to Jefferson, 15 January 1781.

94. Campbell to Jefferson, 15 January 1781. For documents in Oconostota's archive, see "Instructions" of George III, 4 July 1763 ("rights and possessions"); Taitt to Oconostota, 24 January 1777; John Stuart to Oconostota, 6 February 1777; Patrick Henry to Brother Oconostota, 3 March 1777; Treaty of 20 July 1777; sequentially in PCC, roll 85, item 71, vol. 2:150, 189–192, 201–203, 205, 207–208, 213, 220–222.

95. For Jefferson's struggles, see Noble Cunningham, *In Pursuit of Reason: The Life of Thomas Jefferson* (Baton Rouge: Louisiana State University Press, 1987), 66–71. For Jefferson's advocacy of a Cherokee peace, see Jefferson to Campbell, 17 February 1781, TJ, 4:634–635; Jefferson to Samuel Huntington. 10 October 1780, TJ, 4:25.

96. Martin to Jefferson, 7 February 1781, TJ, 4:551–552. For Hanging Maw's plight, see Downes, "Cherokee-American Relations," 37; Raven's Talk, 15 June 1777, Henderson, "Treaty of Long Island," 82–83.

97. Martin to Jefferson, 31 March 1781, TJ, 5:304–305; Campbell to Jefferson, 25 April 1781, TJ, 5:552–553 ("several hundred"). Martin halted his own expedition against Native militants when his men declined to head further south toward Chickamauga. See Martin to Campbell, 22 April 1781, in Campbell to Jefferson, 25 April 1781.

98. On the arrival of Cherokee women and children, see Martin to Campbell, 4 June 1781, CVSP, 2:143. Martin believed there were three hundred Cherokees on the way at the time. See also Campbell to Jefferson, 15 June 1781, TJ, 6:94. On Cherokee attendees, see Christian to Governor [Thomas Nelson], 5 July 1781, CVSP, 2:199.

99. Quoted in Cumfer, "Nan-ye-hi (Nancy Ward)," 10.

100. Cumfer, "Nan-ye-hi (Nancy Ward)," 10. For children of mixed ancestry, usually born of Native women by "white" fathers, see Cumfer, *Separate Peoples*, 72–73, 112–113, 160. William McLoughlin estimates "mixed-blood" children at about 15 percent circa 1805. See McLoughlin, *Cherokee Renascence*, 69.

101. Quoted in Williamson, *Tennessee*, 201.

102. Nichols, "Alexander Cameron," 95, 113.

12. Bloodshed and Quests for Peace

1. Substance of a Talk from Little Turkey [to Thomas Brown], 17 November 1783, CO 5/82.

2. Talk from the Chiefs of the Upper Creeks to Lt. Colonel Thomas Brown, 30 December 1783, CO 5/82.

3. Kathleen DuVal, *Independence Lost: Lives on the Edge of the American Revolution* (New York: Random House, 2015), 350–351. See also Colin G. Calloway, *The American Revolution in Indian Country* (Cambridge: Cambridge University Press, 1995), 288; James H. Merrell, "Declarations of Independence: Indian-White Relations in the New Nation," in *The American Revolution: Its Character and Limits*, ed. Jack P. Greene (New York: New York University Press, 1987), 197–198; Alan Taylor, *American Revolutions: A Continental History, 1750–1804* (New York: Norton, 2016).

4. Cynthia Cumfer, *Separate People, One Land: The Minds of Cherokees, Blacks, and Whites on the Tennessee Frontier* (Chapel Hill: University of North Carolina Press, 2007), 105–112; Tyler Boulware, *Deconstructing the Cherokee Nation: Town, Region, and Nation among Eighteenth-Century Cherokees* (Gainesville: University Press of Florida), 162–176.

5. Gregory Evans Dowd, *A Spirited Resistance: The North American Indian Struggle for Unity, 1745–1815* (Baltimore: Johns Hopkins University Press, 1992), ch. 5; Calloway, *American Revolution in Indian Country*, 280–285; Kevin T. Barksdale, *The Lost State of Franklin: America's First Secession* (Lexington: University Press of Kentucky, 2009). On limited federal authority, see Gregory Ablavsky, *Federal Ground: Governing Property and Violence in the First U.S. Territories* (Oxford: Oxford University Press, 2021), 32–40.

6. For settler population, see John R. Finger, *Tennessee's Frontiers* (Bloomington: Indiana University Press, 2001), 53; Malcolm J. Rohrbough, *The Trans-Appalachian Frontier: People, Societies, and Institutions* (1978; reprint, Belmont, CA: Wadsworth, 1990), 16. See also Kristofer Ray, *Middle Tennessee, 1775–1825* (Knoxville: University of Tennessee Press, 2007), 14. The Black population in three western counties of pre-state Tennessee was 2,466 in 1795. The total non-Indian population in the area was above 11,900 persons. See the census in TP, 4:404; Anita S. Goodstein, "Black History on the Tennessee Frontier, 1780–1810," *Tennessee Historical Quarterly* 38 (Winter 1979): 401–420.

7. Patrick Griffin, *American Leviathan: Empire, Nation, and Revolutionary Frontier* (New York: Hill and Wang, 2007), 187. For population figures, see Rohrbough, *Trans-Appalachian Frontier*, 16.

8. Peter H. Wood, "The Changing Population of the Colonial South: An Overview by Race and Region, 1685–1790," in *Powhatan's Mantle: Indians in the Colonial Southeast*,

Notes to Pages 362–366 551

ed. Gregory A. Waselkov, Peter H. Wood, and Tom Hatley, rev. ed. (Lincoln: University of Nebraska Press, 2006), 86 ("Seminolies"), 90–92; Paul Kelton, *Cherokee Medicine, Colonial Germs: An Indigenous Nation's Fight against Smallpox, 1518–1824* (Norman: University of Oklahoma Press, 2015), 159–173; Russell Thornton, *The Cherokees, A Population History* (Lincoln: University of Nebraska Press, 1990), 37–40. On Chickamauga diversity, see William G. McLoughlin, *Cherokee Renascence in the New Republic* (Princeton: Princeton University Press, 1986), 20.

9. On Robertson's background, see A. M. Goodpasture, "The Watauga Association," *American Historical Magazine* 3 (April 1898): 107–110; Samuel Cole Williams, *Tennessee during the Revolutionary War* (1944; reprint, Knoxville: University of Tennessee Press, 1974), 10–12, 33, 53, 68–73.

10. On Henderson's collaboration with Robertson, see Archibald Henderson, "Richard Henderson: The Authorship of the Cumberland Compact and the Founding of Nashville," *Tennessee Historical Magazine* 2 (September 1916): 155–174. On Henderson and company's settlement plans, see statement, 26 June 1776, CVSP, 1:271–272.

11. For the conference, see St. George L. Sioussat, "Journal of General Daniel Smith, one of the Commissioners to Extend the Boundary Line between the Commonwealths of Virginia and North Carolina, August 1779, to July 1780," *Tennessee Historical Magazine* 1 (March 1915): 50.

12. Talk of Corn Tassel, 25 September 1779, in Sioussat, "Journal," 51.

13. Talk of Virginia commissioners, 27 September 1779, in Sioussat, "Journal," 52. The Cherokee response to Henderson's talk, 26 September 1779, is noted in "Journal," 51.

14. Richard Douglas Spence, "John Donelson and the Opening of the Old Southwest," *Tennessee Historical Quarterly* 50 (Fall 1991): 157–172.

15. Donelson Journal [22 December 1779–4 March 1780], Tennessee Historical Society, ID#33635, Virtual Archive: https://teva.contentdm.oclc.org/digital/collection /tfd/id/600/; transcript: https://tsla.tnsosfiles.com/digital/teva/transcripts/33635.pdf. See also Spence, "John Donelson," 163–165.

16. Donelson Journal, 1–2; Spence, "John Donelson," 164–165. For conflict along the Tennessee and Cumberland, see Natalie Inman, *Brothers and Friends: Kinship in Early America* (Athens: University of Georgia Press, 2017), ch. 3.

17. The Virginia assembly's award of 200,000 acres to Henderson and Company is quoted in George W. Rank, *Boonesborough: Its Founding, Pioneer Struggles, Indian Experiences, Transylvania Days, and Revolutionary Annals* (Louisville: John P. Morton, 1901), 254. For Henderson and North Carolina, see Samuel C. Williams, "Henderson and Company's Purchase in the Limits of Tennessee," *Tennessee Historical Magazine* 5 (April 1919): 3–27; Finger, *Tennessee's Frontiers*, 83; A. Henderson, "Richard Henderson," 169–172.

18. On the Watauga Association, see Ben Allen and Dennis T. Lawson, "The Wataugans and 'the Dangerous Example,'" *Tennessee Historical Quarterly* 26 (Summer 1967): 137–147, 139–142; Finger, *Tennessee's Frontiers*, 45–48, 58–63. See also Peter S. Onuf, "Settlers, Settlements and New States," in Greene, *American Revolution*, 171–196.

19. For the attack on Nashborough, see Williams, *Tennessee during the Revolutionary War*, 177–179; John Haywood, *The Civil and Political History of the State of Tennessee* (1823; reprint: Nashville: W. H. Haywood, 1891), 131–133. A meticulous listing of those killed by Indians in 1780–1781 is in Paul Clements, *Chronicles of the Cumberland Settlements*,

1779–1796 (Self-published, 2012), 555–556. See also Finger, *Tennessee's Frontiers*, 91–92; James P. Pate, "The Chickamauga: A Forgotten Segment of Indian Resistance on the Southern Frontier" (Ph.D. diss., Mississippi State University, 1969), 114–118.

20. Stephen B. Weeks, "General Joseph Martin and the War of the Revolution in the West," *Annual Report of the American Historical Association for the Year 1893* (Washington, DC: GPO, 1894), 411–419.

21. Weeks, "General Joseph Martin," 423–425, 473–475. See also Pat Alderman, *Nancy Ward: Cherokee Chieftainess, Dragging Canoe, Cherokee-Chickamauga War Chief*, 2nd ed. (Johnson City, TN: Overmountain Press, 1978), 75.

22. Talk to Oconostota, 21 May 1779, PCC, roll 85, item 71, vol. 1:259. On Scolacutta's migration to Chickamauga, see John P. Brown, *Old Frontiers, The Story of Cherokee Indians from Earliest Times to the Date of Their Removal to the West, 1838* (Kingsport, TN: Southern Publishers, 1938), 162. "Scolacutta" in Cherokee meant "his stomach hangs down." See James Mooney, *Myths of the Cherokee* (1900; reprint, New York: Dover, 1995), 543.

23. On Scolacutta and the Boone family, see John Mack Faragher, *Daniel Boone: The Life and Legend of an American Frontiersman* (New York: Henry Holt, 1992), 131–140.

24. For Martin's view of "old towns," see his letters to Jefferson, 12 December 1780 and 7 February 1781, TJ, 4:200–201 ("old towns"), 551–552. See also Williams, *Tennessee during the Revolutionary War*, 182–184, 189–192.

25. On the attempted prisoner exchange, see Arthur Campbell to Benjamin Harrison, 26 August 1782, CVSP, 2:272–273. On North Carolina's policy, see Alexander Martin to General Charles McDowell, 23 July 1782, CSRNC, 16:682–683; Alexander Martin to Charles McDowell, John Sevier, and Waightstill Avery, 20 September 1782, CSRNC, 16:710–711. On Sevier's campaign, see Brown, *Old Frontiers*, 200–202.

26. Finger, *Tennessee's Frontiers*, 108 ("land grab"). On boundaries, see the Act for Opening the Land Office (April 1783), CSRNC, 24:478–485. On Blue Licks, see Faragher, *Daniel Boone*, 217–224.

27. Martin to Henry, 21 May 1788, in *Patrick Henry: Life, Correspondence, and Speeches*, 3 vols., ed. William Wirt Henry (New York: Scribner's, 1891), 2:243–244.

28. Robert S. Cotterill, "The Virginia-Chickasaw Treaty of 1783," *Journal of Southern History* 8 (November 1942): 483–496. On Virginia's instructions, see Harrison to Joseph Martin, John Donelson, and Isaac Shelby, 11 January 1783, in *Official Letters of the Governors of the State of Virginia*, 3 vols. (Richmond, 1926), 3:425–427; Martin to Harrison, 16 February 1784, CVSP, 3:560–561. See also William H. Masterson, *William Blount* (Baton Rouge: Louisiana State University Press, 1954), 71–80; Arthur P. Whitaker, "The Muscle Shoals Speculation, 1783–1789," *Mississippi Valley Historical Review* 13 (December 1926): 365–386.

29. On the treaty authorization, see Gov. Alexander Martin to all the Warriors of the Friendly Towns of the Cherokee Nation, and Gov. Martin to Joseph Martin, 4 August 1783, CSRNC, 16:855–857. See also Masterson, *William Blount*, 91–95.

30. The exchange between Oconostota and Martin of 12–13 January 1783 is in Draper Mss., 12S 10–13, WHS. See also James C. Kelly, "Oconostota," *Journal of Cherokee Studies* 3 (Fall 1978): 221–238, 232. Kelly maintains that Oconostota died in the spring of 1783. For Oconostota's burial, see Duane H. King and Danny E. Olinger, "Oconastota," *American Antiquity* 37 (April 1972): 222–228. In 1785, Martin noted

Notes to Pages 372–375   553

Oconostota's death, but was vague about when it occurred. See Martin to Patrick Henry, 19 September 1785, CVSP, 4:54.

31. There is a very considerable literature on Alexander McGillivray. On his background, see DuVal, *Independence Lost*, 24–34; Linda Langley, "The Tribal Identity of Alexander McGillivray: A Review of the Historic and Ethnographic Data," *Louisiana History* 46 (Spring 2005): 231–239. On Brant, whose leadership met internal opposition as did McGillivray's, see Alan Taylor, *The Divided Ground: Indians, Settlers, and the Northern Borderland of the American Revolution* (New York: Knopf, 2006), 88–89, 119–128, 253–260, 275–277, 335–346.

32. McGillivray to O'Neill, 5 February 1784, PPC, legajo 197; Martin to Harrison, [1784], CVSP, 3:608. (This letter, not clearly dated, has an enclosure of 10 July 1784. The story of Americans "Lost" in the woods initially came to Indians from a Spanish source.)

33. Barksdale, *Lost State of Franklin*; Kristofer Ray, "Leadership, Loyalty, and Sovereignty in the Revolutionary American Southwest: The State of Franklin as a Test Case," *North Carolina Historical Review* 92 (April 2015): 123–144; Finger, *Tennessee's Frontiers*, 111–117. See also Samuel Cole Williams, *History of the Lost State of Franklin* (1924; rev. ed. 1933; reprint, Philadelphia: Porcupine Press, 1974).

34. Extract of a letter from Caswell County, in the State of Frankland, 26 May 1785, to a gentleman in Washington, Virginia, *Freeman's Journal* (Philadelphia), 6 October 1785 ("useful citizens" and "poor creatures"); David Campbell to Arthur Campbell, 27 December 1784, Campbell Papers, FHS.

35. Campbell to Madison, 28 October 1785, James Madison Papers, Series 1: General Correspondence, Library of Congress, https://www.loc.gov/item/mjm012588/. For Campbell's view of the French Revolution and his revulsion at Indians, see his letter of 23 February 1795 to Washington, GW: Presidential, 17:561–563. See also Peter Kastor, "'Equitable Rights and Privileges': The Divided Loyalties in Washington County, Virginia, during the Franklin Separatist Crisis," *Virginia Magazine of History and Biography* 105 (Spring 1997): 193–226.

36. For a record of the conference, 18 July 1785, see Draper Mss., 12S 28–33. On Franklin's commercial aims, see Extract of a letter, Sullivan County, Frankland, 20 August 1785, *Freeman's Journal* (Philadelphia), 28 October 1785; Sevier to Patrick Henry, 19 July 1785, CVSP, 4:42.

37. David Narrett, *Adventurism and Empire: The Struggle for Mastery in the Louisiana-Florida Borderlands, 1762–1803* (Chapel Hill: University of North Carolina Press, 2015), 120–133.

38. Sami Lakomäki, *Gathering Together: The Shawnee People through Diaspora and Nationhood, 1600–1870* (New Haven: Yale University Press, 2014), 117–118.

39. Francisco Cruzat to Esteban Miró, 23 August 1784, in *Spain in the Mississippi Valley, 1765–1794*, Pt. 2, *Post-War Decade, 1782–1791*, vol. 3, ed. Lawrence Kinnaird (Washington, DC: Government Printing House, 1949), 117–119. For the westward migration of Native peoples, see Sami Lakomäki, *Gathering Together: The Shawnee People through Diaspora and Nationhood, 1600–1870* (New Haven: Yale University Press, 2014), 167–172; Stephen Aron, *American Confluence: The Mississippi from Borderlands to Border State* (Bloomington: Indiana University Press, 2006), 80–81.

40. Pickens to McGillivray, 23 July 1785; McGillivray to O'Neill, 8 November 1785, in John Walton Caughey, *McGillivray of the Creeks* (1938; reprint, Norman: University of

Oklahoma Press, 1959), 96–97, 99–100. See also Hawkins, Pickens, and Martin to Henry, 10 June 1785, CVSP, 4:33.

41. Rod Andrew Jr., *The Life and Times of General Andrew Pickens: Revolutionary War Hero, American Founder* (Chapel Hill: University of North Carolina Press, 2017), 174, 188–193; R. S. Cotterill, *The Southern Indians: The Story of the Civilized Tribes Before Removal* (Norman: University of Oklahoma Press, 1954), 63–70. For Seneca (Esseneca), see Tom Hatley, *The Dividing Path: Cherokees and South Carolinians through the Revolutionary Era* (New York: Oxford University Press, 1995), 232.

42. Report of Congress of 28 May 1784, Colin G. Calloway, ed., *Confederation and Revolution*, EAID, 18:381.

43. Commissioners' statement to the Cherokees, 18 November 1785, EAID, 18:393–394.

44. Conference record, 18–29 November 1785, EAID, 18:393–402. On treaties as failures for Native peoples, see David Andrew Nichols, *Red Gentlemen and White Savages: Indians, Federalists, and the Search for Order on the Early American Frontier* (Charlottesville: University of Virginia Press, 2008), 44–54.

45. Speech of the Cherokee "War-woman of Chota" (Nan-ye-hi), 23 November 1785, EAID, 18:395.

46. Speech of Corn Tassel, 26 November 1785, EAID, 18:398. See also Lucas P. Kelley, "'It Is Right to Mark Our Boundaries on the Map': Native Sovereignty and American Empire in the Tennessee and Cumberland Valleys, 1770–1820" (Ph.D. diss., University of North Carolina, 2021), 87–97.

47. Speech of Corn Tassel, 26 November 1785.

48. Talks of Chescoenwhee and Nowota, resepectively 24 and 29 November 1785, EAID, 18:396 ("justice"), 402.

49. Blount to the commissioners, 28 November 1785, EAID, 18:402–403. (Blount wrote two letters to the commissioners that day; the second letter is the most expansive in complaint. See also Downes, "Cherokee-American Relations," 43–46; Cotterill, *Southern Indians*, 66–70. Franklin-Georgia maneuvers are evident in Sevier to Governor Edward Telfair, 14 May 1786, Cuyler Collection, UGA.

50. Martin to Governor Patrick Henry, 26 March 1785, CVSP, 4:18–19.

51. On exchange networks, see Joseph Martin to Alexander Martin, CSRNC, 11 January 1784, 16:924; Martin to Harrison, 22 July 1784, CVSP, 3:601–602; Martin to Edmund Randolph, 28 June 1787, PCC, roll 85, item 1, vol. 2:575; Arthur Campbell to the president of Congress, 18 November 1784, PCC, roll 62, item 48, 277–279. See also Pate, "The Chickamauga," 132–138, 147–150, 175–177; Christina Snyder, *Slavery in Indian Country: The Changing Face of Captivity in Early America* (Cambridge, MA: Harvard University Press, 2010), 136, 182–186.

52. For McGillivray's connection to Panton and Leslie, see William S. Coker and Thomas D. Watson, *Indian Traders of the Southeastern Spanish Borderlands: Panton, Leslie and Company and John Forbes and Company, 1783–1847* (Pensacola: University Presses of Florida, 1986), 69–72, 101–110, 129; David Narrett, "William Panton, British Merchant and Politico: Negotiating Allegiance in the Spanish and Southern Indian Borderlands, 1783–1801," *Florida Historical Quarterly* 96 (Fall 2017): 135–173.

53. McDonald to Joseph Martin, 6 September 1785, CSRNC, 17:519. The correspondent was clearly John McDonald even though he evidently signed his letter "James."

Notes to Pages 380–383   555

See Martin to Patrick Henry, 19 September 1785, CVSP, 4:54–55. On McDonald, see Colin G. Calloway, *White People, Indians, and Highlanders: Tribal Peoples and Colonial Encounters in Scotland and America* (Oxford: Oxford University Press, 2008), 152–154.

54. Information of Abner Hammond, 20 April 1786, Cuyler Collection, UGA; Martin to Caswell, 11 May 1786, CSRNC, 18:604–606.

55. McGillivray to O'Neill, 12 May 1786, in Caughey, *McGillivray*, 109.

56. Cumberland settlers killed by Native attack are meticulously listed in Clements, *Chronicles of the Cumberland*, 555–572. For Sevier's criticism, see Sevier to Alexander Martin, 22 March 1785, CSRNC, 22:640–642; Bledsoe to Caswell, 12 May 1786, CSRNC, 18:608.

57. Davenport to Telfair (the Governor of Georgia), 27 May 1787 ("only Pretends"), Cuyler Collection, Series 1: Historical Manuscripts, box 78, folder 12, doc. 13, SNAD, UGA, https://dlg.usg.edu/record/dlg_zlna_tcc214#item. For the Bear Creek concession, see Atkinson, *Splendid Land*, 129–133.

58. On settler casualties, see Clements, *Chronicles of the Cumberland*, 555–558. See also Bledsoe to Caswell, 12 May 1786, CSRNC, 18:607–608. On the Spanish arrest of American boat traffic, see Davenport to Telfair, 1 November 1786, Cuyler Collection, UGA.

59. Pekka Hämäläinen, *The Comanche Empire* (New Haven: Yale University Press, 2008), 101–106.

60. For the fear that the settlements would "break up," see Joseph Martin, to Caswell, 11 May 1786, CSRNC, 18:605; Martin to Patrick Henry, 15 November 1786, CVSP, 4:183. See also Pate, "The Chickamauga," 131–136, 172–177.

61. Speech (Letter) of Moluntha to "Brothers the thirteen states," recorded by Major John P. Wyllys, 8 June 1786, PCC, roll 164, item 150, vol. 1:431–433. Colonel Levi Todd, who authorized the expedition, described the Cherokee village as one of "the Chickamoggies." See Logan to Governor Randolph, 30 April 1787; Harry Innes to Randolph, 21 July 1787, CVSP, 4:277, 322. See also Dowd, *A Spirited Resistance*, 93–94: Lakomäki, *Gathering Together*, 121–123.

62. On Outlaw's demand and Corn Tassel's response, see J. G. M. Ramsey, *The Annals of Tennessee to the End of the Eighteenth Century* (Philadelphia: Lippincott, 1860), 345–346.

63. For Donelson's death in April 1786, see Spence, "John Donelson," 167–168. For a notice of Christian's death, see Notice, Lincoln County (Kentucky), 18–19 April 1786, in the *Massachusetts Spy*, 15 June 1786. Corn Tassel's praise of Christian is in Ramsey, *Annals of Tennessee*, 345–346.

64. Campbell to the Great Warrior [Corn Tassel] of the Cherokees, 3 March 1787, CVSP, 4:249–250. Campbell's intent is in his letter to Randolph, 9 March 1787, CVSP, 4:254. On Franklin settlers, see Ablavsky, *Federal Ground*, 43–45.

65. Old Tassel to Randolph, 25 March 1787, PCC, roll 85, item 71, vol. 2:571.

66. Ramsey, *Annals of Tennessee*, 464–471, and Robertson to Caswell, 2 July 1787, 470. See also Brown, *Old Frontiers*, 263–265; Atkinson, *Splendid Land*, 136; David Narrett, "Kentucky at the Crossroads: George Rogers Clark, James Wilkinson, and the Danville Committee, 1786–1787," *Ohio Valley History* 16 (Spring 2016): 3–23.

67. The story is told in A. W. Putnam, *History of Middle Tennessee, or the Life and Times of Gen. James Robertson* (Nashville, 1859), 246–247.

68. On Martin's opposition to the State of Franklin, see his letter to Randolph, 25 March 1786, PCC, roll 85, item 71, vol. 2:567. For Scolacutta's respect for Martin, see Talk of the Hanging Maw, 24 March 1787, PCC, roll 85, item 71, vol. 2:572.

69. Randolph to the Cherokees, read in Congress [April 1787], PCC, roll 85, item 71, vol. 2:487–488 ("Tomahawk and fire"); Corn Tassel to the Governor, 12 June 1787, CVSP, 4:306–307.

70. Martin to Randolph, 28 June 1787, PCC, roll 85, item 71, vol. 2:575–578. John Watts Sr., served as an interpreter for Alexander Cameron and other officials in talks with the Cherokees. For the elder Watts's death, see Cameron to John Stuart, 4 March 1771, CO 5/72 / Pt. 2 /009.

71. Kingfisher to Randolph, 12 June 1787; Tuskegetchee to Randolph, 12 June 1787, CVSP, 4:307. For Tuskegetchee (Tuskegateehee), see Cumfer, *Separate Peoples*, 106.

72. Record of 7 September 1787, *Pennsylvania Archives*, vol. 11, ed. Samuel Hazard (Philadelphia, 1855), 182.

73. See Katteuha's transcribed talk to Franklin, 8 September 1787, *Pennsylvania Archives*, vol. 11, ed. Samuel Hazard (Philadelphia, 1855), 181–182. The letter or its envelope carried the names and marks of Corn Tassel and Scolacutta. Franklin's letter to the Cherokees is evidently not extant.

74. Alexander Dromgoole to Arthur Campbell, 15 September 1787, Randolph Papers, box 3, LVA. For Davenport's death, see Atkinson, *Splendid Land*, 134, 276n28; Caughey, *McGillivray of the Creeks*, 34. For the truce, see McGillivray to Anthony Bledsoe and James Robertson, 14 April 1788, in PCC, roll 85, item 71, vol. 2:619–621; James Robertson to Joseph Martin, 7 May 1788, Robertson Papers, VUSC.

75. Pate, "The Chickamauga," 178, 182.

76. For Sevier's military plan, see his letter to Colonel Gilbert Christian, 28 November 1787, Sevier Papers, box 1, folder 3, TSLA; Major George Elmholm to George Walton, 23 October 1787, Cuyler Collection, UGA. On internal violence in Franklin, see Williams, *History of the Lost State*, 202–203. A contemporary report is in Lt. John Armstrong to Major John P. Wyllys, 28 April 1788, PCC, roll 85, item 150, vol. 3: 551–552.

77. Martin to Randolph, 25 March 1787, PCC, roll 85, item 71, vol. 2:567; Evan Shelby to Brigadier-General Russell, 27 April 1787, PCC, roll 85, item 71, vol. 2:535–537. The North Carolina legislature recognized as brigadier-general on 13 December 1787, *State Records of North Carolina*, ed. Walter Clark (Goldsboro, NC, 1902), 20:416.

78. Martin to Randolph, 16 January 1788, CVSP, 4: 395–396. The death of one William English and capture of his wife and four children was later confirmed. See Thomas Hutchings to Martin, 3 June 1788, PCC, roll 164, item 150, vol. 2:435. Martin to Randolph, 13 March 1788 ("in great confusion"), roll 85, item 71, vol. 2:597. For scalping, horse stealing, and the killing of cattle, see the letters enclosed in Hutchings to Martin, April 1788 ("Double Games" in Hutchings's letter), in box 5: 1788 January–May, Randolph Papers, LVA.

79. Martin to Randolph, 17 April 1788, CVSP, 4:428. On the deteriorating situation and Martin's departure, see Martin to Randolph, 11 June 1788 ("stay in their Towns," "without any provocation"), PCC, roll 85, item 71, vol. 2:623–624. (Martin wrote this last letter from Abingdon, Virginia.)

Notes to Pages 389–393

80. For Sevier's role, see Martin to Henry Knox, 10 July 1788, PCC, roll 164, item 150, vol. 2:444–445. The Black Dog of Notoly stated that nine were killed in the attack, and one prisoner taken. Black Dog to Pickens, 11 June 1788, enclosed with the Hanging Maw (Scolacutta) and John Watts to Pickens, 25 June 1788, PCC, roll 69, item 56:433–434. Second-hand reports placed the dead at twenty or more. See Hutchings to Martin, 11 July 1788, PCC, roll 165, item 150, vol. 3:401–402. The Kirk family dead are listed as a mother and six children. See Hutchings to Martin, 3 June 1788, roll 164, item 150, 435. Some histories indicate eleven murdered in the Kirk household, suggesting the family had several Black slaves or others who were unspecified victims. See Ramsey, *Annals of Tennessee*, 420.

81. Downes, "Cherokee-American Relations," 46–49; Cumfer, *Separate Peoples*, 51. For Hubbard's reputed words, see Brown, *Old Frontiers*, 277. On Sevier's apparent actions, see the depositions of Nathaniel Evins [sic] and James Hubbert [*sic*], John McMahen, James Mahan and Benjamin Mooney, 25 October 1788, in *Sevier Family History*, Cora Bales Sevier and Nancy S. Madden (Washington, DC: Kaufmann Printing Co., 1961), 98–100.

82. For the murders of Cornstalk and Moluntha, see Dowd, *A Spirited Resistance*, 76, 95. Farragher, *Boone*, 155–156, 253–254.

83. Black Dog of Notoly to Pickens, 11 June 1788, enclosed with the Hanging Maw (Scolacutta) and John Watts to Pickens, 25 June 1788, PCC, roll 69, item 56: 433–434. See also Andrew, *Andrew Pickens*, 215.

84. Hanging Maw and Watts to Pickens, 25 June 1788, PCC, roll 69, item 56:433.

85. Justices of Abbeville County . . . to the people living on Nolichuckie [*sic*] French Broad and Holstein [*sic*], 9 July 1788 PCC, roll 69, item 56:438–440. See also Andrew, *Andrew Pickens*, 216–217.

86. Justices of Abbeville County, 9 July 1788, PCC, roll 69, item 56:438–440 ("bad men").

13. An Unbroken People

1. George Whitefield to Handley, 10 July 1788, *City Gazette* (Charleston), 9 October 1788. Whitefield (not to be confused with the famed evangelist of the name) was an American trader who delivered McGillivray's account, with a request that the report be published.

2. McGillivray to Whitefield, 12 August 1788, *City Gazette* (Charleston), 29 September 1788.

3. For population shift and geography, see Tyler Boulware, *Deconstructing the Cherokee Nation: Town, Region, and Nation among Eighteenth-Century Cherokees* (Gainesville: University Press of Florida, 2011), 153–155, 162–168, 175–177. For the distance between Chota and Knoxville, estimated at between 25 to 30 miles, see Information, 3 November 1792, in Blount to Knox, 8 November 1792, ASPIA, 1:319; Blount to Knox, 20 March 1793, ASPIA, 1:436.

4. "Description of the Five Cherokee Towns," in Blount to Knox, 20 March 1792, ASPIA, 1:263–264. See also James P. Pate, "The Chickamauga: A Forgotten Segment of Indian Resistance on the Southern Frontier" (Ph.D. diss., Mississippi State University Press, 1969), 129–133. It is nearly 200 miles between two Chickamauga villages—Creek Path Town (Guntersville, Alabama) and Sautee (Georgia).

558   *Notes to Pages 394–398*

5. Jeffrey Ostler, "'To Extirpate the Indians': An Indigenous Consciousness of Genocide in the Ohio Valley and Great Lakes, 1750s–1810s," *William and Mary Quarterly*, 3rd ser. 72 (October 2015): 587–622.

6. St. Clair to Knox, 2 September 1788, PCC, roll 165, item 150, vol. 3:389–391.

7. Martin to Knox, [?] June 1788, with enclosure of 3 June; and letters of 10 July 1788, PCC, roll 164, item 150, vol. 2:435, 446; 25 July 1788, PCC, roll 165, item 3:413.

8. Knox to Washington, 28 July 1788, GW: Confederation, 6:105–106. Knox's report of 18 July 1788, PCC, roll 165, item 151, vol. 3:351–357.

9. Black Dog (Prince of Notoly) to Pickens, 11 June 1788, PCC, roll 69, item 56, 432–433.

10. Scolacutta (Hanging Maw) and Watts to Pickens, 25 June 1788 ("spoil the Towns here"). Martin did not identify the place where Watts and Scolacutta composed the written talk. Nor did he specify an interpreter involved in Cherokee messaging. On Little Turkey's purported peace inclinations at Ustanali, see Jobber's Son to Pickens, 30 June 1788, PCC, roll 69, 432–433 (first talk of 20 June 1788), 435–437 (30 June 1788).

11. For the attack by the Hiwassee, see Thomas Hutchings to Martin, 11 July 1788, PCC, roll 164, item 150, vol. 2:435. On the killings in the orchard, see Martin to Knox, 23 August 1788, PCC, roll 165, item 150, vol. 3:361. The list of the dead white men, evidently slain on 8 August, is from a Winchester, Virginia, notice in the *Maryland Journal* (Baltimore), 16 September 1788. The report on murdered Cherokee women is in Pickens to Richard Winn, 6 August 1788, PCC, roll 165, item 150, vol. 3:377.

12. Martin to Knox, 10 July 1788, PCC, roll 164, item 150, vol. 2:449–451; Martin to Knox, 25 July and 23 August, PCC, roll 164, item 150, vol. 3:413. The attack on the river-boat is in Martin to Knox, 10 July 1788, PCC, roll 164, item 150, vol. 2:443–445.

13. Martin to Knox, 23 August 1788 ("a permanent peace"), PCC, roll 165, item 150, vol. 3:409; General Maxwell to Martin, 9 July 1788, PCC, roll 165, item 150, vol. 3:409 ("consummate your character"). On the goal of raising a thousand men, see Council of Officers, Washington District, 19 August 1788, PCC, roll 165, item 150, vol. 3:357.

14. On Knox's voyages to Boston and Maine, see notices, 6 and 23 August 1788, *Massachusetts Centinel* (Boston).

15. J. G. M. Ramsey, *The Annals of Tennessee to the End of the Eighteenth Century* (Philadelphia: Lippincott, 1860), 517–518; Albert V. Goodpasture, "Indian Wars and Warriors of the Old Southwest, 1730–1807," ch. 11, "The Rise of John Watts," *Tennessee Historical Magazine* 4 (September 1918): 170–176, 170.

16. David Narrett, *Adventurism and Empire: The Struggle for Mastery in the Louisiana-Florida Borderlands, 1762–1803* (Chapel Hill: University of North Carolina Press, 2015).

17. For the attack and the number killed, see Richmond (VA) notice, *Pennsylvania Journal* (Philadelphia), 22 November 1788. This article, printed in several newspapers, spread a false rumor that 1,000 Indians were then attacking near White's Fort (Knoxville).

18. The written words were said to be those of Bloody Fellow speaking for the whole. The letter of the four Cherokee leaders, "Bloody Fellow," "Categiskey" (Kaytagusta), John Watts, and Glass, is transcribed in Ramsey, *Annals of Tennessee*, 519.

Notes to Pages 400–405   559

19. Talks of Cherokee Headmen and Warriors to Richard Winn, 12 October and 20 November 1788, ASPIA, 1:45–46; By the United States in Congress Assembled, A Proclamation, 1 September 1788. Congress did not recognize a Cherokee right to "punish" settlers who may have crossed into Indian territory between the forks of the Holston and French Broad Rivers.

20. The Act of Cession not only guaranteed the rights of all legitimate warrant-holders in North Carolina's military reserve, which straddled the Cumberland watershed, but declared that such persons might stake their claims outside the reserve, and implicitly in Indian territories, if there was insufficient acreage in the designated area to satisfy their claims. See Act of Cession, December 1789, TP, 4:4–5. See also John R. Finger, *Tennessee's Frontiers* (Bloomington: Indiana University Press, 2001), 126–127.

21. "Copy of a letter from young Kirk, the noted Indian killer, to John Watts, now Chief War Captain of the Cherokee nation," 17 October 1788, in the *Pennsylvania Packet* (Philadelphia), 22 January 1789. The letter's date, 17 October 1788, corresponding to the attack on Gillespie's Station, seems to have been intentional. Emphasis in original removed.

22. Jackson is quoted in David S. Heidler and Jeanne T. Heidler, *Old Hickory's War: Andrew Jackson and the Quest for Empire* (Mechanicsburg, PA: Stackpole Books, 1996; reprint Baton Rouge: Louisiana State University Press, 2003), 17. For Sevier's bitter clash with Jackson, which reached a height in 1803, see Gordon T. Belt, *John Sevier: Tennessee's First Hero* (Charleston, SC: History Press, 2014), 131–142.

23. "Copy of a letter from Governor Sevier, to the Privy Council of the new state of Franklin," 12 January 1789, in the *Essex Journal* (Newburyport, MA), 12 April 1789. Sevier's attack on the Chickamauga-Creek encampment, said to be headed by John Watts, occurred by Flint Creek (now South Indian Creek), in Unicoi County, Tennessee. See John P. Brown, *Old Frontiers: The Story of the Cherokee Indians from Earliest Times to Their Removal to the West, 1838* (1938; reprint, New York: Arno Press, 1971), 297–299.

24. One rendition of Joseph Brown's recollection is in Ramsey, *Annals of Tennessee*, 508–512. See also C. Somers Miller, "The Joseph Brown Story: Pioneer and Indian in Tennessee History," *Tennessee Historical Quarterly* 32 (Spring 1973): 22–41, 23–25. For Martin's report, which also mentions Vann's role, see *Kentucky Gazette*, 14 November 1788, Draper Mss., 33S 54–55, WHS.

25. Cotteotoy is also spelled Cutleotoy or Cotetoy in some accounts. Ramsey, *Annals of Tennessee*, 511–513. See also "Early History of the South-west. Sketch of the Captivity of Colonel Joseph Brown . . . by the Indians," *South-western Monthly* (1852): 10–16 and 72–78, 12–15, available at https://digital.lib.niu.edu/islandora/object/niu -prairie%3A2004; Brown, *Old Frontiers*, 273–274.

26. A composite of Brown narratives is found in Paul Clements, *Chronicles of the Cumberland Settlements, 1779–1796* (Self-published, 2012), 278–282.

27. For Sevier's role in capturing Cherokee women and children for a prisoner exchange, see "Early History of the South-west. Sketch of the Captivity of Colonel Joseph Brown," 15–16, 72–77; Miller, "The Joseph Brown Story," 27. Clements, *Chronicles*, 278–282.

28. For Knox's involvement with the Cherokees, see Knox to Charles Thompson (secretary of Congress), 6 December 1787, PCC, roll 69, item 56:213. Keenehteteh of

Ellijay, a Cherokee elder, sent a talk to Washington, his "greate & Beloved Brother," with hope that the "Great spirit above will Put it your harte to Do us all the good you can." See Keenehteteh (Rising Fawn) to General Washington, 25 May 1789, PCC, roll 97, item 78:360.

29. Colin G. Calloway, *The Indian World of George Washington: The First President, the First Americans, and the Birth of the Nation* (New York: Oxford University Press, 2018), 330–333. See Knox's lengthy memorandum to Washington, 7 July 1789, ASPIA, 1:53.

30. Calloway, *Indian World of George Washington*, 380–392. R. Douglas Hurt, *The Ohio Frontier: Crucible of the Old Northwest, 1720–1830* (Bloomington: Indiana University Press, 1996), 101–118. For Chickamauga celebration at St. Clair's defeat, see notice, Charleston, 30 January 1792, *Dunlap's American Daily Advertiser* (Philadelphia), 5 March 1792. For Native attacks on Ohio River traffic and in Kentucky, see George Thompson to James Madison, 1 June 1790, *The Papers of James Madison*, Congressional Series, vol. 13, 20 January 1790–31 March 1790, ed. Charles F. Hobson and Robert A. Rutland (Charlottesville: University Press of Virginia, 1981), 235–238; Extract of a letter from a gentleman of Kentucky District, 4 April 1790, in the *Herald of Freedom* (Boston), 25 May 1790.

31. Citizens of the Mero District to Washington, 30 November 1789, GW: Presidential, 4:345–347. The slain of the Cumberland and vicinity were 286 persons from the beginning of 1787 through 1794. The greatest concentration of killings, 165 (57.8 percent) occurred from 1792 through 1794. See the meticulous list in Clements, *Chronicles*, 557–562.

32. Robertson to Miró, 29 January 1789, in Arthur P. Whitaker, "Letters of James Robertson and Daniel Smith," *Mountain Valley Historical Review* 12 (December 1925): 409–412, 410–411; Miró to Robertson, 20 April 1789, Robertson Papers, VUSC. See also Narrett, *Adventurism and Empire*, 164–177, 192–203, 238–240.

33. For Blount's appointment of June 8, 1790, see TP, 4:24. Calloway, *Indian World of George Washington*, 339. Blount's paper holdings grew to about one million acres in the Southwest Territory during his governorship. See Christopher Magra, "Blount's Bunko: Private Fortune Through Public Office in the Southwest Territory," in *A Republic of Scoundrels: The Schemers, Intriguers and Adventurers Who Created a New American Nation*, ed. David Head and Timothy C. Hemmis (New York: Pegasus, 2023), 55–65.

34. For the establishment of the Southwest Territory, which followed North Carolina's Act of Cession of December 1789, see An Act for the Government of the Territory South of the River Ohio, 26 May 1790, see TP, 4:18–19.

35. On Blount's appointment and assumption of duties, see William H. Masterton, *William Blount* (Baton Rouge: Louisiana State University Press, 1954), 183–194, 208. On his speculative land maneuvers, see also Gregory Ablavsky, *Federal Ground: Governing Property and Violence in the First U.S. Territories* (Oxford: Oxford University Press, 2021), 33–35, 209–212.

36. The Georgia Act of 21 December 1789 is in ASPIA, 1:114–115. For the proclamation of 26 August 1790, see GW: Presidential, 6:342. The Cherokee letter, written in Blount's hand and without Native marks, is "[Letter] 1791 Jan. 28, Highwassey [i.e. Hiwassee], to Governor William Blount/Headmen of the Cherokees," SNAD, UGA, https://dlg.usg.edu/record/dlg_zlna_krc004#item.

Notes to Pages 409–413

37. For Cox's venture to Muscle Shoals, see Blount to Daniel Smith, 6 June 1791, TP, 4:55. Judge David Campbell's Charge to the Grand Jury, August term 1791, is printed in the *Boston Gazette*, 19 December 1791. For the grand jury's verdict, see Blount to Robertson, 3 September 1791, TP, 4:79. See also Ablavsky, *Federal Ground*, 53–57, 197–200.

38. For Cherokee fears, see J. Whitney to Abraham Tatum and William Lytle, 28 June 1791, Steele Papers, SHC. Robertson offered assurances to Watts, Scolacutta, and Bloody Fellow who were then at Scolacutta's house at Chota. See Robertson to Blount, 5 June 1791, TP, 4:59. See also Steele to Alexander Martin, 19 February 1789, Steele Papers, SHC.

39. For the Treaty of Holston, or the U.S.-Cherokee "Treaty of Peace and Friendship," 2 July 1791, see TP, 4:60–67. The Cherokee chiefs' address is quoted in Cynthia Cumfer, "Local Origins of National Indian Policy: Cherokee and Tennessean Ideas about Sovereignty and Nationhood, 1790–1811," *Journal of the Early Republic* 23 (Spring 2003): 21–46, 27. See also Ablavsky, *Federal Ground*, 24–29. Blount's attempt to purchase Muscle Shoals was relayed by Cherokee chiefs to Knox when they visited Philadelphia. See Talk of Bloody Fellow, 7 January 1792, ASPIA, 1:204.

40. Holston Treaty, TP, 4:63–64. Finger, *Tennessee's Frontiers*, 133–135.

41. For the Treaty of New York (7 August 1790), and its ratification by the Senate, 12 August 1790, see Proclamation of Washington, 14 August 1790, GW: Presidential, 6:248–254 (note 5 includes the treaty terms with the secret articles). For the Holston treaty and "civilization," see TP, 4:64. For the treaty's ratification by the Senate with the $1,500 annuity, see ASPIA, 1:135. For Knox's policy, see Calloway, *Indian World of George Washington*, 329–335. On federal expenditures to buy peace with Indians, see Ablavsky, *Federal Ground*, 180–187.

42. The Carondelet-McGillivray accord of 6 July 1792 is in AHN. Carondelet's demands on McGillivray were sent via agent Pedro Olivier. See Carondelet to Olivier, 30 March 1792, AHN. See also John Walton Caughey, *McGillivray of the Creeks* (Norman: University of Oklahoma Press, 1938).

43. For Cherokee complaints about the Holston treaty terms, see British agent George Welbank's information passed to Jacob Lindley, a Pennsylvania Quaker touring the west in 1793. See "Jacob Lindley's Account," *Collections of the Michigan Pioneer and Historical Society* 17 (1892): 611–612. Scolacutta told a white confidant of Chickamauga fighters who had brought home scalps from St. Clair's defeat. See Samuel Newell to Arthur Campbell, 1 February 1792, Draper Mss., 9DD67-69, WHS.

44. For Doughty's account of the attack, 17 April 1790, and his evident instructions to establish the post at Bear Creek (Ochappo), fifty miles west of Muscle Shoals, see "Up the Tennessee in 1790: The Report of Major John Doughty to the Secretary of War," ed. Colton Storm, *East Tennessee Historical Society Publications* 17 (1945): 121–126. See also James R. Atkinson, *Splendid Land, Splendid People: The Chickasaw Indians to Removal* (Tuscaloosa: University of Alabama Press, 2004), 131.

45. Bloody Fellow's brother had a price on his head for killing white settlers. Bloody Fellow was also known as Nentooyah and later Iskagua. For the name "Bloody Fellow," see *The Journal of Major John Norton*, ed. Carl F. Klinck and James J. Talman, reissued with notes by Carl Benn (Toronto: Champlain Society, 1970), 155. The Cherokees arrived in Philadelphia on 28 December 1791. See ASPIA, 1:203.

46. Bloody Fellow to Knox, 7 January 1792, ASPIA, 1:204. Bloody Fellow did not list the four nations. The Chickasaws and Creeks were certainly among the four. Cherokee headmen had previously told Blount that they did not own the Shoals "for it belongs to all the Red people." "[Letter] 1791 Jan. 28, Highwassey [i.e. Hiwassee], to Governor [Blount]" from "Headmen of the Cherokees," SNAD, UGA.

47. For the medal and boundary issues, see McDonald to Panton, 7 June 1792, Fondo Floridas, MF 6, legajo 1, THNOC; Knox to Blount, 22 April 1792, ASPIA, 1:252–253. Bloody Fellow cited Washington's assurances on the land issue when protesting white settler "encroachments." See his message to Blount, 10 September 1792, ASPIA, 1:280.

48. Knox to Washington, 22 February and 30 May 1792, GW: Presidential, 7:402–415, 8:220–225. For the Southwest Territory militia, see Richard M. Lytle, *The Soldiers of America's First Army, 1791* (Lanham, MD: Scarecrow Press, 2004), 253.

49. Alexander McKee to Dragging Canoe, 22 July 1791, in Philip M. Hamer, "The British in Canada and the Southern Indians, 1790–1794," *East Tennessee Historical Society Publications* 2 (1930): 107–134, 114.

50. Henry Thompson Malone, *Cherokees of the Old South: A People in Transition* (Athens: University of Georgia Press, 1956), 54–55.

51. J. Leitch Wright Jr., *William Augustus Bowles: Director General of the Creek Nation* (Athens: University of Georgia Press, 1967), chs. 1–2.

52. For the Cherokee petition, "To His Majesty George the Third King of Great Britain &,c &,c, &c." 6 May 1789; the Creek petition of the same date is addressed "To His Majesty George III King of Great B[ritain] France and Ireland &c &c &c"; both documents are in FO 4 / 7. See also McGillivray to Vicente Folch, 14 May 1789, in Caughey, *McGillivray of the Creeks*, 230.

53. See the petitions cited above. See also David Narrett, "William Augustus Bowles, the Pretender: A Tory Adventurer as Native American Leader," in Head and Hemmis, *A Republic of Scoundrels*, 191–224; James L. Hill, *Creek Internationalism in an Age of Revolution, 1763–1788* (Lincoln: University of Nebraska Press, 2022), 92–96; See also William C. Sturtevant, "The Cherokee Frontiers, the French Revolution, and William Augustus Bowles," in *The Cherokee Nation: A Troubled History*, ed. Duane H. King (Knoxville: University of Tennessee Press, 1979), 61–91, 74.

54. Guy Carleton, former British general, was ennobled as 1st Baron Dorchester after the Revolutionary War. Wright identifies Richard Justice as of mixed Cherokee-British ancestry, but some historians believe he was entirely Cherokee by heritage. See Wright, *William Augustus Bowles*, 42. The name "Justice" may reflect a Cherokee notion of a "just" man as rendered in English. On "Dick Justice," see Cephas Washburn, *Cherokees "West": 1794 to 1839* (Claremont, OK: Emmet Starr, 1910), 101.

55. The London press commented on Bowles's ambition to conquer Spanish "New World" colonies. See, for example, *General Evening-Post* (London), 28–30 October 1790. For Covent Garden, see the *Public Advertiser* (London), 2 November 1790.

56. The Representation of Wm. Augustus Bowles . . . Deputed from the United Nation of Creeks and Cherrokees [*sic*] to His Britannic Majesty, in Bowles to Grenville, 3 January 1791, FO 4/9. For Grenville's concession, see his letter to Dorchester, 7 March 1791, CO 42/73.

Notes to Pages 415–419

57. Knox to Washington, 17 January 1792, TP, 4:113.

58. Report of David Craig to William Blount, 15 March 1792, ASPIA, 1:264. For the scalp dance, see Frank G. Speck and Leonard Broom, *Cherokee Dance and Drama* (1951; new ed., Norman: University of Oklahoma Press, 1983), 64.

59. Report of Craig to Blount, 15 March 1792, ASPIA, 1:264.

60. Report of Craig to Blount, 15 March 1792. For Price (Wosseo), see Sturtevant, "The Cherokee Frontiers," 66.

61. Craig to William Blount, 15 March 1792, ASPIA, 1:264.

62. Little Turkey ("Kahanetah") to Alexander McKee, 20 May 1793, in Hamer, "British in Canada," 122. For Bowles's capture, see Gilbert C. Din, *War on the Gulf Coast: The Spanish Fight against William Augustus Bowles* (Gainesville: University Press of Florida, 2012), 42–54.

63. On St. Clair's defeat, see Wilkinson to Miró, 4 November 1791; Carondelet to Floridablanca, 25 February 1792, AHN. On Indian policy, see Carondelet to Florida-blanca, 25 February 1792 (no. 9, reservado), THNOC.

64. Knox to Blount, 18 August 1792, TP, 4:76 ("defensive protection"). The two militia companies, as subsequently mandated by Blount, were together not to have more than 152 noncommissioned officers and men, and to be summoned for no longer than a three-month period. They were not to cross "the Indian Boundary." See Blount to Robertson, 1 April 1792, TP, 4:133. Knox's assertion of congressional authority is in his letter to Blount, 9 October 1792, TP, 4:194.

65. On Watts, see Blount to Knox, 20 March 1792, ASPIA, 1:263. See also Thomas Glass and Dick Justice to Blount, 5 March 1792, with postscript by Justice, ASPIA, 1:263–264.

66. Blount to McGillivray, 17 May 1792, ASPIA, 1:269.

67. Blount to the Cherokee chiefs (with Cherokee replies), 23 May 1792, ASPIA, 1:269–270. Bloody Fellow had now adopted the name Iskagua, often translated "Clear Sky" though it may have meant "Great Day." See James Mooney, *Myths of the Cherokee* (1900; reprint, New York: Dover, 1995), 522.

68. For Blount's description of the scene, see his letters to James Robertson, 20 and 26 May 1792 (quotations, 20 May), Robertson Papers, box 1, folder 7, VUSC. See also conference record, 23 May 1792, ASPIA, 1:269.

69. McDonald to Panton, 6 October 1792, Fondo Floridas, legajo 1, THNOC.

70. Dragging Canoe's son also accompanied Watts. Carey identified Talotiskee as a headman of the Lower Creek town of Broken Arrow. See Information of James Carey to Blount, 3 November 1792, in Blount to Knox, 8 November 1792, ASPIA, 1:329.

71. Since Finnelson was illiterate, Blount wrote a detailed account of his testimony, to which Finnelson attested in Philadelphia. See Information by Richard Finnelson [Findleston], 1 November 1792, ASPIA, 1:288–292. Blount's summary of Finnelson's account is enclosed in his letter to Knox, 27 September 1792, ASPIA, 1:291–292. By coincidence, William Panton was in New Orleans during Finnelson's stay there. Panton knew Finnelson and invited him and Deraque to board his vessel bound for Mobile and Pensacola. On Fagot, see A. P. Whitaker, "Spanish Intrigue in the Old Southwest: An Episode, 1788–1789," *Mississippi Valley Historical Review* 12 (September 1926): 155–176.

564   *Notes to Pages 419–424*

72. Information by Richard Finnelson, 1 November 1792, ASPIA, 1:290.

73. Information by Finnelson, 1 November 1792.

74. On Walker and Fields as warriors, see Information by James Carey to Blount, 3–5 November 1792, in Blount to Knox, 8 November 1792, ASPIA, 1:330–331. Blount attested to the report on 5 November 1792. For Carey, see Little Turkey's statement at a Cherokee council, 26 June 1792, ASPIA, 1:271.

75. Bloody Fellow to Blount, 10 September 1792; Blount to Bloody Fellow, 13 September 1792, ASPIA, 1:280–281. Other peace messages came from Little Turkey and Watts via Glass and Bloody Fellow. See ASPIA, 1:280.

76. Information given by Red Bird, 13 September 1792, ASPIA, 1:282.

77. For an account of the attack on Buchanan's Station, see ASPIA, 1:294. See also Notice, Knoxville, 10 October 1792, *Dunlap's American Daily Advertiser* (Philadelphia), 1 November 1792; "Intelligence from the Cherokee nation, respecting the attack on Buchanan's Station," Winchester, VA, 12 November 1792, *Diary* (New York), 23 December 1792; Brown, *Old Frontiers*, 358–361. There was another Cherokee headman with the name Talotiskee who lived well after the Creek-Chickamauga leader's death. See *Journal of Major John Norton*, 143.

78. "Early History of the South-west. Sketch of the Captivity of Colonel Joseph Brown," 74; "Narrative of John Carr," *South-Western Monthly* 2 (1853): 79–80. The Cumberland dead in 1792–1794 included Clements, *Chronicles*, 559–562. On Joseph Brown and Buchanan's Station, see Natalie Inman, *Brothers and Friends: Kinship in Early America* (Athens: University of Georgia Press, 2017), 1–3, 67–72.

79. Carondelet to Aranda, 28 November 1792 ("salvaje"); Carondelet to Aranda, 20 November 1792; Carondelet to the Chiefs, Warriors and others of the Cherokee Nation, 24 November 1792, AHN. See also James Carey's information, in Blount to Knox, 20 March 1793, ASPIA, 1:436.

80. For Cocke's public letter, 8 September 1792, from the *Knoxville Gazette*, 10 October 1792, in the *New Jersey State Gazette*, 7 November 1792. For the rebuttal by "Hanging Maw," who accused Cocke of being a coward and having a "squaw's heart," see the *Knoxville Gazette*, 22 October 1792, in the *Boston Gazette*, 17 December 1792.

81. The proclamation of 28 January 1793 is in TP, 4:235. For the murders, see Blount to Knox, 24 and 28 May 1793, TP, 4:261–263. Blount appeased Native men after the shooting death of Noonday, a Cherokee man, whom he claimed was mistakenly killed by white gunmen. See Blount to Scolacutta (Hanging Maw) and John Watts, 17 April 1793, ASPIA, 1:450.

82. Minutes of a conference at Henry's Station, 6 February 1793, ASPIA, 1:447; Information of David Gilliland to Blount, 2 April 1793, ASPIA, 1:446. John McKee, a Blount agent to the Cherokees, was aided on a risky visit to the Lower Towns by William Elders and Unakata (White-Man Killer). McKee believed that Watts was responsible for saving his life at Willstown. See McKee to Blount, 28 March 1792, ASPIA, 1:444–445.

83. Blount to Knox, 9 April 1793, TP, 4:250–251 ("jocular").

84. Major King and David Carmichael to Smith, 12 June 1793, ASPIA, 1:459; Extract of a letter from a gentleman in the Southern territory of the United States, Knoxville, 17 June 1793, in *Dunlap's Daily Advertiser* (Philadelphia), 22 July 1793. See also Ore to Isaac Shelby, 26 June 1793, Draper Mss., 11DD50, WHS.

Notes to Pages 425–429

85. Smith to Knox, 13 June 1793, TP, 4:27; Smith to Scolacutta (Hanging Maw), 13 June 1793, ASPIA, 1:459.

86. Scolacutta to Smith, 15 June 1793, ASPIA, 1:460; Ore to Isaac Shelby, 26 June 1793, Draper Mss., 11DD50, WHS. Doublehead ridiculed Smith's advice to Scolacutta to seek satisfaction directly from Washington. Beard's men, he stated, "did not ask any advice when they came and killed our people." See Doublehead to Smith, 15 June 1793, ASPIA, 1:460.

87. Piomingo to Robertson, 17 June 1793, ASPIA, 1:466. See also Wendy St. Jean, "How the Chickasaws Saved the Cumberland Settlement in the 1790s," *Tennessee Historical Quarterly* 68 (Spring 2009): 2–19.

88. Charles H. Faulkner, *Massacre at Cavett's Station: Frontier Tennessee during the Chickasaw Wars* (Knoxville: University of Tennessee Press, 2013), 76–86. Benge, also known as "the Bench" to whites, was probably a son of Corporal John Bench, who served as an interpreter in British-Cherokee peace talks in 1761. See Standing Turkey [Kanagatucko] to Byrd [September 1761], in Stephen to Amherst, 5 October 1761, Amherst Papers, DCAR.

89. Smith to Knox, 27 September 1793, TP, 4:306. For the uncertain size of Sevier's force, which may have ranged from 600 to 1,100 men, see Craig Symonds, "the Failure of America's Indian Policy on the Southwest Frontier, 1785–1793," *Tennessee Historical Quarterly* 35 (Spring 1976): 29–45, 40–43.

90. Letter of Efau Hadjo (the Mad Dog of Tuckabatchee), White Lieutenant of the Okfuskees, Alexander Cornell, and Charles Weatherford to U.S. agent James Seagrove, 14 June 1793, ASPIA, 1:396. For Creek discord, see Claudio Saunt, *A New Order of Things: Property, Power, and the Transformation of the Creek Indians, 1733–1816* (Cambridge: Cambridge University Press, 1999), 104–110. On Blount and Pickens, see Calloway, *The Indian World of George Washington*, 429.

91. Robertson to Blount, 8 October 1794, TP, 4:358–359; Knox to Blount, 29 December 1794, ASPIA, 1:634–635; Pickering to Blount, 22 March 1795, TP, 4:386–392.

92. For Whitley's account, see his Memorial to the Representatives of the people of Kentucky in General Assembly [1795?], Military Papers, FHS. For settlers' war recollections, found in the Draper Mss., see the accounts of General James White, James Collier, Jonathan Ramsay, and Maclin Cross, cited in Clements, *Chronicles*, 441–444.

93. On Creek discord, see Saunt, *A New Order of Things*, 104–110. For Blount and Pickens, see Calloway, *Indian World of George Washington*, 429.

94. Washington to Cherokee Chiefs and Warriors, 14 June 1794, GW: Presidential, 16:222–224. On the annuity's increase, see Articles of a Treaty, 26 June 1794, ASPIA, 1:543.

95. Notice, Richmond, 6 May 1794, *Columbia Herald* (Charleston), 4 June 1794.

96. Robertson to Watts, 20 September 1794, ASPIA, 1:531; Notice, *Knoxville Gazette*, 17 July 1794, in the *Philadelphia Gazette*, 23 August 1794. For the number of whites killed in one boat and a Cherokee retrospective account of the boat attack, see Myers, "Cherokee Pioneers," 136–137.

97. Robertson to Watts, 20 September 1794.

98. All quotations from the peace talks are drawn from the official record: "At a conference held on the 7th and 8th November 1794 at Tellico Blockhouse," Robertson

Papers, MSS.0366.0220, VUSC. See also Talk of Watts, 8 November 1794, ASPIA, 1:537. For the printed conference record, see ASPIA, 1:536–538.

99. Talk of Watts, 7–8 November 1794, ASPIA, 1:536–537.

100. Talk of Scolacutta, 7–8 November 1794, ASPIA, 1:537–538. On Watts's support of the Upper Cherokees, see his talk of November 1794, ASPIA, 1:537. On Scolacutta's role in ordering the death of the Creek men, see John McKee to Blount, 27 May 1795, in "Cherokee Council Minutes, 1795," ID 1000-189, E99.C5C53 1795 Ovrsz, Department of Special Collections, McFarlin Library, University of Tulsa, https://utulsa.as.atlas-sys.com/repositories/2/resources/735.

101. Talk of Scolacutta, 7–8 November 1794, ASPIA, 1:537.

102. Conference record, 8 November 1794, ASPIA, 1:538.

103. For the attack on Joseph Sevier's home, see letters of Anthony Crutcher and John Easten, 12 November 1794, in Robertson to Blount, 15 November 1794, ASPIA, 1:542; Blount to Robertson, 4 December 1794, Robertson Papers, box 1, folder 10, VUSC. On Doublehead's likely involvement, see Brown, *Old Frontiers*, 439–441.

104. On Blount's failure to enlist Cherokees against the Creeks, see his letter to Robertson, 10 January 1795, ASPIA, 1:556. On the Chickasaw peace, see Little Turkey and Black Fox to Robertson, 10 April 1795, (quotations); Little Turkey to Blount, 10 April 1795, both in Robertson Papers, box 1, folder 11, VUSC. For Piomingo's relationship to the Cherokees, see Atkinson, *Splendid Land*, 126.

Conclusion

1. Washington to the Cherokee Nation, 29 August 1796, GW: Presidential, 20:626–630.

2. Washington to Pickering, 2 September 1796, GW: Presidential, 20:650–651; McHenry to Dinsmoor, 29 August 1796, "Detailed Instructions for the Execution of the Plan for Civilizing the Cherokee," Papers of the War Department, 1784–1800, Roy Rosenzweig Center for History and New Media, George Mason University, https://wardepartmentpapers.org/s/home/item/54744.

3. Washington to the Cherokee Nation, 29 August 1796.

4. Washington to the Cherokee Nation, 29 August 1796.

5. Connecorte to Glen, 29 April 1752, DRIA, 1:258.

6. Connecorte to Glen, 29 April 1752.

7. Journal entry, 28 November 1796, *The Letters of Benjamin Hawkins, 1796–1806*, in *Collections of the Georgia Historical Society*, vol. 9 (Savannah: Morning News, 1916), 18.

8. Journal entries, 30 November–1 December 1796, in *Letters of Hawkins*, 20–21; Theda Perdue, *Cherokee Women* (Lincoln: University of Nebraska Press, 1998), 129–132.

9. For the disbursement to Scolacutta's widow, see Receipts, 16 August 1801, RCIAT. By 1809, Cherokees possessed more than 1,000 sheep, 6,500 horses, 19,000 black cattle, and nearly 20,000 swine. See William G. McLoughlin, *Cherokee Renascence in the New Republic* (Princeton: Princeton University Press, 1986), 171. On the stolen horses and compensation, see Report, 31 December 1801, Correspondence and Misc. Records, 185, RCIAT; Receipt, 10 November 1802, Journal, 62, RCIAT. The black woman's return is in 7 September 1803, Fiscal Records, 120, RCIAT.

Notes to Pages 435–446

10. McLoughlin, *Cherokee Renascence*, 20; Gary E. Moulton, *John Ross: Cherokee Chief* (Athens: University of Georgia Press, 1978), 2–7.

11. Theda Perdue, *"Mixed Blood" Indians: Racial Construction in the Early South* (Athens: University of Georgia Press, 2005), 43. On Doublehead, see "Cherokee Council Minutes, 1795," ID 1000-189, E99.C5C53 1795 Ovrsz, Department of Special Collections, McFarlin Library, University of Tulsa, https://utulsa.as.atlas-sys.com/repositories/2/resources/735.

12. Tiya Miles, *The House on Diamond Hill: A Cherokee Plantation Story* (Chapel Hill: University of North Carolina Press, 2010), 41–44, 57–63, 73–74, 87. On slave ownership over time, see McLoughlin, *Cherokee Renascence*, 171, 174; Theda Perdue, *Slavery and the Evolution of Cherokee Society, 1540–1866* (Knoxville: University of Tennessee Press, 1979), 56–60.

13. For slavery's impact, see Celia E. Naylor, *African Cherokees in Indian Territory: From Chattel to Citizens* (Chapel Hill: University of North Carolina Press, 2008); Miles, *The House on Diamond Hill*, 104–107. On Shoe Boots, see Tiya Miles, *Ties That Bind: The Story of an Afro-Cherokee Family in Slavery and Freedom* (Berkeley: University of California Press, 2005), 126–127.

14. In 1813, Meigs wrote that nine Cherokee men had been murdered, and two others wounded by whites since 1801 when his agency began. See Robert M. Owens, "'Between Two Fires': Elusive Justice on the Cherokee-Tennessee Frontier, 1796–1814," *American Indian Quarterly* 40 (Winter 2016): 38–67; McLoughlin, *Cherokee Renascence*, 48–53, 61–78.

15. For the Cherokee cession, see ASPIA, 1:637–638; Gregory Ablavsky, *Federal Ground: Governing Property and Violence in the First U.S. Territories* (Oxford: Oxford University Press, 2021), 218–224. On acreage totals in successive treaties, see Charles C. Royce, *The Cherokee Nation of Indians: A Narrative of Their Official Relations with the Colonial and Federal Governments* (Washington, DC: GPO, 1887), 371. On the community ethic, see Julie L. Reed, *Serving the Nation: Cherokee Sovereignty and Social Welfare, 1800–1907* (Norman: University of Oklahoma Press, 2016), 25–27, 57–59.

16. On "Red-headed Will," see Sevier to Blount, Jackson, and Cocke, 29 January 1797, in "Executive Journal of Gov. John Sevier," *East Tennessee Historical Society Publications* 1 (1929): 131; Sevier to the Cherokee Nation, 8 June 1797, in "Executive Journal," *East Tennessee Historical Society Publications* 2 (1930): 138. On Blount's conspiracy, see David Narrett, *Adventurism and Empire: The Struggle for Mastery in the Louisiana-Florida Borderlands, 1762–1803* (Chapel Hill: University of North Carolina Press, 2015), 235–241.

17. On Cherokee debate over emigration, see *The Journal of Major John Norton, 1816*, ed. Carl F. Klinck and James J. Talman, reissued with notes by Carl Benn (Toronto: Champlain Society, 2011), 71. On women's needs, see Cherokee Nation to Jefferson, 5 January 1809 ("pitied their Children"), Thomas Jefferson Papers, Early Access Document, National Archives, https://founders.archives.gov/documents/Jefferson/99-01-02-9498.

18. On the issue of "reserves" and controversy over the treaties of 1806, see McLoughlin, *Cherokee Renascence*, 110–122. Cherokee men controlled the annuity's use, and women asked their male kin to make sure their needs were met. See Perdue, *Cherokee Women*, 131, 137; Cynthia Cumfer, *Separate Peoples, One Land: The Minds of Cherokees,*

Blacks, and Whites on the Tennessee Frontier (Chapel Hill: University of North Carolina Press, 2007), 122–123.

19. On Doublehead's slaying, carried out by The Ridge and Alexander Saunders, see Thurman Wilkins, *Cherokee Tragedy: The Story of the Ridge Family and the Decimation of a People* (New York: Macmillan, 1970), 39–40. On the Cherokee resolve, see Chiefs and Warriors to the President of the United States, 24 January 1808. This letter was forwarded in Pickens to James Vann, 18 February 1808, RCIAT. See also McLoughlin, *Cherokee Renascence*, 125–126.

20. Letter enclosed in Pickens to James Vann, 18 February 1808, RCIAT.

21. For the declaration, see Chiefs of the Cherokee Nation to Jefferson, 21 December 1808, Thomas Jefferson Papers, Early Access Document, National Archives, https://founders.archives.gov/documents/Jefferson/99-01-02-9361. Senior deputies of the Lower Towns favored cession and emigration, while the opponents were a coalition of Upper Town leaders and their allies in other areas. See McLoughlin, *Cherokee Renascence*, 143–150.

22. Jefferson to Deputies of the Cherokee Upper Towns, 9 January 1809, in the Andrew Jackson Papers, Series 1, Mss. 27352, vol. 8, LC. This letter includes the advice on governance and landholding. On emigration, see Jefferson to Deputies of the Upper and Lower Towns, 9 January 1809, Jefferson Papers, Early Access Document, https://founders.archives.gov/documents/Jefferson/99-01-02-9498. To dwell in "the bosom of the country," is in Chiefs of the Cherokee Nation to Jefferson, 21 December 1808.

23. Letter from the National Council at Wills Town to Meigs, 27 September 1809, RCIAT. For the festival, see *Journal of Major John Norton*, 71.

24. Michelene E. Pesantubbee, "When the Earth Shakes: The Cherokee Prophecies of 1811–1812," *American Indian Quarterly* 17 (Summer 1993): 301–317. On Ridge's role in Chickamauga attacks on white settlements, see Wilkins, *Cherokee Tragedy*, 22–25.

25. Pesantubbee, "When the Earth Shakes," 305–313. See also Gregory A. Waselkov, *A Conquering Spirit: Fort Mims and the Redstick War of 1813–14* (Tuscaloosa: University of Alabama Press, 2006), 74–80.

26. See Claudio Saunt, *A New Order of Things: Property, Power, and the Transformation of the Creek Indians, 1733–1816* (Cambridge: Cambridge University Press, 1999), 249–270; Robbie Ethridge, *Creek Country: The Creek Indians and Their World* (Chapel Hill: University of North Carolina Press, 2003), 237–240; Daniel S. Dupre, *Alabama's Frontiers and the Rise of the Old South* (Bloomington: Indiana University Press, 2018), 229–243; Waselkov, *A Conquering Spirit*, 83–92, 127–142.

27. Susan Abram, *Forging a Cherokee-American Alliance in the Creek War: From Creation to Betrayal* (Tuscaloosa: University of Alabama Press, 2015), 53; Wilkins, *Cherokee Tragedy*, 39–40, 68–79.

28. Abram, *Forging a Cherokee-American Alliance*, 76–82. Of two identified Cherokee friends of Tecumseh, one was killed in the same battle in which the famed warrior fell. See John Norton (Teyoninhokarawen of the Mohawks) to John Thompson, 8 June 1818, RCIAT.

29. Dupre, *Alabama's Frontiers*, 242–243; McLoughlin, *Cherokee Renascence*, 199–204.

30. On Cherokee-Osage tensions, see Kathleen DuVal, *The Native Ground: Indians and Colonists in the Heart of the Continent* (Philadelphia: University of Pennsylvania

Notes to Pages 449–453

Press, 2006), 198–200, 208–226. On Cherokee emigrant lobbying for the employment of missionaries, see chief John Jolly to Meigs, 28 January 1818, RCIAT.

31. McLoughlin, *Cherokee Renascence*, 225 (Cherokee law of May 1817), 229–233 (treaties of 1816–1817).

32. The women's petition is printed in Theda Perdue and Michael D. Green, *The Cherokee Removal: A Brief History with Documents*, 2nd ed. (Boston: Bedford/St. Martin's, 2005), 131–132. See also Katy Simpson Smith, "'I Look on You . . . as My Children': Persistence and Change in Cherokee Motherhood, 1750–1835," *North Carolina Historical Review* 87 (October 2010): 403–430, 424–429: Tiya Miles, "'Circular Reasoning': Recentering Cherokee Women in the Antiremoval Campaigns," *American Quarterly* 61 (July 2009): 221–243, 224.

33. Governor McMinn was then a federal commissioner to the Cherokees. On the bid for "separate" recognition, see Cherokee deputation to James Monroe, 14 January 1818, BIA, M271, roll 2. On the clash over annuities, see Gregory D. Smithers, *The Cherokee Diaspora: An Indigenous History of Migration, Resettlement, and Identity* (New Haven: Yale University Press, 2015), 95–98.

34. Speech of Talohnteskee [Tolluntuskee], 21–22 February 1818, drafted by Return J. Meigs, and intended for "WC" [William Clark, Governor of Missouri Territory], RCIAT. On Arkansas Cherokees, see Joseph Patrick Key, "Indians and Ecological Conflict in Territorial Arkansas," *Arkansas Historical Quarterly* 59 (Summer 2000): 127–146, 138–146.

35. John Jolly to Izard, 18 August 1825, TP, 20:105. Treaty of cession of 6 May 1828, ASPIA, 2:288–289. Duval is quoted in Stanley W. Hoig, *The Cherokees and Their Chiefs in the Wake of Empire* (Fayetteville: University of Arkansas Press, 1998), 140. On U.S. policy and private ambition in Indian expulsion, see Claudio Saunt, *Unworthy Republic: The Dispossession of Native Americans and the Road to Indian Territory* (New York: Norton, 2020).

36. On George Lowrey, see Henry Thompson Malone, *Cherokees of the Old South: A People in Transition* (Athens: University of Georgia Press, 1956), 84, 105, 125, 166–167.

37. McLoughlin, *Cherokee Renascence*, 139–142, 285–290, 335. On witchcraft or sorcery, see Alan Kilpatrick, *The Night Has a Naked Soul: Witchcraft and Sorcery among the Western Cherokee* (Syracuse, NY: Syracuse University Press, 1997), 8–13, 14–30; Rennard Strickland, *Fire and the Spirits: Cherokee Law from Clan to Court* (Norman: University of Oklahoma Press, 1975), 30–31.

38. Stan Hoig, *Sequoyah: The Cherokee Genius* (Oklahoma City: Oklahoma Historical Society, 1995), 45–48, 71–72; McLoughlin, *Cherokee Renascence*, 353–354.

39. Hoig, *Sequoyah*, 17–20.

40. On Ahyokah, see *Cherokee Phoenix*, 13 August 1828; Hoig, *Sequoyah*, 41. Smithers, *Cherokee Diaspora*, 77–82. On the syllabary's "mystery," see the contemporary observation of Samuel Lorenzo Knapp, in *Cherokee Editor: The Writings of Elias Boudinot*, ed. Theda Perdue (Athens: University of Georgia Press, 1983), 55. "Spiritual regeneration" is discussed in Rose Gable, "Talisa Woni—'Talking Leaves': A Re-examination of the Cherokee Syllabary and Sequoyah," *Studies in American Indian Literatures* 24 (Winter 2012): 47–76, 60.

41. "Treaty between the United States and the Cherokee Indians Signed at the Chickasaw Council House," 14 September 1816, Indigenous Digital Archive, https:// digitreaties.org/treaties/treaty/100220764/. See also McLoughlin, *Cherokee Renascence*, 210–211.

42. "1828. Treaty with the Cherokees West of the Mississippi," concluded 6 May 1828, ratified 28 May 1828, Indigenous Digital Archive, https://digitreaties.org /treaties/treaty/185842557/. See also Charles C. Royce, *The Cherokee Nation of Indians* (Reprint, Chicago: Aldine Press, 1975), 114–121.

43. See Hoig, *Cherokees and Their Chiefs*, 139–140. In the 1828 treaty, Cherokee negotiators managed to have the Arkansas western boundary redrawn 40 miles to the east, thereby gaining vital land for their people in Indian Territory. See Cane West, "'They Have Exercised Every Art': Ecological Rhetoric, a War of Maps, and Cherokee Sovereignty in the Arkansas Valley, 1812–1828," *Journal of the Early Republic* 40 (Summer 2020): 297–328.

44. John Ridge was born in 1803 and Gallegina in 1804. See Wilkins, *Cherokee Tragedy*, 33–34, 98–108; Boudinot, *Cherokee Editor*, 3–5; Smith, "Persistence and Change in Cherokee Motherhood," 414–424.

45. This story is well told in *To Marry an Indian: The Marriage of Harriet Gold and Elias Boudinot in Letters, 1823–1829*, ed. Theresa Strouth Gaul (Chapel Hill: University of North Carolina Press, 2005), 8–23. John Ridge left Cornwall in 1822, convalesced after an injury, and then returned to Cornwall to marry.

46. See law of 10 November 1825, *Laws of the Cherokee Nation, Adopted by the Council at Various Periods [1808–1835]* (Tahlequah, Cherokee Nation: Cherokee Advocate Office, 1852), 57. There were nearly 150 white men married to Cherokee women in the nation at the time. David Brown is quoted in Gaul, *To Marry an Indian*, 17. The Ridge is quoted in Perdue, *Cherokee Women*, 150.

47. Elias Boudinot, *An Address to the Whites. Delivered in the First Presbyterian Church, on the 26th of May 1826* (Philadelphia, 1826), 12. "Boudinot" was mistakenly spelled "Boudinott" on the title page. For an insightful summation of Boudinot's views, see Perdue, in *Cherokee Editor*, 10–21. For John Ridge and Boudinot, see also Smithers, *Cherokee Diaspora*, 63–74, 83–92, 107–108.

48. "Strictures," *Cherokee Phoenix*, 13 March 1828. John Ridge used the pseudonym Socrates for this piece. For his authorship and argumentation, see Kelly Wisecup, "Practicing Sovereignty: Colonial Temporalities, Cherokee Justice, and the 'Socrates' Writings of John Ridge," *Native American and Indigenous Studies* 4 (Spring 2017): 30–60.

49. For the Georgia compact, see Articles of Agreement and Cession, 24 April 1802, ASPPL, 1:114. On Georgia's policy, see Saunt, *Unworthy Republic*, 30–41, 45–49, 98–100.

50. See law of 26 October 1829, *Laws of the Cherokee Nation*, 136–137. This last law, which mandated death for the above-mentioned crime, was enacted to confirm previous decisions of the same kind. See Perdue and Green, *Cherokee Nation*, 91–113, 150; Wilkins, *Cherokee Tragedy*, 289 ("death warrant").

51. Saunt, *Unworthy Republic*, 185–200, 205–226.

52. Perdue and Green, *Cherokee Nation*, 131–140; Saunt, *Unworthy Republic*, 276–281; Carolyn Lynn Johnson, *Cherokee Women in Crisis: Trail of Tears, Civil War and*

Notes to Pages 459–464

Allotment, 1838–1907 (Tuscaloosa: University of Alabama Press, 2003), 66–78; Daniel Blake Smith, *An American Betrayal: Cherokee Patriots and the Trail of Tears* (New York: Henry Holt, 2011), 210–236; Perdue, *Slavery and the Evolution of the Cherokee Nation*, 71–72. Blacks died, too, if in uncertain numbers, through the ordeal of Cherokee removal.

53. Sam W. Haynes, *Unsettled Land: From Revolution to Republic, The Struggle for Texas* (New York: Basic Books, 2022), 270–274; Diana Everett, *The Texas Cherokees: A People between Two Fires, 1819–1840* (Norman: University of Oklahoma Press, 1990), 99–116.

54. John R. Finger, *The Eastern Band of Cherokees, 1819–1900* (Knoxville: University of Tennessee Press, 1984), 7–8, 23–40, 178. For folklore and culture, see Sandra Muse Isaacs, *Eastern Cherokee Stories: A Living Oral Tradition and Its Cultural Continuance* (Norman: University of Oklahoma Press, 2019).

55. William McLoughlin, *After the Trail of Tears: The Cherokees' Struggle for Sovereignty, 1839–1880* (Chapel Hill: University of North Carolina Press, 1993), 41–53, 70–85, 153–161: Andrew Denson, *Demanding the Cherokee Nation: Indian Autonomy and American Culture, 1830–1900* (Lincoln: University of Nebraska Press, 2004), 39–51.

56. On John Silk's story, see Clint Carroll, *Roots of Our Renewal: Ethnohistory and Cherokee Environmental Governance* (Minneapolis: University of Minnesota Press, 2015), 61–62.

57. Wilma Mankiller and Michael Wallis, *Mankiller: A Chief and Her People, An Autobiography of the Principal Chief of the Cherokee Nation*, rev. paperback ed. (New York: St. Martin's Griffin, 1999), xxi. For a recent Keetoowah view, see Corey Still, "The Path of a Modern Warrior: Leadership Perspectives through Cultural Teachings," in *Indigenous Leadership in Higher Education*, ed. Robin Minthorn and Alicia Fedelina Chavez (New York: Routledge, 2015), 196–203. See also Smithers, *Cherokee Diaspora*, 263–266; Circe Sturm, *Becoming Indian: The Struggle over Indian Identity in the Twenty-first Century* (Santa Fe: School for Advanced Research Press, 2011), 15–17, 56–61, 132. On "gadugi," see Reed, *Serving the Nation*, 3–6.

Acknowledgments

My foremost thanks goes to Maxine Levy, my companion, who has listened patiently and with keen interest, seemingly at all hours, to many stories of the Cherokees and their world. Maxine has shared the journey with me, and I am most fortunate. My brothers have contributed significantly. I am grateful to Seth for reading the entire manuscript and sharing valuable thoughts as I progressed. Zach and Matt offered insightful comments on several chapters in a most encouraging way. My son, Isaac, is a great booster. Alan Berolzheimer was extraordinarily helpful in thoroughly reviewing the manuscript and providing feedback. Many others have helped along the path.

I have benefited from the professional assistance and courtesy of archivists and librarians at numerous venues. I am especially thankful to Kevin Graffagnino, former director of the William L. Clements Library at the University of Michigan. Gregory Dowd generously shared his thoughts with me at dinners in Ann Arbor. Cameron Strang offered valuable feedback on two of my chapters. John Garrigus helped as friend and colleague by expertly reviewing translations of several French historical documents. Christopher Morris also lent encouragement as friend in the History Department of the University of Texas at Arlington. I am appreciative of support from UTA's College of Liberal Arts, which awarded me a Faculty Development Leave in spring 2019 and also granted a Research Award in 2023 to aid in the drafting of professional maps by Gabriel Moss, whom I thank. My work builds on well above a generation of outstanding scholarship in Cherokee and

Native American history, which has enriched our perspectives on interconnected American pasts.

I am grateful beyond words to the late Michael Kammen, my mentor, friend, and an extraordinary historian and teacher to whose memory I dedicate this book.

Index

Note: Page numbers in *italics* indicate maps and figures.

Abbeville County, SC, public letter of justices of, 395–396

Abeikas Creeks: British-Cherokee War and, 264, 265; Charles Town Conference of 1726, 90, 92, 496n64; Cherokee-Creek peace talks and, 80, 81, 83, 85, 86, 88, 179, 180; influence of, 74; killing of traders, 264; peace path, 133; relations with Cherokees, 81, 176; towns of, 75, 80, 176, 264; war with Choctaws, 148

Abenakis, *42,* 142, 379, 517n13

Abraham (Black courier), 249

Acadia, Nova Scotia, 221

Acorn Whistler of Little Okfuskee, 180, 184

Act of Union 1707, 44

Adair, James: on appearance of Native people, 2; on Cherokee customs, 19, 27; on Cherokee visit to London, 110, 501n41; on hostage-taking, 528n66; on scalps, 31; on Virginia killings of Cherokee Indians, 525n24

Ahyokah (daughter of Sequoyah), 458

Alabama River, 127, 145, 323, 431, *463*

Alabamas, 36, 54–55, 127, 178, 271, 272, 431

Alabama Territory, establishment of, 453

Algonquians, 277, 517n13

Altamaha River, *42,* 95, 123, *225*

American Civil War, 465

American Revolutionary War: Blacks and, 355; British forces in, 333–334, 347–348, 356; British-Indian alliance in, 355–356; Catawbas and, 343; Cherokees in, 6, 331, 332–336, 340–341, 348, 349, 356–357, 364–365; Chickamaugas and, 366; Creeks and, 340, 356, 366; frontier militia in, 288, 331–333,

340–343, 348, 355–356; Jefferson and, 336; Long Island talks of 1777, 350–353; Loyalists in, 348, 353–354, 355–356; Native diplomacy during, 332–333, 338–340, 349–350, 357; significance of, 363; struggle for Kentucky, 326; Whigs, actions in, 338

Amherst, Jeffrey: British-Cherokee War and, 259, 261, 262, 274–275; campaign in French Canada, 245; instructions on gift distribution, 296; James Grant and, 274–275, 277, 278; John Stuart and, 293; protection of white settlers, 256; replacement of, 303

Ammouiscossitte of Great Tellico, 150, 151, 179, 209, 509n84

Anglo-Spanish War in Florida, 121, 124, 125–126

Ani-Kituwagi, 17

Ani-Kutani, 24

Ani-Tsalagi, 15

Ani-Yunwiya, 9, 15

Apalachees, 46, 48–49, 57, 489n29

Appalachian Mountains, 3, 17–18, 36, 87, 97, 101, 127, 154, 166, 299, 312, 466, 515n78

Archdale, John, 44

Arkansas, Cherokee settlers in, 379, 448, 450, 453–456, 458–460, 465

Arkansas River, *463*

Articles of Confederation, 375

Asaquah (Nottawega headman), 166

Ashley River, 44

Askiyvgvsta, 32

Atkin, Edmund, 220–221, 222, 228, 262, 263

Attakullakulla ("The Little Carpenter"): as adopted captive, 10; artistic representation of, 110, *111*, 500n30; attitude to French propaganda, 210; audience with Fauquier, 229, 231, 305; at Augusta Congress, 297, 298–299; boundary negotiations, 315, 320–321; during British-Cherokee War, 266, 270, 272–273, 274, 275–277, 280–281, 283, 288–290; Byrd on, 228–229, 266, 532n24, 533–534n37; Charles Town delegation, 193, 197, 214–218, 229, 231; as Cherokee "emperor," 272–273; Christian and, 345; on Connecorte, 199; correspondence with Bull, 276, 277; diplomatic skills, 215–216, 217, 228–229, 288; Dragging Canoe and, 328; Dunmore's letter to, 327; on execution of Cherokee offenders, 281; Forbes and, 230, 231; gift of wampum strings for eleven towns, 289; Glen and, 107, 185, 186, 187–188, 189, 193–194, 195, 197, 198, 217, 525n21; Goudy's testimony about, 185–186; Grant and, 276, 280, 281, 288, 289; on help to Upper Towns, 217–218; interpretation of the treaty of 1730, 189; at Lochaber conference, 318–319; Lyttelton's march and, 245; Mackintosh and, 288–289; Montgomery's negotiation with, 259, 260; Nan-ye-hi and, 350; Oconostota and, 272–273; peace diplomacy of, 2, 185, 187, 230–231, 242, 245–246, 247, 287, 294–295, 444, 477n4, 533n37, 539n31, 547n50; personality of, 202, 216, 290; on political rift in Overhill country, 216–217; Pontiac's War and, 300; on preservation of people's ways of life, 318; pro-English attitude, 118, 191, 194, 223, 229, 230; raid on Creeks, 185; raid on Illinois tribes, 327; recollections of Cuming, 106–108; request for troops from Raymond Demere, 202; request to reward his warriors, 223; return from Ohio-Tennessee warfare, 223; rivals among Cherokees, 282; sale of Indian lands and, 327; Settico's attack and, 234; Settico visit, 236; at South Carolina council chamber, 289; Southern state invasions of 1776 and, 345, 346; Henry Stuart and, 346; John Stuart and, 209, 262, 265, 280–281, 298–299, 327, 346, 532n24; Sycamore Shoals treaty and, 330; talks with Demere, 205; talks with Lyttelton, 214–218, 229, 231–232, 246–247, 522n72; talks with Six Nations, 307–308, 317; Turner and, 229–230; Virginia-Cherokee clashes and, 227; Virginia mission, 185, 229, 231, 305–306, 339, 350; visit to Fort Prince George, 275–276; visit to London, 99, 100, 106, 107–108, 110, 185, 187, 419, 499n18

Atwood, James, 250–251

Augusta Boys, 304–306, 314, 539n28
Augusta Congress of 1763: boundary issues and, 309–310, 322; British promises at, 297, 299; Cherokee delegation, 296–297; Creeks and, 299–300; importance of, 297; John Stuart and, 296, 297; Native rights issue, 297, 298–299
Augusta County massacre, 304, 305, 539n30

backdoor deals, 184, 208, 237, 376, 424
Barnwell, John ("Tuscarora Jack"), 51, *63*, 127, 406, 503n17
Bartram, William, 19
Batz, Alexandre de, 133
Baudouin, Michel, 130
Beamer, Thomas, 528n68
Beamor (Beamer), James, 165, 289
Bean, Lydia, 349
Beard, John, 429–430, 436, 566n86
Beauharnois, marquis de, 139
beaver skins, 37, 62, 76, 492n74
Bell, John, 253
Bench, John, 1, 566n88
Bend of the Tennessee Company, 374, 382
Benge (the Bench), Captain, 430, 434, 446, 566n88
Benn, Samuel, 185
Berkeley, William, 43
Betsy (daughter of Nancy Ward), 349, 358, 372, 389, 390, 429
Bienville, Jean Baptiste Le Moyne, sieur de: armed forces of, 130; Choctaws and, 131, 132, 136, 505n32; establishment of Mobile, 45; grand campaign of 1739–1740, 133, 135; Native allies of, 82; as provincial governor in New Orleans, 129; return to France, 143
Big Sawney, 542n83
Biloxi Bay, 45
Bird clan, 22
black beads, 3, 232, 238, 246, 305, 306
Black Dog, 153, 401, 558n80
Black Fox, 437
Black slaves: as aides to colonials, 61, 152, 249, 277, 341; American Revolutionary War and, 355; Cherokee acquisition of, 446–447, 458; customs duties on, 48, 159; escape of, 56, 74, 167, 355; freed by Indians, 56, 167; in Grant's army, 278; population of, 45, 55, 122, 147, 159, 366, 551n6; rewards for capture of runaway, 174, 217; in South Carolina militia, 57, 61; stealing or capture of, 156, 383, 408, 434
blankets: as currency, 40, 66, 97, 492n74
Bledsoe, Anthony, 336, 384, 387
blood, as life source, 20–21, 30, 362, 454
bloodstained offerings, 148, 156, 262
blood vengeance, 23, 33–34

Bloody Fellow (Nentooyah, Iskagua): cooperation with Watts, 435; diplomacy of, 417, 423, 427, 562n45, 563nn46, 47; names of, 423, 562n45, 564n67; negotiations with New Orleans, 427; Philadelphia talks and, 415–416; as war leader, 386, 405, 424–425

Blount, William: attempt to purchase Muscle Shoals, 376, 413, 562n39; backdoor intrigues, 376; cession of Native territories, 374–376, 412; Chickamauga militancy and, 422–423; on death of Noonday, 565n81; on Finnelson testimony, 564n71; governorship of Southwest Territory, 411–412, 413, 561n33; head of Bend of the Tennessee Company, 374; Holston parley and, 412–415, 425; Knox's instruction to, 422; lobby for war on Creek Indians, 429, 431; McGillivray and, 423; militia companies of, 564n64; opposition to Hopewell Treaty, 382; political career of, 448; portrait of, *411*; spies of, 424; talks with Native leaders, 412, 413, 423, 425–426, 427, 428, 436, 437, 564n71

Blue Ridge Mountains, *xi*, 3, 16, 18, 35, 44, 62, 140, 156, 159, 181, *258*, 310, 312, 347, 365

Board (Council) of Trade and Plantations: approval of Indian presents, 514n58; assessment of French threat, 127, 503n17; reaction on frontier attacks, 304–305, 308; rulings of, 158, 192; treaty with Cherokees, 113–117, 127, 501nn37, 40

Bonnefoy, Antoine, 137, 138

Boone, Daniel, 294, 324, 329, 367, 372–373

Boone, James, 324

Boone, Jemima, 372–373

Boone, Richard, 503n17

Boone, Thomas, 297

Bosomworth, Mary, 184

Bosomworth, Thomas, 184

Botetourt, Norborne Berkeley, Baron de, 316

Boudinot, Elias (Gallegina), 460, 461–462, 463, 571n44

Boulware, Tyler, 483n29

Bouquet, Henry, 295

Bowles, William Augustus, 417–419, 421, 423, 424, 434

Braddock, Edward, 194, 195, 196, 206

Brant, Joseph (Thayendanegea of the Mohawks), 375

Breath (Cherokee chief), 408, 423, 427

breechclout, 109–110

Brims (Ochese Creek chief): Cherokee-Creek peace talks and, 83, 87; diplomatic influence of, 60, 147; negotiations with English, 60, 74, 75–76; Nicholson's commission and, 71; relations with Spaniards, 87, 96; younger brother of, 86

British-American colonialism, 326–327

British Board of Trade. *See* Board (Council) of Trade and Plantations

British-Cherokee Treaty of 1730: affirmation of, 116–117; Cherokee attitude to, 115–116; conditions of, 114–115; Cuming's approval of, 117–118; on justice system, 115; negotiations of, 113–114; provision on return of runaway slaves, 115; on resolution of disputes, 115

British-Cherokee War (1760–1761), 6, *258*, 444; Abeikas and, 264, 265; Amherst and, 259, 261, 262; Attakullakulla's quests, 228–232; British captives, 273; Cane Creek assault, 261–262, 265–267, 277; casualties of, 288; causes of, 238; ceremony of peace treaty, 289; Cherokees in, 260–261, 278–279; Creeks and, 262–265; destruction of Cherokee towns in, 257–259, 279, 288, 530n2; diplomatic deadlock, 238–246; espionage, 269–270, 530n82; Fort Loudoun surrender, 268, 274, 531n10; French position in, 269; Grant's campaign, *258*, 259, 274–278, 279; Montgomery's campaign, 257–259, *258*, 260–261, 263, 267, 278; onset of, 246–256; peace talks, 1–2, 259, 261, 267–268, 275–276, 280–283, 286, 287; prelude to, 224–246; prisoner exchange, 259, 260, 267, 269, 273, 275, 287–288, 289–290; resistance to the British, 278; Settico's attack, 232–238; sexual abuses during, 288; Shenandoah violence, 226, 227, 229, 233; trigger points of, 238; women in, 10

British-U.S. peace treaty of 1783, 363, 412, 421

Broad River, 344

brotherhood, spiritual notion of, 29, 226

Broughton, Thomas, 124

Brown, Billy, 155, 156, 157, 160

Brown, David, 460

Brown, Joseph, 407–409, 426

Brown, Samuel, 521n57

Brown, Thomas, 353, 356, 364, 549n84

Buchanan's Station, *399*, 426–427

Buffalo Skin (Oxinaa, Cherokee woman), 207, 237, 238

Bull, William: Attakullakulla and, 272–273, 276, 277; on Cane Creek massacre, 531n11; Grant and, 259, 279; Montgomery and, 261; peace talks with Cherokees, 267, 268, 272, 273, 275, 277, 281, 283; plea to Major-General Amherst, 274; prisoner release, 289–290

Bull, William (the elder), 138–139, 141, 146

Bunning, Robert: conflicts with French Indians, 145; as interpreter during London visit, 8, 108, 112, 113–114, 117; panic of 1751 and, 164, 171

Butler, James, 161

Index

577

Butler, Nancy, 208–209, 269, 521n59
Butrick, Daniel S., 482n26
Byrd, William: Attakullakulla and, 228–229, 266, 532n24, 533–534n37; Cherokee entourage of, 228; Kanagatucko and, 535n62; negotiation with Cherokees, 266, 268, 269, 270, 272; resignation of, 282; talks with Catawbas, 198, 199; travel to Keowee, 228; trip to Charles Town, 228–229

Cahokias, 65, 491n59
Calloway, Colin, 412
Cameron, Alexander ("Scotchie"): in American Revolutionary War, 347–348, 353–354; on Campbell, 355; death of, 363; Dragging Canoe and, 328, 341, 346, 348; efforts to strengthen British-Cherokee bonds, 337; estate of, 317, 329, 544n5; gift of land, 321–322; Henderson's land grab and, 329, 330; on hostilities between Indians and whites, 324, 325, 326; letters to white settlers, 337; Lochaber conference and, 319–320; move to Florida, 348; nickname of, 294; Ostenaco and, 320; peace diplomacy, 306, 335; relations with Cherokees, 294, 310, 311, 312, 315, 320, 330, 348, 354–355; son of, 321; talk with Ketagusta, 301–302; talk with Tistoe, 303; on Virginia offensive, 353; Whigs' threats to, 334, 345, 354; Willanawa and, 320; on Williamson, 354
Campbell, Arthur: disrespect for the king's law, 326; Jefferson's correspondence with, 358, 359, 360; letter to Corn Tassel, 387; march on Chota, 358; Nan-ye-hi and, 358, 550n86; on Oconostota, 359; peace negotiations, 361; as power broker, 365; raids on Cherokees, 326, 359, 360–361, 363, 373; State of Franklin and, 376; support of western citizens' quest for self-governance, 377; troops of, 358
Campbell, David, 376
Campbell, John, 355
Canada, British control of, 263, 264, 274
Canadian Iroquois, 142
Canassatego (Iroquois spokesman), 142
captives: French colonials, 58, 64; ransom paid for, 126; torture and execution of, 9–10, 33; tradition of adoption of, 10, 33, 137–138, 302, 408
Carey, James, 424, 425, 564n70
Carondelet, Francisco Luis Héctor, barón de, 410, 414, 421, 422, 424, 427
Carroll, Edward, 161, 162
Carter, John, 337
Castillo de San Marcos, 48
Caswell, Richard, 388

Catawba River, 227
Catawbas: aid to English war effort, 199, 245, 257, 276, 278; American Revolutionary War and, 343; Augusta Congress and, 296; Glen's praise of, 510n10; Moytoy's attack on, 232; Nottawegas, attacks on, 157, 166; peace diplomacy, 141; population in piedmont, 158; Yamasee War and, 54, 56, 95
Caughnawagas, 307, 308, 309
Cavett's Station, 399, 430–431
Cesar (Cherokee headman): Chestowe massacre and, 53; commercial schemes of, 64–65; influence of, 58, 65; panic of 1751 and, 171; peace diplomacy of, 269, 533n31; slave trade and, 53, 64
Charitey-Hagey ("the Conjuror"): death of, 67; negotiation with British, 58, 61, 62; reward for delivering French prisoner, 64; trade negotiations and, 65, 67; Tugaloo massacre and, 60
Charles II (king), 43
Charles Town, 42, 225; Cherokee diplomacy in, 8, 57, 70–71, 82, 158, 163, 242; colonial trade, 61, 62, 66, 67; French threat to, 127; governors of, 192; greeting of Glen, 146–147; Indian Trade Commissioners, 50, 61; location of, 44; Lyttelton-Attakullakulla meeting in, 214–218; population of, 109; response to Native unrest, 122; slave trade in, 41, 47, 48; Tuscarora war and, 51–52
Charles Town Conference of 1726: Abeika delegation, 90, 92, 496n64; Cherokee delegation, 90–91; Chigelly's talks at, 91, 92, 93; Choctaw issue, 93; council meetings with Native delegations, 91, 93; Creek delegation, 90–91; gifts exchange, 90–91; Long Warrior's talks at, 91–92, 93–94; Middleton's talks at, 91, 92–93; Muscogee stance on migration, 93; outcome of, 94; Yamasee issue at, 93
Charles Town conference of 1751: accord conditions, 174–175; Cherokee delegation, 173; distribution of presents, 175; Glen and, 173, 174–175
Charles Town conference of 1753, 188–189
Charles Town treaty of 1761, 287
Charley (Tsali), Cherokee prophet, 451
Chartier, Peter, 145–146, 149–150, 151, 176, 180, 185, 223
Chattooga River, xi
Chatuga (Chatooga) town, xi, 550n92
Chattahoochee region, 60, 89, 95; towns, 74, 84, 88, 93, 179, 180, 431
Chattahoochee River, 42, 225, 258, 399, 417; trade on, 46, 54, 60; villages on, 58; Yamasee War and, 54
Chauga town, 160

578   *Index*

Chavis, Ben, 479n22
Cherokee "Ball Play," 168, 346
Cherokee bearers, 63, 65, 66, 67
Cherokee Booger Dance Mask, *213*
Cherokee conflicts and wars: with American
    forces, 402–405, 409–410, 422–427, 429–433;
    with Apalachees, 57; with Catawbas, 279;
    with Chestowe, 53; with Chickasaws,
    83–84; with Choctaws, 68; with Creeks,
    36–37, 38–39, 43, 59, 65, 67, 76, 83–84,
    170, 175–176, 180–181, 182–183, 300; with
    Cussita, 84; with Delawares, 301; with
    French colonials, 58, 300; with "French
    Indians," 81, 82; geography of, 301; with
    Great Lakes tribes, 65; with Illinois tribes,
    58, 65, 301; with Iroquois, 51, 90, 295, 301;
    levels of, 32–33; with Mohawks, 279; with
    Muscogees, 59–61, 68, 70; with northern
    Indians, 178, 301–302, 538n26, 539n30;
    with Nottawegas, 155, 157; with Ocheses,
    60; with Osage, 453; with Ottawas, 300;
    panic of 1751 and, 170–171; with Savannah
    Indians, 47; with Shawnees, 301; with
    Virginia, 227, 229; with white settlers,
    303–306, 314, 323–326, 400–402, 404–406,
    539n28; with Yamasees, 6, 56–57, 58; with
    Yuchi, 57. *See also individual wars*
Cherokee constitution (1827), 456–457
Cherokee country, *xi;* American invasions of,
    343–344; collapse of British authority in,
    329; growth of white settlements in, 325;
    land grab, 373; Southern states' invasion of,
    331–332, *332;* terrain, 278
Cherokee-Creek peace talks of 1725–1726:
    Charles Town Conference, 90–94; Chero-
    kees' position, 82–83, 88; Chickasaw issue,
    89; Chicken's role in, 68, 77–79, 80–81, 82,
    83, 84, 85, 88, 97–98; Creeks' position,
    83–84, 85, 86–87; English mediation of,
    85–86, 87, 88–89; Fitch's role in, 86–87;
    gift exchange, 87; Muscogees and, 87;
    Native initiative, 89
Cherokee-Creek peace talks of 1749: boundary
    issues, 174, 176, 178–179; disease spread
    during, 180; English mediation in, 176,
    178, 179, 180; Fort Moore talks, 179; gift
    exchange, 178, 179; Native delegation,
    179–180; women's role in, 178
Cherokee-Creek peace talks of 1750, 181–182
Cherokee-Creek peace talks of 1753–1754,
    183, 189–190
Cherokee-Creek truce of 1727, 442
Cherokee diplomacy: Americans and, 8,
    403–404, 412, 413, 422, 425–426; British
    mediation and, 70–71, 305, 308, 309; docu-
    ments and sources on, 8–9; European

officials and, 8; foundations of, 24, 29;
    gift-giving tradition, 3, 175; historical
    memory as part of, 4; important figures,
    460; land and boundary issues, 314–315;
    local and regional underpinnings, 188, 442;
    metaphoric speech, 1–2, 4; performance
    and protocol, 4; personal conferencing,
    399; pluralism of, 442; priest-chiefs' role
    in, 32; pro-French, 206, 208–209, 442; role
    of warriors in, 32; women's role in, 4, 26,
    27, 178, 308, 435
Cherokee Keetowah Society, 466
Cherokee lands: cession of, 159–160, 299, 310,
    311–312, 321–322, 367–368, 370, 446, 448,
    459, 460, 462; colonial intrusions into, 160,
    313–316, 515n78, 519n44; congressional
    legislature on, 405–406; hunting grounds,
    315–316; laws, 463–464, 571n50; private
    purchase of, 326–327; Proclamation Line
    and, 313
Cherokee Nation, 71, 466
Cherokee Phoenix, 456, 462
Cherokee relations: with British, 122, 150, 205;
    with Chickasaws, 154; with Creeks, 7–8,
    192; with Delawares, 525n16; with French
    colonists, 53, 135–136, 137, 143, 144, 191,
    196, 207, 269–272; with Hurons and
    Ottawas, 523n93; with Muscogees, 240;
    with Natchez, 131–132, 154; with outsiders,
    441; with Shawnees, 207, 517n17; with Six
    Nations, 306–309; with South Carolina,
    197, 293; with Virginia, 196–197, 293; with
    white settlers, 254–255, 341, 366, 373, 379,
    393; with Yamasees, 46. *See also* English-
    Cherokee relations
Cherokee Renascence in the New Republic
    (McLoughlin), 456
Cherokees: adoption of captives, 137–138;
    alliance-building practices, 72–73, 81–82;
    American Revolutionary War and, 332–333,
    334–336, 338–340, 349–350, 356–357,
    360–361, 365; ammunition, 255; Anglo-
    Spanish war in Florida and, 121; anti-English
    stance, 206; attacks of pro-French Indians
    on, 192–193; attacks on Canadian traders,
    136; authority in social relations, 9, 24–25,
    28, 449; backdoor plotting, 208; British
    colonials and, 5, 219–220; clans, 22–24;
    clothing of, 26, 109–110; colonialization
    and, 6–7, 11, 38–39, 50, 158, 159–160, 193,
    199–202; communal gathering, 26;
    connections to place and tradition, 17;
    council, 25–26; crime, 458; customs and
    rituals, 9, 21, 27–28, 280, 457; deaths from
    alcohol, 125; development of ethnicity, 34;
    diseases, 5–6, 37–38, 125, 149, 180, 229, 303,

Index   579

Cherokees (*continued*)
549n84; division among, 278, 285–286, 331, 348, 349, 447, 465; early accounts of, 15; elite, 10; English recruitment of, 124, 125; with European ancestry, 446; federal agents to, 445; first contact with the English, 17; first periodical, 456; Florida venture, 125–126; forced removal in 1838–1839, 5, 446, 462, *463*, 464, 465; gender roles, 16, 27, 33, 450; genealogies, 446; geography, 18, 71–72, 315; historical literature on, 5–6; hunting grounds, 369; in imperial war, 196–203; indebtedness, 168; intertribal clashes, 149; invention of a syllabary of, 456, 458–459; Iroquois and, 139–142; Jefferson's idea of relocation, 449–450; justice, 162; kinship relations, 1, 23, 69, 72; land cultivation, 15; language, 34; livestock, 445–446, 567n9; local loyalties of, 28–29, 72, 79, 278; masks, 212, *213*; matrilineal descent, 23, 28; migration, 17, 34, 346–347, 357, 379, 398, *399*, 444, 448–449, 450, 451, 547n52; mixed marriages with white people, 460–461; mystical meaning of place names, 19–20; myths of, 9, 20–21, 30, 108; names of, 9, 15, 17, 24; National Council, 451, 457; Native enemies of, 139; nature in life of, 19, 102, 351, 369; need for security, 193, 309–313; non-state societies, 24–29; notable figures, 446; notion of correct human behavior, 27; occupations, 15; origins of, 15; perception of skin color, 2; perception of strangers, 29; pipe smoking, 22; police force, 457–458; population of, 15–16, 37, 50, 149, 316, 366, 398–399; property-holding, 446, 458; purification rites, 19, 21, 32; religion, 290; respect for personal autonomy, 273; sacred number seven, 22; self-governance, 440–441; self-identification, 69, 466; sense of common peoplehood, 9–10, 22, 29, 72, 98, 209, 441–442; significance of color, 3; slave ownership, 10; superstitions, 452; sympathy among the U.S. public, 461–462; territory, 16–17, 316; trade, 241; traditional practice of listening, 23–24; violence, 396, 449, 454; warfare practices, 7, 41, 64, 69, 220, 260, 278, 279, 301, 348, 442; warriors, estimated number of, 503n11, 515n78; Washington's address to, 439–440, 444–445; welcoming ceremony, 21–22; wheeler-dealers, 64; "white" and "red" social orders, 24–25; worldview, 20, 222. *See also* Cherokee women
Cherokee-Shawnee collaboration, 152–153
Cherokee towns and villages, *63*, *73*; attack of "northern Indians" on, 295; colonization and, 35; council house, 25, 36; destruction of, 343–344, 380–381; dispersed situation of, 3, 6; "mother" towns, 17; population of, 16; summer and winter dwellings, 26; types of, 18–19
Cherokee-U.S. peace of 1794, 448
Cherokee visit to London (1730), 100–118; Board of Trade and Plantations and, 113; Cherokee delegation, 107–108, *111*, 499n23; Cuming's role in, 101–102, 104, 105, 108–109; dinner at Windsor inn, 110–111; diplomacy, 113–118; disturbances during, 112; entertainments in London, 111–112, 500n32; gift presentation, 107; interpreters, 107, 108, 112, 113–114, 117; newspaper coverage of, 109–111; ocean crossing, 108; public attention to, 112; reception in Windsor Castle, 100, 109; recollections of, 201; return trip, 118; review of British cavalry regiments, 111; royal audience, 101, 109; signing of British-Cherokee treaty during, 103, 501nn37, 40
Cherokee visit to London (1790), 418–419
Cherokee women: abuses of, 288; annuity pay to, 568n18; anti-removal campaign, 454; childbirth, 21; clothes of, 189; diplomacy of, 4, 10, 26, 27, 178, 189, 266–270, 276, 283, 308, 350, 356–357, 361–362, 381, 390–391, 433–435; at Fort Ninety-Six, 251; hospitality of, 445; liaisons with white traders, 27–28, 72, 571n46; menstruating, 20, 21; occupations of, 16, 445; political activism, 251, 443, 454; response to hostage crisis of 1760, 250–251; right to speak at town councils, 26, 72; sexual freedom, 27–28; survival skills of, 344, 347, 360–361, 402, 432
Chescoenwhees, 382
Chester, Peter, 334
Chestowe massacre, 52–53, 57, 490n43, 550n92
Cheulah (Fox) of Settico, 21–22
Chickamauga region: Cherokee migrations to, 346–347, 357, *399*, 547n52; Donelson's voyage through, 369
Chickamaugas: American Revolutionary War and, 366; assault on Nashborough, 371; attacks on white settlers, 371, 386; conflicts with Americans, 6, 352, 353, 354, 361, 363, 398, 409–410, 422–423, 424–425, 432; connections to Creeks, 382–388, 400, 428, 429, 431–432; exchange with traders, 415; Martin's offensive against, 402–403, 404–405; Muscogee militants and, 429; opposition to Cumberland settlement, 410; relations with British, 366, 421–422; relations with northern tribes, 416; relations with Spanish, 410, 424; Servier's offensive

580   *Index*

against, 431; Shawnee militants and, 429; state formation, 370–371; towns, 347, 365, 378; white captives of, 407

Chickasaws: alliance-building practices, 81–82, 131; attacks on Indian foes, 47, 81, 84, 170, 210; Augusta Congress and, 296; British-Cherokee conflict and, 245; Cherokee-Creek peace talks and, 89; Choctaws, attacks on, 82, 158; deerskin map of, 133; in Grant's army, 278, 279; impact of colonialization on, 38; map of friendly and unfriendly nations, 133, *134*; migration, 82, 379; names for warriors, 32; population in piedmont, 158; raids on white settlers, 371; redemption of women from slavery, 97; refugees, 154; relations with Americans, 391, 430; relations with Creeks, 437; relations with French, 8–9, 130–131, 132, 133, 135; relations with Iroquois, 505n39; relations with Muscogees, 176, 437; relations with Natchez, 129, 131; relations with Nottawegas, 157; relations with Shawnees, 517n17; status of women, 28; territory of, *42*; trade, 47, 385; traditions, 126; warfare, 41, 47, 130

Chicken, George: on Cahokias, 491n59; Catawba war party and, 56; Cherokee-Creek peace talks and, 77–79, 83, 88, 90, 97–98; communication with Middleton, 493n1; on Creek captive, 491n64; Creek war captive woman and, 80–81; death of, 97; diplomatic mission of, 68–69; journals of, 58, 62, 495n48; Long Warrior and, 79–80, 90, 94; mission to Cherokee country, 58–60, 77–79, 82, 84, 85, 101

Chicken, George, Jr., 101

Chigelly of Coweta: Altamaha River killings and, 95; Cherokee-Creek peace talks and, 86–87, 88, 89, 90, 91, 92, 496nn54, 64; talks with Fitch, 86, 87–88, 89; talks with Glen, 179, 184; talks with Glover, 96; talk with Long Warrior, 90, 93

Child, James, 50

Chilhowee town, *xi, 399;* American Revolutionary War and, 339; destruction of, 358, 381; massacre at, 394–396; rebuilding of, 347; support of British, 214

chilokee, 15

Chinisto of Conasatchee, 323, 325, 543n86

Chinisto of the Lower Towns, 543n86

Chipacasi of Coweta, 86, 496n53

Chitimacha tribe, 45

Choctaws: attacks on Cherokees, 68; attacks on Chickasaws, 79, 82, 221; Augusta Congress and, 296; Cherokee-Creek peace talks and, 93, 179; civil war, 149; diseases and, 38; with European ancestry, 446;

impact of colonialization on, 38; migration to Spanish territories, 379; population of, 38, 50; relations with Creeks, 323; relations with French, 8–9, 45, 130, 213; relations with Natchez, 129; status of women, 28

Chota town, *73, 225, 258, 322, 399;* Campbell's march on, 358; Christian's offensive on, 344; destruction of, 359; French influence in, 184–185, 273; influence of, 3; location of, 146; negotiation with Virginia, 270, 282; peace negotiations in, 175, 179, 319–320, 443; peace talks with Six Nations, 307; as "peace" town, 230, 491n60; relations with Charles Town, 215–216, 298; Shawnee friends, 185, 188; threat to Fort Loudoun and British surrender, 238, 261, 266

Chottee (Cherokee town in today's Georgia), 58, 64–65

Christian, William: death of, 372, 386; diplomacy of, 350–352, 361, 387; offensive of 1776, *332, 343, 344, 344–345*

clan system, 22–24, 485n62

Clark, George Rogers, 353

Clark, William, 456

Clarke, George, 140, 141

Clinch River, 294, *332, 399*

Clinch Valley, 341

Clinton, George, 166

Cloud, Isaac, 167

Cloud, Mary, 167

coats, as currency, 64, 165, 492n74

Cocke, William, 427, 428

Coffee, John, 452

Colbert, Jean-Baptiste, 133

"Coldwater," 388, *399*

Collins, Hezekiah, 323–324, 542n83

colonial era, 16, 34, 370; early colonial era, 7, 40

colonialization, 6–7, 11, 37–39, 45

colonial settlers: abduction and killings of, 155–156, 161–162, 167, 168–169, 369, 405–406, 427, 430, 526nn25, 37, 527n44; animosity toward "red" men, 324–325; attacks on Indians, 156, 308, 314, 323–324, 400–401, 539n28; in Carolina piedmont, 158–159; Cherokee and, 254, 339, 341–342; emigration to Virginia, 512n34; expansion of settlements, 158–162; panic of 1751 and, 169–170; population of, 366; violence of, 304, 394–396, 399–400, 401, 403–404, 428; women among, 349, 404, 426

colonial trade: Cherokee bearers and, 66; embargos, 66, 76, 156, 513n50, 526n38; exchange networks, 62, 63; French, 296; Native dependency on, 52, 53–54, 512n41; practice of selling goods on credit, 53–54, 61, 173; regulations of, 44, 50, 61–63, 66;

Index

581

colonial trade (*continued*)
unfair practices, 72; Yamasee War and, 54–55. *See also* deerskin trade; gun trade
compass, story of, 388–389
Conasatchee village ("Sugar Town"), *xi, 258;* American military offensive on, 343; attacks on colonists, 247; destruction of, 257–259; intelligence, 237; Moytoy's visit to, 232
Conasauga (Spring Place), 460
Conestogas, 166, 303–304
confidence games, 166
Connecorte of Chota ("Old Hop"): Attakullakulla and, 231, 245–246; authority of, 230; British-Cherokee War and, 267; British nickname, 165; as Cherokee "emperor," 198, 272; death of, 246, 252; diplomacy of, 179, 205, 238, 443; fear of English defeat, 209; intelligence reports on Cherokee conspiracy, 238; letter to Glen, 165–166, 442–443; loyalty to British, 165, 223; meaning of name, 516n3; personality of, 205; pro-French attitude of, 184–185; Saluda River conference (1775), 194; sense of time, 443; Settico's attack and, 234; Shawnee connections, 193; talks with Demere, 205–206; talks with Hurons and Ottawas, 523n92; Virginia-Cherokee clashes and, 227
Continental Army, 288
Cooper, Joseph, 77–78, 79, 101, 103
Cooper River, 44
Coosa River, *42, 73, 399, 463;* American forces on, 431; British forces on, 346; British trade on, 47; French forces on, 127, 128, 144; hunting ground on, 176
Coosa town, *42,* 80–81, 181, 431
Coosawattee River, 178, 354, 401
Coosawattee town, 58–59, 81, *399*
Coosawattee Valley, 80
corn bread, 57
cornfields, destruction of, 343, 344
Corn Tassel (Utsidsata, Old Tassel): authority of, 353, 392; as Cherokee spokesman, 350; on death of William Christian, 386–387; gifts for, 390–391; at Hopewell conference, 381; map of the river valleys, 381; Martin and, 389; meeting with Sevier, 394; murder of, 394, 395, 400, 401, 402, 405, 406; names of, 548n67; negotiations with Americans, 332, 333, 350–352, 380; peace diplomacy, 367, 379, 380, 387, 389–390, 396; on Richard Henderson's deeds, 381; talks with Governor Randolph, 387, 389–390
Cornwallis, Charles, Lord, 356
Cotteotoy, 408
council houses, 25–26, 36
Countryman, Edward, 5

Cowee town, *xi,* 381
Cowetas: attacks on Cherokees, 65, 180–181, 183; attacks on traders, 323; Cherokee-Creek peace talks and, 86, 91, 95, 173, 179; English influence among, 74–75, 85, 201; petitions addressed to George III, 417–418; relations with Senecas, 87–88
Coweta town, *73;* British-Cherokee War and, 262; Carolina trade and, 46, 60, 65, 96, 184; political alliances, 98, 124; status of, 71, 74, 88
Cox, Zachariah, 412, 413
Coyatee town, 386, *399,* 423, 429, 430
Coytmore, Richard: accusation of rape, 243; assault on, 253; Cherokee attitude to, 241; death of, 528n68, 529n78; defense of Fort Prince George, 249–250; disrespect for Indian men, 243–244; Estatoe women and, 236–237, 251–252; Moytoy and, 526n25; Nequassee's plea to, 250; Oconostota and, 253; Seroweh and, 237, 241; Tistoe and, 248; Wawhatchee and, 232, 239
Crabtree, Isaac, 324, 325
Craig, David, 420, 421, 426
Creeks: alliance-building practices, 73–74, 75, 96; Altamaha River killings and, 95; American Revolutionary War and, 340, 348, 353–354, 356, 366; attacks on white settlers, 385; Augusta Congress and, 296; British-Cherokee conflict and, 245, 262–265; Carolina trade and, 65; cession of land at Savannah River and, 322–323; Chickamaugas, connections to, 382–383, 400, 428, 429, 431; clan system, 22–23, 485n62; cultural traditions, 36; Cumberland settlement and, 410, 423; diplomacy of, 3, 88; diseases and, 38, 549n84; English-Yamasee conflicts and, 76, 96; ethnolinguistic group of, 36; with European ancestry, 446; French negotiations with, 8–9; impact of colonialization on, 38; influential communities of, 36, 73–74; killing of traders, 59, 98; Nottawegas, attacks on, 157; opposition to McGillivray's leadership, 410; origin of name, 36; population of, 38, 183, 366; relations with Americans, 397, 409–410, 432; relations with Cherokees, 3, 7–8, 38–39, 63, 65, 76, 80–81, 170, 175–176, 180–181, 182–183; relations with Choctaws, 323; relations with English, 84–85, 262–265, 364; relations with French, 94; relations with Georgia, 323, 378, 385; relations with Seminoles, 421; relations with Spaniards, 94, 96, 397; territory of, *42;* torture of enemy captives, 10; towns and villages, 3, *73;* trade routes, *73;* Tugaloo massacre and, 59–61; warfare, 41, 383; women's status, 28

582

Index

Crow (Keowee headman), 68–69, 77
Crowe, J. A., 112
Crow town, 398, *399*
Cruzat, Francisco, 379
Cumberland Compact of 1780, 370, 371
Cumberland Gap, 324, 326, *332*, 339, 351, 371, 373, 383, *399*, 420
Cumberland region: communication and trade, 385; land speculation in, 367–368; Native attacks on, 371, 385–386, 410, 423, 426, 427, 430, 431; negotiations over land and boundaries in, 368–369; white settlers, 369–370, 371
Cumberland River, *225*, 357, 366, 367
Cuming, Alexander: account of mission to Cherokees, 101–102, 103–106, 108, 151, 499n23; Attakullakulla's account of, 106–107; background of, 105; British-Cherokee Treaty of 1730 and, 117–118; Cherokee respect for, 105–106, 117, 192; Cherokee voyage to England and, 99, 102, 104, 108–109, 113; end of life, 118, 502n47; Grant and, 103, 499n10; on mineral riches of "Cherokee" Mountains, 101, 102; Moytoy and, 104, 136; on Native ceremonial gestures, 104; personality of, 102, 103; on Tanasee warriors, 104; Wigan and, 104, 107
currency: blankets as, 40, 66, 97, 492n74; coats as, 64, 165, 492n74; cutlass as, 64, 103
Cusabo of Cussita, 74
Cussita town, 46, 75, 84, 85, 87, 180
Cussoes, 95
cutlass, as currency, 64, 103

Dartmouth, William Legge, Earl of, 326
Datleyastai, 19
Davenport, William, 385, 391
Davidson, James, 435
Davies, Ambrose, 253
Davis, Donald Edward, 16
Dean, Anthony, 169, 171
Declaration of Independence, 336
deerskin trade, 44, 52, 55, 62, 65, 68, 76
Delawares: anger at British, 296; attacks on white settlers, 371, 373; Cherokees and, 301, 304, 319, 525n16; conflicts with Americans, 338, 409; diseases, 303; Forbes's diplomacy toward, 230; migration to Spanish territories, 379; Pontiac's War and, 301; Proclamation Line and, 313
Delisle, Guillaume: *Carte de Louisiane et du cours du Mississipi*, 127
Demere (Demeré), Paul, 261–262, 264, 520n48, 521n59, 523n98
Demere (Demeré), Raymond: Black courier of, 249; dealing with Cherokees, 212–214;

diplomacy of, 205–206, 210, 223, 234; letters to Lyttelton, 212, 240; Mankiller of Tellico and, 211, 212; march on Fort Prince George, 200, 201
Deraque, Jacques, 424, 425, 564n71
Detroit River, 296
Diamond, Jared, 38
Dinsmoor, Silas, 439
Dinwiddie, Robert: Cherokees and, 202, 219, 220, 518n28; as chief magistrate at Williamsburg, 218; diplomacy of, 198; fort building in Overhill country, 199; Glen and, 191; Lewis and, 203; return to England, 218; unofficial agent of, 196; view of Cherokee-British alliance, 203
diseases, 34–35, 37–38, 125, 149, 251–252, 288, 303. *See also* smallpox
Dobbs, Arthur, 245
Donelson, John: Blount's patronage, 374; death of, 386; on Lochaber treaty, 542n75; Native land cession, 374; Virginia-Cherokee negotiations, 317, 320; voyage through Chickamauga territory, 369–370
Dorchester, Guy Carleton, Earl of, 418
Doublehead (Cherokee headman): assassination of, 449; Black slaves of, 446–447; Cavett's Station attack and, 430; North Carolina commissioners and, 340; purchase of Black slaves, 446; relations with Americans, 428, 433, 566n86
Dougherty (Doharty), Cornelius, 171, 251, 253
Dougherty, Jean, 415
Doughty, John, 415
Dowd, Gregory, 169
Downing, John, 268
Dragging Canoe: during American Revolutionary War, 334, 338–339, 367; Attakullakulla and, 328; Cameron and, 345–346; Chickamauga movement, 395, 444; Coweta conference and, 417; death of, 404, 421; diplomacy of, 329, 333, 350, 352, 353, 405, 547n50; Henry Stuart and, 335–336; influence of, 328, 363, 392; John Stuart and, 345–346; Martin's offensive and, 403; migration of, 370, 398; Mohawk gift to, 338; protection of English supply line, 334; raids against Americans, 330, 331, 340–341, 347, 416; relations with British, 416; Southern state invasions of 1776, 344, 345–346; at Sycamore Shoals conference, 329, 330, 333; travels of, 329, 346
Drayton, William Henry, 334, 345
Dromgoole, Alexander, 390, 391
Dunmore, John Murray, Earl of, 320, 324, 326, 327, 417, 542n75
Duwali (Cherokee chief), 465

Index   583

eagle tail dance, 21–22
Eastern North America, *42*
Echoe (Lower Cherokee town), 181
Ecuiy (headman), 543n83
Edistos, 95
Elders, William, 565n82
Ellijay town, *xi, 258, 332,* 344, 381
Elliott, John, 249–250, 529n69
Ellis, Henry, 239, 263–264, 265
encampment tradition, 31
English-Cherokee relations: "bad talks," 164,
    166; Cherokee pleas for munition, 182–183;
    distrust in, 166–167, 168–169; English view
    of, 113, 419; killing of farm animals, 167;
    mutual theft of goods, 170; tensions in,
    155–157, 168, 323–326; unlicensed rum sale
    and, 169; war alliances, 56–58, 60, 300
Enostanakee (Gun Merchant), 181, 182, 210, 265
Erneville, Lieutenant, 131
Estatoes, 183, 236–237, 238, 241, 526n37
Estatoe town, *xi,* 68, 181, 257–259, 268
Etchoe town, *xi, 258,* 260, 264, 278
Ethridge, Robbie, 23
Etowah River, 431
Euphasee town, 53
Euseteestee village, 161, 162
Eyre, Thomas, 125

Fagot, André, 424
Fallen Timbers, Battle of, 432
Fauquier, Francis, 229, 231, 239, 304, 305,
    306, 315
Federal Convention of 1787, 412
Ferguson, Patrick, 355
Fields, John, 425
Figg, James, 112
fig leaf of peace, 180, 314
Finnelson, Richard, 424, 425, 564n71
Fitch, Tobias: communication with Chicken,
    68, 85, 89; on Coweta, 88; mission to
    Muscogees, 77, 83, 84–85, 86; report on
    Cherokee attacks on Abeikas, 81; talks with
    Chigelly, 86, 87–88, 89, 496n64
Five Nations of the Iroquois League, 37,
    100–101
Flint (Cherokee man), 53
Flint Creek, 406
flints, 41, 62
Florida: American loyalist emigration to, 334,
    337; Anglo-Spanish clashes in, 121; British
    possession of, 333; emergence of, 45;
    Moore's campaign against, 49; trade and
    commerce, 416–417; Yamasees in, 46
Floridablanca, José Moñino, conde de, 422
Fogelson, Raymond, 24
Forbes, John, 224, *225,* 230

Forks of the Ohio, 190, 194, 216, 224, 296
Fort Assumption (Fort de l'Assomption), 133
Fort Augusta (GA), 125, 144, 254, *258,* 297,
    356, 360
Fort Caswell (NC), 341
Fort Duquesne, 190, 222, 224, 225–226, 231
Fort Frederica (GA), 139
Fort Frederick (MD), 196, 219
Fort Jackson, Treaty of, 453
Fort Loudoun: Cherokee siege of, 260, 267,
    271; construction of, 203, 260, 519n44,
    520n48; Native allies of, 210, 211, 229;
    provision of, 208, 240, 527n47; surrender
    and destruction of, 265, 268, 274, 296,
    531n10; as threat to Natives, 222–223,
    240–241
Fort Massiac (Massac), 269, 518n30
Fort Moore (SC), 179
Fort Necessity, 190
Fort Ninety-Six, *258;* Cherokees hostages in,
    244; colonial settlement, 159, 160; conflicts
    with Cherokees, 254, 288, 341; female
    informant in, 251; Francis's raid on, 170;
    Glen in, 161, 200; peace talks in, 151; prisoner
    exchange in, 273; trade in, 212
Fort Patrick Henry, *332,* 349, *399,* 428
Fort Pitt, 264, 295, 296
Fort Prince George: collection of military
    intelligence, 197; commander of, 200, 236;
    construction of, 191, 519n44; exchange
    of captives in, 269, 275, 528n63, 533n31;
    female informants in, 251, 530n82, 533n33;
    Grant's troops in, 279; hostage crisis in,
    227, 245, 246–249, 251–254, 255, 260, 265,
    268, 529n79; Lyttelton's advance guard at,
    245; munitions for Cherokees at, 229,
    239–240, 525n13; peace talks at, 200–202,
    245–246, 252–253, 275–276; Seroweh's
    attack on, 249; smallpox in, 245, 247, 251,
    252, 265–266, 529n79; traders in, 241, 251
Fort Randolph, 394
Fort Stanwix, 313, 316, 317
Fort Toulouse, 127, 131, 138, 139, 147–148, 206
Fox (mythic warrior), 31
Francis, James, 167, 170, 254
Franciscan missions, 46
Franklin, Benjamin, 313, 390–391
French Alabama fort ("Le Post aux Alibamons"
    or Fort Toulouse), 127, 147, 203, 207, 208,
    237–238, 240, 264
French and Indian War (1754–1763), 190,
    196–203, 221, 222, 295
French colonials: relations with Natives, 4,
    8–9, 121–122, 131, 132, 133, 142–143, 191,
    221, 517n13; settlements in North America,
    45, 293; traders, 137, 296; war with Great

584   *Index*

Britain, 127–128, 133, 135, 157, 203, 205; war with Virginia, 191
"French John," 223, 519n32, 520n56, 523n98
French Lick settlement, 367, 369, 370
French Louisiana, 38, *42*, 82, 127–129, 132, 144, 147, 207, 270, 272
French-Natchez War (1729–1730), 121, 128–129

gadugi, 448, 466
Gage, Thomas, 300, 303–304, 305, 306–307, 316–317, 333
Gakatiyi, 20
Gallay, Alan, 41
Gallegina. *See* Boudinot, Elias
Galloway, Patricia, 38
Galphin, George, 340
Ganaghquiesn of the Oneidas, 309
Gardiner, John, 123
George I (king), 105
George II (king), 101, 102, 104, 107, 109, 126, 142
George III (king), 284–285, 297, 298, 301, 311, 312, 319, 417
Georgia: ban on African slavery, 124; British invasion of, 353; Cherokee and, 163, 293, 322–323, 343; emergence of, 45; jurisdiction over Natchez region, 377; "Pretended State of Franklyn" and, 392; private land companies, 412; relations between South Carolina and, 123, 124; territorial expansion, 158, 322, 462
Germain, George, 348
German settlers, 155–156, 158–159, 241
Germany, Billy, 262
Germany, James, 262
gift-giving tradition, 3, 4, 145, 175, 177, 178, 179
Gilchrist, Robert, 56, 57
Gillespie's Station, 405, 406
Gilliland, David, 428
Gist, Nathaniel, 349, 351
Glass (Cherokee chief), 341, 403, 405, 420, 425, 435
Glen, James: on Acadian deportees, 523n93; Attakullakulla and, 185, 186, 187–188, 193–194, 197, 198, 525n21; Cherokee-Creek peace talks and, 176, 179, 180, 182, 183–184, 189; crisis management in 1751, 172–173, 442; Cuming and, 106, 107; fort building, 190, 191, 192, 200, 511n23, 517n15, 519n38; as governor of South Carolina, 146, 147, 192, 200; Indian allies, 190; letter to Governor Clinton of New York, 166; on Nottawega situation, 166–167; portrait of, *177*; relations with Catawbas, 158, 510n10; relations with Cherokees, 149–153, 156, 157, 158, 159, 163–166, 191, 192, 197–198, 260, 525n21;

relations with Choctaws, 148, 179; reports to London, 162; at Saluda River conference, 151–152, 194–195, 518n24; on surrender of French army deserters, 198; on tension between colonials and Natives, 159; trade regulations, 156, 161
Glover, Charlesworth, 96
Gold, Harriet, 460
Gooch, William, 140
gorgets, 264, 390, 416
Goudy, Robert, 169, 185, 212
"Granny Maw," 445, 446
Grant, James: Amherst's orders to, 274–275, 277; army of, 277–278; Attakullakulla and, 276–277, 280–281, 281–282, 288, 289; campaign against Cherokees in 1761, *258*, 274–278, 279, 280, 343, 535n59, 540n37; diplomacy of, 277, 281–282; duel with Middleton, 279–280; Montgomery's campaign and, 258, 259; relations with Cherokees, 274, 287, 340
Grant, Ludovick, 94, 103, 138, 139, 145, 146, 168, 499n10
Gray, Edmund, 167
Great Britain: North American colonies, 45; war with France, 157
Great Buzzard story, 20
Great Island of the Holston. *See* Long Island of Holston
Great Kanawha River, 268, 314, 315, 320
Great Lakes, 45–46, 264
Great Miami River, *225*
Great Tellico (Tellico), *xi, 63, 73, 332*; attacks on French Indians, 104; Chicken's mission to, 79, 81; destruction of, 381, 550n92; diplomacy of, 98, 181, 206–207; fort building near, 153; location of, 98; population of, 79; prisoners in, 137–138; pro-French orientation, 203, 207, 217, 237, 269, 443; trade depots in, 62
"Great Water" (the Atlantic), 8, 99, 101, 104
Greenbrier Company, 314
Green Corn Festival, 21, 224
Grenville, William, Lord, 418, 419
guerrilla warfare, 356, 426, 442
Guess, George. *See* Sequoyah
Gulf Coast, 34, 45, 47, 50–51, 221, 336, 346, 364, 400, 416, 419, 421, 422
gun trade, 40–41, 55

Hahn, Steven, 3, 36
Haig, Elizabeth, 156, 161
Haig, George, 155–156, 157, 160, 163
Hammerton, William, *63*
Hammond, Abner, 384
Handsome Fellow (Creek militant leader), 265

Index   585

Hard Labour, Treaty of, 312
Harlan, Ellis, 357
Harmar, Josiah, 409
"harmony ideal," 27, 483n33
Harrison, Benjamin, 374
Hastings, Theophilus, 62, 74
Hatley, Tom, 518n25
Hatton, Rachel, 268
Hatton, William, 66, 67, 76, 78, 268, 492n81, 533n28
Hawkins, Benjamin, 379, 445
Henderson, Richard: land purchase, 324, 326–327, 339, 357, 367, 368, 370; Martin and, 371; at Sycamore Shoals conference, 329–330, 333, 352, 367
Henry, Patrick, 349, 350, 353, 359, 373, 444
Henry's Station, 428
Herbert, John, 98
Hillsborough, Wills Hill, Earl of, 314
Hitchiti town, 36, *73*
Hiwassee River, *xi, 258, 332*
Hiwassee town, *xi*, 181, *258, 332*, 381, 550n92
Hiwassee Valley Cherokees, 347, 365
H.M.S. *Fox*, 102, 108–109
Hobohatchey (Abeika chief), 85, 90, 92, 496n64
Holm, Tom, 479n22
Holston River, 266, 294, 313, 314, 315, *399*
Holston, Treaty of 1791, 413–415, 425, 562nn41, 43
Holston Valley, 315, 341, 356, 546n36
Hopewell, Treaty of 1785, 380, 381–382, 387, 400, 405, 414
horses: for carrying goods, 521n57; conflicts over, 85; as food, 196, 261, 287, 518n28; importance to Cherokees, 189; as reward to spies, 345; stealing of, 166, 167, 169, 170, 217, 226, 251, 255, 383, 385–386, 388, 393, 433; as war trophy, 348, 353, 359, 360, 368, 416, 423, 428
Horseshoe Bend, Battle of, 452
Hubbard, James, 394
Hudson, Charles, 22, 35
Hughes, Bernard, 170
Hunt (English trader), 72
Hunter, George, 101
hunting, 29–31
Hurons, 357, 517n13, 523n93

Illinois country, 47, 300
Illinois tribes, 327
influenza, 37
Iroquois: Catawbas and, 140–141, 142; Cherokees, negotiations with, 139–142, 222, 307, 308–309, 357; Confederacy, 87; conflicts with Americans, 409; Johnson's peace

negotiation, 317, 319; raids on Native people, 45–46, 47, 51, 140, 295, 301, 302, 505n39; relations with English, 140, 309; relations with French, 8–9, 65, 142, 517n13, 518n29; site of council fire, 141. *See also* Five Nations of the Iroquois League; Six Nations
Ishempoaphi (Creek headman), 240
Iskagua ("Clear Sky"), 562n45, 564n67. *See also* Bloody Fellow
Izard, George, 456

Jackson, Andrew, 406, 446, 452, 453–454
James River, *225*
James II (king), 105
Jay, John, 378, 389
Jefferson, Thomas, 336, 358, 359, 360, 449–450, 462
Jemmy (shaman of Estatoe), 236–237
Jews: arrival in South Carolina, 44; Cuming's plan of Jewish settlement, 118
Johnny (Jonnie) of Tanasee (Cherokee headman), 172, 180, 487n17, 497n73
Johnson, Nathaniel, 50, 51
Johnson, Robert: appointment as royal governor, 101; Cherokee visit to London and, 113, 117, 118; death of, 123; relations with Cherokees, 65–66, 101, 122; on Yamasee War, 490n48
Johnson, William: Cherokee-Iroquois peace and, 317, 319; Cherokee–Six Nations negotiations and, 221–222, 305, 306, 307–308, 309, 313–314; communication with John Stuart, 302; diplomacy of, 294; Proclamation Line and, 313
Jolly, John, 456
Joly Coeur (former French soldier), 153
Jonesboro town, 377
Joree town, *xi*, 102, 103, 169, 171, 172, *332*, 525n15
Junaskala (regional chief), 465
Justice, Richard, 405, 418, 420, 421, 423, 434, 563n54

Ka'ati (daughter of Nancy Ward), 349, 357
Kahanetah. *See* Little Turkey
Kahnungdatlageh. *See* Ridge, The
Kai-a-tee town, 550n92
Kanagatucko (Standing Turkey): anti-British attitude of, 266, 267; as Chota's priest-chief, 246; commitment to surrender future malefactors, 282; diplomacy of, 1–3, 227, 535n62; influence of, 2–3; negotiations with Virginians, 282–283, 284; relations with French, 238; winter "hot-house" of, 26
Kanati ("the Lucky Hunter"), 20, 29
Katteuha (Cherokee woman), 391

586   *Index*

Keith, William, 113
Kelly, John, 249
Kenneteag. *See* Little Turkey
Kenoteta, 207, 209
Kentucky, 366, 377
Keowee River, 19, 251
Keowee town, *73*, 81; American military
offensive on, 343; British fort near, 174,
188, 238, 251, *252*; Chicken's mission in,
68–69, 77–78; concerns over settlement
near, 159–160; Coytmore in, 237–238;
Cuming in, 101–102, 103–104; destruction
and recovery of, 19, 257, 258, 286; Glen's
diplomacy in, 163, 166, 168, 173, 175, 191,
200–201; Haig's abduction and, 157, 160;
head warrior of, 71, 72; meaning of name,
19; northern Indian friends, 156; relations
with British, 125, 152, 276, 286; relations
with Creeks, 69, 89; smallpox in, 245; trade
depots in, 62; treaty of 1747 and, 160
Kerlérec, Louis Bouillart de, 207, 221, 270,
271, *271*, 272, 517n19, 520n54
Ketagusta of Chota (Prince of Chota): at
Augusta Congress, 297, 298; meeting
with Cameron, 322; on northern enemies,
301–302; peace diplomacy of, 289, 290,
294–295; talks with Six Nations, 307
Kiatchatalla of Nickjack, 408, 426
Kiateh, 377
Kickapoos, 131, 145
Kiewah town, 394
King George's War, 142–146, 149
King's Mountain, Battle of, 355–356, 358
kinship relations, 1, 23, 69–70
Kirk, John, Jr., 393–394, 406, 407, 426, 558n80
Kirk family household, Cherokee attack on,
393–394
Kituwah (Kituhwa) town, 17–18, 35, 171, 172,
279, 328
Knox, Henry (secretary of war), 400, 409, 415,
419, 439
Knoxville, 393, 398, 404, 412, 421, 424,
430–431, 454
Knoxville Gazette, 427
Konontroy town, 171, 172
Kosati (Coushatta), 36
Kunoskeskie. *See* Watts, John

Lake George, Battle of, 221
Lancaster (PA), 142
land grab, 113, 329, 330, 373
land speculation, 377, 404
Lantagnac, Antoine de, 206, 269, 270, 273,
521n57
Lawson, John, 28
lead, 40, 41, 136

Lee, Charles, 342
Lee, E. Wayne, 33
Lee, Thomas, 185, 516n83
Le Moyne, sieur d'Iberville, Pierre, 45, 82
Lewis, Andrew: British-Cherokee War and,
266, 304, 305, 313–314; expedition against
Shawnees, 196; expedition to Chota, 199;
land engrossment scheme, 314; mission to
Overhill country, 202–203; recruitment of
Cherokee warriors, 218
liquor: bans of sale, 50, 53, 173–174, 202; as
gift distribution to Indians, 161, 296; unli-
censed trafficking, 169
"Little Deer" (mythic chief), 30
Little Rock, *463*
Little Tellico, *xi*, *73*, 178, 344, 381, 494n31
Little Tennessee River, 343
Little Tennessee Valley, *204*
Little Turkey (Kahanetah), 408; on British
defeat in war with Americans, 364; Coweta
conference and, 417; Knox and, 419; Mar-
tin's offensive and, 403; Native conference
at Tuckabatchee and, 397; negotiations with
Americans, 401, 405, 421, 425, 427, 437
Little Tuskegee town, 359
Lochaber conference of 1770, 317–318,
541n68, 544n5
Lochaber treaty line, 542n75
Long Cane Creek, 160
Longe, Alexander, 26–27, 34, 52–53, 57,
64–65, 490n42
Long Island of Holston, 315–316, 318, *332*,
350, 351, 352, 361–362, 398, *399*
Long Warrior of Tanasee: attitude toward
English, 80, 94, 97, 103; attitude toward
French, 97, 98; Cherokee-Creek peace
talks and, 72–73, 79–80, 85–86, 88–89, 90,
91–93, 98; Chicken and, 90, 94; death of, 99;
diplomacy of, 67, 73, 82–83, 106, 279, 308,
442; influence of, 456; last years of, 97–98;
on Muscogees, 98; on red people, 69, 154;
Wigan and, 495n50
Lookout Mountain Town, *332*, 346, 398, *399*,
403, 418, 420, 428, 434, 446
"Lord Dunmore's War," 326
Lords Proprietors, 43, 44, 55
Louisa River, 320
Louisiana: administration of, 129; American
purchase of, 448; Cherokee negotiation
with, 270–272; French immigrants, 128;
frontier garrisons, 128; population of,
128–129; slavery in, 128; Spanish control
of, 296, 410
Louis XIV (king), 47
Louis XV (king), 296
Lower Mississippi Valley, 127–128

Index   587

Lower Towns, *xi;* aid to Tuckasegee Valley villages, 198; American Revolutionary War and, 353; British-Cherokee War of 1760–1761 and, 278, 279; Chickasaws and, 133; colonial garrisons near, 160; Cowetas and, 323; Creek raid on, 180–181; division between Upper Towns and, 447; hunting lands, 286; impact of Anglo-Spanish war on, 121; land cession to South Carolina, 442; location of, 18; negotiations with North Carolina, 310–311; peace diplomacy, 179, 242, 323, 324, 435; plan of centralizing Cherokee authority and, 71–72; talks with Virginians, 352; violence in, 155, 161; war with Americans, 343, 428

Lowrey, George, 456, *457*

Loyalists: American Revolutionary War and, 348, 353–354, 355–356; migration to West Florida, 334, 337

Lucas, Henry, 251

Ludwell, Philip, 47

Luna, Tristán de, 35

Lyttelton, William Henry: Attakullakulla and, 214–218, 231–232, 246–247, 522n72; attitude to Settico, 233; correspondence of, 200, 528n56; dealing with deserters, 246; demand for justice for killing English men, 233–234; distrust of Oconostota, 244; as governor of Charles Town, 192; governor's post of Jamaica, 256; hostage-taking, 246, 247, 254, 259, 263, 340; at Keowee, 203; Lewis and, 203; mediator in Virginia-Cherokee talks, 226–227; Middle Town headmen, letter to, 234, *235;* move toward the war, 242, 243; negotiations with Cherokees, 242–243, 247–248, 339–340; quarantine against smallpox, 245; reliance on Demere intelligence, 203; rewards for French and enemy Indian scalps, 217; Tistoe and, 107; trade embargo on Cherokees, 239; troops of, 244–245, 246; on women, 215, 216, 522n76

MacCormack, John, 284

Mackintosh (McIntosh), Lachlan, 231, 236, 275–276, 286, 288–289

Madison, James, 377

Mad Turkey, 322

Mahican, 100, 112

Malatchi of Coweta, 147, 179, 181, 184

Manhattan peace conference, 307–309

Mankiller, Wilma, 466

Mankiller of Tellico (Outacite), 32, 206, 207, 208, 210, 211–212, *271,* 521n57

Marshall, John, 462

Martin, Alexander, 373

Martin, Joseph: adventures of, 371–372; attitude to Indians, 372, 427; background of, 371; on Blacks captured by Cherokees, 407; Blount's patronage, 374; on Chickamauga region, 382; Corn Tassel and, 387, 389; correspondence with John McDonald, 383; departure from Cherokee country, 393; as federal agent to Cherokees, 400; intelligence on Chickamauga and Creek forays, 384; Knox and, 402; as mediator between white settlers and Cherokees, 358, 360–361, 371, 372, 373, 374, 379, 392–393; Native land cession, 373–374; Oconostota and, 374–375, 553n30; offensive against Chickamaugas, 402–403, 404–405, 406; peace diplomacy, 361, 375, 390, 395; prisoner exchange with Chickamaugas, 373; promotion to major, 373; reports on Cherokees, 401–402, 550nn97, 98; reputation among Cherokees, 390; storehouse at Long Island, 372; wives, 372, 389

Martin, Josiah, 327

Maryland, 167, 219

Mascoutens, 131, 145

Mathews, George, 397

Maxwell, James, 169, 171, 512n36

McCarter, General, 406

McDonald, John, 346, 383, 416, 424, 446

McDonald, Mollie, 446

McGary, Hugh, 394

McGillivray, Alexander: background of, 375; Blount and, 423; on Cherokees, 397, 398, 417; continental perspective of, 384; on Creek population, 366; Davenport's activities and, 391; death of, 415, 429; distrust of the Chickasaws, 385; influence of, 384; letter to O'Neill, 379; McDonald's correspondence with, 383; message to Handley, 397; negotiations with the United States, 410, 414; opposition to, 410; as power broker, 375; prestige of, 397–398, 421; report on Native conference at Tucka-batchee, 397; retaliation against Creeks, 391; on Sevier, 397–398; Spanish alliance, 383–384, 414; vision of the future of Native nations, 384–385

McHenry, James, 439

McKee, John, 420, 436, 565n82

McLemore, Charles, 267

McLoughlin, William, 551n100; *Cherokee Renascence in the New Republic,* 456

McMinn, Joseph, 454, 570n33

measles, 37

Meigs, Return J., 445, 450, 451, 568n14

menstruating women, 20, 21

Merrell, James, 3

Mialoquo town, 328, 335, 344, 550n92

Miamis, 132, 378, 409, 508n72

Mico (Creek civil chief), 71, 88

Middleton, Arthur: as acting chief magistrate, 77; at Charles Town Conference, 90, 91, 93–94; communication with Chicken, 493n1; information on Yamasees, 487n17

Middleton, Thomas, duel with Grant, 279–280

Middle towns, *xi;* American military offensive on, 343, 347; destruction of, 279; location of, 18–19; peace diplomacy, 234, *235,* 324, 352; plan of centralizing Cherokee authority and, 71–72

militia companies: in American Revolutionary War, 288, 331–333, 340–343, 348, 355–356, 422; assault on Coyatee, 430; assault on Nickjack town, 403, 409, 426, 432–433, 434, 435; assault on Running Water town, 403, 433, 434, 435; raids on Cherokees, 331–333, 341, 342–343, 344, 348, 353, 354, 359; raids on Chickamauga, 353; scorched-earth tactics, 344, 399–400, 432; in Yamasee War, 56

Miln, Alexander: Fort Prince George hostage crisis and, 253–255, 259, 275, 530n5; Oconostota and, 268, 529n78, 533n31; reports of, 528n68, 529nn78–79; spies of, 269–270

Minggáshtàbe, 31–32

Mingo Ouma (Chickasaw headman), 131, 132, 133

Mingos, 301, 319

Miró, Esteban, 384, 410, 422

Mississippi River, 46, *463*

Mississippi Valley, 47, 334

"mixed-blood" children, 362, 391, 398, 446, 551n100

Mobile town, *42,* 45, 49, 55, 132, 139, 261, 274

Mohawk River, 39, 222

Mohawks: American Revolutionary War and, 338; Cherokees and, 139, 302, 307; in Grant's army, 278, 279; visit to London, 100, 112

Mohawk Valley, 307, 314, 317

mollusk shells, 145

Moluntha (Shawnee chief), 386, 394

Monongahela, Battle of, 194, 221

Monongahela River, *225*

Monroe, James, 454

Montgomery, Archibald: Bull's letter to, 261; campaign against Cherokees in 1760, 257–259, *258,* 260–261, 278; forces of, 256; peace negotiation, 259; ultimatums to Cherokees, 340

Mooney, James, 19

Moore, James, 48–49, 341, 489n29

Moore, James, Jr., 51, 62

Moore, Maurice, 57, 61

Morris, John, 428

Mortar ("Wolf Warrior"): anti-English position, 210, 263, 264, 300; British-Cherokee War and, 262–263, 264, 265; death of, 323

Moytoy of Great Tellico: as Cherokee "emperor," 104, 105–106, 272; Cherokee visit to London and, 114; death of, 139, 506n53; son of, 150; as war leader, 136–137

Moytoy of Settico: attack on the North Carolina frontier, 232–233, 526n25; attacks on whites, 242; gift for Connecorte, 237–238; meeting with Mortar, 233; relation to Oconostota, 234; spread word of the "Dutch," 233

Murphy, Daniel, 170

Muscle Shoals: attempts to purchase land at, 374, 376, 382, 389, 412–413, 562n39; colonial settlement of, 369–370, 376, 385; military post near, 415, 562n44; Native attack at, 384–385, 387–388, 407, 413; trading house near, 385

Muscogees: attacks on Apalachees, 48–49; British-Cherokee War and, 262, 263; Cherokee-Creek peace talks and, 85, 87, 90, 93, 176; Chickamaugas, connections to, 429; Chickasaw attacks on, 86, 176; conflicts with Cherokees, 59–61, 68, 70, 86, 170, 452; dialects, 496n58; English-Yamasee conflicts and, 96; French and, 127; migration, 36; northern Indian attacks on, 176; offensive on Charles Town, 83; relation with English, 46, 47; Spanish attacks on, 46; status among Creeks, 73–74; towns and villages of, 46–47, 74; Tugaloo massacre, 59–61; violence of, 67, 264; warriors' honorifics, 32; women's status, 26; Yamasee War and, 54–55

Musgrove, John, 60, 492n67

muskets, 40–41, 61

Muskogean (language or speech). *See* Muscogees

Muskogees. *See* Muscogees

Nacoochee town: Chicken in, 58; Chicken's mission to, 58; Creek attack on, 77

Nairne, Thomas, 48, 49–50, 51, 54, 64

Nanatlugunyi ("Spruce Tree Place"), 325

Nantas, 197

Nantoogas. *See* Nottawegas

Index 589

Nan-ye-hi (Nancy Ward): character of, 444; colonial authorities and, 389; daughter of, 372; diplomacy of, 333, 350, 357; English traders and, 357; family of, 349, 357, 358; *Guighau* ("Supreme Beloved Woman") status of, 349, 548n62; healing powers, 349; Martin and, 358; negotiations with Americans, 358–359, 360, 361–362, 454; as peace broker, 10–11, 381, 387; residence of, 358; as spy for Americans, 550n86; statue of, *455*

Nashborough (Nashville) settlement, 370, *399*, 409–410, 415, 426, 435

Natchez people: eviction from Chickasaw territory, 129, 130–132; French-allied Indians and, 191; life among Cherokees, 131–132, 154; uprising against French, 128–129, 193–194

Natchez region: Georgia's jurisdiction over, 377; white colonization in, 334

Native diplomacy: acquisition of trade goods and munitions, 7; during American Revolutionary War, 338–340, 349–350, 357; French and English intolerance to, 130; gift-giving tradition, 3, 145, 175, 177, 178, 179; intermediaries in, 144; peace feelers, 60, 80; speech-making, 1–2, 4, 477n4, 483n33; traditional practices of, 93, 148; women's involvement in, 4, 181, 266–270, 283, 308, 454

Native peoples: alliance-building practices, 81–82; American Revolution and, 365; colonists and, 52–53; communal fields, 483n29; concern for security, 210; conflicts between, 5; deerskin map of, 132–133; dependence on Indian slave trade, 38, 44, 46–48; diseases of, 303, 549n84; economies, 40, 516n7; elite, 447; ethnolinguistic groups, 36; European trade and, 38, 40, 441; French colonials and, 121–122, 296, 517n13, 518n29; governance of, 9, 482n26; historical literature on, 5–6; imperial powers and, 121; land cession, 54, 158, 294, 299, 310, 313–316, 325, 326–327, 453; localism and regionalism of, 28, 53; migration patterns, 17–18, 35, 36, 379; physical appearance, 2; retributive justice, 10; sense of nature, 19–20; Indian slave trade, 41, 52, 58, 63–64; spirituality, 21, 296; tension between colonials and, 143, 163; towns and villages, 3–4, 478n9, 496n58, 550n92; ways of war, 30, 31, 136, 278–279, 302–303, 320, 324, 327, 338, 344–345, 484n45; weapons, 40–41

Native women: capture and killing of, 191, 344; involvement in diplomacy, 4, 10–11, 27–28, 181, 207, 266–270, 283, 454; liaisons with colonials, 28, 362, 492n67;

occupations of, 15, 26, 64, 347; social status of, 20, 26, 27, 323, 448–449; as spies, 269–270, 530n82. *See also* Cherokee women

Nelson, William, 542n72

Nentooyah. *See* Bloody Fellow

Neolin of the Delawares, 296

Nequassee town, 104, 268, 381, 530n81, 540n37

Neuse River, *225*

New Echota, Treaty of, 462

New Orleans, 133, 136, 261, 274, 296, 427

New York, Treaty of (1790), 410, 414

New York City, Cherokee visit, 306

Niagara River, 296

Nicholson, Francis, 70–71, 74, 75, 76, 77

Nickjack town, *399*; captives in, 407–408; Chickamauga militancy at, 398, 403; militia assault on, 403, 409, 426, 432–433, 434, 435

Nipissings, 10, 142, 517n13

Nittawiga Nation, 166

Nolichucky River, 294, 325, *332*

Nolichucky settlers: British warning to, 337–338; Cherokee raids on, 357; King's Mountain Battle and, 355–356; North Carolina jurisdiction over lands, 351

Noonday (Cherokee man), 565n81

North America: Anglo-French rivalry, 126–128; collapse of British authority, 329–330; imperial clashes in, 6; map of the southeastern part of, *63*

North Carolina: boundaries, 310–312, 368; Council of Safety, 342; discontented settlers, 376; emergence of, 43; Regulator Movement, 313; representative assembly, 43; territorial demands, 310, 353, 373, 376, 448; white frontiersmen of, 400

Northrop, Sarah, 460, 461

Notoly town, *xi*, 171, *258*, *332*, *399*, 401, 558n80

Nottawegas: attacks on colonists, 155, 157, 160, 166–167, 169; Creek-Cherokee diplomacy and, 176, 182; relations with Cherokees, 170, 319, 351; tribal identity, 155, 166, 193, 497n76; violent reputation of, 157, 168

Nowota of Chickamauga, 382

Nunna-da-ul-tsun-yi (Trail of Tears), 5, 446, 447, *463*, 464–465

Nunnehi (spirit people), 20, 481n15

Nuntaweas (Nuntaways), 197, 205

Nutsawi (Cherokee man), 24–25

Oatis, Steven, 60, 74

Ocheses, 60

Ocmulgee River, 36, 54, *73*, *225*

Oconee River, *73*

Oconostota: American Revolutionary War and, 339, 359; Attakullakulla and, 272–273, 444; at Augusta Congress, 297; boundaries

590   *Index*

negotiations, 315, 320; British-Cherokee War and, 229, 266, 267–269, 273, 280; Cameron's meeting with, 322; Christian and, 345; commission granted by Governor Kerlérec to, *285*; death of, 375, 554n30; Fort Prince George hostage crisis and, 252–253, 255, 267; on hostilities between whites and Cherokees, 322, 325–326; John Stuart and, 266, 306, 527n47; on killing of Russell and Boone, 324; letter from colonial leaders to, 339; at Lochaber conference, 318, 319; Martin and, 374–375; Miln and, 529n78, 533n31; Nan-ye-hi and, 350; negotiations with French, 270–272, 273; negotiations with Six Nations, 307, 308–309; negotiations with Virginia, 198, 270, 283–284, 332, 350, 359; peace diplomacy of, 241, 294–295, 353, 359; personal archive, 359–360; Pontiac's War and, 300; relations with South Carolina, 273; relation to Moytoy of Settico, 234; reputation of, 252; royal instructions of 1763, 538n13; sale of Indian lands and, 327; siege of Fort Loudoun, 260, 267; on surrender of killers of whites, 248; Sycamore Shoals treaty and, 330; talk with Dougherty, 253; visit to New Orleans, 427

Oglethorpe, James, 123, 124, 125–126

Ohio country: boundary issues, 313, 316–317; British military presence, 263, 296, 324, 517n16; conflict with Virginia, 326; Indian resistance in, 409; settlers' attacks on Cherokee in, 304

Ohio River, *42, 225*; attacks on Canadian traders on, 132, 135–136, 137; confluence with the Tennessee River, 18, 370

Ohio Valley, 46, 47, 64, 79, 87, 313

Ojibwas, 409

Okchai town, 176, 181, 210, 237, 265

Okfuskee town: British-Cherokee War and, 262; Cherokee-Creek peace diplomacy and, 176, 178; Red Coat king of, 189–190; relations with Cherokees, 180, 182, 183, 184; relations with English, 265

Oklahoma, Cherokee communities in, 466

Old Warrior of Estatoe, 259

Old Warrior of Tomotley, 208

Oliphant, John, 530n5

Onatoy of Toqua, 265–266, 289

Oneidas, 309

O'Neill, Arturo, 375, 424

Onitositah, 548n67. *See also* Corn Tassel

Onondaga, 141

Ore, James, 430, 432

Osage, 379, 453, 456

Oskuah (Abram) of Chilhowee, 394

Ostenaco ("Judd's Friend" or "Judge's Friend"): American offensive and, 353; Attakullakulla and, 275; at Augusta Congress, 297; boundary issue and, 315; Cameron and, 320, 322; Cane Creek assault and, 266–267; Cherokee-Creek negotiations and, 179; Glen and, 189; as guide of Lewis, 199; letter from colonial leaders to, 339; negotiations with British, 196, 267–269, 282, 283; negotiations with North Carolina, 310–312, 314; peace diplomacy of, 209, 210, 241, 242, 294–295, 297, 307, 311; Pontiac's War and, 301; portraits of, *271, 297, 298*; support for building of British fort, 153–154; on threat of the French, 209–210; Timberlake and, 284, 285; travel to England, 284–285, 296

Ottawas, 142, 300, 338, 409, 517n13, 523n93

Ouachita River, 138

Ouiatenons (Weas), 538n17

Ouletta (Creek chief), 74, 75, 86, 496n53

Oustenali town, 173

Outacite. *See* Mankiller of Tellico

Outerbridge, White, 240

Outlaw, Alexander, 386

Overhill Cherokees: Fauquier's apology to, 305; guerrilla warfare, 442; hunting ground, 314; relations with Chickasaws, 133; relations with Euseteestee, 162; reputation of, 278; talks with Virginia and North Carolina, 185, 368

Overhill towns. *See* Upper Towns

Owl (mythic warrior), 31

Oxinaa. *See* Buffalo Skin

Pacolet River, 527n44

Pakana, "Captain" (Alabama chief), 132–133, 148

Palmer, John, 95

panic of 1751, 169, 170, 171–175

Panton, Leslie and Company, 383, 416–417

Panton, William, 416, 424, 564n71

Pardo, Juan, 35

Parga, Juan de, 49

Paris, Treaty of, 300

Partridge (Cherokee man), 65

Pawley, George, 152–154, 176

Paxton Boys, 303, 304

Pearis, Richard, 196

Pearson, J. Diane, 479n22

Peggy (Cherokee woman), 64, 78, 168, 533n28

Peggy's Corn House, 64, 492n77

Pendleton, Edmund, 342

Pennsylvania, 140, 142, 145, 156, 166–167, 296, 303, 308

Pensacola town, 415, 417, 424

peoplehood, 9, 22, 29, 72, 98, 173, 209, 331, 423, 441, 453, 479n22

Index 591

Perdue, Theda, 21, 446
Peyton, John, 388–389
Philadelphia, 304, 415–416, 419, 424, 427–429, 431, 433
Pickens, Andrew, 379, 395, 397, 401, 402, 431
Pickering, Timothy, 439
Piomingo (Mountain Leader), 377, 385, 387, 389, 430, 437
pipes, 22, 145
pipe tomahawk, *418*
Pitt, William, 263
Pocotaligo town, 54
Pontiac's War (1763–1766), 296, 300–301, 306
potato fields, 22, 137, 344
Potawatomis, 409
Powell River, 294, *399*
Powell Valley, 341, 434
Priber, Christian Gottlieb, 138–139
Price, Moses (Wosseo), 391, 418, 420, 421, 427
priest-chiefs, 2–3, 25, 30, 32, 484n45
Proclamation Line of 1763, 294, 299, 311, 313, 318, 321, *332*
Pumpkin Boy, 428
Purrysburg (SC), 123

Qualatchee town, *xi*, 257, 343
Quanassee town, *xi*
Quapaws, 379
Quebec, 351, 418
Queen Anne's War, 47
Quetua, 35

Randolph, Edmund, 387, 389–390
Randolph, Peter, 198, 199
Raven (mythic warrior), 31
Raven of Chota, 330, 344, 350, 351, 357, 360, 372
Raven of Hiwassee: on Creeks attacks, 182; death of, 209; fort building and, 190; peace diplomacy, 164–165, 171–172, 173, 175, 178, 179; white packhorseman's killing and, 162
Raven of Tugaloo, 307
Read, Clement, 219
Red Bird, 426
red color, symbolism of, 3–4, 478nn8, 9
"Red-Headed Will." *See* Webber, Will
red people, *vs.* white people, 2, 69, 154, 493n4
Red Shoe (Soulouche Oumastabé), 129–130, 148, 149
Red Stick War, 452–453, 459, 464
Reese, Susanna, 460
Reynolds, Joshua, 297, *298*
Richter, Daniel, 6
Ridge, John, 460–461, *461*, 462, 463, 571nn44, 45, 48
Ridge, Major, 462, 463

Ridge, The (Kahnungdatlageh), 449, 451, 452, 559n19
Robertson, Charles, 338
Robertson, James: background of, 367; Cherokee land cession, 367; diplomacy of, 365, 410, 413, 436–437; expedition to Cumberland, 357, 369–370, 387; letter to Watts, 434–435; Nashville settlement, 370; raid on Chickamaugas, 432; spies of, 424, 430
Ross, Daniel, 446
Ross, John, 446, 464
Round O (Stecoe's head warrior), 234, 244, 246–247, 248, 251–252, 265, 526n28, 529n75
Running Water town, 398, *399*, 403, 433, 434, 435
Russell, Henry, 324, 325, 326
Russell, William, 324
Rutherford, Griffith, *332*, 343

Sacred Fire, 30, 484n45
Salisbury, Neal, 18
Salisbury town, 312
Sally (wife of Sequoyah), 459
Saluda River, 160, 174, 254, 257, *258*, 321–322
Saluda River conference (1775), 151–152, 194, 195, 286, 518n24
Savannah Indians, 47, 343. *See also* Shawnees
Savannah River, *xi*, 73, 225, *258*; cession of Indian land on, 321, 322; Cherokee towns on, 18, 50; freed slaves on, 49
Savannah settlement, 123, 125, 129, 353
Savano town, 89
Scaliloskern Ketagusta (Tasetchee warrior), 108, 110, 116, 117
Scalioskie of Great Tellico, 174
scalps/scalping, 31, 33, 69, 95, 236–237, 420
Scantie (Cherokee chief), 429
Scioto River, 316, 386
Scolacutta (Hanging Maw): Coyatee conference and, 423; death of, 445; escape to southwest, 395; gifts for, 391; Martin and, 360, 372–373, 393; meaning of name, 553n22; Morris's murder and, 428; negotiations with Americans, 401, 405, 417, 423, 427, 428, 429–430, 435–436, 559n10; negotiations with Robertson, 562n38; negotiations with Virginians, 360, 361, 401, 559n10; peace diplomacy, 386, 387, 405, 464; on St. Clair's defeat, 562n43; Watts and, 401; widow of, 567n9; wound of, 429
Scott, Robert, 255
Scott, Winfield, 464
Seed of Settico, 268, 302–303
Selu (first human mother), 20, 30
Seminoles, 348, 353, 421

592   *Index*

Seneca River, *xi*

Senecas, 65, 87–88, 141, 179, 308, 518n29

Seneca (Esseneca), Cherokee town, *xi*, 354, 380, 542n81, 552n41

Sequoyah (George Guess), 458–460

Seroweh ("Young Warrior" of Estatoe): attacks on whites, 236–237, 241, 242, 250; at Augusta Congress, 297; brother of, 236; conflicts with Native peoples, 301; Fort Prince George hostage crisis and, 249, 251, 276; gift of land to Cameron, 321; as military leader, 260, 528n68; negotiations with North Carolina, 310–311, 314; pro-French position of, 269–270

Settico town, *xi, 332;* attacks on North Carolina frontier, 232–234, 239, 302, 406; Attakullakulla's visit of, 236; destruction of, 359; peace overtures and, 268, 280; rebuilding of, 347; relations with English, 280

seven, as sacred number in Cherokee culture, 22

Seven Years' War (1756–1763), 293, 295. *See also* French and Indian War

Sevier, John: assault on Chickamaugas, 405, 430–431, 432; captive-taking, 408; concern over Cherokee alliance with Spain, 448; federal measures against, 401, 402–403; as governor of Franklin, 365, 376; killing of Corn Tassel, 406; land engrossment agenda, 365; meeting with Chickasaw headmen, 377; nicknames of, 406; offensive against Creeks, 392; raids on Cherokees, 358, 359, 360, 363, 373, 394, 400–402, 406–407, 431–432; reputation of, 397, 406; St. Clair's expedition and, 416; use of newspaper publicity, 406–407

Sevier, Joseph, 436

Sewees, 44

Sharp, John, 64, 76

Sharpe, Horatio, 219

Shawnees: American Revolutionary War and, 338; attacks on white settlers, 167, 168, 324, 329, 371, 373; concern over settlement at Fort Pitt, 296; dispersal of, 47; hostility toward Kentucky and Ohio Valley settlers, 378; hunting grounds, 315; Iroquois Confederacy and, 87–88; liaison to southern Indians, 145; migration, 144, 379; Pontiac's War and, 301; Proclamation Line and, 313; relations with Americans, 409, 415; relations with Cherokees, 6, 152–153, 168, 193, 207, 295, 301, 304, 316–317, 319, 517n17; relations with Chickamaugas, 386, 429; relations with Chickasaws, 153, 207, 517n17; relations with Creeks, 87; relations with English, 72, 196; relations with French, 72, 517n19, 520n54; at Saluda River conference,

152; slaughter of prisoners, 394; territory of, *42,* 47; warfare, 207

Shelburne, William Petty, Earl of, 306

Shelby, Evan, 353, 369

Shenandoah killings, 229, 232, 233, 525n24

Shenandoah's "Great Wagon Road," 140, 158

Shenandoah Valley, 226

Shettroe, David, 341

Shorey, Anne, 416, 446

Shorey, William, 266, 446, 532n24

Silk, John, 466

Silverman, David, 41

Six Nations, 141, 222, 302–303, 306–309

Skalioski (chief speaker), 32

Skaygusta Oukah Ulah (Tasetchee warrior), 108, 109, 110, 111, 112, 117, 118, 500n23

"skiagusta" (Askiyvgvsta), 32

Skiagusta ("Old Warrior") of Keowee: approval of building of English fort, 188, 190; Charles Town conference of 1751 and, 174–175; concern about colonial settlement, 159–160; death of, 190; diplomacy of, 157, 188; talks with Glen, 150–151, 188–189

Slave-Catcher of Tanasse, 284

slave trade, 41, 46, 47, 52, 53, 58, 63–64, 128

Slim Tom, 406

Sludders, William, 181

smallpox: in Fort Prince George, 245, 247, 251–252, 529n79; in Native communities, 34, 125, 149, 266, 303, 529n74, 549nn78, 84; spread of, 37, 303

Smith, Abraham, 168

Smith, Daniel, 368, 429, 430–431, 566n86

Smith, Richard, 512n41

Soquee town, 58

Soto, Hernando de, 34–35

South Carolina: bid for Creek support against Yamasees, 70, 74–75, 93, 95–96; boundary defined by Cherokee treaty of 1747, 160, 174; conflict between Georgia and, 123, 124; economic development of, 49; emergence of, 43–45; English colonization of, 35, 144; financial situation, 147; imperial ambitions, 49–50; landscape, 44–45; militarily weakness, 122; Natives-colonials tensions, 163; pleas for imperial aid, 256; population of, 45, 48, 49, 55, 122, 158–159; prohibition of liquor sales, 202; relations with Cherokees, 65, 122, 239, 282, 293; relations with Creeks, 74, 75, 76; representative assembly, 43, 52, 95, 172, 301; slave trade, 44, 45, 46, 49; St. Augustine campaign, 48; threat of French invasion, 126–127, 192; trade, 76, 122, 200; war on Florida, 124; Whigs, revolution in, 333–334

Index

593

South Carolina Indian trade: decline of Indian slave trade, 95; embargo on Creek towns, 76; in Georgia, 124; height of Indian slave trade, 41, 46–50; public monopoly over, 61–62; regulations of, 50, 61, 62–63, 66; reliance on Native peoples, 46–47; trade depots, 62

South Carolina Yazoo Company, 412

Southeastern Indigenous societies, 35

Southwest Territory, 411–412

Spain: attacks on Muscogee towns, 46; Cherokee diplomatic relations with, 422, 425; military forces, 383; North American colonies, 45, 293, 296, 422, 427

Spears, Susanna, 428

spies, 269–270, 424, 430, 530n82

spirit world, 30–31

sport, 31

Spotswood, Alexander, 127

Squirrel King (Chickasaw chief), 170

Standing Turkey. *See* Kanagatucko

State of Franklin: collapse of, 402; elected governor of, 376; foundation of, 365, 376; negotiation with Georgia, 382; relations with Natives, 376–377, 405; territorial expansion of, 377, 389, 392, 400

St. Augustine (FL), 48, 95, 126

St. Clair, Arthur (general), 400, 409, 416, 420, 422, 562n43

Stecoe (Stickoe) town, *xi*, 171, 172

Stephen, Adam, 1, 282–283, 284, 535n63

Stephens, William, 125, 163

St. Francis River, 379

St. Johns River, 125

St. Louis town, 379, *463*

Stono Rebellion, 124–125

Stuart, Henry: Attakullakulla and, 346; Dragging Canoe and, 334, 335–336; efforts to strengthen British-Cherokee bonds, 337; forged letter of, 336–337, 338; interest in colonization scheme, 334; warning letters to white settlers, 336, 337–338

Stuart, John: Attakullakulla and, 209, 262, 266, 280, 327, 346, 532n24; at Augusta Congress, 296, 297, 298; boundary line talks, 310, 311, 312–313, 314–316, 319–320; Cane Creek assault and, 262, 265–266, 267, 289; on Cherokee refugees in Chickamauga, 347; on Cherokee ways of war, 348; death of, 353; Dragging Canoe and, 346; on English-Cherokee relations, 325–326; Gage instructions to, 300, 333; intelligence on northern Indian attacks, 302, 538n26, 539n30; Johnson and, 302; letter to Baron de Botetourt, 316; at Lochaber conference, 317–318, 321, 541n68; mission to Fort

Loudoun, 527n47, 531n10; on Mortar, 323; move to Florida, 333; nickname of, 266; Oconostota and, 266, 306, 359, 527n47; as peace mediator, 293, 296–298, 303, 317–318; personality of, 293; replacement of, 356; on root cause of Native discontent, 316; as superintendent, 293–294, 329, 333; supply of ammunition to Cherokees, 241; sympathy for Native peoples, 293; Whigs, suspicion of, 333, 345

Stump, Frederick, 308

Sunderland, Charles Spencer, Earl of, 50, 51

Susquehanna River, *42*, 47, 144, 166, *225*, 308

Susquehanna Valley, 87, 166, 318

Sycamore Shoals conference, 327, 329, 330, 331, 352, 367, 544n3

Sycamore Shoals town, *332, 399*

Taghtaghquisera (chief of Caughnawaga Mohawks), 307–308

Taitt, David, 359

Tallapoosa River, 47, 54, *73*

Tallapoosas: Cherokee-Creek peace talks and, 83, 85, 86, 91, 179, 431; Yamasee War and, 74, 75–76

Tallassee town, *xi*, *73*, 80, 214, *258, 332*, 364

Talohnteskee (Arkansas Cherokee warrior), 455–456

Talotiskee (headman of Broken Arrow), 424, 426, 564n70, 565n77

talwas (towns), 3, 36

Tanaghrisson (Seneca leader), 156

Tanasee (Tunisee) town, *17*, 62, *63*, 68, 98, 146, 153, 176, *332*, 493n3

Tasetchee (Tasache) village, *xi*, 108, 499n23

Tassel. *See* Corn Tassel

Tate, John, 55

tattoos, 91, 109

Taylor, John, 427

Tea Act, 323

Tecumseh (Shawnee leader), 451–452, 453, 569n28

Tellico. *See* Great Tellico

Tellico Blockhouse, *399*; and peace accord of 1794, 433–434, 435, 436, 445, 566n98

Tellico River, 18

Tennessee: Cherokee offensive on white settlements of, 340; land cession, 448; name of state and Cherokee town, 16; population of, 366, 551n6; statehood, 366; white settlers, 366

Tennessee Company, 412

Tennessee River, *xi*, 18, *73*, 135, *225*, *258*, 313, *332*, 374–375, 382, 392, *399*

Terrapin (Cherokee man), 341

Texas, expulsion of Cherokees from, 465

594   *Index*

Theyanoguin ("Hendrick"), 100, 498n1
Thomas, George, 142
Thomas, Isaac, 339, 357
Thomas, Robert, 483n33
Thomson, William, 512n41
Timberlake, Henry, 21–22, 25, 26, 284, 285
Tistoe of Hiwassee, visit to London, 107
Tistoe of Keowee: at Augusta Congress, 297; Cameron and, 303, 321; complaints about Coytmore, 243–244; hostage crisis in Fort Prince George and, 247, 248, 250, 259, 260; letter to Captain Mackintosh, 286; peace diplomacy of, 165, 242–244, 250–251, 255, 275, 286–287, 294–295, 310–311, 499n22; raid on Northern enemies, 302–303; resettlement by Keowee, 276, 286; talks with Six Nations, 307
Tolluntuskee. See Talohnteskee
Tomahitans, 87, 487n16
Tomasee town, xi
Tombigbee River, 47, 144
Tomotley town, xi, 76, 284, 444
Toqua town, 348, 550n92
Tortora, Daniel J., 536n75
Toxaway town, 257–259, 343, 530n2
traders. See white traders
Trail of Tears. See Nunna-da-ul-tsun-yi
Transylvania Company, 329, 330, 367, 370
Tryon, William, 310, 311, 312, 313, 314
Tryon Mountain, 312
tsalagi (Cherokee people and dialects), 15, 480n1
Tsali (Cherokee headman), 427, 429
Tsali (Cherokee prophet), 451
Tsi-yugunsini. See Dragging Canoe
Tuckabatchee town, 73, 86, 263, 390, 397, 451
Tuckasegee River, xi, 17, 19, 258
Tuckasegee town, xi, 85, 171, 258, 279
Tuckasegee Valley, 170, 171, 173, 198
Tugaloos, 181, 497n72
Tugaloo town, xi; alliance with South Carolina, 343; Cameron in, 348; Chicken mission to, 58, 59, 78; colonials in, 57; Creeks, attacks on, 497n72; killing of Creek emissaries in, 59–61; negotiation with British, 58, 62; as sacred town, 445, 451; trade in, 76
Turner, George, 229–230
"Tuscarora Jack." See Barnwell, John
Tuscarora War, 28, 51–52, 82, 90, 443
Tuskegee town, xi, 332, 359
Tuskegetchee (Cherokee headman), 390
Tuwekee (Chickamauga head warrior), 353

uktenas, 19
Ukwaneequa. See Attakullakulla
Unakata ("White Man Killer"), 417, 565n82
unega, 18

Unicoi Mountains, 18, 104
United States: Cherokee relations with, 396, 405–406, 448–451, 453–456, 459; formation of, 400; Indian policy, 378, 380, 412–413; territorial expansion of, 376; threat of dissolution of, 378; weakness of, 375, 409–410
Upper (Overhill) Towns, xi, 63; colonization and, 294; fort-building, 199; French threat to, 121, 174; geopolitical position, 18, 378; lack of defense, 217–218; local loyalties, 71; Native attacks on, 106, 178–179; peace diplomacy, 227, 352, 365, 435–436; population of, 366; Southern State offensives of 1776, 344–345; trade depots in, 62; white frontier citizens and, 428
U.S.-Cherokee treaty of 1819, 456, 459
U.S. Congress, 375, 377–378, 379
U.S. Constitution, 398, 400, 403
Ustanali town, 399, 401, 405, 423, 431
Ustutli (mythic monstrous horned foot snake), 102
Utsidsata. See Corn Tassel
Uwenahi. See Justice, Richard

Valley Towns, 18–19
Van Buren, Martin, 464
Vann, James, 430, 447
Vann, John, 407
Vann, Joseph, 329
Vattel, Emmerich de, 462
Vaudreuil-Cavagnial, Pierre François de Rigaud, marquis de: as governor of Louisiana, 143–144, 149, 153; as governor of New France, 207, 221; relations with Natives, 144, 149, 153, 518n29; support of Indian guerrilla warfare, 207; troops of, 147
vigilantism, and frontier whites, 304–305, 325–326, 394–396, 399, 426–427
Virginia: boundary settlements, 316, 320, 368; British invasion of, 360; cession of western territories to the Union, 376; Cherokee relations with, 185, 199, 219, 226–227, 270, 282, 293, 313, 315, 320, 359, 525n24; colonial settlements, 167; conflict with Ohio Indians, 326; diplomacy, 139, 280; land grants, 313; militia, 190, 342, 344–345; Native looting of, 226; territorial expansion, 373; trade, 66
Virginia Company, 412

Wabash River, 89, 225, 409
Wade, Robert, 233
Walker, Thomas, 313–314, 368, 371
Wall, Robert, 211–212

Index   595

wampum belts and beads, as sign of peace accord, 3, 21, 141, 145, 146, 156, 205, 211, 221, 222, 280, 283, 305, 307, 308, 319, 435

Ward, Bryant, 11, 349

Ward, Nancy. *See* Nan-ye-hi

War of 1812, 451–453

War of the Austrian Succession, 142

War of the Spanish Succession, 47–48

warriors, 31–32, 33

Washington, George: Blount and, 411; Cherokees and, 352, 439, 440, 444–445, 451; diplomacy of, 412, 563n47; Indian policy, 409, 410, 422, 429, 431, 433, 439–440; presidency of, 403; proclamation on national sovereignty, 413; surrender of Fort Necessity, 190

Wassamassaw swamp, 56

Watauga Association, 370

Watauga massacre, 324–326

Watauga River, 294, 324, 325, 327, 329, 330, 351

Watauga settlements, 336, 337–338, 341, 347, 351, 355, 356, 357, 367

Waters, Sally, 445

Watts, John (Kunokeskie): Cavett's Station attack and, 430; Coyatee conference and, 423; diplomacy of, 390, 395; Martin's offensive and, 403; McKee and, 565n82; mixed parentage of, 390, 446; negotiations with Americans, 401, 422–423, 425, 428–429, 434–436, 459, 464; relations with Chickamaugas, 423; Robertson's letter to, 434–435; visit to Pensacola, 424, 426; as war leader, 398, 404–405, 421, 422, 424–425, 426

Watts, John, Sr., 305, 307, 346, 390, 541n62

Wawhatchee of Keowee, 190, 198, 219, 220–221, 239, 242

Wayne, Anthony, 432, 433, 436

Weas, 132, 508n72, 538n17

Webber, Will, 398, 448

Weiser, Conrad, 142, 156

Welbank, George, 421

Welsh, Jack, 302

Welsh, James, 251, 270

Whigs, 333–334, 337, 338, 342, 345

White, Andrew, 167–168, 430, 512nn36, 40

White, James, 432

White, Richard, 4–5, 46

white color, symbolism of, 3–4, 478nn8, 9

White Owl (Ukwaneequa). *See* Attakullakulla

White Owl (Overhill warrior), 306

white people, *vs.* red people, 2, 69, 154, 493n4

white settlers. *See* colonial settlers

White's Fort. *See* Knoxville

white traders: abuses and killings of, 53, 55, 59, 95, 98, 249–251, 264, 302, 512n41; Chero-

kees and, 170, 178, 401; reliance on Native peoples, 72; spy on Spanish maneuvers, 424

Whitley, William, 432

Wickett, Susanna, 460

Wigan, Eleazar: background of, 97; Cherokee diplomacy and, 56–57, 107; Chestowe massacre and, 52–53, 57, 490n42; Chicken and, 77–78; Cuming and, 104, 107; as interpreter, 64; James Adair and, 501n41; journey to Appalachian highlands, 56; Long Warrior and, 85, 98, 495n50; nickname of, 53; talks with Tugaloo men, 497n72

Wild Boy, 20, 29–30

Wilkinson, James, 410, 422

Will (Cherokee man), 324, 325

Willanawa (Willanawaw) of Toqua: at Augusta Congress, 297; Cameron and, 320; on Cherokee action in Virginia, 227; military intelligence, 197; peace diplomacy of, 214, 217, 246, 294–295, 297, 346, 536n65

Williamsburg, 8, 185, 272, 282, 283, 284, 295, 304–305, 316, 349–350

Williamson, Andrew, 343, 345, 352, 353–354

Willstown (Will's Town), 398, *399*, 424, 434, 565n82

Winn, Richard, 405

Wolf (mythic warrior), 31

Wolf of Keowee, 267, 286, 321

women. *See* Cherokee women; Native women

Woodward, Henry, 15

Worcester v. Georgia, 462

Wosseo. *See* Price, Moses

Woyi (Pigeon), 350

Wright, James, 322, 324

Wrightknower, William, 155

Wyandots, *42*, 357, 386, 409

Yadkin River, 227

Yahatastanage ("Wolf Warrior"). *See* Mortar

Yamasees: assault on Tuscaroras, 51–52; attacks on colonists, 56, 70, 74, 75, 95; attacks on Franciscan missions, 46; relations with Cherokees, 57, 93; relations with English, 47, 48, 51, 70; slaving warfare, 41, 43, 48, 52; South Carolina campaigns against, 95–96; territories of, *42*, 46; tribal identity of, 46

Yamasee War: English-Cherokee alliance, 6, 56–58, 60; impact on trade, 63, 66; militia forces in, 56; Native allies, 54–55, 56, 75–76; outbreak of, 54; Spanish and French involvement, 55; violence of, 54–55; white colonists and, 55–56

Yazoo land companies, 412–413

Yellow Bird of Keowee, 180, 239

Yuchis, 36, 52, 57, 490n43